AMERICAN INDIAN BIOGRAPHIES

MAGILL'S CHOICE

AMERICAN INDIAN BIOGRAPHIES

Revised Edition

Edited by

Carole Barrett

University of Mary

Harvey Markowitz

Washington and Lee University

Project Editor

R. Kent Rasmussen

SALEM PRESS, INC.

Pasadena, California   Hackensack, New Jersey

Library of Congress Cataloging-in-Publication Data

American Indian biographies / edited by Harvey Markowitz, Carole Barrett.–Rev. ed.

    p. cm.

    "Essays originally appeared in American Indian biographies (1999), Dictionary of world biography, Great lives from history: the Renaissance & early modern era, 1454-1600 (2005), and American ethnic writers (2000). New material has been added"–T.p. verso.

    Includes bibliographical references and index.

    ISBN 1-58765-233-1 (alk. paper)

    1. Indians of North America–Biography. 2. Indians of North America–Kings and rulers–Biography. 3. Indian women–North America–Biography. I. Markowitz, Harvey. II. Barrett, Carole A. III. Title.

E98.A46 2005

920'.009297–dc22

2004028872

First Printing

Table of Contents

Table of Contents

Table of Contents

Publisher's Note

This volume is a revised and expanded edition of Salem Press's *American Indian Biographies*, which was published in 1999. The majority of the essays in that first edition were taken from Salem's *Ready Reference: American Indians* (1995), and 32 new essays were added. *American Indian Biographies, Revised Edition* includes all the subjects covered in the first edition and adds 60 entirely new essays and longer versions of other essays from Salem's *Great Lives from History* series and *American Ethnic Writers* (2000), bringing the new total to 391 essays. Essays on living figures have been brought up to date, essay bibliographies have been updated through 2004 publications, and several new appendices have been added.

As the core curricula at the middle school, high school, and college levels have expanded to encompass the diversity of American peoples and wider historical perspectives, so has the need for such high-quality reference works on American Indians as *American Indian Biographies*. Indeed, the ongoing demand for such works has been demonstrated by the popularity of other Magill's Choice reference sets on Indians: *American Indian Tribes* (2 vols., 2000), *American Indian History* (2 vols., 2002), and *American Indian Culture* (3 vols., 2004). Biographical encyclopedias, which are among the cornerstones of any library reference collection, have not always been able to fill the need for reliable reference covering key personages previously overlooked. *American Indian Biographies, Revised Edition* provides an affordable and authoritative resource for librarians seeking to fill such gaps in their collections.

Coverage

American Indian cultures hold a fascination for Americans of all ages and ethnicities. The essays in this volume examine the lives of the American Indians who are most widely studied in secondary schools, colleges, and universities in the United States and Canada and who have had the greatest impact on popular culture. Ranging in length from 200 to 3,000 words, the 391 alphabetically arranged articles profile religious, social, and political leaders, warriors, and reformers from the past, as well as modern activists, writers, artists, entertainers, scientists, and athletes. The best-known and most important figures are covered in articles ranging from 1,000 to 3,000 words in length, with the longer formats allowing for greater biographical depth and the presentation of full historical and cultural contexts.

While the volume includes portraits of such well-known historical figures as Powhatan, Pocahontas, Sitting Bull, Crazy Horse, and Geronimo, it also covers such modern political activists as Dennis Banks, Russell Means, and Elouise Cobell—who may yet prove to be the most important Indian figure in U.S. history. The chronological coverage ranges from mid-sixteenth century to present day figures. More than 310 of the 391 people profiled were born before the twentieth century, and more than 110 before the nineteenth century. Of the figures born in the twentieth century, more than 50 were still living as this book went to press.

Although the sixty new articles added to this edition cover many traditional leaders, they also include a number of contemporary figures whose names and faces will be especially familiar to young-adult readers. These figures include actors Adam Beach, Irene Bedard (famous as both the voice and the model for the title character in Disney's *Pocahontas*), and Wes Studi. There is also a new article on actor Iron Eyes Cody, who may not have been a real Indian by heritage but who presented himself to the world as the son of Cherokee and Cree parents and came to symbolize to millions of Americans the face of authentic Native Americans as the Indian who gazed over a polluted river and wept in television environmentalism spots.

In addition to those essays already mentioned, there are long pieces on such major figures from the past as Pontiac, Tecumseh, John Ross, Sacagawea, Sequoyah, Cochise, Joseph the Younger (Chief Joseph), Black Elk, Red Jacket, and Red Cloud, as well as such twentieth century personages as Cherokee chief Wilma Mankiller, humorist Will Rogers, and Osage prima ballerina Maria Tallchief. Among the hundreds of other figures profiled are Major Ridge, Isatai, Kamiakin, Kicking Bear, Little Turtle, Osceola, Mangas Coloradas, Massasoit, Metacomet, Crashing Thunder, Naiche, Oshkosh, Ely Samuel Parker, Popé, Pleasant Porter, Seattle, Spotted Tail, Squanto, Black Kettle, Captain Jack, Henry Roe Cloud, and nineteenth century physicians Carlos Montezuma and Susan La Flesche. Religious leaders include Handsome Lake, Neolin (the Delaware Prophet), John Slocum, Tenskwatawa, and Wovoka.

Notable twentieth century political figures include Charles Curtis, the first Native American U.S. senator and vice president; five-term congressman Ben Reifel; Senator Ben Nighthorse Campbell; and the first Native Canadian senator, James Gladstone; as well as Bureau of Indian Affairs commissioners Louis R. Bruce and Ada Elizabeth Deer and the controversial Navajo leader Peter MacDonald. Among the modern activists discussed are Leonard Peltier, Mary Crow Dog, John Trudell, and LaDonna Harris.

Writers covered here include Sherman Alexie, Vine Deloria, Jr., Michael Dorris, Louise Erdrich, Joy Harjo, Linda Hogan, N. Scott Momaday, Gerald Vizenor, playwrights Tomson Highway and Seth Riggs, and others. Artists profiled include silversmith Delgadito, potters Popovi Da and Nampeyo, weavers Datsolalee and Hosteen Klah, as well as a number of painters, such as Awa Tsirah, James Bear Heart, Acee Blue Eagle, R. C. Gorman, Oscar Howe, Fritz Scholder, Jerome R. Tiger, Spencer Asah, and the other members of the Kiowa Five group. Entertainment industry figures include Cher, Dan George, Graham Greene, Will Sampson, Jay Silverheels, Robbie Robertson, Wayne Newton, and Buffy Sainte-Marie. There are also articles on record-setting athletes Jim Thorpe and Billy Mills and scientists Mary Ross and Freda Porter-Locklear.

Organization

Each essay provides essential information at its beginning: the individual's birth and death places and dates, alternative names, tribal affiliations, and significance. Many articles contain cross-references to other personages who are subjects of their own articles in the set; cross-referenced names are printed in SMALL CAPITAL LETTERS. Reference features at the end of the volume include a time line of events in North American Indian history from 15,000 B.C.E. to the early twenty-first century, a list of personages categorized by tribe, a list of personages arranged by the dates of their birth, and a comprehensive subject index.

One of the major changes in this edition has been a significant expansion of bibliographical material. Nearly 250 articles now contain individual bibliographies—a five-fold increase—and wherever possible, these bibliographies have been updated to include books and articles published as recently as 2004. Approximately 110 essays are illustrated with portraits—photographs, engravings, or drawings.

Acknowledgments

Salem Press extends thanks to all the contributors—many of whom are Native Americans—to this volume. A list of the contributors, who are mostly academicians in anthropology, history, ethnic studies, and other fields, appears following the Publisher's Note. We also offer special thanks to the project's Editors, Harvey Markowitz of Washington and Lee University and Carole Barrett of the American Indian Studies program at North Dakota's University of Mary.

List of Contributors

Jeff Abernathy
Illinois College

McCrea Adams
Independent Scholar

Richard Adler
University of Michigan, Dearborn

Thomas L. Altherr
Metropolitan State College of Denver

Richard J. Amundson
Columbus College

T. J. Arant
East Central College

Tanya M. Backinger
Jackson Community College

John W. Bailey
Carthage College

Carl L. Bankston III
Tulane University

Susan Barfield
Montana State University, Billings

Carole A. Barrett
University of Mary

Alvin K. Benson
Utah Valley State College

George R. Bent III
Washington and Lee University

Robert L. Berner
University of Wisconsin at Oshkosh

Joy A. Bilharz
State University of New York College at Fredonia

Terry D. Billhartz
Sam Houston State University

Nicholas Birns
New School University

Pegge Bochynski
Salem State College

Larry W. Burt
University of Utah

Byron D. Cannon
University of Utah

Jack J. Cardoso
State University of New York College at Buffalo

Emmett H. Carroll
Seattle University

Thomas Patrick Carroll
John A. Logan College

Ward Churchill
University of Colorado at Boulder

Cheryl Claassen
Appalachian State University

C. B. Clark
Oklahoma City University

David A. Crain
South Dakota State University

LouAnn Faris Culley
Kansas State University

Ronald J. Duncan
Oklahoma Baptist University

Robert P. Ellis
Worcester State College

Edward A. Fiorelli
St. John's University

C. George Fry
Winebrenner Theological Seminary

Constance M. Fulmer
Pepperdine University

Lynne Getz
Appalachian State University

Larry Gragg
University of Missouri, Rolla

Gretchen L. Green
Rockhurst College

Jennifer Padgett Griffith
Independent Scholar

Robert Haight
Kalamazoo Valley Community College

Robert M. Hawthorne, Jr.
Independent Scholar

Carl W. Hoagstrom
Ohio Northern University

Hal Holladay
Simon's Rock College of Bard

John R. Holmes
Franciscan University of Steubenville

Tonya Huber
Wichita State University

Raymond Pierre Hylton
Virginia Union University

M. A. Jaimes
University of Colorado at Boulder

Jennifer Raye James
Independent Scholar

Helen Jaskoski
California State University, Fullerton

Jeffry Jensen
Independent Scholar

Bruce E. Johansen
University of Nebraska at Omaha

Robert Jones
Granite School District

Sondra Jones
Brigham Young University

Charles Louis Kammer III
College of Wooster

Richard S. Keating
*United States Air Force
Academy*

Lynne Klyse
Independent Scholar

Janet Alice Long
Independent Scholar

Ronald W. Long
*West Virginia University
Institute of Technology*

William C. Lowe
Mount St. Clare College

Richard B. McCaslin
High Point University

Ron McFarland
University of Idaho

Paul Madden
Hardin-Simmons University

Harvey Markowitz
*Washington and Lee
University*

Thomas D. Matijasic
*Prestonsburg Community
College*

Anne Laura Mattrella
Southeastern University

Howard Meredith
*University of Science and
Arts of Oklahoma*

Michael R. Meyers
Shaw University

David N. Mielke
Appalachian State University

Laurence Miller
*Western Washington
University*

Bruce M. Mitchell
*Eastern Washington
University*

Robert E. Morsberger
*California State Polytechnic
University, Pomona*

Molly H. Mullin
Duke University

Bert M. Mutersbaugh
Eastern Kentucky University

Eric Niderost
Chabot College

Patrick M. O'Neil
Broome Community College

Sean O'Neill
Grand Valley State University

Andrea Gayle Radke
Brigham Young University

P. S. Ramsey
Independent Scholar

R. Kent Rasmussen
Independent Scholar

Jon Reyhner
*Montana State University,
Billings*

S. Fred Roach
Kennesaw College

Moises Roizen
West Valley College

John Alan Ross
*Eastern Washington
University*

Constance B. Rynder
University of Tampa

Richard Sax
Madonna University

Glenn J. Schiffman
Independent Scholar

Lee Schweninger
*University of North Carolina,
Wilmington*

Burl E. Self
*Southwest Missouri State
University*

Jennifer Shannon
Cornell University

R. Baird Shuman
*University of Illinois at
Urbana-Champaign*

Michael W. Simpson
Independent Scholar

James Smallwood
Oklahoma State University

Daniel L. Smith-
Christopher
*Loyola Marymount
University*

Ruffin Stirling
Independent Scholar

Trey Strecker
Ball State University

Darlene Mary Suarez
*University of California,
Riverside*

Glenn L. Swygart
Tennessee Temple University

Teresa Neva Tate
Smithsonian Institution

Susan Daly Vinal
University of Texas

Mary E. Virginia
Independent Scholar

Kelly C. Walter
Southern California College

Harry M. Ward
University of Richmond

Raymond Wilson
Fort Hays State University

Sharon K. Wilson
Fort Hays State University

Shawn Woodyard
Independent Scholar

Joanna Yin
University of Hawaii

Adair, John L.

Born: 1828; northern Georgia
Died: October 21, 1896; Tahlequah, Indian Territory (now in Oklahoma)
Tribal affiliation: Cherokee
Significance: John L. Adair played an important role in Cherokee affairs during the difficult years following the Trail of Tears.

John Lynch Adair was born in 1828 in the original Cherokee Nation, which included northern Georgia. The Adair family, originally from Ireland, had intermarried with the Cherokee and produced numerous part-Cherokee Adairs, of whom John was one.

When John was ten years old, the Cherokee were forcibly moved to the Indian Territory west of the Mississippi River. Reaching manhood there, John Adair provided needed leadership in helping the Cherokee adjust to a new environment.

In 1871, as a result of the Cherokee Treaty of 1866, Adair was appointed Cherokee boundary commissioner to work with a U.S. government commissioner in determining the boundaries between the Cherokee Nation and surrounding states. In later years, he compiled the constitution and laws of the Cherokee Nation; published in 1893, they were the major references for Cherokee law until Oklahoma became a state in 1907. Adair died in the Cherokee capital of Tahlequah in 1896.

Glenn L. Swygart

FURTHER READING

McLoughlin, William G. *After the Trail of Tears: The Cherokees' Struggle for Sovereignty, 1839-1880.* Chapel Hill: University of North Carolina Press, 1993.
Wardell, Morris L. *A Political History of the Cherokee Nation, 1838-1907.* Norman: University of Oklahoma Press, 1938.
Woodward, Grace Steele. *The Cherokees.* Norman: University of Oklahoma Press, 1963.

Adario

Born: c. 1650; Ontario, Canada
Died: August 1, 1701; Montreal, Canada
Also known as: Kondiaronk, Sastaretsi, Gaspar Soiga, Le Rat

Tribal affiliation: Petun
Significance: Adario skillfully thwarted a late seventeenth century French-Iroquois alliance.

Acting under a 1688 treaty, the Petun leader Adario embarked on a French-sponsored military expedition against the powerful Iroquois Confederacy. Unbeknown to Adario, however, the French simultaneously were courting an Iroquois alliance. While he was en route, Adario received intelligence of an Iroquois delegation led by the Onondaga DEKANISORA, who was traveling to Montreal for negotiations; Adario ordered his men to ambush them. Later he claimed he was acting under French orders. As an ostensible gesture of goodwill toward Dekanisora, Adario released his Onondaga prisoners except one hostage, whom he surrendered to the French fort commander at Michilimackinac. Ignorant of machinations by the French and Adario, the commander executed the captive. Retaliating, the Iroquois launched a massive attack on August 25, 1689, catching the French unprepared. They inflicted heavy casualties and burned Montreal.

Adario died in 1701 in Montreal while leading a treaty delegation of Huron chiefs. Unaware of Adario's duplicities, the French buried him with military honors.

Mary E. Virginia

Alexie, Sherman

Born: October 7, 1966; Spokane Indian Reservation, Wellpinit, Washington
Tribal affiliation: Spokane/Coeur d'Alene
Significance: Sherman Alexie is one of the most prolific and accomplished of Native American writers; he has received widespread critical acclaim for his poetry, short stories, and novels.

Sherman Alexie is a Spokane-Coeur d'Alene Indian who grew up on a reservation in Wellpinit, Washington. He acknowledges that his origin and upbringing affect everything that he does in his writing and otherwise. His father retired from the Bureau of Indian Affairs and his mother worked as a youth drug and alcohol counselor. The first of their five children to leave the reservation, Alexie attended Gonzaga University in Spokane for two years before entering Washington State University, where he studied creative writing with Alex Kuo. He was graduated in 1991.

Among the five books Alexie produced between 1992 and 1995, the seventy-seven-line free verse poem "Horses," from *Old Shirts and New Skins* (1993), typifies the passion, anger, and pain in some of his most effective poems. Focused on the slaughter of a thousand Spokane horses by General George Wright in 1858, the long lines echo obsessively: "1,000 ponies, the U.S. Cavalry stole 1,000 ponies/ from the Spokane Indians, shot 1,000 ponies & only 1 survived." The poem is one of Alexie's favorites at readings, where it acquires the incantatory power of the best oral poetry.

Sherman Alexie. (© Marion Ettlinger)

Alexie's *First Indian on the Moon* (1993) is largely composed of prose poems. "Collect Calls" opens with an allusion to CRAZY HORSE, who appears often as a mythic figure in his writing: "My name is *Crazy Horse*, maybe it's *Neil Armstrong* or *Lee Harvey Oswald.* I am guilty of every crime; I was the first man on the moon." As in his fiction, Alexie tempers the anger and pain of his poems with satiric wit, as in "The Marlon Brando Memorial Swimming Pool," from *Old Shirts and New Skins,* in which activist Dennis BANKS is imagined as "the first/ Native American real estate agent, selling a 5,000 gallon capacity dream/ in the middle of a desert." Not surprisingly, there is no water in the pool.

Alexie's initial foray into fiction (except for a few stories sprinkled among his poems), *The Lone Ranger and Tonto Fistfight in Heaven* (1993) appeared before his twenty-seventh birthday and was awarded a citation from the PEN/Hemingway Award committee for best first book of fiction in 1993. Praising his "live and unremitting lyric energy," one reviewer suggested that three of the twenty-two stories in the book "could stand in any collection of excellence."

Critics have noted that the pain and anger of the stories are balanced by his keen sense of humor and satiric wit. Alexie's readers will notice certain recurring characters, including Victor Joseph, who often appears as the narrator, Lester FallsApart, the pompous tribal police chief,

David WalksAlong, Junior Polatkin, and Thomas Builds-the-Fire, the storyteller to whom no one listens. These characters also appear in Alexie's first novel, *Reservation Blues* (1995), so the effect is of a community; in this respect, Alexie's writings are similar to the fiction of William Faulkner. One reviewer has suggested that *The Lone Ranger and Tonto Fistfight in Heaven* is almost a novel, despite the fact that Alexie rarely relies on plot development in the stories and does not flesh out his characters. It might more aptly be said that the stories come close to poetry, just as Alexie's poems verge on fiction. The stories range in length from less than three to about twenty pages, and some of the best, like "The First Annual All-Indian Horseshoe Pitch and Barbecue," leap from moment to moment, from one-liner to quickly narrated episode, much like a poem.

Alexie's novel, *Reservation Blues,* was published before his thirtieth birthday and after the striking success of *The Business of Fancydancing,* a collection of poems and stories published by a small press when he was twenty-six. By the time his novel was being reviewed, nearly eight thousand copies of *The Business of Fancydancing* were in print, along with two additional collections of poetry, *Old Shirts and New Skins* and *First Indian on the Moon,* and a heralded book of short stories, *The Lone Ranger and Tonto Fistfight in Heaven,* all published in 1993.

In his novel, Alexie reasserts an equation that he formed in "Imagining the Reservation," from *The Lone Ranger and Tonto Fistfight in Heaven:* "Survival = Anger + Imagination. Imagination is the only weapon on the reservation." *Reservation Blues* is arguably the most imaginative of his works to date, blending, among other things, the Faust myth with life on the "rez" and the dream of making it big in the music world. Alexie has performed in his own blues band.

In 1998, stories from Alexie's collections were adapted in the film *Smoke Signals.* Alexie has continued to produce works in poetry and fiction, such as the poetry collection *One Stick Song* (2000). His works of fiction include *The Toughest Indian in the World* (2000) and *Ten Little Indians: Stories* (2003). Alexie also wrote and directed the film *The Business of Fancydancing: The Screenplay* in 2003.

Ron McFarland

FURTHER READING

Bellante, John, and Carl Bellante. "Sherman Alexie, Literary Rebel." *Bloomsbury Review* 14 (May-June, 1994): 14-15, 26.

Grassian, Daniel. *Understanding Sherman Alexie.* Columbia: University of South Carolina Press, 2005.

Silko, Leslie Marmon. "Big Bingo." *Nation* 260 (June 12, 1995): 856-858, 860.

Teters, Charlene. "Poet, Novelist, Filmmaker Sherman Alexie: Spokane, Coeur d'Alene." *Indian Artist* 4, no. 2 (Spring, 1998): 30-35.

Alford, Thomas Wildcat

Born: July 15, 1860; near Sasakwa, Oklahoma
Died: August 3, 1938; Shawnee, Oklahoma
Also known as: Gaynwawpiahsika
Tribal affiliation: Shawnee
Significance: Drawing on knowledge of white customs gained from his education with whites, Thomas Wildcat Alford counseled Indians about their land rights and helped them to cope with rapid cultural changes.

Born in Indian Territory, Thomas Wildcat Alford was the grandson of the pantribal Indian leader TECUMSEH. Educated in tribal customs until age twelve, he thereafter attended a mission school. In 1879, he earned a scholarship to Virginia's Hampton Institute, where he adopted Christianity. Upon returning to Indian Territory, Alford initially was shunned by Indian traditionalists. Nevertheless, the following year, he was appointed principal of a federally funded Shawnee school, a position he occupied for five years.

In 1893, Alford chaired a federally sponsored committee designed to supersede Shawnee tribal government. Utilizing his knowledge of U.S. law, he assisted Indians in safeguarding their land rights during implementation of the allotment system. He also made trips to Washington, D.C., lobbying on behalf of his tribe. In addition, he was employed by the Bureau of Indian Affairs. Until his death, Alford continued advising his people, working to meliorate social problems exacerbated after Oklahoma achieved statehood in 1907.

Mary E. Virginia

FURTHER READING

Nabokov, Peter. *Native American Testimony: A Chronicle of Indian-White Relations from Prophecy to the Present, 1492-2000.* Foreword by Vine Deloria, Jr. New York: Viking, 1991.

Allen, Paula Gunn

Born: October 24, 1939; Cubero, New Mexico

Tribal affiliation: Laguna Pueblo

Significance: Paula Gunn Allen's prolific works of poetry, fiction, and literary criticism have brought an influential lesbian and feminist perspective to American Indian literature.

Paula Gunn Allen, as an American Indian woman, sees her identity in relation to a larger community. She is proud to be part of an old and honored tradition that appreciates the beautiful, the harmonious, and the spiritual. She also recognizes that since in the United States there are more than a million non-Indians to every Indian, she must work to stay connected to her Native American heritage.

Allen frequently refers to herself as "a multicultural event"; people of many ethnicities are related to her. Her mother was a Laguna Indian whose grandfather was Scottish American. Allen says that she was raised Roman Catholic, but living next door were her grandmother, who was Presbyterian and Indian, and her grandfather, who was a German Jew. Her father's family came from Lebanon; he was born in a Mexican land-grant village north of Laguna Pueblo. She grew up with relatives who spoke Arabic, English, Laguna, German, and Spanish. Her relatives shared legends from around the world.

Even with such cultural diversity in her family, as a teenager Allen could find no Native American models for her writing. Consequently, she read Charlotte Brontë's *Jane Eyre: An Autobiography* (1847) about twenty times; her other literary favorites were Louisa May Alcott, Gertrude Stein, and the Romantic poets John Keats and Percy Bysshe Shelley. When she went to the University of New Mexico and wanted to focus on Native American literature in her doctoral program in English, it was impossible. The scholarship was not there to study. She came to write the books that she wanted to read and teach the courses that she wanted to take.

Allen has taught at San Francisco State University, at the University of New Mexico, in the Native American Studies Program at the University of California at Berkeley, and at the University of California, Los Angeles.

In enumerating the influences that have made her who she is, Allen first honors her mother, who taught her to think like a strong Indian woman and that animals, insects, and plants are to be treated with the deep respect one customarily reserves for high-status humans. She hon-

Paula Gunn Allen. (© Tama Rothschild)

ors her father for teaching her how to weave magic, memory, and observation into the tales she tells. Finally, the Indian collective unconscious remains the source of her vision of spiritual reality.

The collection of essays *The Sacred Hoop: Recovering the Feminine in American Indian Traditions* (1986) documents the continuing vitality of American Indian traditions and the crucial role of women in those traditions. The title comes from a lesson Allen learned from her mother: that all of life is a circle, a sacred hoop, in which everything has its place. These essays, like tribal art of all kinds, support the principle of kinship and render the beautiful in terms of the harmony, relationship, balance, and dignity that are the informing principles of Indian aesthetics. Indians understand that woman is the sun and the earth: She is grandmother, mother, thought, wisdom, dream, reason, tradition, memory, deity, and life itself.

The essays are all characterized by seven major themes that pertain to American Indian identity. The first is that Indians and spirits are always found together. Second, Indians endure. Third, the traditional tribal lifestyles are never patriarchal and are more often woman-centered than not. Tribal social systems are nurturing, pacifist, and based on ritual and spirit-centered, woman-focused worldviews. The welfare of the young is paramount, the complementary nature of all life forms is stressed, and the centrality of powerful, self-defining, assertive, decisive women to social well-being is unquestioned. Fourth, the physical and cultural destruction of American Indian tribes is and was about patriarchal fear and the inability to tolerate women's having decision-making capacity at every level of society. Fifth, there is such a thing as American Indian literature, and it informs all American writing. Sixth, all Western studies of American Indian tribal systems are erroneous because they view tribalism from the cultural bias of patriarchy. Seventh, the sacred ways of the American Indian people are part of a worldwide culture that predates Western systems.

Spider Woman's Granddaughters: Traditional Tales and Contemporary Writing by Native American Women (1989), edited by Allen, is a collection of two dozen traditional tales, biographical writings, and short stories by seventeen accomplished American Indian women writers. All the women follow the tradition of Grandmother Spider, who, according to the Cherokee, brought the light of thought to her people, who were living as hostages in their own land. These stories are war stories, since all American Indian women are at war and have been for five hundred years.

Some of the selections are old-style stories; others deal with contemporary issues. All are by women intimately acquainted with defeat, with being conquered, and with losing the right and the authority to control their personal and communal lives. They have experienced the devastating destruction of their national and personal identities. They powerfully demonstrate the Indian slogan: We shall endure.

Allen's other works of poetry include *Life Is a Fatal Disease: Collected Poems, 1962-1995* (1997). In 2003, she published *Pocahontas: Medicine Woman, Spy, Entrepreneur, Diplomat*, a well-rounded examination of the life of Pocahontas that delves into many areas ignored in other biographies of the early seventeenth century Powhatan woman.

Constance M. Fulmer

FURTHER READING

Albers, Patricia, and Beatrice Medicine. *The Hidden Half: Studies of Plains Indian Women*. Lanham, Md.: University Press of America, 1983.

Allen, Paula Gunn, ed. *Studies in American Indian Literature*. New York: Modern Language Association of America, 1983.

Bataille, Gretchen M., and Laurie Lisa, eds. *Native American Women: A Biographical Dictionary*. 2d ed. London: Routledge, 2001.

Bataille, Gretchen M., and Kathleen M. Sands, eds. *American Indian Women: Telling Their Lives*. Lincoln: University of Nebraska Press, 1984.

Bataille, Gretchen M., Kathleen Mullen Sands, and Charles L. P. Silet, eds. *The Pretend Indians: Images of Native Americans in the Movies*. Iowa City: University of Iowa Press, 1980.

Brandon, William. *The Last American: The Indian in American Culture*. New York: McGraw-Hill, 1974.

Bruchac, Joseph, ed. *Survival This Way: Interviews with American Indian Poets*. Tucson: University of Arizona Press, 1987.

Chapman, Abraham. *Literature of the American Indians: Views and Interpretations*. New York: New American Library, 1975.

Coltelli, Laura. *Winged Words: American Indian Writers Speak.* Lincoln: University of Nebraska Press, 1990.

Deloria, Vine, Jr. *God Is Red.* New York: Grosset & Dunlap, 1973. Reprint. New York: Dell Books, 1983.

Etienne, Mona, and Eleanor Leacock, eds. *Women and Colonization: Anthropological Perspectives.* New York: Praeger, 1980.

Fisher, Dexter, ed. *The Third Woman: Minority Women Writers of the United States.* Boston: Houghton Mifflin, 1980.

Hanson, Elizabeth I. *Paula Gunn Allen.* Boise State University Western Writers Series 96. Boise, Idaho: Boise State University Press, 1990.

Keating, Ana Louise. *Women Reading Women Writing: Self-Invention in Paula Gunn Allen, Gloria Anzaldúa, and Audre Lorde.* Philadelphia: Temple University Press, 1996.

Swann, Brian, and Arnold Krupat, eds. *I Tell You Now: Autobiographical Essays by Native American Writers.* Lincoln: University of Nebraska Press, 1987.

Alligator

Born: c. 1795; northern Florida
Died: c. 1865; Seminole reservation, Indian Territory (now part of Oklahoma)
Also known as: Halpata Tastanaki, Halpatter Tustenuggee
Tribal affiliation: Seminole
Significance: Chief Alligator was considered among the bravest and most capable Seminole leaders during the Second Seminole War.

The Seminole Indians originated among the Lower Creeks living along the Chattahoochee River in Georgia. With encroachment by whites during the late eighteenth century, they began moving down the Florida peninsula and adopted the name Seminole, which meant "separate." Eventually comprising some twenty villages, the Seminoles fought against the U.S. Army several times during the first decades of the nineteenth century. The fighting in 1817 became known as the First Seminole War. General Andrew Jackson invaded Florida, then under Spanish rule, with some three thousand men and forced the Seminoles to cede most of their lands to the United States. In 1819, Spain ceded all of Florida to the United States.

An 1832 treaty forced the Seminoles to move beyond the Mississippi River, but a large portion of the people refused to adhere to the treaty's terms. In December, 1835, the Seminoles killed Charley Emathla, a chief who had signed the treaty and supported emigration, as well as the American agent, General A. R. Thompson. In response, General Winfield Scott, then commander of the U.S. Army, ordered three columns of troops to attack Seminole villages and enforce the treaty. One army of one hundred men was led by Major Frank Dade. On December 28, 1835, Dade's men were ambushed by Seminoles under the command of Chief Alligator and Little Cloud near the Wythlacooche River. Dade and all but one of his men were killed. That attack began the Second Seminole War.

Though information on Alligator is scarce, he appears to have been born in the village known as Halpata Telofa (Alligator Town). His ancestry may have been Eufaula, one of the Creek tribes from southeastern Alabama. He along with Chief OSCEOLA, were the principal commanders of the Indian warriors during the war and proved to be a match for the American armies sent against them.

During the first months of 1836, Seminoles under Alligator and Osceola's leadership fought American armies commanded by Generals Duncan Clinch and Edmund Gaines to draws. Osceola was eventually betrayed and died in prison, but Alligator continued to fight for another year. In December, 1837, Alligator attacked an army led by future U.S. president Colonel Zachary Taylor, killing twenty-six soldiers and leaving more than one hundred men wounded in what became known as the Battle of Okeechobee.

Realizing that continued resistance against overwhelming forces would be ultimately futile, Alligator surrendered shortly afterward. He, along with most members of the Seminole nation, was removed to Oklahoma, where he died sometime in 1865. Meanwhile, the Second Seminole War dragged on for several more years and cost the United States fifteen hundred lives and approximately thirty million to forty million dollars. After the Seminoles were defeated, white settlers occupied the town of Halpata Telofa. For a time, it retained the name of Alligator Town but was later renamed Lake City.

Richard Adler

American Horse

Born: c. 1840; Black Hills area (now in South Dakota)
Died: December 16, 1908; Pine Ridge, South Dakota
Also known as: Wasechun-tashunka
Tribal affiliation: Oglala Lakota (Sioux)

Significance: A skilled orator and negotiator, American Horse advocated peace between whites and Sioux during the Sioux Wars of the late nineteenth century.

American Horse, the Younger, was probably Sitting Bear's son; American Horse, the Elder's nephew; and RED CLOUD's son-in-law. As a young warrior, he fought white encroachment on Sioux hunting grounds during the Bozeman Trail War of 1866. In 1888-1889, after an extended and exhaustive negotiation with General George Crook, American Horse signed a treaty by which the Sioux ceded approximately half of their land in Dakota territory.

As tensions between whites and Sioux escalated, culminating in the Ghost Dance uprising of 1890, American Horse continued to advocate peace. Prior to the Wounded Knee Massacre in 1890, American Horse persuaded BIG FOOT's band to return to the Pine Ridge Reservation. In 1891, he led the first of several Sioux delegations to Washington, D.C., to negotiate for better Sioux-white relations. After Wounded Knee, American Horse was one of several Indian leaders who toured with Buffalo Bill Cody's Wild West show.

Mary E. Virginia

American Horse. (Library of Congress)

FURTHER READING
Ostler, Jeffrey. *The Plains Sioux and U.S. Colonialism from Lewis and Clark to Wounded Knee.* New York: Cambridge University Press, 2004.

Annawan

Born: Unknown
Died: August 12, 1676; place unknown
Tribal affiliation: Wampanoag
Significance: Annawan led the war chiefs during King Philip's War.

Leader of the war chiefs under King Philip (METACOMET) during King Philip's War (1675-1676) in the New England colonies, Annawan was a trusted adviser and strategist. He was acknowledged as a valiant soldier in this decisive war for the future of Indian-white relations in the Northeast.

After the death of Philip in August, 1676, Annawan became the leader of a short-lived continued Indian resistance, leading attacks on the towns of Swansea and Plymouth. Conducting guerrilla-style warfare and shifting campsites nightly, Annawan was able to evade colonial forces under Captain Benjamin Church for two weeks. Then a captive Indian led Church and a small party of soldiers to Annawan's camp, now known as Annawan's Rock. Church misled the Indians into believing that they were outnumbered, and Annawan surrendered the tribe's medicine bundle, which included wampum belts telling the history of the tribe and of the Wampanoag Confederacy.

Church respected his defeated adversary so much that he asked for clemency for Annawan. During Church's absence, however, Plymouth residents seized Annawan and beheaded him, ending the last vestige of Wampanoag resistance.

Thomas Patrick Carroll

FURTHER READING
Drake, James D. *King Philip's War: Civil War in New England, 1675-1676.* Amherst: University of Massachusetts Press, 2000.
Kawashima, Yasuhide. *Igniting King Philip's War: The John Sassamon Murder Trial.* Lawrence: University Press of Kansas, 2001.
Schultz, Eric B., and Michael J. Tougias. *King Philip's War: The History and Legacy of America's Forgotten Conflict.* Woodstock, Vt.: Countryman Press, 1999.

Antonio, Juan

Born: c. 1783; Mt. San Jacinto region, California
Died: February 28, 1863; San Timoteo Cañon, California
Also known as: Cooswootna, Yampoochee (He Gets Mad Quickly)
Tribal affiliation: Cahuilla
Significance: A powerful Cahuilla chief, Juan Antonio aided whites on several occasions in California during the turbulent 1850's.

Several competing forces vied for control of California during the 1850's, including ranchers, Mexicans, miners, Mormons, outlaws, and Indians. In 1842, Juan Antonio, leader of the Cahuillas of Southern California, greeted explorer Daniel Sexton at the San Gorgino Pass, granting him permission to explore the region. Antonio likewise assisted Lieutenant Edward F. Beale of the U.S. Army in his explorations of the region, defending Beale's men against raids from Ute warriors led by Walkara. In appreciation for his aid, Beale presented Antonio with a pair of military epaulets.

Antonio continued to assist white Californians. After the outlaw John Irving and his men raided the area, stealing cattle and killing local settlers, Antonio swiftly ended the raid by killing all but one of Irving's men. White settlers, although relieved at Irving's death, nevertheless were ambivalent about Antonio's killing of whites. Consequently, Antonio was officially deposed by white Californians as chief; his Indian followers, however, ignored the white mandate and continued to view him as their leader.

As white migration increased during the Gold Rush, a Cupeño shaman named Antonio GARRA organized Indian tribes to drive whites from the region. Both whites and Indians sought Antonio's assistance. Electing to help white settlers, Antonio captured Garra in 1851, thereby suppressing the uprising. In appreciation, Commissioner O. N. Wozencraft designed a treaty that would enable the Cahuilla to retain their ancestral lands. The California Senate refused to ratify the treaty, however, leading to discontent among the Cahuilla.

Between 1845 and 1846, violence erupted but resistance to whites was largely ineffectual. Furthermore, by 1856 anti-Mormon sentiments had eclipsed the Indian issue, and land speculators and squatters forced Indians from their land. Already facing dispossession and inadequate provisions, California Indians were suddenly devastated by smallpox. The last of the Cahuilla leaders, Antonio died of the disease and was buried in San Timoteo Cañon. During a 1956 archaeological expedition, Antonio's body was exhumed, identified by his epaulets, and later reburied with military honors.

Mary E. Virginia

FURTHER READING
Bean, Lowell J. *Mukat's People: The Cahuilla Indians of Southern California.* Berkeley: University of California Press, 1972.

Apes, William

Born: January 31, 1798; Colrain, Massachusetts
Died: April, 1839; New York, New York
Also known as: William Apess
Tribal affiliation: Pequot
Significance: William Apes, a nineteenth century political protest writer, produced the first published autobiography by an American Indian.

Little is known of William Apes outside his own account in his autobiography, *A Son of the Forest* (1829), which recounts his youth and early adulthood. He spent his first four years with intemperate grandparents, who reportedly often beat him and his siblings. While growing up, he recalled, his indenture was sold several times to different families in Connecticut. He had only six years of formal education, took part in the War of 1812, had bouts with drinking, and was reformed by his introduction to Christianity. In 1829, he was ordained as a Methodist minister.

In May, 1833, he traveled to the Massachusetts community of Mashpee, where he immediately took part in a revolt against the Massachusetts Commonwealth. In the context of organizing and leading this revolt, he published an account of Indians' grievances against whites in *Indian Nullification of the Unconstitutional Laws of Massachusetts, Relative to the Mashpee Tribe* (1835). Like the earlier "An Indian's Looking-Glass for the White Man" (1833), this book turns on his political astuteness and sense of fairness. At the Odeon in Boston in 1836, Apes preached *Eulogy on King Philip*, a political and historical account of the Indian wars of the previous century; it was published the same year. Apes returned to autobiography in *The Experiences of Five Christian Indians* (1837), in which he accuses whites of racism. After about 1838, Apes disappeared from the public eye, and nothing is known of his later life.

Lee Schweninger

FURTHER READING

Apess, William. *A Son of the Forest and Other Writings.* Edited and introduced by Barry O'Connell. Amherst: University of Massachusetts Press, 1997.

_____. *On Our Own Ground: The Complete Writings of William Apess.* Edited by Barry O'Connell. Amherst: University of Massachusetts Press, 1992.

Walker, Cheryl. *Indian Nation: Native American Literature and Nineteenth-century Nationalisms.* Durham, N.C.: Duke University Press, 1997.

Arapoosh

Born: c. 1790; northern Wyoming
Died: August, 1834; place unknown
Also known as: Rotten Belly, Sour Belly
Tribal affiliation: Crow
Significance: Revered for his extraordinary spiritual powers, Arapoosh was believed to be virtually invincible in battle.

Known to whites as Rotten Belly or Sour Belly, Arapoosh apparently earned his name through his disposition: He was surly, ill-tempered, and impatient. He was also known to be extraordinarily brave. The foremost warrior among the River Crow who lived along the Big Horn, Powder, and Wind Rivers in present-day northern Wyoming and southern Montana, Arapoosh led his people against their traditional Indian enemies, the Blackfeet, Sioux, and Northern Cheyennes.

After receiving a guardian spirit vision from the "Man in the Moon," Arapoosh adopted that symbol, painting it on his medicine shield. Before battle, Arapoosh would roll his shield along a line of tipis, using its position as it fell as an omen for the coming battle. If it landed with his insignia facing down, the project was doomed and consequently abandoned; face up, however, augured well for the engagement and the battle was waged.

Believing his tribe's future was threatened by the proposed reservation, and voicing his suspicions of the ultimate intentions of whites, Arapoosh in 1825 refused to sign a treaty of friendship negotiated between the Crow and the United States. Instead he continued to protect the lush Crow territory from other tribes as well as from whites.

At Pierre's Hole, Idaho, Arapoosh met the trader and Hudson's Bay Company representative William Sublette, who was much impressed with his bearing and reputation.

During a war between the Crow and the Blackfeet in 1834, Arapoosh prophesied his own death. Resting his shield on a pile of buffalo chips, he claimed that he would die in the coming battle if his shield rose into the air of its own volition. Purportedly it did just that, rising to a height level with his head. Arapoosh died in the battle.

Mary E. Virginia

FURTHER READING
Hoxie, Frederick E. *Parading Through History: The Making of the Crow Nation in America, 1805-1935.* New York: Cambridge University Press, 1995.

Arpeika

Born: c. 1760; Georgia
Died: 1860; Florida
Also known as: Aripeka, Apayaka Hadjo (Crazy Rattlesnake), Sam Jones
Tribal affiliation: Seminole
Significance: Arpeika was the only Seminole leader successfully to resist removal to the West.

Arpeika probably was born in Georgia and moved into Florida in the late eighteenth century as part of the migration of Creeks that created the Seminole Nation. A *hillis haya*, or medicine man, he became a revered figure among the Seminoles and was an ardent opponent of attempts by the U.S. government to remove the tribe to Indian Territory (modern Oklahoma). During the Second Seminole War (1835-1842), he became a military leader despite his advanced age, leading his warriors in a number of battles while unsuccessfully warning OSCEOLA and other Seminole leaders not to trust the American flags of truce.

While most Seminoles were being removed to the West after the war, Arpeika led his band into the Everglades and eluded U.S. forces. In the Third Seminole War (1855-1858), he again fought to avoid removal, fighting beside Billy BOWLEGS. The only major Seminole leader to survive the Seminole Wars and remain in Florida, Arpeika died near Lake Okeechobee in 1860. He was thought to be one hundred years old.

William C. Lowe

FURTHER READING
Missall, John, and Mary Lou Missall. *The Seminole Wars: America's Longest Indian Conflict.* Foreword by Raymond Arsenault and Gary R. Mormino. Gainesville: University Press of Florida, 2004.

Asah, Spencer

Born: c. 1908; Carnegie, Oklahoma
Died: May 5, 1954; Norman, Oklahoma
Also known as: Lallo (Little Boy)
Tribal affiliation: Kiowa
Significance: Spencer Asah was one of a group of Kiowa artists who initiated the flat style of easel painting, or traditional American Indian painting.

Spencer Asah was the son of a medicine man. He completed six years of schooling at Indian schools in the Anadarko area, including St. Patrick's Mission School. He, along with other Kiowa youths, joined Susan C. Peters's Fine Art Club. She was the U.S. Indian Service field matron stationed in Anadarko who, with the assistance of Willie Lane, gave the students formal instruction in the arts, including drawing, painting, and beadwork. Peters took Asah to the University of Oklahoma to explore the possibility of his receiving further art instruction. Asah, Jack HOKEAH, Stephen MOPOPE, and Monroe TSATOKE began private lessons in painting in the fall of 1926 with Edith Mahier of the art department, using her office as a studio. They publicly performed dances to raise money for expenses. The four boys were joined by James AUCHIAH in the fall of 1927. This group is often known as the Kiowa Five; it is also referred to as the Kiowa Six when Lois Smoky, who came to the university in January of 1927, is included.

The Kiowa flat style that the Kiowa Six created was illustrative watercolor, with little or no background or foreground and with color filling in outlines, depicting masculine activities. Asah depicted recognizable people. The group's work was shown nationwide and at the 1928 First International Art Exhibition in Prague. Asah was hired to paint murals for various Oklahoma buildings during the Depression. Later he farmed. Asah fathered four children.

Cheryl Claassen

FURTHER READING
Berlo, Janet C., and Ruth B. Phillips. *Native North American Art.* New York: Oxford University Press, 1998.

Atotarho

Born: fl. 1500's; present-day New York State
Also known as: Tadodaho (Snaky-Headed, or His House Blocks the Path)
Tribal affiliation: Onondaga
Significance: Atotarho was one of three central figures who established the Iroquois Confederacy.

Atotarho is a historical figure for whom there is almost no historical record. Oral tradition stories hold that Atotarho was a brutal, evil sorcerer. These stories relate that Atotarho had snakes growing out of his head, that he was a cannibal, and that he was soothed by magical birds sent by DEGANAWIDA (the Peacemaker) and HIAWATHA, the other two principal architects of the Iroquois Confederacy. It is probably true that he was a cannibal.

Atotarho was bitterly opposed to the formation of the confederacy. He insisted that certain conditions be met before the Onondagas would join. The Onondagas were to have fourteen chiefs on the council, the other nations only ten. It was also a condition that Atotarho be the ranking chief on the council—only he would have the right to summon the

European depiction of the sachem Atotarho (right), one of the founders of the Iroquois Confederacy in the sixteenth century. (Library of Congress)

other nations. In addition, he demanded that no act of the council would be valid unless ratified by Onondagas.

The Onondagas were given the role of central fire-keepers of the confederacy, and to this day they retain not only that role but also the role of keepers of the wampum belt, which records and preserves the laws of the confederacy.

Glenn J. Schiffman

FURTHER READING

Wilson, Edmund. *Apologies to the Iroquois.* New York: Farrar, Straus, Cudahy, 1960.

Auchiah, James

Born: 1906; Medicine Park, Oklahoma Territory
Died: December 28, 1974; Carnegie, Oklahoma
Tribal affiliation: Kiowa
Significance: James Auchiah was one of the Kiowa artists who created the Oklahoma style of Native American painting in the early to mid-twentieth century.

James Auchiah was a Kiowa and a grandson of Chief SATANTA. He was an authority on Kiowa history and culture and also a leader of the Native American Church. He took noncredit art classes with the Kiowa Five group at the University of Oklahoma in 1927.

In 1930, Auchiah won an award at the Southwest States Indian Art Show in Santa Fe, New Mexico, which led to commissions to paint murals in a number of public buildings, including the Fort Sill Indian School, Muskogee Federal Building, Northeastern State University (Oklahoma), and St. Patrick's Mission School. The most important of his murals was a commission in Washington, D.C., for the Department of the Interior, in which the Bureau of Indian Affairs is located. This mural, which is 8 feet high and 50 feet long, represents the theme of the Harvest Dance.

Auchiah's work is included in public and private collections, including the National Museum of the American Indian (Smithsonian), University of Oklahoma Museum of Art, and the Castillo de San Marcos National Monument (Florida). He served in the U.S. Coast Guard during World War II and later worked for the U.S. Army Artillery and Missile Center Museum, Fort Sill, Oklahoma.

Ronald J. Duncan

FURTHER READING
Berlo, Janet C., and Ruth B. Phillips. *Native North American Art.* New
  York: Oxford University Press, 1998.

Awa Tsireh

Born: February 1, 1898; San Ildefonso Pueblo, New Mexico
Died: March 12, 1955; San Ildefonso Pueblo, New Mexico
Also known as: Alfonso Roybal
Tribal affiliation: San Ildefonso Pueblo
Significance: Alfonso Roybal, who signed his paintings Awa Tsireh, gained
  widespread recognition as a painter during the 1920's and 1930's; his
  paintings are included in many major museum collections.

As a child in San Ildefonso Pueblo, Awa Tsireh sometimes painted pottery made by his mother, Alfonsita Martínez. Even before attending San
Ildefonso Day School, where he was given drawing materials, Tsireh
made sketches of animals and ceremonial dances. After completing day
school, he began painting watercolors with his uncle, Crescencio MAR-
TÍNEZ, who, in 1917, was commissioned by anthropologist Edgar Hewett
to paint a series of depictions of ceremonies held at San Ildefonso.

Tsireh's meticulously precise but sometimes whimsical paintings attracted the attention of Hewett, who hired him to paint at the Museum of
New Mexico; in 1920, Tsireh's work was included in exhibitions of Indian
art at the Society of Independent Artists in New York and at the Arts Club
of Chicago. In 1925, his paintings were exhibited in a one-man show at
the Newberry Library in Chicago. In 1931, he won first prize at the opening of the Exposition of Indian Tribal Arts in New York, a show that went
on to tour major cities in the United States and Europe.

Tsireh traveled frequently but made San Ildefonso his home for life.
Around the time of his death, he was still painting and continued to be
among the most popular of Pueblo painters.

Molly H. Mullin

Bad Heart Bull, Amos

Born: c. 1869; present-day Wyoming
Died: 1913; place unknown
Also known as: Tatanka Cante Sica (Bad Heart Buffalo), Eagle Lance
Tribal affiliation: Ite Sica band of Oglala Lakota (Sioux)

Significance: Amos Bad Heart Bull kept an extensive pictographic history of the Oglala Lakota that spanned the second half of the nineteenth century and the beginning of the twentieth century.

Amos Bad Heart Bull was born into a noted Oglala family. His father,
also called Bad Heart Bull, was a band historian who kept a historic record in pictographic form. His uncles, He Dog and SHORT BULL, and
his cousin CRAZY HORSE were noted warriors active in opposing U.S. encroachments on Lakota lands. Born around 1869, during the final years
of the traditional Lakota life, Amos Bad Heart Bull was too young to
take part in the Sioux Wars (1864-1876) but was present at many of the
battles, particularly Little Bighorn. His father and older male relatives
were prominent warriors in these battles.

From 1890 to 1891, Amos Bad Heart Bull served with his uncle Short
Bull as a scout for the U.S. Army at Fort Robinson, Nebraska. During
this time he purchased a ledger book from a clothing store owner in
Crawford, Nebraska, and began to record the recent history of the
Oglala Lakota in the traditional Plains art genre of pictography. Because his father was dead, Bad Heart Bull's primary informants for this
work were his uncles Short Bull and He Dog. Bad Heart Bull's drawings
convey an extensive narrative history of Oglala social and political history, religious ritual and ceremony, methods of warfare, and battles.
This extensive record of more than four hundred drawings is unique in
its scope and in its intent to be a complete historic record. Artistically,
Bad Heart Bull provided greater action, realism, and attention to detail
than previous artists of this genre.

Amos Bad Heart Bull died in 1913, and his manuscript passed to his
sister Dollie Pretty Cloud. In 1926, a graduate student at the University
of Nebraska, Helen Blish, studied and photographed the manuscript in
A Pictographic History of the Oglala Sioux. This photographic record is all
that remains. The original ledger was buried with Dollie Pretty Cloud in
1947 at her request.

Carole A. Barrett

Banks, Dennis

Born: April 12, 1937; Leech Lake Reservation, Minnesota
Tribal affiliation: Ojibwa (Chippewa)
Significance: One of the founders and leaders of the American Indian
   Movement (AIM), Dennis Banks has drawn attention to the plight of
   contemporary Indians.

Dennis Banks, born on the Leech Lake reservation in northern Minnesota, was one of the founders of the American Indian Movement (AIM) in 1968. During the summer of 1972, Banks and about fifty other native activists met in Denver to plan a Trail of Broken Treaties caravan. Their hope was to marshal thousands of protesters across the nation to march on Washington, D.C., dramatizing the issue of American Indian self-determination. Banks was also a principal leader of AIM in 1973 during the occupation of the hamlet Wounded Knee on the Pine Ridge Sioux Reservation.

Banks eluded capture during a Federal Bureau of Investigation (FBI) dragnet following the deaths of two agents at Pine Ridge in 1975. He went underground before receiving amnesty from Edmund G. Brown, Jr., governor of California. Banks earned an associate of arts degree at the University of California's Davis campus and, during the late 1970's, helped to found and direct Deganawida-Quetzacóatl University, a native-controlled college.

After Brown's term as governor ended, Banks was sheltered in 1984 by the Onondagas on their reservation near Nedrow, New York. In 1984, he surrendered to face charges stemming from the 1970's in South Dakota. He served eighteen months in prison, after which he worked as a drug and alcohol counselor on the Pine Ridge Reservation. Banks remained active in Native American politics during the 1990's, although he was not as often in the national spotlight. He also had acting roles in several films, including *War Party, The Last of the Mohicans,* and *Thunderheart* (1992).

In 1996, Banks agreed to lead the "Bring Peltier Home" Campaign, which fought for clemency for Leonard PEL-TIER. Banks continued his po-

Dennis Banks chats with students on the Oxford campus of the University of Mississippi in 1999.
(AP/Wide World Photos)

litical activism into the twenty-first century by remaining involved in
AIM activities, lecturing around the world, and providing alcohol and
drug counseling. He also wrote with Richard Erdoes, *Ojibwa Warrior:
Dennis Banks and the Rise of the American Indian Movement* (2004).

Bruce E. Johansen

FURTHER READING

Banks, Dennis, with Richard Erdoes. *Ojibwa Warrior: Dennis Banks and
the Rise of the American Indian Movement.* Norman: University of Oklahoma Press, 2004.
Smith, Paul Chaat, and Robert Allen Warrior. *Like a Hurricane: The Indian Movement from Alcatraz to Wounded Knee.* New York: New Press,
1996.

Barboncito

Born: c. 1820; Canyon de Chelly, present-day Arizona
Died: March 16, 1871; Canyon de Chelly, present-day Arizona
Also known as: Barbon, Bislahani (The Orator), Hastín Daagii (Man
with Whiskers), Hozhooji Naata (Blessing Speaker)
Tribal affiliation: Navajo
Significance: Barboncito was a major war chief during the 1863-1866
Navajo War, and he signed the 1868 treaty establishing the Navajo
Reservation.

At the age of twenty-six, Barboncito agreed to terms of friendship with
whites when he signed a treaty with the American representative to the
New Mexico territory during the Mexican War. Barboncito came to the
attention of American army officers when, in April of 1860, he joined
forces with MANUELITO on the attack of Fort Defiance. After the skirmish, Barboncito and his brother DELGADITO tried to work for peace.
During the campaign for "resettlement" to Bosque Redondo, in eastern
New Mexico, however, the brothers defiantly rejoined Manuelito.

In 1864, Barboncito was captured and forced to resettle at the
Bosque. Unbearable living conditions forced him and five hundred followers to escape. In November of 1866, he surrendered for the second
time. In 1868, while signing the treaty establishing the Navajo Reservation, Barboncito eloquently articulated the desires of his people when
he said, "We do not want to go to the right or left, but straight back to
our country."

Moises Roizen

FURTHER READING

Iverson, Peter. *Dine: A History of the Navajos.* Albuquerque: University of New Mexico Press, 2002.

Beach, Adam

Born: November 11, 1972; Ashern, Manitoba, Canada
Tribal affiliation: Saulteaux
Significance: During the 1990's, Adam Beach achieved prominence as a film actor without having to compromise his Native American heritage.

Adam Beach was reared on the Dog Creek Indian Reserve. Both his parents died in 1981, when he was eight years old. First, his mother—who was carrying another child—was killed by a drunk driver; two months later, his alcoholic father drowned in a boating accident. Afterward, Beach and his two brothers went to live with an aunt and uncle in Winnipeg. It was not an easy childhood for him, and when he was fourteen, another aunt and uncle became the guardians of him and his brothers. Beach took out some of the anger he felt as a teenager by joining a gang.

At the age of sixteen, Beach enrolled in a drama class at Gordon Bell High School. He found an outlet for his emotions in acting, which served as a kind of symbolic "sweat lodge" for him. He eventually was able to let go of his bitterness and find peace. Meanwhile, he continued to take advantage of acting opportunities by performing in local theater productions. After being offered a lead role at the Manitoba Theatre for Young People, Beach decided to drop out of school. At the age of eighteen, he earned a

Adam Beach at a Maxim *magazine party in New York in 2003.* (AP/Wide World Photos)

chance to play a small role in the television miniseries *Lost in Barrens*.

By the early 1990's, Beach was making guest appearances, such American television series as *Walker, Texas Ranger, Touched by an Angel*, and *Lonesome Dove*. Disney cast him as the sixteenth-seventeenth century New England Indian SQUANTO in the 1994 family film *Squanto: A Warrior's Tale*. In 1995, First Americans in the Arts recognized Beach's outstanding performance in the television movie *My Indian Summer* by giving him their best-actor award. By the late 1990's, Beach was winning recognition in the entertainment industry as a rising star.

Beach gained even more acclaim with his lead role in the 1998 film *Smoke Signals*—the first film in which the writing, production, direction, and acting were done entirely by Native Americans. In that poignant coming-of-age story, Beach played a bitter young Coeur d'Alene man who goes from Idaho to Arizona to pick up the ashes of the father who abandoned his family, accompanied by another young Indian who helps him come to terms with his father's memory. The film touched an international audience and won both the Audience Award and the Filmmaker's Trophy Award at the Sundance Film Festival.

After *Smoke Signals*, Beach was offered roles in such films as *Mystery, Alaska* (1999), *Joe Dirt* (2001), and *Windtalkers* (2002). For *Windtalkers*— a big-budget film set in the Pacific theater of World War II—Beach learned to speak Navajo to play the part of a Navajo codetalker. In 2002 and 2003, he starred in the Public Broadcasting System's (PBS) adaptations of the Tony Hillerman's mysteries *Skinwalkers, Coyote Waits*, and *A Thief in Time*.

Jeffry Jensen

Bear Hunter

Born: c. 1830; present-day Utah
Died: January 27, 1863; near present-day Preston, Idaho
Also known as: Wairasuap, Bear Spirit
Tribal affiliation: Shoshone
Significance: War chief Bear Hunter was killed during the Bear River Campaign, which secured the Great Basin for white expansion.

Located along the Bear River in southeastern Idaho, Bear Hunter's village was near the Great Salt Lake, which had become the focal point for Mormon expansion. The village was crossed by the Central Overland Mail Route and the Pony Express, each bearing stagecoaches carrying mail to California. Although some Shoshone leaders, including

WASHAKIE of the Wind River Shoshone and TENDOY of the Lemhi Shoshone, were friendly toward whites, Bear Hunter led his people in active
resistance to white encroachment into the Great Basin.

Largely unimpeded by sparsely stationed federal troops during the
early years of the Civil War, on several occasions Shoshone war parties
attacked mail carriers and emigrants. In order to protect the telegraph
lines and mail coaches, their only communication with the east, the
Third California Infantry under Patrick E. Connor and a portion of the
Second California Cavalry, a volunteer force of more than one hundred
troops, traveled to Utah to reinforce federal troops at several forts.

In January, 1863, Connor led more than three hundred men 140
miles through deep snow from Fort Douglas north to Bear Hunter's village. Although Bear Hunter's people had fortified their village with bar-
ricades of rock, they were unable to defend themselves against Connor's superior manpower and arms. After four hours of relentless
shelling, 224 Indians including Bear Hunter were killed and more than
150 women and children were taken captive. Following the Bear River
Campaign, Indians were forced to cede most of their lands in the Great
Basin.

Mary E. Virginia

Bear's Heart, James

Born: 1851
Died: January 25, 1882; Darlington, Indian Territory (now in Okla-
    homa)
Also known as: Nock-ko-ist
Tribal affiliation: Cheyenne
Significance: A prolific artist, James Bear's Heart combined Indian sym-
    bolism with formal Western techniques.

Young James Bear's Heart was a noted warrior who fought against the
Utes, Texans, Mexicans, and U.S. Rangers. During the Red River War of
1875, he was accused of complicity in the murder of white settlers in Indian Territory and sent to the Fort Marion military prison in St. Augustine, Florida. He was confined for three years as a prisoner of war. While
imprisoned, he participated in an educational and vocational program
designed by U.S. Army Lieutenant Richard Henry Pratt. For their artistic pursuits, AMERICAN HORSE and fellow warriors Cohoe, HOWLING
WOLF, and Paul ZOTOM became known as the Florida Boys. Bear's Heart
discovered a substantial market for his artwork.

After release from prison in 1878, Bear's Heart attended Virginia's Hampton Institute, where he converted to Christianity and adopted the name James. In 1881, Bear's Heart returned to Indian Territory, where he practiced carpentry, another skill learned under Pratt's tutelage while imprisoned. Bear's Heart died of tuberculosis in 1882.

Mary E. Virginia

Bedard, Irene

Born: July 22, 1967; Anchorage, Alaska
Also known as: Goodiarook
Tribal affiliation: Inupiat/Cree
Significance: After winning fame as the voice of Pocahontas in Disney's 1995 animated film about the Powhatan princess, the multitalented Irene Bedard went on to become one of the most successful female Native American actors in film history. By 2004, she had appeared in two dozen films and a number of television programs.

Irene Bedard has an ethnic heritage almost as diverse as the Native American characters whom she has played on screen. Born in Alaska, she is the oldest of four children of an Inupiat Eskimo mother and a father who was half Cree and half French Canadian. Her father worked for the Alaskan state government in the field of Native American land rights, and Bedard grew up in a family that took pride in its cultural heritage and made her acutely aware of Native American issues. While she was still a child, her family moved to the state of Washington, where her parents went into business. They bought and operated a motel, which they later traded for an apartment building, which, in turn, they later traded for a roller-skating rink. Bedard helped out with the family business, performing such chores as cleaning and painting. Meanwhile, she developed an interest in storytelling and acting and often organized and performed in small-scale dramas.

Bedard's interest in acting led her to Philadelphia, where she earned a bachelor's degree at the University of the Arts. Afterward, she went to New York City and helped to found an ensemble theater for Native American actors. Her first major acting job was the title role in the 1994 cable-television film *Lakota Woman: Siege at Wounded Knee,* a story adapted from the autobiography of Mary Crow Dog. Bedard's portrayal of Crow Dog in that film earned her a Golden Globe nomination (best actress in a television movie or miniseries) and caught the attention of the Disney Company, which cast her in the historical drama *Squanto: A Warrior's Tale*

*Irene Bedard at the Thunder in the Desert powwow
in Tucson, Arizona, in 2004.* (AP/Wide World Photos)

(1994), which starred Adam
BEACH as the famous colonial-
era New England Indian.

In 1995, Bedard's career
took another major step forward when Disney cast her as
the voice of another colonial-
era American Indian icon, the
Powhatan princess POCAHON-
TAS, in its animated film of the
same title. In addition to providing Pocahontas's voice,
Bedard served as the artists'
model for the film's animated
character. While critics could
justly charge that the historical
Pocahontas never looked re-
motely like the willowy beauty
who appeared in the Disney
film, Bedard herself looked remarkably like her cartoon
counterpart. The editors of
People magazine concurred, as
they named her one of the
fifty most beautiful people in
the world in 1995. In 1998, Bedard reprised her voice role in Disney's
Pocahontas II: Journey to a New World. She later also supplied the voices of
completely fictional Native American characters in such animated television series as *The Real Adventures of Jonny Quest* (1996) and *Starship
Troopers* (2000-2001).

An outspoken advocate of supporting Native American rights and
correcting popular misconceptions about Indians, Bedard has portrayed both Native American and nonnative characters in her many
film, television, and stage roles. Her most important films, however,
have been about Indians, and she has portrayed women from a wide variety of Native American cultures, including another Lakota woman in
Crazy Horse (1996), a Navajo in *Navajo Blues* (1996), and a Mohawk in
Song of Hiawatha (1997).

Bedard had only a supporting role in *Smoke Signals* (1998), but it was
one of her more important films, as it was the first feature film to be an
entirely Native American production, and it broke away from the stereo-

typed depictions of Indians typical of past Hollywood films. In *Naturally Native* (1998), another Native American-produced film, Bedard played one of three sisters of Indian ancestry who had been adopted and raised by white families. As adults, the sisters attempt to start a business together, running a cosmetics company, "Naturally Native," that caters to Native Americans.

After achieving stardom, Bedard continued to donate her time to doing readings for children. A singer and dancer, as well as an actor, she has performed and recorded with her musician husband, Denny Wilson (Deni), whom she married in 1993. She is also one of the founders of Guardians of Sacred Lands, an organization dedicated to cleaning up coastal rivers in Southern California.

R. Kent Rasmussen

FURTHER READING

Graber, Janna. "Irene Bedard." *Cowboys & Indians* 6, no. 1 (March, 1998).

Schneider, Wolf. "Irene Bedard: At Home in Ojai with the Most Successful Native American Actress Working Today." *Cowboys & Indians* (November, 1999).

Bellecourt, Clyde H.

Born: May 8, 1936; White Earth Reservation, Minnesota
Also known as: Nee-gon-we-way-we-dun
Tribal affiliation: Ojibwa (Chippewa)
Significance: Long an activist for the civil and spiritual rights of Native Americans, Clyde Bellecourt is a founder and director of the American Indian Movement (AIM) and has played major roles in many other organizations.

Clyde H. Bellecourt became inspired to organize a movement for spiritual rights for Native Americans while serving time in Stillwater Prison, Minnesota. Along with another young prisoner, a medicine man named Edward Benton Banai, he started a class on American Indian culture in which nearly fifteen Indian prisoners participated.

After getting out of prison, Bellecourt was part of an Indian group called the United Indians of All Tribes that seized Alcatraz Island in San Francisco Bay in late 1969. The group seized the former federal prison island, claiming it as unused federal land, in the name of Native Nations. The first Indian radio broadcasts—Radio Free Alcatraz—were heard in the San Francisco Bay Area. Bellecourt also helped to establish the Legal Rights Center to give Indian people legal representation.

Concerned about the high rate of suicide attempts among Indian children, he helped found the Heart of the Earth Survival School in Minneapolis in 1972. The Minnesota city's first culturally based alternative school, the kindergarten-through-twelfth-grade school was designed particularly to address the high drop-out rate among American Indian students. It offered a student-centered, culturally correct curriculum operating under parental control.

Clyde Bellecourt speaks during a rally at the University of North Dakota to protest the university's continued use of the nickname "Fighting Sioux." (AP/Wide World Photos)

In 1972, Bellecourt helped to lead the Trail of Broken Treaties caravan that drew members of Indian tribes throughout the United States to Washington, D.C. There, caravan participants converged on the Bureau of Indian Affairs building, which they occupied for six days. The Nixon administration agreed to consider a list of twenty Indian demands, including examination of many broken treaties and reform of the government on the Pine Ridge Reservation in the Dakotas. Although most of the demands were never met, during that same year, Congress passed the American Indian Freedom Act (AIF), which restored religious freedom to Indian people.

In 1973, Bellecourt and other AIM leaders, including his brother Vernon BELLECOURT, Russell MEANS, Dennis BANKS, and Eddie Benton Banai, led a violent seventy-one-day standoff with federal authorities at the village of Wounded Knee in Pine Ridge Reservation, where the U.S. Cavalry had killed more than 250 Lakota people in 1890. The confrontation arose from Indian demands for a review of the broken treaties between the tribes and the federal government. The AIM takeover of Wounded Knee had great symbolic value that drew attention to the social, legal, and economic conditions of modern Indians.

In 1978, Bellecourt helped lead the Longest Walk, from San Francisco Bay to Washington, D.C., to oppose anti-Indian legislation calling for the abrogation of treaties. The marchers set up a tipi on the White House grounds, and the proposed legislation was defeated.

Bellecourt played an important part in the 1974 creation of the International Indian Treaty Council (IITC), which represents Indian peoples throughout the Western Hemisphere. In 1977, the United Nations formally recognized the council as a nongovernmental organization that was qualified to participate in the U.N. Commission on Human Rights. Bellecourt also founded and has served as chairman of the board of the American Indian Opportunities and Industrialization Center (OIC), an innovative job program that has helped to moved more than fifteen thousand people from welfare to full-time employment.

In 1989, Bellecourt helped found the Peacemaker Center for Indian Youth in Minnesota as well as the AIM Patrol, which addresses issues of police brutality and develops collaborative partnerships that create and maintain communities free from violence. In 1992, Bellecourt helped establish the National Coalition on Racism in Sports and the Media (NCRSM) to educate Americans about misused Indian images and names in team names, logos, symbols, and mascots in professional and collegiate sports. The organization charges that such caricatures often desecrate native spirituality by using feathers, paint, dances, and music for entertainment and in inappropriate contexts.

Joanna Yin

FURTHER READING

Deloria, Vine, Jr. *Behind the Trail of Broken Treaties.* Austin: University of Texas Press, 1991.

Bellecourt, Vernon

Born: October 17, 1931; White Earth Reservation, Minnesota
Tribal affiliation: Ojibwa (Chippewa)
Significance: During the last decades of the twentieth century, Vernon
Bellecourt emerged as a prominent Indian rights activist and a
leader of the American Indian Movement.

Born on the White Earth Reservation in Minnesota, Vernon Bellecourt
belongs to the Crane clan of the Anishinabe-Ojibwa nation. He comes
from a family of twelve children that includes his equally renowned
younger brother, Clyde H. BELLECOURT. Like many marginalized Indian youths who grew up experiencing poverty, racism, and a culturally
irrelevant white educational system, the Bellecourt brothers spent some
time in prison. Reading, reflection, and sharing thoughts with fellow Indian inmates led Clyde to embrace traditional spiritual and cultural renewal as a means of revitalization for Native Americans suffering from,
despair, alcoholism, and alienation from their heritage and its values.
Soon, Vernon also took up this cause.

One result of a cultural awakening among urban Indians who left reservations to seek employment was the creation during the late 1960's of
the American Indian Movement (AIM) in the Minneapolis/St. Paul
area. Vernon was a close collaborator with his brother and Dennis
BANKS, another Ojibwa activist, in building AIM to combat police ha-
rassment, to defend Indian rights, and to foster cultural renewal. He
and other AIM members traveled to reservations in the Minnesota region to consult with traditional elders and spiritual leaders who taught
them the history, traditions, and ceremonies of their suppressed heritage.

During the late 1960's and early 1970's, Bellecourt was at the center
of nearly all the actions involving AIM that drew national attention to
Native American rights issues. He assisted in drafting the twenty-point
manifesto of the Trail of Broken Treaties caravan to Washington, D.C.,
in 1972 and was an influential figure during the ensuing takeover of the
Bureau of Indian Affairs office. During the seventy-two-day armed
standoff between AIM supporters and federal forces at Wounded Knee,
South Dakota, in early 1973, Bellecourt supported the occupation by
departing to serve as a spokesperson, and raise money for supplies in
other parts of the country. His attempt to bring food and medical supplies into the besieged site, contributed to a federal indictment against
him.

From that time into the early twenty-first century, Bellecourt was a tireless crusader for the rights of indigenous peoples on both the national and international scene. In 1974, he helped organize the first International Indian Treaty Council (IITC). During the 1980's, he was arrested for throwing blood on the Guatemalan embassy to protest the Guatemalan government's killing of 100,000 Maya Indians. Bellecourt later focused on the issue of using Indian stereotypes as logos and team mascots in sports and led high-profile protests at sporting events. He became president

Vernon Bellecourt, national director of the American Indian Movement (AIM), speaks at a news conference in 1973. (AP/Wide World Photos)

of the National Coalition on Racism and Sports in the Media, and special representative of the International Indian Treaty Council.

Bellecourt's various honors include the city of Phoenix's Martin Luther King, Jr., Human Rights Award for 1993. In January of 2000, the St. Paul *Pioneer Press* listed Bellecourt and his brother Clyde among its "famous Minnesotan activists of the twentieth century."

David A. Crain

Bent, George

Born: July 7, 1843; near Bent's Old Fort, Colorado
Died: May 19, 1918; Colony, Oklahoma
Also known as: Ho-my-ike, Beaver
Tribal affiliation: Southern Cheyenne
Significance: A warrior, hunter, diplomat, interpreter, and source for the nation's first generation of cultural anthropologists of Native Americans, George Bent participated in some of the nineteenth century's most important events and lived to tell of them well into the twentieth century.

George Bent was the son of William Bent—one of the most famous white traders of the day—and his Southern Cheyenne wife, Owl Woman. Through the first ten years of his life, he moved with his family between the trading posts built by his father along the Arkansas River, including the impressive adobe structure dubbed Bent's Old Fort. His childhood was divided almost equally between time among the Cheyenne and time among white people, and he grew up learning the language and ways of his mother's people. However, around the time he reached the age of eleven, his preference for Cheyenne customs was alarming his father, who moved his family to Missouri to provide educational and cultural opportunities that he regarded as more fitting for his children.

After the Civil War began in early 1861, Bent witnessed a clumsy Union effort to suppress a mild rebel uprising in St. Louis. During the spring, he enlisted in the Confederate Army. Thanks to the equestrian skills he had learned as a Cheyenne, he was assigned to a cavalry unit in the western theater. The following year, he was captured by Union troops but was spared the degradations of being sent to a prisoner-of-war camp when a family friend serving in the Union Army heard of his detainment and arranged for his quick release.

Grateful for the chance to escape from military service unscathed, Bent spent the next two years traveling with his father between St. Louis and Bent's Old Fort. As he learned his father's trading business, he also reconnected with the Cheyenne people whom he had once considered his family. Deeply affected by the lure of his mother's people, he finally left his father's side in order to live among the Cheyenne along the Arkansas River. Only days after joining the Sand Creek Cheyenne community in late November, 1864, Bent witnessed Colonel John Chivington's massacre of the federally protected community. He was wounded in the hip but managed to escape with his life—and with stories that he would tell to eager listeners in later years.

Over the next twelve months, Bent rode with Cheyenne, Lakota, and Arapaho warriors avenging the deaths of those slaughtered at Sand Creek. However, this campaign merely drew more government troops after them. After the conclusion of the Civil War, Bent and his brethren soon realized they could no longer compete with the hordes of white settlers—and Army regulars—streaming west. Convinced that war would lead to the destruction of the Southern Cheyenne, Bent participated in peace conferences between the U.S. government and Indian tribes, serving both as an interpreter and as a diplomatic liaison between the two negotiating parties. He played a major role in persuading many Indian leaders to comply with federally initiated treaties.

Bent's success in persuading leaders of the Dog Men to sign the 1868

Medicine Lodge Treaty, in which they ceded lands they had used for generations, so impressed U.S. officials that the government engaged Bent to serve as a Cheyenne interpreter for their agents. At the age of twenty-six, he became one of the most highly respected leaders in the American Southwest and was one of only a handful of people enjoying the admiration of both white and Indian communities. However, this success came at a price.

Bent soon began to regret his role in isolating the Cheyenne people on reservations. His influence as a federal interpreter and Cheyenne advisor gradually dissipated as agreements between the Southern Cheyenne and the federal government quickly unraveled. Bent initially persuaded other Cheyenne to embrace President Ulysses S. Grant's new policies of assimilation through Christianization and farming but later looked on in horror as governmental decrees pushed the Southern Cheyenne onto arid reservations and away from the hunting grounds they craved. As the Cheyenne increasingly rejected the conditions forced on them, Bent's reputation among both Indians and government officials declined.

The burdens of Bent's trying to live in two opposing worlds took their toll on him personally. He struggled to support the eight children he fathered with his three wives—Magpie (niece of BLACK KETTLE), Kiowa, and Standing Out Woman. His reputation within the U.S. government was tainted by his blinding alcoholic binges, which ultimately cost him his job, and his naïve belief that the Southern Cheyenne could be spared annihilation through a policy of appeasement damned him in the eyes of his Indian peers. By 1889, he was in disgrace, fired from his government position and ostracized by his Cheyenne friends and many of his own family members. Through the last thirty years of his life, he scratched out a living on a humble farm in Colony, Oklahoma, where he worked as a school administrator, translator, and interpreter, and tried to repair his damaged reputation while laboring to sustain the legacy of the people he loved best.

In the last endeavor, at least, Bent seems to have succeeded, and with remarkable prowess. Fearing a total loss of cultural identity among his own people, he energetically participated in a series of studies conducted by eastern anthropologists after 1890. He acted as an eyewitness recorder, gave personal interviews, persuaded friends to recall stories and moments from their shared experiences, and conducted long correspondences with a group of scholars, whom he impressed as a person of enormous intelligence and vast knowledge—and as one who had lived the very life they were trying to capture in print. Bent had seen much and had an innate ability to remember specific details of events that had happened decades earlier. The stories he told of the days of Bent's Old Fort, of the age of the clans in Cheyenne culture before Sand Creek, and of the Cheyenne movements along the Arkansas river directly shaped the impressions and analyses of the first modern scholars of Native American culture. Using Bent as their main source of information, George Hyde and George Grinnell wrote books and articles on Cheyenne history and culture (including Bent's own account of the Sand Creek Massacre), with the latter's classic, *The Cheyenne Indians*, coming largely on the heels of almost two decades of interviews and epistolary communications with him. In many ways, modern thinking about the Southern Cheyenne, their history, and their ritual traditions has come down by way of the memories and anecdotes of George Bent, whose life served as the template for much of what is now known about his people.

George R. Bent III

FURTHER READING

Hoebel, E. Adamson. *The Cheyennes: Indians of the Great Plains*. New York: Holt, Rinehart and Winston, 1978.

Hoig, Stan. *The Peace Chiefs of the Cheyennes*. Norman: University of Oklahoma Press, 1980.

_____. *The Sand Creek Massacre*. Norman: University of Oklahoma Press, 1961.

Betzinez, Jason

Born: 1860; Monticello, Mexico
Died: 1960; place unknown
Also known as: Nah-dethy (Going-to-Run)
Tribal affiliation: Mimbres (Warm Springs) Apache
Significance: A tireless advocate for the rights and welfare of his Apache people, Jason Betzinez promoted their interests with government officials.

Jason Betzinez's extended family lived in the region that became the Warm Springs Reservation in New Mexico, he himself was born in Monticello, Mexico, while his mother and father were visiting friends in that community. Two years later, his sister Ellen was also born in Monticello during a family visit there. Betzinez's father, Tudeevia (later called Nonithian), was a member of the Mimbres Apache tribe, and his mother, Nah-thle-tla, was a Chiricahua Apache.

From Betzinez's boyhood until 1886, he lived mostly on the San Carlos and Warm Springs Reservations. In 1882, his family left the San Carlos Reservation under GERONIMO's leadership. Betzinez was still too young to fight at that point. Two years later, the family returned to the reservation. When Geronimo fled the reservation a second time in 1885, Betzinez and his family chose to remain behind rather than accompany their family leader. Nevertheless, after Geronimo surrendered to General George Crook in 1886, all the Chiricahua Apaches—including Betzinez's family—were sent to Fort Marion in St. Augustine, Florida.

In 1886, Captain Richard Pratt included Betzinez among a small group of young Apaches whom he sent from Florida to Carlisle Indian Industrial Boarding School in Pennsylvania. During his years at Carlisle, Betzinez attended academic classes in the mornings and trained in blacksmithing during the afternoons.

At the beginning of his ninth year at Carlisle, when Betzinez was thirty-six years old, he asked Pratt for permission to quit school so he could look for employment. Pratt wanted Betzinez to remain at Carlisle one more year so he could graduate but agreed to allow him to leave. In 1897, Betzinez took a job with the Pennsylvania Steel Mill Company in Steelton, where he earned one dollar for each eighteen-hour workday. However, he worked so hard work that his wages soon jumped to forty-five cents an hour. In his spare time, Betzinez played baseball and was a fullback on a local football team.

By this time, Betzinez had converted to Christianity and was selected as a delegate to the national convention of the Christian Endeavor Society in Washington, D.C. While he was there, he visited the federal government's commissioner of Indian affairs to speak on behalf of Apache prisoners of war.

After only one year working at the steel mill, Betzinez was diagnosed with incipient tuberculosis. Friends urged him to move to the drier climate near Fort Sill, in what later became Oklahoma, where many Apache prisoners of war—including his mother and sister—were being held. Heeding Pratt's advice, he applied for and was hired as a blacksmith at the nearby Darlington Agency. Betzinez wanted to be even closer to his family and other Apache prisoners, so eighteen months later he applied for the position of blacksmith at Fort Sill. However, in order to get that position, he had to give up his freedom and return to the status of prisoner of war. In 1900 Betzinez agreed to these terms.

Two years later the Apaches at Fort Sill entered into negotiations with the government over their possible resettlement on the Mescalero Reservation in New Mexico. However, some of the Apaches, including Betzinez, wished to stay in Oklahoma on lands that the Kiowas and Comanches had donated for this purpose. Eventually, the commissioner of Indian Affairs called Betzinez to Washington. D.C., to help plead the case for those who preferred to remain near Fort Sill, and Betzinez's efforts in that endeavor were successful.

In 1914, Betzinez moved into his own home. Five years later, he married Anna Heersma, a missionary who had worked among the Apaches since 1907. Toward the end of his life, Betzinez wrote an autobiography, *I Fought with Geronimo*, that was published in 1959, a year before he died at the age of one hundred years.

Teresa Neva Tate

FURTHER READING
Betzinez, Jason, with Wilbur Sturtevant Nye. *I Fought with Geronimo*. Reprint. Lincoln: University of Nebraska Press, 1987.

Big Bear

Born: 1825; near Fort Carlton in present-day Saskatchewan, Canada
Died: 1888; near Fort Pitt in present-day Saskatchewan, Canada
Also known as: Mistahimaskwa
Tribal affiliation: Cree
Significance: Big Bear was a war chief during the Second Riel Rebellion of 1885.

At a council of two thousand Indians in 1876, Big Bear denounced the newly formed Canadian government for dishonesty and urged armed resistance. He joined Louis RIEL, Jr., leader of the Métis uprisings against white encroachment. The Métis were people of mixed French, Scottish, and Indian ancestry whose land and trade rights had been guaranteed after the First Riel Rebellion. Unremitting white encroachment, particularly during the construction of the Canadian Pacific Railway, precipitated a second rebellion.

Big Bear's warriors raided a settlement at Frog Lake on April 2, 1885. Although Big Bear attempted to prohibit violence, there were several white mortalities, provoking retaliation by Canadian Mounties. On May 28, Big Bear's group was attacked near Fort Pitt, escaped, and was relentlessly pursued northward, where they were attacked at Lake Loon. On June 18, Big Bear released several white prisoners, who bore his request for mercy to the commander at Fort Pitt. He surrendered on July 2 and was sentenced to three years' imprisonment. He died while imprisoned.

Mary E. Virginia

FURTHER READING
Flanagan, Thomas. *Riel and the Rebellion: 1885 Reconsidered.* 2d ed. Buffalo: University of Toronto Press, 2000.

Big Bow

Born: c. 1830; Elk Creek, Indian Territory (now in Oklahoma)
Died: c. 1900; place unknown
Also known as: Zipkoheta
Tribal affiliation: Kiowa
Significance: During the Central Plains Indian wars, Big Bow was the most militant Kiowa chief and the last to surrender to reservation settlement.

Big Bow's parentage and heritage are unknown. He gained an early reputation as one of the most hostile and violent Indian war chiefs after killing and scalping countless whites. With BIG TREE, SATANTA, Satank, and LONE WOLF, he fought settlers in Texas, Kansas, and Oklahoma.

Big Bow refused to honor the Medicine Lodge Treaty (1867), which assigned Indians to two reservations in southern Kansas and which was endorsed by leaders of the Arapaho, Kiowa, Comanche, and Kiowa-Apache (Apache of Oklahoma). Instead, he continued attacking settlers and battling U.S. troops. After an aggressive U.S. Army campaign to subdue the Kiowa in 1870-1871, Big Bow was the last major war chief to capitulate. In 1874, he joined the Comanches in the Red River War. Later in 1874, at the urging of the peace leader, Kicking Bull, he moved his people to the reservation. Subsequently he was granted amnesty and served as an army Indian scout.

Mary E. Virginia

Big Foot

Born: c. 1825
Died: December 29, 1890; South Dakota
Also known as: Si Tanka, Spotted Elk

Tribal affiliation: Miniconjou Lakota (Sioux)
Significance: Big Foot was the leader of the band of nearly two hundred
    men, women, and children who were killed by the U.S. Seventh Cav-
    alry at Wounded Knee Creek, South Dakota, on December 29, 1890.
Big Foot is primarily remembered as a central figure in the 1890 massacre
at Wounded Knee Creek. Born around 1825, he became a tribal leader
upon the death of his father in 1874. Shortly after the Sioux wars of 1876,
he began farming and was one of the first Sioux to raise corn. In the year
1889, however, conditions for the Sioux became nearly intolerable, with
failed crops and threats from the U.S. government to take over much of
the remaining Sioux land. Into this situation came the hope offered by
the Ghost Dance of the prophet WOVOKA. The Ghost Dance was among
the things that struck fear into white settlers in the area.

A resolution by the citizens of Chadron, Nebraska, in November,
1890, requested that the secretary of war order all Sioux in the area be
disarmed and deprived of their horses (Chadron is on the border with
South Dakota). The Sioux people of the Pine Ridge, Rosebud, and

Standing Rock reservations
frequently visited the town.
The suggestion of the Chadron citizens' committee initiated a chain of events that
included the murder of SIT-
TING BULL by reservation police, the flight of his people to
Big Foot's camp, and the
tragic massacre of Sioux who
were under the leadership of
Big Foot by the U.S. Seventh
Cavalry at Wounded Knee
Creek, South Dakota, on December 29, 1890.

Many have tried to deci-
pher what happened that day.
Most accounts agree that Big
Foot was dying of pneumonia.
One thing is certain: In the
confusion of the military
chain guard that surrounded
the Sioux council that day,

Big Foot. (Library of Congress) military gunfire took the lives of nearly two hundred Sioux men, women, and children. Twenty-five soldiers died as well—many of whom fell in the crossfire, killed by comrades. The inscribed monument erected at Wounded Knee Cemetery by survivor Joseph Horn Cloud bears the names of 185 Indian people killed that day. Other estimates, however, have placed the number at three hundred or higher.

Tonya Huber

FURTHER READING

Mooney, James. *The Ghost-Dance Religion and the Sioux Outbreak of 1890.* Introduction by Raymond J. DeMallie. Lincoln: University of Nebraska Press, 1991.

Ostler, Jeffrey. *The Plains Sioux and U.S. Colonialism from Lewis and Clark to Wounded Knee.* New York: Cambridge University Press, 2004.

Big Tree

Born: c. 1847; Texas
Died: November 13, 1929; Anadarko, Oklahoma
Also known as: Adoltay, Adouette
Tribal affiliation: Kiowa
Significance: Big Tree ambushed General William Tecumseh Sherman's wagon train as it was en route to Fort Sill, Texas, during the Kiowa raids.

As a young Kiowa war chief, Big Tree raided soldiers and settlers in present-day Texas. After ambushing William Tecumseh Sherman's wagon train on May 18, 1871, chiefs Big Tree, SATANTA, and SATANK were arrested for murdering seven white men. Satank was killed while attempting escape; Big Tree and Satanta were tried and sentenced to die. Leaders of the Kiowa militants, as well as of the peace faction, protested their sentence. During negotiations in Washington, D.C., LONE WOLF negotiated the men's prison release subject to their agreeing to remain in Texas. After violating their parole during a hunting trip to Kansas, Big Tree was imprisoned at Fort Sill, Texas; Satanta apparently committed suicide. Following his release in 1875, Big Tree married Omboke, a Kiowa woman, and settled peacefully on the Kiowa reservation, where he farmed and ran a supply train between Kansas and Texas. After converting to Christianity, he became a Baptist deacon and Sunday school teacher.

Mary E. Virginia

Big Warrior

Born: ?
Died: March 8, 1825; Washington, D.C.
Also known as: Tustennugee Thlucco
Tribal affiliation: Creek
Significance: Big Warrior's decision to fight on the American side in the Creek War of 1813-1814 contributed to the defeat of the Red Sticks.

Of Shawnee ancestry, by 1802 Big Warrior had become principal chief of the important Upper Creek town of Tukhabahchee. In 1811, as a religious revival and resentment at white encroachments swept through Indian country, Big Warrior hosted the Shawnee pan-Indian leader Tecumseh at Tukhabahchee. Many thought that he would join the anti-American Red Stick faction. In 1812, however, his warriors carried out the order of the Creek National Council to punish Creeks who had attacked white settlers. This helped to bring on a Creek civil war, in which Big Warrior became a target of the Red Sticks. Tukhabahchee was besieged, but Big Warrior was able to escape and fight on the American side of the Creek War.

Big Warrior signed the Treaty of Fort Jackson in 1814. He was angered, however, at the American demand for a large land cession that penalized friendly Creeks as severely as Red Sticks. Opposing further land cessions, he died in Washington in 1825 while arguing against ratification of the Treaty of Indian Springs.

William C. Lowe

FURTHER READING
O'Brien, Sean Michael. *In Bitterness and in Tears: Andrew Jackson's Destruction of the Creeks and Seminoles.* Westport, Conn.: Praeger, 2003.

Black Elk

Born: December, 1863; On the Little Powder River, Wyoming
Died: August 17, 1950; Pine Ridge Reservation, South Dakota
Also known as: Hehaka Sapa
Tribal affiliation: Lakota (Sioux)
Significance: Black Elk, one of the greatest of Lakota holy men, witnessed and described many of the most important events of nineteenth century Lakota history.

At the time of Black Elk's birth, the Lakota and other Indian peoples were already suffering from the encroachment into their territory by European Americans. In spite of the constant threat of conflict between the U.S. Army and the Indians, Black Elk lived in traditional Lakota fashion until he became a young adult. His was the last generation to live in that way.

When he was about five years old, Black Elk had a vision in which two men came down from the clouds, "headfirst like arrows slanting down." There was thunder that sounded like drumming, and the two men sang a song, telling Black Elk, "A sacred voice is calling you." Black Elk did not know what to make of his vision, and he was afraid to tell anyone what had happened. From that point on, however, he could hear and see things that no one else could perceive. He sometimes heard voices; he had the feeling that the voices wanted him to do something, but he did not know what.

When he was nine years old, Black Elk had a great vision that was to shape his life for many years. The vision was long and complex; it is described in detail in *Black Elk Speaks* (1961), by John Neihardt. In the vision, Black Elk was summoned by the six grandfathers: the powers of the four directions, of the sky, and of the earth. Black Elk was made to understand that he was being given abilities that would enable him to help the Lakota people in times of trouble. He still did not know what to do, however, and it was not until he was seventeen that he began to put what he had learned in his vision into practice.

Black Elk became a warrior by 1876, and he fought in the famous Battle of the Little Bighorn, which is called the Battle of the Greasy Grass by the Lakota, during which George Armstrong Custer and all his troops were killed. Custer had moved, on June 25, 1876, to attack the camps of CRAZY HORSE (Black Elk's second cousin) and his followers, but the Indians far outnumbered Custer's troops, and they responded quickly and effectively to Custer's attack. Black Elk's account of the battle, as given by John Neihardt in *Black Elk Speaks*, is one of the most important descriptions of that famous event.

On September 5, 1877, Crazy Horse was arrested and taken to Fort Robinson, where he was murdered when he refused to enter a jail cell. With his death, serious resistance to the U.S. Army ended. It was clear that the traditional Lakota way of life was coming to an end, but Black Elk's family stayed away from the Indian agencies that had been set up by the U.S. government and lived as they always had.

It was during this period that Black Elk told another holy man of his great vision and learned that the vision had to be performed as a dance by the Lakota people. A horse dance based on his vision was performed when Black Elk was about seventeen. Other visions and dances followed, and Black Elk began to work as a healer, using the understanding that had come to him in his visions.

In 1886, Black Elk joined the performing troupe organized by Buffalo Bill Cody. He traveled to England, France, and Germany, where he hoped to learn more about the ways of white people in order to help the Lakotas. Once, he performed for Queen Victoria of England, who impressed him as a good woman.

When he returned to South Dakota in 1889, Black Elk continued to work as a healer. He was frustrated, however, because he believed that he had not lived up to the requirements that his vision had made of him. He was convinced that he had been given the opportunity to save his people but that he had not been strong enough to do so.

On December 29, 1890, a band of 250 to 350 Indians led by the Miniconjou chief BIG FOOT was massacred by troops commanded by Colonel James W. Forsyth. Black Elk witnessed and fought in this one-sided engagement, which marked the end of the traditional way of life for the Lakota and the other tribes in the area, who from that point on lived as they were directed by the U.S. government.

In 1904, when Black Elk was attempting to heal a sick boy, he was interrupted by a Roman Catholic priest, Father Lindebner, who had baptized the boy. Lindebner caught the healer by the neck and said, "Satan, get out!" The priest gave the boy Communion and prayed with him, after which he took Black Elk to the Holy Rosary Mission, where he gave him clothing and religious instruction. Black Elk stayed there for two weeks, and on December 6, 1904, he willingly accepted the Catholic faith.

For the next forty-five years, Black Elk was a devout Catholic. He did his best to convert other Lakotas and to encourage them to live virtuous lives, although he respected those who adhered to traditional Lakota belief. He was most disturbed by those people who had no belief of any kind. Until the end of his life, Black Elk served as a catechist, assisting the priests and teaching Catholicism.

Black Elk died on August 17, 1950, apparently of old age. He had told Joseph Epes Brown, "You will know when I am dying, because there will be a great display of some sort in the sky." Indeed, after his wake, a spectacular phenomenon was observed in the night sky. The Jesuit brother William Siehr, who attended the wake, described it as follows: "There were different formations in the sky that night which, to me, looked like spires, like tremendous points going up—then flashes. And it seemed like they were almost like fireworks in between. It was something like when a flare goes off in the sky—some sparkle here and there, but spread over such a vast area. And it was not just momentary. We all seemed to wonder at the immensity of it."

Shawn Woodyard

FURTHER READING

Black Elk, and John G. Neihardt. *Black Elk Speaks: Being the Life Story of a Holy Man of the Oglala Sioux.* 21st century ed. Lincoln: University of Nebraska Press, 2000.

Brown, Joseph Epes, ed. *The Sacred Pipe: Black Elk's Account of the Seven Rites of the Oglala Sioux.* Baltimore: Penguin Books, 1971.

DeMallie, Raymond. *The Sixth Grandfather: Black Elk's Teachings Given to John G. Neihardt.* Lincoln: University of Nebraska Press, 1984.

Holler, Clyde. *The Black Elk Reader.* Syracuse, N.Y.: Syracuse University Press, 2000.

_____. *Black Elk's Religion: The Sun Dance and Lakota Catholicism.* Syracuse, N.Y.: Syracuse University Press, 1995.

Neihardt, John G. *Black Elk Speaks: Being the Life Story of a Holy Man of the Oglala Sioux.* Lincoln: University of Nebraska Press, 1961.

Petri, Hilda Neihardt. *Black Elk and Flaming Rainbow: Personal Memories of the Lakota Holy Man and John Neihardt.* Lincoln: University of Nebraska Press, 1995.

Powers, William K. *Oglala Religion.* Lincoln: University of Nebraska Press, 1975.

Steltenkamp, Michael F. *Black Elk: Holy Man of the Oglala.* Norman: University of Oklahoma Press, 1993.

Black Hawk

Born: 1767; Saukenak, Virginia Colony (now near Rock River, Illinois)
Died: October 3, 1838; near the Des Moines River, Iowa
Also known as: Makataimeshekiakiak
Tribal affiliation: Sauk
Significance: Black Hawk led a band of Sauk and Fox against the Americans in an attempt to regain their traditional village sites along the Rock River in Illinois; the destruction of his band marked the end of armed Indian resistance in the region known as the "Old Northwest."

Black Hawk was born near the mouth of the Rock River in Illinois. He took his name early in life, after realizing that his guardian spirit would be the sparrow hawk. Little is known about Black Hawk's early life. He

Engraving of Sauk leader Black Hawk made in 1836. (Library of Congress)

earned his right to be considered a warrior at the age of fifteen; after demonstrating his valor, he joined his father in a war against the Osages. It was during this war that Black Hawk killed and scalped the first of his opponents. By the time he reached his mid-thirties, Black Hawk was recognized as one of the most able war chiefs of the Sauk nation.

Black Hawk's hostility toward European Americans began in 1804, when a party of five Sauk and Fox leaders journeyed to St. Louis to negotiate the release of a Sauk brave accused of murder. Governor William Henry Harrison of the Indiana Territory took advantage of the situation. After encouraging the Indian leaders to drink heavily, Harrison managed to get their signatures on a treaty under which the two tribes ceded all their land east of the Mississippi River. Most of the money promised to the delegation was used to pay for the whiskey they drank. The Sauk and Fox were permitted to use the ceded land until American settlers moved into the region.

When the Sauk and Fox delegation returned to their homeland, they told their people little about the treaty. Upon learning of the terms the following year, more than 150 natives went to St. Louis to protest that the chiefs sent to the city the previous year had no power to sell land.

Inspired by the anti-American message of TECUMSEH, Black Hawk led an attack on Fort Madison in 1811. When the War of 1812 began, Black Hawk assembled more than two hundred Sauk and Fox warriors and led them to Green Bay in order to fight alongside the British.

During the War of 1812, Black Hawk and his warriors fought with distinction in Tecumseh's Indian army. The Sauk warriors participated in the battles of the Raisin River, Fort Meigs, and Fort Stephenson. During Black Hawk's absence, many Sauk moved west of the Mississippi in order to seek the protection of the United States. Those who remained at Saukenuk, east of the river, chose KEOKUK as their new war chief. When Black Hawk and his warriors returned to their homes in 1814, they were surprised by the election of Keokuk.

In spite of Keokuk's new position, it was Black Hawk who rallied the Indians of the region in their efforts to turn back two American invasion forces. Black Hawk was stunned to learn of the Treaty of Ghent. For a time, the Sauk warrior continued his personal war against the Americans. Both Black Hawk and Keokuk traveled to St. Louis with a delegation of civil chiefs in May, 1816. The civil chiefs signed a document reaffirming the Treaty of 1804.

By the 1820's, the U.S. government was placing an increased amount of pressure on the Sauk to abandon their Rock River villages and move west. Keokuk urged cooperation with the Americans, but Black Hawk protested the increasing encroachment by pioneer settlers.

When the Sauk returned from their winter hunt in the spring of 1829, they discovered that white families had established themselves in Saukenuk. Most of the Sauk decided to move to new homes along the Iowa River. Black Hawk refused to abandon his village, and his followers took up residence in lodgehouses not occupied by white families. Black Hawk's band returned again in the spring of 1830.

When the British returned to Saukenuk in the spring of 1831, Illinois governor John Reynolds called out the militia. After a futile meeting between General Edmund Gaines and Black Hawk, the militia army destroyed Saukenuk. Black Hawk's people escaped across the Mississippi. Black Hawk was forced to sign a promise never to return.

The Black Hawk War occurred during the summer of 1832. Inspired by WHITE CLOUD, a Winnebago prophet, Black Hawk attempted to forge an alliance of tribes against the Americans. When he recrossed the Mississippi with six hundred Sauk and Fox warriors in April, 1832, his allies failed to come to his aid. Black Hawk's reappearance in Illinois sparked alarm among the settlers, and a militia army, supplemented by several regiments of the U.S. Army, quickly assembled.

Black Hawk's band was forced to fight their way up the Rock River into southern Wisconsin. Facing near-starvation in the marshes of Wisconsin, Black Hawk attempted to lead what remained of his band west across the Mississippi. The Sauk attempted to cross the river on August 1, 1832, near the mouth of the Bad Axe River. The Indians were forced to battle the armed steamboat *Warrior* during most of the day.

The Battle of Bad Axe occurred on August 2. General Henry Atkinson's force of more than sixteen hundred men attacked the Sauk. An estimated two hundred Indians were killed, including women and children. Many who managed to get across the Mississippi were attacked by Sioux warriors. Black Hawk managed to escape to a Winnebago village, but he soon surrendered to the Americans at Prairie du Chien. Placed in chains, he was transported by the *Warrior* to Fort Armstrong. A treaty ending the war was signed on September 21, 1832.

After several months of confinement, Black Hawk was taken to meet President Andrew Jackson. The president confined him in prison at Fortress Monroe for a year, then sent him on a tour of the East Coast. The old warrior lived out his remaining years on the Sauk reservation in Iowa. He made a second trip to Washington, D.C., in 1837 and was invited to speak at a banquet in Madison, Wisconsin, a year later. The power within his own nation had passed to his rival, Keokuk.

Thomas D. Matijasic

FURTHER READING

Black Hawk. *Black Hawk: An Autobiography.* Edited by Donald Dean Jackson. Urbana: University of Illinois Press, 1964.

Drake, Benjamin. *The Great Indian Chief of the West: Or, Life and Adventures of Black Hawk.* Cincinnati: H. M. Rulison, 1856.

Eby, Cecil. *"That Disgraceful Affair," the Black Hawk War.* New York: W. W. Norton, 1973.

Josephy, Alvin M., Jr. *The Patriot Chiefs: A Chronicle of American Indian Resistance.* New York: Viking Press, 1961.

Tebbel, John W. *The Compact History of the Indian Wars.* New York: Hawthorn Books, 1966.

Waters, Frank. *Brave Are My People: Indian Heroes Not Forgotten.* Santa Fe, N.Mex.: Clear Light Publishers, 1993.

Black Kettle

Born: 1803?; present-day South Dakota

Died: November 27, 1868; village on the Washita River, Indian Territory (now in Oklahoma)

Also known as: Moketavato

Tribal affiliation: Southern Cheyenne

Significance: Cheyenne leader Black Kettle, who struggled to maintain peace with white settlers and soldiers, was one of the few survivors of the Sand Creek Massacre.

Black Kettle was one of the most noted of the traditional chiefs of the Cheyenne Nation, who were known as "peace chiefs." The Cheyenne were originally part of the larger complex of Algonquian-speaking peoples of the Canada/Minnesota region surrounding the Great Lakes. They were encountered in this region as late as 1667 by French explorers but were soon driven southward by British distribution of guns to more northern peoples.

Cheyenne oral tradition holds that the first such peace chief was appointed by Sweet Medicine, who left a code of conduct for the peace chiefs. A peace chief was to abandon all violence, even in the face of imminent danger to himself or his family. Yet he was also to stand firm, even if nonaggressively, against opponents of his people, even when the soldier societies among the Cheyenne had retreated. He was to persist in peacemaking efforts despite total opposition by the soldier societies of the younger Cheyenne warriors—seeking peace with native and settler alike in all circumstances. Finally, he was to show generosity in dealing with his own people, particularly toward the poor.

From U.S. military sources, Black Kettle appears to have been recognized as the main leader of the Cheyenne people of the western Plains by 1860. Therefore, he was the main authority in the crisis years of 1860 until his death in 1868. Reports of his age at death vary from fifty-six to sixty-one. Little is known about his early life except that he was an able warrior in the traditional Cheyenne manner.

Black Kettle was distinguished in his dealings with white settlers by his courage in the face of superior firepower and his willingness to negotiate release of captives, often by purchasing them at his own expense (even the chief was subject to Cheyenne economic law) in order to present them to white authorities.

In the midst of serious hostilities and severe food shortages, Black Kettle traveled to Fort Lyon, where he was refused food rations by Major Scott Anthony and Colonel John Chivington. He was instructed to take his people to Sand Creek village, where he had assurances that they would be allowed to hunt and would not be endangered by American military operations. On November 28, 1864, American soldiers attacked the Sand Creek village. Severely injured, Black Kettle was among the few survivors. During the attack, Black Kettle tried to hoist an American flag presented to him by American authorities, believing that these were soldiers who did not know about the agreement at Fort Lyon. He was to discover, however, that it was Anthony and Chivington themselves who led the unprovoked massacre of the Cheyenne people at Sand Creek.

There followed a period of serious warfare, and for the next eight years, Black Kettle was frequently involved in attempting to mediate disputes between the Cheyenne and the American military. The constant movements imposed upon the Cheyenne made it increasingly difficult for Black Kettle to control the younger soldiers, as was also often the case with the lack of central control of the American military raiding parties. On November 27, 1868, George Armstrong Custer led a surprise attack at dawn on the encampment at Washita River, where Black Kettle's band was located. Black Kettle and his wife were killed.

Daniel L. Smith-Christopher

FURTHER READING

Hatch, Thom. *Black Kettle: The Cheyenne Chief Who Sought Peace but Found War.* Hoboken, N.J.: John Wiley & Sons, 2004.

Hoig, Stan. *The Peace Chiefs of the Cheyennes.* Norman: University of Oklahoma Press, 1980.

_____. *The Sand Creek Massacre.* Norman: University of Oklahoma Press, 1961.

Blackbird, Andrew

Born: c. 1822; Muskegon River, Michigan
Died: September 8, 1908; Brutus, Michigan
Also known as: Mack-aw-de-be-nessy (Black Hawk), Mukatapenaise
Tribal affiliation: Ottawa, Potawatomi
Significance: The son of an Ottawa chief, Andrew Blackbird wrote a history of the Ottawa and Chippewa peoples and a grammar of their language and served as a government interpreter.

Andrew Blackbird grew up in a family of Ottawa chiefs on the northwest shore of Michigan's lower peninsula. He journeyed to Ohio for education among whites. He was raised as a Roman Catholic but converted to Protestantism. In 1861 he was appointed to the post of interpreter for the federal government and held that position into the 1870's. After the Civil War, he looked after claims of widows and orphans for both soldiers and Indians. He was the first postmaster of Little Traverse, Michigan (now Harbor Springs).

In 1887, Blackbird wrote *A History of the Ottawa and Chippewa Indians of Michigan and a Grammar of their Language,* which included stories from native legends, including tales about a great flood and a giant fish that swallowed a man who came out alive. Blackbird's book also covered such historical episodes as the Ottawa alliance with the French against the British during the mid-eighteenth century French and Indian War, in which the British started a smallpox epidemic among the Ottawa.

Both the Ottawa and Ojibwa peoples speak Ojibwa (which they call Anishinabe), an Algonquian language. The Ottawa (traders) lived on the north shores of Lake Huron as traders. Like the Ojibwa, the Ottawa refer to themselves as Anishinabe (original people). The Ojibwa and Ottawa and Patawotomi tribes had formed an historical alliance called the Council of the Three Fires, who clashed with the Iroquois Confederation and Lakota. Most Ottawa live on their traditional lands in Michigan and Ontario.

Joanna Yin

FURTHER READING
Blackbird, A. J. *A History of the Ottawa and Chippewa Indians of Michigan and a Grammar of their Language.* 1887. Petoskey, Mich.: Little Traverse Regional Historical Society, 1977.

Blacksnake

Born: c. 1760; Cattaraugus, New York
Died: December 26, 1859; Cold Spring, New York
Also known as: Thaonawyuthe, Chain Breaker
Tribal affiliation: Seneca
Significance: Blacksnake was present at, and later recalled in memoirs, many significant events involving the Iroquois between 1775 and 1850.

A principal chief of the Seneca, Chain Breaker, or Governor Blacksnake, was an honored warrior and leader in combat, but he was not one of the fifty sachems of the confederacy. The exact date of his birth is not known, but he is thought to have lived almost a hundred years. He was present on the English side at the Battle of Oriskany, New York, in 1777, and his memoirs discuss the Wyoming and Cherry Valley, Pennsylvania, "massacres" of 1778 and the Sullivan-Clinton campaign against the Iroquois in 1779. He fought on the American side in the War of 1812. Blacksnake's autobiographical account of his war experiences, dictated at the age of ninety-six and told to a Seneca native with limited English, contains unique insights into Indian character and thought during the American Revolution. His opinions of Joseph Brant, Old Smoke, Cornplanter, Handsome Lake, Red Jacket, and well-known British loyalists are especially perspicacious.

Blacksnake was present when the prophet Handsome Lake fell into the trance that provided the visions for the Longhouse religion, and his perspective tempers the force of those revelations. Among the Americans Blacksnake met were George Washington and possibly Thomas Jefferson. Some of Blacksnake's war accounts are quite lurid and graphic; in other cases he sets the record straight, especially regarding the "massacre" at Cherry Valley.

Because Cornplanter, Handsome Lake, and Red Jacket were related to him through his mother (an important relationship in a matrilineal society), Blacksnake was allowed to be present at nearly every council meeting, treaty negotiation, and battle undertaken by the Seneca during his active years. Blacksnake was in a central position to relate the historical events of the time from the Indian perspective. His story is one of violence and war, of military alliances, and finally of building peace. Fortunately, Blacksnake was often in the right place at the right time, and he was a careful observer.

Glenn J. Schiffman

FURTHER READING

Ables, Thomas, ed. *Chainbreaker: The Revolutionary War Memoirs of Governor Blacksnake as told to Benjamin Williams.* Lincoln: University of Nebraska Press, 1989.

Adler, Jeanne Winston, ed. *Chainbreaker's War: A Seneca Chief Remembers the American Revolution.* Hensonville, N.Y.: Black Dome Press, 2002.

Caswell, Harriet. *Our Life Among the Iroquois.* Chicago: Congregational Sunday School and Publishing Society, 1892.

Graymont, Barbara. *The Iroquois in the American Revolution.* Syracuse, N.Y.: Syracuse University Press, 1972.

Hodges, F. W., ed. *Handbook of American Indians North of Mexico.* New York: Pageant Books, 1959.

Stone, William L. *The Life of Joseph Brant—Thayendanega.* 2 vols. 1838. Reprint. St. Clair Shores, Mich.: Scholarly Press, 1970.

Bloody Knife

Born: c. 1840; Dakota Territory (now North Dakota)
Died: June 25, 1876; Little Bighorn, Montana
Tribal affiliation: Arikara, Hunkpapa Lakota (Sioux)
Significance: A skilled army scout, Bloody Knife served with George Armstrong Custer and fought at the Battle of the Little Bighorn.

Bloody Knife was born around 1840 to a Hunkpapa Sioux father and an Arikara mother. Taunted by his peers because of his mixed heritage, he returned at the age of twelve with his mother to her people in Missouri. He carried a hatred for the Hunkpapa, especially GALL and SITTING BULL. By 1860, he was carrying mail to forts and settlements along the Missouri River, where he developed skills in avoiding Sioux patrols. He enlisted as an army scout and received the commendation of several generals. In 1865, while at Fort Berthold, North Dakota, he led an army patrol to Gall's encampment. Gall was shot as he emerged from his dwelling and pronounced dead. To be certain, Bloody Knife put his shotgun to Gall's head and fired. An army officer kicked the gun and it discharged harmlessly in the snow. Gall recovered.

By 1876, Bloody Knife had become one of Custer's best scouts. He rode with Custer from Fort Abraham Lincoln as Custer set out in search of Gall and Sitting Bull. Bloody Knife expressed concern about the possible size of the Sioux party they were pursuing and recommended against attack. On June 25, he was deployed with Major Marcus A. Reno's detachment as Custer split his command. Bloody Knife rode

Bloody Knife. (Library of Congress)

with the advance attack, which Custer had hoped would disperse the Sioux in panicked flight. The Sioux, however, counterattacked. Early in the fighting, Bloody Knife's skull was shattered by a shot from Gall's warriors, causing Reno's detachment to disperse in their own chaotic retreat. Bloody Knife was then beheaded and his head paraded among the victorious Sioux.

Following his death, it took his wife, She Owl, four years to collect the less than one hundred dollars the army owed Bloody Knife in back wages.

Charles Louis Kammer III

FURTHER READING

Libby, Orin G. *The Arikara Narrative of Custer's Campaign and the Battle of the Little Bighorn.* Introduction by D'Arcy McNickle. Norman: University of Oklahoma Press, 1998.

Scott, Douglas D., P. Willey, and Melissa A. Connor. *They Died with Custer: Soldier's Bones from the Battle of the Little Bighorn.* Norman: University of Oklahoma Press, 1998.

Welch, James, with Paul Stekler. *Killing Custer: The Battle of the Little Bighorn and the Fate of the Plains Indians.* New York: W. W. Norton, 1994.

Blue Eagle, Acee

Born: August 17, 1907; Wichita Reservation, Oklahoma
Died: June 18, 1959; Muskogee, Oklahoma
Also known as: Chebona Bula (Laughing Boy), Alex C. McIntosh
Tribal affiliation: Pawnee, Creek
Significance: The flamboyant Acee Blue Eagle is probably Oklahoma's best-known Indian painter; he also taught and lectured widely.

Acee Blue Eagle was reared by a guardian in Henryetta, Oklahoma. His education included coursework at Bacone College, University of Oklahoma, and Oxford University (1935). His art career began during the 1920's. Acee studied with Oscar Jacobson at the University of Oklahoma and continued to paint in the Kiowa flat style. He created numerous murals, including those for a commission from the Works Progress Administration (1934), in addition to many canvases.

In 1935, Acee toured the United States and Europe, lecturing and exhibiting on the life, dances, and stories of American Indians, often in costume. He spent three years in the Air Force during World War II. From 1947 until 1949, he freelanced in New York and Chicago and then was artist-in-residence at Oklahoma Technical College from 1951 to 1952. From 1950 to 1954, he hosted a television program. He toured the West Coast, lecturing about improving television programs for children. Blue Eagle wrote and illustrated *Ecogee, the Little Blue Deer* (1972), a children's book, drew a cartoon carried in Oklahoma newspapers, and edited *Oklahoma Indian Painting-Poetry* (1959). Referred to as flamboyant and as the foremost living Indian painter, he was named "Outstanding Indian in the United States" in 1958.

Cheryl Claassen

Blue Jacket

Born: c. 1745; probably Michigan
Died: c. 1810; probably near Detroit, Michigan
Also known as: Weyapiersenwah, Jim Blue Jacket
Tribal affiliation: Shawnee

Significance: A Shawnee war chief, Blue Jacket organized pan-Indian resistance against white expansion into Ohio Country during the 1780's and 1790's.

Blue Jacket was born at a time of intensive trade between his Shawnee people and both the French and British, mainly in furs. After the British won the French and Indian War in 1763, they assumed control over the former French lands east of the Mississippi River.

In 1774, Blue Jacket participated in Lord Dunmore's War, during which militiamen from Pennsylvania and Virginia tried to force the Ohio territory peoples to cede some of their lands. The British defeated the Shawnee in the Battle of Point Pleasant, but Blue Jacket emerged as a Shawnee leader.

Like most Shawnee, Blue Jacket fought on the side of the British during the American Revolution. During a raid into Kentucky in 1778, he and his party captured Daniel Boone. Blue Jacket continued to defend the Shawnee hunting grounds but lost those in Kentucky by 1782. After the Revolution, he settled along the Maumee River.

As the principal architect of pan-Indian resistance during the 1780's and 1790's, Blue Jacket paved the way for future pan-Indian confederacies. Along with Chief LITTLE TURTLE of the Miamis, he organized some of the most decisive setbacks that Native Americans ever administered to U.S. forces. These included routs of armies led by General Josiah Harmar in 1790 and General Arthur St. Clair in 1791 by a confederation of Shawnees, Miamis, Wyandots, and Delawares.

In retaliation for the U.S. defeats, President George Washington ordered General "Mad" Anthony Wayne to prepare to defeat the Native American confederation. Fearing lack of support by British allies, Chief Little Turtle conceded overall leadership to Blue Jacket, whose confederation was defeated on August 20, 1794, at the Battle of Fallen Timbers, near present-day Toledo, Ohio. This conflict ended in the Treaty of Greenville (1795), which ceded the southern half of Ohio to the U.S. government. In 1805, Blue Jacket signed the Treaty of Fort Industry—named after a fort built by General Wayne on the site of present-day Toledo—which ceded parts of northern Ohio to the United States.

Joanna Yin

FURTHER READING
Sugden, John. *Blue Jacket: Warrior of the Shawnees.* Lincoln: University of Nebraska Press, 2000.

Bonnin, Gertrude Simmons

Born: February 22, 1875; Pine Ridge Reservation, South Dakota

Died: January 26, 1938; Washington, D.C.

Also known as: Zitkala Sa (Red Bird)

Tribal affiliation: Lakota (Sioux)

Significance: In the early twentieth century, Gertrude Bonnin became an author and an advocate of Indian policy reform.

Gertrude Bonnin in 1899. (National Archives)

Gertrude Bonnin belonged to a generation of Indian leaders who survived an educational process whose aim was to assimilate Indian youth into European American life. Bonnin put her education to use by urging tolerance for Indian cultural differences and by trying to reform prevailing policy regarding Indians.

The daughter of a Sioux, Ellen Simmons, and a European American settler, Bonnin left Sioux country at the age of eight to attend a Quaker missionary school for Indians in Indiana and went on to attend Earlham College. As a young woman, Bonnin taught at the Carlisle Indian School, studied violin at the Boston Conservatory of Music, and began a career as a writer. She published autobiographical essays and stories based on tribal legends in *The Atlantic Monthly* and *Harper's*. Bonnin's publications include two books, *Old Indian Legends* (1901) and *American Indian Stories* (1921).

After returning to live among the Sioux in the early twentieth century, Bonnin married a Sioux employee of the U.S. Indian service, Raymond Talesfase Bonnin, and joined the Society of American Indians. In 1916, she moved to Washington, D.C., where she spent the rest of her life as an activist, writer, and lecturer. During the 1920's and 1930's, Bonnin worked with numerous groups involved in reforming Indian policy, and in 1926, she organized the National Council of American Indians.

Molly H. Mullin

FURTHER READING

Edmunds, R. David, ed. *The New Warriors: Native American Leaders Since 1900.* Lincoln: University of Nebraska Press, 2001.

Perdue, Theda, ed. *Sifters: Native American Women's Lives.* New York: Oxford University Press, 2001.

Boudinot, Elias

Born: c. 1803; near Rome, Georgia
Died: June 22, 1839; Park Hill, Indian Territory (now in Oklahoma)
Also known as: Galegina
Tribal affiliation: Eastern Cherokee
Significance: Elias Boudinot was editor of, and a frequent contributor to, the Cherokee newspaper, the *Cherokee Phoenix*; he collaborated in translating parts of the New Testament into Cherokee and was a signer of the Treaty of New Echota.

Elias Boudinot was born Galegina or Kilakeena Watie in northwestern Georgia in 1803, to a full-blooded Cherokee father and a half-blood mother. He became a Christian and attended the Moravian mission school at Spring Place. Upon graduation in 1818, he and his cousin John RIDGE, with Leonard Hicks, enrolled at the Foreign Mission School at Cornwall, Connecticut. At this time, Galegina adopted the name Elias Boudinot from one of the benefactors of the school.

After graduation, Boudinot attended the Andover Theological Seminary. When he became engaged to Harriet Gold of Cornwall, townspeople hostile to racial intermarriage burned them in effigy, but Harriet married Elias on March 28, 1826. They had six children, one of whom (Elias Cornelius Boudinot) became a noted lawyer. En route back to Georgia, Boudinot delivered a notable address at the First Presbyterian Church of Philadelphia in which he spoke of the progress and prosperity of the Cherokees and their desire to live in friendship with their white neighbors. Part of that progress was SEQUOYAH's devising an eighty-six-character syllabary, which soon enabled many Cherokees to read and write their own language. Consequently, the Cherokees started a newspaper, the *Cherokee Phoenix*, printed partly in English and partly in Cherokee, which Boudinot edited from February 21, 1828, until its suppression by the Georgia Guard in October, 1835. Boudinot frequently wrote for the paper and, in 1833, published in Cherokee a book, *Poor Sarah: Or, The Indian Woman.* With the Reverend Samuel Worcester, a close friend and neighbor, Boudinot worked on translating the New Testament into Cherokee.

When gold was discovered in Cherokee lands in the late 1820's, Georgia began an intense effort, supported by President Andrew Jackson, to force the Indians to give up their lands and move west. The principal chief of the Eastern Cherokees, John Ross, stubbornly resisted removal, even after his own plantation was confiscated and sold at lottery. Eventually, Boudinot, John Ridge, and Boudinot's uncle, Major RIDGE, concluded that it might be better to go west and make a new start, free from persecution. Despite a "blood law" decreeing death for anyone selling Cherokee lands without the full consent of the nation, Boudinot and the Ridges signed the Treaty of New Echota in December, 1835, selling the Cherokee land in Georgia for five million dollars, comparable land in Indian Territory, and transportation there. John Ross and most Cherokees were not at New Echota and did not endorse the treaty, so the Ridge party was subject to the death penalty. In 1836, Harriet Boudinot died as a complication of childbirth. Boudinot married Delight Sargent and shortly thereafter journeyed with the Ridges to what is now eastern Oklahoma. When Ross and his followers continued to resist removal, President Martin Van Buren in 1838 sent troops to collect the remaining seventeen thousand or so Cherokees in concentration camps until they could be marched under armed guard to Indian Territory west of the Mississippi. The Trail of Tears in the autumn and winter of 1838-1839 became a death march in which about a third of the Cherokees died. In retaliation, militants of the Ross faction, without Ross's knowledge, carried out the blood law by murdering Boudinot, Major Ridge, and John Ridge on June 22, 1839.

Robert E. Morsberger

FURTHER READING

Dale, Edward Everett, and Gaston Litton. *Cherokee Cavaliers: Forty Years of Cherokee History as Told in the Correspondence of the Ridge-Watie-Boudinot Family.* Foreword by James W. Parins. 1939. Reprint. Norman: University of Oklahoma Press, 1995.

Peyer, Bernd C. *The Tutor'd Mind: Indian Missionary-Writers in Antebellum America.* Amherst: University of Massachusetts Press, 1997.

Wilkins, Thurman. *Cherokee Tragedy: The Ridge Family and the Decimation of a People.* 2d rev ed. Norman: University of Oklahoma Press, 1986.

Boudinot, Elias Cornelius

Born: August 1, 1835; near Rome, Georgia
Died: September 27, 1890; place unknown
Tribal affiliation: Cherokee
Significance: Elias Cornelius Boudinot, a lawyer and tobacco factory owner, was involved in a U.S. Supreme Court case with far-reaching implications.

The son of Elias Boudinot, one of the signers of the Treaty of New Echota, Elias Cornelius Boudinot was one of the first relocated Cherokees to realize the possibility of great profits in Indian Territory. As a young man, Boudinot worked briefly as an engineer, but he soon changed careers. Settling in Arkansas, he studied law and was admitted to the bar in 1856. He also worked as a journalist, writing editorials for newspapers in Arkansas. During the Civil War, he served in the Confederate Army.

The Treaty of 1866 between the U.S. government and the Cherokees allowed manufacturing and merchandising to proceed on Cherokee land without excise tax being levied by the U.S. government. In the late 1860's, Boudinot and his uncle, Stand WATIE, created the Watie and Boudinot Tobacco Company. They found that the cost of manufacturing chewing tobacco was forty-three cents per pound. Competing firms' product, after federal excise taxes were added to the price, sold at seventy-five cents per pound. Boudinot realized that he could sell his product at significantly lower prices. He used his profits to stake out extensive land claims of his own.

On December 20, 1869, however, U.S. marshals seized the Watie and Boudinot Tobacco Company after compet-

Elias Cornelius Boudinot. (Library of Congress)

itors claimed that the company had an unfair advantage. The case came before the U.S. Supreme Court, which ruled in 1871 that an act of Congress can supersede any treaty previously entered into and that the Watie and Boudinot Tobacco Company could be held *post facto* for unpaid excise taxes. This court decision ended one of the few economic advantages held by the Cherokees.

In the years after the case, Boudinot was a controversial figure, disliked by many Cherokees, as he advocated dividing Indian lands into individual allotments. He continued to farm and practice law in Indian Territory into the 1880's.

T. J. Arant

FURTHER READING

Dale, Edward Everett, and Gaston Litton. *Cherokee Cavaliers: Forty Years of Cherokee History as Told in the Correspondence of the Ridge-Watie-Boudinot Family.* Foreword by James W. Parins. 1939. Reprint. Norman: University of Oklahoma Press, 1995.
Wilkins, Thurman. *Cherokee Tragedy: The Ridge Family and the Decimation of a People.* 2d rev ed. Norman: University of Oklahoma Press, 1986.

Bowl

Born: 1756; North Carolinia
Died: July 16, 1839; near present-day Overton, Texas
Also known as: Diwali, Colonel Bowles
Tribal affiliation: Cherokee
Significance: The leader of a large band of Cherokee militants, Bowl fought Americans throughout his life.

The son of a Cherokee woman and a Scots-Irish trader named Bowles, Bowl was born in North Carolina and grew up in Chickamauga, Tennessee.

While most Cherokee sided with the Americans or remained neutral during the American Revolution, Bowl aided the British. In 1794, at the Massacre of Muscle Shoals, he attacked a white settlement along the Tennessee River in present-day Alabama. Thereafter, rather than surrendering to the Cherokee Council, which demanded his arrest, Bowl conducted his people across the Mississippi River to Spanish Territory. In 1824, after his new home in the Louisiana territory became a U.S. possession, Bowl again led his people westward, settling on the Angelina River in Texas, where Mexican authorities encouraged Indian settlement as a buffer to American expansion. Bowl's band was granted land near Overton, Texas, and in 1827, Bowl was commissioned a lieutenant colonel in the Mexican army. With Texan independence in 1835, white settlers demanded removal of Indians to reservations. Bowl retreated to Indian Territory, where he was killed in a battle against Texas troops in 1839.

Mary E. Virginia

Bowlegs, Billy

Born: c. 1810; near Cuscowilla, Florida
Died: April, 1859; Indian Territory (now in Oklahoma)
Also known as: Holatamico, Halpatter-Micco
Tribal affiliation: Seminole
Significance: Billy Bowlegs was the principal leader of the Seminoles in Florida during the Third Seminole War, 1855-1858.

Billy Bowlegs was a Miccosukee, or Hitchiti-speaking Seminole, who was related to other prominent leaders of the tribe. His Indian name, Holatamico, is a Creek corn dance title for a leader with influence over several villages.

Bowlegs first emerged as a leader in 1832, when he signed the Treaty of Payne's Landing. He led other Seminole warriors during the Second Seminole War and remained in the field after OSCEOLA was captured. In 1839, he directed a force of two hundred in an attack on a federal trading post, killing most of the garrison. He surrendered in 1842 and was given a grant of land in Florida. By this

Engraving of Seminole leader Billy Bowlegs that appeared in Harper's Weekly *in 1858.*
(Library of Congress)

time he was recognized as the most prominent leader of the Seminoles who remained in Florida, and as such he went to Washington, D.C., to speak with federal officials in 1842.

Government officials in 1850 began pressuring Bowlegs to take his people to the Indian Territory. They offered him $215,000 and sponsored him on a tour of several cities, including a stop in Washington, D.C., where he met President Millard Fillmore. Bowlegs would not move, so the government in 1853 declared that all Indians in Florida were outlaws.

The Third Seminole War erupted in 1855 when a party of federal surveyors and soldiers penetrated the region inhabited by Bowlegs and his people. Bowlegs led an attack on the intruders, and three years of guerrilla warfare ensued. The federals greatly outnumbered Bowlegs's tiny force, but they never inflicted a decisive defeat.

In 1858, Bowlegs accepted a large financial settlement from the government and moved his followers—thirty-three warriors, eighty women and children—to the Indian Territory, where he remained a prominent leader. When the Civil War began, he spurned the Confederates and led his group to Kansas, where he became a captain in a Union regiment mustered from among the Indians. He died of smallpox while still serving in the army.

Richard B. McCaslin

FURTHER READING
Missall, John, and Mary Lou Missall. *The Seminole Wars: America's Longest Indian Conflict.* Foreword by Raymond Arsenault and Gary R. Mormino. Gainesville: University Press of Florida, 2004.

Brant, Joseph

Born: 1742; the Ohio country
Died: November 24, 1807; near Brantford, Ontario (now in Canada)
Also known as: Thayendanegea (Two Sticks of Wood Bound Together for Strength)
Tribal affiliation: Mohawk
Significance: An unofficial leader of the Mohawk tribe and of the Six Nations Iroquois Confederacy, Joseph Brant led most of the Iroquois in siding with the British during the American Revolution.

Born into the matrilineal and matrilocal Mohawk tribe and into a leading political family, Joseph Brant's status as a chief or "sachem" of the

Mohawk leader Joseph Brant. (Library of Congress)

Mohawk tribe was unorthodox. Because of his position within his family, he had no chance of inheriting a formal position as sachem. Instead, Brant was the most famous of the "pine tree chiefs," men whose political power rested on recognition by European American and European Canadian political or military leaders rather than from within their own nation or tribe.

Brant was born in 1742, while his family was on a seasonal hunting trip in the Ohio Valley. His older sister was Molly Brant (Degonwadonti), who inherited the political office of matron from her family line. While growing up at Canajoharie, the Mohawk village on the Mohawk River in present-day upstate New York, both Joseph and Molly Brant were exposed to two worlds and two cultures. They lived in the Mohawk village but may have attended an Anglican mission school and church nearby. A close family friend was Sir William Johnson, Superintendent of Indian Affairs for the British colonial administration from the 1750's to the 1770's. Molly Brant married Johnson according to Mohawk rite, probably in 1758, and young Joseph, now Johnson's brother-in-law, became William Johnson's protégé.

With his mentor leading the way, thirteen-year-old Joseph Brant experienced the terrors of battle at Lake George, New York, in 1755. Johnson led a group of Mohawk warriors, including Brant, in a victory over the French in this important engagement of the French and Indian War (1754-1763), in which the British defeated the French. In 1757, Brant was commissioned as a captain in His Majesty's Royal American Regiment. In this capacity, he and other Mohawks accompanied Johnson on a campaign to capture Forts Oswego, Miami, Duquesne, Detroit, and Niagara from the French. Brant proved a courageous warrior during this campaign.

At the close of the war, Sir William sponsored Brant's continued formal education at Moor's Charity School (later to become Dartmouth College). The school curriculum emphasized English, Latin, Greek, and mathematics, as well as practical training courses. Christianity was also emphasized; Brant attended Bible study and catechism classes and was baptized, probably in 1763. In that year he returned to his homeland to rally support among the Mohawks and the other Iroquois tribes (Oneidas, Onondagas, Cayugas, Tuscaroras, and Senecas) for a steadfast alliance with the British. This support was needed against the confederacy of tribes rallying around PONTIAC for war against the British. Although Joseph Brant was gaining in reputation as an accomplished warrior and unofficial leader of the Mohawks, his popularity within the Iroquois Confederacy at large was limited because many of them sided with Pontiac. Many non-Mohawk Iroquois leaders such as CORNPLANTER, a Seneca, were growing wary of Brant.

Brant first married an Oneida woman with whom he had two children, Isaac and Christine. Isaac inherited his mother's fiery temper, and when she died of tuberculosis, he blamed his father. Brant then married his deceased wife's half-sister, but she also died of tuberculosis within a year. In 1775, a year after the death of his mentor, William Johnson, Joseph married Catharine Croghan, the daughter of a Mohawk woman and an Irish man. She was to bear him seven children during the 1780's and 1790's. Before he could start a family, however, the American Revolution took up much of Brant's time and proved to be extremely disruptive not only to the Brant family but also to the Mohawk and Iroquois nations in general.

As the patriots and loyalists formed sides around 1775, few of the former wooed Iroquois leaders to their side. Most were disdainful of Indians, seeing them as a nuisance to be gotten rid of to make way for European American farms. Consequently, and also perhaps because leaders such as Brant were hand-in-glove with the British Indian Department, most sided with the British. Guy Johnson, Sir William's nephew and successor in his post as head of the Indian Department, made Brant his secretary. The Indian Department operated during the American revolutionary war mostly as a military force for fighting non-Indians. Brant was also recognized as a leader of the Mohawk warriors, and in that capacity British officials invited him to Montreal in 1774 to persuade him into solid support of the British cause against the Americans. Sir Guy Carleton, governor of the colony of Quebec, and Major-General Frederick Haldimand, commander in chief of the military forces, displayed the power of the British army for Brant and others. Haldimand even promised that the Iroquois would not lose their lands at the end of the war. Brant and others wanted assurances directly from the British crown, so they journeyed to England in 1775 and held meetings with King George III. These combined efforts persuaded the Mohawks to promise Iroquois support for the British in the impending war. Brant returned to the Mohawk Valley convinced of British victory.

Brant's sister Molly also lobbied among all the Iroquois nations for a strong contingent of warriors to join the British forces. Eventually most, except one large faction of the Oneidas, agreed. During the war, Joseph Brant was extensively involved in military operations in the Mohawk Valley, most notably at Oriskany, Cherry Valley, and German Flats. Patriot legend had it that Brant participated in a British raid on Wyoming, a hamlet south of the Mohawk River, committing horrible atrocities against American settlers there; it was later proved that he had not been there. In fact, he was known for his humanity in the face of war, more than once sparing innocent women and children from the brutality of his fellow non-Indian officers (such as Walter Butler, Jr.).

When the Clinton-Sullivan expedition invaded Iroquois territory and wreaked havoc on Seneca towns and food supplies in the far west of

Iroquoia, RED JACKET, a Seneca chief long opposed to Brant for his too-close ties to the British, blamed Brant's policies for the revenge of the Clinton-Sullivan patriots. Red Jacket even attempted to engineer a separate peace with the Americans. Brant heard of the plan and headed it off, only to discover that during the treaty negotiations between the Americans and the British in 1783 the Iroquois Confederacy had been forgotten.

Brant spent much of his time after the American Revolution trying to rectify this injustice. Most of the Iroquois people took refuge at British Fort Niagara at the end of the war, and holding onto Haldimand's promise, Brant persuaded him to grant a huge tract of land west of the fort, in a newly formed British colony (Upper Canada, now Ontario), to the Six Iroquois Nations. In 1784, the Iroquois were granted a large tract of land along the Grand River: about six miles wide from the river's source to its mouth on Lake Erie. The town which grew up near this reserve became known as Brant's Ford—Brantford. Brant, in order to make the reserve a success, sold parcels of it to non-Indians to raise money for needed supplies. Many Mohawks and other Iroquois who settled there criticized him for this, as they did for his grandiose style (he dressed and furnished his estate in the manner of an English gentleman) and for his posturing with British colonial and American officials. Brant had personally received from the British government a tract of land at Burlington Bay, east of Grand River, for an estate of his own, and therefore was distanced geographically as well as in outlook from his people. While many of them wanted to maintain as much of their traditional culture as possible, Brant arranged for English-language schools, Christian missionaries, and other elements of European culture at Grand River.

Brant remained a controversial figure until his death in 1807. He was seen by many Iroquois as a self-promoter who sold out his people to the British. Nevertheless, he was an extremely influential figure in a turbulent period of North American history.

Gretchen L. Green

FURTHER READING

Baughman, Mike. *Mohawk Blood.* New York: Lyons & Burford, 1995.

Graymont, Barbara. *The Iroquois in the American Revolution.* Syracuse, N.Y.: Syracuse University Press, 1972.

Hamilton, Milton W. *Sir William Johnson: Colonial American, 1715-1763.* Port Washington, N.Y.: Kennikat Press, 1976.

Johnson, Charles. *The Valley of the Six Nations.* Toronto: Champlain Society, 1964.

Kelsay, Isabel Thompson. *Joseph Brant, 1743-1807: Man of Two Worlds.* Syracuse, N.Y.: Syracuse University Press, 1984.

O'Donnell, James H. "Joseph Brant." In *American Indian Leaders: Studies in Diversity,* edited by R. David Edmunds. Lincoln: University of Nebraska Press, 1980.

Stone, William L. *The Life of Joseph Brant—Thayendanegea.* 2 vols. 1838. Reprint. St. Clair Shores, Mich.: Scholarly Press, 1970.

Brant, Molly

Born: 1736; Canajoharie, New York
Died: April 16, 1796; Kingston, Ontario, Canada
Also known as: Mary Brant, Degonwadonti (Many Opposed to One), Gonwatsijayenni
Tribal affiliation: Mohawk
Significance: Molly Brant was a leading Mohawk political figure during the time of the American Revolution. She was instrumental in convincing the Mohawks and the Iroquois Confederacy to side with the British.

Little is known of Molly Brant's early childhood, except that she lived with her family at the Mohawk village of Canajoharie and frequently traveled to the Ohio Valley for winter hunting trips. Brant's childhood was one of mixed Mohawk and English/Dutch influences; she may have attended an Anglican mission school at Canajoharie and therefore learned how to read and write English, since her letters written in later years displayed excellent penmanship. Her family was prominent within Mohawk society; consequently, she was destined to become a matron (a female political role in traditional Iroquois culture). Her younger brother, Joseph BRANT, was to become a prominent politician and war leader.

Brant's stepfather was a close personal friend of Sir William Johnson, Superintendent of Indian Affairs for the British colonial administration in North America from the 1740's to the 1770's. Brant married Johnson according to Mohawk marriage customs, probably in 1758, and although he was against female involvement in politics, Brant stubbornly refused to let her marriage prevent her from exercising her political power. In addition to bearing eight children with Johnson, Brant took advantage of the opportunities available at her new residence, Johnson Hall, which was also the headquarters of the British Indian Department. She used these opportunities, some of them in the form of access to information, some in the form of material goods, to increase her own political influence among the Iroquois people. After her husband's death in 1774, she was said to be the heir of his influence among the Iroquois. Patriot revolutionary war politicians and military strategists feared this influence, since Brant was loyal to the British.

When hostilities broke out between the British and the Americans, Brant refused to leave her homeland. She aided the British cause by informing British rangers of an impending American attack on a New York village, as well as by working to convince the Mohawk tribe and the Iroquois Confederacy that their interests could best be served by siding with the British against the Americans. Most were reluctant to agree with her, although gradually they were forced by circumstances to make a decision. Most decided to ally with the British; both Molly Brant and her brother Joseph played large roles in this outcome.

Brant received a military pension from the British government following the American Revolution, and lived, courtesy of the British, in a substantial European-style house in Kingston, Ontario. She attended the local Anglican church, which she had helped to establish, until her death in 1796. Despite Brant's apparent assimilation, she preferred native dress throughout her life, and often insisted on speaking only Mohawk, even though she could speak English. Her legacy among the Mohawk people is controversial, however. She is viewed by some as having sold out her people by convincing them to fight on the British side in the American Revolution, after which they were forgotten at the treaty negotiations in 1783. She did protest this omission, and the treatment of Iroquois people by the British, on numerous occasions after 1783, but her influence among her people had declined by that time. Brant may not have been popular among her kinspeople after the Revolutionary War, since she chose not to live on one of the two Mohawk reserves set up in Upper Canada (Ontario) by the British government during the 1780's.

Gretchen L. Green

FURTHER READING

Kenny, Maurice. *Tekonwatonti, Molly Brant, 1735-1795: Poems of War.* Fredonia, N.Y.: White Pine Press, 1992.

Thomas, Earle. *The Three Faces of Molly Brant: A Biography.* Kingston, Ontario: Quarry Press, 1996.

Bronson, Ruth Muskrat

Born: 1897; Whitewater, Indian Territory (now in Oklahoma)
Died: May 14, 1982; Tucson, Arizona
Tribal affiliation: Cherokee
Significance: Ruth Muskrat Bronson educated Native American youth
  in their culture and heritage.

Beginning her career as a playground supervisor, Ruth Muskrat Bronson went on to obtain an A.B. degree from Mount Holyoke College in
Massachusetts. She taught at the Haskell Institute in Kansas in 1935. She
also worked with the Bureau of Indian Affairs, starting in 1931 as director of the bureau's scholarship program, a position she held until 1943,
after which she was executive secretary of the National Congress of
American Indians. From 1957 until she retired in 1962, she was health
education specialist for the San Carlos Apache Reservation in Arizona.
After retirement, she continued her work as an educator, serving the
Tohono O'odham and Yaqui in Arizona as a representative of the Save
the Children Foundation. She died in a nursing home in Tucson.

FURTHER READING
Perdue, Theda, and Michael D. Green. *The Columbia Guide to American
  Indians of the Southeast.* New York: Columbia University Press, 2001.

Bruce, Louis R.

Born: December 30, 1906; Onondaga Reservation near Syracuse, New
  York
Died: May 20, 1989; Arlington, Virginia
Also known as: Agwelius (Swift)
Tribal affiliation: Mohawk, Oglala Lakota (Sioux)
Significance: Louis R. Bruce served as commissioner of the Bureau of
  Indian Affairs (BIA) during a time of considerable Native American
  activism.

Louis R. Bruce was reared on the Saint Regis Mohawk reservation in upstate New York; his father was a Methodist minister there. Bruce's
mother was an Oglala Sioux, and he considered himself a Sioux; his paternal grandfather was a Mohawk chief. Bruce was graduated from Syracuse University in 1930; in 1935 he was appointed the New York state
director of Indian projects for the National Youth Administration, a position he held for seven years.

Louis R. Bruce. (Library of Congress)

Bruce was named commissioner of the Bureau of Indian Affairs by President Richard M. Nixon in 1969. He set out to "Indianize" the bureau by appointing Native Americans to influential positions. His policies encountered considerable opposition from interests that had benefited from keeping Indians in subordinate positions. Bruce's tenure coincided with Indian activist movements in the late 1960's and early 1970's; in 1972, for example, the BIA building in Washington was occupied by native militants. Bruce and most of his top assistants were subsequently fired by Nixon, less than a week before the 1972 presidential election.

Bruce E. Johansen

FURTHER READING

Johnson, Troy, Joane Nagel, and Duane Champagne, eds. *American Indian Activism: Alcatraz to the Longest Walk.* Urbana: University of Illinois Press, 1997.

Bruchac, Joseph

Born: October 16, 1942; Saratoga Springs, New York
Also known as: Joseph E. Bruchac III
Tribal affiliation: Abenaki
Significance: Joseph Bruchac is widely known as a children's author, short-story writer, and novelist who works with traditional Native American tales and has described his work as creating a bridge between Native American oral traditions and contemporary written literature.

Joseph Bruchac grew up in the Adirondack Mountain region of New York State. His father's family was of Slovak descent, but his mother was from a mixed Abenaki and European background. Bruchac was especially close to his maternal grandfather, a dark-skinned man whom Bruchac has described as Native American in appearance. According to Bruchac, the grandfather was reluctant to talk about his Indian heritage. The mystery of his family inheritance, and his feelings for his grandfather, inspired Bruchac to take an interest in exploring Native American traditions.

Bruchac attended Cornell University, where he began writing poems on Native American themes. After graduating, he entered graduate school at Syracuse University, where he earned a master's degree in 1966. From 1966 to 1969, he lived and taught in Ghana, sponsored by the Teachers in West Africa Program. He learned enough of a local Ghanaian language to do some translating, and he was impressed by the similarities between Native American and West African tribal literatures.

On his return to the United States, Bruchac moved into the house built by his grandfather in the small village of Greenfield Center in the foothills of the Adirondacks. There, he founded and edited the *Greenfield Review*. Bruchac then became involved in the movement opposing the war in Vietnam and came into contact with other antiwar writers, such as poet Robert Bly. While doing graduate work at the State University of New York at Albany and simultaneously teaching at Skidmore College, Bruchac coedited, with William Witherup, an anthology of prison writings that was published by Bruchac's own Greenfield Review Press. He also published poetry, two novellas, and essays in a variety of periodicals and edited a special issue of the *Small Press Review* on the small presses of Africa. In 1975, Bruchac received a doctoral degree from Union Graduate School.

Bruchac's interest in prison life led him to establish creative writing programs in a number of prisons during the early 1970's. In 1975, he was awarded a National Endowment for the Arts grant to expand these programs, and to found the Prison Project newsletter. However, most of his own writing continued to spring from his Native American background. He became well known as a poet and a short-story writer, and began producing children's literature based on the tales he collected.

With coauthor Michael J. Caduto, Bruchac published the best-selling children's books *Keepers of the Earth* (1988) and *Keepers of the Animals* (1991). These books attempted to employ Native American stories to express concern for the environment. Bruchac's fascination with Native American stories also led him to write his first full-length novel, *Dawn Land*, which was published in 1993. Drawn from stories of the Abenaki and Iroquois peoples, *Dawn Land* tells a story of prehistory of the region that is now New England. Bruchac's young adult novel *Skeleton Man* (2001) recasts a traditional Abenaki story in the form of long fiction.

Carl L. Bankston III

Buffalo Hump

Born: c. 1800; Indian Territory (now in Oklahoma)
Died: 1870; Kiowa-Comanche Reservation, near Fort Cobb, Indian Territory (now in Oklahoma)
Also known as: Bull Hump, Pochanaquarhip, Pochanaw-quoip, Ko-cho-naw-quoip
Tribal affiliation: Comanche
Significance: A leader in the early Comanche Wars, Buffalo Hump was most active from the 1830's through the 1850's.

With the exception of his exploits as a leader during the early Comanche Wars, little is known of Buffalo Hump's life. After proving himself in battle against Mexicans, Texans, Cheyennes, and Arapahos, Buffalo Hump became principal chief of the Penateka band of Comanches in 1849.

During the 1830's, he led more than one thousand men on raids for horses and slaves in Chihuahua, Mexico. During the same period, he also raided other Indians, particularly the Southern Cheyenne under YELLOW WOLF. In 1840, Buffalo Hump participated in establishing peace between the Cheyennes, Kiowas, and Comanches.

After an incident in 1838 known as the Council House Affair, in which Texas Rangers attempted to force Comanche release of several white hostages by seizing chiefs who had gathered under truce at San Antonio, Buffalo Hump led his forces to the Gulf of Mexico. After raiding several villages and coming under attack by Rangers, Buffalo Hump returned north.

Texas Rangers led a coordinated campaign against the Comanches during the 1850's. Although his band was badly defeated at Rush Springs, Oklahoma, Buffalo Hump escaped. With representatives from other Southern Plains tribes, including the Comanches, Kiowas, Cheyennes, and Arapahos, Buffalo Hump, in October, 1856, signed the Little Arkansas Treaty, by which a reservation was established in Kansas and Indian Territory. The resulting peace was short-lived, however, as the promised reservation was never established. Buffalo Hump's son, also named Buffalo Hump, fought with war chief Quanah PARKER.

Mary E. Virginia

FURTHER READING
Fehrenbach, T. R. *Comanches: The History of a People.* New York: Anchor Books, 2003.

Bull Bear

Born: c. 1840; Kansas
Died: after 1875; Cheyenne Reservation, Indian Territory (now in Oklahoma)
Tribal affiliation: Cheyenne
Significance: One of the principal leaders of the elite Cheyenne Dog Soldiers, Bull Bear participated in numerous battles during the Cheyenne Wars for the Great Plains.

With TALL BULL and White Horse, Bull Bear led the society of warriors known as the Dog Soldiers. Functioning partially as an internal Cheyenne police force, the Dog Soldiers were also known for their battles against the U.S. Army during the wars for domination of the Great Plains. After his brother, peace chief LEAN BEAR, was murdered in 1864, Bull Bear became increasingly militant and thereafter was arguably the most powerful Dog Soldier.

Although he negotiated with Colorado governor John Evans at Camp Weld in 1864, Bull Bear nevertheless continued raiding whites. He participated in the Hancock Campaign of 1867, which sought to eliminate all nonreservation Indian presence in Kansas, and (although he signed the Medicine Lodge Treaty in 1867) he fought against the Sheridan Campaign, including the Battle at Summit Springs, Colorado, on July 11, 1868, during which Tall Bull was killed. In 1869, he led his people to Indian Territory, but returned in 1871. During the Red River War of 1874-1875, he aided the Comanches and Kiowas, thereafter retiring to the Cheyenne Reservation.

Mary E. Virginia

FURTHER READING
Afton, Jean. *Cheyenne Dog Soldiers: A Ledgerbook History of Coups and Combat.* University Press of Colorado, 2000.

Bull Lodge

Born: 1802; unknown
Died: 1886; unknown
Also known as: Buffalo Lodge, Buffalo Bull Lodge
Tribal affiliation: Gros Ventre
Significance: A great medicine man of the Gros Ventre tribe, Bull Lodge was a powerful spiritual leader, who was the last shaman to hold the powers of the tribe's sacred Feathered Pipe.

Little is known about the early life of Bull Lodge, but much of his later life was documented by his daughter Garter Snake, who was born in 1868. Bull Lodge was the son of a Gros Ventre woman and a French trader whom he never meet. He grew up among the Gros Ventre (A'aninin) people in the vicinity of Milk River, a tributary of the Missouri River, in what is now northern Montana. He became known as a fierce warrior and respected political leader of the tribe but is best known as a great spiritual leader and healer of his people. He was one of the White Clay people, members of the Gros Ventre who held possession of the sacred Feathered Pipe of the tribe.

Late in his life, Bull Lodge told his daughter Garter Snake numerous stories about the tribe and his role as their medicine man and spiritual healer. His daughter memorized most of the stories and also observed at first hand many of the ceremonial and healing events participated in by her father. Over an extended period of time, young Bull Lodge received seven visions on seven different buttes in what is now northern Montana. During his visions, he was given the powers of the supernatural and was awarded the healing rituals, animal helpers, and magical artifacts that would allow him to perform as the tribe's medicine man (shaman). In the last vision, Bull Lodge received instructions on how to raise the dead.

One of Bull Lodge's primary doctoring implements was a woodpecker feather, which he used on occasion to open a patient's body to extract the source of the disease. According to Garter Snake, he used that technique to heal a respected Gros Ventre woman known as Wind Woman. During healing rituals, Bull Lodge also used a therapeutic whistle and a shield that protected him from his enemies.

Garter Snake later recounted many intriguing stories about her father, including how he turned dirt into sugar, initiated and stopped storms, and healed numerous sick individuals, many on the verge of death. Bull Lodge was the last medicine man of the White Clay people to hold the sacred powers associated with the tribe's Feathered Pipe. Shortly before he died, Bull Lodge heard the voice of a spirit telling him that he had eight days left to live. He was given instructions for a ceremony that needed to be performed in order for him to be resurrected. He died as predicted, but due to the overhunting of the buffalo by white men, the ceremony could not be held. According to legend, Bull Lodge gracefully accepted his fate and died a natural death in 1886.

With the passing of Bull Lodge and other spiritual leaders, many of the Native American traditions began fading into memory. A Jesuit mission established near Fort Belknap in 1862 led some members of the Montana tribes, including the Gros Venture, to convert to Christianity. This furthered the loss of the sacred ceremonies and left the surviving tribe members with little knowledge of their own history.

During the late 1930's, the federal government established the Works Progress Administration (WPA) to create jobs during the Great Depression. One WPA programs was the Federal Writers' Project, one of whose many projects was the hiring of unemployed writers to document the lives of ordinary Americans. One such writer was Fred P. Gone, a member of the Gros Ventre tribe. Gone interviewed Garter Snake, who related details about her father's life as a spiritual leader and described many of the ceremonies he performed. She also said that her father had foretold that she would be the one to tell the story of his life.

After the Depression ended, many WPA programs, including the Federal Writers' Project, were eliminated. The approximately ten thousand manuscripts created by the project were turned over to the Library of Congress and largely forgotten. Forty years later, Gros Ventre scholar George Horse Capture found a reference to Gone's interview with Garter Snake while researching the history of his tribe. He obtained the transcripts, edited them, and published them as *The Seven Visions of Bull Lodge* in 1980. Until that book was published, little was known about the history of the Gros Venture. The recovery of Garter Snake's manuscript thus provided a vital link to the tribe's spiritual history.

Alvin K. Benson
P. S. Ramsey

FURTHER READING

Harvey, Graham. *Shamanism: A Reader.* New York: Routledge, 2002.

Horse Capture, George. *The Seven Visions of Bull Lodge: As Told by His Daughter, Garter Snake.* Reprint. Lincoln: University of Nebraska Press, 1992.

Kalweit, Holger. *Shamans, Healers, and Medicine Men.* Translated by Michael H. Kohn. Boston: Shambhala, 2000.

Bushotter, George

Born: 1864; near Moreau River, Dakota Territory (now in South Dakota)
Died: February 2, 1892; Hedgesville, West Virginia
Also known as: Oteri (Trouble), George Bush
Tribal affiliation: Lakota (Sioux)
Significance: Working with James Owen Dorsey of the Smithsonian Institution's Bureau of Ethnology, George Bushotter translated more than three thousand pages of texts written in the Teton language.

George Bushotter was the son of a Yankton man and a Miniconjou Lakota. While he was still a young boy, his father was killed by whites. Despite this introduction to white civilization, Bushotter developed a curiosity about white culture, as well as a strong desire to become educated at white schools. His opportunity came after he turned fourteen, when he was enrolled at the Hampton Institute in Virginia. Founded by General Samuel Chapman Armstrong, Hampton was noted for educating Native Americans and freed slaves and was the alma mater of the influential African American educator and spokesman, Booker T. Washington.

James Owen Dorsey from the Smithsonian Institution apparently first met Bushotter when the latter was enrolled at Hampton. Bushotter attended the institute until 1881, and after a brief return to Dakota Territory, was admitted to the Theological Seminary of Virginia in 1885. Dorsey, himself a graduate of the seminary, most likely encouraged Bushotter to enroll there. Bushotter's plans were to become an ordained minister, but difficulties with the Greek and Latin languages resulted in his leaving after two years.

Despite Bushotter's failure to complete his seminary education, Dorsey continued to hold him in high regard. As a member of the Bureau of Ethnology at the Smithsonian, Dorsey was considered one of the outstanding scholars in the study of the Sioux culture. Among his works were attempts to translate Indian languages into English. When Bushotter became available, it was logical for Dorsey to recruit him with the purpose of translating the Teton language for the bureau.

In March, 1887, Bushotter was hired to carry out several tasks, primarily the preparation of a dictionary for the Teton language, as well as putting into writing myths, games, customs and ceremonies carried out by the tribe. The hot and humid Washington summer only served to aggravate Bushotter's health, so he and Dorsey decided to carry out the work in the mountains of Hedgesville, West Virginia, the home of Dorsey's in-laws. For the next ten months, Bushotter worked on the project, eventually producing nearly 3,300 pages of texts in 258 stories. The ethnography project represented the first translation of the Lakota story.

Bushotter's health had never been good. While attending school in the East, he contracted tuberculosis. The disease, which would eventually prove fatal, limited his opportunities in the teaching field. His marriage to a white woman, Evalina Hull, in 1888, aggravated his financial hardships. In March of that year, he accepted a teaching position at a school in Fort Stevenson, North Dakota. However, a dispute with the school superintendent resulted in his resignation. In November, 1889, Bushotter was offered a position on the Rosebud Reservation in South Dakota, but by this time his health had deteriorated to the point where he could no longer teach. He returned to Hedgesville, where he died in 1892.

The Bushotter manuscripts were rediscovered in the early part of the twentieth century, when they were translated by Ella Cara Deloria (1889-1971), a Dakota Sioux who was fluent in all three Sioux dialects (Dakota, Lakota, and Nakota), as well as English. While studying at Columbia University, Deloria became acquainted with the anthropologist Franz Boass; at his request, she began translating the manuscripts into English. Deloria graduated from Columbia in 1915 and spent several years as a teacher in Native American schools before returning to Columbia in 1927 to teach and to complete the translation of the Bushotter manuscripts.

Richard Adler
P. S. Ramsey

Further Reading
Liberty, Margot, ed. *American Indian Intellectuals of the Nineteenth and Early Twentieth Centuries.* Norman: University of Oklahoma Press, 2002.

Bushyhead, Dennis Wolf

Born: March 18, 1826; near Cleveland, Tennessee
Died: February 4, 1898; Talequah, Oklahoma
Also known as: Unáduti
Tribal affiliation: Cherokee
Significance: Dennis Wolf Bushyhead was one of the leading political
figures of the Cherokee Nation during the second half of the nine-
teenth century.

Dennis Wolf Bushyhead, a mixed-blood Cherokee, was born near the
present-day town of Cleveland, Tennessee, in 1826. When he was twelve
years old, he and his family were rounded up and sent west on the infamous Trail of Tears with thousands of other Cherokees. Bushyhead
reached manhood in the Indian Territory of present-day eastern Oklahoma.

Bushyhead assumed a leadership role in helping the Cherokees solve
the numerous problems related to their forced move to a strange land.
During the 1870's, Dennis helped found the National Independent
Party, partly to challenge an attempt by full-bloods to take control of all
Cherokee affairs.

In 1879, Bushyhead began serving two elected four-year terms as
principal chief. His major goal was to preserve Cherokee sovereignty,
which was becoming increasingly difficult to do. The General Allotment Act, passed by Congress in 1887, led to denationalizing the tribes
in the Indian Territory and eventually to the establishment of the state
of Oklahoma in 1907.

Glenn L. Swygart

FURTHER READING
McLoughlin, William G. *After the Trail of Tears: The Cherokees' Struggle for
    Sovereignty, 1839-1880.* Chapel Hill: University of North Carolina
    Press, 1993.

Campbell, Ben Nighthorse

Born: April 13, 1933; Auburn, California
Tribal affiliation: Northern Cheyenne
Significance: Elected to the U.S. Senate in 1992, Ben Nighthorse Campbell was successful in the jewelry business before winning elective office in Colorado.

Ben Campbell is the son of Portuguese immigrant Mary Vierra and Albert Valdez Campbell, of Scottish-Mexican descent; his paternal grandmother is said to have been Yellow Woman, a Southern Cheyenne. He was entered on the Northern Cheyenne tribal roll in 1980.

After stints as a U.S. Air Force military policeman during the Korean War, a San Jose State University student, and a member of the 1964 U.S. Olympic judo team, Campbell taught martial arts near Sacramento. Thereafter, he married, worked as a shop teacher, moonlighted in law enforcement, and began making jewelry with American Indian motifs. In 1970, he first announced his identity as a "closet Indian" and took the name "Nighthorse." In 1977, with his jewelry business an established success, Campbell and his wife moved to a ranch near Durango, Colorado. They raised quarter horses and opened a gallery to display and sell his work. Campbell had become a millionaire by 1980.

Campbell was elected to the Colorado state legislature in 1983 and served until 1986. He was also an adviser to the Colorado Commission

on International Trade and the Arts and Humanities. He was elected to the U.S. House of Representatives in 1987. During his time in the House he was a member of the House Committee on Agriculture and the Committee on Interior and Insular Affairs. He was elected to the U.S. Senate in 1992; Campbell was the first Native American since Charles CURTIS to be elected to the U.S. Senate.

In 1995, Campbell switched from the Democratic Party to the Republican Party, and three years later, he was re-elected to the Senate as a Republican. As a legislator, Campbell has been a proponent of preserving public lands and natural resources. In 2001, he succeeded in having the site of the 1864 Sand Creek massacre

Senator Ben Nighthorse Campbell speaks to supporters in downtown Denver in 2004.
(AP/Wide World Photos)

of Cheyenne in eastern Colorado designated a national historic site. Citing health problems, Campbell announced in March, 2004, that he would not seek reelection to the U.S. Senate.

Ward Churchill

FURTHER READING

Edmunds, R. David, ed. *The New Warriors: Native American Leaders Since 1900.* Lincoln: University of Nebraska Press, 2001.

Viola, Herman J. *Ben Nighthorse Campbell: An American Warrior.* New York: Orion Books, 1993.

Canonchet

Born: c. 1630; place unknown
Died: April, 1676; Stonington, Connecticut
Also known as: Nanuntenoo
Tribal affiliation: Narragansett
Significance: Canonchet is best known for his interactions with the British colonists during King Philip's War.

Initially the settlers persuaded Canonchet, sachem of the Narragansett, to remain loyal to the British cause. He signed a treaty in July, 1675, promising to turn over to the British their enemies and agreeing to fight against those Indians the colonists deemed enemies. Canonchet evidently agreed, however, to shelter women and children of the Wampanoag tribe, thereby breaking the agreement. The following December (1675), in retaliation, the British attacked and killed about one thousand Narragansett. Canonchet survived and, in March, 1676, led an ambush of about forty of Captain Michael Pierce's troops.

While organizing an effort to replace the corn the British had destroyed, Canonchet was spotted in April by Captain George Denison, who chased and captured him. Upon learning that he was to be executed, Canonchet is reputed to have replied that he "liked it well, that he should die before his heart was soft, or had spoken anything unworthy of himself." The sachem was turned over to the Pequots and Mohegans, who shot and beheaded him. Canonchet's execution in 1676 coincides with the dispersal of the Narragansett and essentially signals the end of what was formerly the strongest tribe in New England.

Lee Schweninger

FURTHER READING

Drake, James D. *King Philip's War: Civil War in New England, 1675-1676.* Amherst: University of Massachusetts Press, 1999.

Drake, Samuel G. *The Book of the Indians.* 1832. Reprint. New York: AMS, 1976.

Hubbard, William. *The History of the Indian Wars in New England.* Reprint. New York: Kraus, 1969.

Schultz, Eric B., and Michael J. Tougias. *King Philip's War: The History and Legacy of America's Forgotten Conflict.* Woodstock, Vt.: Countryman Press, 1999.

Canonicus

Born: c. 1565
Died: June 4, 1647; place unknown
Tribal affiliation: Narragansett
Significance: Canonicus kept the Narragansetts at peace with the British colonists for the twenty-seven years between their arrival in 1620 and his death; he befriended Roger Williams, giving him the land on which stands present-day Providence, Rhode Island.

Canonicus shared the leadership of the Narragansetts with his nephew MIANTONOMO at the time of English arrival. While Miantonomo dealt with the colonists and the other tribes, Canonicus ruled at home. Colonist Edward Winslow gives an account of how Canonicus had a bundle of arrows wrapped in snake skin delivered to the Plymouth pilgrims, a gesture the pilgrims interpreted as hostile. No hostilities came of the act, however, nor did hostilities result from Canonicus's 1632 threat of three settlers near Plymouth. Besides maintaining peace with the pilgrims, Canonicus befriended Roger Williams and his fellow outcasts in 1636, giving them the land that is now Providence, Rhode Island.

Despite the Narragansetts' having been betrayed by the colonists in the death of Miantonomo, Canonicus remained faithful to a peace compact, though his tribe did avenge the death of Miantonomo by UNCAS in June, 1644. Also in 1644, Canonicus made a treaty accepting the sovereignty of England and its king.

Noting his death, New England historian John Winthrop wrote: "Canonicus, the great sachem of Narrangansett [*sic*], died, a very old man." Roger Williams recalled Canonicus as a great and benevolent friend to him and the British.

Lee Schweninger

FURTHER READING

Drake, Samuel G. *The Book of the Indians.* 1832. Reprint. New York: AMS, 1976.

Hodge, Frederick W., ed. *Handbook of American Indians.* 2 vols. 1907-1910. Reprint. Totowa, N.J.: Rowman and Littlefield, 1975.

Rubertone, Patricia E. *Grave Undertakings: An Archaeology of Roger Williams and the Narragansett Indians.* Washington, D.C.: Smithsonian Institution Press, 2001.

Winslow, Edward. *Good News from New England.* London: John Dawson, 1624.

Captain Jack

Born: c. 1840; Lost River, Northern California
Died: October 3, 1873; Fort Klamath, Oregon
Also known as: Kintpuash (Having Indigestion)
Tribal affiliation: Modoc
Significance: A chief during the Modoc War of 1872-1873, Captain Jack engaged in a lifelong struggle to preserve Modoc independence.

Born near the California-Oregon border, Kintpuash (nicknamed Captain Jack by whites) became a Modoc chief when his father was killed by whites. Believing in peace, he encouraged trade with the white settlers. In 1864, however, Schonchin Jim surrendered Modoc lands and moved the Modoc to the Klamath Reservation in Oregon. The Modoc were denied food and supplies, and disputes developed with the more favorably treated Klamath Indians. In 1865, denied permission for a separate Modoc reservation, Kintpuash led his people back to California. In November, 1872, troops ordered to return the Modoc to Oregon were engaged in a skirmish. Captain Jack led the main group to a natural rock sanctuary in the

Captain Jack. (National Archives)

lava beds near Tule Lake. HOOKER JIM led a separate group, which took revenge by killing white settlers. Seeking refuge, Hooker Jim joined Captain Jack.

During January, 1873, soldiers tried unsuccessfully to dislodge the Modocs. General Edward Canby was then ordered to end the uprising. He convened peace talks that included Kintpuash's cousin, WINEMA. While the talks proceeded, Canby surrounded the Modoc with a thousand soldiers. On February 28, Kintpuash requested a separate Modoc reservation and amnesty for Hooker Jim's band. Both requests were refused. Believing that Canby was stalling for time, Hooker Jim convinced the majority of warriors that they needed to kill Canby. Facing tribal pressure, Captain Jack agreed. At a meeting on April 11, Kintpuash and his warriors drew hidden pistols, killing Canby and several others.

In an act of betrayal, Hooker Jim later agreed to lead soldiers to Captain Jack in exchange for amnesty. On June 1, surrounded, Kintpuash surrendered. The resisting Modocs were tried without legal defense. Kintpuash and three of his warriors were sentenced to death and hanged on October 3. His body was stolen from its grave and displayed by an eastern carnival.

Charles Louis Kammer III

FURTHER READING

Quinn, Arthur. *Hell with the Fire Out: A History of the Modoc War.* Boston: Faber & Faber, 1997.

Riddle, Jefferson C. Davis. *The Indian History of the Modoc War.* Introduction by Peter Cozzens. Mechanicsburg, Pa.: Stackpole Books, 2004.

Catahecassa

Born: c. 1740; Florida
Died: c. 1831; Wapakoneta, Ohio
Also known as: Black Hoof
Tribal affiliation: Shawnee
Significance: A principal chief and spirited orator, Catahecassa fought against white settlers during several Indian rebellions.

Although forced to move north because of white expansion, Catahecassa was originally from Florida. During the French and Indian war, Catahecassa aided the French, thereby helping ensure General Edward Braddock's defeat at Fort Duquesne in 1755. Following the ultimate French defeat, Catahecassa supported PONTIAC in his pantribal rebel-

lion against the British in 1763. He also aided Shawnee chief CORN-
STALK and TARHE of the Wyandots during Lord Dunmore's War, 1773-
1774, in which Indians unsuccessfully fought to retain their land rights
in Kentucky.

During the American Revolution, Catahecassa assisted the British
against the Americans. With the Shawnee BLUE JACKET, he again fought
Americans during LITTLE TURTLE's War, 1790-1794. After General
"Mad" Anthony Wayne marshaled two thousand highly disciplined
troops, Indians suffered a devastating loss at the Battle of Fallen Timbers, August 20, 1794. On August 3, 1795, the allied leaders signed the
Treaty of Fort Greenville, by which their territory, including more than
half of Ohio, was ceded for lands farther west.

Thereafter, Catahecassa sought to maintain peace. To that end, like
the Wyandot Tarhe, he refused to join TECUMSEH in his rebellion during 1809-1811.

Mary E. Virginia

Catches, Pete

Born: March 17, 1912; South Dakota
Died: December 3, 1993; South Dakota
Also known as: Petaga Yuha Mani (Walks with Hot Coals)
Tribal affiliation: Lakota (Sioux)
Significance: A Lakota medicine man, Pete Catches is credited with re-
viving the outlawed Plains Indian Sun Dance ceremony among the
Lakota.

Pete Catches was born into a Lakota family of hereditary medicine men.
After being orphaned, he was reared in a Roman Catholic mission
school. Despite his rearing, he grew up devoted to traditional beliefs
and ways and became a Lakota healer and adviser. He grew to shun all
aspects of Western culture and formally ended his involvement with Catholicism during the 1970's.

In 1964, Catches performed the Sun Dance, which had been outlawed by the U.S. government in 1881 but had been kept alive secretly.
The most solemn and important ritual of the Plains Indians, the Sun
Dance is performed at midsummer near the summer solstice at the time
of the year's fullness and fertility. After purification in a sweat lodge, the
Lakota Sun Dancer approaches the dance site. The camp circle represents the universe. At its center is a two-branched cottonwood tree cut
first by a Lakota virgin and carried by Lakota men who never let it touch

the ground. The tree's crotch signifies the legendary nest of the Thunderbirds, huge eagle-like birds who produce thunder, lightning, and rain. The tree is placed at the center of the circle in a hole filled with buffalo fat. This pole represents the Tree of Life that links earth and sky, people and Grandfather Spirit. It is also the sun pole that signifies the regenerative power of the sun, necessary for the grass that the buffalo eat. From this pole are hung thongs of buffalo hide and figures of a man and a buffalo made of buffalo hide, formerly endowed with exaggerated male organs that signify the fertility of both humans and animals.

The Sun Dancers wear head garlands made of sage, medicine bundles around their necks, and long kilts, usually red, and blow eagle bone whistles. High-flying eagle are regarded as closest to the sun and are thus seen as messengers that delivers prayers to god. When an eagle appears at the start of a ceremony, its presence blesses the occasion.

Participants in the Sun Dance do their dancing with the sun pole from sunrise to sunset, without eating or drinking, on the fourth day of the ceremony. Often their chests are cut and pierced with wooden or bone skewers that are attached to the rawhide thongs on the poles. Each participant then stretches the pierced skin until it breaks free. In addition, some dancers have their backs pierced and tied to buffalo skulls that pull their flesh as they walk. This sacrificial ceremony makes offerings for the welfare of the tribes or individual tribal members who need aid. Buffalo give of themselves to provide food, shelter, clothes and utensils. In reconciliation to the wise and powerful buffalo, humans give of themselves to help maintain the cycles of regeneration.

Catches also was an Eagle Power medicine man, one of the few who conducted the Eagle Power Ceremony. This sacred and secret healing ceremony draws its curing skills from the eagle, red hawk, or red-tailed hawk. Although Catches had earlier rejected the use of peyote, he became a peyote roadman, performing all-night Half-Moon peyote ceremonies. During the 1970's, he lived close to the natural world with few material possessions. He avoided white-introduced objects, including metal, glass, and automobiles, and walked great distances while rejecting mechanical forms of transportation. A devout holy man, he conducted regular fasts at Bear Butte and other sacred sites and frequent sweat-lodge purifications.

Catches's son, Peter V. Catches, wrote *Oceti Wakan* (sacred fireplace), a book that describes the experiences and wisdom of his father and generations of Lakota medicine men.

Joanna Yin

FURTHER READING

Catches, Pete, and Peter V. Catches. *Oceti Wakan: Life and Teaching of a Lakota Medicine Man*. Pine Ridge, S.Dak.: Oceti Wakan, 1997.

Erdoes, Richard. *Crying for a Dream: The World Through Native American Eyes*. Rochester, Vt.: Bear & Company, 2001.

Charcoal

Born: 1856; near Oldman River, western Canada
Died: March 16, 1897; Macleod, Alberta, Canada
Also known as: Opee-o'wun (Palate), Paka'panikapi (Lazy Young Man), Si'k-okskitsis (Charcoal)
Tribal affiliation: Blood Indian Blackfoot
Significance: In what is regarded as a classic conflict between Indian and white society's laws, Charcoal was arrested and hanged for murder.

The Blood Indians of Canada's Alberta province represented the westernmost division of the Blackfoot Indian tribes. Under the terms of an 1877 treaty with the Canadian government, the Bloods, numbering about two thousand persons, were resettled on land known as the Blood Reserve. As a young man, Charcoal and others in the tribe hunted buffalo, while protecting their lands from other tribes, such as the Cree and Crow. However, under the new treaty, the Bloods were restricted to their reserve and could no longer control their own destinies.

Charcoal was the son of Red Plume, a respected warrior among the Blood Indians. By the time he reached adulthood, however, disease, whiskey and Canadian laws had significantly reduced both the numbers and the freedom of his tribe. Food which was ostensibly supplied under terms of the treaty was often inedible. During the winter of 1883, Charcoal and some of his friends stole and butchered cattle from nearby white ranchers. Charcoal was arrested for theft and spent a year in jail. Following tribal custom, Charcoal had by this time married twice. One wife he left in near-starvation, and a second wife died.

In 1891, Charcoal married Pretty Wolverine Woman, a widow nine years younger than him who had been previously married four times. Five years later, Charcoal learned that his wife had been guilty of adultery with a prominent man from his tribe named Medicine Pipe Stem. When Charcoal caught his wife and Medicine Pipe Stem in bed together, he shot his rival in the head. Under Indian law, the killing may have been justified. However, Canadian law was in force, and Major

Samuel Steele of the Northwest Mounted Police was sent to arrest Charcoal. Charcoal spent weeks eluding the police while hiding in the hills. While the Mounted Police had little luck in finding Charcoal's trail, Indian scouts were adept at locating small signs of his movements, and they ultimately tracked him down, to his camp near the Oldman River. Sergeant William Wilde led a police patrol that cornered Charcoal, but in a shootout, Wilde was killed and Charcoal escaped.

Charcoal's shooting of Wilde was more than simply a means for Charcoal to escape. In Charcoal's religious view, Wilde was an officer and "chief" who would serve as a messenger to the spirit world, providing proof of Charcoal's leadership and bravery. Hence, when Charcoal himself later entered that world, he would be welcomed as a great leader.

Meanwhile, tired and without food, Charcoal returned to his village in November, 1896, where he was betrayed by two brothers and handed over to the police. In the ensuing murder trial, he argued that he had been justified in shooting Medicine Pipe Stem and Wilde but was nevertheless convicted. On March 16, 1897, he was hanged.

Richard Adler

FURTHER READING
Dempsey, Hugh. *Charcoal's World.* Lincoln: University of Nebraska Press, 1978.

Charlot

Born: c. 1831; northern Idaho
Died: 1900; Jocko Reservation, Montana
Also known as: Clem-hak-kah (Bear Claw)
Tribal affiliation: Flathead/Salish (possibly Kalispel)
Significance: Charlot fought against removal by white settlers.

Charlot (sometimes called Martin Charlot) was among the Flathead/Salish people in the Bitterroot Mountains of Montana who created fertile farms only to have them seized by immigrants. In the early 1890's, he was among those who were told to move to less fertile land on the Pend d'Oreille reservation. The dissident band of Flathead/Salish led by Charlot managed to delay relocation for several years. Charlot even traveled to Washington, D.C., in 1884 with Indian Agent Peter Ronan to discuss the issue. He still refused to cooperate in removal to a reservation. As whites usurped their homeland, many of Charlot's followers

A 1908 photograph of Chief Charlot, taken at the Flathead Indian Reservation in Montana. (Library of Congress)

moved during the 1880's, but he and a few followers held out until 1900, when they were finally removed by force.

Bruce E. Johansen

FURTHER READING

Marks, Paula M. *In a Barren Land: American Indian Dispossession and Survival.* New York: William Morrow, 1998.

Chatto, Alfred

Born: 1854; place unknown

Died: August 13, 1934; Mescalero Apache Reservation, Ruidoso, Lincoln County, New Mexico

Also known as: Chato (Flat Nose)

Tribal affiliation: Chiricahua Apache

Significance: Alfred Chatto is best known for his service as a scout for the U.S. Army. Although he received a medal from the U.S. government for his service, he was sent to Florida as a prisoner of war.

Alfred Chatto. (National Archives)

Shortly after the U.S. government's forced removal of Chiricahua Apaches to Arizona's San Carlos Reservation in 1881, Alfred Chatto joined many others in fleeing south into Mexico's Sierra Madre Mountains. However, in 1883 he surrendered to General George Crook and afterward became a scout for the U.S. Army. In June, 1886, Chatto and other prominent Apaches who had aided the U.S. military in its campaigns against GERONIMO were called to Washington, D.C., to discuss the future of their people. During this trip the secretary of war awarded Chatto a silver peace medal bearing the likeness of former president Chester A. Arthur for his service.

On July 26, 1886, Captain John G. Bourke, who was well acquainted with Chatto and the scouts, arranged for them to meet with Secretary of War William C. Endicott. Chatto spoke of his trust in the secretary, and he believed that his medal was a sign that the federal government would allow the Chiricahuas to remain in Arizona. On the following day, Bourke escorted Chatto and the entire delegation of scouts to meet with President Grover Cleveland. However, Cleveland did not meet with the scouts, as he had already made up his mind in favor of Apache removal. On July 31, the president met with several cabinet members, including Endicott, and Bourke and Captain Joseph Dorst, who had accompanied Chatto's delegation, to devise a strategy for Apache removal. At the same time, he made sure that Chatto and the other scouts did not return to Arizona. Bourke spoke out against this scheme, arguing that the

Chiricahuas who were then living on the reservation represented no threat to neighboring whites. In the end, however, there was no swaying Cleveland and Endicott from their course.

By the time that Chatto and the scouts finally left Washington, D.C., the only remaining concern of federal officials was how to conduct the removal. General Philip Sheridan, who believed that Chatto was already aware of the government's plan to expel the Chiricahuas from Arizona, wanted to act swiftly. He was worried that if the Apache scouts were to return to their reservation, they would spread word of the government's intentions, thereby causing unrest and a potential breakout. On July 30, Sheridan advised that Chatto and the scouts be sent, as prisoners of war, directly to Fort Marion in Florida. At the same time, the remaining Chiricahua men at San Carlos were to be arrested and placed on a train to Fort Marion. On August 11, Dorst received orders to take Chatto and the scouts to Fort Leavenworth, Kansas. The following month they proceeded to Fort Marion, arriving on September 17. They were then reassigned to Fort Sill in Oklahoma.

In 1902, Chatto once again visited Washington, D.C., accompanied by Jason BETZINEZ and Rogers Toclanny. Their wished to meet with Secretary of War William H. Taft to discuss the possibility of relocating Chiricahuas to the Mescalero Reservation in New Mexico. It was not until 1913, however, that Chatto and most other Chiricahuas were released from their prisoner-of-war status and allowed to establish homes in New Mexico.

Teresa Neva Tate

FURTHER READING
Ball, Eve. *Indeh, An Apache Odyssey.* Utah: Brigham Young University Press, 1980.

Cher

Born: May 20, 1946; El Centro, California
Tribal affiliation: Cherokee
Significance: One of the most adaptable celebrities of her time, Cher has been a recording artist, performer/comedian, and award-winning serious actress.

Cher was born Cherilyn Sarkisian. Her mother, Jackie Jean Crouch, later known as Georgia Holt, was part Cherokee and part French. Her father, John Sarkisian, was of Armenian descent. Cher's parents were divorced

Cher. (Hulton|Archive by Getty Images)

soon after her birth. One of her mother's other husbands, Gilbert LaPiere, adopted Cher and her sister Georgeanne.

Cher left school and then left home when she was about sixteen. She soon met Salvatore "Sonny" Bono, an aspiring songwriter and record producer. Cher and Sonny wrote songs and began to perform in Los Angeles nightclubs under the name Caesar and Cleo before changing the name of their act to Sonny and Cher. The couple was married on October 27, 1964.

In 1965 Sonny and Cher's single "I Got You Babe" sold more than three million records and reached the top of the pop charts. The couple, with their colorful, hip outfits (including fringed vests, patterned pants, and boots), became pop icons. They released a number of hit singles, including "Bang, Bang (My Baby Shot Me Down)" (1966) and "The Beat Goes On" (1967). By 1968, out of favor with the young people who had been their record-buying public, Sonny and Cher began performing in nightclubs in glittering evening wear. In 1969 their daughter, Chastity, was born.

In 1971 Sonny and Cher began a successful comedy-variety show for CBS that lasted until 1974. In the wake of her newfound popularity as a television star, Cher recorded solo hit records, including "Gypsies, Tramps, and Thieves" (1971), "Half-Breed" (1973), and "Dark Lady" (1974). Cher has not been notably active in American Indian causes or culture, but the song "Half-Breed"—and the fact that she sometimes performed it wearing a stage version of Indian attire—was an acknowledgment of her part-Indian ancestry.

By 1974 Sonny and Cher were divorcing. Three days after her divorce from Sonny Bono was final in 1975, Cher married rock musician Gregg Allman. Nine days later, she filed for divorce from the alcoholic, drug-addicted Allman. The couple attempted several reconciliations, but none was successful. Cher and Gregg Allman had one child, a son, Elijah Blue Allman, born in 1976. (Sonny Bono's show business career never recovered after his divorce from Cher. He went on to become a successful restaurateur and politician. He was elected mayor of Palm Springs, California, in 1988 and U.S. Congressman in 1994. Bono died in a skiing accident in 1998.)

In the late 1970's Cher was performing her solo act in Las Vegas and looking for acting jobs. Robert Altman cast her in his 1982 filmed version of the play *Come Back to the Five and Dime Jimmy Dean, Jimmy Dean.* She then appeared in *Silkwood* (1983), with Meryl Streep, for which she was nominated for an Academy Award for Best Supporting Actress. In *Mask* (1985) she played the unconventional biker mother of a son afflicted with craniodiaphyseal dysplasia, a disease that causes facial deformity and enlargement of the head.

Cher also continued as a recording artist. In 1987 she released the album *I Found Someone* and made music videos for three of its songs. The year 1987 also saw the release of three Cher films: *The Witches of Eastwick, Suspect,* and *Moonstruck. Moonstruck* won her the Academy Award for Best Actress. Cher released another album, *Heart of Stone,* in 1989. The same year, in collaboration with nutritionist Robert Haas, she published *Forever Fit,* a diet and exercise book. *Mermaids,* Cher's next film, was released in 1990.

Cher became involved in environmental and charitable causes during the 1980's and 1990's. She became active in the International Craniofacial Foundation after learning of the organization during her work in *Mask.* She arranged for facially deformed children and their parents to attend her concerts as guests, and she contributed significant amounts of money to the foundation and to individual patients who needed expensive surgeries.

In 1998, Cher published her autobiography. Meanwhile, she continued to release albums, make television appearances, and perform on-stage.

Jennifer Padgett Griffith
Jennifer Raye James

FURTHER READING

Bego, Mark. *Cher: If You Believe.* Introduction by Mary Wilson. New York: Cooper Square Press, 2001.

Cher, and Jeff Coplon. *The First Time.* New York: Simon and Schuster, 1998.

Chisholm, Jesse

Born: c. 1805; southeastern Tennessee
Died: March 4, 1868; near Norman, Indian Territory (now in Oklahoma)
Tribal affiliation: Cherokee
Significance: Jesse Chisholm's work as a trader and his ability as an interpreter carried his influence far beyond the reach of his own Cherokee tribe.

Jesse Chisholm, a half-blood Cherokee born in Tennessee, traveled to the western Indian Territory before the Trail of Tears of 1838-1839. After marrying a Creek woman, he traded with the Plains Indian tribes of the West. In the course of that work, he learned fourteen different languages, which enabled him to become an interpreter.

Chisholm's language abilities made him a vital part of Creek efforts to establish peace among the tribes of the Great Plains. In 1853, he was sent to the Comanche to help make arrangements for the Grand Council, which was held at the Salt Plains in June, 1853. Here Creek leaders met with delegations from many of the Great Plains tribes. Chisholm was the interpreter for all of the tribes.

Chisholm had a trading post near Wichita, Kansas. In 1865, he drove a wagon from Texas to his trading post. Texas cattlemen followed the ruts left by Chisholm's wagon to get their cattle to Wichita, and the route became the famous Chisholm Trail. Jesse Chisholm died in 1868.

Glenn L. Swygart

FURTHER READING
Cushman, Ralph B. *Jesse Chisholm: Trail Blazer, Sam Houston's Troubleshooter Friend, Kin to the Cherokee.* Austin, Tex.: Eakin Press, 1992.
Hoig, Stan. *Jesse Chisholm: Ambassador of the Plains.* Niwot: University of Colorado, 1991.

Chona, Maria

Born: c. 1845; Mesquite Root, Arizona
Died: 1936; Santa Rosa, Arizona
Tribal affiliation: Tohono O'odham
Significance: An important spiritual healer among her people, Maria Chona was the subject of an work of autobiography written during the 1930's.

Maria Chona was born in what is now the Tohono O'odham (formerly Papago) Indian Reservation in southwestern Arizona. During the early 1930's, when she was nearly ninety years old, she collaborated with anthropologist Ruth Underhill on *Papago Woman*, an as-told-to autobiography that is still considered one of the finest examples of its genre. In her introduction to the book, Underhill explained that she chose Chona as the subject for the autobiography partly because of her personal friendship with Chona and partly because of Chona's prior service to her as an informant and guide, to Tohono O'odham culture. Underhill added that a crucial factor in her decision was Chona's complete acceptance of her culture and her "contact with so many of its important phases."

Chona's presentation of these "important phases" is all the more compelling because, as a woman, she offered what was at the time a rarely documented glimpse of the woman's views of American Indian life. Part of Chona's narrative presents a first-hand account of the typical activities of Tohono O'odham life before it was markedly influenced by white culture, including the tribe's desert subsistence patterns, daily routines, ritual activities, and entertainments. Among the book's highlights are Chona's reminiscences about helping to gather the fruit of the saguaro cactus, which the Tohono O'odham use in their rainmaking ceremony; a war expedition against the Apaches and the ceremonies performed upon the war party's return; rituals surrounding the planting and "singing up" of corn; and customs and attitudes regarding relationships among parents and children, and the genders, including a brief description of transsexuality.

Interspersed among these descriptions are Chona's accounts of major events and crises in her own life. For example, she describes a time when she was a young girl and she and the rest of her family were stricken with "owl sickness" and were cured by village medicine men. She also presents an extended description of her coming-of-age ceremony, which she describes as being as hard for girls as the men's purification rites. She also points out that the girls were given more to eat, "because we are women. And they do not let us sit and wait for dreams. That is because we are women, too. Women must work!"

Dreams, or visions, in Tohono O'odham culture have always been sources of spiritual power. Chona describes how, starting in her childhood, she received such visions, but because of gender proscriptions she was not permitted to pursue her apparent calling to become a medicine woman. Instead, soon after her puberty rite, her parents arranged for her to marry a young medicine man and to follow a life course more typical for Tohono O'odham women. Although she dutifully entered into the union and grew to love her husband, with whom she "had starved so much together." However, she abruptly left him after twelve years when he took a second wife, even though that was an accepted practice for Tohono O'odham medicine men during that period.

Soon after her divorce, Chona's uncle arranged for her second marriage—to a widower who was much older but "had horses" (that is, was wealthy). Following the birth of two sons, the couple moved to Tucson where they worked during the winter. Shortly after they returned home, Chona fell ill and received a vision in which she was given the power to cure childhood diseases. In contrast to her situation during her first marriage, Chona now actively pursued the role of medicine woman, learning additional cures from her medicine man brother and receiving further visions and powers from spirit helpers.

Chona died in Santa Rosa village on the Tohono O'odham Reservation in 1936, the same year that *Papago Woman* first appeared.

Harvey Markowitz

FURTHER READING
Underhill, Ruth Murray. *Papago Woman.* New York: Holt, Rinehart and Winston, 1979.

Clarke, Peter Dooyentate

Born: c. 1810; place unknown
Died: c. 1892 (possibly as early as 1870); Anderdon reserve, Ontario, Canada
Also known as: Peter D. Clark
Tribal affiliation: Wyandot
Significance: An influential chief of the Wyandot tribe, Peter Dooyentate Clarke published an important book that preserves some of the history, customs, and traditions of the Wyandots.

Peter Clarke was the son of a European-Canadian Indian officer and a Wyandot woman. At the time of his birth, his father was stationed at Fort Malden, located in present-day Amherstburg, Ontario, Canada. His mother was the daughter of Huron-Wyandot chief Adam Brown. Clarke spent most of his early life in the Anderdon township on an Indian reserve in southwestern Ontario. In 1841, he moved south to present-day Sandusky, Ohio, onto land granted to the Wyandots by the U.S. government after the War of 1812. While living there, Clarke married a Cherokee woman named Sabra. By 1842, the Wyandots had sold most of their land in Ohio and were moved to Wyandotte County, Kansas.

Around 1865, Clarke moved back to Anderdon to assist his mother who was in failing health. In 1867, he was reinstated into the Anderdon Wyandot tribe. Being the grandson of former chief Adam Brown, he then claimed his hereditary right to be chief of the tribe. His brother, George I. Clark, had been appointed chief of the tribe in 1850 and served for many years. George and Peter were both close friends of William Walker, a leader of the Wyandot nation who was appointed provisional governor of the Nebraska-Kansas Territory in 1853.

In 1871, Clarke was able to refute the claim of Joseph White to be the tribal chief and attain that post himself. While serving as chief of the Canadian (Lorette) Wyandots, Clarke signed numerous treaties. Among the results of these treaties were the surrendering of Little Turkey Island in the Detroit River in 1874, parts of the Anderdon Township in 1877 and 1879, and the Huron Indian reserve in 1892. Near the end of Clarke's tenure as chief, the Wyandots were confined to lands that occupied a reduced region with boundaries that extended from the shores of the Thames River, in the north, to the shores of Lake Erie, in the south.

After returning to Anderdon in the mid-1860's, Clarke undertook the important task of recording the history, customs, and traditions of the Wyandot tribe. He gathered and recorded much of the oral history of the tribe. His *Origin and Traditional History of the Wyandots, and Sketches of Other Indian Tribes of North America* was published in Toronto in 1870. According to North American Indian experts, the book is unreliable in many of its historical statements and conclusions but is accurate in its descriptions of the habits, customs, and traditions of the Wyandots.

Clarke is believed to have died in the Anderdon reserve around 1892. However, historian Penny Petrone records his death as occurring around 1870.

Alvin K. Benson

Cloud, Henry Roe

Born: December 28, 1884; Thurston County, Nebraska
Died: February 9, 1950; Siletz, Oregon
Also known as: Wonah'ilayhunka
Tribal affiliation: Winnebago
Significance: Henry Roe Cloud was instrumental in expanding Indian educational opportunities.

Henry Cloud's parents were Nah'ilayhunkay and Hard to See. He later added "Roe" to his English name in honor of his adoptive parents, missionaries Dr. and Mrs. Walter C. Roe. He was educated at the Indian school in Genoa, Nebraska, the Santee Mission School in Nebraska, and Dwight Moody's Academy at Mt. Hermon, Massachusetts. He was the first Indian to graduate from Yale, in 1910. He went on to receive a Bachelor of Divinity degree from Auburn Theological Seminary in 1913, and was ordained a Presbyterian minister the same year. He received a master's degree from Yale in 1914 and a Doctor of Divinity degree from the College of Emporia. In 1915, he married Elizabeth A. Bender (a Chippewa), a graduate of the Hampton Normal Training School. They had four daughters and a son who died in infancy.

In 1915, Cloud founded the Roe Indian Institute in Wichita, Kansas. He remained the Institute's superintendent until 1931, when he became a special representative of the Bureau of Indian Affairs. Roe Institute, which became the American Indian Institute in 1920, was unique for the time in that it promoted an academic rather than a vocational curriculum, with the aim of developing Indian leaders.

From 1933 to 1936, Cloud was superintendent of Haskell Institute in Lawrence, Kansas. Appointed Haskell's superintendent under the administration of John Collier to help change the direction of Indian education, he was unhappy with Haskell's vocational emphasis and wanted Indian education to help develop Indian leaders. His pioneering work in that direction helped lead to Haskell eventually becoming a junior college in 1970 and Haskell Indian Nations University in 1993. Cloud was appointed assistant supervisor of Indian education at-large for the Bureau of Indian Affairs in 1936. In 1947, he became superintendent of the Umatilla Indian Agency, where he served until his death.

Throughout his life, Cloud was active in Indian affairs. In his twenties he was a leader in the Society of American Indians, which preceded the National Council of American Indians. He served as chairman of the Winnebago delegation to the President in 1912, was a member of the Commission of Federal Survey of Indian Schools in 1914, was a member of the Standing Committee of One Hundred on Indian Affairs in 1920, and was a co-author of the Meriam Report of 1928. While he called for Indian leadership, he also promoted cultural assimilation both as a Presbyterian minister and as a Bureau of Indian Affairs employee.

Jon Reyhner

Cobell, Elouise

Born: 1946; Blackfeet Reservation, Montana

Tribal affiliation: Blackfoot

Significance: The founder of the first Native American-owned bank in the United States, Elouise Cobell has won a national reputation as the initiator of a class-action suit seeking an accounting from the federal government of the vast sums of money held in trust on behalf of Native Americans.

Elouise Cobell has spent most of her life on the Blackfeet Reservation of Montana, where she was born. She was one of eight children in a household with no electricity or running water, and a form of family entertainment was reciting oral histories. The stories that she heard while growing up included anecdotes about the pitifully small government checks the Indians received from the federal Bureau of Indian Affairs (BIA). As Cobell grew up, she became interested in financial matters and would later come to question why it was that Indians received so little money from the government.

After high school, Cobell graduated from Great Falls Commercial College and then studied for two years at Montana State University. Her education at the university was interrupted when she returned to the reservation to take care of her terminally ill mother. In 1968, she went to Seattle, Washington, and worked as an accountant at a local television station. She thought that she would never return to reservation life, but the man she married, Alvin Cobell, was also a Blackfoot, and he soon decided that he wanted to return to the natural environment in which he had grown up. In 1970, the couple returned to the Blackfeet Reservation, where they have since lived on Elouise's family ranch.

As one of the few members of her tribe with training in accounting, Elouise Cobell accepted the position of treasurer of the Blackfeet Nation. She found the tribal's financial records and accounting system in chaos and spent the next thirteen years putting it on a sound footing, while working her ranch with her husband. Her involvement in tribal finances drew her into investigating the tribe's relationship with the BIA and asking the Department of the Interior questions about the many financial discrepancies that she uncovered. She had little success, however, in getting satisfactory answers from the government.

In 1987, Cobell was the primary force behind the creation of a bank owned and operated by the Blackfeet Nation; it was the first tribally owned bank in the country. Since its creation, the bank has provided loans to members of the tribe to help them start businesses that they would otherwise have not been able to create.

In 1887, when the federal government opened Indian reservation land to white settlers with the Dawes Severalty Act, it set up the Individual Indian Trust to handle money earned from leases and the sale of oil, natural gas, coal, timber, and other resources on the Indian-owned lands. Judging that Indians were not capable of managing their own finances, the government made itself responsible for managing their money. Over the next century, the government made payments to individual Indians from the trust funds but provided recipients with little or no explanation of what the payments were based on.

During an average year of the late twentieth century, at least $500 million were deposited into the Individual Indian Trust from companies leasing Native American lands. According to law and financial theory, the money is collected by the Interior Department and sent to the Treasury Department, where is supposed to be placed into individual "trust" accounts for redistribution to the Indian owners of the leased lands. However, over the course of more than century, the Interior Department's records became a shambles, as the BIA lost track of tens of thousands of people entitled to payments. Most of the money was apparently diverted to other government funds, and many records were lost or destroyed.

The checks for small sums of money that members of Cobell's family and their Blackfoot neighbors received from the government were payments from that federal trust fund. One resident of the reservation, for example, wanted to know why her family was receiving less than one thousand dollars per year for the seven thousand acres of family land that the government leased to non-Indians, who were using it to graze cattle and extract timber, oil, and other minerals. When Cobell asked for explanations of such matters, government officials put her off. In addition to having to cope with government mismanagement, Cobell encountered a long BIA tradition of discouraging Indians from rocking the boat.

Around 1991, after having spent a decade badgering federal government officials for explanations of BIA finances, Cobell finally found someone in the Interior Department who was willing to help her— David Matheson, a member of the Coeur d'Alene tribe who was a deputy commissioner of Indian affairs in the George H. W. Bush administration. However, Matheson was about to lose his job when Bill Clinton's administration came into power in 1993. Cobell would have trouble finding anyone in the new administration who was willing to listen to her, but Matheson connected her with an influential Washington, D.C., banking attorney, Dennis Gingold, who took an interest in the question of Indian trust money. Gingold recommended to Cobell that she file a suit against the government, but she was initially reluctant to do so, hoping that the Congress would take action to correct the problems.

Congress did take some steps to force the BIA to account for its finances, but the magnitude of the problem was so great that no tangible progress was made. In 1996, Cobell finally became fed up with government inaction after Attorney General Janet Reno reneged on a promise to look into the matter. With Gingold's help, she initiated the lawsuit against the Department of the Interior that was to become the largest class-action ever filed against the federal government. This suit, known as *Cobell v. Norton,* after Cobell and Secretary of the Interior Gale Norton, eventually involved some 500,000 plaintiffs. Drawing on the services of more than one hundred government lawyers in the Interior and Treasury Departments, the lawsuit grew into the largest single employer of federal legal talent in the history of the United States.

Cobell's goal in filing the suit was to force the Department of the Interior to account for its administration of the Individual Indian Trust and to make appropriate restitution to Indians who had been denied money that was rightfully theirs. The suit was still being litigated in late 2004, and the total amount of money that it involves has been open to conjecture. In 1997, the most commonly accepted figures ranged between two and three billion dollars. By late 2002, however, Gingold, who was leading the plaintiffs' suit, raised the estimate to more than ten billion dollars. A report prepared for the Interior Department in 2004 suggested that the federal government's total liability to Native Americans might eventually reach forty billion dollars—a figure that would work out to about eighty thousand dollars per plaintiff.

In 1997, Cobell was surprised to receive a $300,000 "genius award" from the John D. MacArthur Foundation for her work on the Indian trust funds case. She immediately donated most of her prize to the expensive legal work that the case required. Shortly afterward, J. Patrick Lannan of the Lannan Foundation read about Cobell's MacArthur grant, and traveled to Montana to meet her. Lannan's foundation eventually donated four million dollars to the cause. By mid-2002, the cost of prosecuting the suit had reached eight million dollars—a great deal of money, but a small amount compared to the hundreds of millions of dollars in tax money that the federal government was spending to defend itself.

In December, 1999, federal judge Royce C. Lamberth, who was assigned to conduct the case in the Washington, D.C., federal district court, stated that the federal government had violated its trust responsibilities to Native Americans. The judge ordered the Interior and Treasury Departments to compile an audit of the Individual Indian Trust fund, going back to its origins in 1887. Thanks largely to Cobell's determination to see the case through, the suit continued to achieve victories in the court, but the case was still not fully resolved at the end of 2004, and none of the misappropriated funds had yet been turned over to their rightful recipients.

Bruce E. Johansen

FURTHER READING

Awehali, Brian. "Fighting Long Odds: Government Continues to Shred, Evade, Obstruct, Lie, and Conspire in Indian Trust Case." *LiP Magazine*, December 15, 2003.

Johansen, Bruce E. "The B.I.A. as Banker: 'Trust' Is Hard When Billions Disappear." *Native Americas* 14, no. 1 (Spring, 1997): 14-23.

Kennedy, J. Michael. "Truth and Consequences on the Reservation." *Los Angeles Times Magazine*, July 7, 2002.

Reynolds, Jerry. "Bush Administration Likely Behind Cobell Appropriations Rider." *Indian Country Today*, November 1, 2003.

Cochise

Born: c. 1812; Chiricahua Mountains of present-day southern Arizona
Died: June 8, 1874; Chiricahua Apache Reservation, Arizona Territory
Also known as: Goci (His Nose)
Tribal affiliation: Chiricahua Apache
Significance: As principal chief of the eastern Chiricahua Apaches from 1860 to 1872, Cochise orchestrated and led raids against U.S. and Mexican settlements.

Cochise was born in the Spanish colony of Sonora (in present-day Arizona) during the revolution of 1810-1821, which eventually established the modern nation of Mexico. Although details of his ancestry remain uncertain, Cochise was probably the son of Pisago Cabezon, the leader of one of four bands of the Chiricahua Apaches who ranged over the area that is now southern Arizona and New Mexico and the northern Mexican states of Sonora and Chihuahua. As he grew to manhood, the long peace that had marked Mexican-Chiricahuan relations since around 1790 was coming to an end. By 1830, a bloody cycle of raiding,

Apache Chief Cochise's stronghold in the Dragoon Mountains of Arizona, from which he led raids against the U.S. Army and American settlers. (National Archives)

plundering, and murder had begun between the Apaches and Mexicans that determined the course of Cochise's life.

Virtually nothing is known about Cochise's life before 1835. He almost certainly received the special training his people reserved for the sons of chiefs, who were expected to become leaders when they matured. Such a child learned more discipline than other children, including controlling one's temper, patience with other children, and respect for the property of others. Religious ritual accompanied every phase of the instruction of all Apache children.

Cochise entered the pages of history for the first time in 1835, when Mexican documents mention him as a leader of the Chokonen band of Chiricahua Apaches raiding in Sonora. His name appears again on the lists of those Apaches drawing rations from the Mexican government at Janos in modern Chihuahua in 1842 and 1843. By that time, the Apaches were in an almost perpetual state of war with the Mexican population of the area. Beginning about 1830, raiding (what Cochise called in his later years "making a living"), livestock stealing, and plundering became an integral part of the economies of many Apache tribes.

The man who was most likely Cochise's father died by treachery during the Mexican-Apache wars in 1845 or 1846. Cochise never forgave the Mexicans and continued to raid south of the U.S. border until almost the end of his life.

After the Mexican-American War in 1846-1848, the United States acquired the territory known as the Mexican Cession (modern New Mexico, Arizona, Colorado, Utah, Nevada, and California). The Apache bands quickly learned that they could raid in northern Mexico, flee across the border into Arizona or New Mexico, and have relative immunity from Mexican pursuit. The Apaches also found unscrupulous U.S. citizens eager to buy their Mexican plunder.

The Chiricahuas continued to live in the United States and raid primarily in Mexico for the next eight years, with Cochise probably a subchief in large frequent raiding parties led by his father-in-law, MANGAS COLORADAS. In 1857, the U.S. Army launched its first large-scale campaign against the Apaches in reaction to raids in New Mexico. Cochise joined other Chiricahuas in making a temporary peace with the Mexicans and fled across the border. This began a pattern that continued throughout the next decade: The Apaches would make peace on one side of the border for a while and then raid on the other.

By 1859, Cochise had become the principal chief of the Chokonen band. He negotiated a peace with the U.S. troops that lasted until 1861, although members of his band occasionally raided north of the border. Early in 1861, with the American Civil War only days in the future, an event occurred that launched the so-called Cochise wars between the U.S. government and the Chiricahuas: the Bascom affair.

Although accounts of the affair vary, American troops led by Lieutenant George Nicholas Bascom apparently captured Cochise by treachery during a peace parlay on February 6, 1861, near Apache Pass in southern Arizona. Bascom ordered the execution of three of Cochise's relatives in retaliation for the torture deaths of three U.S. citizens. Cochise escaped and spent the next decade pursuing vengeance against the Americans. For the next four years, the American governments (both U.S. and Confederate) focused most of their attention on fighting each other. As a result of American distraction, the Apaches raided with relative impunity throughout New Mexico and Arizona.

Cochise led or planned many of the Apache raids during this period. He became not only the principal chief of the Chokonen, but of the entire Chiricahua tribe. Apache warriors from other Apache tribes such as the Mescaleros and White Mountain groups often joined his raiding parties because of his reputation as a leader. He became the most famous (or infamous) Indian leader of the 1860's, often mentioned prominently in the American press by newspapers as far away as San Francisco and Missouri. He also continued to plan and lead raids into Mexico. The Mexicans, their attention diverted by the French Emperor

Napoleon III's attempt to establish himself as emperor of Mexico, became easy prey for Apache raids.

After the U.S. Civil War ended and the French were expelled from Mexico, both governments began devoting more men and resources to stopping the Apache depredations in the Southwest. American and Mexican officials began cooperating more closely to eliminate the Apache scourge. As a result of this cooperation, Cochise found it more difficult to make peace with one country and raid in the other. Despite large expenditures by both governments on troops and costly expeditions, Cochise managed to evade the American and Mexican armies for several years. Cochise was growing old, however, and his health was deteriorating. He also supposedly confided to his subchiefs that the Apache way of life was coming to an end. Finally, largely through the efforts of Thomas J. Jeffords, General Oliver Otis Howard negotiated a lasting treaty with Cochise on October 10, 1872, at Cochise's camp in the Dragoon Mountains in southern Arizona.

The terms of the treaty allowed Cochise and his people to live at peace in his beloved Chiricahua Mountains, drawing rations from the U.S. government. In return, he agreed to use all of his influence to halt Apache raids in both the United States and Mexico. For the remainder of his life, the raids virtually ceased in Arizona and New Mexico, but continued sporadically in northern Mexico. On June 8, 1874, Cochise died in bed of a stomach ailment, an ironic end for a man who spent virtually his entire adult life at war.

Paul Madden

FURTHER READING

Aleshire, Peter. *Cochise: The Life and Times of the Great Apache Chief.* New York: Wiley, 2001.

Cremony, John C. *Life Among the Apaches.* Tucson: Arizona Silhouettes, 1954.

Lockwood, Frank C. *The Apache Indians.* New York: Macmillan, 1938.

Sweeney, Edwin R. *Cochise: Chiricahua Apache Chief.* Norman: University of Oklahoma Press, 1991.

Sweeney, Edwin R., and Angie Debo. *Great Apache Chiefs: Cochise and Geronimo.* New York: MJF Books, 1996.

Thrapp, Dan L. *Conquest of Apacheria.* Norman: University of Oklahoma Press, 1967.

Tyler, Barbara Ann. "Cochise, Apache War Leader, 1858-1861." *Journal of Arizona History* 6 (Spring, 1965): 1-10.

Cody, Iron Eyes

Born: April 3, 1904; Fort Gibson, Oklahoma?
Died: January 4, 1999; Los Angeles, California
Also known as: Espera DeCorti, Espera Corti
Tribal affiliation: Cree/Cherokee?
Significance: Iron Eyes Cody was a film and television actor who was probably most familiar to Americans as the crying Indian looking at a polluted river in "Keep America Beautiful" television spots during the early 1970's.

With his omnipresent head feathers and braided wigs, Iron Eyes Cody was a living embodiment of popular images of the noble Indian. He claimed that his mother was a Cree from northern Canada and his father an Oklahoma Cherokee named Thomas Long Plume, a performer in circuses and wild west shows, but it is possible that he had no Native American blood in him at all.

Cody made dozens of films, and his acting credits date back to the silent movie era, when he began making films at the age of twelve with Cecil B. DeMille. His most notable film appearances included *Custer's Last Stand* (1936), *Code of the Redman* (1942), *Sitting Bull* (1954), *The Great Sioux Massacre* (1965), and *Grayeagle* (1977)—in all of which he played Indians. The films' credits sometimes identified him as "Indian Chief," or "Indian Joe." He also had guest appearances on such television shows as *Bonanza, Gunsmoke,* and *Rawhide.* He was a consultant on Indian lore on many shows, teaching such skills as Indian sign language, use of the bow and arrow, and dancing.

In 1996 the *New Orleans Times-Picayune* broke the story

Iron Eyes Cody in 1986. (AP/Wide World Photos)

of Cody's true identity with the aid of members of his family. They claimed that he was actually born in New Orleans to an Italian immigrant family, DeCorti, which later changed its name to Corti. His sister said that he liked to dress as an Indian when he was a child and that he always wanted to be a movie star. After he moved to Los Angeles, he changed his surname to Cody and his first name, Espera, to Iron Eyes, and presented himself to the world as a full-blooded Native American.

Throughout his life, Cody helped Indian charities, especially schools and reservations working to eradicate alcoholism and teach Native American traditions. His Iron Eyes Cody Foundation (IEC) supports scholarships for Indian education for Indian children. With his Native American wife, he adopted two Native American boys.

Joanna Yin

Colorow

Born: c. 1810; northern Mexico, in present-day northern Colorado
Died: December 11, 1888; Uintah Reservation, Utah
Also known as: Colorado (Red)
Tribal affiliation: Ute
Significance: Colorow was an influential chief among northern Colorado Ute bands and a leader in an attack on U.S. troops in 1879; he clashed with game wardens while leading his band to hunt off the reservation in 1887.

Colorow rose to prominence among the isolated northwestern Colorado Ute bands as a chief of the Yampa band, which ranged the Yampa River. After 1868, his band was consolidated with other northern Ute bands as part of the White River Ute agency (White River Utes) near present-day Meeker, Colorado.

Colorow signed as subchief to a treaty in 1863 and as a Yampa Ute chief in 1868. He was one of the prominent Ute leaders who were passed over as spokesman for all Utes when the U.S. government sought a head chief with whom to negotiate and settled on the more conciliatory leader OURAY.

Colorow was known for his large size and often belligerent and threatening manner. In 1879, he joined CAPTAIN JACK and Antelope in ambushing U.S. troops under the command of T. T. Thornburgh as they entered the Ute reservation at the request of White River agent Nathan C. Meeker. The Ute bands feared that the soldiers were coming to transport them forcibly to Indian Territory in Oklahoma. When, after negotiations with Colorow and Captain Jack, the troops crossed the reservation boundaries anyway, the Utes attacked and besieged them for six days. Meanwhile, other Utes attacked the agency and massacred white workers and took their women captive.

As punishment for the massacre, the U.S. government removed the White River Utes from Colorado and resettled them on the Uintah Reservation in Utah; however, Colorow switched his allegiance to the central Colorado Uncompaghre Ute band to avoid removal. Nevertheless, by 1881, this band had been maneuvered out of Colorado too. On the day the Utes were to begin their exodus into Utah, Colorow led his warriors in a charge against U.S. troops, but they were quickly and ignominiously repulsed by a show of power.

While on the Uintah Reservation, Colorow led his band back into northern Colorado for annual fall hunts, as was provided in their 1873 agreement and never rescinded. In 1886, however, Colorado passed legislation binding all Indians to local laws when off reservations; this was interpreted as including game laws, so Colorado game wardens and a posse were waiting for Colorow's band in 1887. Shots were exchanged and a squaw camp burned with its accumulated hides. The Utes fled back toward Utah, chased by state troops and a local posse. The band was engaged in battle just before the Utah border where at least fifteen Indians were killed and a substantial amount of Indian livestock was confiscated. Troops from Fort Duchesne, Utah, eventually arrived and escorted the band home. According to tradition, it was at this battle that Colorow received the wound from which he would die a year later.

Robert Jones
Sondra Jones

FURTHER READING

Decker, Peter R. *"The Utes Must Go!: American Expansion and the Removal of a People.* Golden, Colo.: Fulcrum Publishing, 2004.

Miller, Mark E. *Hollow Victory: The White River Expedition of 1879 and the Battle of Milk Creek.* Niwot: University Press of Colorado, 1997.

Rockwell, Wilson. *The Utes: A Forgotten People.* Ouray, Colo.: Western Reflections, 1998.

Simmons, Virginia McConnell. *The Ute Indians of Utah, Colorado, and New Mexico.* Niwot: University Press of Colorado, 2000.

Comcomly

Born: c. 1765; Northwest Coast, U.S.
Died: 1830; Northwest Coast, U.S.
Tribal affiliation: Chinook
Significance: Comcomly aided white exploration of the Northwest Coast.
A Chinook leader, Comcomly assisted Meriwether Lewis and William
Clark as they traveled to the mouth of the Columbia River in 1805. In
1811, he aided John Jacob Astor's fur traders, who had been ship-
wrecked while traveling on the *Tonquin*. The following year, he wel-
comed Astor's minions, the Overland Astorians, who established the
Astoria trading post at the mouth of the Astoria River. To secure rela-
tions with the traders, he offered his daughter in marriage to Duncan
M'Dougal, leader of the Astorians' expedition.

During the War of 1812, Comcomly extended military support to the
Americans. The following year, when the Americans abandoned their
post, he aided the British who moved into the region.

An extraordinarily wealthy man, Comcomly relished extravagant dis-
plays. During visits to Vancouver, he was accompanied by three hundred
slaves, who carpeted his path from ship to town with beaver and otter
furs. After his death from smallpox in 1830, his skull was stolen by a
white trader, who then sold it in Edinburgh.

Mary E. Virginia

Conquering Bear

Born: ?
Died: August 19, 1854; near Ash Hollow (now in Nebraska)
Also known as: Mahtoiowa, Whirling Bear
Tribal affiliation: Brule Lakota (Sioux)
Significance: Conquering Bear was killed while attempting to accom-
    modate whites; his death precipitated war in the northern Plains.
Conquering Bear's band of Sioux lived along the North Platte River,
which was part of the Oregon Trail. When a party of Mormons passed
through the region in August, 1854, a cow wandered onto Conquering
Bear's land. Its Mormon owner fled to nearby Fort Laramie, reporting
that Indians had stolen his livestock. Meantime, High Forehead, a visiting Miniconjou Sioux, slaughtered the cow. Conquering Bear, who in
1851 had signed the Treaty of Fort Laramie pledging peace along the
Oregon Trail, traveled to the fort offering restitution. The fort com-

mander, however, dispatched a newly commissioned and eager West Point lieutenant, John Grattan, to arrest High Forehead.

Even after cavalrymen murdered one of his men, Conquering Bear restrained his warriors. Grattan, however, ordered his men to attack, and Conquering Bear was killed. Conquering Bear's warriors retaliated, killing all but one of Grattan's detachment. Subsequently, on September 3, 1855, General William S. Harney and his forces attacked a Sioux camp. Thus began the wars of the northern Plains.

Mary E. Virginia

Cook-Lynn, Elizabeth

Born: November 17, 1930; Fort Thompson, South Dakota
Tribal affiliation: Dakota Lakota (Sioux)
Significance: Elizabeth Cook-Lynn is an author, poet, scholar, educator, and journal editor.

Born Elizabeth Irving, Elizabeth Cook-Lynn grew up on the Crow Creek Reservation in South Dakota, a scenic landscape of grasslands, rolling hills, and bluffs near the eastern shore of the Missouri River. She comes from a distinguished Dakota Indian family that includes linguists, writers, and tribal political leaders.

The federal government's past policies of forceful assimilation of Native Americans separated many tribal people from their cultural roots. However, from her traditional Dakota family and reservation community, Cook-Lynn absorbed and retained important elements of her indigenous heritage, such as the language and old stories. As she grew up, she was angered by the lack of Native American content in the materials she read in school and made the cause of indigenous cultural survival and expression her life's work.

In 1952, Cook-Lynn received a bachelor's degree in English and journalism from South Dakota State College (now a university). After nineteen years devoted to marriage, child rearing, and her work as a journalist, editor, and teacher, she obtained a master's degree in education from the University of South Dakota in 1971. From 1972 until her retirement with emeritus status in 1993, he served as an associate professor of English and Native American studies at Eastern Washington University. Meanwhile, she did doctoral work at the University of Nebraska and Stanford University. After retiring from her post at Eastern Washington, she worked as a writer-in-residence and visiting professor at several other institutions. She has also regularly served as a mentor at

South Dakota State University's annual summer retreats for aspiring Native American writers.

The key influences on Cook-Lynn's work have been her Dakota heritage and family, the natural surroundings of her tribal homeland, and the literary techniques employed by the talented Kiowa author, N. Scott MOMADAY. She has expressed herself creatively in a variety of forms: poetry (*I Remember the Fallen Trees*, 1998); combined fiction, poetry, and remembrances (*Then Badger Said This*, 1983); novels (*From the River's Edge*, 1991); and short stories and novelettes (*The Power of Horses and Other Stories*, 1990, and *Aurelia: A Crow Creek Trilogy*, 1999).

Cook-Lynn has also written essays and nonfiction works that reflect her deeply held political convictions. Her father and grandfather's tribal government experience and bitter memories of the Crow Creek tribe's past and ongoing struggles against state and federal encroachment on its sovereignty have also shaped her views. Cook-Lynn has been a forceful and articulate defender of Native American political sovereignty and rights in works such as *Why I Can't Read Wallace Stegner and Other Essays: a Tribal Voice* (1996), *Anti-Indianism in Modern America: A Voice from Tatekeya's Earth* (2001), and *The Politics of Hallowed Ground: Wounded Knee and the Struggle for Indian Sovereignty* (1999) written with Mario Gonzalez. Her articles, stories, and poems have appeared in many journals and at least twenty different anthologies. Cook-Lynn is also the cofounder and editor of *Wicazo Sa Review: A Journal of Native American Studies*, which she bases in the Black Hills community of Rapid City, South Dakota.

David A. Crain

FURTHER READING

Bruchac, Joseph. "As a Dakotah Woman." Interview with Elizabeth Cook-Lynn. In *Survival This Way: Interviews with American Indian Poets*. Edited by Joseph Bruchac. Tucson: University of Arizona Press, 1987.

Copway, George

Born: c. 1818; near the mouth of the Trent River, Ontario, Canada
Died: c. 1863; near Pontiac, Michigan
Also known as: Kahgegwagebow (Stands Fast)
Tribal affiliation: Ojibwa (Chippewa)
Significance: George Copway published a number of books on Ojibwa topics.

George Copway spent his early years in a traditional Ojibwa environment until 1827, when his parents converted to Christianity. Copway attended Ebenezer Manual School in Jacksonville, Illinois, in 1838 and shortly thereafter married Elizabeth Howell. During the 1840's he served as a Methodist missionary to Ojibwas in Wisconsin and Minnesota. His first book was an autobiography, *The Life, History, and Travels of Kah-ge-ga-gah-bowh* (1847), later revised and reissued as *The Life, Letters and Speeches of Kah-ge-ga-gah-bowh, or G. Copway* (1850).

In 1850-1851, Copway represented Christian Indians at a world peace congress in Germany. He subsequently published a book based on his travels, *Running Sketches of Men and Places, in England, France, Germany, Belgium, and Scotland* (1851). For a few months during 1851, Copway also published a newspaper, *Copway's American Indian*. His last book was a history of the Ojibwa that was first published as *The Traditional History and Characteristic Sketches of the Ojibway Nation* (1850); it was later reissued as *Indian Life and Indian History, by an Indian Author* (1858). Copway was baptized Joseph-Antoine in the Roman Catholic Church shortly before he died.

Helen Jaskoski

FURTHER READING

Peyer, Bernd C. *The Tutor'd Mind: Indian Missionary-Writers in Antebellum America.* Amherst: University of Massachusetts Press, 1997.

Walker, Cheryl. *Indian Nation: Native American Literature and Nineteenth-Century Nationalisms.* Durham, N.C.: Duke University Press, 1997.

Cornplanter

Born: between 1732 and 1740; Conewaugus, New York
Died: February 18, 1836; Cornplantertown, Pennsylvania
Also known as: Kayehtwanken (By What One Plants), John Abeel, John O'Bail
Tribal affiliation: Seneca
Significance: Cornplanter achieved prominence as an Iroquois war chief fighting for the British in the American Revolution; at subsequent treaty conferences he emphasized the need for peaceful coexistence between Indians and the United States.

Cornplanter, the son of a Seneca woman and a Dutch trader, John Abeel (or O'Bail), was born at Conewaugus on the Genesee River sometime between 1732 and 1740. Little is known of his childhood except for

Cornplanter. (Library of Congress)

his recollections of being teased because of his light skin.

Along with RED JACKET, he argued for neutrality in the American Revolution, but when his view did not prevail, he joined the British, participating in the Wyoming, Cherry Valley, and Newtown campaigns (1777-1778). During the attack on Canajoharie (1780), he met his father and refused to take him prisoner.

Emerging from the Revolution as a major Seneca war chief, he decided the wisest course for the Senecas was to establish peaceful coexistence with the United States. He was present at the treaty negotiations at Fort Stanwix (1784) and Fort Harmar (1789), which resulted in the loss of Seneca lands to the Americans. He later complained to U.S. officials about the tactics used to exact Seneca concessions. Despite strong opposition from Red Jacket's more conservative faction, he maintained this pro-U.S. policy and mediated with other Indian nations to promote friendship with the Americans. His assistance at the Treaty of Fort Harmar allowed Pennsylvania to acquire the Erie Triangle, and he was given fifteen hundred acres in gratitude. He visited Philadelphia in 1789 to voice complaints before the Pennsylvania Assembly about white incursions on Indian land and remained to meet President George Washington. Cornplanter requested technical assistance for his people, and Washington recommended the Quakers, who established a model farm and school for the Senecas. Thus began an association that would last two centuries.

The land promised by Pennsylvania was patented to Cornplanter in 1796, and many Senecas in the Allegany region lived on his grant pending settlement of reservation boundaries in New York. Among those with him was his half-brother, the prophet HANDSOME LAKE, whose visions were recorded by resident Quakers.

The land was deeded to Cornplanter as an individual and therefore lacked reservation status. When agents tried to collect taxes, he appealed to Pennsylvania, and in 1822 the land was declared tax exempt as long as it was held by Cornplanter or his descendants. Following his death in 1836, the land was partitioned among his heirs. In 1871, Pennsylvania erected the first monument to an Indian in the U.S. in recognition of his friendship and aid.

Cornplanter's descendants continued to live on the land grant until the early 1960's, when most of it was flooded by the backwaters of Kinzua Dam. The descendants organized to fight the dam but lost because of a lack of federal protection. Their association continued into the 1990's, with descendants gathering from throughout the United States for an annual celebration of their Cornplanter heritage.

Joy A. Bilharz

FURTHER READING
Swatzler, David. *A Friend Among the Senecas: The Quaker Mission to Cornplanter's People.* Mechanicsburg, Pa.: Stackpole Books, 2000.

Cornstalk

Born: c. 1720; western Pennsylvania
Died: November 10, 1777; Point Pleasant, Virginia (now in West Virginia)
Also known as: Wynepuechsika
Tribal affiliation: Shawnee
Significance: Cornstalk opposed white settlers in the Ohio Valley and intermittently warred against them from the 1750's to his death in 1777.

Cornstalk was born about 1720 in western Pennsylvania. By the 1750's, he was a Shawnee war chief leading raids against the white settlements being established in Shawnee territory. His most significant battle was in October, 1774, at Point Pleasant, on the south bank of the Ohio River. Cornstalk led an attack to stop a planned invasion of Shawnee territory by the Virginia militia. Although Cornstalk was defeated, he was able to make a peace treaty with the British governor of Virginia.

When the American Revolution began in 1775, Cornstalk said he desired Shawnee neutrality, but this was only a diversionary tactic. In 1776, he attempted to form an Indian alliance to drive all whites back across the Appalachians. Despite eloquent appeals, he was unsuccessful, and neutrality again became his policy. In November, 1777, Cornstalk and his son went to Fort Randolph at Point Pleasant to discuss the rapidly worsening relations between Shawnees and whites. Cornstalk and his son were taken hostage. On November 10, they were murdered by a band of militia men.

Glenn L. Swygart

Costo, Rupert

Born: 1906; probably Southern California
Died: 1989; place unknown
Tribal affiliation: Cahuilla
Significance: From the 1930's through the 1950's, Rupert Costo was active in national and tribal politics, serving both as a vocal critic of the Indian New Deal during the 1930's and as tribal chairman of Southern California's Cahuilla people during the 1950's. He later became an important figure in Native American publishing.

As a football player at Haskell Institute and Whittier College (where he played with future President Richard M. Nixon) during the 1920's,

Rupert Costo demonstrated his athletic and intellectual aptitudes to the Indian and non-Indian world. Through most of his working life, he was employed by the state of California's highway department as an engineer. Upon his retirement, he and his wife, Jeannette Henry Costo (an Eastern Cherokee) founded the San Francisco-based American Indian Historical Society in 1964. The organization was often in the forefront of American Indian issues such as protection of American Indian burial grounds and American Indian human remains, as well as the correction of American Indian textbooks. The Costos sought to develop publications accurately reflected the historical role of American Indians in American society.

Initially, the American Indian Historical Society published three journals: *Wassaja,* a national Indian newspaper; *The Indian Historian,* a respected academic journal; and the *Weewish Tree,* a national magazine for Indian young people. The Costos coedited all three publications. In 1970, the historical society founded another publication arm of the society, the Indian Historian Press, an American Indian-controlled publishing house, which published fifty-two titles. Among its best-known books are *Textbooks and the American Indian,* edited by Rupert Costo (1970), and Donald A. Grinde, Jr., *The Iroquois and the Founding of the American Nation* (1977).

Through his editorial column in *Wassaja,* Costo advocated increased sovereignty for Native American nations in order to enhance their land and water rights. He also worked tirelessly for the protection of American Indian civil, social and religious rights. At the end of his life, Costo endowed the Rupert Costo Chair in American Indian History at the University of California at Riverside. He and his wife also established the Costo Library of the American Indian at the University of California at Riverside, one of the most comprehensive collections of American Indian books in the United States. In 1994, the university renamed its Student Services Building Costo Hall in honor of the outstanding contributions that the Costos had made to the university.

Bruce E. Johansen

Crashing Thunder

Born: c. 1865; place unknown
Died: unknown; place unknown
Also known as: Sam Blowsnake, Big Winnebago, Hágaga
Tribal affiliation: Winnebago

Crazy Horse / 117

Significance: Crashing Thunder's autobiography is filled with cultural information, personal detail, and psychological revelation.

Crashing Thunder and his Winnebago relatives became known to generations of students. His life story—elicited, translated, and published (as *Crashing Thunder: The Autobiography of an American Indian*, 1926) by ethnologist Paul Radin—reveals the day-to-day lives and the fundamental beliefs of the Winnebago. When he was born, Crashing Thunder relates, his mother was told that he would not be an ordinary individual. This prediction came true in the sense that Crashing Thunder, who with great reluctance and after years of avoiding the task, wrote an important social history of his people, despite his and other tribe members' worries that such a record, however valuable to the tribe it might be, would certainly be misunderstood by whites and would lead to trouble.

In another sense, and fortunately for students of Indian culture, Crashing Thunder was ordinary and his life experiences typify those of many of his contemporaries. Reading his book, one learns what childhood, adolescence, and adulthood were like for a Winnebago of his time. His rich and varied life included some of the following experiences: the childhood and adolescent tradition of the vision quest, courtship and sexual experience, marriage, family life (including the murder of a brother), murder, alcoholism, storytelling, ceremonies, migrant work and trouble in the white world, and conversion to the Native American Church and its peyote rituals.

Bruce E. Johansen

FURTHER READING

Radin, Paul, ed. *Crashing Thunder: The Autobiography of an American Indian*. Foreword by Arnold Krupat. Ann Arbor: University of Michigan Press, 1999.

Crazy Horse

Born: 1842?; Black Hills (now in South Dakota)
Died: September 5, 1877; Fort Robinson, Nebraska
Also known as: Tashunca-uitko, Curly
Tribal affiliation: Oglala Lakota (Sioux)
Significance: Crazy Horse, the greatest of the Sioux chiefs, led his people in a valiant but futile struggle against domination by the white culture. Instrumental in the U.S. Army's defeats at Rosebud and the Little Bighorn, he fought to the last to hold native land for his people.

Little is known of Tashunca-uitko's early life; even the date of his birth and the identity of his mother are somewhat uncertain. He was probably born in a Sioux camp along Rapid Creek in the Black Hills during the winter of 1841-1842. Most scholars believe that his mother was a Brule Sioux, the sister of SPOTTED TAIL, a famous Brule chief. His father, also called Crazy Horse, was a highly respected Oglala Sioux holy man. Tashunca-uitko was apparently a curious and solitary child. His hair and complexion were so fair that he was sometimes mistaken for a captive white child by soldiers and settlers. He was known as "Light-Haired Boy" and as "Curly." At the age of ten, he became the protégé of HUMP, a young Miniconjou Sioux warrior.

When he was about twelve, Curly killed his first buffalo and rode a newly captured wild horse; to honor his exploits, his people renamed him "His Horse Looking." One event in Crazy Horse's youth seems to have had a particularly powerful impact on the course of his life. When he was about fourteen, His Horse Looking witnessed the murder of Chief CONQUERING BEAR by the troops of Second Lieutenant J. L. Gratton and the subsequent slaughter of Gratton's command by the Sioux. Troubled by what he had seen, His Horse Looking went out alone, hobbled his horse, and lay down on a high hill to await a vision. On the third day, weakened by hunger, thirst, and exposure, the boy had a powerful mystical experience which revealed to him that the world in which humans live is only a shadow of the real world. To enter the real world, one must dream. When he was in that world, everything seemed to dance or float— his horse danced as if it were wild or crazy. In this first crucial vision, His Horse Looking had seen a warrior mounted on his (His Horse Looking's) horse; the warrior had no scalps, wore no paint, and was naked except for a breech cloth; he had a small, smooth stone behind one ear. Bullets and arrows could not touch him; the rider's own people crowded around him, trying to stop his dancing horse, but he rode on. The people were lost in a storm; the rider became a part of the storm with a lightning bolt on his cheek and hail spots on his body. The storm faded, and a small red-tailed hawk flew close over the rider. By the time he revealed this vision a few years later, His Horse Looking had already gained a reputation for great bravery and daring. His father and Chips, another holy man, made him a medicine bundle and gave him a red-tailed hawk feather and a smooth stone to wear.

When he went into battle thereafter, he wore a small lightning streak on his cheek, hail spots on his body, a breech cloth, a small stone, and a single feather; he did not take scalps. He was never seriously wounded in battle. His Horse Looking's father, in order to honor his son's

A sketch from Frank Leslie's Illustrated Newspaper *that depicts Crazy Horse and his people preparing to surrender to General Crook in Nebraska.* (Library of Congress)

achievements, bestowed his own name, Crazy Horse, upon the young man and asserted to his people that the Sioux had a new Crazy Horse, a great warrior with powerful medicine.

The Gratton debacle had one immediate effect other than the vision: It resulted in brutal reprisals by the Bluecoats. On September 3, 1855, shortly after Crazy Horse had experienced the vision, General William S. Harney attacked the Brule camp in which Crazy Horse was living with Spotted Tail's people. The soldiers killed more than one hundred Indians (most of them women and children), took many prisoners, and captured most of the Sioux horses. Crazy Horse escaped injury and capture but was left with an abiding hatred of the whites.

Since the major white immigration to the West did not begin until after the Civil War, Crazy Horse spent his youth living in the traditional ways: moving with the seasons, hunting, and warring with the other Plains Indians. The solitary boy grew into a man who, according to BLACK ELK,

would go about the villages without noticing people or saying anything. . . . All the Lakotas (Sioux) liked to dance and sing; but he never joined a dance, and they say nobody heard him sing. . . . He was a small man among the Lakotas and he was slender and had a thin face and his eyes looked through things and he always seemed to be thinking hard about something. He never wanted many things for himself, and did not have many ponies like a chief. They say that when game was scarce and the people were hungry, he would not eat at all. He was a queer man. Maybe he was always part way into that world of his vision.

Crazy Horse and the Oglala north of the Platte River lived in relative freedom from white interference until 1864. From the early 1860's, however, there was ever-increasing pressure from white settlers and traders on the U.S. government to guarantee the safety of people moving along the Oregon and Santa Fe trails and to open the Bozeman Trail through the Sioux country.

The military began preparations early in 1865 to invade the Powder River Indian country. General Patrick E. Connor announced that the Indians north of the Platte "must be hunted like wolves." Thus began what came to be known as Red Cloud's War, named for the Sioux chief who led the Sioux and Cheyenne warriors. General Connor's punitive expedition in 1865 was a failure, as were subsequent efforts to force the free Indians to sign a treaty. In 1866, General Henry B. Carrington fortified and opened the Bozeman Trail through Sioux territory. By 1868, having been outsmarted, frustrated, and beaten again and again by RED CLOUD's warriors, the United States forces conceded defeat, abandoned the forts, closed the Bozeman Trail, and granted the Black Hills and the Powder River country to the Indians forever.

Crazy Horse rose to prominence as a daring and astute leader during the years of Red Cloud's War. He was chosen by the Oglala chiefs to be a "shirt-wearer," or protector of the people. All the other young men chosen were the sons of chiefs; he was selected solely on the basis of his accomplishments. Crazy Horse played a central role in the most famous encounter of this war. On December 21, 1866, exposing himself repeatedly to great danger, he decoyed a troop of eighty-one of Colonel Carrington's men, commanded by Captain William J. Fetterman, into a trap outside Fort Phil Kearny. All the soldiers were killed. (The event came to be known among whites as the Fetterman massacre.)

Red Cloud's War ended in November, 1868, when the chief signed a treaty which acknowledged that the Powder River and Big Horn country were Indian land into which white people could not come without permission. The treaty also indicated that the Indians were to live on a reservation on the west side of the Missouri River. Red Cloud and his followers moved onto a reservation, but Crazy Horse and many others refused to sign or to leave their lands for a reservation. Crazy Horse never did sign a treaty.

As early as 1870, driven by reports of gold in the Black Hills, whites were venturing illegally into Indian territory. Surveyors for the Northern Pacific Railroad, protected by U.S. troops, also invaded the Black Hills in order to chart the course of their railway through Indian land. Crazy Horse, who became the war chief of the Oglala after Red Cloud moved onto the reservation, led numerous successful raids against the survey parties and finally drove them away. The surveyors returned in 1873; this time they were protected by a formidable body of troops commanded by George Armstrong Custer. In spite of a series of sharp attacks, Crazy Horse was unable to defeat Custer, and the surveyors finished their task. In 1874 Custer was back in Indian territory, leading an expedition of twelve hundred men purportedly to gather military and scientific information. He reported that the hills were filled with gold "from the roots on down"; the fate of the Indians and their sacred hills was sealed. Neither the military genius of their war chief, their skill and bravery, nor their clear title to the land could save them from the greed and power of the whites.

During the years between the signing of the 1868 treaty and the full-scale invasion of Indian lands in 1876, Crazy Horse apparently fell in love with a Sioux woman named Black Buffalo Woman, but she was taken from him through deceit and married another man, No Water. Crazy Horse and Black Buffalo Woman maintained their attachment to each other over a period of years, causing some divisiveness among the Sioux and resulting in the near-fatal shooting of Crazy Horse by No Water. Crazy Horse eventually married an Oglala named Tasina Sapewin (Black Shawl), who bore him a daughter. He named the child They Are Afraid of Her, and when she died a few years later, he was grief-stricken.

Because of the reports concerning the great mineral wealth of the Black Hills, the U.S. government began to try to force all the Indians in the vicinity to move onto reservations. On February 7, 1876, the War Department ordered General Philip Sheridan to commence operations against the Sioux living off reservations. The first conflict in this deadly campaign occurred on March 17, when General George Crook's advance column under Colonel Joseph J. Reynolds attacked a peaceful camp of Northern Cheyennes and Oglala Sioux who were on their way from the Red Cloud Agency to their hunting grounds. The survivors fled to Crazy Horse's camp.

Crazy Horse took them in, gave them food and shelter, and promised them that "we are going to fight the white man again." Crazy Horse's chance came in June, when a Cheyenne hunting party sighted a column of Bluecoats camped in the valley of Rosebud Creek. Crazy Horse had studied the soldiers' ways of fighting for years, and he was prepared for this battle. General Crook and his pony soldiers were no match for the Sioux and Cheyenne guided by Crazy Horse. Crook retreated under cover of darkness to his base camp on Goose Creek.

After the Battle of Rosebud Creek (June 17), the Indians moved west to the valley of the Greasy Grass (Little Bighorn) River. Blackfoot, Hunkpapa, Sans Arc, Miniconjous, Brule, and Oglala Sioux were there, as well as the Cheyenne—perhaps as many as fifteen thousand Indians, including five thousand warriors. The U.S. soldiers had originally planned a three-pronged campaign to ensnare and destroy the Indians. Crook's withdrawal, however, forced General Alfred Terry to revise the plan. On June 22 he ordered Colonel John Gibbon to go back to the Bighorn River and to march south along it to the Little Bighorn River. Custer and the Seventh Cavalry were to go along the Rosebud parallel to Gibbon and catch the Indians in between. General Terry, with the remaining forces, would trail them and provide whatever support was necessary. General Terry expected that Gibbon and Custer would converge and engage the enemy on June 26.

Custer and his troops arrived on June 25, and Custer decided to attack the Indian encampment without waiting for Gibbon's column. His rash decision was fatal to him and to the Seventh Cavalry. The Sioux and Cheyenne, led by Crazy Horse and GALL, SITTING BULL's lieutenant, crushed Custer. More than 250 soldiers died. Perhaps Crazy Horse and Gall could have defeated the troops of Gibbon and Terry as well, but they were not committed to an all-out war, as were the whites, and they had had enough killing, so they moved on, leaving the soldiers to bury their dead.

The Battle of the Little Bighorn is recognized as a great moment in the history of the Sioux nation, but it also proved to be a sad one, for it confirmed the U.S. government's conviction that in spite of the Treaty of 1868, the free Indians must be either confined to a reservation or annihilated. In the brutal days which were to follow, Crazy Horse clearly emerged as the single most important spiritual and military leader of the Sioux.

The government's response was swift: On August 15, a new law was enacted that required the Indians to give up all rights to the Powder River country and the Black Hills. Red Cloud and Spotted Tail succumbed to what they took to be inevitable and signed documents acknowledging that they accepted the new law. Sitting Bull and Gall fought against the forces of General Crook and Colonel Nelson Miles during the remainder of 1876 but decided to take their people to Canada in the spring of 1877. Crazy Horse alone resolved to stay on his own lands in the sacred Black Hills.

General Crook led an enormous army of infantry, cavalry, and artillery from the south through the Powder River country in pursuit of Crazy Horse, and Colonel Miles led his army from the north, looking for the Oglala war chief. Crazy Horse was forced to move his village from one place to another in order to avoid the Bluecoats. He had little ammunition or food, the winter was bitterly cold, and his people were weary. In December he approached Colonel Miles's outpost and sent a small party of chiefs and warriors with a flag of truce to find out what the colonel's intentions were. The party was attacked as it approached the outpost; only three Sioux survived. Miles's brutal intentions were made quite clear, and Crazy Horse was forced to flee again.

Colonel Miles caught up with the Sioux on January 8, 1877, at Battle Butte; in spite of his lack of ammunition and the weakened condition of his warriors, Crazy Horse was able, through bravery and superior tactics, to defeat Miles. Crazy Horse and his band escaped through the Wolf Mountains to the familiar country of the Little Powder River. The soldiers decided to cease their military operations until spring, but they redoubled their efforts to persuade the Indians to surrender. Numerous emissaries were sent throughout the northern lands with pack trains of food and gifts to tempt the suffering Sioux and Cheyenne into coming in to the security of the agencies. Many small bands yielded to these entreaties, but Crazy Horse only listened politely and sent the messengers home. His fame and his symbolic value to the Indians grew daily; the longer he resisted, the more important he and his followers became to the thousands of Indians now confined to reservations. When Spotted Tail himself came to entice them to give up, Crazy Horse went off alone into the deep snows of the mountains in order to give his people the freedom to decide their own fate. Most chose to stay with their leader, but Spotted Tail did persuade BIG FOOT to bring his Miniconjous in when spring came.

In April, General Crook sent Red Cloud to plead with Crazy Horse and to promise him that if he surrendered, the Sioux would be given a reservation in the Powder River country, where they could live and hunt in peace. At last Crazy Horse gave in; the suffering of his people was so great, the prospects of renewed conflict with Crook and Miles so grim, and the promise of a Powder River reservation so tempting that he led his band to the Red Cloud Agency, arriving in an almost triumphal procession witnessed by thousands on May 5, 1877. Predictably, Crazy

Horse did not like living at the agency, and General Crook did not make good on his promise of a Powder River reservation. Black Shawl died, and Crazy Horse married Nellie Larrabee, the daughter of a trader. The more restive Crazy Horse became, the more concerned the government became, and the more vulnerable the chief was to the plots of his enemies. Wild rumors that Crazy Horse planned to escape or to murder General Crook circulated. Government officials decided that it would be best to arrest and confine the war chief. On September 4, 1877, eight companies of cavalry and four hundred Indians, led by Red Cloud, left Fort Robinson to arrest Crazy Horse and deliver him to the fort. Crazy Horse attempted to flee but was overtaken and agreed to go and talk with Crook. When it became clear to him that he was not being taken to a conference but to prison, Crazy Horse drew his knife and tried to escape. He was restrained by Little Big Man and other followers of Red Cloud, and Private William Gentles bayoneted him. He died in the early hours of September 5; his father was at his side. Crazy Horse's parents rode into the hills and buried their son in a place known only to them.

Later that fall, the Sioux were forced to begin a journey eastward to the Missouri River and a new reservation. Among the thousands of Indians were Crazy Horse's Oglala. After approximately seventy-five miles of travel, the Oglala, two thousand strong, broke from the line and raced for Canada and freedom. The small cavalry contingent could only watch as these Sioux fled to join Sitting Bull—manifesting, in their refusal to submit to the whites, the spirit of Crazy Horse.

Crazy Horse seems to have been a truly exceptional and admirable man; he was the greatest warrior and general of a people to whom war was a way of life. He provided a powerful example of integrity and independence for the Sioux during a very difficult period of their history: He never attended a peace council with the whites, never signed a treaty. To quote Black Elk:

> He was brave and good and wise. He never wanted anything but to save his people, and he fought the Wasichus (the whites) only when they came to kill us in our own country. . . . They could not kill him in battle. They had to lie to him and kill him that way.

Hal Holladay

FURTHER READING

Ambrose, Stephen E. *Crazy Horse and Custer: The Parallel Lives of Two American Warriors.* New York: Anchor Books, 1996.

Andrist, Ralph K. *The Long Death: The Last Days of the Plains Indians.* New York: Macmillan, 1964.

Brown, Dee. *Bury My Heart at Wounded Knee: An Indian History of the American West.* New York: Holt, Rinehart and Winston, 1971.

Connell, Evan S. *Son of the Morning Star: Custer and the Little Bighorn.* San Francisco: North Point Press, 1984.

Friswold, Carroll. *The Killing of Chief Crazy Horse.* Lincoln: University of Nebraska Press, 1988.

Hinman, Eleanor. "Oglala Sources on the Life of Crazy Horse." *Nebraska History* 57, no. 1 (1976).

Josephy, Alvin M., Jr. *The Patriot Chiefs: A Chronicle of American Indian Resistance.* New York: Viking Press, 1958.

Lazarus, Edward. *Black Hills, White Justice.* New York: HarperCollins, 1991.

Marshall, Joseph. *The Journey of Crazy Horse.* New York: Viking, 2004.

Neihardt, John G. *Black Elk Speaks.* Lincoln: University of Nebraska Press, 1961.

Olson, James C. *Red Cloud and the Sioux Problem.* Lincoln: University of Nebraska Press, 1965.

Sajna, Mike. *Crazy Horse: The Life Behind the Legend.* New York: Wiley, 2000.

Sandoz, Mari. *Crazy Horse: The Strange Man of the Oglalas.* 50th anniversary ed. Introduction by Stephen B. Oates Lincoln: University of Nebraska Press, 1992.

Crow Dog

Born: c. 1835; Horse Stealing Creek, Montana
Died: 1911; Pine Ridge Reservation, South Dakota
Also known as: Kangi Sunka, Jerome Crow Dog
Tribal affiliation: Brule Lakota (Sioux)
Significance: Crow Dog was an important figure in the Ghost Dance phenomenon of 1890.

Crow Dog was present when CRAZY HORSE was killed at Fort Robinson, Nebraska, in 1877; he helped prevent a retaliatory attack on soldiers at the fort. He was police chief at the Rosebud Reservation in 1879-1880, during which time he assassinated SPOTTED TAIL.

Crow Dog was born at Horse Stealing Creek, Montana Territory, into a family of esteemed warriors. Before submitting to reservation life, he made his reputation in battle. As the Sioux were confined on reserva-

Brule Sioux war chief Crow Dog around 1900.
(Library of Congress)

tions following the Battle of the Little Bighorn, dissension rose between some of their leaders. On one occasion, RED CLOUD accused Spotted Tail of pocketing the proceeds from a sale of tribal land. Crow Dog heard rumors that Spotted Tail was selling Lakota land to the railroads and building himself an enormous white-styled mansion with the proceeds. In mid-July of 1880, Spotted Tail was called before the general council by Crow Dog's White Horse Group, where he denied the charges. The council voted to retain him as head chief, but Crow Dog continued to assert the chief's complicity in various crimes against the people. Crow Dog carried out his own sentence on Spotted Tail, executing him on August 5, 1881. Blood money was paid in traditional Brule fashion for the crime. Crow Dog was convicted of murder in a Dakota Territory court, but he was later freed on order of the U.S. Supreme Court when it ruled that the territorial government had no jurisdiction over the crime (*Ex parte Crow Dog*, 1883).

Later, Crow Dog was one of the leaders in spreading the Ghost Dance among the Lakota; he had adopted the religion from Short Bull. Crow Dog vociferously opposed army occupation of South Dakota Indian reservations and was one of the last holdouts after the massacre at Wounded Knee during December of 1890. He spent the last years of his life in relative peace on the Rosebud Sioux reservation in South Dakota.

Bruce E. Johansen

FURTHER READING
Crow Dog, Leonard, and Richard Erdoes. *Crow Dog: Four Generations of Sioux Medicine Men*. New York: HarperCollins, 1995.

Mooney, James. *The Ghost-Dance Religion and the Sioux Outbreak of 1890.* Introduction by Raymond J. DeMallie. Lincoln: University of Nebraska Press, 1991.

Crow Dog, Henry

Born: 1901; Rosebud Reservation, South Dakota
Died: February 2, 1985; Rosebud Reservation, South Dakota
Tribal affiliation: Brule Lakota (Sioux)
Significance: Henry Crow Dog introduced peyote use into Sioux religion.

The father of Leonard CROW DOG and the son of CROW DOG, Henry Crow Dog is best known for having introduced peyote use to his Oglala Sioux people. His father was the last of the Ghost Dancers of the late nineteenth century, and all three Crow Dog men are descendants of a long lineage of traditional medicine men seeking to find new ways to deal with the onslaught of American civilization in order to preserve their traditions. They have done this through the vision quest, seeking new ways to pray and to relate to the ancient spirits of their tribal religion.

Many important Sioux Indian ceremonies were forbidden by the federal government in the late nineteenth century, and the prohibition lasted for nearly a full century. Before Europeans arrived in North America, members of the Sioux used the poisonous mescal bean, a vine native to the northern Great Plains, to induce visions in ceremonial rituals. As a medicine man, Crow Dog created a way to replace the mescal bean with the peyote cactus, which is native to the southern Plains and northern Mexico.

Crow Dog was inspired by his father, Crow Dog, who was the first Native American to take a case to the U.S. Supreme Court and win. Determined to maintain tribal traditions, he taught his son Leonard Crow Dog the ways of traditional medicine men, including the Sun Dance and the Ghost Dance. He hid his son from U.S. government agents when they came to take him away to a government boarding school, instead raising him in the ways of their Sioux ancestors. He lived to see Leonard revive the Ghost Dance in modern times during the 1973 siege of Wounded Knee.

Crow Dog thought that the U.S. government was brutal and unjust in its actions toward the Sioux during the times when the tribe was being hunted down and forced onto the Rosebud Reservation, in what became South Dakota, during the late nineteenth century. His people had for centuries been freely living, hunting the buffalo and practicing their unique culture until the coming of the white men. Henry did not trust the invaders, and rightfully so. With what he saw as great vindictiveness and prejudice, the U.S. government rounded up the remainder of the tribe, which had been dramatically reduced when the coming of the railroads during the 1850's led to the near extinction of the buffalo, and forced them to sign a treaty limiting their movements to the reservation lands. They were disarmed, and their traditional culture was suppressed from 1890 to 1972.

A life-long resident of South Dakota's Rosebud Reservation, Crow Dog died in his home, apparently from exposure to the cold, at the age of eighty-four.

Michael W. Simpson

FURTHER READING

Crow Dog, Leonard, and Richard Erdoes. *Crow Dog: Four Generations of Sioux Medicine Men*. New York: HarperCollins, 1995.

Crow Dog, Leonard

Born: 1942; Rosebud Reservation, South Dakota
Tribal affiliation: Brule Lakota (Sioux)
Significance: Leonard Crow Dog acted as a spiritual adviser to the American Indian Movement (AIM) during the period of its greatest activism during the 1960's and 1970's.

Leonard Crow Dog is best known for his book, *Crow Dog: Four Generations of Sioux Medicine Men* (1995), which chronicles the lives of Sioux medicine men from the time of the Indian surrender to the federal government during the 1890's until his own time. He was born on the Rosebud Reservation in South Dakota, where his father, Henry CROW DOG, hid him from U.S. government agents to prevent his being taken from them and sent to a government boarding school, where he would have lost his language, culture, and Sioux identity.

Crow Dog is of the Crow Dog lineage of Sun Dance medicine men going back to the time of SITTING BULL. Their original family name was actually Crow Coyote, but in translation into English, the word for Coyote was misinterpreted to mean "dog," by a U.S. census taker. Crow Dog himself became a medicine man at the age of thirteen. When he was twenty-nine, he became well known as a Native rights activist affiliated with the American Indian Movement during the siege of Wounded Knee. He served some time in prison because of his political activities.

Crow Dog married his second wife, Mary Brave Bird, when he was thirty-one, and she was seventeen, after they met at an AIM meeting in 1972. Mary became the stepmother to the two children from his first marriage, and they had four more children together. His family was against this marriage, as Mary was not a full-blood Sioux, as his first wife had been. She had been raised, like her mother before her, at a Roman Catholic mission school, where she lost her native language and culture. Emily Brave Bird, Mary's mother, eventually became a nurse, then a teacher on the Rosebud Reservation. Mary's father, Robert Brave Bird, was descended from the warrior lineage of Iron Shell.

Crow Dog had to reteach Mary the language, rituals, and sacred traditions of the Sioux, including the traditional uses of healing plants and herbs. Mary later became well known in her own right for her autobiographical book *Lakota Woman* (1990).

In 2003, at the age of sixty-four, Crow Dog opened up the Sun Dance to non-Indians during the ceremony held near Hallam, Nebraska. He there stated his view that all races should be allowed to participate. He afterward distanced himself from both traditionalists and AIM, believing that preservation and sharing of culture are more important than politics. Meanwhile, he has continued to perform sacred ceremonies and serve as a sweat lodge leader.

Michael W. Simpson

FURTHER READING

Crow Dog, Leonard, and Richard Erdoes. *Crow Dog: Four Generations of Sioux Medicine Men.* New York: HarperCollins, 1995.
Crow Dog, Mary, and Richard Erdoes. *Lakota Woman.* New York: Grove Weidenfeld, 1990.

Crow Dog, Mary

Born: 1953; Rosebud Sioux Reservation, South Dakota
Also Known as: Mary Brave Bird, Ohitika Win
Tribal affiliation: Brule Lakota (Sioux)
Significance: Mary Crow Dog has been active in the American Indian Movement (AIM), and her literary works present the concerns and realities of contemporary Indian women.

Also known as Mary Brave Bird and Ohitika Win, Mary Crow Dog describes herself as a "half-breed" who struggled to fit into the Indian world. The daughter of Emily Brave Bird, she was removed from her home and put into a mission school, where she lost much of her culture and language. Two volumes of autobiography, *Lakota Woman* (1990, covering the years from her birth to 1977) and *Ohitika Woman* (1993, describing events until 1992), portray an environment of poverty, alcoholism, and despair in her community. In 1994, *Lakota Woman* was made into a television movie, with Irene BEDARD portraying Crow Dog.

In the American Indian Movement, she found a sense of hope and pride, and discovered a vehicle for cultural recovery. She became an AIM activist and participated in the takeover of the Bureau of Indian Affairs building in Washington, D.C., in 1972, and the Wounded Knee occupation in 1973. Through AIM, she met Leonard CROW DOG, a Lakota medicine man whom she married. She became stepmother to his children, and together they had four more children. In their shared life, she became an activist for the recovery of Indian traditions. Leonard Crow Dog traveled frequently and always took his family with him. They were later divorced, and in 1991, Mary Crow Dog married Rudi Olguin.

Crow Dog's books present the hardships of an Indian woman struggling against the oppression and subservience of women in the Indian community while working to improve the political and economic situation for all Indian peoples.

Charles Louis Kammer III

FURTHER READING
Crow Dog, Mary, and Richard Erdoes. *Lakota Woman.* New York: Grove Weidenfeld, 1990.

Crowfoot

Born: c. 1830; Blackfoot Crossing, near present-day Calgary, Alberta, Canada
Died: April 25, 1890; Canada
Also known as: Isapo-Muxika, Astoxkomi (Shot Close)
Tribal affiliation: Blackfoot
Significance: Crowfoot was a skillful chief who led his people through the twenty-year transition from nomadic freedom to reservation life.
Crowfoot, who was born a Blood Indian, became a Blackfoot by adoption when his widowed mother married a man from that tribe. Because the Blackfoot were a hunting and raiding people, buffalo and horses were

important fixtures in their existence, and life revolved around the acquisition of both. Crowfoot matured and excelled in this environment, earning his place as chief because of his bravery in fighting and hunting.

As the white settlers advanced westward across the land, the ways of the Blackfoot suffered. Although Crowfoot was the leader of a particular Blackfoot tribe, the whites thought him to be the supreme leader of the entire Blackfeet Confederacy. Thus, he had great influence with the whites, particularly with the North West Mounted Police, who were organized in 1873 in the service of Queen Victoria.

Crowfoot signed a treaty in 1877 giving reservation lands to the Blackfeet Confederacy and ceding some fifty thousand acres to the whites. He also kept the Blackfoot out of the unsuccessful Riel Rebellion of 1885, maintaining his position as a trusted and peace-seeking leader. His overwhelming concern was the welfare of the Blackfoot people in the face of advancing white authority. Thus, he also led his tribe in the shift to agriculture as a primary means of subsistence.

Ruffin Stirling

FURTHER READING
Dempsey, Hugh A. *Crowfoot: Chief of the Blackfeet.* Foreword by Paul F. Sharp. Norman: University of Oklahoma Press, 1974.

Curly

Born: c. 1859; along the Rosebud River, Montana
Died: May 22, 1923; probably in Montana
Also known as: Ashishishe
Tribal affiliation: Crow
Significance: Curly served as scout for George A. Custer at the Battle of the Little Bighorn; after Custer's defeat, he escaped and reported the annihilation of Custer's army, but questions later arose concerning his involvement in the battle.

Curly was born in Crow country along the Rosebud River in Montana. There is little knowledge of the thin young brave with long black braids prior to his service as an Indian scout for the Seventh Cavalry. In April of 1876 Curly and several other young Crows were recruited for the famed Yellowstone expedition. Enlisted for their intimate knowledge of the region, their mission was to aid in the search for hostile tribes. Curly and five of his Crow scouts were assigned to George Armstrong Custer's ill-fated detachment.

Curly. (Library of Congress)

Like Custer's ominous battle, Curly has become embroiled in controversy. None of Custer's men escaped the Battle of the Little Bighorn; however, the Crow scouts did, including the seventeen-year-old Curly. He claimed to have remained with the battle until it appeared hopeless, then, tying his hair similar to the Sioux and wrapping himself in a fallen Sioux's blanket, rode away undetected to the fork of the Bighorn and Yellowstone Rivers where an Army supply boat, waited. There he delivered the first news of Custer's defeat.

The other Crow scouts tell a different story. They claim they were instructed before the battle began to remain in the rear; they watched from a distance as Custer led his troops to their death, and when the outcome seemed apparent, Curly rode to the supply boat while the rest rode home. Many historians, in search of the true story, sought Curly in his later years; unfortunately, his reluctance to talk and seeming inconsistencies only added to the debate. Curly died in 1923 and was buried in Montana at the National Cemetery on the Custer Battlefield.

Andrea Gayle Radke

Curtis, Charles

Born: January 25, 1860; Topeka, Kansas
Died: February 8, 1936; Washington, D.C.
Tribal affiliation: Kansa
Significance: Charles Curtis was the first American of Indian descent to serve in the U.S. Senate and the first to become vice president of the United States.

Charles Curtis was born and spent much of his childhood in Topeka, Kansas. In 1881, Curtis established a law practice in Topeka. He soon won

election to become the prose-
cuting attorney of Shawnee
County, serving from 1885 to
1889. Curtis won election to
the U.S. House of Representatives in 1893, serving until
1907, when he was elected to
the U.S. Senate. As the first Native American to serve in the
Senate, Curtis took an active
role in Indian matters, chair-
ing the Committee on Indian
Depredations. Curtis was a
member of the U.S. Senate
from 1907 to 1913, and again
from 1915 to 1929. During
that period, Curtis was the Republican whip, responsible for
gathering and counting votes,
from 1915 to 1924, but then he
ascended to the position of

Charles Curtis. (Library of Congress)

Senate majority leader, considered to be the most powerful leadership
role in the Senate, which he held from 1925 to 1929.

Curtis was elected vice president of the United States in 1928, serving
under President Herbert Hoover from 1929 to 1933. After failing to win
reelection, he resumed the practice of law in Washington, D.C., where
he died on February 8, 1936. His remains are interred at the Topeka
Cemetery in Topeka, Kansas.

Susan Daly Vinal

FURTHER READING

Edmunds, R. David, ed. *The New Warriors: Native American Leaders Since
1900.* Lincoln: University of Nebraska Press, 2001.

Moses, L. G., and Raymond Wilson, eds. *Indian Lives: Essays on Nineteenth
and Twentieth Century Native American Leaders.* Albuquerque: University of New Mexico Press, 1985.

Seitz, Don Carlos. *From Kaw Teepee to Capitol: The Life Story of Charles
Curtis, Indian, Who Has Risen to High Estate.* New York: Frederick A.
Stokes, 1928.

Unrau, William E. *Mixed Bloods and Tribal Dissolution: Charles Curtis and
the Quest for Indian Identity.* Lawrence: University Press of Kansas, 1989.

Datsolalee

Born: November, 1835; Carson Valley, Nevada
Died: December 6, 1925; Carson City, Nevada
Also known as: Louisa Keyser, Dabuda (Wide Hips)
Tribal affiliation: Washoe
Significance: Datsolalee (Louisa Keyser) was an accomplished Washoe designer and basketmaker.

Datsolalee was widely recognized in the art world for the beautiful design and weaving of her baskets. Basketry had long been a fine art among the Washoe, and she was recognized as its most accomplished practitioner. She was married twice (her first husband died), both times to Washoe men, and had two children by her first marriage, but it seemed to those who knew her that her primary concern was her work.

In 1895, Datsolalee first arranged to sell her baskets to the proprietor of a clothing store in Carson City. He was a basket collector as well, and he was delighted that she had kept the tradition alive; for many years, because of the outcome of a dispute with the Paiute, the Washoe were legally prohibited from making baskets. The store owner, Abram Cohn, actively found markets for her basketry and kept written records of the sales of her work. About forty of her baskets are considered major pieces; one sold for ten thousand dollars in 1930.

It was said that Datsolalee often saw designs in her dreams before doing her weaving. Her technical expertise impresses weavers to this day. One of her most famous works (she entitled it "Myriads of Stars Shine over the Graves of Our Ancestors") took more than a year to weave and contains more than thirty-six stitches per inch. Her designs reflected both Washoe tribal tradition and her own deep involvement with her art. She continued to work nearly until her death in 1925.

Richard S. Keating

FURTHER READING

Berlo, Janet C., and Ruth B. Phillips. *Native North American Art.* New York: Oxford University Press, 1998.
Porter, Frank W. III, ed. *The Art of Native American Basketry: A Living Legacy.* Westport, Conn.: Greenwood Press, 1990.

Decora, Spoon

Born: c. 1730; place unknown
Died: 1816; Portage, Wisconsin
Also known as: Choukeka, DeKaury, Choukelea
Tribal affiliation: Winnebago
Significance: Spoon Decora was a Winnebago leader who played a lead-
ing role in negotiating the St. Louis Treaty of 1816.

Also called Choukeka, Spoon Decora was one of the first of several
Winnebago leaders to carry the name "Decora." He was born to a
French trader, Joseph des Caris, and a Winnebago named Hopokaw.
He married a daughter of Nawkaw and had six sons and five daughters
with her. Decora took a leading role in the Winnebagos' conflicts with
the Chippewas and, shortly before his death, in negotiating the St.
Louis Treaty of 1816. He generally refrained from becoming involved
in conflicts with whites. Spoon Decora's son, Konoka, became the
Winnebagos' principal chief in 1816 following the death of the elder
Decora.

Bruce E. Johansen

FURTHER READING
Radin, Paul. *The Winnebago Tribe.* Lincoln: University of Nebraska Press,
1990.

Deer, Ada Elizabeth

Born: August 7, 1935; Keshena, Wisconsin
Tribal affiliation: Menominee
Significance: Ada Deer was appointed commissioner of the Bureau of
Indian Affairs (BIA) by President Bill Clinton in 1993.

Born in Keshena, Wisconsin, Ada Deer earned a bachelor's degree at
the University of Wisconsin, Madison, in 1957 and a master's degree in
social work at Columbia University in 1961. Her first interest after graduation was social work, including lecturing in the fields of social work
and Native American studies at the University of Wisconsin's Madison
campus.

Deer also became involved in political action and organizing, working as a lobbyist for the Menominees in Washington in the early 1970's.
She chaired the Menominee Restoration Committee between 1973 and
1976; that group was primarily responsible for the restoring of federally

Ada Elizabeth Deer (right). (AP/Wide World Photos)

recognized tribal status to the Menominees (the tribe had been "terminated" in 1954). During the late 1970's, she was a member of the American Indian Policy Review Commission. President Bill Clinton appointed her commissioner of the Bureau of Indian Affairs in 1993.

Deer resigned from the Bureau of Indian Affairs in 1997. She was appointed director of the American Indian Studies program at the University of Wisconsin, Madison in January, 2000.

Bruce E. Johansen

FURTHER READING

Edmunds, R. David, ed. *The New Warriors: Native American Leaders Since 1900.* Lincoln: University of Nebraska Press, 2001.

Perdue, Theda, ed. *Sifters: Native American Women's Lives.* New York: Oxford University Press, 2001.

Deganawida

Born: c. 1550; near present-day Kingston, Ontario, Canada
Died: c. 1600; place unknown
Also known as: The Peacemaker
Tribal affiliation: Huron

Significance: Deganawida enlisted the aid of an orator and diplomat, HIAWATHA, to spread his vision of a united and peaceful Iroquois Confederacy, formed of separate nations, which had suffered from internal wars and feuds that nearly destroyed Iroquois civilization.

Little is known of the early life of Deganawida, whose name means, roughly, "two rivers flowing together." Oral accounts maintain that he was the product of a virgin birth that surprised his mother and grandmother, both poor women who lived alone in the forest. They feared that the virgin birth might portend evil, so they tried to drown him three times in an icy river, only to find Deganawida safe at home after each attempt. His mother then came to realize that he was meant to live.

As a young man, Deganawida is said to have possessed *orenda*, a force or energy that enabled him to unite all things. He had dreamed of a mighty white pine tree, whose reaching roots united warring tribes as an eagle soared overhead. Deganawida had proposed that the weapons of war be buried under the roots of this white pine. He was a stutterer who could hardly speak, a manifestation that Iroquois oral history attributes to a double row of teeth.

Deganawida mourned the waste of war and the pain of torture. He asked the Huron, the tribe to which he was a part, to cease warfare, but they did not listen, so he set off to visit the Iroquois nations to the south and to the east. Oral tradition relates that Deganawida arrived in Iroquois country in a stone canoe.

Deganawida traveled for many years through Iroquois land, presenting his vision of peace, but no one seemed ready to listen to a stuttering prophet. As he despaired, Deganawida met Hiawatha, who supported Deganawida's vision, and they joined forces. With Hiawatha advancing their vision of peace, both men won agreement from each of the five Iroquois nations, one by one, over several years.

The toughest to convert from the ways of war were the Onondagas, who were led by an evil, twisted leader, the wizard ATOTARHO, who used magic to make birds fall dead from the sky and to kill members of Hiawatha's family. After an epic battle, Atotarho agreed to follow the path of peace. Eventually, he became the chief executive of the grand council. The last of the five nations to agree to follow Deganawida's law of peace was the Senecas, who came into the fold after a "sign on the sky," probably a total eclipse of the sun, in what is now western New York State.

Deganawida sought to replace blood feuds that had devastated the Iroquois with peaceful modes of decision making. The result was the Great Peace and Power and Law (sometimes called the Great Binding Law, or *Kaianerekowa*) of the Iroquois, which endures to this day as one

of the oldest forms of participatory democracy. The confederacy originally included the Mohawks, Oneidas, Onondagas, Cayugas, and Senecas. Deganawida's confederacy was founded before first European contact in the area, possibly as early as 900, or as late as 1550; debate has
continued for many years about the confederacy's age.

The Great Peace has been passed from generation to generation by
use of wampum, a form of written communication using strings of shell
beads, which outlines a complex system of checks and balances between
the confederacy's nations. A complete oral recitation of the Great Peace
can take several days; encapsulated versions have been translated into
English for more than one hundred years, but a close-to-complete version was not developed until the 1990's.

Each of the five Iroquois nations in Deganawida's confederacy maintained its own council, whose sachems, or loved ones, were nominated
by the clan mothers of families holding hereditary rights to office titles.
The grand council at Onondaga was drawn from the individual national
councils. The rights, duties, and qualifications of the sachem were outlined explicitly, and the women could remove (or impeach) a sachem
who was found guilty of any of a number of abuses of office, from missing meetings to murder. A sachem was given three warnings, then removed from the council if he did not mend his ways, and a sachem
guilty of murder lost not only his title but also deprived his entire family
of its right to representation. The female relatives holding the rights to
the office lost those rights, and the title transferred to a sister family.

The Iroquois Great Peace and Power and Law has been cited frequently, along with European precedents, as a forerunner of modern
democratic traditions. Deganawida, for example, said that leaders'
skins must be seven spans thick to withstand the criticism of their con-
stituents. The law pointed out that the sachem should take pains not to
become angry when people scrutinized their conduct in governmental
affairs. Such a point of view pervades the writings of Thomas Jefferson
and Benjamin Franklin.

Under Deganawida's law, the sachem was not allowed to name its
own successors, nor could it carry its title to the grave. The Great Peace
provided a ceremony to remove the "antlers" of authority from a dying
chief. The Great Peace also provided for the removal from office of a
sachem who could no longer function in office adequately, a measure
remarkably similar to the twenty-fifth amendment to the U.S. Constitution (1967), which provides for the removal of an incapacitated president or a president who dies while in office.

In some ways, the grand council operates like the U.S. House of Representatives and the U.S. Senate, which have conference committees. As it was designed by Deganawida, debating protocol in the grand council calls for debate to begin with the elder brothers. After debate by the older brothers, the younger brothers debate in much the same manner. Once consensus is achieved by the younger brothers, the discussion is then given back to the elders for confirmation. Next, the question is laid before a "judicial" council for its review and decision.

At this stage, the judicial reviewer can raise objections to the proposed measure if it is believed inconsistent with the Great Peace. Essentially, the "legislature" can rewrite the proposed law on the spot so that it accords with established law. When the reviewers reach consensus, a sachem who presides over debates between the delegations, is asked to confirm the decision.

Deganawida's Great Peace also included provisions guaranteeing freedom of religion and the right of redress before the grand council. It also forbade unauthorized entry of homes—all measures that sound familiar to U.S. citizens through the Bill of Rights. Public opinion is of great importance within the League of the Iroquois. Iroquois people can have a direct say in the formulation of government policy, even if a sachem chooses to ignore the will of the people. The Great Peace stipulates that the people can propose their own laws even when leaders fail to do so, adding them to the rafters of the metaphorical longhouse. This provision resembles provisions for popular initiatives in several states of the United States, as well as the mechanism by which the federal and many state constitutions may be amended.

Bruce E. Johansen

FURTHER READING

Colden, Cadwallader. *The History of the Five Nations.* Ithaca, N.Y.: Great Seal Books, 1958.

Mann, Barbara A., and Jerry L. Fields. "A Sign in the Sky: Dating the League of the Haudenosaunee." *American Indian Culture and Research Journal* 21, no. 2 (1997): 105-163.

Wallace, Paul A. W. *The White Roots of Peace.* Santa Fe, New Mexico: Clear Light, 1994.

Wilson, Edmund. *Apologies to the Iroquois.* 1959. Reprint. Syracuse, N.Y.: Syracuse University Press, 1992.

Woodbury, Hanni, Reg Henry, and Harry Webster, comps. *Concerning the League: The Iroquois League Tradition as Dictated in Onondaga.* Algonquian and Iroquoian Linguistics Memoir 9. Winnipeg, Canada: University of Manitoba Press, 1992.

Dekanisora

Born: c. 1650; near present-day Onondaga, New York
Died: c. 1732; Albany, New York
Tribal affiliation: Onondaga
Significance: Dekanisora was the leading Iroquois orator of his era and a noted neutralist politician and diplomat in Iroquois dealings with the English and French in the Northeast.

Respected and admired by both his own people and the French and English, Dekanisora masterfully played these two European powers in the Iroquois backyard off against each other. Devoted to the cause of neither imperial power but rather to the cause of the Onondagas and the Iroquois Confederacy, he forced both the English and the French to court him. In 1700, when his wife died accidentally, he was so overcome with grief that he resolved to mourn her indefinitely by giving up his activities as negotiator and statesman for the Iroquois confederacy and retiring as a recluse. So great was his influence that the English at Albany, New York, pleaded with him not to do so, but rather to attend peace talks in Montreal. It was highly unusual for English officials to ask an Iroquois politician to negotiate with the French; this request underscores the fact that the English believed their interests would be much better served by Dekanisora's diplomacy than that of another Iroquois negotiator.

Dekanisora played a leading role in engineering the major peace settlement of 1701 between the Iroquois, French, and French-allied tribes. He continued in this role of diplomat for the Iroquois confederacy until it became apparent that he was suffering memory loss associated with old age; he was replaced as chief orator of the Onondaga nation in 1721, but was still active as a sachem ("chief") of the Onondagas. Dekanisora most likely died in the early summer of 1732, as James Logan, negotiator for the Pennsylvania colonial government, mentioned soon after that the politician's son had taken his deceased father's place as an Iroquois representative to English colonial officials.

Gretchen L. Green

FURTHER READING
Snow, Dean R. *The Iroquois*. Cambridge, Mass.: Blackwell, 1994.

Delgadito

Born: c. 1830; near Nazlini, New Mexico Territory
Died: c. 1870; near Chinle, New Mexico Territory
Also known as: Atsidi Sani (Old Smith), Beshiltheeni (Knife Maker)
Tribal affiliation: Navajo
Significance: Delgadito was the first Navajo metalsmith; his pride in craftsmanship continues to influence Navajo smiths, and silverwork has become the single most important source of individual income to the tribe.

Like his older brother, BARBONCITO, Delgadito was a medicine man and ceremonial singer of the Ma'iidee-shgiizhnii (Coyote Pass) clan at Canyon de Chelly. He learned silversmithing from a Mexican craftsman during the 1850's. Later he learned other metal techniques from an American blacksmith, and still later he taught the craft to other Navajos, thus establishing the silversmithing tradition among his people. His artistic talents did not keep him from participating in the Navajo War of 1863-1866. Delgadito and Barboncito supported MANUELITO's efforts against the American army at Fort Defiance. When the "resettlement" policy was announced and eventually implemented by Colonel Christopher (Kit) Carson, Delgadito and Barboncito sent a third brother, El Sordo, as an envoy to negotiate a truce. He offered to construct hogans near Fort Wingate and settle there. El Sordo's proposal was rebuffed and he was told instead that all Navajo nation members were to "resettle" to Bosque Redondo. Delgadito resisted, but he and a large number of women and children were the first Navajos to be taken to the Bosque. On June 1, 1868, Delgadito was a signatory of the treaty allowing the Navajos to return to their ancient lands.

Moises Roizen

FURTHER READING
Iverson, Peter. *Dine: A History of the Navajos.* Albuquerque: University of New Mexico Press, 2002.

Deloria, Ella Cara

Born: January 30, 1888; Yankton Sioux Reservation, South Dakota
Died: February 12, 1971; Tripp, South Dakota
Also known as: Anpetu Waste (Beautiful Day)
Tribal affiliation: Yankton Lakota (Sioux)

Significance: Ella Deloria collected and translated numerous traditional Sioux stories and beliefs; she was a leading authority on Sioux
culture, and posthumously she was recognized as a novelist.

When Ella Cara Deloria was born in 1888 on the Yankton Sioux Reservation in South Dakota, the Sioux population was nearing its nadir.
(The Wounded Knee Massacre in South Dakota occurred the following
year.) Deloria's parents were determined that the Sioux culture would
thrive in their household. Deloria's mother, Mary (Sully Bordeaux),
reared the family in the tribal traditions and language even though she
was only one-quarter Sioux. These Dakota views, along with Christian
beliefs (Deloria's father was an Episcopalian minister), strongly influenced Deloria's life.

The year following her birth, Deloria's father transferred to St. Elizabeth's Church on the Standing Rock Sioux Reservation in South Dakota. There Deloria attended St. Elizabeth's School until 1902, when
she transferred to All Saints Boarding School in Sioux Falls, South Dakota. Graduating in 1910, Deloria then studied at Oberlin College in
Ohio, the University of Chicago and Columbia Teachers College in New
York.

Awarded a bachelor's degree in 1915, Deloria returned to All Saints
Boarding School to teach. Four years later, she moved to New York City
to work for the Young Women's Christian Association (YWCA) as its
health education secretary for native schools, a position that afforded
Deloria exposure to several western reservations. In 1923, Haskell Indian School in Lawrence, Kansas, offered Deloria a teaching job in an
experimental program designed to explore the spiritual aspects of physical education within native traditions.

Recognizing her work with native culture, Franz Boas, the preeminent American anthropologist of that time, recruited Deloria in 1927 to
translate traditional Sioux stories. As an ethnographer and linguist,
Deloria worked with Boas until his death in 1942.

With a mission to explain Dakota insights to nonnatives, Deloria published several books. *Dakota Texts* (1932) contains a bilingual collection
of traditional Sioux stories. In *Dakota Grammar* (1941), she collaborated
with Boas to show Dakota linguistic rules. She explored native and non-
native differences in an effort to dispel cultural misunderstandings in
Speaking of Indians (1944). In her writings, Deloria stressed that native
philosophy was rooted in complex patterns and that nonnative educators should work with these traditional designs and not against them.

During the 1940's, Deloria was America's major authority on Sioux
culture. To generate further public awareness, she traveled extensively

to give lectures and to present pageants with Sioux songs and dances. In 1955, Deloria returned to St. Elizabeth's to be its director for three years. During the 1960's, Deloria worked on linguistic projects at the University of South Dakota in Vermillion, where she spent her final years.

Upon her death on February 12, 1971, Deloria left hundreds of pages of unpublished manuscripts. Seventeen years later, in 1988, her novel *Waterlily*, drafted during the early 1940's, was published. *Waterlily* focuses on women's roles in traditional native life. Even though Deloria was never formally trained as an anthropologist, her research on Sioux culture and her transcriptions of oral histories have recovered voices from a fading culture.

Tanya M. Backinger

FURTHER READING

Deloria, Ella Cara. *Speaking of Indians*. Introduction by Vine Deloria, Jr. Lincoln: University of Nebraska Press, 1998.

Rice, Julian. *Lakota Storytelling: Black Elk, Ella Deloria, and Frank Fools Crow*. New York: Peter Lang, 1989.

Sligh, Gary Lee. *Study of Native American Women Novelists: Sophia Alice Callahan, Mourning Dove, and Ella Cara Deloria*. Lewiston, N.Y.: Edwin Mellen Press, 2003.

Deloria, Philip Joseph

Born: 1853; near Grand River, Dakota Territory (now in South Dakota)
Died: May 8, 1931; Mission, South Dakota
Also known as: Tipi Sapa
Tribal affiliation: Yankton Lakota (Sioux)
Significance: Philip Deloria was one of the first American Indians to become an Episcopal priest and was an important facilitator of Sioux adjustment to American culture and Christianity.

Philip Joseph Deloria was born during an era of Yankton Sioux history in which European-American culture and Christianity were posing increasing challenges to the traditional beliefs and practices of tribal life. Members of his generation faced the necessity of working out how to participate in the two competing worlds. Some Yanktons adamantly refused to have anything to do with white lifeways and religion. At the other extreme were Yanktons who, for pragmatic or philosophical reasons, chose to travel the road of accommodation by adopting many of the beliefs and practices of European-American culture. Although frequently condemned as "sellouts," many such Sioux were guided by the traditional Indian value of acting according to what they deemed best for their own communities—in this case, by finding ways to usher their people into the new social order with as little trauma as possible.

Throughout his life, Deloria dedicated himself to cushioning the impact of imposed culture change upon the Sioux. The son a mixed-blood Yankton sub-chief and shaman, Saswe, and a Blackfeet Lakota woman, Sihasapawin, Deloria seemed destined to inherit the mantels of traditional Sioux political and religious leadership worn by his father. The headman's decision to name his child Tipi Sapa after the black lodge where he received curing power in a vision, only seemed to confirm the direction the young Deloria's life would take. However, by the early 1860's, Saswe's sense of the growing dominance of white culture impelled him to begin attending Episcopal services and to encourage his then teenage son to take advantage of that denomination's religious and educational resources. Although Deloria initially resisted his father's advice, when he was seventeen years old, he decided to convert to Christianity. He enrolled in the church-run school on the Yankton reservation and later studied at the Shattuck Military Academy in Faribault, Minnesota.

After returning to the Yankton Reservation in 1874, Deloria took up the duties of a headman, including negotiating agreements for his band with the federal government and the railroad company that was moving into Sioux territory. He also began serving as an Episcopal lay reader and catechist. His growing involvement in the church eventually led him to forsake his political activities and dedicate himself exclusively to Sioux missionary work. In 1883, Episcopal bishop William Hare, made him a deacon; nine years later, Deloria was ordained one of the first American Indian Episcopal priests.

Through more than thirty years of his ministry, Deloria was stationed on the Standing Rock Reservation, home to Yanktonai and Lakota Sioux. One of his major duties at this post was to oversee the construction of St. Elizabeth's Boarding School in 1892. In this and all his priestly activities, he sought what was best—as he understood it—for the spiritual and social welfare of his congregation.

Deloria died in Mission, South Dakota, in 1931. Five years later, in gratitude for his many years of service, the Episcopal Church named him one of the sixty "Saints of the Ages" and erected a statue of him in its National Cathedral in Washington, D.C.

Harvey Markowitz

Deloria, Vine, Jr.

Born: March 26, 1933; Martin, South Dakota
Tribal affiliation: Yankton or Standing Rock Lakota (Sioux)
Significance: Vine Deloria, Jr., is the most prolific of Indian protest writers and an advocate of education for American Indians.

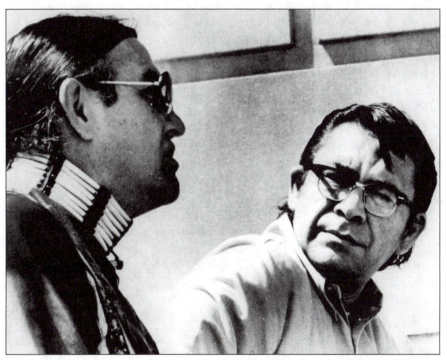

Vine Deloria, Jr. (right). (AP/Wide World Photos)

After receiving a bachelor's degree in science from Iowa State University, Vine Deloria, Jr., studied for a career as a minister, earning a master's in theology from the Lutheran School of Theology in Illinois. Then he earned a J.D. from the University of Colorado law school that enabled him to serve as the executive director of the National Congress of American Indians. He taught political science and Native American studies at the University of Arizona, which he left to direct the Indian studies program at the University of Colorado.

Much of the power of Deloria's writing comes from his sharp-witted political satire, as manifested especially in two books on contemporary Indian life. His first book, *Custer Died for Your Sins: An Indian Manifesto* (1969), indicts the U.S. government's treatment of Indians and has served as a manifesto for Indian activists. In *We Talk, You Listen: New Tribes, New Turf* (1970), he pleads for a return to tribalism, by which he means a return to a balanced relationship among people, land, and religion. He has written much about political and legal issues concerning Indian-white relations, including *Behind the Trail of Broken Treaties: An Indian Declaration of Independence* (1974); *American Indians, American Justice* (1983); and *American Indian Policy in the Twentieth Century* (1985). Best-known of his books on Indian religion is *God Is Red* (1973), in which he argues that Indian religions that promote an ecologically sound relationship with the environment are more appropriate in contemporary America than Christianity. He also edited *A Sender of Words: Essays in Memory of John G. Neihardt* (1984), a volume that contains essays on *Black Elk Speaks.* Deloria's later works include *Tribes, Treaties, and Constitutional Tribulations* (1999), *Documents of American Indian Diplomacy* (2000), and *Power and Place: Essays in American Indian Education* (2001).

Lee Schweninger

FURTHER READING

Deloria, Barbara, Kristen Foehner, and Sam Scinta. *Spirit and Reason: The Vine Deloria, Jr., Reader.* Golden, Colo.: Fulcrum Publishing, 1999.

Warrior, Robert Allen. *Tribal Secrets: Recovering American Indian Intellectual Traditions.* Minneapolis: University of Minnesota Press, 1994.

Delshay

Born: c. 1835; present-day Arizona
Died: c. 1874; Arizona
Tribal affiliation: Apache
Significance: Delshay was murdered by a bounty hunter, and his head was publicly displayed as a warning to other Apaches who raided white settlements.

Following their uprisings between 1861 and 1863, Apache bands continued raiding neighboring whites. In 1868, Chief Delshay agreed to peace and resettled his band at Camp McDowell on Arizona's Verde River. In 1871, after the Camp Grant Massacre, in which members of ESKIMINZIN's peaceful band of Aravaipa Apache were attacked after having been granted sanctuary, Delshay requested permission to move his band from the region.

Meanwhile, with settlers calling for military action, the U.S. army under General George Crook launched a massive campaign against the Apaches, winning decisive battles at Skull Cave, December 28, 1872, and Turret Peak, March 27, 1873. Delshay surrendered in April, 1873, and his band was relocated to Fort Apache on the White Mountain Reservation. Later he was granted permission to settle at Camp McDowell in return for promises that he cease hostilities. For a time, peace was maintained. After Delshay was joined by Apache fugitives, however, Crook ordered his arrest. When he eluded capture for several months, a bounty was offered for his head; two rival claims were honored, and the heads were displayed at Camp Verde and at the San Carlos Reservation.

Mary E. Virginia

FURTHER READING

Cozzens, Peter, ed. *Eyewitnesses to the Indian Wars, 1865-1890.* Mechanicsburg, Pa.: Stackpole Books, 2001.

Lockwood, Frank C. *The Apache Indians.* Foreword by Dan L. Thrapp. 1938. Reprint. Lincoln: University of Nebraska Press, 1987.

Dodge, Henry Chee

Born: February 22, 1860; Fort Defiance, Arizona
Died: January 7, 1947; Ganado, Arizona
Also known as: Hastin Adiits'a'ii (Mr. Interpreter)
Tribal affiliation: Navajo
Significance: Henry Chee Dodge played a central role as an interpreter, businessman, and tribal chairman in more than half a century of dealings between the U.S. government and the Navajos.

Henry Chee Dodge's father was a captured Mexican who was killed in the conflict between the Navajos and New Mexicans shortly after Henry's birth. His mother was Jemez (Pueblo) and Navajo, and since Navajos trace family lineage through the mother, he was considered a member of the Navajo Maii'deshgizhnii (Coyote Pass People) Clan. His family hid during the Navajo Wars, but they nevertheless went hungry—victims of the U.S. Army's scorched-earth policy. His mother left him with a family that had more food, but he was subsequently abandoned by them.

An aunt took charge of Henry at about the age of five, moving him first to Fort Sumner and then to Fort Defiance. She married a white man who adopted the child, and his contact with his stepfather as well as the soldiers helped him to develop a masterful command of English.

This ability served him well throughout his life, despite his having had only a few months of formal schooling.

With the rare skill of speaking both Navajo and English, Dodge was employed as a teenager at the Fort Defiance Indian Agency. At twenty, he was promoted from clerk to official interpreter for the U.S. government, and he continued in that position for ten years. During this time he assisted Washington Matthews in collecting Navajo legends and chants. In 1884, Indian Agent Dennis Riordan appointed him "head chief" of the Navajos, and he escorted three medicine men to meet President Chester A. Arthur in Washington, D.C.

Dodge saved his wages, and at the age of thirty, he entered into a partnership to operate the Round Rock Trading Post. He married Asdzaan Tsinnijinnie and settled at what is now Crystal, New Mexico, on the Arizona-New Mexico border, where he opened a store in his house. Dodge divorced his first wife because she was a gambler and then married two sisters with whom he had a total of four children. He stressed education and sent his children to school in Salt Lake City.

In 1892, Dodge helped save an Indian agent from angry Navajos who objected to having their children sent to boarding schools. Dodge's trading post was attacked for three days as the agent barricaded himself inside.

In 1922, Dodge became a member of the Tribal Business Council; he became the tribe's first elected chairman the following year, serving until 1928. His son Tom became tribal chairman in 1932, and another son, Ben, served on the tribal council. Dodge went on to direct the tribal police force and was reelected tribal chairman in 1942. His daughter, Annie Dodge WAUNEKA, became an important health educator.

Jon Reyhner

FURTHER READING

Moses, L. G., and Raymond Wilson, eds. *Indian Lives: Essays on Nineteenth and Twentieth Century Native American Leaders.* Albuquerque: University of New Mexico Press, 1985.

Dohasan

Born: c. 1805
Died: c. 1866; Indian Territory, present-day Oklahoma
Also known as: Little Mountain, Little Bluff, Dahauson, Tohauson

Tribal affiliation: Kiowa

Significance: Dohasan forged an alliance among independent Kiowa bands, making the tribe a major power in the southern Plains during the 1840's.

After the Kiowas were defeated in war by the Osage in 1833, Dohasan was chosen to replace the deposed chief, Adate. Dohasan quickly proved his worth by uniting the several bands of Kiowa into a cohesive and formidable tribe. He likewise negotiated peace with the Osage.

During the 1840's, as the Kiowas were devastated by cholera and smallpox and were increasingly threatened by white migration onto their lands, Dohasan led numerous raids against the white intruders. After army retaliation, Dohasan signed the Treaty of Fort Atkinson in 1853, by which the Kiowa were paid an annuity in exchange for promising to cease their raiding. Hostilities continued virtually unabated, however, until Dohasan agreed to the Little Arkansas Treaty of 1865, by which the Kiowas agreed to settle on a reservation in the Oklahoma panhandle in Indian Territory.

After his death in 1866, Dohasan was succeeded by LONE WOLF, the tribe's compromise choice, over the war leader SATANTA and the peace faction's leader, KICKING BIRD.

Mary E. Virginia

Donnaconna

Born: ?
Died: c. 1539; France
Tribal affiliation: Huron
Significance: Donnaconna was the first Indian leader of note to resist the French incursion into tribal territory in present-day Canada.

When the French explorer Jacques Cartier erected a cross at the Iroquoian village of Stadacona (present-day Quebec City) in July, 1534, the village chief, Donnaconna, strenuously objected. Cartier forced him aboard his French ship on the banks of the St. Lawrence River adjacent to Stadacona; after some negotiations, Cartier released him but took Donnaconna's two sons, Domagaya and Taignoagny, captive. They were taken to France to become interpreters for Cartier, whose plans included exploring further up the St. Lawrence River to the Iroquoian village of Hochelaga (now Montreal) and beyond.

Cartier returned from France the following year with Donnaconna's sons, feasted with the chief, and planned an expedition to Hochelaga with his two young interpreters. The boys, however, intrigued against Cartier in an attempt to prevent French penetration of the interior of the continent. Cartier ventured without them and relations between the French and Stadaconans worsened. Donnaconna told Cartier of the "kingdom of the Saguenay" along the river of that name in what is now eastern Quebec, where he would find "immense quantities of gold, rubies and other rich things." Donnaconna was trying to divert the explorer from the St. Lawrence Valley and from his nation's territory. Although Domagaya inadvertently saved the French crew of more than one hundred from death by scurvy through a white cedar bark cure, Cartier connived with Donnaconna's rival Agona to oust Donnaconna from his role as chief. Cartier seized the deposed leader, his two sons, and seven other Stadaconans.

On May 6, 1536, Cartier left for France with these ten captives. None of them returned to their homeland; all but one died soon after arrival in France. Before his death, however, Donnaconna received an audience with King François I and told him of great gold and silver mines and spices such as nutmeg, cloves, and pepper, which existed in northern North America. Donnaconna probably concocted this fiction in the hope that he would be released and allowed to return home. The former chief also was interviewed by the monk and cosmologist André Thevet, who later wrote extensively about Donnaconna's homeland. When Cartier next ventured to Stadacona in 1541 without Donnaconna, his sons, or any of the other captives, the Stadaconans, including chief Agona, grew increasingly wary. War broke out between them and the French in 1542.

Gretchen L. Green

FURTHER READING
Trigger, Bruce G. *The Children of Aataentsic: A History of the Huron People to 1660.* Montreal: McGill-Queen's University Press, 1976.

Dorris, Michael

Born: January 30, 1945; Louisville, Kentucky
Died: April 11, 1997; Concord, New Hampshire
Tribal affiliation: Modoc
Significance: Writer and educator Michael Dorris had a significant impact on Native American studies as an academic discipline and on the general public's awareness of fetal alcohol syndrome (FAS).

Michael Dorris's involvement with Native American affairs came quite naturally. The only child of a non-Native American mother and a Modoc father, Dorris spent childhood vacations with relatives who lived on reservations in Montana and Washington. His disdain for being called a Native American writer stemmed from these early experiences; he learned to think of people as human beings rather than as members of particular ethnic groups.

After his father's death, Dorris was raised by his mother, aunts, and grandmothers. The result of this feminine influence is apparent in his novel *A Yellow Raft in Blue Water* (1987), a story about three generations of women, narrated in their own voices.

In 1981, Dorris married Louise ERDRICH, another author of mixed ancestry. Dorris attributed much of his literary success to Erdrich, making her another of his women-as-mentors. Dorris and Erdrich collaborated as they wrote, producing works that authentically showcase Native Americans.

After his adopted son, Abel, was diagnosed with fetal alcohol syndrome, a preventable but debilitating condition caused by alcohol consumption during pregnancy, Dorris began writing *The Broken Cord: A Family's Ongoing Struggle with Fetal Alcohol Syndrome* (1989). The book includes a touching autobiographical account provided by Abel.

The Broken Cord's focus on alcohol abuse reflects Dorris's concern that U.S. government policies are driving Native Americans into a health and education crisis. While a professor at Dartmouth, Dorris founded the Native American Studies Program and was recipient of the Indian Achievement Award. His empathy for Native Americans is apparent in his literary characters, who dramatize the often difficult living conditions of contemporary tribal members.

Despite the focus on Native Americans in his works, the common experiences of humanity fueled Dorris's passion

Michael Dorris with Louise Erdrich. (© Jerry Bauer)

for writing. As an anthropologist who valued differences, Dorris used his literary voice to promote acceptance of diversity, touching on the basic elements of life that connect all people.

A Yellow Raft in Blue Water, Dorris's first novel, chronicles incidents in the lives of his three women narrators. Readers have embraced the book, finding the story to be a compelling look at mothers and daughters. The novel opens with Rayona, a fifteen-year-old girl who is part Native American and part black. When her mother moves her to Montana to stay with her grandmother on a reservation, Rayona's mixed heritage makes her the target of prejudiced teens, damaging her already fragile self-esteem.

Eventually Rayona leaves the reservation and meets an understanding couple, who invite her to live with them. In Sky and Evelyn's modest home, Rayona feels accepted and begins to value commitment, self-sacrifice, and honesty as prime ways to define oneself. By the novel's end, Rayona develops the confidence and self-respect she needs to function in the tribal community and to be accepting of its diverse members.

In 1995, Dorris and Erdrich separated after their children brought sexual abuse charges against Dorris. The allegations were never proven, but Dorris committed suicide in 1997.

Lynne Klyse

FURTHER READING

Beattie, L. Elisabeth, ed. *Conversations with Kentucky Writers.* Lexington: University Press of Kentucky, 1996.

Chavkin, Allan, and Nancy Feyl Chavkin, eds. *Conversations with Louise Erdrich and Michael Dorris.* Jackson: University Press of Mississippi, 1994.

Rosenberg, Ruth. *Louise Erdrich and Michael Dorris.* New York: Twayne, 1995.

Weil, Ann. *Michael Dorris.* Austin, Tex.: Raintree Steck-Vaughn, 1997.

Dozier, Edward Pasqual

Born: April 23, 1916; Santa Clara Pueblo, New Mexico
Died: May 2, 1971; Tucson, Arizona
Also known as: Awa Tside
Tribal affiliation: Santa Clara Pueblo
Significance: One of the first American Indian professors of anthropology, Edward Dozier published many important articles and books based on his research among Pueblo people and in the Philippines.

Although American anthropologists have often studied Indian people, very few have been Indian themselves. Such an imbalance has meant that, within the educational system, the authorities on the history and cultural experiences of Indian people have tended to be outsiders to Indian communities. As an Indian, Edward Pasqual Dozier is a major exception in the history of American anthropology.

Dozier grew up in Santa Clara Pueblo and learned to speak Tewa, Spanish, and English. As an adolescent during the 1930's, he worked as a research assistant for Elizabeth Sergeant, a journalist and ethnographer conducting research among the Pueblos.

Dozier applied his diverse linguistic and cultural experience to his academic studies in anthropology. In 1952, Dozier received a doctorate in anthropology from the University of California, Los Angeles. After conducting research in a community of Tewa people living among the Hopi in Arizona, Dozier went on to teach anthropology and linguistics at the University of Oregon, Northwestern University, and the University of Arizona. His books include *The Tewa of Arizona* (1954), *Hano: A Tewa Village in Arizona* (1966), *Mountain Arbiters: The Changing Life of a Philippine Hill People* (1966), and *The Pueblo Indians of North America* (1970).

Throughout his career, Dozier attempted to further the interests of Indian people. At the University of Arizona, he established an American Indian studies program. Between 1957 and 1971, he served on the board of the Association on American Indian Affairs.

Molly H. Mullin

Dragging Canoe

Born: c. 1730; Running Water Village on the Tennessee River (now in Tennessee)
Died: March 1, 1792; Running Water Village, Southwest Territory (now in Tennessee)
Also known as: Cheucunsene, Kunmesee, Tsungunsini
Tribal affiliation: Cherokee
Significance: Cherokee leader Dragging Canoe violently opposed white expansion into Indian land.

Unlike his father, Chief Attakullakulla, the peace leader for the Cherokee who sought accommodation with whites, Dragging Canoe was opposed to any form of white encroachment on Cherokee lands. Angered by the 1775 agreement through which the Cherokee sold all of Kentucky and part of Tennessee, he prophesied that the Cherokee would eventually be banished to some distant land. Dragging Canoe led a dissident group who refused to sign the treaty.

While Attakullakulla and most Cherokee sided with the Americans during the revolutionary war, Dragging Canoe sided with the British, using British-supplied weaponry to attack settlers in Tennessee. Although betrayed by his cousin Nancy WARD, who warned settlers of pending attacks, his band inflicted several white casualties. When the Cherokee were driven from the region in 1782, Dragging Canoe established a new home near Chickamauga, Tennessee, from which he continued to attack white settlers. In retaliation, the Americans destroyed all Chickamauga villages. As the Cherokee continued signing away their land, Dragging Canoe maintained his policy of armed resistance. In 1782, he again led his people to a new settlement downriver, though in 1784, these new villages were also destroyed. Afterward, Dragging Canoe finally agreed to peace.

Mary E. Virginia

FURTHER READING

Ehle, John. *Trail of Tears: The Rise and Fall of the Cherokee Nation.* New York: Doubleday, 1988.

Dull Knife

Born: c. 1810; Rosebud River (now in Montana)
Died: c. 1883; Pine Ridge Reservation, South Dakota
Also known as: Wahiev, Morning Star, Tamela Pashme
Tribal affiliation: Northern Cheyenne
Significance: Dull Knife, with LITTLE WOLF, led the 1,500-mile journey of the Cheyenne from their exile in Indian Territory to their northern home in Montana.

As a soldier chief, Dull Knife had a reputation for never sending anyone ahead of him, and he often counted the first coup. Dull Knife and Little Wolf are both noted in connection with an incident in 1856 at the Upper Platte Bridge, which according to historian Stan Hoig, was the first significant conflict between Cheyennes and U.S. troops.

Prior to the killing of BLACK KETTLE and his people in 1864, Dull Knife had been a noted warrior and respected chief. He fought alongside Sioux and Northern Arapahos in many of the major engagements of the northern Plains. During the War for the Bozeman Trail (or Red Cloud's War), 1866-1868, and the Fetterman massacre of December,

Dull Knife. (Library of Congress)

1866, Dull Knife allied with Sioux leaders CRAZY HORSE, GALL, and HUMP. Dull Knife's participation in negotiations at Fort Laramie, however, and his subsequent signature on an agreement to allow a fort in the Powder River country may have permanently affected his role as a leader. In May, 1868, Dull Knife was one of the signers of the Fort Laramie Treaty. In November of 1873, Dull Knife and Little Wolf led a delegation of Cheyenne and Arapaho chiefs in negotiations with the commissioner of Indian affairs in Washington, D.C. The leaders explained that they had never given up their homelands and that they did not want to move south to Indian Territory. The differing interpretations of the treaty arrangements provided another four years of freedom for the Cheyenne people, but the Battle of the Little Bighorn in 1876 changed that. Following the defeat of George Armstrong Custer, the government was determined to move the Sioux and Cheyenne peoples to Indian Territory.

At dawn on November 25, 1876, eleven hundred cavalrymen under Colonel R. S. Mackenzie attacked the village of Dull Knife and Little Wolf in a canyon of the Bighorn Mountains. Forty Cheyennes died. As deadly was the destruction of tipis, clothing, and the entire supply of winter food—burned by the soldiers. When the temperature dropped to thirty below zero that same night, more lives were lost. The Cheyenne who surrendered were sent to Indian Territory. Of the one thousand people sent to the Darlington Agency in August, 1877, six hundred became ill in the first two months, and forty-three died. After several failed attempts to convince the authorities that they should be returned to their Montana homeland, Dull Knife—with Little Wolf and about 350 people—set out for Montana in September, 1878. The group included

92 men, 120 women, and 141 children. After six weeks of flight, the group split, part following the leadership of Little Wolf, who wanted to continue north to the Tongue River, and part following Dull Knife, who wanted to seek shelter with RED CLOUD. Dull Knife did not know that the Red Cloud Agency had been moved.

During a blizzard in October, Dull Knife's 149 Cheyenne followers were surrounded by troops from Fort Robinson; they surrendered and initially were lodged at the fort until the Indian bureau could determine their disposition. On January 3, 1879, the bureau determined that the Cheyenne people should be returned to Indian Territory. When Dull Knife said his people would rather fight than go back, the doors to the barracks they were housed in were chained shut. Food and firewood were denied in an effort to freeze and starve them into submission. On January 9, after six days without provisions, the Cheyenne people broke from the barracks building. In the first moments of gunfire, those jumping from the windows were shot, but the confusion allowed some to escape. Even so, in that first half-mile to freedom, more than half of the Cheyenne fighting men were killed.

On January 21, the so-called Cheyenne Outbreak ended with one last battle at Antelope Creek. Of the 149 people who had fled the prison barracks, 64 had been killed in the fighting and 78 were recaptured. Dull Knife was one of the seven who escaped. He was captured later when he went to the Red Cloud Agency for help. He was later returned to the Northern Cheyenne reservation secured by Little Wolf in the Rosebud Valley. The Northern Cheyenne were officially granted the Tongue River Reservation in Montana in 1884, the year following Dull Knife's death.

Dull Knife had one son, the warrior Bull Hump. Dull Knife Memorial College in Lame Deer, Montana, recognizes the Cheyenne leader's encouragement to acquire an education to learn a new way of life.

Tonya Huber

FURTHER READING
Boye, Alan. *Holding Stone Hands: On the Trail of the Cheyenne Exodus*. Lincoln: University of Nebraska Press, 1999.
Dockstader, Frederick J. *Great North American Indians: Profiles in Life and Leadership*. New York: Van Nostrand Reinhold, 1977.
Grinnell, George Bird. *The Cheyenne Indians: Their History and Ways of Life*. 2 vols. New Haven, Conn.: Yale University Press, 1923. Reprint. Lincoln: University of Nebraska Press, 1972.
_____. *The Fighting Cheyennes*. New York: Charles Scribner's Sons, 1915.

Hoebel, E. Adamson. *The Cheyennes: Indians of the Great Plains.* New York: Holt, Rinehart and Winston, 1978.

Hoig, Stan. *The Peace Chiefs of the Cheyennes.* Norman: University of Oklahoma Press, 1980.

Maddux, Vernon A. *In Dull Knife's Wake: The True Story of the Northern Cheyenne Exodus of 1878.* Norman, Okla.: Horse Creek Publications, 2003.

Sandoz, Mari. *Cheyenne Autumn.* New York: McGraw-Hill, 1953.

Utley, Robert M. *The Indian Frontier of the American West, 1846-1890.* Albuquerque: University of New Mexico Press, 1984.

Dumont, Gabriel

Born: 1837 or 1838; Winnipeg, Manitoba, Canada
Died: 1906; Batoche, Saskatchewan, Canada
Tribal affiliation: Métis
Significance: Gabriel Dumont was an expert buffalo hunter, guide, and tribal military leader during the Second Riel Rebellion in Saskatchewan.

Gabriel Dumont was the grandchild of a French Canadian who settled on the western prairie during the 1790's and married a Sarcee woman. An outgrowth of the fur trade, the Méti (mixed) people represented a new mixed-blood nation with a culture that combined French Roman Catholic and indigenous ways. Several thousand Métis ranged over the plains of western Canada, North Dakota, and Montana. They hunted buffalo, made pemmican (concentrated food), traded, and served as guides.

Dumont's family left the Red River settlement (now Winnipeg), where he was born, and moved further west, eventually settling in what is now Saskatchewan. Gabriel Dumont, who received his first rifle before he reached the age of ten, became an expert marksman with both firearms and the bow and arrow. He quickly gained a reputation as a hunter, canoeist, interpreter, guide, and a fighter in two Métis-Indian clashes. Although illiterate, he become fluent in six Indian languages in addition to French. In 1862, he was elected leader of a band of three hundred Méti hunters who operated along the North Saskatchewan River. A few years later, they established the small settlement of Batoche on the South Saskatchewan River. Near there, Dumont and his wife of Scottish and Indian descent operated a ferry crossing at a site that still bears his name.

Increasing Anglo-Canadian settlement from the east and the progressive slaughter of the buffalo herds threatened the Méti way of life and jeopardized their land claims. The latter situation produced the Riel Rebellion of 1869-1870 in Manitoba. Fifteen years later, dissatisfaction reached the boiling point in Canada's Northwest Territories when the government in Ottawa neglected the area and did not respond to concerns of both Métis and white settlers.

In 1884, Dumont led a Méti delegation to Montana to enlist the help of Louis RIEL, Jr., a Méti leader living there in exile. After the government ignored Riel's representations, violence broke out in a new rebellion in 1885. Small groups of Indians joined with the Métis. While Riel headed a provisional government, Dumont served as military leader of the resistance. Under Dumont, the rebels routed a detachment of Mounted Police and white settlers at Duck Lake, won other minor victories, and delayed the advance of Canadian forces. The more cautious Riel opposed Dumont's plan of harassing the approaching inexperienced Canadian troops with guerrilla-style ambushes, preferring to rest on divine help while awaiting a confrontation in Batoche. Eventually, a force of eight hundred government soldiers equipped with artillery and a Gatling gun, overran the three hundred poorly armed Méti defenders, who were short of ammunition.

Riel was eventually captured and executed, while Dumont escaped to Montana. In 1886, Dumont joined the traveling Wild West show of Buffalo Bill Cody and entertained crowds with his marksmanship. He also earned money from lectures. Gabriel returned to Saskatchewan in 1893 and settled again in Batoche, where he dictated his memoirs, traded, and hunted until his death in 1906.

David A. Crain

FURTHER READING

Dumont, Gabriel. *Gabriel Dumont Speaks*. Translated by Michael Barnholden. Vancouver: Talonbooks, 1993.

Woodcock, George. *Gabriel Dumont: The Métis Chief and His Lost World*. Edited by J. R. Miller. Peterborough, Ont.; Orchard Park, N.Y.: Broadview Press, 2003.

Eastman, Charles Alexander

Born: February 19, 1858; near Redwood Falls, Minnesota
Died: January 8, 1939; Detroit, Michigan
Also known as: Ohiyesa (The Winner)
Tribal affiliation: Santee Lakota (Sioux)
Significance: Through his many publications and participation in Indian-related activities, Charles Eastman became a leading advocate of Indian reform during the early twentieth century.

Charles Alexander Eastman was born at a time when the Santee Sioux were facing the hardships of reservation life. He later became recognized as the most highly educated Indian in the United States and devoted his entire career to helping Indians adjust to the dominant white society.

Eastman's mother, who died giving birth to him, was the mixed-blood daughter of Captain Seth Eastman, a noted artist. His father, Many Lightnings, belonged to the Wahpeton band of the Santee Sioux. Eastman received the name Ohiyesa to represent symbolically a victory by his band over another in a lacrosse game. After the ill-fated Santee Sioux uprising in Minnesota in August, 1862, Eastman was among those who fled to Canada. He believed his father, had been killed during the uprising.

Eastman's paternal grandmother and uncle reared him in the traditional ways of a Sioux boy. He became a skilled hunter and anxiously awaited his initiation as a warrior. His traditional upbringing abruptly ended in 1872 when his father appeared in Canada to reclaim him. Many Lightnings had been imprisoned for his actions in the Sioux uprising and became a Christian while in confinement. After his release, he established a home at Flandreau, Dakota Territory. Many Lightnings persuaded Eastman to return with him to Flandreau and later to adopt an English name and to begin his formal education in white schools.

For the next seventeen years, Eastman attended several schools. In 1887, he received his bachelor's degree from Dartmouth College, and in 1890, he obtained his medical degree from Boston University. The Indian Rights Association and the Lake Mohonk Conference of Friends of the Indian, two powerful reform groups, praised his accomplishments and used him as a model for other Indians. Eastman was now thirty-two years old and ready to begin a career dedicated to helping Indian people.

Eastman's adult years paralleled an important period of federal Indian policies—from the Dawes Severalty Act of 1887 to the Indian New Deal of the 1930's. During that time, he held several federal jobs and became a nationally known author, lecturer, and reformer.

Eastman served as government physician at Pine Ridge Academy, South Dakota, 1890-1893, witnessing the Ghost Dance and the Wounded Knee tragedy; administrator at Carlisle Indian School, Pennsylvania, 1899; government physician at Crow Creek, South Dakota, 1900-1903; head of the revision of the Sioux allotment rolls, 1903-1909; and Indian inspector, 1923-1925. Eastman frequently clashed with his white superiors during his employment with the federal government. For example, white Indian agents often felt threatened by an educated Indian and suspected him of undermining their authority.

Eastman's nongovernment jobs included establishing a brief medical practice in St. Paul, Minnesota, in 1893; serving as the Indian secretary of the International Committee of the YMCA, 1894-1898; and representing the Santee Sioux claims in Washington, D.C., for many years.

Eastman became a prolific writer, authoring eleven books and numerous articles. Elaine Goodale Eastman, his wife, who was also a writer and reformer, helped him with his work.

Eastman's autobiographical writings included *Indian Boyhood* (1902) and *From the Deep Woods to Civilization* (1916). *The Soul of the Indian* (1911) and *The Indian Today* (1915) addresses Indian history and culture as well as Indian-white relations His books usually received good reviews, sold well, and were translated into foreign editions. Although Eastman tended to be romantic in his writings, he wrote about Indians from his perspective as an Indian—a unique situation in the early twentieth century. He was also in demand as a lecturer.

As a reformer, Eastman

Charles Alexander Eastman. (Library of Congress) helped to organize and later served as president of the Society of American Indians, a pan-Indian organization formed in 1911. He worked hard to protect Indians from injustices and to improve reservation conditions. He initially supported the Dawes Act, but later, like many other reformers, began criticizing its elimination of Indian-owned lands. Eastman called for improved health and educational programs on reservations; disapproved of the use of peyote by Indians; supported the Indian Citizenship Act of 1924, believing that suffrage would help Indians to achieve equality; and condemned the Bureau of Indian Affairs for not doing its job. As an acculturated Indian, Eastman most likely supported the acculturation approaches of the Indian New Deal, which allowed Indians to be Indians and still operate in the dominant society.

Eastman spent his last years separated from his wife. He purchased a cabin in Canada in the late 1920's and continued to lecture and do research. In 1933, the Indian Council Fire, a pan-Indian organization, honored Eastman as their first recipient of an annual award that recognized his many achievements in improving Indian and white relations.

Charles Eastman believed that Indians did not have to discard their Indianness to survive in the dominant society. He developed, as did many Indians, a special syncretism, or blending of cultures, which allowed him to operate in two different worlds.

Raymond Wilson

FURTHER READING
Eastman, Charles Alexander [Ohiyesa]. *From the Deep Woods to Civilization: Chapters in the Autobiography of an Indian.* 1916. Reprint. Lincoln: University of Nebraska Press, 1977.
_____. *Indian Boyhood.* New York: McClure, Phillips, 1902. Reprint. New York: Dover, 1971.
_____. *The Indian Today: The Past and Future of the First Americans.* Garden City, N.Y.: Doubleday, 1915.
_____. *The Soul of the Indian: An Interpretation.* 1911. Reprint. New York: Johnson Reprint, 1971.
Fitzgerald, Michael Oren, ed. *Light on the Indian World: The Essential Writings of Charles Eastman (Ohiyesa).* Introduction by Janine Pease Pretty on Top. Bloomington, Ind.: World Wisdom, 2002.
Wilson, Raymond. *Ohiyesa: Charles Eastman, Santee Sioux.* Urbana: University of Illinois Press, 1983.

Erdrich, Louise

Born: June 7, 1954; Little Falls, Minnesota
Tribal affiliation: Turtle Mountain Chippewa (Ojibwa)
Significance: One of the most widely acclaimed Native American writers of fiction and poetry, Louise Erdrich tells of intertwining relationships and histories among an extended family of twentieth century Chippewas.

Louise Erdrich was born in Little Falls, Minnesota, across the Red River from Wahpeton, North Dakota, the small town that later served as a model for Erdrich's fictional town of Argus. Her father, Ralph Erdrich, was a German immigrant; her mother, Rita Journeau Erdrich, was a three-quarters Chippewa. Both her parents were employed by the Wahpeton Bureau of Indian Affairs boarding school. Louise grew up in Wahpeton, the oldest of seven children, and was exposed to the cultures of both her parents. Maintaining a close bond with her German Roman Catholic grandmother, she was also on familiar ground with her extended Chippewa family on the Turtle Mountain reservation. Her maternal grandfather was a tribal chairman there, and the North Dakota plains reservation eventually became the setting for much of Erdrich's fiction.

Erdrich later claimed that she had never given serious attention to her Native American background while growing up, had never thought about "what was Native American and what wasn't." In 1972, she entered Dartmouth College in New Hampshire and majored in creative writing. Her parents had encouraged her interest in writing since her childhood, binding her stories into homemade books. At Dartmouth, she began to garner awards for her poetry and stories. After her graduation from Dartmouth, she worked a variety of odd jobs, compiling a personal archive of experiences for use in her writing. While pursuing her master's degree at Johns Hopkins University, which she earned in 1979, she composed many of the poems that would be collected in her first published book. *Jacklight* (1984) received critical praise, but it was her short stories, appearing in literary magazines, that produced a sense of anticipation among literary critics. "The World's Greatest Fisherman," set on the reservation and centering on the death of June Kashpaw, won first prize in the Nelson Algren fiction competition in 1982. Introducing the various members of the Kashpaw, Lamartine, and Nanapush families, this story became the starting place for a number of related novels reaching back in history as far as 1912.

Erdrich's marriage to Michael Dorris in 1981 coincided with her burgeoning interest in her Chippewa heritage. Dorris, the founder and director of the Native American Studies program at Dartmouth, shared Erdrich's writing ambitions and a similar ethnic background. He had previously adopted a son, whose struggle with fetal alcohol syndrome (FAS) led Dorris to write *The Broken Cord* (1989). Dorris had also adopted two more children; when they married, Erdrich adopted all three of Dorris's children, and together Erdrich and Dorris produced three more. In addition to rearing their large family, Erdrich and Dorris collaborated on all their writing during the 1980's and early 1990's and campaigned together against the increasing incidence of FAS. Dorris committed suicide in 1997; the couple had previously separated.

When Erdrich's *Love Medicine* first appeared in 1984, two of its stories had already been honored: "Scales," which was anthologized in *Best American Short Stories, 1983* (1983); and the 1982 Nelson Algren competition winner, "The World's Greatest Fisherman." Among the awards Erdrich received for *Love Medicine* were the National Book Critics Circle Award and the *Los Angeles Times* Award for Fiction. Erdrich was hailed as an original and powerful talent, and her second novel, *The Beet Queen* (1986), confirmed her place among contemporary authors.

A distinctive yet difficult element of Erdrich's fiction, for which she has been criticized, is the apparent disjointedness of her narratives: cross-cutting points of view, circular plotting, jarring shifts in time. Casual, linear reading produces an impression of a beautifully written but incoherent patchwork of short stories. A more careful approach reveals a deliberate and artful weaving of tales, all related—some more distantly than others—but all essential to the whole.

While *Love Medicine* dealt with the extended family of the Kashpaws on the reservation, *The Beet Queen* told the

Louise Erdrich. (Michael Dorris)

somewhat more tightly plotted story of the Adares: siblings Mary and Karl and Karl's daughter Dot. Dot is the intersection at which the worlds of the white Adares and Erdrich's Chippewas overlap. Celestine, Karl's lover and Dot's mother, is half-sister to Russell Kashpaw; Gerry Nanapush is the adult Dot's lover.

Tracks appeared in 1988, continuing the histories of characters begun in the two previous works. The action in this novel is concentrated in the years 1912 through 1924, though its repercussions travel backward through *Love Medicine* and *The Beet Queen* (and forward through time), filling in crucial details and enriching the saga. A vibrant and complex picture of the Matchimanito reservation emerges. Erdrich depicts a mature and many-branched family tree. Nanapush and Pauline Puyat alternate their narratives, each revealing from strikingly different perspectives the life of Fleur Pillager, an alluring and mystical figure. In 1993, Henry Holt issued an expanded edition of *Love Medicine* that included five new sections. Erdrich believed that the new stories belonged with the earlier work. Then in 1994, she released *The Bingo Palace*, bringing the latest generation of her characters to adulthood.

It is easy to draw comparisons between Erdrich's fictional community and William Faulkner's Yoknapatawpha County. Erdrich herself has named Faulkner as an influence. Matchimanito is based on Turtle Mountain reservation, where Erdrich spent much of her youth; the off-reservation town of Argus is a re-creation of her hometown of Wahpeton. The complicated family network that binds her fiction into a comprehensive whole is certainly inspired by the author's own Chippewa relatives. Her familiarity with the more sinister aspects of Roman Catholic mysticism and the dangers posed by its mingling with Indian superstition appears especially in the dark, twisted reasoning of Pauline, a fanatical nun.

The themes raised in Erdrich's fiction are universal: the value and potency of hope and love and the importance of home and family. The issues that illustrate these themes stem from the condition of Native Americans in the twentieth century. The reservation is a blighted residue left over from previous centuries of decline, a place of concentrated despair; yet it is also a community where ties among members are strong and the connection of its people to the land is ancient and sacred. Poverty, alcoholism, abandoned or distorted faith are balanced against self-worth, endurance, and love. Erdrich's plots also involve a variety of contemporary issues, including the erosion of land rights, the education of children in both the government schools (in which Indian children endured forced assimilation and the attempted erasure of their own language and culture) and in the wilds, tribal politics, religious conflict, generational conflict, and intermarriage.

In addition to giving expression to the trauma of the Chippewa experience, Erdrich has presented the lives of American Indians not as defeated but as determined and vital. She has also brought to the storytelling tradition a literary artistry that is both challenging and refreshingly original. Critical opinion, however, does not confine Erdrich to the narrow category of Indian writer. She is among the most important novelists of the twentieth century. In addition to her fiction she has published works of poetry and folktales, including *Baptism of Desire* (1989). Her collaborative relationship with Michael Dorris resulted in other works of fiction, including *A Yellow Raft in Blue Water* (1987) and *The Crown of Columbus* (1991), as well as Dorris's autobiographical work *The Broken Cord.*

Erdrich and Dorris's campaign against fetal alcohol syndrome, which afflicts many reservation children because of the high rate of alcoholism among Native Americans, helped to draw the nation's attention to the dangerous effects of alcohol on fetuses. Legislation was eventually passed requiring the posting of warnings to pregnant women anywhere liquor is sold.

In 2000, after relocating with her three youngest children, Erdrich and her sister opened Birchbark Books, Herbs, and Native Arts in Minneapolis. Erdrich continued writing and produced such books as *The Last Report on Miracles at Little No Horse* (2001), *The Master Butchers Singing Club* (2003), and *Four Souls* (2004).

Janet Alice Long

FURTHER READING

Owens, Louise. "Acts of Recovery: The American Indian Novel in the '80's." *Western American Literature* 1 (May 22, 1987): 53-57.

Rainwater, Catherine. "Reading Between Worlds: Narrativity in the Fiction of Louise Erdrich." *American Literature* 62 (September, 1990): 405-422.

Sergi, Jennifer. "Storytelling: Tradition and Preservation in Louise Erdrich's *Tracks.*" *World Literature Today* 66 (Spring, 1992): 279-283.

Smith, Jeanne Rosier. *Writing Tricksters: Mythic Gambols in American Ethnic Literature.* Berkeley: University of California Press, 1997.

Towery, Margie. "Continuity and Connection: Characters in Louise Erdrich's Fiction." *American Indian Culture and Research Journal* 16 (1992): 99-122.

Wong, Hertha D. "An Interview with Louise Erdrich and Michael Dorris." *North Dakota Quarterly* 55 (Winter, 1987): 196-218.

Eskiminzin

Born: c. 1825; Gila region, present-day Arizona
Died: 1890; San Carlos Agency, Arizona
Also known as: Big Mouth, Hackibanzin
Tribal affiliation: Apache
Significance: Although a proponent of peace, Eskiminzin was victimized by white settlers seeking retaliation for Apache raids.

Born a Pinal Apache, Eskiminzin married an Aravaipa Apache, eventually becoming the Aravaipa principal chief. During the Apache wars, Eskiminzin's people were peaceful agave farmers. Seeking asylum, in 1871 Eskiminzin led his people to Camp Grant near Tucson, where Lieutenant Royal Whitman allowed them to settle rather than forcing their relocation to a reservation.

In retaliation for Apache raids in March and April, 1871, Tucson settlers assaulted Eskiminzin's band. In what became known as the Camp Grant massacre, 150 Apache, including eight members of Eskiminzin's family, were murdered. After the raiders were tried and acquitted, Apache hostility escalated. Thereafter, Eskiminzin was arrested on several occasions; each time he escaped or was released after brief incarcerations. In 1886, at the cessation of hostilities, he traveled to Washington, D.C., for negotiations. He was again arrested in 1888 and was imprisoned in Florida and Alabama; returning home in 1888, he died shortly thereafter. Although he counseled peace, Eskiminzin frequently was a scapegoat for white anger—a convenient target, though an innocent one.

Mary E. Virginia

FURTHER READING
Cozzens, Peter, ed. *Eyewitnesses to the Indian Wars, 1865-1890*. Mechanicsburg, Pa.: Stackpole Books, 2001.

Flat Mouth

Born: 1774; Leech Lake (now in Minnesota)
Died: 1860; Leech Lake, Minnesota
Also known as: Guelle Plat, Wide Mouth, Eshkebugecoshe
Tribal affiliation: Ojibwa (Chippewa)
Significance: Flat Mouth was a principal chief during the struggles for control of the Upper Mississippi Valley region.

Flat Mouth, an Ojibwa principal chief during the nineteenth century. (National Archives)

Flat Mouth succeeded his infamous shaman father, Wasonaunequa, who, as village chief of the Leech Lake Chippewas, attained his position by poisoning his enemies. As a young man, Flat Mouth traveled extensively, living for a time among various tribes, including the Cree and Assiniboine.

With HOLE-IN-THE-DAY, Noka, and Curling Hair, Flat Mouth led

Chippewa warriors against the Sioux, who were battling for domination of land surrounding the Mississippi headwaters.

Apparently influenced by TECUMSEH's brother, the Shawnee Prophet, TENSKWATAWA, Flat Mouth denounced poison as a means for eliminating rivals. Despite Tenskwatawa's influence, however, Flat Mouth refused aid to Tecumseh during his pan-Indian rebellion in 1809-1811, choosing instead to remain friendly to white Americans. Similarly, Flat Mouth spurned British entreaties to attack Americans during the War of 1812, occasionally aiding Americans during the war. Flat Mouth's Chippewas were among the few Indian tribes to resist relocation, remaining on tribal lands.

Mary E. Virginia

Fools Crow, Frank

Born: December, 1890; Pine Ridge Reservation, South Dakota
Died: November, 1989; Pine Ridge Reservation, South Dakota
Tribal affiliation: Oglala Lakota (Sioux)
Significance: A holy man and civic leader, Frank Fools Crow was instrumental in preserving traditional tribal customs, as well as denouncing the social ills that were eroding his native culture.

A nephew of the Lakota visionary BLACK ELK, Fools Crow was raised in the traditional Sioux manner. When he was thirteen, a holy man named Stirrup took him on his first vision quest. In 1923, Fools Crow formally began his training as a medicine man and eventually became adept at the sweat lodge and Yuwipi ceremonies. Because he often did not receive payment for his services, he worked at a variety of occupations, including railroad lineman, jockey, actor, and performer in wild west shows.

In 1925, Fools Crow succeeded his father, Eagle Bear, as chief of the Porcupine District in Pine Ridge Reservation. Two years later, he experienced his first crisis as district leader when reservation agents asked him to lead the Sun Dance for the benefit of white tourists. He refused to allow sacred Sioux traditions to become a sideshow for non-Indian spectators. His struggle was emblematic of the challenges that Native American tribes faced as they tried to blend their traditional ways with the harsh realities of government-controlled reservations.

During the Great Depression of the 1930's, conditions on the reservation became intolerable as non-Indians living in and around it benefited from government work programs, while Native Americans—especially those like Fools Crow, who could not read or write English—

were unable to secure jobs. Widespread use of alcohol among the Sioux increased, which further eroded traditional life. Discouraged, Fools Crow resigned as district leader.

During the 1960's, the tribe appointed Fools Crow a ceremonial chief—a position that qualified him to lead religious and civil ceremonies, as well as install tribal officials. As a result of a vision quest he performed in 1965, he claimed that his power to heal greatly increased and that he could cure diabetes, cancer, and gallstones. His fame as a medicine man spread beyond the reservation, and even non-Indians consulted him.

Fool Crow's leadership was tested in 1973 during the seizure at Wounded Knee by the members of American Indian Movement (AIM). He was asked by federal marshals to present a peace proposal to AIM officials. At a critical point in the negotiations, a young Sioux threatened to kill him, but Fools Crow managed to talk the young man out of his rash behavior. Eventually both sides signed the document ending the siege as a result of Fool Crow's intervention.

In 1975, Fools Crow traveled to Washington, D.C., seeking a meeting with President Gerald Ford concerning reservation issues. During his visit, he became the first Native American holy man to lead the opening prayer before the U.S. Senate. In 1976, he returned to Washington and addressed the Senate Subcommittee in Interior and Insular Affairs, charging that the government had illegally confiscated the sacred Black Hills. Although his plea failed, he remained active in tribal affairs and was highly esteemed by the Sioux until his death.

Pegge Bochynski

FURTHER READING
Mails, Thomas E. *Fools Crow.* New York: Doubleday. 1979.
_____. *Fools Crow: Wisdom and Power.* Tulsa, Okla.: Council Oak Books, 1991.

Foreman, Stephen

Born: October 22, 1807; Rome, Georgia
Died: December 8, 1881; Park Hill, Indian Territory (now in Oklahoma)
Tribal affiliation: Cherokee
Significance: A fully ordained Presbyterian minister, Stephen Foreman served as a spiritual and political leader to the Cherokee.

Stephen Foreman was one of twelve children of a Scottish trader and a Cherokee woman. When he was a boy, his family moved to Tennessee, where young Foreman attended a missionary school. When his father died, Foreman was sponsored by the Congregational minister Samuel Worcester at New Echota, Georgia. He also attended the College of Richmond, Virginia, and Princeton Theological Seminary, where he was ordained in 1835. Afterward he returned to live among the Cherokee and immediately became embroiled in the Cherokee resistance to removal. For a time he was imprisoned for his antiremoval activities. In 1841, he led one of the last Cherokee detachments on the Trail of Tears, continuing his ministry in Oklahoma.

With Worcester, Foreman translated the Bible into Cherokee using the syllabary created by SEQUOYAH. He also served as associate editor of the Cherokee newspaper, the *Cherokee Phoenix*. In 1841, Foreman organized a public school system for Cherokee children and in 1844 was elected to the Cherokee Supreme Court. From 1847 through 1855, he served as executive councilor of the Cherokee tribe. During the Civil War, Foreman lived in Texas, where he continued proselytizing, returning to Indian Territory at war's end. There he purchased the former home of Cherokee leader Elias BOUDINOT and established a church, where he preached until his death.

Mary E. Virginia

Francis, Josiah

Born: ?
Died: c. 1818; St. Marks River, Florida
Also known as: Francis the Prophet, Hayo, Hillis, Hillishago
Tribal affiliation: Creek, Seminole
Significance: Josiah Francis traveled the Mississippi Valley with TECUMSEH, seeking allies for Tecumseh's Rebellion.

Although Josiah Francis's ancestry was an unknown mix of Indian and white, his affiliation was with the Red Stick Creeks and with the Seminoles. Francis's daughter was Milly Hayo Francis, best known for saving the life of a Georgia militiaman, George McKinnon (also known as Duncan McKrimm), whom Francis was about to order executed during the First Seminole War.

When Tecumseh attempted to recruit the Creeks for his pan-Indian alliance, most of the Creek White Sticks from the Lower Creek villages were unresponsive. The traditional Creek warriors, the Red Sticks, including Francis, joined Tecumseh. In 1811, Francis traveled with Tecumseh throughout the Mississippi Valley, recruiting tribes for the new confederacy.

In the Creek War of 1813-1814, Francis fought against General Andrew Jackson, who referred to him as the "prophet." In 1814, Jackson forced the defeated Creeks to sign the Treaty of Fort Jackson, by which the Creeks lost twenty-three million acres of their land. Afterward, many Creeks, including Francis, settled among the Florida Seminoles. In 1815, Francis journeyed to England to solicit aid for Indians against the Americans. He participated in the First Seminole War in 1817-1818 and was captured in 1818, after being lured onto a gunboat in the St. Marks River. There Jackson ordered his execution.

Mary E. Virginia

FURTHER READING

Missall, John, and Mary Lou Missall. *The Seminole Wars: America's Longest Indian Conflict.* Foreword by Raymond Arsenault and Gary R. Mormino. Gainesville: University Press of Florida, 2004.

Francis, Milly Hayo

Born: c. 1802; Florida
Died: c. 1848; Muskogee, Indian Territory (now near Oklahoma)
Tribal affiliation: Creek, Seminole
Significance: In an incident reminiscent of the legend of POCAHONTAS and John Smith, Milly Francis is known for having intervened to save the life of a white soldier.

Milly Hayo Francis was the daughter of the Seminole prophet Josiah FRANCIS, who traveled throughout the Mississippi Valley seeking allies for TECUMSEH's pantribal rebellion. According to legend, Josiah Francis, during the First Seminole War (1817), ordered the death of Georgia militiaman George McKinnon. After he was tied to a stake in preparation for burning, Milly Francis intervened, begging for McKinnon's release, claiming she would also die if he burned. After Josiah Francis relented, McKinnon lived with the tribe. He was eventually sold to the Spanish as a slave.

When a band of starving women and children, including Milly Francis, appeared at an army post after Josiah Francis's death, newly escaped McKinnon spared her life. Legend holds he offered her marriage, which she refused, believing he only asked out of a sense of obligation.

After relocating to Indian Territory, in 1844 Milly Francis was granted a pension by the U.S. government in gratitude for her actions during the First Seminole War. She died fours years later without having received any of the funds.

Mary E. Virginia

FURTHER READING

Missall, John, and Mary Lou Missall. *The Seminole Wars: America's Longest Indian Conflict.* Foreword by Raymond Arsenault and Gary R. Mormino. Gainesville: University Press of Florida, 2004.

Gall

Born: c. 1840; near Moreau River in present-day South Dakota
Died: December 5, 1894; Oak Creek, South Dakota
Also known as: Pizi, Man Who Goes in the Middle, Red Walker
Tribal affiliation: Hunkpapa Lakota (Sioux)
Significance: Gall was a noted warrior and military tactician in the wars for the Bozeman Trail and the Black Hills; he was the principal Indian military strategist at the Little Bighorn.

Gall was born about 1840 along the Moreau River in Dakota Territory. His father died when Gall was a young boy, and he was reared by his widowed mother and relatives. SITTING BULL took him as a younger brother, and for many years these two were close allies. He was most commonly called Pizi. According to family legend, as a child he tried to eat the gall of an animal. He was also known as Red Walker because as a child his father once dressed him entirely in vermillion clothing. Gall was also known as Man Who Goes in the Middle, and although the origin of this name is unclear, it probably refers to a battle exploit.

Gall rose to prominence during the 1860's and 1870's as a noted leader in the wars for the Bozeman Trail and the Black Hills. These battles were fought in present-day Montana, Wyoming, and South Dakota. He allied closely with Sitting Bull and was committed to resisting government attempts to confine the Lakota people to the Great Sioux Reservation after the 1868 Treaty of Fort Laramie.

Gall's greatest fame came from his participation in the Battle of the Little Bighorn on June 25, 1876. Major Marcus Reno's command was the first to approach the Indian village, and they attacked the Hunkpapa camp. Gall's two wives and three children were killed in this foray, and Gall later said, "It made my heart bad." Gall led the counterattack

Gall. (National Archives)

that drove Reno from the village, and then he joined Crazy Horse in repelling George Armstrong Custer's forces. Gall gained great notoriety in the American press for his military prowess at the Battle of the Little Bighorn, and a newspaper labeled him "the worst Indian living."

After Indian defeats following the Battle of the Little Bighorn, Gall accompanied Sitting Bull to Canada in 1877. Hungry and destitute, he reluctantly returned to the United States in 1881 with about three hundred people and surrendered at Poplar Agency in present-day eastern Montana. Gall was relocated to the Standing Rock Agency in North Dakota. There he was befriended by Indian agent James McLaughlin, who urged him to denounce Sitting Bull for his uncompromising attitude toward the reservation system. The early reservation period was difficult for the Lakota people, and Gall believed that it was best to compromise with the government officials; Sitting Bull did not. Gall became a favorite of Agent McLaughlin's and in 1889 was appointed a judge of the court of Indian Offenses and a spokesman in the negotiations that brought about the breakup of the Great Sioux Reservation.

During his last years, Gall was an envoy to Washington, D.C., on behalf of his band. He became a strong proponent of education, and he enjoyed considerable prestige among whites. He took no part in the Ghost Dance religion when it spread to Standing Rock; some years before he had become a staunch Episcopalian. Gall's relationship with the U.S. government was not well received by other Indians, especially those who fought with him years earlier. This rejection was clear when KICKING BEAR did a pictographic drawing of the Battle of the Little Bighorn in 1898 and left a blank space where Gall should have been.

Carole A. Barrett

FURTHER READING
Welch, James, with Paul Stekler. *Killing Custer: The Battle of the Little Bighorn and the Fate of the Plains Indians.* New York: W. W. Norton, 1994.

Ganado Mucho

Born: c. 1809; near present-day Klagetoh, Arizona
Died: 1893; near Klagetoh, Arizona
Also known as: Tótsohnii Hastiin (Man of the Big Water)
Tribal affiliation: Navajo
Significance: Ganado Mucho was a Navajo leader during the tribe's difficult transition to reservation life.

Ganado Mucho, which means "many cattle," was born into the Tótsohnii (Big Water) Clan of the Navajo, or Diné ("the people"). His father was a Hopi captured by the Navajos. A successful cattle grower and sheepman all his adult life, he worked with other Navajo headmen such as MANUELITO to keep the peace with whites. He cooperated with U.S. Indian agents to return livestock stolen from New Mexicans. In February, 1861, he attended a council with Colonel Edward R. S. Canby to sign a treaty of peace along with other Navajo headmen. Unfortunately, the outbreak of the Civil War forced the abandonment of Fort Defiance and ended any chance for the treaty's success.

Soon it became impossible to meet the peacekeeping demands of the U.S. government while at the same time protecting his people from raids initiated by other Indians and Mexicans. Kit Carson's scorched-earth campaign was the final straw, and Ganado Mucho moved his people near the Grand Canyon. Eventually, he was forced to surrender to avoid starvation. On the journey to the government's desolate resettlement camp at Fort Sumner (Bosque Redondo), Mexicans kidnapped two of Ganado's daughters. After he arrived there in July of 1866, his son was killed by Comanche raiders. Ganado escaped the following year, but hunger again forced his return.

In 1868, he and seventeen other traditional leaders signed a peace treaty allowing the Navajo to return home. At the treaty council he stated:

> Let us go home to our mountains. Let us see our flocks feeding in the valley, and let us ride again where we can smell the sage and know of hidden hogans by the smell of piñon smoke. . . . We have learned not to kill and not to steal from the flocks of others. Here we have nothing. Our children grow up in ugliness and death. Let us go home.

Ganado was appointed a subchief for the western side of the reservation by the Indian agent and settled near what was to become the reservation town of Ganado. The transition to reservation life without raiding was difficult. In 1878, Ganado Mucho helped kill an estimated forty Navajo "witches" who continued to raid white cattlemen.

Jon Reyhner

Garakontie, Daniel

Born: c. 1600; present-day Onondaga, New York
Died: c. 1676; present-day Onondaga, New York
Also known as: Harakontie
Tribal affiliation: Onondaga
Significance: Daniel Garakontie was a highly skilled negotiator between the Onondaga (and other Five Nations Iroquois) and the French in New France.

Not much is known of Garakontie's early life. He was first noted in European records for attempting to prevent war between the Iroquois and the French, and for sheltering Jesuits in Iroquois towns from attack by anti-French forces. He enjoyed warm personal relationships with several French Jesuit missionaries. Garakontie engineered a truce between the Iroquois and the French in 1661 and attempted in 1665 and 1666 to do the same. There were strong anti-French factions arrayed against him within the Iroquois tribes, which often foiled his efforts.

Following the 1667 French-Iroquois peace, Garakontie greatly encouraged the work of Jesuit missionaries in Iroquoia, although not until 1669 did he express his wish to be baptized. Political alignments clearly preceded his religious convictions. He was baptized in 1670 in the cathedral at Quebec City. The colonial governor, Daniel de Rémy de Courcelle, who served as his godfather, hosted a feast for the attending Indians following the ceremony. Garakontie remained devoted to his adopted faith, learned to read and write, and on a visit to New Netherlands, scolded Protestant Dutchmen who criticized his theological convictions.

Garakontie did not always enjoy popularity and support among his own people; many of them denounced him for accepting Christianity and for allying closely with the French. He was not, however, a mere tool of the French. Garakontie believed that his people could learn some useful things from the French, and that Iroquois interests would be best served in most cases by siding with the French rather than with the Dutch or the English in Albany. This cost him dearly at times, but he was at all times highly respected among his own people, and his oratory, political skills, and honesty were unquestioned.

Gretchen L. Green

FURTHER READING

Richter, Daniel K. *The Ordeal of the Longhouse: The Peoples of the Iroquois League in the Era of European Colonization*. Chapel Hill: University of North Carolina Press, 1992.

Garra, Antonio

Born: c. 1800; Southern California
Died: December, 1852; Southern California
Tribal affiliation: Cupeño
Significance: A leader of the Garra Uprising, Antonio Garra attempted to halt white migration into California.

As chief of the Cupeño Indians living in Southern California at the headwaters of the San Louis Rey River, Antonio Garra opposed white expansion into California. As migration into the California region of white miners and ranchers, as well as of Mexicans and Mormons, intensified during the Gold Rush era, Garra sought to organize a united Indian revolt. Claiming that he could transform his enemies' bullets into water, Garra and his Cahuilla, Chemehuevi, Cocopa, Kamia, Luiseño, Mojave, and Quechan supporters raided ranchers and sheepherders. Garra's son, also named Antonio Garra, fought with his father during the Garra Uprising.

Several other California bands elected to remain neutral, however, and some, including the Luiseños under Manuelito Cota, actively aided whites. The influential Cahuilla, Juan Antonio, was courted by both Indians and whites. Electing to assist white settlers, Antonio captured Garra in 1851, thereby ending the Garra Uprising. Antonio released Garra to the California militia, who convened a court martial that tried and hanged him.

Mary E. Virginia

FURTHER READING

Secrest, William B. *When the Great Spirit Died: The Destruction of the California Indians, 1850-1860.* Sanger, Calif.: Word Dancer Press, 2003.

Garry, Spokane

Born: 1811; near the junction of the Latah Creek and Spokane River (now in Washington)
Died: January 14, 1892; Indian Canyon, near Spokane, Washington
Tribal affiliation: Spokane (Salish)
Significance: Spokane Garry both led his tribe in battle against whites and sought to Christianize his people.

Spokane Garry went to a Hudson's Bay Company school in Canada (1825-1830). On returning home, he built a tule mat church and commenced teaching English, agriculture, and the Christian religion. As a pacifist, he opposed the Hudson's Bay Company policy of encouraging chiefs to flog Indians who committed crimes. He also restrained the Spokanes from joining the Yakimas and other Plateau groups in warfare against the whites during the Yakima War of 1855-1856. Yet because of the absence of treaties, increasing Spokane grievances against white incursion, and the military expedition by Colonel Edward Steptoe, Spokane Garry was forced to join other Indian warriors in the 1858 Battle of

Four Lakes, losing to Colonel George Wright. He continued, however, to encourage the Spokanes to negotiate treaties to avoid violence in relation to what he believed was inevitable domination by whites.

Garry became disillusioned with Calvinistic revivalists Cushing Eells and Elkahah Walker and their establishment of Tshimakain Mission (1838), which increased religious factionalism. Eventually he gave up his teaching and preaching and joined the Spokane in hunting buffalo on the Great Plains. In middle age he was considered wealthy, having many horses and a productive farm. He was known for his abilities as a skillful negotiator.

John Alan Ross

General, Alexander

Born: c. 1889; Six Nations Reserve, near Brantford, Ontario, Canada
Died: September, 1965; Brantford, Ontario, Canada
Also known as: Deskahe, Shao-hyowa (Great Sky)
Tribal affiliation: Cayuga, Oneida
Significance: Alexander General worked with anthropologists to promote understanding of traditional Iroquois beliefs and the cause of Iroquois nationalism.

Alexander General was born on the Six Nations Reserve near Brantford, Ontario, in 1889 and given the name Shao-hyowa, or "Great Sky." Previously a faithkeeper, in 1917 he became the principal speaker for the Upper Cayuga Turtle Moiety at the Sour Springs longhouse. He was elevated to a confederacy chieftainship in 1925 and received the title Deskahe.

Strongly opposed to Canada's imposition of an elected council on the Six Nations in 1924, he traveled to England in 1930 to argue unsuccessfully for Iroquois sovereignty in Canada. He was instrumental in the organization of the Indian Defense League and the Mohawk Workers, early nationalist movements. Through various jobs in nearby cities, he learned English and earned enough to establish himself as a successful farmer. For three decades, he worked closely with anthropologists in interpreting Iroquois ritual and ideology, emphasizing the close ties between the confederacy and the longhouse. He is best known for his collaboration with Frank Speck on *The Midwinter Rites of the Cayuga Longhouse* (1949), but he also worked with many other scholars.

Joy A. Bilharz

George, Dan

Born: July 24, 1899; North Vancouver, British Columbia, Canada
Died: September 23, 1981; Vancouver, British Columbia, Canada
Tribal affiliation: Salish
Significance: After entering acting late in his life, Dan George played
   Indian roles in a number of films during the 1970's.

Dan George began his acting career when he was in his sixties. Previously
he was a laborer and musician, and from 1951 to 1963 he was chief of his
Tell-lall-watt band of the Burrard Salish. In 1959 George had a part in a
Canadian television series entitled *Caribou Country.* He appeared in the
film *Smith* in 1969. His best-known film role was as Old Lodge Skins in the
unusual 1970 Western *Little Big Man,* starring Dustin Hoffman. George
won the New York Film Critics Circle Award for Best Supporting Actor
and was nominated for an Academy Award in the same category.

   George also appeared in the original stage production of George
Ryga's *The Ecstasy of Rita Joe,* a drama about contemporary Indian life, and
a number of other films, including *Harry and Tonto* (1974), *The Outlaw
Josie Wales* (1975), and *Shadow of the Hawk* (1976). He did not support the
radical Indian activism of the
1970's, but he worked to support native rights, to counter
derogatory depictions of Indians, and to argue that Indian
roles should be played by Indian actors.

McCrea Adams

FURTHER READING
Kilpatrick, Jacquelyn. *Celluloid
   Indians: Native Americans
   and Film.* Lincoln: University of Nebraska Press, 1999.
Rollins, Peter C., and John E.
   O'Connor. *Hollywood's Indian: The Portrayal of the
   Native American in Film.* Expanded ed. Lexington: University Press of Kentucky,
   2003.

Dan George. (Hulton|Archive by Getty Images)

Geronimo

Born: June, 1829; near present-day Clifton, Arizona
Died: February 17, 1909; Fort Sill, Oklahoma
Also known as: Goyathlay (One Who Yawns)
Tribal affiliation: Chiricahua Apache
Significance: For two decades Geronimo was the Indian leader most feared and vilified by whites in the Southwest. His misunderstood and maligned struggle epitomized the troubles of a withering Apache culture attempting to survive in a hostile modern world.

While the precise location of Geronimo's birth is not known, he most likely was born near the head of the Gila River in a part of the Southwest then controlled by Mexico. Named Goyathlay (One Who Yawns) by his Behonkohe parents, the legendary Apache warrior later came to be called Geronimo—a name said to have been taken from the terrified cries of Mexican soldiers calling on the Roman Catholic saint Jerome to protect them from his relentless charge.

Geronimo's early life, like that of any Apache youth, was filled with complex religious ritual and ceremony. From the placing of amulets on his cradle to guard him against early death to the ceremonial putting on of the first moccasins, Geronimo's relatives prepared their infant for Apache life, teaching him the origin myths of his people and the legends of supernatural beings and benevolent mountain spirits that hid in the caverns of their homeland. Geronimo learned about Usen, a remote and nebulous god who was the life giver and provider for his people. Geronimo's religious heritage taught him to be self-sufficient, to love and revere his mountain homeland, and never to betray a promise made with oath and ceremony.

Geronimo grew into adulthood during a brief period of peace among the chronic wars between the Apache and Mexican peoples. Even in times of peace, however, Apache culture placed a priority on the skills of warfare. Through parental instruction and childhood games, Geronimo learned how to hunt, hide, track, and shoot—necessary survival skills in an economy based upon game, wild fruits, and booty taken from neighboring peoples.

Geronimo heard the often-repeated stories of the conquests of his heroic grandfather, Mahko, an Apache chief renowned for his great size, strength, and valor in battle. Like his grandfather, Geronimo had unusual physical prowess and courage. Tall and slender, strong and quick, Geronimo proved at an early age to be a good provider for his

Geronimo in a posed studio portrait shortly after his capture. (National Archives)

mother, whom he supported following his father's premature death, and later for his bride, Alope, whom he acquired from her father for "a herd of ponies," stolen most likely from unsuspecting Mexican victims. By his early twenties, Geronimo (still called Goyathlay) was a member of the council of warriors, a proven booty taker, a husband, and a father of three.

In 1850, a band of Mexican scalp hunters raided an Apache camp while the warriors were away. During the ensuing massacre, Geronimo's mother, wife, and three children were slain. Shortly after this tragedy, Geronimo had a religious experience that figured prominently in his subsequent life. As he later reported the incident, while he was in a trancelike state, a voice called his name four times (the magic number among Apaches) and then informed him, "No gun can ever kill you. I will take the bullets from the guns of the Mexicans, so they will have nothing but powder. And I will guide your arrows." After receiving this gift of power, Geronimo's vengeance against Mexicans was equaled by his confidence that harm would not come his way.

While still unknown to most Americans, during the 1850's, Geronimo rose among the ranks of the Apache warriors. A participant in numerous raids into Mexico, Geronimo fought bravely under the Apache chief COCHISE. Although wounded on several occasions, Geronimo remained convinced that no bullet could kill him. It was during this period that he changed his name from Goyathlay to Geronimo.

War between the U.S. government and the Apaches first erupted in 1861 following an incident in which the government charged Cochise with kidnapping. The war lingered for nearly a dozen years, until Cochise and General O. O. Howard signed a truce. According to the terms of the agreement, the mountain homeland of the Chiricahua (Geronimo's tribe, one of the tribes that made up the Apache) was set aside as a reservation, on which the Chiricahua promised to remain.

Following Cochise's death in 1874, the United States attempted to relocate the Chiricahua to the San Carlos Agency in the parched bottomlands of the Gila River. Although some Apache accepted relocation, Geronimo led a small band off the reservation into the Sierra Madre range in Mexico. From this base, Geronimo's warriors conducted raids into the United States, hitting wagon trains and ranches for the supplies needed for survival.

In 1877, for the first and only time in his life, Geronimo was captured—by John Clum of the U.S. Army. After spending some time in a guardhouse in San Carlos, Geronimo was released, being told not to leave the reservation. Within a year, however, he was again in Mexico.

While a fugitive, he was blamed in the American press for virtually all crimes committed by Apache "renegades" of the reservation.

Upon the promise of protection, Geronimo voluntarily returned to the San Carlos Agency in 1879. This time he remained two years until an unfortunate incident involving the death of Noch-ay-del-klinne, a popular Apache religious prophet, triggered another escape into the Sierra Madre. In 1882 Geronimo daringly attempted a raid into Arizona to rescue the remainder of his people on the reservation and to secure for himself reinforcements for his forces hiding in Mexico. This campaign, which resulted in the forced abduction of many unwilling Apache women and children, brought heavy losses to his band and nearly cost Geronimo his life. The newspaper coverage of the campaign also made Geronimo America's most despised and feared villain.

In May, 1883, General George Crook of the U.S. Army crossed into Mexico in search of Geronimo. Not wanting war, Geronimo sent word to Crook of his willingness to return to the reservation if his people were guaranteed just treatment. Crook consented, and Geronimo persuaded his band to retire to San Carlos.

Geronimo, however, never adjusted to life on the reservation. Troubled by newspaper headlines demanding his execution and resentful of reservation rules (in particular, the prohibition against alcoholic drink), Geronimo in the spring of 1885 planned a final breakaway from the San Carlos Agency. With his typical ingenuity, Geronimo led 144 followers off the reservation. Cutting telegraph lines behind him, he eluded the cavalry and crossed into Mexico, finding sanctuary in his old Sierra Madre refuge. Although pursued by an army of five thousand regulars and five hundred Apache scouts, Geronimo avoided capture until September, 1886, when he voluntarily surrendered to General Nelson Miles. (He had agreed to a surrender to General George Crook in March but had then eluded his troops.)

Rejoicing that the Apache Wars were over, the army loaded Geronimo and his people on railroad ears and shipped them first to Fort Pickens in Florida and then to the Mount Vernon Barracks in Alabama. Unaccustomed to the warm, humid climate, so unlike the high, dry country of their birth, thousands of the Apache captives died of tuberculosis and other diseases. In 1894, after the government rejected another appeal to allow their return to Arizona, the Kiowa and Comanche offered their former Apache foes a part of their reservation near Fort Sill, Oklahoma.

Geronimo spent the remainder of his life on the Oklahoma reservation. Adapting quickly to the white economic system, the aged Apache warrior survived by growing watermelons and selling his infamous signature to curious autograph seekers. While the government technically still viewed him as a prisoner of war, the army permitted Geronimo to attend, under guard, the international fairs and expositions at Buffalo, Omaha, and St. Louis. In 1905 Theodore Roosevelt invited him to Washington, D.C., to attend the inaugural presidential parade. Wherever Geronimo went, he attracted great crowds and made handsome profits by selling autographs, buttons, hats, and photographs of himself.

In February, 1909, while returning home from selling bows and arrows in nearby Lawton, Oklahoma, an inebriated Geronimo fell from his horse into a creek bed. For several hours, Geronimo's body lay exposed. Three days later, the Apache octogenarian died of pneumonia. As had been promised many years before, no bullet killed him.

Terry D. Billhartz

FURTHER READING

Adams, Alexander B. *Geronimo: A Biography.* New York: G. P. Putnam's Sons, 1971.

Betzinez, Jason, with Wilbur Sturtevant Nye. *I Fought with Geronimo.* Harrrisburg, Pa.: Stackpole, 1960.

Brown, Dee. "Geronimo." *American History Illustrated* 15 (May, 1980): 12-21; 15 (July, 1980): 31-45.

Clum, Woodworth. *Apache Agent: The Story of John P. P. Clum.* Boston: Houghton Mifflin, 1936. Reprint. Lincoln: University of Nebraska Press, 1978.

Davis, Britton. *The Truth About Geronimo.* Edited by M. M. Quaife. 1929. Reprint. New Haven, Conn.: Yale University Press, 1963.

Debo, Angle. *Geronimo: The Man, His Time, His Place.* Norman: University of Oklahoma Press, 1976.

Faulk, Odie B. *The Geronimo Campaign.* New York: Oxford University Press, 1969.

Geronimo. *Geronimo: His Own Story.* Edited by S. M. Barrett and Frederick Turner. New York: Duffield, 1906. Rev. ed. New York: Meridian, 1996.

Kraft, Louis. *Gatewood and Geronimo.* Albuquerque: University of New Mexico Press, 2000.

Sweeney, Edwin R., and Angie Debo. *Great Apache Chiefs: Cochise and Geronimo.* New York: MJF Books, 1996.

Wood, Leonard. *Chasing Geronimo: The Journal of Leonard Wood, May-September 1886.* Edited by Jack C. Lane. Albuquerque: University of New Mexico Press, 1970.

Giago, Tim

Born: July 12, 1934; Pine Ridge Reservation, South Dakota
Also known as: Nanwica Kciji (Defender)
Tribal affiliation: Oglala Lakota (Sioux)
Significance: Tim Giago is an award-winning newspaper editor, publisher, columnist, and author.

Tim Giago was born on the Pine Ridge Reservation in South Dakota. Besides his Lakota Sioux heritage, he has some Pueblo background. Much of his childhood experience was linked with the Holy Rosary Indian Mission School (now Red Cloud School), a Jesuit school with strict discipline. Giago came deeply to resent the school's policy of cultural genocide that forbade students to speak Lakota or practice their cultural beliefs. On the other hand, his attendance at the school instilled in him a strong work ethic that would later aid his successful career in journalism.

After serving in the U.S. Navy and seeing action in the Korean War, Giago attended San Jose College and the University of Nevada at Reno. He then worked at various jobs over about a fifteen-year period before beginning his career as a journalist in 1979. He worked first as an Indian affairs columnist, then as a full-time reporter for the *Rapid City Journal* in South Dakota. He quit following a disagreement with the paper's management over coverage of Indian news.

In 1981, Giago launched his own Rapid City-based publication, the *Lakota Times,* a weekly newspaper with an Indian staff covering local reservation news. His newspaper's coverage and readership eventually grew beyond the local level, and its circulation increased from 3,000 copies to 50,000 copies. In 1992, Giago renamed the paper *Indian Country Today.* Under his direction, *Indian Country Today* became the nation's largest Indian newspaper. By 1997, its circulation reached 125,000, and it was distributed in all fifty states and seventeen foreign countries.

In 1998, Giago sold *Indian Country Today* to the Oneida tribe, which soon moved its operation to New York. However, Giago reentered the field of newspaper publishing and editing in 2000 by founding the weekly *Lakota Journal* in Rapid City. After the Santee Sioux tribe of Flandreau, South Dakota, bought this newspaper in 2004, Giago stayed on as its editor.

Giago has written extensively on Indian issues in his own newspapers and through his syndicated column, *Notes from Indian Country,* which is carried in hundreds of papers by the Knight-Ridder news service. He

Tim Giago. (Lakota Times)

has been an outspoken advocate of various sensitive issues of concern to Indians and has frequently appeared on radio and television talk shows and given presentations around the country. Giago is the author of two books, *The Aboriginal Sin: Reflections on the Holy Rosary Mission School* (1978), and *Notes from Indian Country* 1 (1984); 2 (1999). He also coedited *The American Indian and the Media Handbook* (1994).

Giago has garnered numerous honors in recognition of his professional contributions and defense of Indian and minority rights. In 1992, Harvard University granted him a prestigious Nieman Fellowship in journalism. He also is a recipient of the Golden Quill Award for outstanding editorial writing and the *Baltimore Sun*'s H. L. Mencken Award. In 1994, he was inducted into the South Dakota Hall of Fame.

David A. Crain

Gilcrease, William Thomas

Born: February 8, 1890; Robeline, Louisiana
Died: May 6, 1962; Tulsa, Oklahoma
Tribal affiliation: Creek
Significance: William Thomas Gilcrease devoted his life to American Indian art and history, gathering a large collection of artifacts, documents, and artwork.

Born into the Creek Nation in Louisiana, Thomas William Gilcrease moved with his family to Indian Territory as a young boy. Each member of his family received 160 acres of tribally allotted land before Oklahoma was granted statehood. Gilcrease's Indian land allotment was located south of modern Glenpool, Oklahoma's first major oil-producing field. He attended Bacone Indian College at Muskogee by using royalty money. He later transferred to Emporia State College, Emporia, Kansas. Gilcrease, however, was mostly self-educated; his early formal education consisted primarily of intermittent attendance at rural schools in Louisiana and Indian Territory.

In 1922, he organized the Gilcrease Oil Company, later moving to San Antonio, Texas. He had a long-term fascination with learning about, understanding, and collecting Native American art, artifacts, and literature. In the process of satisfying his interest in Native Americans, he also developed a preoccupation with the general collecting of historical Americana.

In 1942, he established the Tulsa-based Gilcrease Foundation, whose corporate charter was "to maintain an art gallery, museum, and library devoted to the preservation for public use and enjoyment the artistic, cultural and historical records of the American Indian." In 1949, a museum was opened and, in 1958, deeded in its totality to Tulsa, Oklahoma. Thomas Gilcrease devoted most of his adult life to his love of art and Indian people. Today the Gilcrease Museum is one of the world's largest repositories of Western art, artifacts, and book collections devoted to North American indigenous peoples.

Burl E. Self

Gladstone, James

Born: May 21, 1887; Mountagin Hill, Northwest Territories, Canada
Died: September 4, 1971; Fernie, British Columbia, Canada
Also known as: Akay na muka (Many Guns)
Tribal affiliation: Kainai (Blood)
Significance: James Gladstone was the first aboriginal senator in Canada.

Although of Métis and Cree ancestry, James Gladstone attended an Anglican mission school on the Blood Reserve in Alberta. He spoke fluent Blackfoot and married Janie Healy, a Blood tribe community member, in 1911. It was not until 1920 that he became a treaty member of the Kainai (Blood) tribe. Before he was a political figure, he was a typesetter, then an interpreter and scout for the mounted police on the Blood Reserve. He was then a successful farmer on the reserve, owning some 800 acres.

Gladstone attended his first meeting of the Indian Association of Al-

James Gladstone (right) with Speaker of the Senate Mark Drouin in 1959.
(AP/Wide World Photos)

berta (IAA) in 1946, and four years later he was elected IAA President. As president, he was able to travel outside Alberta and speak out against the oppression caused by the Indian Act.

During the 1950's, members of First Nations (Canadian Indian tribes) were still not allowed to vote in federal elections. Prime Minister John Diefenbaker believed that aboriginal peoples should be represented in the Canadian Senate, and he appointed Gladstone to the Senate in 1958. (First Nation members were given the right to vote in 1960.) As a senator, Gladstone was an advocate for First Nations throughout the country. During his thirteen years in the Senate, Gladstone pursued issues such as increased aboriginal self-governance, improvement of education, and better economic development on First Nations reserves. One of Gladstone's most important contributions was to educate non-Native Canadians about First Nations peoples.

Susan C. Barfield

FURTHER READING
Dempsey, Hugh A. *The Gentle Persuader: A Biography of James Gladstone, Indian Senator.* Saskatoon, Saskatchewan: Western Producer Prairie Books, 1986.

Godfroy, Francis

Born: c. 1788; Kekionga (now Ft. Wayne, Indiana)
Died: May, 1840; Mount Pleasant Trading Post, Indiana
Tribal affiliation: Miami
Significance: Francis Godfroy was an ally of TECUMSEH during Tecumseh's Rebellion and fought on the side of the British in the War of 1812.

Francis Godfroy was born of a French father (Jacques Godfroy) and a Miami mother. He grew up near the present-day site of Fort Wayne, Indiana. He won renown as a war chief and as an ally of Tecumseh in Tecumseh's 1809-1811 attempt to stop white immigration into the Old Northwest. Godfroy was a large, stout man. Late in his life he weighed more than four hundred pounds.

Godfroy allied with the British during the War of 1812, and at one point he commanded a Miami force of three hundred men that routed troops sent against Miamis under the command of William Henry Harrison. With the defeat of the British, Godfroy accommodated the American advance as he moved to the site of his father's former trading post on the Wabash River and became a prosperous trader. He also benefited from grants of cash and land as he signed away much of the Miamis' homelands to the United States.

FURTHER READING
Anson, Bert. *The Miami Indians.* Norman: University of Oklahoma Press, 1970.
Rafert, Stewart. *The Miami Indians of Indiana: A Persistent People, 1654-1994.* Indianapolis: Indiana Historical Society, 1996.

Gorman, R. C.

Born: July 26, 1932; Chinle, Arizona
Tribal affiliation: Navajo
Significance: One of the most commercially successful Indian painters, R. C. Gorman altered the non-Indian standard of Indian art; he was the first Indian artist to own a gallery.

R. C. Gorman. (AP/Wide World Photos)

Rudolph Carl Gorman, or R. C. Gorman, has been called the "Picasso of Indian artists," "the Reservation Dali," and "the Vargas of Indian art," but he began life in a hogan during the Depression and herded sheep in Canyon de Chelly. At the private Ganado High School, volunteer teacher Jenny Lind influenced his drawing. After four years in the Navy, he won a scholarship from the Navajo tribe to study at Mexico City College in 1958. The muralists of Mexico profoundly shaped his art. In 1962, he moved to San Francisco and then, in 1968, to Taos, New Mexico, opening his Navajo Gallery. His unconventional paintings rapidly changed the Indian art market starting in 1965.

Apolitical images of strong, large women strolling or sitting, often with a child or pottery, drawn with a single line, are his hallmark. He carried these images into lithographs in 1966, posters in 1975, etchings in 1976, silk-screening, bronze sculpture, and ceramics in 1977, cast paper and glass etching in 1985—while continuing to draw and paint with charcoal and pastels. His work enjoys worldwide sales, and he has established a scholarship fund for Indians. Honors include the first one-man show for an Indian both in Taos and at the Heye Foundation, honorary doctorate degrees, and the Harvard Humanitarian Award in Fine Arts in 1986.

Cheryl Claassen

FURTHER READING
Parks, Stephen. *R. C. Gorman, a Portrait.* Boston: Little, Brown, 1983.
Reno, Dawn E. *Contemporary Native American Artists.* Brooklyn, N.Y.: Alliance Publishing, 1995.

Grass, John

Born: c. 1837; place unknown
Died: May 10, 1918; Standing Rock Reservation, North Dakota
Also known as: Pezi (Grass Field), Mato Watakpe (Charging Bear)
Tribal affiliation: Teton Lakota (Sioux)
Significance: John Grass was a diplomat and political leader of the Sioux in their long struggle against the United States.

John Grass's English name came from the Dakota "Pezi," meaning "field of grass"; he also was sometimes called Mato Watakpe (Charging Bear). He was a son of Grass, a Sioux leader of the early nineteenth century. He spoke a number of Dakota dialects as well as English, so he was one of few people in the Dakotas who could communicate with nearly everyone else.

In an attempt to break SITTING BULL's influence over the Sioux, Indian Agent Major James ("White Hair") McLaughlin set up Grass, GALL, and other Sioux as rival chiefs to Sitting Bull after the latter had surrendered in 1881. Over the objections of Sitting Bull, Grass signed an agreement in 1889 which broke up the Great Sioux Reservation. He probably was bowing to threats by McLaughlin that the U.S. government would take the land with or without Sioux consent. Even after the land was signed over, the government reduced the food allotments on northern Plains reservations, intensifying the poverty and suffering that helped increase tensions just before the massacre at Wounded Knee in 1890.

For more than three decades, Grass served as head judge in the Court of Indian Offenses of the Standing Rock Reservation. He died at Standing Rock in 1918.

Bruce E. Johansen

FURTHER READING
Ostler, Jeffrey. *The Plains Sioux and U.S. Colonialism from Lewis and Clark to Wounded Knee.* New York: Cambridge University Press, 2004.

Great Sun

Born: ?
Died: c. 1730; place unknown
Tribal affiliation: Natchez
Significance: The Great Sun who is known to history was the leader of the Natchez Revolt of 1729.

Among the Natchez, "Great Sun" was the hereditary title bestowed upon the tribe's principal chief. The Great Sun who was the head of the tribe in the early eighteenth century had to face the problems that resulted when the French began to settle along the Lower Mississippi River. He was the brother of Tattooed Serpent and the son of Tattooed Arm.

The Great Sun's family was strongly pro-French, but when Tattooed Serpent died, the anti-French faction began to gain influence. Trouble ensued when the governor of Louisiana demanded the Great Sun's village site for a plantation; the Great Sun refused, and the governor demanded payment in the form of crops. On November 30, 1729, Natchez warriors attacked French settlements along the Mississippi and inflicted more than five hundred casualties. French and Choctaw forces soon recaptured the main French fort (Fort Rosalie), and the captured Great Sun agreed to a peace. He escaped, however, and fought against French forces again in 1730. Again overpowered, he surrendered and was probably executed, perhaps in New Orleans. In the aftermath of the revolt, the tribal identity of the Natchez was destroyed.

Bruce E. Johansen

FURTHER READING

Cushman, H. B. *History of the Choctaw, Chickasaw, and Natchez Indians.* Edited by Angie Debo. Introduction by Clara Sue Kidwell. Norman: University of Oklahoma Press, 1999.

Ethridge, Robbie, and Charles Hudson, eds. *The Transformation of the Southeastern Indians, 1540-1760.* Jackson: University Press of Mississippi, 2002.

Oswalt, Wendell H. *This Land Was Theirs: A Study of Native Americans.* New York: Oxford University Press, 2005.

Green, Rayna

Born: July 18, 1942; Dallas, Texas
Tribal affiliation: Cherokee
Significance: Rayna Green is a literary pioneer who has presented new perspectives on American Indian women's issues.

As a child Rayna Green was taught Cherokee cultural traditions by her paternal grandmother, a member of the BUSHYHEAD family. After receiving her bachelor's degree in American literature from Southern Methodist University in 1963, she joined the Peace Corps and served as a history instructor in Ethiopia. In 1966, she resumed her education at Indiana University, where she received a master's and doctoral degrees in folklore. She was the first American Indian to earn a doctorate in that field.

Throughout her career, Green has taught English, social sciences, American studies, folklore, and Native American studies courses at such institutions as the University of Arkansas, the University of Maryland, Yale University, George Washington University, and Dartmouth College. As a professional writer, she has held numerous editorial positions and has written books, articles, and poems. Among the books she has written or edited are *The British Museum Encyclopedia of Native North America* (1999), *Native American Women: A Contextual Biography* (1983), *That's What She Said: Contemporary Poetry and Fiction by Native American Women*

(1984), *Women in American Indian Society* (1992), and *Encyclopedia of the First Peoples of North America* (1999). She has also worked on several films documenting Native American life.

Several of Green's poems deal with themes relating to the struggle of Native American women to preserve their culture. While encompassing the daily and ceremonial aspects of Indian life, her poems express the courage and strength, sorrows, and joys experienced by women. Her writings express the struggles of women resisting the Western forms of patriarchy imposed upon them. Green emphasizes and celebrates the ways women persist by reclaiming and redefining their roles in traditional Native cultures.

Among Green's numerous articles are "Traits of Indian Character: The 'Indian Anecdote' in American Vernacular Tradition" and "The Pocahontas Perplex." These essays investigate the misconceptions and mistreatment of Indians and the symbolic icon of the Indian princess. Her article "Nanye (Nancy Ward), the Last Beloved of the Cherokees, 1738-1822" presents the history of a prominent female Cherokee leader who is often forgotten. This story discusses the dispossession of women caused by the transformation of the Cherokee nation into a patriarchal society.

In recognition of her work to improve the health, educational, and economic conditions of members of the Cherokee Nation of Oklahoma, Green has received many civic awards, including the prestigious Jessie Bernard Wise Women Award. She has also held fellowships from the Ford Foundation and the Smithsonian Institution, where she was chair of the Division of Cultural History and Director of the American Indian Program for the National Museum of American History in 2004.

Teresa Neva Tate

Greene, Graham

Born: 1952; Six Nations Reserve, near Brantford, Ontario, Canada
Tribal affiliation: Oneida
Significance: One of the most visible contemporary Native American
    actors, Graham Greene is probably best known for his film roles in
    Dances with Wolves (1990), *Thunderheart* (1992), *Maverick* (1994), and
    Education of Little Tree (1997) and his television roles in *L.A. Law* and
    Northern Exposure.

The second of six children born to working-class parents, Graham Greene dropped out of school at the age of sixteen and worked at vari-

Graham Greene.
(Hulton|Archive by Getty Images)

ous jobs as a laborer, builder of railway cars, rock-band roadie, high-steelworker, landscape gardener, factory laborer, bartender, and carpenter. His first acting role, in 1974, was as part of a Toronto theater company. His first film role cast him as a friend of the Native American track star Billy MILLS in *Running Brave* (1982). In 1989 he played a Lakota Vietnam veteran in *Pow-Wow Highway*. The same year he received the Dora Mavor Moore Award of Toronto for Best Actor in his role as St. Pierre in the play *Dry Lips Oughta Move to Kapuskasing* (by Canadian Cree playwright Tomson HIGHWAY).

Greene's role as KICKING BIRD in *Dances with Wolves* brought him an Academy Award nomination for best supporting actor in 1991. In the same year, he gained popularity as Native American activist Arthur in the Canadian film *Clearcut*. Green undertook two major roles in 1992: ISHI in *The Last of His Tribe* and Lakota tribal policeman Walter Crow Horse in *Thunderheart*.

Greene appeared in more than twenty stage productions and more than eighty films and television shows between 1974 and 2004. During the 1990's, he made Toronto his main home.

Tonya Huber

FURTHER READING

Kilpatrick, Jacquelyn. *Celluloid Indians: Native Americans and Film.* Lincoln: University of Nebraska Press, 1999.

Rollins, Peter C., and John E. O'Connor. *Hollywood's Indian: The Portrayal of the Native American in Film.* Expanded ed. Lexington: University Press of Kentucky, 2003.

Hagler

Born: c. 1690; present-day South Carolina
Died: August 30, 1763; South Carolina
Also known as: Haiglar
Tribal affiliation: Catawba
Significance: Hagler was the most significant of the eighteenth century Catawba chiefs; he established peace with the white colonists and unified his people.

From the time of first contact with the English, the Catawba Indians conferred the title of king on their chiefs. No precise date can be fixed for Hagler's birth, but it is known that he was murdered on August 30, 1763, by Shawnee warriors. It is assumed that, following the death of chief Young Warrior in 1749, Hagler became leader of the Catawbas. Though Catawba chiefs were elected and served with a tribal council, both Young Warrior and Hagler were absolute in their rule.

The Catawbas and other tribes warred constantly during the first half of the sixteenth century. This constant conflict was considered a threat by whites, and in 1750 Governor De Witt Clinton of New York called for a meeting of Indian nations in Albany, New York. Hagler and five headmen sailed from Charles Town on May 23, 1751, and arrived in New York on May 30. The negotiations in New York were successful, and the Catawbas returned to the South believing a permanent peace was at hand. Their optimism was short-lived, however: Within two years, tribes from the north were making forays into Catawba territory, taking property and attacking people.

The Cherokees also continued to attack the Catawbas. By 1759, Hagler expressed solidarity with the white people against the Cherokees. He and forty other Catawbas served in the "Indian Corps" of an army commanded by Captain Quentin Kennedy and fought in the second Battle of Etchoe. It is clear that it was the alliance forged by Hagler with white South Carolinians that enabled the Catawbas to survive.

The greatest enemy of the Catawbas, though, was smallpox. Warriors brought the disease to the tribe when they returned from Fort Duquesne. Hagler survived by having his own encampment separate from the tribe. He was able to keep the tribe together, and by 1787 the Catawbas were the only organized Indian tribe in South Carolina.

Hagler was very much opposed to alcohol and the harm it seemed to be doing to his people. In 1754 he attended a "treaty"—a time to list grievances between whites and Indians. There, he told the white state authorities that they were to blame for the illness and crime among his people by making and selling strong drink to them. This speech has been referred to as "the first temperance lecture in the Carolinas." Though an absolute ruler, Hagler was concerned for the welfare of his people—even demanding that the white community provide food for them. He also had a keen sense of justice, as evidenced by the return of stolen property and his punishment of Catawbas for crimes against the whites.

In 1760 the Catawbas, ravaged by smallpox, were moved to Pine Tree Hill. Hagler and his headmen negotiated a treaty which provided a 15-square-mile tract of land for the Catawbas. A fort was built for security, and the friendship with whites continued.

In 1763, Hagler was returning home to Twelve Mile Creek with a slave when he was shot six times by a party of seven Shawnee. The slave escaped and told the story. Following the murder, the Catawbas were so taken with grief and enmity that they perpetrated atrocities against the Shawnee. One of the murderers was captured with a group of Shawnees. He was hacked to death; the others were beaten senseless with hickory switches and then given over to the young Catawba boys for target practice. The scalps were presented to the South Carolina governor, who told the warriors to give them to their Catawba boys so they would be brave men. He told the party, "We loved King Hagler because he was a friend to the English and we are glad that the man that killed him was killed by the Catawbas." Hagler was buried with his personal possessions, including a silver-mounted rifle, gold, and other items of value. His grave was robbed less than a month after his death.

David N. Mielke

FURTHER READING
Merrell, James H. *The Indians' New World: Catawbas and Their Neighbors from European Contact Through the Era of Removal.* Chapel Hill: University of North Carolina Press, 1989.

Hale, Janet Campbell

Born: January 11, 1947; Riverside, California
Tribal affiliation: Coeur d'Alene
Significance: Janet Campbell Hale's fiction and nonfiction reflect the troubled and difficult lives of contemporary Native Americans, struggling with poverty and the effects of alcoholism.

Janet Campbell Hale's childhood was spent first on the Coeur d'Alene Reservation in Idaho, then in Washington—in Tacoma and on the Yakima Reservation. Her father was an abusive alcoholic, and her mother moved frequently, hoping to leave him behind. Hale's early schooling was therefore somewhat sporadic, and she dropped out before the ninth grade. Her relations with her mother and older sisters were often troubled. She attended high school for a time but never graduated. At eighteen she married and had a son; the marriage was abusive, however, and she was divorced about a year later. She was a poor single mother with an incomplete education, but she believed that she could make her life better.

Hale began taking college classes at the City College of San Francisco, which did not require a high school diploma for enrollment. She did well enough to transfer to the University of California, Berkeley, the next year, and she graduated in 1972. Hale had been writing in some form or another since she was a small child, and now she was writing in earnest. Her first novel, *The Owl's Song*, was published in 1974.

In 1984 she received a master's degree from University of California, Davis. Her second novel, the well-reviewed *The Jailing of Cecelia Capture*, was published in 1987. Nominated for the Pulitzer Prize, it tells of a Native American woman put in jail for drunk driving and welfare fraud; the experience leads her to reflect on her troubled life. *Bloodlines: Odyssey of a Native Daughter* (1993), her first nonfiction book, is a combination of autobiography and stories of her family and ancestors. *Women on the Run* (1999) is a collection of short fiction about Native American women. In addition to her writing, Hale has been active as a teacher and lecturer.

McCrea Adams

FURTHER READING
Hale, Frederick. *Janet Campbell Hale.* Boise, Idaho: Boise State University, 1996.

Half-King

Born: c. 1700; near present-day Buffalo, New York
Died: October 4, 1754; present-day Harrisburg, Pennsylvania
Also known as: Tanacharison
Tribal affiliation: Oneida
Significance: Half-King joined the British forces during the French and Indian War.

Half-King, or Tanacharison, was one of a number of Iroquois who lived in the Ohio Valley area during the eighteenth century. Some of these Iroquois, who were often called "Mingos" by the whites, had been delegated power from the Iroquois Grand Council to conduct diplomacy with local tribes. The whites called such delegates "half-kings," so the designation was more a title than a personal name.

Born a Catawba, Tanacharison was captured at an early age and reared as a Seneca near the eastern shore of Lake Erie. He was a valued ally of the British in the French and Indian War and held councils with several officials, including Conrad Weiser, George Croghan, and a young George Washington, who was serving in his first combat situation. Tanacharison fought as an ally of Washington in the Battle of Great Meadows (1754), the opening salvo of the final British war with the French in North America, which ended in 1763. As a result of this battle, in which Tanacharison killed at least one French officer, Washington surrendered Fort Necessity to the French.

Tanacharison later moved to Aughwick (now Harrisburg), Pennsylvania, where he died of pneumonia in 1754.

Bruce E. Johansen

FURTHER READING
White, Richard. *The Middle Ground: Indians, Empires, and Republics in the Great Lakes Region, 1650-1815.* New York: Cambridge University Press, 1991.

Hancock

Born: fl. early 1700's
Also known as: King Hancock
Tribal affiliation: Tuscarora
Significance: Hancock led his tribe in North Carolina's bloody Tuscarora War against white settlers.

Little is known about Hancock except that, in 1711, he ordered his tribe to retaliate for the abusive treatment of his people at the hands of the English colonists in the Carolina colony. The tribe was located primarily in eastern North Carolina, in the rich and fertile lands along the Roanoke, Tar, Pamlico, and Neuse Rivers. Population estimates put their numbers at about five thousand during Hancock's reign.

Throughout the first two decades of the eighteenth century, the Tuscaroras were abused by English settlers in the Carolinas. Slave traders raided their settlements and settlers took their most fertile lands away from them. The colonists' most incendiary act occurred in 1711, when more than four hundred Swiss colonists under the command of the opportunistic Baron Christoph Von Graffenreid drove a number of families off a large tract of Indian land. Hancock ordered retaliatory raids throughout eastern North Carolina, which led to Von Graffenreid's capture and the death of the colony's surveyor-general, John Lawson, author of the famous narrative *A New Voyage to Carolina* (1709). The raids escalated so that the war involved the Coree, Pamlico, and Machapunga tribes as well as the Tuscarora. Nearly 140 settlers, mostly Swiss, died in the initial attacks.

In 1712, North and South Carolina sent a combined force under the leadership of Colonel John Barnwell against Hancock, destroying his main village of Cotechney. Hancock finally agreed to a peace plan, which was quickly broken by the colonists. Tuscarora raids began again. Hancock fled to Virginia with a considerable supply of booty but was captured by a band of Tuscaroras who remained allied to the whites. The chief was turned over to colony officials and executed.

In 1713, Colonel James Moore of South Carolina, with one thousand Indian allies, attacked the remaining Tuscarora force and quickly overcame them. To finance the campaign, Moore ordered all Tuscarora prisoners, about four hundred, to be sold into slavery. Survivors fled north and joined their Iroquoian brethren in New York. The Tuscaroras were formally accepted as the sixth Iroquois nation in 1722.

Richard S. Keating

Handsome Lake

Born: c. 1735; Canawaugus Village on the Genessee River near Avon, New York
Died: August 10, 1815; Onondaga, New York
Also known as: Kaniatario, Ganeodiyo
Tribal affiliation: Seneca
Significance: Handsome Lake was the Seneca (Iroquois) prophet whose visions became the basis for the Longhouse religion, or the *Gaiwiio*, the Good Word. This Seneca traditional religious movement is still practiced in Canada, New York, and Oklahoma, where the Seneca people are concentrated.

Handsome Lake was born at the Seneca village, Canawaugus, near Avon, New York. He was a recognized Seneca chief. In June, 1799,

Handsome Lake was seriously ill and fell unconscious. He reported having a vision during this state. In this vision he saw three men holding berry bushes, who then offered berries to Handsome Lake. The berries had a healing effect, and as he recovered, he began to talk with the men. It was understood that there was one man missing, a fourth whom Handsome Lake later identified with the Great Spirit, who would come again at a later time. During his conversations with the three men, Handsome Lake heard them condemn alcoholism, pronounce a death sentence on a witch, and condemn witchcraft generally. Handsome Lake himself was told not to drink anymore. Furthermore, he was given to understand that his sins were not unforgivable and that he was to teach his people the proper way to live.

Handsome Lake had many such visions after the initial one, and over more than sixteen years of activity, a code of teachings was gathered and became a part of Seneca oral tradition. The code, which sounds very similar to apocalyptic biblical visions such as those found in the books of Daniel and Revelation, includes descriptions of heaven and hell. It involves a conversation between Handsome Lake and a being who describes what Handsome Lake is seeing and verifies its important message.

Among the more significant of the visions of Handsome Lake are his reports of punishments in hell for specific sins, such as stinginess, alcoholism, witchcraft, promiscuity, wife beating, gambling, and quarrelsome family relations. Each of these sins was associated with a particularly graphic punishment in hell.

The religious visions of Handsome Lake were the basis for a nearly complete transformation in the religion and practice of the Seneca. By the the start of the U.S. Civil War (1861), nearly all Seneca considered themselves members of either a Christian church or the Longhouse religion, and many considered active participation in both to be acceptable. The Longhouse religion of Handsome Lake was similar to other prophetic movements, such as Wovoka's and John Slocum's.

Daniel L. Smith-Christopher

FURTHER READING

Handsome Lake. *The Code of Handsome Lake.* Edited by Arthur C. Parker. Albany: University of the State of New York, 1913.

Swatzler, David. *A Friend Among the Senecas: The Quaker Mission to Cornplanter's People.* Mechanicsburg, Pa.: Stackpole Books, 2000.

Wallace, Anthony F. C. *Death and Rebirth of the Seneca.* New York: Alfred A. Knopf, 1973.

_____, ed. "Halliday Jackson's Journal to the Seneca Indians, 1798-1800." Part 1. *Pennsylvania History* 19, no. 2 (1952): 117-147.

_____, ed. "Halliday Jackson's Journal to the Seneca Indians, 1798-1800." Part 2. *Pennsylvania History* 19, no. 3 (1952): 325-349.

Harjo, Chitto

Born: 1846; Indian Territory (now near Boley, Oklahoma)
Died: April 11, 1912; near Smithville, Oklahoma
Also known as: Crazy Snake, Wilson Jones
Tribal affiliation: Creek
Significance: The leader of the traditionalist faction of the Creek Nation, Chitto Harjo—who was also well known as Crazy Snake—led an unsuccessful uprising to prevent the allotment of tribal lands in 1901.

Chitto Harjo rose to prominence during the late nineteenth and early twentieth centuries as leader of the traditionalist faction within the Creek Nation, making him the successor to OPOTHLEYAHOLO, Oktarharsars Harjo (Sands), and ISPARHECHER. Traditionalist Creeks, many of whom were full-bloods, sought to maintain the old tribal religion and lifestyle; in addition, they resisted assimilation and the settlement of whites on tribal lands. They distrusted tribal leaders, who were often of mixed blood and thus more acculturated. One vital aspect of traditional Creek life, namely the communal ownership of land, came under direct threat during the 1890's when Congress established the Dawes Commission to extend the policy of allotment (the division of tribal lands among individual Indians) to the Creeks and the rest of the Five Civilized Tribes.

Chitto Harjo. (Library of Congress)

In opposition to allotment, Harjo and his followers (called "Snakes") organized a rival government in opposition to the recognized tribal authorities, who were reluctantly cooperating with the federal government. Harjo's "government" called on the United States to keep its treaty obligations. It issued decrees forbidding the acceptance of allotments, and organized its own tribal police (lighthorse) to enforce its policies. In 1901, this campaign of interference with allotment policy developed into a full-scale rebellion; Indians who had accepted allotments—as well as white settlers—were attacked. Harjo and sixty-six of his followers were arrested and convicted, but were allowed to return home under suspended sentences. Thereafter, Harjo generally found more peaceful ways—such as lobbying—to oppose allotment. He was also a vocal opponent of Oklahoma statehood.

In 1907, after Oklahoma became a state and the Creek government was dissolved, Harjo became involved in a skirmish known as the Smoked Meat Rebellion, in which traditionalist Creeks were accused by whites of sheltering a thief. Fighting erupted, and Harjo spent the rest of his life as a fugitive.

William C. Lowe

Harjo, Joy

Born: May 9, 1951; Tulsa, Oklahoma
Tribal affiliation: Creek
Significance: Joy Harjo has published poetry, written screenplays, lectured, and taught in creative writing programs; she is also a jazz musician and artist.

Joy Harjo's collections of poetry express a close relationship to the environment and the particularities of the Native American and white cultures from which she is descended. She is an enrolled member of the Creek tribe, the mother of two children (a son, Phil, and a daughter, Rainy Dawn), and a grandmother. Various forms of art were always a part of her life, even in childhood. Her grandmother and aunt were painters. In high school, she trained as a dancer and toured as a dancer and actress with one of the first Indian dance troupes in the country. When her tour ended, she returned to Oklahoma, where her son was born when she was seventeen years old. She left her son's father to move to New Mexico, enrolling at the university as a premed student. After one semester, she decided that her interest in art was compelling enough to engage in its formal study.

Educated at the Institute of American Indian Arts in Santa Fe, New Mexico, where she later worked as an instructor, Harjo received a bachelor's degree from the University of New Mexico and a master's degree

Joy Harjo.

in fine arts from the University of Iowa. She was a professor of English at both the University of Arizona and the University of New Mexico.

Harjo has received numerous awards for her writing, including the William Carlos Williams award from the Poetry Society of America, the Delmore Schwartz Award, the American Indian Distinguished Achievement in the Arts Award, and two creative writing fellowships from the National Endowment for the Arts. Harjo's poetry has been increasingly influenced by her interest in music, especially jazz. She plays the saxophone in a band, Poetic Justice, that combines the musical influences of jazz and reggae with her poetry. Many of her poems are tributes to the various musicians who have influenced her work, including saxophonists John Coltrane and Jim Pepper.

The history and mythology of her people and the current state of their oppression also are prominent themes in her work. As she states in the explanation of her poem "Witness," "The Indian wars never ended in this country . . . we were hated for our difference by our enemies."

In Mad Love and War (1990) is composed of two sections of poems expressing the conflicts and joys of Harjo's experiences as a Native American woman living in contemporary American culture. The poems draw on a wealth of experiences, including those relating to tribal tradition and sacredness of the land. Such positive experiences are compared with the sometimes grim realities inherent in the modern society in which Harjo lives. Many of the poems in "The Wars" are political in nature, containing stark images of violence and deprivation, most notably her poem dedicated to Anna Mae PICTOU AQUASH, a member of the American Indian Movement whose murdered body was found on the Pine Ridge Reservation.

The Woman Who Fell from the Sky (1994), Harjo's seventh collection of poetry, consists primarily of prose poems. The collection is divided into two sections, "Tribal Memory" and "The World Ends Here," which express the lore of Harjo's Native American ancestry and her observations of contemporary life. These poems show a concern for content over style. The poetry is presented without conventions of patterned rhyme or meter; the imagery is stark and unadorned.

Each poem is followed by an explanation that contextualizes the piece by offering a brief history of the genesis of the poem or commenting on themes elucidated by the writing. The majority of the book's poems are narrative, developing stories that explain the destinies of Native American characters who retain identity despite the onslaught of European culture, which strips away their language, lore, and religion. The poems create a universe of oppositions: darkness and light, violence and peace. Other poems relate stories of ancestry on a more personal level, illuminating a view of many worlds existing at once, interconnected and affecting one another.

Harjo's later works include *A Map to the Next World: Poetry and Tales* (2000) and *How We Became Human: New and Selected Poems, 1975-2001* (2002).

Robert Haight

FURTHER READING

Leen, Mary. "An Art of Saying." *American Indian Quarterly* 19, no. 1 (Winter, 1995): 1-16.

Pettit, Rhonda. *Joy Harjo*. Boise, Idaho: Boise State University Press, 1998.

Smith, Stephanie. "Joy Harjo." *Poets and Writers* 21, no. 4 (July/August, 1993): 23-27.

Harper, Elijah

Born: March 3, 1949; Red Sucker Lake, Manitoba, Canada
Tribal affiliation: Cree
Significance: Elijah Harper, the only native member of Manitoba's legislative assembly, blocked the adoption of the Meech Lake Accord in June, 1990, because it failed to mention native peoples.

Elijah Harper was born on the Red Sucker Lake Reserve in Manitoba, Canada, on March 3, 1949, and educated at the University of Manitoba. From 1975 to 1977 he served as an analyst and legislative assistant to the minister of northern affairs. He served as Chief of the Red Sucker Lake Reserve from 1978 until his election to the Manitoba Legislative Assembly in 1981 as its sole native member, representing the northern riding (district) of Rupertsland. Reelected as a New Democratic Party candidate in 1986, 1988, and 1990, he served as minister of native affairs from 1986 to 1988.

Harper became a national hero to Canada's native peoples by delaying consideration of the Meech Lake Accord in the Assembly, thus blocking its adoption as Canada's constitution in 1990. Holding an eagle feather for spiritual strength, he quietly refused the necessary unanimous consent required for introduction of the accord because it made no mention of aboriginal peoples. He was awarded the Stanley Knowles Humanitarian Award in 1991 and was elected to the House of Commons as a member of the Liberal Party in 1993.

Joy A. Bilharz

FURTHER READING
Miller, J. R. *Skyscrapers Hide the Heavens: A History of Indian-White Relations in Canada.* 3d ed. Buffalo: University of Toronto Press, 2000.
_____, ed. *Sweet Promises: A Reader on Indian-White Relations in Canada.* Buffalo: University of Toronto Press, 1991.

Harris, LaDonna

Born: February 15, 1931; Temple, Oklahoma
Tribal affiliation: Comanche
Significance: LaDonna Harris has been an outspoken leader in the fight for native rights and an advocate of native self-determination.

LaDonna Harris was born to a Comanche mother and an Irish American father. Reared by her grandparents, she spoke only Comanche until she started school. The mother of three, her husband is Fred Harris, former U.S. senator from Oklahoma.

Harris has been a leader in the fight for the rights of under-represented people and for social reform, serving as one of the first members of the National Women's Political Caucus during the 1970's. During the 1972 take-over of the Bureau of Indian Affairs building by the American Indian Movement (AIM) in Washington, D.C., Harris supported AIM by spending a night with the demonstrators. She actively protested the U.S. government policy of terminating Indian tribes and tribal lands and has been instrumental in forming coalitions involving native people and organizations, such as Oklahomans for Indian Opportunity.

Harris founded Americans for Indian Opportunity (AIO) in 1970 in Washington, D.C., and serves as executive director of AIO, which promotes economic self-sufficiency for indigenous people and supports self-determination projects for native people at the local, national, and international levels. She has been appointed to various national boards, including that of the National Organization for Women. In 2000, she published her autobiography.

FURTHER READING

Edmunds, R. David, ed. *The New Warriors: Native American Leaders Since 1900.* Lincoln: University of Nebraska Press, 2001.

Harris, LaDonna, and H. Henrietta Stockel. *LaDonna Harris: A Comanche Life.* Lincoln: University of Nebraska Press, 2000.

Hatathli, Ned

Born: October 11, 1923; Coal Mine Messa, near Tuba City, Arizona
Died: October 12, 1972; Many Farms, near Tsaile, Arizona
Tribal affiliation: Navajo
Significance: As the founder of the first community college for Native Americans, Ned Hatathli was a pioneer in indigenous education.

Ned Hatathli had a thorough education in both his own indigenous Navajo (Diné) traditions and mainstream American culture. However, as a young man he was more interested in the latter. He graduated from Tuba City High School, where he was the valedictorian of his class. He volunteered for the Navy after the U.S. entry into World War II and served until the war ended in 1945.

After the war, Hatathli returned to Flagstaff and attended Northern Arizona University, obtaining bachelor and doctoral degrees in education. He never lost touch with his own people on the Navajo Reservation, to which he returned after completing his degrees. There, he began to energize the Navajo in their drive for greater social opportunity. He became the director of the Navajo Arts and Crafts Guild in Window Rock and in 1955 was elected to the tribal council.

During the 1960's, the federal government's growing attention to problems of poverty symbolized by President John F. Kennedy's New Frontier and President Lyndon B. Johnson's Great Society programs began to direct attention to the educational plight of the Navajos, and federal money became available for innovative programs designed to better the lives of indigenous people. Hatathli took advantage of this development and was instrumental in founding the Rough Rock Demonstration School, which was a trial run for his ultimate vision of a college run for and by the Navajo.

With the help of leaders of his generation in the Navajo community, such as Allen Yezzie and Dillon Platero, as well as with supportive non-Navajo such as Robert Roessel, Hatathli worked with Arizona State University to set up Navajo Community College. In 1969, the college opened in temporary quarters in Many Farms; three years later, it moved east to its permanent home in Tsaile. Roessel served as its first president, but Hatathli quickly succeeded him as the institution's first Native American president.

As Hatathli became more involved in indigenous education, he became less convinced of his earlier belief that its primary goal should be to accelerate his people's acculturation into mainstream American life. Instead, he came to value and to know more of Navajo traditions. He also began to envision the college as a force not only in addressing immediate educational needs but also in addressing the health problems and widespread poverty of the Navajo, for instance fostering the start of a nursing program at the college.

Hatathli died from an accidental gunshot wound just as he was achieving prominence as a Navajo leader. The college was later renamed Diné College, after the name by which the Navajo call themselves. Two of its prominent attractions are the Ned Hatathli Cultural Center and the Ned Hatathli Museum.

Nicholas Birns

FURTHER READING

Magnetite Kapeahiokalani Padeken, AhNee-Benham, Wayne J. Stein, eds. *The Renaissance of American Indian Higher Education: Capturing the Dream.* Mahwah, N.J.: Lawrence Erlbaum, 2003.

Hayes, Ira Hamilton

Born: January 12, 1923; Bapchule, near Sacaton, Arizona
Died: January 24, 1955; Bapchule, Arizona
Tribal affiliation: Pima
Significance: Ira Hayes was one of the American soldiers helping to raise the flag of the United States in a famous photograph taken on Iwo Jima during World War II.

Ira Hamilton Hayes was born in the small village of Bapchule, near Sacaton, southeast of Phoenix, Arizona. Before he was twenty years old, Ira joined the Marines, and he was soon sent to serve in the Pacific theater during World War II. The turning point in Hayes's life occurred when he was discovered to be one of the servicemen in the famous photograph recording the flag-raising on Iwo Jima Island.

After the war, Hayes was often invited to appear at public events. He knew that he was being exploited as a patriotic icon even as the Pima people and other Indians were suffering discriminatory treatment, and he spoke out against mistreatment of Indians whenever he could. With limited education, it was hard for Hayes to find work, and he struggled throughout his life with alcoholism. His last job was picking cotton at three dollars per hundred pounds. Shortly after his thirty-second birthday, he was found dead of exposure in a field not far from his birthplace.

Helen Jaskoski

Ira Hayes (far left) is best remembered as one of the Marines in this famous World War II photograph. (National Archives)

Heat-Moon, William Least

Born: August 27, 1939; Kansas City, Missouri
Also known as: William Trogdon
Tribal affiliation: Osage
Significance: William Least Heat-Moon is a veteran reporter and an astute chronicler of ordinary events whose works provide intimate journeys to self-discovery for all Americans.

William Least Heat-Moon, best-selling author and noted lecturer, was born on August 27, 1939, in Kansas City, Missouri, to Ralph G. Trogdon and Maurine Davis Trogdon. His surname, Trogdon, comes from Irish and English ancestors. His pen name, Least Heat-Moon, comes from an Osage Indian ancestor who was born in July—the Moon of Heat. His father is known as Heat-Moon. His older brother is called Little Heat-Moon. Because William is the youngest and last, he took the name Least Heat-Moon. Heat-Moon credits his Osage ancestry as being the influential force in inspiring and shaping his works.

Heat-Moon received his degrees from the University of Missouri at Columbia: a bachelor's degree in literature in 1961, a master's degree in literature in 1962, and a doctorate in literature in 1973. He also earned a bachelor's degree in photojournalism in 1978. He taught literature at Stephen's College in Columbia, Missouri, from 1965 to 1978. Heat-Moon was also a lecturer at the University of Missouri School of Journalism from 1985 to 1987. Since the late 1980's, his main occupation has been that of writer and lecturer.

Although Heat-Moon contributes articles to a variety of prestigious magazines, such as *Esquire, Time,* and *The Atlantic Monthly,* he is best known for his nonfiction best-sellers, *Blue Highways* (1983) and *Prairy-Erth* (1991).

Blue Highways, his first book, is the culmination of a 13,000-mile automobile trek along the backroads of thirty-eight states. Acclaimed by critics nationwide as the greatest travel memoir since John Steinbeck's *Travels with Charley, Blue Highways* became an immediate success. In 1983, *The New York Times* named it a notable book, and *Time* listed it as one of the five best nonfiction books of the year. In 1984, it received both the Christopher Award and the Books-Across-the-Sea Award for literary excellence.

Hailed with the same critical acclaim as *Blue Highways, PrairyErth,* an old geologic term for the soils of the central grasslands, was published in 1991. Heat-Moon's exploration of 774 square miles of the tall grass prairies and grasslands of Chase County, Kansas, culminated in a meticulous, poetic narrative that celebrates the beauty and richness of the ordinary in America's heartland. The book combines natural history, social history, and ecology with life-affirming vignettes of common people who live in the heart of the Kansas Flint Hills. Valuable information is provided on the Kaw (Kansa) tribe and numerous plants Native Americans once used for food.

Heat-Moon's later books include *This Land Is Your Land: Across America by Air* (1997), *River-Horse: A Voyage Across America* (1999), and *Columbus in the Americas* (2002).

Raymond Wilson

FURTHER READING
Heat-Moon, William Least. *Blue Highways: A Journey into America.* Boston: Little, Brown, 1982.

Hewitt, John N. B.

Born: December 16, 1859; Lewiston, New York
Died: October 14, 1937; Washington, D.C.
Tribal affiliation: Tuscarora
Significance: John N. B. Hewitt, who was perhaps as much as one-quarter Tuscarora, was a leading authority on the Iroquois League and the ceremonials and customs of the Six Nations.

John Napoleon Brinton Hewitt was born in Lewiston, Niagara County, New York, in 1859. He was of French, English, Tuscarora, and Scottish heritage. Hewitt hoped to become a physician, but poor health prevented him from completing preparatory schooling. He continued his scholarly pursuits, however, and in 1880 was employed to collect Iroquoian Indian myths from residents of the Grand River and Onondaga reservations. In 1886, the Bureau of American Ethnology began sponsoring his work, and he continued with the same institution and line of research to the end of his life.

Hewitt was fluent in Tuscarora, Mohawk, and Onondaga; he also became well versed in several Algonquian dialects and successfully established the connection of the Cherokee language to the Iroquoian family. After 1896, although Hewitt gathered information on Chippewa, Ottawa, and Delaware languages, he concentrated primarily upon Iroquoian. He was painstakingly thorough and slow; thus only a small part of his research was printed before his death. In the bureau's archives there are 250 entries under his name, consisting of eight thousand manuscript pages, ten thousand notecards, more than one hundred articles submitted to the *Handbook of American Indians,* and twenty-five submissions to *American Anthropologist.*

Glenn J. Schiffman

Hiawatha

Born: c. 1525; Mohawk River Valley, New York
Died: c. 1575; Mohawk River Valley, New York
Also known as: Hienwentha, Ayonwatha (He Who Combs), Aiionwatha, A-yo-went-ha
Tribal affiliation: Mohawk
Significance: Hiawatha was instrumental in founding and organizing the Iroquois Confederacy with the prophetic peacemaker Deganawida. Through his skills of oratory and diplomacy, he helped establish peace among the Iroquois in precolonial North America.

Not much is known about the life of Hiawatha before he became a chief. Some oral histories relate that he had another name before meeting the visionary DEGANAWIDA, and that it was the visionary who named him Hiawatha.

There are no written references to Hiawatha before the seventeenth century, and the first complete story of his life was written from oral tradition by the eighteenth century Mohawk chief and statesman Joseph BRANT shortly before the latter's death. A more complete version by Seth Newhouse (1842-1921) in 1885 became the "official" version of the Iroquois Nations when the council of chiefs redacted it in 1900 and again in 1912. The story itself, however, suggests great antiquity. The exact date, or even century, of the founding of the Iroquois Confederacy might never be known, though recent archaeological evidence suggests a union of the five nations much earlier than the fifteenth century date that has become standard.

Before his meeting with Deganawida, Hiawatha was a prosperous chief with seven beautiful daughters (in some versions of the story, three). An enemy of Hiawatha, ATOTARHO, whom some narratives describe as a wizard and a cannibal, killed the daughters, one at a time, when they would not marry him. Inconsolable with grief for his daughters, Hiawatha exiled himself in the woods. It was there that the meeting with Deganawida would change his life and make Hiawatha the first *royaneh* (chief) to accept the visionary's message of peace and consolation.

While recent historians and ethnographers have rightly emphasized the greater role of Deganawida in bringing peace to the five nations of the Iroquois (Mohawk, Cayuga, Oneida, Onandaga, and Seneca), and uniting them in a confederacy (to which the Tuscaroras were added in 1712 after their defeat by English colonial forces), One cannot overstate Hiawatha's role as the first tribal leader to embrace and have validated, because of his influence, Deganawida's vision of peace. Deganawida had been exiled from his own nation, the Huron, for his pacifist tendencies, and though he was presented in the narrative and religious tradition as divinely appointed, he met nothing but rebuffs until he met Hiawatha in the forest. The meeting of Deganawida and Hiawatha was mutually beneficial.

Deganawida had a message of peace to deliver to the warring tribes of Iroquoia (the geological term for central and western New York state), yet he was afflicted, some say, with a stutter or similar speech impediment. Hiawatha was gifted in eloquence, yet his debilitating grief isolated him from the people whom he should have served as hereditary leader. Deganawida healed Hiawatha by teaching him a series of rituals that remain part of the ceremonial life of the six nations: the sequential use of wampum, the condolence ceremony, and the requickening ceremony.

The use of wampum (Algonquian *wampumpeag*, white shell beads) represents a genuine collaboration between Hiawatha and Deganawida. The wampum were used for ceremonies, to record a treaty or other agreement, as tribute, and as gifts for exchange. The wampum in the case of Hiawatha came to represent his grief and reconciliation as he wandered through the forest. One story is as follows: On the third day of his exile (or perhaps the third leg of the journey), Hiawatha reached a deserted village on the Susquehanna River. He traced the river to its source and found a pond or lake filled with ducks. The ducks were startled by him, and then flew away, taking the water of the pond with them. Hiawatha then collected white and purple shells from the exposed dry bed of the pond, and strung them on threads made from hemp to serve as reminders of the coming together of the Iroquois nations. Given the sacredness of the wampum to the Iroquois, and given that the wampum, by definition, is used to mark significant events, Hiawatha's collecting these sacred objects became legend.

Upon meeting Hiawatha on his journey to spread the gospel of peace, Deganawida used Hiawatha's strings of shells as a mnemonic (memory) device to guide his oration in a prototype of what would become the condolence ceremony. The concept of "condolence" is vital to the Iroquois concept of "peace." The warring nations, which had been familiar with an intricate system of retaliation and revenge that characterized their cultures at war, needed an alternate system of compensation to replace it. Hiawatha learned that by ritually mourning the deaths of his daughters, instead of seeking consolation through retaliation alone, he could return to the concerns of the living; he soon became an advocate of Deganawida's message of peace by mourning his daughters through a ritual of condolence.

The requickening ceremony takes the compensatory nature of condolence one step further by ritually adopting a member of another tribe as a reembodiment of a slain member of one's own tribe. That these surrogates were often seized in raids on the tribe responsible for the death of a loved one (usually a chief or sachem) indicates that the Iroquois definition of "peace" is not necessarily the cessation of all violence. It is, instead, a spiritual balance.

Hiawatha's total absorption of Deganawida's doctrine of peace is suggested by his reconciliation even with the evil Atotarho. The Onandaga shaman is depicted as having a crooked back and having snakes in his hair. In many cultures, including Iroquoian, straightness is an emblem of righteousness. Hiawatha straightened Atotarho's body and combed the snakes out of his hair. (Combs made of antlers are common archaeological finds at Iroquois sites, and a possible etymology of the word *hiawatha* is "he who combs.") The combing and straightening represented the re-formation of an evil wizard who would, as a now-righteous advocate of peace, become the first titular head of the Iroquois Confederacy.

The formation of the Iroquois Confederacy is the last great event of Hiawatha's life. Under his leadership, and that of the re-formed Atotarho, the five great nations—from east to west Seneca, Cayuga, Onandaga, Oneida, and Mohawk—became a loose confederacy with the central nation, the Onondagas, having the final voice. The Onondaga's leadership was more spiritual than political, and all five (later six) nations still functioned independently.

The original wampum record of the confederacy—with four squares, two on either side of a central pine tree (which on the reverse appears as a heart), representing the union of five nations—can be seen in New York's state museum.

As the primary carrier of Deganawida's message of peace, Hiawatha deserves a place not only in the history of the Iroquois but also in the history of world peace. As a Mohawk chief, he has come to stand for what was thought to be an unfamiliar (or unlikely) tolerance for peace, for like many Native American tribal names, the word "Mohawk" is derived from the slur of a neighboring tribe. In this case, "Mohawk" means "those who eat human flesh."

Some versions of the Hiawatha and the Iroquois Confederacy stories make Hiawatha a cannibal in a grieving phase—compounding his divorce from society—and other versions make Atotarho the cannibal. In either case, Hiawatha is the agent of reform, either himself repenting, or reforming another of cannibalism. For a great chief like Hiawatha to subordinate himself to a former enemy is the epitome of the humility that is necessary for peace to flourish.

The survival of Hiawatha's name and legend (though with a great deal of inevitable variation) across half a millennium or more is itself indicative of his historical significance. As one of the facilitators of the Great Peace and Power and Law that helped inspire the founders of American federalism, Hiawatha's historical importance goes beyond just Seneca or Native American history; he deserves to be an icon of democratic principles.

John R. Holmes

FURTHER READING

Fenton, William N. *The Great Law and the Longhouse: A Political History of the Iroquois Confederacy.* Norman: University of Oklahoma Press, 1998.

Hale, Horatio. *The Iroquois Book of Rites.* Toronto, Canada: University of Toronto Press, 1963. This reprint of Hale's 1883 classic preserves some of the earliest versions of the Hiawatha legend.

Parker, Arthur C. *Parker on the Iroquois.* Syracuse, N.Y.: Syracuse University Press, 1968. A reprint of three of an Iroquois ethnologist's early twentieth century monographs that includes the Newhouse text of the Hiawatha story.

Richter, Daniel K. *Ordeal of the Longhouse: The Peoples of the Iroquois League in the Era of European Colonization.* Chapel Hill: University of North Carolina Press, 1992. A thorough history of the Iroquois people and their confederacy before and after the arrival of the Europeans.

Higheagle, Robert Placidus

Born: c. 1873; place unknown
Died: c. 1950; place unknown
Also known as: Kohektakoya
Tribal affiliation: Teton Lakota (Sioux)

Significance: Robert Higheagle served as an interpreter of both language and culture for researchers documenting the songs and history of the people of the Standing Rock Reservation in South Dakota.

Robert Placidus Higheagle was born around 1873, when the traditional way of life among the Lakota Sioux, which centered on the buffalo, was disappearing. His mother was from the Miniconjou band of Lakota and his father was a Hunkpapa Lakota. His parents' bands were closely related; their people shared a common language, government system, and social organization. During the heart of the Indian wars on the northern Plains, from about 1868 to 1876, Higheagle's family was allied with SITTING BULL, who was a relative of Higheagle's father.

After the Battle of the Little Bighorn (1876) the various Indian bands involved in the conflict dispersed in many directions. Federal policy required that all Indians report to their reservations and remain there. Those that refused to follow government orders were hunted down by the U.S. Army. By the fall of 1876, most Indians had returned to their reservations, their horses and guns had been seized, and it was clear that a new way of life was about to begin for the people.

Some tribal people, notably those under CRAZY HORSE and Sitting Bull, resisted moving to their agencies, and so they were pursued by the soldiers. In early 1877, Sitting Bull and many of his followers crossed into Canada, and Higheagle's family accompanied him. Over the next few years, many families drifted back to their agencies, and all were repatriated in 1881.

The members of Higheagle's family adapted well to reservation life. They converted to Christianity, and his father farmed. Robert Higheagle, as the boy came to be known after baptism, attended Hampton Institute in Virginia during the mid-1880's. There he learned to speak English. When he completed his studies at Hampton in 1895, he was the school's first graduate from the Standing Rock Reservation. Meanwhile, his family was deeply affected by Sitting Bull's death in 1890, because his father and uncle were members of the Indian police.

After Higheagle returned to Standing Rock, he taught school. Frances Densmore, an expert in tribal music, came to the Standing Rock Reservation in 1911 to record music on wax cylinders. She wanted to preserve the old buffalo hunting songs, war songs, and others before the old people died. Higheagle served as her assistant for several years. He contacted the elderly men who knew the old songs, translated the songs from Lakota into English, and also described Lakota culture and the meaning of the songs to Densmore.

From 1928 to 1932 Higheagle worked in much the same way with Walter Stanley Campbell (who wrote under the name Stanley Vestal). Campbell was interested in writing a book about Sitting Bull. Higheagle set up and conducted interviews, took notes, translated for him, and explained various Lakota customs, especially those connected with warfare.

Carole Barrett

FURTHER READING

Densmore, Frances. *Teton Sioux Music and Culture.* Reprint. Lincoln: University of Nebraska Press, 1992.

Vestal, Stanley. *Sitting Bull: Champion of the Sioux.* Reprint. Norman: University of Oklahoma Press, 1989.

Highway, Tomson

Born: December 6, 1951; northern Manitoba, Canada
Tribal affiliation: Cree
Significance: Tomson Highway is an award-winning playwright whose works dramatize Canadian Native life, particularly reservation life.

Tomson Highway spoke the Cree language in his early years living in rural northern Manitoba. He began learning English after being sent away to boarding school at the age of six. He later attended high school in Winnipeg, then went on to the University of Western Ontario. He worked for a number of years for native organizations, working on cultural programs, traveling extensively, and experiencing a variety of cultures.

At the age of thirty he decided to try to dramatize native life. It was not until 1986 that one of his plays, *The Rez Sisters,* was first performed, in Toronto. It was a surprise success, winning the 1987 Dora Mavor Moore Award for Outstanding New Play. In the play, seven native women on the fictional Wasayshigan Hill Reserve fantasize about winning a million-dollar bingo jackpot and in the process reveal much about their lives. *Dry Lips Oughta Move to Kapuskasing* was performed (and published) in 1989. It examines cultural issues such as sexism among native men. Highway's characters, despite their generally bleak situations, manage to maintain their courage, humor, and sense of community. Their conversations combine farcical and sorrowful elements and are peppered with references to native culture, present and sometimes past.

Highway's other writings include the plays *The Sage, the Dancer, and the Fool* (1989) and *New Song . . . New Dance* (1988) and the novel *Kiss of the Fur Queen* (1998). He has also served as the artistic director of Toronto's Native Earth Performing Arts group. The organization has fostered the artistic development of many indigenous actors and writers.

McCrea Adams

FURTHER READING

Brask, Per, and William Morgan, eds. *Aboriginal Voices: Amerindian, Inuit, and Sami Theater.* Baltimore: Johns Hopkins University Press, 1992.

Hogan, Linda

Born: July 16, 1947; Denver, Colorado
Tribal affiliation: Chickasaw
Significance: Through her fiction and poetry, Linda Hogan develops unique perspectives on Indian history, nature, and feminism.

Born of a working-class Chickasaw father and a white mother of an immigrant family, Linda Hogan learned the history and legends of her

people through oral narrative. She received a bachelor's degree and a master's degree from the University of Colorado and was associate professor of American Indian and American studies at the University of Minnesota before turning to full-time writing. In 1989, she began teaching creative writing and American Indian studies at the University of Colorado.

Hogan's first novel, *Mean Spirit* (1990), set in an Oklahoma Indian community during the oil boom of the 1920's, describes the devastation that results from greed and corruption. *That Horse* (1985) contains several of her short stories.

Linda Hogan.

Hogan has published several volumes of poetry. Her first, *Calling My-self Home* (1978), includes many poems about family and Indian iden-tity; as she has said, "A lot of my poems come from family stories." *Daughters, I Love You* (1981), reprinted in *Eclipse* (1983), is a protest against destruction of the land. Both *Seeing Through the Sun* (1985) and *Savings* (1988) include numerous poems about a kinship with nature and a speaker's (Indian's) interaction with it. Like her novel, which de-scribes especially the plight of Indian women during the oil boom, Ho-gan's poetry often includes feminist perspectives.

Hogan's later books include *The Woman Who Watches Over the World: A Native Memoir* (2001) and collections of short works by other writers that she has edited.

Lee Schweninger

FURTHER READING

Balassi, William, et al., eds. *This Is About Vision: Interviews with Southwest-ern Writers.* Albuquerque: University of New Mexico Press, 1990.

Bruchac, Joseph. *Survival This Way: Interview with American Indian Poets.* Tucson: University of Arizona Press, 1987.

Hogan, Linda. "The Two Lives." In *I Tell You Now,* edited by Brian Swann and Arnold Krupat. Lincoln: University of Nebraska Press, 1987.

_____. *The Woman Who Watches Over the World: A Native Memoir.* New York: W. W. Norton, 2001.

Hokeah, Jack

Born: c. 1900; Caddo County, Indian Territory (now in Oklahoma)
Died: December 14, 1969; Fort Cobb, Oklahoma
Tribal affiliation: Kiowa
Significance: Jack Hokeah was one of the original members of the Ki-owa Five, a group of painters who instituted a style of painting based on traditional cultural scenes.

Jack Hokeah was orphaned as a young child; he was reared by his grand-parents. His grandfather, White Horse, was known as a warrior. Starting in 1926, Hokeah attended the special noncredit courses for the Kiowa Five at the University of Oklahoma. By 1930, he and other Kiowa paint-ers were attending the Gallup Inter-Tribal Ceremonials in New Mexico to sell their work and compete for prizes. During these visits to New Mexico, Hokeah met Julián and María Antonía MARTÍNEZ, the famous potters of San Ildefonso Pueblo. They became close friends, and he stayed there a number of years. In 1932, he worked on murals for the buildings of the Santa Fe Indian School.

Hokeah was a champion dancer; he also led dance groups. His painting is most known for strong images of dancers in motion. He portrayed details of designs in the costumes and caught the dramatic quality of the dancing. He worked with flat colors, and the dancers were presented against a plain background. After considerable initial success he ended his art career. He experimented with acting for a period in New York and was later employed by the Bureau of Indian Affairs. His work is in the collections of the National Museum of the American Indian, Mabee-Gerrer Museum of Art, Denver Art Museum, Museum of New Mexico, and others.

Ronald J. Duncan

FURTHER READING
Berlo, Janet C., and Ruth B. Phillips. *Native North American Art.* New York: Oxford University Press, 1998.

Hole-in-the-Day

Born: c. 1825; Sundy Lake Village (now in Minnesota)
Died: June 27, 1868; Crow Wing, Minnesota
Also known as: Bugonegijig
Tribal affiliation: Ojibwa (Chippewa)
Significance: A controversial figure, Hole-in-the-Day made a number of agreements for his people that brought him considerable personal gain.

There were two Chippewa (Ojibwa) leaders named Hole-in-the-Day; they were father and son. The elder Hole-in-the-Day (a more accurate translation of the Indian name is "Opening in the Sky") was a war leader who waged war against the Sioux, playing a major role in pushing them westward. He also fought with the Americans against the British in the War of 1812. He died in 1846.

The younger Hole-in-the-Day, born in 1825, became head chief of the Chippewa Bear Clan after his father died. He visited Washington, D.C., several times, and at one point, he married a white newspaper reporter there. He was known as a bargainer and a person who would take a percentage of any agreement made on behalf of his people. Many Chippewas complained that Hole-in-the-Day was aggrandizing himself at the expense of his people, and in fact he became quite rich. He was

Hole-in-the-Day in 1864. (Library of Congress)

politically prudent, however, and distributed benefits to enough people to gain popular support from "progressive" Chippewas. When his people were compelled to move to the White Earth Reservation in Minnesota, Hole-in-the-Day at first refused to go. He relented, however, just before being murdered by his own people at Crow Wing, Minnesota.

Bruce E. Johansen

FURTHER READING

Diedrich, Mark. *The Chiefs Hole-in-the-Day of the Mississippi Chippewa*. Minneapolis: Coyote Books, 1986.

Hollow Horn Bear

Born: 1850; Sheridan County, Nebraska
Died: March 15, 1913; Washington, D.C.
Also known as: Matihehlogego
Tribal affiliation: Brule Lakota (Sioux)
Significance: Hollow Horn Bear favored peace with whites, and he became something of a celebrity; his image appeared on a U.S. postage stamp and on a five-dollar bill.

Hollow Horn Bear in 1907. (Library of Congress)

Hollow Horn Bear fought with the leading chiefs of the Great Plains against subjugation until the 1870's; after that, he favored peace with the whites and became something of a celebrity along the East Coast. His likeness appeared on a fourteen-cent stamp as well as on a U.S. five-dollar bill.

Born in Sheridan County, Nebraska, a son of the chief Iron Shell, Hollow Horn Bear earned his early fame as a warrior. He raided the Pawnees at first, then aided other Sioux leaders in harassing forts along the Bozeman Trail between 1866 and 1868, when the Treaty of Fort Laramie was signed. During this time, he gained fame as the chief who defeated Lieutenant William Fetterman (who had bragged that he would cut through Sioux country with a handful of troops). Hollow Horn Bear also led raids on Union Pacific railroad workers' camps.

In 1905, Hollow Horn Bear was invited to take part in the inauguration of Theodore Roosevelt. In 1913, he led a group of Indians in the presidential inauguration parade for Woodrow Wilson. On that visit, Hollow Horn Bear caught pneumonia and died.

Bruce E. Johansen

Hooker Jim

Born: c. 1825; California
Died: 1879; Quapaw Agency, Indian Territory (now in Oklahoma)
Also known as: Hakar Jim
Tribal affiliation: Modoc
Significance: As a leader of the Modoc War, Hooker Jim resisted relocation to an Oregon reservation.

After relocating to the Klamath Reservation in Oregon, several Modocs returned to California requesting their own reservation. In November, 1872, while resisting army efforts to return them to Oregon, several Modoc men, a woman, and a child were killed. In retaliation, Hooker Jim raided a white ranch, killing twelve settlers. Thereafter he retreated to the California lava fields seeking the protection of the leader of the rebellion, CAPTAIN JACK, who refused to surrender him to white authorities. Hooker Jim persuaded Captain Jack to kill General Edward Canby, commander of the U.S. forces seeking to roust the Modocs. Although mobilizing for war, Canby was also a member of a peace commission. In the midst of negotiations, Captain Jack murdered Canby; there was substantial white retaliation.

After arguing with Captain Jack over strategy, Hooker Jim led U.S.

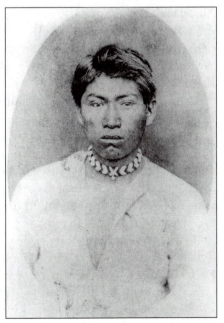

Hooker Jim. (National Archives)

forces to Captain Jack's hideout. Bargaining to spare his own life, Hooker Jim testified against his past protector, who was subsequently hanged. Thereafter, Hooker Jim and his followers relocated to a reservation in Indian Territory.

Mary E. Virginia

FURTHER READING

Quinn, Arthur. *Hell with the Fire Out: A History of the Modoc War.* Boston: Faber & Faber, 1997.

Riddle, Jefferson C. Davis. *The Indian History of the Modoc War.* Introduction by Peter Cozzens. Mechanicsburg, Pa.: Stackpole Books, 2004.

Hopocan

Born: c. 1725; Pennsylvania
Died: 1794; Captain Pipe's Village (now in Upper Sandusky, Ohio)
Also known as: Captain Pipe, Konieschguanokee
Tribal affiliation: Lenni Lenape (Delaware)
Significance: A hereditary war chief, Hopocan battled Americans during the French and Indian War, PONTIAC's Rebellion, and the American Revolution.

Allied with the French during the French and Indian War, Hopocan led the war faction of his tribe against Gelelemend's peace faction. He participated in Pontiac's Rebellion in 1763 and was captured at Fort Pitt. With the cessation of hostilities, Hopocan settled on the Muskingum River in Ohio.

During the American Revolution, Hopocan led several raids on American settlers. After Colonel William Crawford's forces were defeated by Indians at Sandusky, Ohio, in 1782, Crawford was captured and relinquished to Hopocan. In retaliation for his troops' massacre of peaceful Moravian Delawares at Gnaddenhutten, Pennsylvania, Crawford, a friend of General George Washington, was tortured and executed. His murder was avenged through escalating warfare on the western frontier.

As an orator and diplomat, Hopocan participated in several councils, signing treaties at Fort Pitt (1778), Fort McIntosh, Ohio (1785), and Fort Harmer (1787). After relocating several times during the revolution, Hopocan and his band settled on the Upper Sandusky River at what became known as Captain Pipe's Village.

Mary E. Virginia

FURTHER READING

Dowd, Gregory Evans. *A Spirited Resistance: The North American Indian Struggle for Unity, 1745-1815*. Baltimore: Johns Hopkins University Press, 1992.

_____. *War Under Heaven: Pontiac, the Indian Nations, and the British Empire*. Baltimore: Johns Hopkins University Press, 2002.

Howe, Oscar

Born: May 13, 1915; Joe Creek, South Dakota
Died: October 7, 1983; Vermillion, South Dakota
Also known as: Nazuha Hoksina (Trader Boy)
Tribal affiliation: Yankton Lakota (Sioux)
Significance: Oscar Howe successfully eschewed the prevailing Native American style with his modernist canvases, initiating the modern Indian art movement.

Oscar Howe has been called "the father of the new Native American art." His painting career began under Dorothy Dunn at the Santa Fe Indian School and continued under Oscar Jacobson at the University of Oklahoma. In Howe's career he was a Works Progress Administration (WPA) commissioner, five-time winner of the Philbrook's Grand Award, professor at the University of South Dakota, 1966 Waite Phillip's Award recipient, Artist Laureate of South Dakota, and holder of several honorary doctorates. Howe's life was a tapestry of difficulties. Health problems included an ugly facial skin disease, trachoma, and tuberculosis. Social problems included ostracism, loneliness, slow advancement through schools (he started high school at the age of twenty), joblessness, and shyness.

Howe's artistic subjects were Sioux stories, hunts, and myths—images shaped by his use of line and color. Before World War II, he painted in the Santa Fe style, using pastels and shapes bounded by lines. After the war, he moved away from pastels to use bold reds, and he painted straight lines between points in addition to sinuous lines. His stylized postwar art has been called cubist, which Howe denied, explaining that his influence was, instead, Plains Indian hide painting. Howe also painted a number of murals.

Cheryl Claassen

FURTHER READING
Hoover, Herbert T., and Larry J. Zimmerman, eds. *South Dakota Leaders: From Pierre Chouteau, Jr., to Oscar Howe.* Vermillion: University of South Dakota Press, 1989.

Howling Wolf

Born: c. 1850; Indian Territory (now in Oklahoma)
Died: July 2, 1927; Waurika, Oklahoma
Also known as: Honanisto
Tribal affiliation: Cheyenne
Significance: Howling Wolf was a warrior, war chief, and artist.

The son of Eagle Head, principal Cheyenne chief, Howling Wolf as a young man proved himself an able warrior, eventually becoming a war chief during the wars for the Great Plains. Following the Red River War of 1874-1875, Howling Wolf surrendered and was sent to Fort Marion, a military prison in St. Augustine, Florida. While imprisoned, Howling Wolf and fellow prisoners James BEAR'S HEART, Cohoe, and Paul ZOTOM, were encouraged by Lieutenant Richard Henry Pratt to become artists. The artistic Indians became known as the Florida Boys.

After being released in 1878, Howling Wolf returned to Indian Territory, where he labored as a school janitor, converted to Christianity, and became a farmer. Although initially supporting peace, he quickly abandoned his white sympathies after witnessing recurrent treaty violations.

In 1884, he became chief of the Dog Soldiers, a self-styled Cheyenne reservation police force. He opposed the 1887 General Allotment Act, which provided for the redistribution of tribal lands to individual Indians. Howling Wolf died in 1927, the victim of a car accident.

Mary E. Virginia

FURTHER READING
Szabo, Joyce M. *Howling Wolf and the History of Ledger Art.* Albuquerque: University of New Mexico Press, 1994.

Hump

Born: c. 1848; near Bear Butte, western South Dakota
Died: December, 1908; Cherry Creek, South Dakota
Also known as: Etokeah

Tribal affiliation: Miniconjou Lakota (Sioux)
Significance: An important leader in the Sioux Wars of the 1860's and
   1870's, Hump later became a Ghost Dancer; in 1890, he went to
   Washington, D.C., on behalf of his people.

Little is known about Hump's parentage, date of birth, or early life. He
gained prominence in 1866 leading the attack that killed Captain William Fetterman and eighty soldiers outside Fort Kearney in Wyoming.
Refusing to sign the Treaty of Fort Laramie, he joined CRAZY HORSE,
RED CLOUD, and other Sioux war chiefs. A distinguished warrior, he was
present at Little Bighorn in 1876.

   Forced to surrender in 1877, Hump left to join SITTING BULL in Canada but eventually returned to the Cheyenne River Reservation in
South Dakota. In 1890, he participated with fellow Miniconjou, BIG
FOOT, in the Ghost Dance movement. Warned of danger, he led his fol-
lowers to the safety of the Pine Ridge Agency. Shortly thereafter, Big
Foot and the remaining Ghost Dancers were massacred by the U.S.
Army at Wounded Knee Creek. Hump and other Sioux chiefs then went
to Washington, D.C., to negotiate for better treatment of the Sioux peo-
ple. He returned to reservation life and died in 1908 at Cherry Creek,
South Dakota.

Charles Louis Kammer III

FURTHER READING

Mooney, James. *The Ghost-Dance Religion and the Sioux Outbreak of 1890.*
   Introduction by Raymond J. DeMallie. Lincoln: University of Nebraska Press, 1991.
Ostler, Jeffrey. *The Plains Sioux and U.S. Colonialism from Lewis and Clark
   to Wounded Knee.* New York: Cambridge University Press, 2004.

Hunt, George

Born: c. 1854; Fort Rupert, British Columbia, Canada
Died: September 5, 1933; Fort Rupert, British Columbia, Canada
Tribal affiliation: Kwakiutl
Significance: George Hunt worked with anthropologist Franz Boas to
   record Kwakiutl traditions and lifeways.

As an ethnologist, George Hunt had a major impact on the study of the
Kwakiutls. He was a major contributor to the work of Franz Boas, the pioneer ethnologist of the Northwest Coast. During his lifetime, Hunt
supplied Boas with more than six thousand pages of ethnographic ma-

terial. He also appeared as coauthor with Boas on *Kwakiutl Tears* (1905) and *Ethnology of the Kwakiutl* (1921).

Born in 1854 at Fort Rupert, British Columbia, Hunt was a son of Robert Hunt, a Scotsman who worked for the Hudson's Bay Company in British Columbia. Hunt's mother was Mary Ebbetts, a Tlingit or Tsimshian. Hunt was reared in the traditional Indian manner and had little contact with white immigrants until he was in his twenties. Hunt is famous for acting as a guide and interpreter for the Adrian Jacobsen expedition along the North Pacific Coast between 1881 and 1883.

Hunt first met Franz Boas in 1886, after which he assumed a major role in recording Kwakiutl history and customs in English. Boas taught Hunt to write the native language in a phonetic script which could be precisely translated into English. To support himself while he did scholarly work (which began in earnest about the turn of the century), Hunt worked in canneries and as an expedition guide. As he became an elder, Hunt also became a political leader among his people. He was one of few native informants who maintained the respect of both academicians and his own people. Hunt also worked as a consultant to the American Museum of Natural History. He died at Fort Rupert in 1933.

Bruce E. Johansen

Ignacio

Born: 1828; near present-day San Juan, Colorado
Died: December 9, 1913; Ute Mountain Reservation, Colorado
Also known as: John Lyon
Tribal affiliation: Wiminuche Ute
Significance: Ignacio was leader of the Southern Ute during negotiations with the U.S. government for a Ute reservation.

The Southern Ute, comprising the Wiminuche, Muache, and Capote bands, occupied land in the San Juan Mountains of southwestern Colorado, venturing into New Mexico, Utah, and the San Luis Valley of Colorado on hunting and trading forays. In 1849, they signed a treaty recognizing the authority of the U.S. government. During the 1860's, mining discoveries attracted white prospectors to the Colorado mountains; in 1863 the Capote, Wiminuche, and Tabeguache Utes agreed to accept a large reservation in western Colorado. Pressure from white settlers and miners resulted in reductions of the Ute reservation in 1868 and 1873. In 1878 the Southern Utes accepted a smaller reservation in southwestern Colorado and received their own agency in the San Juan basin.

A member of the Wiminuche band of the Southern Ute, Ignacio was born in the San Juan Mountains in 1828. His father, also a medicine man, was killed by a dying man's family after he failed to cure him. Ignacio exacted revenge by killing all twelve members of the family of the dead man. He grew to be a peace-loving man, however, and a chief of the Wiminuche. He counseled cooperation with whites and abided by all treaties between his people and the United States. Although OURAY of the Tabeguache (or Uncompaghre) band was considered the chief of all the Utes by the U.S. government, the Southern Ute recognized Ignacio, Kaniache, and Ankatosh as their major chiefs. Ignacio would have little to do with Ouray because the Tabeguache chief received a stipend from the U.S. government for his services. Ouray deferred to Ignacio on matters having to do with the land of the Southern Utes, especially the 1878 land settlement. After the death of Ouray in 1880, Ignacio was recognized as the chief of all the Southern Utes. He died at the Ute Mountain Reservation on December 9, 1913. The town of Ignacio, Colorado, was named for him.

Lynne Getz

FURTHER READING

Decker, Peter R. *"The Utes Must Go!: American Expansion and the Removal of a People.* Golden, Colo.: Fulcrum Publishing, 2004.

Rockwell, Wilson. *The Utes: A Forgotten People.* Ouray, Colo.: Western Reflections, 1998.

Simmons, Virginia McConnell. *The Ute Indians of Utah, Colorado, and New Mexico.* Niwot: University Press of Colorado, 2000.

Inkpaduta

Born: c. 1815; South Dakota
Died: 1881; Manitoba, Canada
Tribal affiliation: Wahpekute Lakota (Sioux)
Significance: Inkpaduta was the Sioux leader of a bloody outbreak in Iowa in 1856-1857, during a time of increasing settlement by whites.

Inkpaduta (Sioux for "scarlet point") was among the Wahpekute Santee Sioux cast out about 1828 after his father, Wamdesapa, killed principal chief Tasagi. Inkpaduta became the leader of the renegades in 1848, after his father's death. In 1849, he led a raid on the Wahpekutes' principal village, killing their leader Wamundeyakapi and seventeen others.

After his brother was murdered by a white liquor dealer, Inkpaduta turned his rage on settlers; during the Spirit Lake (Iowa) Uprising of 1856 and 1857, warriors under Inkpaduta's leadership killed forty-seven colonists and kidnapped four women, only one of whom was later released. Inkpaduta also engaged in skirmishes with other Indians, notably with the Mdewakanton Sioux LITTLE CROW, who killed three of his warriors in a battle at Lake Thompson.

Inkpaduta may have played a minor role in the Sioux Uprising of 1862-1863 in Minnesota, after which reports indicate that he and a few supporters moved westward. Inkpaduta was reported to have allied with the Sioux and Cheyenne at the Battle of the Little Bighorn, after which he fled to Canada with Sitting Bull's people. Various accounts place his death between 1878 and 1882.

Bruce E. Johansen

FURTHER READING

Bakeman, Mary Hawker, comp. and ed. *Legends, Letters, and Lies: Readings About Inkpaduta and the Spirit Lake Massacre.* Roseville, Minn.: Genealogical Books, 2001.

Irateba

Born: c. 1814; near present-day Needles, California
Died: June 17, 1878; probably in California
Also known as: Arateva, Yaratev, Beautiful Bird
Tribal affiliation: Mojave
Significance: During initial white explorations of the Mojave region of California, Irateba was the principal Indian guide.

Irateba, hereditary chief of the Huttoh-pah band, welcomed white explorers into California. In 1849-1850 and again in 1856-1858, he aided Lieutenant Joseph Ives's exploration of the Colorado River. Irateba also guided Lieutenant Lorenzo Sitgreaves's expedition to San Diego, 1854, and Lieutenant Amiel Whipple's trek to Los Angeles.

Dismayed by advancing white settlement, in 1858, militant Mojaves ambushed a wagon train and in 1859 attacked the newly constructed Fort Mojave. When the Mojave chiefs surrendered, Irateba played a key role in negotiations. The chiefs were imprisoned at Fort Yuma and held as hostages to ensure the cooperation of their people. When principal chief Cairook died attempting escape, Irateba assumed leadership of the Mojave. Until the discovery of gold in 1862, Irateba's Mojave enjoyed relative peace.

On a federally sponsored trip in 1862-1863, Irateba traveled to several eastern cities, met with President Abraham Lincoln, and returned with accounts of white wealth and might. Considered exaggerations, his stories were discounted, and Irateba lost influence with the militant chief, Hojmoseah Quahote, who advocated violent resistance. Irateba died in 1878, probably from smallpox.

Mary E. Virginia

Isatai

Born: c. 1850; northwest Texas
Died: c. 1900; northwest Texas
Tribal affiliation: Comanche
Significance: When Isatai was a young warrior, his claims of supernatural power at first brought hope to his discouraged people.

A Quahadi Comanche, Isatai was born in Texas about 1850. In 1873, with the Comanche on a reservation, Isatai claimed to have communed with the Great Spirit, who revealed to him how the Comanche could return to their past ways. Isatai reportedly demonstrated his supernatural power by belching a wagonload of cartridges and then swallowing them.

In early 1874, Isatai announced that only a Sun Dance could produce the medicine needed to preserve the buffalo and traditional Comanche life. Although the Sun Dance was not common to the Comanche, they often witnessed it performed by neighboring tribes. In June, the dance was performed. For the only time in their history, the scattered bands of Comanche were united.

Using the medicine that Isatai said would protect them in battle, and joined by Kiowa, Cheyenne, and Arapaho warriors, the Comanche were ready to reclaim their heritage. Led by war chief Quanah PARKER and the other war chiefs, on June 24, 1874, the united force attacked Adobe Walls, an old trading post then occupied by white buffalo hunters. Isatai's medicine proved useless against the high-powered buffalo rifles of the hunters. After twelve men had been killed, nine of them Indians, the united force terminated the attack. With his supernatural power discredited, Isatai all but disappeared into historical obscurity.

Quanah Parker and other Comanche leaders never again trusted the power of medicine men. Even the Ghost Dance movement of the late 1880's, which involved many of the Plains Indians tribes, could not restore that confidence.

Glenn L. Swygart

Ishi

Born: c. 1862; near Deer Creek, Northern California
Died: March 25, 1916; San Francisco, California
Tribal affiliation: Yahi
Significance: After all his fellow Yahi people in Northern California had died off or been killed, Ishi became known throughout America as the "last wild Indian."

In 1911, when the man known as Ishi appeared in the corral of a slaughterhouse near Oroville, in Northern California, the Yahi were all thought to have been annihilated many years before. After resisting the invasion of their territory, the Yahi were hunted down and massacred by settlers

Ishi. (American Museum of Natural History)

in the latter part of the nineteenth century. During the 1890's, Ishi and the few remaining members of his community concealed themselves along Deer Creek and successfully hid any trace of their existence from their European American neighbors. After his last remaining relatives died in 1908, Ishi entirely lived alone until his appearance at the Oroville slaughterhouse.

Ishi immediately became a media sensation and an object of scientific inquiry. To the popular press, he was the "last wild Indian." To anthropologists, Ishi was an important source of scientific knowledge. From Oroville, anthropologists Alfred Kroeber and Thomas Waterman took Ishi to live at the Museum of Anthropology at the University of California, Berkeley. When Ishi, in keeping with Yahi etiquette, would not reveal his name to probing journalists, Kroeber bestowed on him the name "Ishi"—a Yana term for "man."

In the years before his death from tuberculosis in 1916, Ishi made a home for himself at the museum, patiently educating anthropologists about Yahi life and language, demonstrating skills such as fire making and stone toolmaking for museum visitors (sometimes as many as several thousand in the course of an afternoon) and working as a janitor.

Although Ishi won the respect and sincere affection of anthropologists such as Kroeber, in many ways he was treated more as a scientific specimen and object of curiosity than as a friend, fellow human being, and refugee of war. Many scholars, therefore, have come to see that Ishi's story holds important lessons about the relationship between science and tribal peoples. Since the 1960's, Ishi has been the subject of a biography by Theodora Kroeber, documentary and feature films, and essays by native studies scholar Gerald VIZENOR.

Molly H. Mullin

FURTHER READING

Kroeber, Karl, and Clifton Kroeber, eds. *Ishi in Three Centuries.* Lincoln: University of Nebraska Press, 2003.

Kroeber, Theodora. *Ishi in Two Worlds: A Biography of the Last Wild Indian in North America.* Foreword by Lewis Gannett. Berkeley: University of California Press, 1961.

Starn, Orin. *Ishi's Brain: In Search of America's Last "Wild" Indian.* New York: Norton, 2004.

Isparhecher

Born: 1829; Alabama
Died: December 22, 1902; Creek Nation, present-day Oklahoma
Also known as: Spahecha (Whooping While Taking off Scalp)
Tribal affiliation: Creek
Significance: The leader of the traditionalist faction in the Creek Nation, Isparhecher led an attempt to overthrow the tribal government in 1882.

Born in Alabama, Isparhecher (pronounced "Spi-e-che") moved as a child to Indian Territory, losing both parents on the Trail of Tears. A full-blooded Creek, he grew up steeped in tribal tradition and never learned English. Enlisting in the Confederate Army at the outbreak of the Civil War, he later switched sides and joined the Union forces. After the war, he became active in tribal politics as a follower of the traditionalist Oktarharsars Harjo (Sands). He served in the Creek legislature and was elected a district judge in 1872.

Less acculturated Creeks, many of them full-bloods such as Isparhecher, distrusted the tribal leadership. Not only had it disastrously allied the tribe with the Confederacy, but also traditionalists regarded a centralized tribal government as yet another imported white practice, one inconsistent with the Creek tradition of local autonomy.

Isparhecher became the leader of the conservative opposition during the 1880's. Violence erupted in 1882, when two Creek Light Horsemen (tribal police) arrested a traditionalist leader. Other full-bloods rescued him, killing the two troopers. Soon a rebellion was under way, with Isparhecher leading a rival government. Known as Isparhecher's War, or the Green Peach War, the uprising was eventually put down after Principal Chief Samuel Checote called out the Creek militia. Isparhecher fled to the Cherokee Nation, eventually returning under an amnesty.

Isparhecher continued to be the leader of tribal conservatives and enjoyed some political success. He served as chief justice and was elected principal chief in 1895. He was widely respected by Creeks of all factions for his honesty and dignified personal presence. At the time of his death, he was working to prevent the individual allotment of tribal lands and the opening of the Creek Nation to white settlement.

William C. Lowe

Johnson, Emily Pauline

Born: March 10, 1861; Six Nations Reserve, near Brantford, Ontario, Canada

Died: March 7, 1913; Vancouver, B.C., Canada

Also known as: Tekahionwake

Tribal affiliation: Mohawk

Significance: One of Canada's leading poets of the late nineteenth century, Emily Pauline Johnson is notable because she celebrated her Mohawk heritage at a time when it was not fashionable; she wrote about the Canadian landscape from a native perspective.

Emily Pauline Johnson grew up in a bicultural environment, the youngest of four children of George Henry Martin Johnson, a Mohawk leader of his Six Nations Iroquois community, and Emily Howells, originally from Bristol, England. Her father was an influential leader of the Iroquois community, receiving guests from England and other countries at his home on the Six Nations reserve. Her mother encouraged her to read widely and to become interested in literature. Johnson attended the Brantford Model School and, as a teenager, sent her written verses to periodicals in Canada, the United States, and England. Many of these were published. She also spent much of her time while still living at Six Nations canoeing on the Grand River, which she thoroughly enjoyed and at which she excelled.

In 1892, Johnson began reciting her works in public before an audience of literary highbrows at the Young Men's Liberal Club of Toronto. After success with this event, she became a frequent platform entertainer before both fashionable Toronto audiences and audiences in bars in small-town Ontario. She traveled to England, where she received many invitations to recite her poetry and other written works and became a minor celebrity. This was in part because of her warmth and attractive personality and in part because of her Mohawk ancestry, which she highlighted in her work and in her appearance. She usually wore buckskin clothing, a bear-claw necklace, traditional Iroquois trade silver brooches, and beaded moccasins for her performances. English audiences particularly found this intriguing.

Johnson soon became well known in Canada as well as in England, and high-level politicians and Canadian officials sponsored her work. She found it difficult, however, to be a traveling writer at the turn of the twentieth century because of the vagaries of train and ship travel, and it was particularly difficult for women because of sexism. In fact, Johnson's own sister disapproved of her career and lifestyle, causing a rift between the two. Most family members, however, supported her.

Johnson's first published volume of verse was *The White Wampum*, published in 1895 and followed by *Canadian Born* (1903). She also published prose: *Legends of Vancouver* (1911), *The Moccasin Maker* (1913), and *The Shagganappi* (1913). Her most famous poem, "The Song My Paddle Sings," which generations of Canadian schoolchildren have learned, earned her only three dollars. Her collected poems have been published, with a biographical sketch, under the title *Flint and Feather* (Toronto, no date).

In 1909, Emily Pauline Johnson settled in Vancouver after years of travel had taken their toll on her health. She was tired from her years of touring but had also contracted cancer. Her last years were spent in much physical pain, and she died on March 7, 1913. At her request, her ashes were interred in Vancouver's spectacular Stanley Park. Succeeding generations of British Columbians have revered her with memorials.

Johnson successfully blended two cultures artfully and fearlessly when no one else was doing so. She is remembered as one of Canada's and Native North America's leading female voices in poetry.

Gretchen L. Green

FURTHER READING
Wiget, Andrew, ed. *Dictionary of Native American Literature.* New York: Garland, 1994.

Jones, Florence

Born: November 28, 1907; at McCloud River, Shasta County, California
Died: November 22, 2003; near Redding, California
Tribal affiliation: Wintu (Winnemem band)
Significance: Florence Jones served for many years as the foremost Winnemem Wintu healer and was a leader in the band's attempts to protect its sacred sites; her renown extended far beyond her tribal homeland.

As is common with many Northern California Indian tribes, the role of traditional doctoring among the Wintu people has generally been performed by women. For nearly three quarters of a century, Florence Curl Jones served as one of the Winnemem (Middle Water) band of Wintus principle curers and religious leaders.

Soon after Jones was born in 1907, six Wintu healers visited her and pronounced that she possessed the special spiritual gifts that were characteristic of shamans. While she was still a child, her mother, grandmother, and aunt (all of whom were noted curers) began the long process of teaching her the special language and ceremonies of Wintu shamanism. As her instruction proceeded, Jones was visited by animal spirits that would continue to serve as her helpers and guides throughout her life.

However, the road leading Jones to her destiny as a Wintu curer was anything but straight. When she was only five years old, federal officials ordered that she be sent to a boarding school in Greenville, California. There she was to be stripped of her tribal customs and religion and re-educated in European-American lifeways and Christianity. Five years later, a fire at the school allowed Jones to return home to the Winnemem's territory along the McCloud River. However, her homecoming proved to be short-lived, as she was sent back to Greenville after the school was rebuilt. It was not until Jones was seventeen that she was finally at liberty to return to her people and recommence in earnest her training as a Wintu doctor and spiritual leader. Her curing abilities and knowledge of herbal plants eventually brought her renown as the leading Wintu doctor. Born Florence Curl, she took the name Jones when she married Andrew Jones.

In addition to her role as healer, Jones was a leader in the ongoing Winnemem fight to regain federal recognition. During the 1980's she also spearheaded the band's efforts to protect a sacred spring located on national forest lands at Bulyum Puyuik (Great Mountain), or Mount Shasta. The Wintus protested that tourists and New Age devotees were desecrating the spring and that plans to build a ski resort at a nearby location would lead to the site's ruin. This struggle, and the complicated issues concerning the protection of Indian sacred sites on public lands, were highlighted in the 2001 documentary film *In the Light of Reverence.*

In 1987, Jones announced her retirement as a healer, and her intention to pass on the role to her great-niece, Caleen Sisk-Franco. However, she continued to play an active role in Winnemem spiritual life until her death in 2003, six days before she would have turned ninety-seven.

Harvey Markowitz

Jones, Peter

Born: January 1, 1802; Burlington Heights, Ontario, Canada
Died: June 29, 1856; Brantford, Ontario, Canada
Also known as: Kahkewaquonaby, Kahkewagwonnaby

Tribal affiliation: Ojibwa (Chippewa)

Significance: As missionary, author, and political activist, Peter Jones worked tirelessly on behalf of his people in southern Ontario and New York State.

Peter Jones's father, Augustus Jones, was a Welshman and a Canadian government surveyor who married Tuhbenahneeguay, the daughter of Wahbanosay, a Missisauga chief. The influential Mohawk Joseph BRANT was Augustus Jones's close friend.

Although reared in traditional Indian fashion, Jones was baptized an Episcopalian and given the English name Peter at the age of sixteen. In 1823, he converted to Methodism at a Methodist mission. Serving initially as a church deacon, Jones was later sent on missionary tours. After being ordained in 1830, he lived the remainder of his life working tirelessly as an itinerant minister. As a missionary and also as a political lobbyist, Jones traveled extensively throughout Ontario and New York State.

Jones also wrote numerous religious tracts and hymnbooks and translated Ojibwa texts into English. Two of his most important works are *The Life and Journals of Kah-ke-wa-quona-by* (1860) and *A History of the Ojebway Indians* (1861), which remains a source for information on Ojibwa customs.

One of Peter Jones's sons by his English wife—his son was also known as Peter Jones—continued his father's missionary work after the elder Peter Jones died.

Mary E. Virginia

Joseph the Younger

Born: c. 1840; Lapwai Preserve, Wallowa Valley, northeastern Oregon

Died: September 21, 1904; Colville Indian Reservation, Washington

Also known as: Chief Joseph, Hinmaton Yalatkit (Thunder in the Mountains)

Tribal affiliation: Nez Perce

Significance: The leader of his people in the Nez Perce War of 1877— actually a brilliant tactical retreat—Joseph the Younger, generally known simply as Chief Joseph, attempted to retain for his people the freedoms they had enjoyed prior to white American interest in their lands.

Joseph the Younger (Hinmaton Yalatkit in his native tongue, which translates as Thunder in the Mountains) was born to Old Joseph (Tuekakas) and Asenoth. He is believed to have been baptized Ephraim

Joseph the Younger, chief of the Nez Perce during the 1870's, when he tried to lead his people to Canada to escape confinement on a U.S. reservation. (National Archives)

by a Presbyterian missionary at Lapwai, in the heart of Nez Perce country. This area, which comprises parts of Idaho, Oregon, and Washington, contains some of the most desirable land in the United States. White Americans soon wanted the land upon which the Nez Perce and other bands of Indians lived.

In 1855 the U.S. government greatly reduced the holdings of all tribes and bands in the northwestern United States in a series of treaties at the Council of Walla Walla, called by the governor of the Washington Territory, Isaac Stevens. In those treaties, the Neemeepoo (meaning "the people"), or Nez Perce (pronounced "nez purse"), agreed to what amounted to a 50 percent reduction of their territory. The Nez Perce were able to keep this much of their land because the whites were not yet interested in the wild and remote country of west-central Idaho and northwestern Oregon. The Nez Perce had been exposed to Christianity as early as 1820, and the existence of Christian names indicates that many practiced that religion.

The troubles of the Nez Perce developed in 1861, when gold in significant quantities was discovered along the Orofino Creek, a tributary of the Clearwater. Old Joseph attempted to keep the prospectors from the land but finally accepted the inevitable and sought to supervise rather than prohibit the activity. This plan failed. Once the area had been opened, many whites entered. In violation of the agreements, and of the treaties of 1855, which prohibited such white encroachments, some whites turned to farming. The results were surprising. The government, rather than forcing the whites to leave, proposed an additional reduction of the Nez Perce lands. The federal government indicated that as much as 75 percent of the holdings should be made available for white settlement. Old Joseph refused; his refusal apparently split the Nez Perce peoples. Some of them agreed to the reduction. Aleiya, called LAWYER by the whites, signed the agreement that the Joseph faction of the Nez Perce would refer to as the thief treaty. Hereafter, the Nez Perce were divided into the treaty and nontreaty bands. Old Joseph refused to leave the Wallowa Valley, where his nontreaty Nez Perce bred and raised Appaloosa horses.

Old Joseph died in 1871. At his parting, he reminded his eldest son, Joseph the Younger, "Always remember that your father never sold his country. You must stop your ears whenever you are asked to sign a treaty selling your home. . . . This country holds your father's bones. Never sell the bones of your father and your mother." Chief Joseph was as adamant in his refusal to sell or part with the land as his father has been, but he realized the power and inconstancy of the U.S. government. In 1873, President Ulysses S. Grant issued an executive order dividing the area that the whites were settling between the whites and the Nez Perce. In 1875, however, Grant reversed the order and opened the entire region to white settlement. In 1876 he sent a commission to see Chief Joseph. The decision had been made to offer Joseph's band of nontreaty Nez

Perce land in the Oklahoma Indian Territory for all their Idaho holdings.

What transpired as a result of this decision was termed by Jacob P. Dunn, Jr., in *Massacres in the Mountains* (1886), "the meanest, most contemptible, least justifiable thing that the United States was ever guilty of." Chief Joseph refused the offer to move to Oklahoma. General Oliver Otis Howard arrived with orders to enforce the presidential decision. Howard proposed a swift compliance with those orders. Joseph realized that his Nez Perce could not long stand against a government and an army determined to take their land and move them. Accordingly, a council of chiefs, including Joseph's younger brother Ollokot (a fine warrior), WHITE BIRD, LOOKING GLASS, and the Willowa prophet Toohoolhoolzote reached the decision to go to Canada rather than to Oklahoma. General Howard, however, declared that "the soldiers will be there to drive you onto the reservation."

The Nez Perce War of 1877 may be misnamed. It might be more appropriate to label it a chase. It is the story of Chief Joseph's attempt to lead his people to the safety of Canada, where the geography and the climate were more similar to their traditional lands than were those of Oklahoma. The U.S. Army, under orders to deliver the Nez Perce to the Indian Territory, would pursue Chief Joseph's band during the 111-day chase that eventually found Joseph winding for more than fourteen hundred miles through the mountains. His attempt to elude the military failed because of the technology of the U.S. forces rather than his lack of ability.

Hostilities began when a member of White Bird's band of Nez Perce, a man named Wahlitits, wanting to avenge the death of his father and two others at the hands of white men, killed four white men. The men killed by Wahlitits had been the first white men killed by any Nez Perce in a generation.

Joseph's reaction to the killings was regret. He realized that only flight would preserve his people. General Howard's reaction was to move immediately not only against White Bird's people but also against all the nontreaty Nez Perce. The initial engagement on June 17, 1877, was between two troops of the First Cavalry (about ninety men) under Captains David Perry and Joel Trimble. The cavalry was accompanied by eleven civilian volunteers. One of those civilian volunteers fired at the Nez Perce truce team. This action led to a short, unplanned, disorganized fight during which the Nez Perce, under Ollokot, killed thirty-four cavalry. (Important also was the capture of sixty-three rifles and many pistols.)

This initial defeat led Howard, fearing a general uprising of all Nez Perce—treaty and nontreaty alike—to call for reinforcements. Troops from all over the United States were quickly dispatched, including an infantry unit from Atlanta, Georgia, to the Washington Territory. Joseph's strategy was to seek protection from the Bitterroot Mountain range, where traditional cavalry tactics would be neutralized. Leading his approximately 500 women and children and 250 warriors, he moved over the Lolo Trail, crossed the Bitterroots, and then, hoping to avoid detection, moved southward to the vicinity of Yellowstone National Park, which he crossed in August, 1877. Joseph then swung northward into present-day Montana, hoping to reach Canada undetected. Seeking the security of the Bearpaw Mountains, Joseph moved his people as quickly as the women and young could travel. They were not quick enough, however: The Bearpaws would be the location of the final encounter with the military.

Joseph was probably not a military strategist, but Ollokot was. Joseph urged that they try to reach Canada. Ollokot, Toohoolhoolzote, Looking Glass, and other chiefs preferred to fight. Battles had been joined several times along the route. At the Clearwater (July 11), at Big Hole (August 9-10), at Camas Meadows (August 16), at Canyon Creek (September 13), and at Cows Creek (September 23), sharp engagements were fought. Each resulted in Joseph's band eluding capture but with irreplaceable losses. The military, meanwhile, was receiving reinforcements in large numbers. Especially important was the arrival of Colonel Nelson Miles with nearly six hundred men, including elements of the Second and Seventh Cavalries.

About thirty miles from the Canadian border, the Nez Perce halted, Joseph believing that they had succeeded in eluding the army and had the time to rest. Joseph was wrong: Technology—the telegraph and the railroad—had enabled the cavalry forces to outflank him. Colonel Miles caught the Nez Perce unprepared on September 30, on the rolling plains of the Bearpaw Mountains. Joseph's band, hopelessly outnumbered, held out until October 4. After a hastily convened, makeshift council, Joseph decided to surrender. On October 5 he rode to the headquarters of Miles and Howard (who had arrived in force the day before) and handed his rifle to Howard, who, in turn, passed it to Miles—still in command of the operation. Joseph said, through translators,

Tell General Howard I know his heart. What he told me before I have in my heart. I am tired of fighting. Our chiefs are killed. Looking Glass is dead. Toohoolhoolzote is dead. The old men are all dead. It is the young men who say yes or no. He who led the young men [Ollokot] is dead. It is cold and we have no blankets. The little children are freezing to death. My people, some of them, have run away into the hills, and have no blankets, no food; no one knows where they are—perhaps freezing to death. I want time to look for my children and see how many I can find. Maybe I shall find them among the dead. Hear me, my chiefs. I am tired; my heart is sick and sad. From where the sun now stands I will fight no more forever.

Joseph's surrender may have been based on an assumption that the Nez Perce could return to the Lapwai. This was not to be. The Nez Perce were loaded onto boxcars and transported to the Oklahoma Indian Territory. In this new climate and country, many of the remaining Nez Perce died. Joseph repeatedly begged for permission to return to the northwestern hunting grounds. Partial success came in 1885, when Joseph was allowed to return with his people to the Colville Reservation in Washington. Thereafter, every attempt on Joseph's part to effect a return to the Lapwai was unsuccessful. Joseph died on September 21, 1904, on the Colville Reservation.

Joseph's failure marked the end of the wars of the Northwest and was the last important Indian resistance except for the Battle at Wounded Knee Creek. The removal of the Nez Perce to reservations marked the end of freedom as the American Indians had known it. As Joseph said, "You might as well expect the rivers to run backward as that any man who was born free should be content when penned up and denied liberty."

Richard J. Amundson

FURTHER READING
Allard, William Albert. "Chief Joseph." *National Geographic* 151 (March, 1977): 408-434.
Andrist, Ralph K. *The Long Death: The Last Days of the Plains Indians.* New York: Macmillian, 1964.
Beal, Merrill D. *"I Will Fight No More Forever": Chief Joseph and the Nez Perce War.* Seattle: University of Washington Press, 1963.
Brown, Dee. *Bury My Heart at Wounded Knee: An Indian History of the American West.* New York: Holt, Rinehart and Winston, 1970.
Chalmers, Harvey. *The Last Stand of the Nez Perce: Destruction of a People.* New York: Twayne, 1962.
Dunn, Jacob P., Jr. *Massacres of the Mountains: A History of the Indian Wars of the Far West.* New York: Harper and Brothers, 1886.

Hampton, Bruce. *Children of Grace: The Nez Perce War of 1877.* Lincoln: University of Nebraska Press, 2002.

Josephy, Alvin M., Jr. *The Patriot Chiefs: A Chronicle of American Indian Leadership.* Harmondsworth, England: Penguin Books, 1958.

Miles, Nelson A. *Personal Recollections and Observances.* Chicago: Werner, 1896.

Moeller, Bill, and Jan Moeller. *Chief Joseph and the Nez Perces: A Photographic History.* Missoula, Mont.: Mountain Press, 1995.

Park, Edwards. "Big Hole: Still a Gaping Wound to the Nez Perce." *Smithsonian* 9 (May, 1978): 92-99.

Journeycake, Charles

Born: December 16, 1817; Ohio
Died: January 3, 1894; Indian Territory (now in Oklahoma)
Also known as: Neshapanasumin
Tribal affiliation: Lenni Lenape (Delaware)
Significance: Charles Journeycake fought for the rights of his people during a number of relocations.

Charles Journeycake was one of the founders of Bacone College, an Indian school in Oklahoma. Born in the Upper Sandusky region of Ohio to the Lenni Lenape (Delaware) chief Solomon Journeycake and a French-Indian mother, Charles Journeycake was baptized at the age of sixteen. He learned English as a young man and moved with ease between the white and Indian worlds. He served simultaneously as a preacher and as head of the Wolf Clan. He strenuously opposed liquor sales to Indians.

Journeycake led his people during a number of relocations—first to Kansas, then to land formerly allocated to the Cherokees in northeastern Oklahoma. He was also a principal figure in the Indian Defense Association.

Bruce E. Johansen

Juh

Born: c. 1825; probably northern Sierra Madre Mountains, Mexico
Died: September 21, 1883; Casas Grande River, Chihuahua, Mexico
Also known as: Yah Natch Cln, Ju, Ho, Whoa, Hoo, Tandinbilnojui (He Brings Many Things with Him)
Tribal affiliation: Chiricahua Apache

Significance: Juh was a principal Chiricahua headman who was respected for his ability as a war leader.

Juh was a prominent Chiricahua Apache, a leader of fighting men. His name is mentioned throughout U.S. military reports of government hostilities with the Apache during the nineteenth century, especially in the conflicts that took place on the border area near the Chihuahua-Sonora line, in southwestern New Mexico, and southeastern Arizona. On occasion his band joined with that of the Mimbreño chief VICTORIO.

Reports of numerous battles and campaigns credited to Juh indicate he killed First Lieutenant Howard Bass Cushing on May 5, 1871, south of the Whetstone Mountains. Cushing had assembled an outstanding record in Arizona through his relentless pursuit of Indians. According to the memoirs of Chiricahua Ace Daklugie, Juh killed the lieutenant after the latter led an army massacre of an Apache camp at Guadalupes.

In June, 1876, the federal government attempted to relocate the Chiricahua Apaches from their Warm Springs Reservation in New Mexico to the San Carlos Reservation in Arizona. Although Juh and GERONIMO had agreed to move on the eleventh day of that month, they fled with their bands a few days before the removal was to take place. In 1879, after they had evaded the U.S. Army for several years, Geronimo and Juh negotiated with Captain Harry L. Haskell and settled on the San Carlos Reservation. However, only two years later, they and their followers escaped and headed south into Mexico's Sierra Madre. Their flight may have been provoked in part by the addition of twenty-three extra army troops, companies, and batteries flooding into Arizona to thwart any attempted uprising by the Apaches. While remaining on the reservation, Loco, Nani, and their communities repeatedly received urgent messages to join the other groups in the south.

In late March, 1882, Juh, and several other Apache leaders, including Geronimo, slipped back onto the reservation to encourage the remaining Apaches to follow them into Mexico. An estimated four hundred to seven hundred Apaches then escaped the reservation and evaded the vast number of troops spread throughout Arizona. After fighting in several battles, Juh and his followers separated from Geronimo. Juh's band withdrew into the depths of the Sierra Madre and did not emerge when General George Crook penetrated the mountains and encouraged Geronimo to return to San Carlos in 1883.

Around this same time, When Juh was nearly sixty years old, he died after falling off his horse. With the death of Juh, one of the great Apache leaders passed from the scene

Teresa Neva Tate

FURTHER READING

Ball, Eve. *Indeh, An Apache Odyssey.* Provo, Utah: Brigham Young University Press, 1980.

Thrapp, Dan L. *Juh: An Incredible Indian.* El Paso: Texas Western Press, 1973.

Jumper

Born: ca. 1790; Seminole territory, Florida
Died: April 18, 1838; New Orleans, Louisiana
Also known as: Ote Emathla (Home Warrior), John Jumper
Tribal affiliation: Seminole (Red Stick Creek)
Significance: Jumper was among the most outstanding leaders during the Second Seminole War of 1835-1842.

Little is known of the early life of Jumper. Born a Red Stick Creek, he first became known for his leadership during the First Seminole War in Florida conducted by General Andrew Jackson from 1816-1818. The treaty of 1823 eventually signed between the Seminoles and the U.S. government restricted the Indians to what was essentially inhospitable land.

By the 1830's, pressure from U.S. expansion into Seminole territory aggravated a division among the Seminoles; some wanted to stay on their remaining territory, and others wanted to move west of the Mississippi River. To decide the question, a delegation of Indians that included Jumper met with government representatives at Payne's Landing on the Ocklewaha River. The treaty they signed provided for the removal of the Seminoles to the west. However, rather than simply accept the government's word on the suitability of their new homeland, seven Indians, along with an agent, went to visit the land. They discovered the settlement was already occupied by members of the Creek Nation, traditional enemies of the Seminoles. The Seminoles were nevertheless forced to sign the treaty, and all but approximately two hundred of them were moved.

Because of the threat of another Seminole outbreak. General D. L. Clinch and an army of some 540 men were authorized to face a combined Indian force of more than 1,000 warriors. In December, 1835, Seminole warriors led by OSCEOLA, ALLIGATOR and Jumper simultaneously carried out several raids. At Fort King, the Indian agent and several troops were killed, while a column of 100 men under Major Frank Dade was practically annihilated near Wahoo Swamp. These hostilities represented the beginning of a Second Seminole War. A third attack three days later killed additional soldiers, resulting in a total of some 160 U.S. casualties during that period.

In January, 1836, General Winfield Scott, commander of the Eastern Department of Florida, was authorized to raise a force of 3,700 volunteers to put down the Seminole rebellion. At the same time, General Edmund Gaines, commander of the Western Department attempted to surprise the Seminole force. The lack of coordination proved a disaster; Osceola and Jumper, along with other chiefs, proved adept at guerrilla warfare. The Seminole force caught Gaines's command at the bend of the Withlacoochee River near the end of February and forced a siege. Only the arrival of fresh troops saved the detachment.

On March 5, emissaries from the army met with Osceola, Jumper and Alligator. The Indians agreed to lift the siege and cross over the river, but only if they were allowed to remain in their villages. However, the talks broke down, and the war continued.

While the Seminoles had arguably fought the American troops to at least a draw in the war, Jumper's loss of men and a lack of food supplies ultimately forced him to surrender, which he did in December, 1837. He agreed to be moved along with the remaining Seminoles to territory west of the Mississippi River. However, he died on the journey and never reached the destination. Meanwhile, the war would continue for another five years.

Richard Adler

FURTHER READING
Waldman, Carl. *Who Was Who in Native-American History.* New York: Facts on File, 1990.

Jumping Bull

Born: c. 1800-1810; place unknown
Died: 1858; place unknown
Also known as: Returns Again, Sitting Bull
Tribal affiliation: Hunkpapa Lakota (Sioux)
Significance: The father of the great warrior and leader SITTING BULL, Jumping Bull is remembered by the Hunkpapa Lakota for his bravery, skills as a sacred man, and the care with which he raised his son.

As a young warrior, Jumping Bull was known as Returns Again, a name he earned from his exploits on the warpath. The name Returns Again indicated that he was never afraid to jump into the heat of battle, but he always returned unharmed to his family and people. However, it was common among Plains Indians for adult names to change to reflect deeds in battle, special visions, or other notable events.

Returns Again and his wife, Her Holy Door, had a son in the spring of 1831. As was expected among the Lakota, Returns Again and his brothers took great care in raising their sons and teaching them the many skills they would need as adult men. According to Lakota custom, parents fed people and gave gifts to mark their children's accomplishments, as Returns Again did when his son Sitting Bull killed his first buffalo at the age of ten and again to honor the boy's accomplishments on his first war party at the age of fourteen.

Returns Again was known as a brave warrior and also a sacred man among his people. It was said that he had the ability to understand the speech of certain animals that provided him with guidance. One time after a day of hunting buffalo, he and three men were in camp far from their people when they heard a noise that made them think someone was coming. The men were alert to the possibility of danger. When they investigated they saw a huge buffalo bull slowly moving toward them. It continued making noises, but only Returns Again could understand the buffalo's message: Sitting Bull, Jumping Bull, Bull Standing with Cow, and Lone Bull. Returns Again recognized that this corresponded to both the four life stages of the buffalo and the four stages of human life—infancy, youth, maturity, and old age. Meanwhile, the hunters stood in awe as the bull slowly walked past them and disappeared over a hill. Returns Again understood he had received four powerful names that were his to use and to bestow to others. He then changed his own name to Sitting Bull, a name that he eventually gave to his son to honor his deeds on his first war party. He then took for himself the name Jumping Bull, which he kept until his death.

In the summer of 1858, when Jumping Bull's people were moving their camp, they were attacked by Crow warriors. Although Jumping Bull was past his warrior days, he joined the younger Hunkpapa in chasing down the enemy. During the skirmish that followed, he challenged a bold and brave Crow to hand-to-hand combat but died from gunshot and stab wounds delivered by this young warrior.

Jumping Bull exemplified the courage expected of Lakota men; he raised his son carefully, gave him a strong name, and laid the groundwork for Sitting Bull's bravery and future leadership among the Lakota people.

Carole A. Barrett

Kalicho

Born: c. mid-1500's; Arctic region (now Baffin, Nunavut, Canada)
Died: Late 1577; Bristol, England
Also known as: Calichough, Collichang, Callicho
Tribal affiliation: Inuit

Significance: Kalicho was an Inuit abducted by explorer Martin
Frobisher's crew during the explorer's second voyage to the New
World. He, along with an Inuit woman and her child, were taken to
England and exhibited as curiosities from the land that Queen Eliza-
beth I designated "meta incognita."

Kalicho probably belonged to one of the Baffin Inuit tribes, nomadic
hunters and fishermen who moved throughout the region adjusting to
the season and the animals they hunted. They lived traditionally in extended families of five or six members, which would band together in
groups of six to ten families for hunting.

During the winter, the Baffin Inuit lived in coastal encampments,
spearing seal and whale. They traveled by dog sled, often over great distances, and lived in igloos and homes of sod, stone, and whalebone.
They moved inland during the summer in smaller groups, where they
hunted caribou and caught fish in stone weirs. They lived in skin tents,
traveled on foot, and subsisted on an all-meat diet.

Nothing is known of Kalicho's life prior to his abduction by British
explorer Martin Frobisher's crew. His tribe had spent the summer on
the outer islands at the northeast entrance to what came to be called
Frobisher's Bay. A woman and child, who were captured later, came
from a tribe on the southern shore, more than 62 miles (100 kilometers) away. The woman had a tattooed face—blue streaks down her
cheeks and around her eyes—and would have carried her baby in her
hood or under her coat in the traditional manner. It is unlikely that she
and Kalicho had met prior to their captivity, but Frobisher's crew expected them to live as husband and wife.

Martin Frobisher was one of the first English explorers to locate and
navigate the Northwest Passage. The Inuit that Frobisher encountered
on his first and subsequent voyages were familiar with explorers and
their ships. The Inuit called them *qadlunaat*, which originally denoted
the Norse explorers they had encountered during the previous three
hundred years. The Inuit greeted Frobisher's crew and seemed to welcome the opportunity to trade with them. They traded fish, seal and
bearskin coats, and received bells, mirrors, and other trinkets.

The language barrier proved to be a problem between the two groups, which might have led to the disappearance of five of Frobisher's men and their only landing boat. The men went ashore with an Inuit they believed to have been hired to be their guide but were never seen again.

Without a landing boat, Frobisher was unable to search for his missing crewmen. After several days, a group of Inuit came out to the ship, presumably to trade. The first to reach the ship was plucked from the ocean, kayak and all, and held as hostage against the return of the five missing men. When this failed, again because of the language barriers, Frobisher was forced to abandon his men and return to England, bringing with him the Inuit and his kayak as proof of the success of his mission. This Inuit's name is unknown, and he died shortly after they reached home.

During the second voyage in 1577, Frobisher and his men were more wary of the indigenous peoples they encountered, but still expected to rescue, or at least obtain word of, their missing crewmen. Frobisher decided to obtain an Inuit to use as an interpreter. The Englishmen pretended to discuss trade with two Inuit who had approached, then attempted to capture them. The Inuit escaped and fled to their boat, and Frobisher was wounded by an iron-bladed Inuit arrow in the struggle. The sailors ultimately succeeded in capturing one as an interpreter, an Inuit man named Kalicho.

They then sailed to the southwest, exploring the southern shore of Frobisher's Bay. Items of English clothing were found in an abandoned Inuit settlement, and despite being more than 125 miles (200 kilometers) from the place the men were last seen, the sailors believed they had found traces of their missing crewmen. They decided the men were being held captive and made plans to attack a nearby Inuit camp.

During the battle, the Englishmen found two Inuit women hiding among the rocks. Suspecting the older woman might be a witch, they left her behind and took the younger woman and her infant son hostage. The woman was known as Ignoth, a variation on the Baffin Island Eskimo word for "woman." Likewise, the infant Nutiok was called by the Inuit word for "child."

In later encounters with the Inuit, Kalicho acted as a translator for Frobisher, though he had been in captivity for a period of just weeks and could not have gained a full command of the English language in that time.

A group of Inuit attempted to rescue the hostages, presumably told of their plight by Kalicho during his translating sessions. The English responded by wounding the Inuit in order to show the power of their weapons. Hostility between the two groups prevented any further trading. At the end of August, Frobisher and his crew left the New World and sailed for home, carrying the three hostages with them.

Despite the severity of the situation, the hostages were not mistreated. The group was provided with a cabin and expected to live as a family. The English were surprised by the behavior of their Inuit captives because they had believed them to be savages. According to an account by George Best, Frobisher's second in command, the Inuit people were very eager to communicate with their captors and taught the seaman the names of things in their native language. They loved music and would keep time with their heads, hands, and feet, and they eventually grew attached to each other. According to Best, the woman acted as wife to Kalicho by caring for him or preparing his food, but the relationship was never consummated. Records indicate the Inuit killed and ate dogs (believed to have been stolen) while aboard the ship. Traditionally, Inuit only ate dog when nothing else was available; Kalicho and Ignoth may have found the English food unsuitable.

The trio arrived in Bristol, England, in the fall of 1577. The mayor of Bristol held a celebration in honor of the event. Kalicho demonstrated the use of his kayak and used his bird spear to hunt ducks on the Avon River. The Inuit were no longer considered hostages and, according to Best, they achieved a level of respect and admiration with their hosts.

During the first month, Kalicho fell ill but refused to have his blood let by a surgeon. His hosts, some of them Frobisher's people, supported his decision. The surgeon attributed Kalicho's death to their kindness in providing too much food and preventing medical care. The actual cause of death may have been pneumonia, aggravated by two broken ribs that had not healed properly and may have occurred during his initial capture. There was no burial ceremony because the English did not want to confuse Ignoth with the strange rituals; they feared that she would believe Kalicho had been sacrificed. They also had her watch him being buried, so she would know that he was not being used for food.

Ignoth died the following week. She had a skin rash, which may have been measles. Her child was sent to London in care of a nurse, where he died shortly thereafter, despite receiving medical care. Kalicho and Ignoth were buried at St. Stephen's Church in Bristol. Nutiok was buried in St. Olave's Church, in London, as was the unnamed Inuit from Frobisher's first voyage.

Frobisher's disregard for the Inuit was typical of the period. For the most part, the indigenous peoples encountered by the early explorers were considered subhuman, without a society, religion, or even emotions. Kalicho and the other two hostages were brought to England to be displayed, like animals or like a mummy looted from an Egyptian tomb. Most such "visitors" died within weeks or months of their arrival because they lacked immunity to the diseases prevalent in crowded English seaports.

P. S. Ramsey

FURTHER READING

McDermott, James. *Martin Frobisher: Elizabethan Privateer.* New Haven, Conn.: Yale University Press, 2001.

McGhee, Robert. *The Arctic Voyages of Martin Frobisher: An Elizabethan Adventure.* Seattle: University of Washington Press, 2001.

Mason, Peter. *Infelicities: Representations of the Exotic.* Baltimore: John Hopkins University Press, 1998.

Ruby, Robert. *The Unknown Shore: The Lost History of England's Arctic Colony.* New York: H. Holt, 2001.

Kamiakin

Born: c. 1800; near present-day Yakima, Washington
Died: 1877; Rock Lake, Washington
Also known as: Camaekin (He Will Not Go)
Tribal affiliation: Yakima
Significance: Chief Kamiakin led the Yakima Nation during the Yakima War of 1855-1856.

Chief Kamiakin was the most famous leader of the Yakima tribe in south-central Washington. He led the Yakimas at a time in history when they were being overrun by European American settlers, who flocked into the region in search of gold and a better life. Kamiakan was extremely concerned about false accusations against his people and even dictated a letter to Father Pandosy of the St. Joseph's Mission. In the letter he protested hangings without even "knowing if we were right or wrong." He offered to grant European Americans a parcel of land if they would agree not to "force us to be exiled from our native country" onto reservations.

During the summer of 1853, Chief Kamiakin coordinated a meeting of tribal groups in the central and western portion of Washington to make plans for dealing with the white settlers. During June, 1855, Kamiakin and several other tribes and bands attended a grand treaty council in the Walla Walla area. Eventually, treaties were signed by five area tribes, including the Cayuse, Walla Wallas, Nez Perces, and Uma- tillas. The treaty with the Yakimas was signed by Chief Kamiakin, Owhi, Skloom, and eleven other delegates. After being persuaded to sign the treaty, Chief Kamiakin said, "Don't offer me any presents. I have not yet accepted one from a white man. When the government sends the pay for these lands, I will take my share."

After the treaty was signed, an Indian agent was killed by an unidenti- fied band of Indians in Yakima territory. The murdered agent, Andrew J. Bolon, was on his way to confer with Kamiakin about an ambush of miners in Yakima territory. Major Granville O. Haller led an expedition against Chief Kamiakin and the Yakimas to avenge Bolon's death. Haller was defeated at Toppenish Creek, and Major General Gabriel Rains went to Yakima territory to settle the score with Kamiakin. Rains burned a Roman Catholic mission at Ahtanum Creek after a skirmish with the Yakimas. Colonel George Wright wanted a meeting with Kamia- kin. The Yakima chief had decided that further conflict was futile.

Chief Kamiakin lived a quieter life after the termination of the Yakima War. He moved north to Rock Lake, Washington, where he and his family farmed until his death in 1877.

Bruce M. Mitchell

FURTHER READING
Ruby, Robert H., and John A. Brown. *Indians of the Pacific Northwest: A History.* Foreword by Alvin M. Josephy, Jr. Norman: University of Okla- homa Press, 1981.

Katlian

Born: late 1700's
Died: mid-1800's
Tribal affiliation: Tlingit
Significance: Katlian led Tlingit resistance against Russian colonists in Alaska.

Katlian led his people in a sporadic war with Russian freebooters and colonists in the present-day Alaska panhandle. The Russians arrived in the Aleutian chain after the exploratory voyage of Vitus Bering (1741), where they forced the Aleuts to trap furs for export.

Born in Sitka, Katlian led a native raid there in 1799 that destroyed the first Russian fort in America. The Tlingits held the fort with great tenacity for two years until the Russians retook it with a force of 120 Russians and about 1,000 Aleuts. The Tlingets retreated from the fort in the face of cannon fire and armed assault, but they attacked the Russian fort at Yakutat in 1805. Raids continued after that; by 1818, a Russian warship was delegated to patrol Sitka harbor, after traders there appealed for protection.

Bruce E. Johansen

Kennekuk

Born: c. 1785; along Osage River (now in Illinois)
Died: 1852; along Missouri River in present-day Kansas
Also known as: Kickapoo Prophet
Tribal affiliation: Kickapoo
Significance: As the leader of the peaceful Northern Kickapoo, Kennekuk delayed his tribe's relocation for several years.

Influenced by prior spiritual leaders, particularly the Shawnee TENSK-WATAWA, Kennekuk advocated a return to traditional ways and abstention from alcohol. With the aid of meditation, fasting, and wooden prayer sticks, he urged his tribe to reach a state of holiness and thereby achieve an earthly paradise. He also advocated sedentary agriculture and peaceful relations with whites. For a time, peace prevailed. As the white population increased, however, fertile Indian farm lands were coveted. In the Treaty of Edwardsville, 1819, all Kickapoo, both Kennekuk's peaceful band and the warring southerners, were forced to cede their Illinois lands in exchange for lands in Missouri. Some Kickapoo became militant in their resistance, while Kennekuk's followers passively resisted removal. On several occasions Kennekuk negotiated with white officials, particularly William Clark in St. Louis. After being forced to sign the Treaty of Castor Hill in 1832, Kennekuk's band moved in 1833 to land along the Missouri River in Kansas, where they re-created their farming village. There, he continued his preaching.

Mary E. Virginia

Keokuk

Born: c. 1783; Saukenuk (now in Rock Island, Illinois)
Died: April, 1848; Franklin County near Pomona, Kansas
Tribal affiliation: Sauk

Significance: Keokuk led the peace band of Sauk Indians in the Rock
River Valley of Illinois; often in active opposition to BLACK HAWK, he
proved willing to exchange Sauk and Fox land for personal gain.

Keokuk was born into the Fox clan at Saukenuk. His blue eyes and flat
cheeks reveal evidence of European ancestry. Keokuk gained a degree
of notoriety because of his ability as a horseman. He had a striking physical appearance and demonstrated great oratorical skills.

Keokuk took advantage of the crisis caused within the Sauk Nation by
the War of 1812. The Sauk and Fox were divided in their response to the
conflict. Many Sauk and Fox migrated across the Mississippi River to
Missouri in order to seek the protection of the U.S. government. Others, led by Black Hawk, joined the British. Those who remained behind
in the villages along the Rock River felt pressure from both sides.

When rumors circulated that an American army was approaching
Saukenuk, the village council prepared to abandon their homes. Keokuk was invited to speak, and he advocated organizing a defense before
making plans to flee. The council chose him as war chief, but the much-
feared American army never arrived.

In June, 1821, Keokuk was instrumental in the apprehension
of two warriors accused of murder. From that time forward, U.S.
Indian agents Thomas Forsyth
and William Clark promoted the
ambitions of Keokuk for prestige
among his people. His growing
influence with the Americans allowed him to speak in councils
with great authority. In 1825, the
Americans sponsored a great
peace council at Prairie du Chien,
Wisconsin. Keokuk served as the
spokesman for the Sauk and Fox
nations.

In May, 1828, Forsyth informed
the Rock River Sauk that they
would have to abandon their
lands east of the Mississippi in order to comply with earlier treaties.
Keokuk led the peace band that
advocated cooperation with the

Keokuk. (Library of Congress)

American demand. Black Hawk and his followers refused to acquiesce. Keokuk's peace band established new homes along the Iowa River in 1829 while Black Hawk's band continued their struggle to occupy Saukenuk.

When open warfare erupted in 1832 between Black Hawk's warriors and the American army, Keokuk offered his services to the Americans. They refused his offer, but, following the destruction of Black Hawk's band during the course of the Black Hawk War, Keokuk emerged as the dominant figure among the Sauk. At the conclusion of the conflict, Keokuk obliged the Americans by negotiating a treaty in which the Sauk, Fox, and Winnebago sold much of their land west of the Mississippi. The Sauk and Fox nations were left with a small reservation along the Iowa River. Keokuk was empowered to distribute an annuity among his people.

Keokuk accompanied Black Hawk on grand tours of the eastern United States in 1833 and 1837. During his 1837 trip, Keokuk participated in negotiations in Washington, D.C., in which 26,500,000 acres of Indian land were ceded to the United States.

In 1845, Keokuk sold the remaining Sauk lands in Iowa, and the Sauks were forced to relocate in Kansas. Keokuk died at the Sauk Agency in Kansas. A bronze bust of Keokuk was placed in the U.S. capitol.

Thomas D. Matijasic

Kicking Bear

Born: c. 1846; place unknown
Died: May 28, 1904; near Manderson, South Dakota
Also known as: Mato Wanartaka
Tribal affiliation: Oglala, Miniconjou Lakota (Sioux)
Significance: Kicking Bear became an apostle of WOVOKA and claimed that wearing Ghost Dance shirts would protect the wearers from bullets shot by white men.

Born an Oglala, Kicking Bear married into the Miniconjou band and became a chief. He fought in the Battles of the Little Bighorn and Rosebud, and in the Black Hills War of 1876-1877. He was a medicine man and is best known as an apostle of Wovoka's Ghost Dance religion. The message of this messianic religion included the idea that God made earth and all people on it; He sent Christ to teach, but white men treated him badly, so he returned to Heaven. Christ, now an Indian

Kicking Bear. (Library of Congress)

(Wovoka), reappeared to let all living and dead Indians inherit the earth. The earth would be filled with grasses, game, and buffalo herds; Indians would live in harmony, avoiding alcohol and the ways of whites. Preparatory rituals included meditation, prayers, chanting, and dancing the Ghost Dance, which would levitate the Indians into space while a great flood drowned all the whites.

Anticipating negative reactions by whites to the Ghost Dance, Kicking Bear claimed that wearing special ghost shirts would stop bullets. Throughout the Great Plains, Indians wearing ghost shirts danced, the whites attacked, and the shirts did not stop the bullets. The Ghost Dance religion essentially died on December 29, 1890, with the massacre at Wounded Knee.

Moises Roizen

FURTHER READING

Mooney, James. *The Ghost-Dance Religion and the Sioux Outbreak of 1890.* Introduction by Raymond J. DeMallie. Lincoln: University of Nebraska Press, 1991.

Kicking Bird

Born: c. 1835; present-day Oklahoma
Died: May 5, 1875; Cache Creek, Indian Territory (now in Oklahoma)
Also known as: Tene-angop'te, Watohkonk, Eagle Striking with Talons
Tribal affiliation: Kiowa
Significance: Kicking Bird led a peace faction during the 1870's Indian wars on the central Plains.

Kicking Bird's grandfather was a Crow adopted by the Kiowas. Little else is known of his ancestry. He earned his early reputation as a warrior but soon emerged as a leader of the Kiowa peace faction, envisioning peace with whites as the best opportunity for tribal survival. To that end, he signed the Treaty of Little Arkansas River (1865), by which Kiowas were granted reservations in the Indian Territory and Texas. He likewise signed the Medicine Lodge Treaty (1867), establishing reservations in Kansas.

With his warrior's reputation challenged by the war faction, Kicking Bird participated in a raid against the Texas Rangers in 1870 during which he killed a soldier. Nevertheless, he continued to support peace. In 1872, with his cousin STUMBLING BEAR, he acted as spokesman for the Kiowa delegation to Washington, D.C. With Indian agent Thomas C. Battey, Kicking Bird developed an educational program and school for Kiowas. His death was probably caused by strychnine administered by a militant Indian. He was buried at Fort Sill, Oklahoma.

Mary E. Virginia

Kiowa leader Kicking Bird. (Library of Congress)

FURTHER READING

Hoig, Stan. *The Kiowas and the Legend of Kicking Bird.* Niwot: University Press of Colorado, 2000.

Klah, Hosteen

Born: October, 1867; Bear Mountain, New Mexico Territory
Died: February 27, 1937; near Gallup, New Mexico
Also known as: Left Handed
Tribal affiliation: Navajo
Significance: Hosteen Klah was an influential Navajo medicine man; as a weaver, he represented his people at two world's fairs.

Hosteen Klah was born in October, 1867, at Bear Mountain, near Fort Wingate, as his family returned home from captivity at Bosque Redondo. As was Navajo tradition, he was called *Away Eskay* (Baby Boy) until some characteristic suggested a nickname—"Klah" (Left Handed). The ceremonial name given to babies at their naming rites is considered personal property and is seldom known outside the immediate family.

Navajo custom dictates that one studies chants and ceremonies only with teachers belonging to the clans of one's mother, father, or grandmother. In Klah's case, many of his kinsmen were shamans and he began studying at an early age. By age ten, he knew the full ceremony of the Hail Chant; then he learned the Wind Chant and the Bear Chant, which lasts for nine days and includes hundreds of chants, prayers, and several elaborate sand paintings.

When not studying, Klah tended sheep and helped his mother and sister with their weaving. He became an accomplished weaver himself and, in 1892, exhibited his weaving at the World's Columbian Exposition in Chicago as a representative of the New Mexico Territory.

As a youth, Klah began learning the Yeibichai Ceremony from its leading chanter, Hathile Nah-Cloie (Laughing Chanter). There were seven forms of this long and complicated ceremony and Klah eventually knew five of them. Altogether, Klah studied for twenty-six years before holding his first Yeibichai Ceremony as principal chanter. He sent invitations to this nine-day ceremony throughout the Navajo Reservation and, at its conclusion, was acknowledged as the greatest Yeibichai chanter.

In 1916, Klah wove a rug illustrating several Yeibichai dancers. Other medicine men objected, demanding that the rug be destroyed, but the furor died out once the rug was sold and off the reservation. In 1919-1920, Klah wove the first rug based on a sand painting; it was called "The Whirling Log," from the Yeibichai Ceremony. Again, other Navajos protested, thinking that an accurate and permanent representation of a sand painting would bring disaster to the tribe. Klah's status as a medicine man allowed him to do as he pleased, however, and he exhibited the rug at the Gallup Ceremonial, where it won a blue ribbon. The rug was sold to a tourist, who asked Klah to weave two more to complete the set of Yeibichai sand paintings. This was the beginning of Klah's career as a weaver of ceremonial rugs, and between 1919 and 1937, he wove twenty-five sand-painting tapestries.

In 1934, Klah again represented the Navajos in the New Mexico exhibit at the Century of Progress Exposition in Chicago, demonstrating sand painting. He died in February, 1937. The Museum of Navajo Ceremonial Art in Santa Fe was built as a memorial to Hosteen Klah and houses many of his sand paintings and weavings.

LouAnn Faris Culley

FURTHER READING
Newcomb, Franc Johnson. *Hosteen Klah, Navaho Medicine Man and Sand Painter.* Norman: University of Oklahoma Press, 1964.

Konkapot, John

Born: c. 1700; Housatonic River Valley, Massachusetts
Died: c. 1775; Stockbridge, Massachusetts
Also known as: Captain Konkapot, Captain John
Tribal affiliation: Mahican
Significance: After converting to Christianity, John Konkapot aided Calvinist missionaries among his band of Mahicans.

After the powerful Mohawks forced the Mahicans to abandon their ancestral lands near Albany, New York, in 1664, the band moved to the Housatonic Valley of western Massachusetts. In 1724, tribal chief Konkapot ceded his land to the British. He remained friendly with the British, aiding them during the French and Indian War. Konkapot was commissioned a captain in 1734.

In 1736, Yale missionary John Sergeant founded the Stockbridge mission among the Mahicans, who then became known as the Stockbridge. Konkapot was soon Christianized, adopting the name John, and assisted Sergeant in his mission. When Massachusetts congregational minister Jonathan Edwards succeeded Sergeant in 1750, he befriended Konkapot. Konkapot died on the eve of the American Revolution. His band, under Samson OCCOM, migrated to Oneida, New York, in 1786, then again, under John W. QUINNEY, to Wisconsin in 1822, where they merged with the Munsee band of Lenni Lenapes (Delawares).

Mary E. Virginia

LaDuke, Winona

Born: 1959; Los Angeles, California
Tribal affiliation: Anishinabe
Significance: Winona LaDuke has become one of the foremost environmental advocates among Native Americans, as well as a major political figure in her role as Ralph Nader's vice presidential candidate on the Green Party ticket in the 2000 election.

Winona LaDuke is a daughter of Vincent LaDuke, who was an Indian activist during the 1950's, and Betty LaDuke, a painter. After being educated at Harvard University during the late 1970's, she moved to the White Earth Reservation in Round Lake, Minnesota, during the early 1980's. There, she became involved in protests against "environmental racism," and in recovery of the Native American land base. With a twenty-thousand-dollar stipend from the first Reebok Human Rights Award, she founded the White Earth Land Recovery Project, which took action to regain land base on her home reservation. By the early 1990's, 92 percent of the land in thirty-six-square-mile reservation was owned by non-Indians.

LaDuke has tirelessly lectured, written, and pressed authorities for answers on environmental issues, ranging from the Navajo uranium mines and Hydro-Quebec's construction sites at James Bay to toxic waste sites on Native Alaskan and Canadian land along the Arctic Ocean. Her findings have been confirmed by environmental scientists. For example, as if to illustrate just how pervasive pollution of the entire earth has become, studies of Inuit women's breast milk in the late twentieth century revealed abnormally high levels of polychlorinated biphenyls (PCBs).

Winona LaDuke, the Green Party candidate for vice president of the United States during the 2000 presidential election. (AP/Wide World Photos)

Studies around the rim of Hudson Bay, conducted by Eric Dewailly of Laval University in 1988, found that the milk of nursing mothers contained more than six times the level of PCBs considered safe by the Canadian government. The fish that most Inuit eat bioaccumulate PCBs, dioxins, mercury, and other toxic materials in the food chain.

Through the last decades of the twentieth century, LaDuke also publicized her findings in numerous newspaper and magazine articles, and as a founder of the Indigenous Women's Network and a board member of Greenpeace.

Bruce E. Johansen

FURTHER READING
Bowermaster, Jon. "Earth of a Nation." *Harper's Bazaar,* April, 1993.

La Flesche, Francis

Born: December 25, 1857; Omaha Reservation, Nebraska
Died: September 5, 1932; near Macy, Nebraska
Also known as: Zhogaxe (Woodworker)
Tribal affiliation: Omaha
Significance: Francis La Flesche joined his sister Susette LA FLESCHE in working with the Poncas in their struggle to regain their homeland during the late 1870's and 1880's.

The son of Omaha chief Joseph La Flesche and Elizabeth Esau, Francis La Flesche traveled with Ponca chief STANDING BEAR and Omaha journalist Thomas H. Tibbles on a tour of several eastern cities to advance the Poncas' cause after they had been given shelter by the Omahas. He worked as an interpreter on the tour. Afterward, he attended National University Law School in Washington, D.C., graduating in 1892. While there, he began working with anthropologist Alice C. Fletcher, and he collaborated with her on *A Study of Omaha Music* (1893).

Recordings made under Fletcher's study are still available. Fletcher and La Flesche also collaborated on *The Omaha Tribe* (1911), published a year after he joined the Bureau of American Ethnology. Francis La Flesche authored *Middle Five: Indian Boys at School* (1900), *Who Was the Medicine Man?* (1904), *A Dictionary of the Osage Language* (1932), and a play entitled *Da-o-ma* (1912).

Bruce E. Johansen

La Flesche, Susan

Born: June 17, 1865; Omaha, Nebraska
Died: September 18, 1915; Walthill, Nebraska
Also known as: Susan La Flesche Picotte
Tribal affiliation: Omaha
Significance: Susan La Flesche practiced medicine, eventually treating almost every member of the Omaha tribe.

The daughter of Omaha principal chief Joseph La Flesche and the sister of Susette LA FLESCHE, Susan La Flesche became a government doctor on the Omaha reservation during a time when cholera, influenza, tuberculosis, and other diseases were reaching epidemic proportions. She blazed an inspiring career through a number of white schools and then worked tirelessly serving her people.

La Flesche attended boarding school in New Jersey, then the Hampton Normal and Agricultural Institute in Virginia. Urged to study medicine by Dr. Martha Waldron, the school physician at Hampton, La Flesche eagerly accepted a scholarship to Woman's Medical College of Pennsylvania. On March 14, 1889, Susan graduated at the head of her class of thirty-six women, becoming the first female Native American to acquire a medical degree.

La Flesche accepted the position of government physician to the Omaha Agency school. Of all the Nebraska tribes, the Omahas were considered the most successful in trying to accommodate to white ideas of "progress." The Omaha Allotment Act of 1882 had divided much of the reservation into individual farms, and more and more Indian families were sending their children to the agency school. Despite this seeming progress, drought, grasshoppers, unscrupulous white neighbors, and inept government agents all combined to create desperate poverty among the Omahas.

With this social upheaval and deprivation came malnutrition and disease. Influenza, dysentery, and tuberculosis were endemic on the reservation, as were periodic outbreaks of cholera, smallpox, diphtheria, and typhoid fever. Within weeks of her arrival, the twenty-four-year-old La Flesche also took on the arduous task of treating the entire adult population, giving her a patient load of more than twelve hundred. The size of the reservation—thirty by forty-five miles—and the absence of paved roads forced La Flesche to travel huge distances by horse and buggy or on horseback, often in severe weather.

By 1892, the intensity of her work was costing La Flesche her health.

She was beset by a number of debilitating illnesses for the rest of her life, as she ministered to the ever-present ills of the Omahas. At one point she wearily departed for Washington, D.C., to testify for the Omahas because people had threatened to convey her against her will, so important was her mission to them. Exhausted and temporarily bedridden by disease, she resigned as agency doctor in October of 1893.

In 1894, her health improving, La Flesche married Henri Picotte, who was part French and part Sioux; she also began a new medical practice for Indians and whites at Bancroft, Nebraska. La Flesche practiced medicine there as long as her own health permitted.

La Flesche was also a temperance crusader, decrying the devastating effects of alcohol abuse among Indian populations. She came to regard "demon rum" as the principal health hazard threatening her people. In temperance lectures, newspaper articles, and letters to government officials, she argued that alcohol abuse not only increased violence and crime but also made people easy prey for all sorts of deadly diseases, especially tuberculosis and pneumonia. Moreover, she charged, local politicians and bootleggers routinely used whiskey to cheat tribal members out of their allotments. She lobbied the Bureau of Indian Affairs (BIA) for stricter enforcement of the 1897 congressional ban on selling liquor to Indians. By 1906, she had persuaded the secretary of the interior to ban all liquor sales in any new town carved out of the Omaha reservation.

La Flesche and her sister Marguerite bought property in the new town of Walthill, where, in 1906, they each built modern homes. Over the next nine years, La Flesche actively participated in the civic and professional life of the community, despite her own failing health. After her death on September 18, 1915, the Walthill *Times* added an extra page in its September 24 issue filled with warm eulogies to her. Friends recalled that hundreds of people in the area, Indian and European American, owed their lives to her care.

As practicing physician, missionary, social reformer, and political leader, Susan La Flesche Picotte had a profound effect on the lives of her people. By 1915, there was scarcely an Omaha alive who had not been treated by her; even those who did not embrace all of her reformist ideals trusted her. As the Omahas' unofficial but clearly recognized spokesperson, La Flesche defended their interests in the white world, even as she devoted her energies to their physical well-being at home. Beyond modern medical care, public health improvements, and vigorous leadership, she provided her tribe—and the larger world—with a vibrant example of what late nineteenth century reformers hoped to accomplish with their assimilationist policies.

Like her father, La Flesche believed that education, Christian principles, and legal rights were the key to her tribe's advancement. That she and her non-Indian mentors underestimated the difficulties facing Native Americans and overestimated the virtues of forced acculturation does not detract from her achievement. Susan La Flesche walked with grace in two worlds: Assimilated into middle-class mainstream American culture, she never abandoned her tribal roots or her overriding concern for her people. Few women, Indian or white, have left such an indelible mark on their communities.

Constance B. Rynder
Bruce E. Johansen

FURTHER READING

Clark, Jerry E., and Martha Ellen Webb. "Susette and Susan La Flesche: Reformer and Missionary." In *Being and Becoming Indian: Biographical Studies of North American Frontiers*, edited by James A. Clifton. Chicago: Dorsey Press, 1989.

Green, Norma Kidd. *Iron Eye's Family: The Children of Joseph La Flesche.* Lincoln, Nebr.: Johnsen, 1969.

Mathes, Valerie Sherer. "Dr. Susan La Flesche Picotte: The Reformed and the Reformer." In *Indian Lives: Essays on Nineteenth and Twentieth-Century Native American Leaders*, edited by L. G. Moses and Raymond Wilson. Albuquerque: University of New Mexico Press, 1985.

Moses, L. G., and Raymond Wilson, eds. *Indian Lives: Essays on Nineteenth and Twentieth Century Native American Leaders.* Albuquerque: University of New Mexico Press, 1985.

Tong, Benson. *Susan La Flesche Picotte, M.D.: Omaha Indian Leader and Reformer.* Foreword by Dennis Hastings. Norman: University of Oklahoma Press, 1999.

Wilson, Dorothy Clarke. *Bright Eyes: The Story of Susette La Flesche, an Omaha Indian.* New York: McGraw-Hill, 1974.

La Flesche, Susette or Josette

Born: 1854; Omaha Reservation, Nebraska
Died: May 26, 1903; Lincoln, Nebraska
Also known as: Inshtatheumba (Bright Eyes)
Tribal affiliation: Omaha
Significance: Susette La Flesche lectured in support of the Poncas' regaining their ancestral land.

Susette La Flesche became a major nineteenth century native-rights advocate through the case of Ponca leader STANDING BEAR. Like her sister Susan LA FLESCHE, Susette La Flesche attended the Presbyterian mission school on the Omaha reservation. She also studied art at the University of Nebraska. In the late 1870's, she traveled with her father, Joseph La Flesche, to Indian Territory (later Oklahoma) to render rudimentary medical attention to the Poncas. Standing Bear's people had been forced to move there from their former homeland along the Niobrara in northern Nebraska. When the Poncas attempted to end this forced exile and return to their homeland, they marched for several weeks in midwinter, finally eating their moccasins to survive and arriving at the Omaha reservation with bleeding feet. The Omahas, particularly the La Flesche family, granted them sanctuary and sustenance.

Susette accompanied her brother Francis LA FLESCHE and Standing Bear on a lecture tour of eastern cities during 1879 and 1880 to support the Poncas' case for a return of their homeland. Newspaper articles by Omaha journalist Thomas H. Tibbles about the Poncas' forced exile helped ignite a furor in Congress and among the public. In 1882, Susette—who often used the name "Bright Eyes" in public—married Tibbles. She also coauthored a memoir with Standing Bear, *Ploughed Under: The Story of an Indian Chief* (1832). During ensuing years, La Flesche and Tibbles also toured the British Isles. Later the couple lived in Washington, D.C., but eventually Susette returned to Lincoln, Nebraska, where she died in 1903.

Bruce E. Johansen

Lame Deer

Born: c. 1895; near Pine Ridge, South Dakota
Died: December 14, 1976; Denver, Colorado
Also known as: Tahca Ushte, John Fire
Tribal affiliation: Miniconjou Lakota (Sioux)
Significance: Lame Deer is remembered for his autobiography, which recounts his life growing up on a reservation and his protest against the white culture that had robbed the Indians of their land and culture.

Named for his grandfather, a Sioux warrior who was killed by the U.S. cavalry during the 1890's, Lame Deer lived his life between two worlds, that of the reservation and that of white America. After the death of his mother in 1920, Lame Deer inherited horses and cattle from his father, who at that time gave up the old ways. Lame Deer too gave up the old life, as he followed the rodeo circuit. He also received instruction from medicine men. Lame Deer moved between the white world and the world of the Indian on a reservation; he was a rancher, rodeo rider, reservation policeman, and holy man.

With the publication of *Lame Deer: Seeker of Visions* in 1976, written with Richard Erdoes, Lame Deer established himself as a spokesperson and a spiritual leader among American Indians. In the book, he describes his ancestors and treaties that were broken, his upbringing on the reservation, and his forced schooling at government schools (where he had no choice but to repeat the third grade six times because there were no teachers beyond that level). He also recounts his experiences as a medicine man. The book evaluates both white and Indian culture, finding the suburban modern American culture spiritless and sterile. Lame Deer laments the loss of the prairie life.

Lee Schweninger

FURTHER READING
Lame Deer, with Richard Erdoes. *Lame Deer: Seeker of Visions.* New York: Simon and Schuster, 1976.

Lawyer

Born: c. 1795; place unknown
Died: January 3, 1876; place unknown
Also known as: Hallalhotsoot, Hollolsotetote (The Talker)
Tribal affiliation: Nez Perce, Flathead
Significance: Lawyer took his English from his work in negotiating Nez Perce land rights with the U.S. government.

Lawyer negotiated treaties in the name of the Nez Perces that were repudiated by Chief JOSEPH THE YOUNGER before his Long March in 1877. Chief Joseph gave Lawyer that name because (as Joseph noted in a speech to Congress in 1879) "he talked too much" and gave away land that did not belong to him.

Lawyer was a son of Twisted Hair, a Nez Perce chief who had greeted Meriwether Lewis and William Clark, and his Flathead wife. Lawyer often worked as a guide and interpreter for missionaries and traders and became well known for his oratorical skill in both the English and Nez Perce languages.

Lawyer. (Library of Congress)

Lawyer was designated as a representative of all the Nez Perces by Washington territorial governor Isaac Stevens at a treaty council in 1855. The outcome of that council was bitterly protested by Old Joseph, his son Chief Joseph the Younger, and other antitreaty Nez Perces. During the ensuing Yakima War of 1855-1856, Lawyer's band protected Stevens from attack by warriors seeking revenge for the death of Peopeomoxmox. In 1863, Lawyer signed another treaty and ceded even more land that Old Joseph insisted was not his to give. By 1868, Lawyer himself was upset at the number of treaties that had been broken, and he traveled to Washington, D.C., to protest. He died in 1876, one year before the Long March of the antitreaty Nez Perces under Chief Joseph the Younger.

Bruce E. Johansen

Lean Bear

Born: c. 1813
Died: May 16, 1864; near Big Creek, Kansas
Also known as: Awoninahku, Starved Bear
Tribal affiliation: Southern Cheyenne
Significance: Lean Bear was one of the principal Plains Indian leaders who strove for peace.

Cheyenne leader Lean Bear, the brother of BULL BEAR, was part of the 1863 delegation to Washington, D.C., that met with President Abraham Lincoln to negotiate a peace. The delegation included TEN BEARS of the Comanche and LONE WOLF of the Kiowa.

The following year, a detachment of troops attacked a group of Cheyenne who had stolen three cattle, thus launching a war with the Cheyenne. In May, 1864, Lieutenant George Eayre entered the Nebraska

Territory with the intent of attacking Cheyenne on sight. Lean Bear's camp at Ash Creek was friendly, but when Lean Bear (the peace chief) and several other leaders, including Star and Wolf Chief, rode forth to offer peace to the soldiers, the troops moved into battle formation and opened fire. Lean Bear was shot on his horse and then shot again as he lay on the ground.

On his chest was the peace medal given to him in Washington; in his hand were the papers signed by Lincoln saying that he was a friend to the whites and a keeper of peace. This attack, and the Sand Creek Massacre soon afterward, led to the Cheyenne-Arapaho War (or the Colorado War) of 1864-1865 and to later fighting on the southern Plains.

Tonya Huber

Left Hand the First

Born: 1820's; present-day eastern Colorado or western Nebraska or Kansas
Died: November 29, 1864; Sand Creek, Colorado
Also known as: Nawat, Niwot
Tribal affiliation: Southern Arapaho
Significance: The first Left Hand was a leading peace chief during the Plains Indian wars.

There were two Left Hands of considerable renown in Southern Arapaho history, a fact which has led to some confusion in the historical record. The first Left Hand learned English from his sister's husband. He became an important translator and leader in Arapaho dealings with whites. He worked with LITTLE RAVEN, the principal chief of the Southern Arapaho at the time, attempting to keep peace as white Americans moved into the Great Plains. Despite his known peaceful intentions, he appears to have been killed in the 1864 massacre at Sand Creek, Colorado.

Carl W. Hoagstrom

FURTHER READING
Coel, Margaret. *Chief Left Hand, Southern Arapaho.* Norman: University of Oklahoma Press, 1981.

Left Hand the Second

Born: c. 1840; present-day eastern Colorado or western Nebraska or Kansas
Died: June 20, 1911; Geary, Oklahoma
Also known as: Nawat, Niwot
Tribal affiliation: Southern Arapaho
Significance: The second Left Hand was a principal chief, and he signed an agreement permitting allotment of Arapaho land.

The second Left Hand replaced LITTLE RAVEN as principal chief of the Southern Arapaho in 1889. Although he could not speak English, he was an important intermediary between his people and the whites, visiting Washington, D.C., on a number of occasions. His reasoning ability and his willingness to compromise helped make the transition to reservation life smoother for the Southern Arapaho than it was for many tribes. In 1890, however, he created considerable enmity when he signed an agreement that allowed the allotment of Arapaho lands in Indian Territory in spite of opposition from the Southern Cheyenne, who shared a reservation with the Arapaho.

Carl W. Hoagstrom

Little Assiniboine

Born: c. 1846; place unknown
Died: December 15, 1890; place unknown
Also known as: Kills Plenty, Stays Back, Jumping Bull
Tribal affiliation: Assiniboine
Significance: Adopted as a brother by the Sioux leader SITTING BULL, Little Assiniboine steadfastly supported Sitting Bull in warring, accompanied him in hunting, and died with him.

Little Assiniboine was a childhood name given to a young boy from the Assiniboine tribe taken captive by the Hunkpapa Lakota (Sioux). In the winter of 1857 a small war party of Hunkpapa Lakota mounted a raid north of the Missouri River in what is now Montana. They came upon a lone tipi and scared the family out. The father and a skinny youth about eleven years old defended the family, while the mother tried to escape across the ice with two children. Despite the family's courageous stand, the gangly youth was soon the only member of the family left, and the Hunkpapa warriors surrounded him and counted coup on him. The boy had one arrow left. He did not cry; rather, he looked at each warrior, and when his eyes fell on one man and he addressed him as "big brother." That warrior was Sitting Bull. Rather than kill him, as the other warriors wanted to do, Sitting Bull hoisted the courageous boy onto his own horse and spared his life.

Sitting Bull formally declared the boy his brother through a making-a-relative ceremony. To celebrate the occasion Sitting Bull fed the people in his camp, gave horses away, and the two men pledged that they would always be closely connected. They would go to war together, hunt together, and provide for each other if their families needed help. After Sitting Bull's father, Jumping Bull, died in 1858, Little Assiniboine received that man's honored name. Relatives of the boy asked him to return to his tribe, but Little Assiniboine refused. When he proclaimed that he was Sitting Bull's brother, he was nicknamed Stays Back. The two men remained close throughout the rest of their lives.

Little Assiniboine became a courageous warrior and took part in many of the battles of the plains war era. At a young age he became the leader of the prestigious Strong Hearts warrior society and rode at the front of warriors in battle and challenged enemies to attack. He admiringly came to be called Kills Plenty by the Hunkpapa.

Little Assiniboine was at Sitting Bull's side in early summer of 1876 when the latter had a vision of soldiers falling into the enemy camp—a premonition of the Indian victory at the Little Bighorn a few weeks later. Little Assiniboine remained at Sitting Bull's side when he went to Canada in early 1877 and when he settled on the Standing Rock Reservation in Dakota Territory in 1883.

On the morning of December 15, 1890, Little Assiniboine and his son Chase Wounded died defending Sitting Bull from arrest by Indian police on the reservation. Sitting Bull and his son Crowfoot were also among the casualties. Afterward, Little Assiniboine's wife and children were detained at Fort Yates for a time. Later, they fled to the Pine Ridge Reservation, where Little Assiniboine's descendants continue to live.

Carole A. Barrett

Little Crow

Born: c. 1820; near present-day South St. Paul, Minnesota
Died: July, 1863; near Hutchinson, Minnesota
Also known as: Cetan Wakan Mani, Tahatan Wakan Mini (Hawk That Hunts Walking), Taoyateduta (His Red People)
Tribal affiliation: Mdewakanton (Dakota) Lakota (Sioux)

Significance: Little Crow was a tribal leader during the Sioux Minnesota Uprising of 1862.

Little Crow was born at Kapoosa, a Mdewakanton Dakota village on the west bank of the Mississippi River. Little is known of his childhood or youth. By the time he was fully grown he was a big man with a powerful, dominant personality.

Accounts differ, but apparently one of Little Crow's brothers was jealous of the chief and tried to kill him in 1846. Little Crow was badly wounded in both arms and never fully regained the use of his hands. The chief had six wives and produced twenty-two children.

Little Crow was one of the signers of the Treaty of Mendota, which ceded most of the Dakota Sioux territories to the whites. In spite of this 1851 pact, Little Crow subsequently spoke out against ceding Indian lands. The chief raised an Indian "posse" against INKPADUTA, a Sioux whose band had killed thirty-four whites at Spirit Lake, Minnesota, in 1857. Though his band was defeated, Inkpaduta escaped.

The Minnesota Sioux lived peacefully for a number of years, but grievances developed. There was pressure for Indian land, government annuities failed to arrive, and merchants refused credit, the latter meaning near-starvation for the Sioux. When a group of young warriors killed some whites, it sparked the great Minnesota Sioux uprising in the summer of 1862.

Little Crow became a major leader in Indian resistance to the whites. It is said that he was against war but changed his mind when accused of cowardice. The chief led a large force against Fort Ridgley, but the warriors were repulsed and Little Crow himself wounded. The brief but bloody uprising was ended when the Sioux were defeated at Wood Lake on September 23, 1862. Little Crow managed to escape with some two hundred followers.

Little Crow returned to Minnesota, where it is alleged

Little Crow around 1862. (Library of Congress)

that he continued his raiding. He was shot and killed by a white farmer near Hutchinson, Minnesota, in July, 1863. Little Crow's skeleton was given to the Minnesota Historical Society, but the remains were turned over to his descendants in 1971. He was laid to rest in a Sioux cemetery near Flandreau, South Dakota.

Eric Niderost

FURTHER READING
Anderson, Gary Clayton. *Little Crow, Spokesman for the Sioux*. St. Paul: Minnesota Historical Society Press, 1986.
Gibbon, Guy E. *The Sioux: The Dakota and Lakota Nations*. Malden, Mass.: Blackwell Publishing, 2003.

Little Priest

Born: Early nineteenth century; place unknown
Died: September, 1866; place unknown
Also known as: Hoonk-hoo-no-kaw, Little Chief
Tribal affiliation: Winnebago
Significance: Little Priest was a tribal representative and warrior.

Little Priest followed his father in the role of chief of his village in 1840. In that same year, the people of the village had relocated from Wisconsin to Iowa. Then, in 1846, he and other Winnebago leaders signed a treaty trading the reservation land in Iowa for land in Long Prairie, Minnesota. He traveled to Washington, D.C., in 1855 to sign the treaty that exchanged the Long Prairie lands for reservation space south of Mankato, Minnesota.

Little Priest supported the Minnesota Uprising of the Sioux that took place from 1862 to 1863. Most Winnebagos did not fully support the Sioux, and Little Priest was arrested for taking part in the uprising in October, 1862; he was tried and acquitted.

In 1863, the Winnebago were once again relocated, this time to a reservation in South Dakota. There was no food at this reservation, however, so the Winnebago left the reservation and reached Nebraska, where the Omaha granted them some land. Little Priest became a scout and company leader for the Omaha, fighting the Sioux between 1866 and 1868 in a war for the control of the Bozeman Trail. In March, 1866, by the Powder River in Montana, Little Priest single-handedly held off a party of advancing Sioux. In September, 1866, he died as a result of the wounds suffered at the engagement.

Little Raven

Born: c. 1825; on the Platte
River, Nebraska
Died: 1889; Cantonment, In-
dian Territory (now in Ok-
lahoma)
Also known as: Hosa, Little
Crow
Tribal affiliation: Arapaho
Significance: As principal
Arapaho chief, Little Raven
supported accommodation
and peace with whites.

After earning his warrior's
reputation in battle against
the Sauk and Fox, Little Raven succeeded his father as
hereditary chief in 1855. Little Raven's intelligence, leadership, and oratorical skills
were admired by Indians and
whites.

Little Raven. (National Archives)

As chief, Little Raven signed the Treaty of Fort Wise (1861), establishing a reservation in Arkansas. Retaliating against white encroachment during the Civil War, he led several raids in Kansas and Colorado.
Distrusting Colorado governor John Evans and militia commander
John Chivington, Little Raven declined their false promises for protection at Sand Creek and led his people farther south.

In 1865 and 1867, Little Raven signed the treaties of Little Arkansas
and Medicine Lodge by which Indians were further relegated to reservations. During a trip in 1871 to several eastern cities, he earned a reputation among whites for oratory. Returning convinced of the president's peaceful intentions, he remained neutral during the Red River
War of 1874-1875. At his death in 1889, Little Raven was succeeded as
chief by Left Hand.

Mary E. Virginia

Little Robe

Born: 1828; place unknown
Died: 1886; place unknown
Tribal affiliation: Southern Cheyenne
Significance: Little Robe succeeded BLACK KETTLE as leading peace chief of the Southern Cheyenne.

As a young man, Little Robe distinguished himself as a warrior against traditional Cheyenne foes including Utes and Pawnees; in 1863 he became a chief. Briefly, following the Sand Creek Massacre, he fought

Little Robe. (Library of Congress)

against whites in the Cheyenne-Arapaho War. Thereafter he advocated peace, joining with Black Kettle and George BENT to bring the militant Dog Soldiers to the signing of the Medicine Lodge Treaty of 1867. After Black Kettle's death in 1868 at the Battle of Washita River, Little Robe succeeded him as principal peace chief and surrendered to General Philip Sheridan at Fort Cobb in the Indian Territory. In 1873 he headed the delegation of Southern Cheyenne and Arapaho chiefs who traveled to Washington to negotiate with the commissioner of Indian affairs. During the Red River War of 1874-1875, Little Robe continued to counsel peace.

Following the war, Little Robe lived on the North Canadian River in Indian Territory. Although he desired peace, he did not readily adapt to "white ways," as evidenced by his refusal to send children from his band to white schools and his work to keep white-owned cattle off reservation lands.

Tonya Huber

Little Turtle

Born: c. 1752; near Fort Wayne, Indiana
Died: July 14, 1812; Fort Wayne, Indiana
Also known as: Michikinikwa
Tribal affiliation: Miami
Significance: Little Turtle led a coalition of Indian forces in an attempt to retain the Ohio River as the southern boundary of their land; he inflicted several defeats upon the U.S. Army during the 1790's.

Little Turtle was born along the banks of the Eel River in Indiana. His father was a powerful Miami chief; his mother was believed to be a Mahican. Little Turtle actively campaigned against the Americans during the American Revolution. He participated in the routing of a small American force led by Colonel Augustin Mottin de la Balme during the summer of 1780 at the Aboite River.

As American settlers pushed north of the Ohio River after the close of the revolution, conflicts with the Indians intensified. A loose coalition of Miami, Shawnee, Potawatomi, and Ojibwa formed to resist the incursion.

On September 26, 1790, General Arthur St. Clair ordered Brigadier General Josiah Harmar northward from Fort Washington (present-day Cincinnati) on a mission to pacify the hostile Indians. As Harmar moved through the wilderness with an armed force of fifteen hundred men, Little Turtle organized a masterful strategy to lure him forward. The Miami towns around Fort Wayne were intentionally destroyed by the Indians in order to convince Harmar that the Indian coalition was in disarray. On October 18 and 19, 1790, Little Turtle's army defeated Harmar's force in two sharp engagements. The Americans suffered more than two hundred casualties and retreated southward.

A second punitive expedition was organized the following year. On October 3, 1791, General St. Clair left Fort Washington, moving toward the Upper Wabash River. On November 4, 1791, Little Turtle's Indian army struck St. Clair's men at dawn. The ferocity of the attack panicked the militia units and delayed the formation of organized battle lines. Desperate fighting allowed a portion of St. Clair's army to escape total annihilation. Of the fourteen hundred American soldiers who participated in the battle, fewer than six hundred survived.

In 1792, General Anthony Wayne was placed in command of the U.S. Army in the West. He managed to raise and train an army of three thousand men. As he moved northward, Wayne built a series of forts, including Fort Recovery on the site of St. Clair's defeat. On June 29, 1794, Little Turtle ordered a probe of Fort Recovery's defenses. Finding them too strong, Little Turtle began to advocate negotiating a peace settlement. The other Indian leaders rejected his counsel, and he was replaced by Turkey Foot (some scholars say BLUE JACKET) as commander of the Indian army.

Following the defeat of the Indian forces at Fallen Timbers (1794), Little Turtle helped to negotiate the Treaty of Greenville. By the terms of that treaty, the Miami and associated tribes ceded their rights to most of modern Ohio and a large portion of Indiana.

Following the Treaty of Greenville, Little Turtle aided William Henry Harrison in his policy of gaining title to additional Indian lands. His influence prevented the Miami from joining the Indian Confederacy being created by TENSKWATAWA and TECUMSEH. In later years, he suffered from gout. He died at Fort Wayne while being treated by an army surgeon.

Thomas D. Matijasic

FURTHER READING
Carter, Harvey Lewis. *The Life and Times of Little Turtle: First Sagamore of the Wabash.* Urbana: University of Illinois Press, 1987.

Little Wolf

Born: c. 1820; near the Eel and Blue Rivers, Montana
Died: 1904; Tongue River Reservation, Montana
Also known as: Ohkom Kakit, Two Tails
Tribal affiliation: Northern Cheyenne
Significance: Little Wolf fought alongside such leaders as CRAZY HORSE
and GALL during the 1860's; along with DULL KNIFE, he led some 350
Cheyennes on a 1,500-mile journey from Indian Territory back to
their Montana homeland.

Little Wolf first distinguished himself as a warrior in battle against other
tribes. In 1864, his generally peaceful attitude toward whites changed
when he learned how BLACK KETTLE and his people were killed. Along
with fellow Cheyenne Dull Knife, Little Wolf fought in many of the major battles against whites that occurred in the northern Plains. He
fought in the Bozeman Trail wars (RED CLOUD's War) in 1866-1868 and
in the Fetterman massacre of December, 1866. Little Wolf was one of
the signers of the 1868 Fort Laramie Treaty. He was also one of the most
active war chiefs in the war for the Black Hills in 1876 and 1877, under
the leadership of SITTING BULL.

The village of Dull Knife and Little Wolf was attacked by eleven hundred cavalry troops under the command of Colonel R. S. Mackenzie
on November 25, 1876. Forty Cheyennes were killed in the attack; just
as devastating was the destruction
of their tipis, clothing, and entire
winter food supply. The night of the
attack, temperatures dropped below zero and many more died. During the course of the fighting, Little
Wolf was erroneously reported to
have been shot a number of times.
He surrendered the following May
and was sent to Indian Territory.
About 1,000 of his people were sent
to the Darlington Agency in August,
1877, with hundreds becoming ill
and 43 dying within the first two

Little Wolf. (National Archives)

months. Little Wolf and Dull Knife failed to persuade authorities to allow them to return home to Montana. Nevertheless, about 350 people,
under their leadership, left for Montana in September, 1878.

The group divided en route, with some following Dull Knife and others going with Little Wolf. The group following Little Wolf eluded the
thousands of troops pursuing them until March, 1879, at which time
Little Wolf surrendered to W. P. Clark near the mouth of the Powder
River. He and his people were returned to Fort Keogh, Montana, with
the promise of a reservation in their homeland. Dull Knife's group did
not fare as well. Captured in October and imprisoned at Fort Robinson,
many lost their lives in a winter attempt to escape.

Little Wolf and many of his warriors enlisted in the army as Indian
scouts for General Nelson A. Miles, perhaps because military life seemed
more familiar to them than reservation life. Little Wolf lived for almost
thirty years on the Tongue River Reservation. Though blind in his old
age, he remained mentally astute.

Tonya Huber

Further Reading
Boye, Alan. *Holding Stone Hands: On the Trail of the Cheyenne Exodus.* Lincoln: University of Nebraska Press, 1999.

Logan, James

Born: c. 1725; Shamokin (now Sunbury), Pennsylvania
Died: 1780; near Detroit, Michigan
Also known as: Logan the Mingo, John Logan, Tahgahjute
Tribal affiliation: Cayuga
Significance: A leader in Lord Dunmore's War, James Logan on several
occasions raided white settlers in the Appalachian region.

James Logan's mother was a Cayuga and his father, SHIKELLAMY, was
probably a Frenchman who was reared by Oneidas. After being elected
by the Iroquois council as representative for Iroquois holdings in Pennsylvania, Shikellamy and his family moved to Shamokin, Pennsylvania.

Logan rose to prominence among the Pennsylvania and Ohio Cayugas, known as Mingos, and was initially friendly toward whites. Indeed,
his name was probably adopted from his friend, James Logan, colonial
secretary of Pennsylvania. In 1774, Logan and his band moved to the
Sciota River in Ohio. There, following an unprovoked attack in which
white settlers killed his wife and several children, Logan became mili-

tant. Aligning himself with the Shawnee leader CORNSTALK in Lord Dunmore's War, Logan conducted retaliatory raids throughout the region. After the Battle of Point Pleasant, 1774, and his refusal to participate in a peace conference, he sustained his raids against white settlers throughout the American Revolution.

Logan was murdered in Detroit in 1780, probably after a quarrel with a nephew.

Mary E. Virginia

Lone Wolf

Born: c. 1820
Died: 1879; near Fort Sill, Indian Territory (now in Oklahoma)
Also known as: Guipago
Tribal affiliation: Kiowa
Significance: Lone Wolf was principal chief of the Kiowa from 1866 to
    1879 and participated in many major battles against whites.

Lone Wolf grew to manhood within the ceremonial life and ritual of his tribe, preparing for the warrior's role. After the death of the great leader DOHASAN, an 1866 Kiowa council acknowledged Lone Wolf's war leadership and selected him to serve as principal chief, although he never achieved the hegemony of his predecessor. He attended the Medicine Lodge Treaty council in 1867 and toured the nation's capital as a guest of the federal government in 1872. Following the death of his son a year later, he led attacks on hide hunters, teamsters, and the U.S. Cavalry, and participated in the Wichita Agency melee in August, 1874, which set off the Red River War on the southern Plains. He fled pursuing army troops, survived

Lone Wolf. (National Archives)

the Palo Duro Canyon disaster, and finally reluctantly surrendered in early 1875.

Because of his prominence, Lone Wolf was singled out as the yard-stick for antiwhite sentiment, and he was among the resisting Indians exiled to Fort Marion, Florida. He died in 1879, shortly after his release from confinement and his return home. Ethnologist James Mooney noted that Lone Wolf's passing marked "the end of the war history of the Kiowa" and the final tribal surrender to reservation assimilation.

C. B. Clark

FURTHER READING

Boyd, Maurice, ed. *Kiowa Voices*. 2 vols. Fort Worth, Tex.: Texas Christian University, 1981, 1983.

Jones, J. Lee. *Red Raiders Retaliate: The Story of Lone Wolf, The Elder.* Seagraves, Tex.: Pioneer, 1980.

Looking Glass

Born: c. 1823; near present-day Asotin, Washington

Died: October 5, 1877; Bear's Paw Battlefield, Bear's Paw Mountains, Montana

Also known as: Allalimya Takanin, Apushwahite

Tribal affiliation: Nez Perce

Significance: Looking Glass, one of the important nontreaty Nez Perce chiefs, served as war leader and guide in the ultimately unsuccessful retreat to Canada in the Nez Perce War of 1877.

Looking Glass was the son of Looking Glass the leader (Apah Wya-kaikt), an illustrious and respected chief. He was reared to be a warrior, buffalo hunter, and chief. He and his father were of the Nez Perce faction that was never Christianized by missionaries and never signed any land treaties with whites. Their faction represented one-third of the Nez Perce people.

In January of 1863, the elder Looking Glass died and his son became chief. He adopted his father's name and, just as his father had done, hung his father's small, round trade mirror around his neck (hence the name Looking Glass). His village was located on the Clearwater River just above the present town of Kooskia, Idaho. The village of about 40 men and 120 women and children raised livestock, planted crops, and generally prospered. In 1863, however, gold was discovered on Nez Perce lands and Looking Glass was a realist concerning the invading

Looking Glass. (National Archives)

whites. Aware of their strength and numbers, at tribal council in 1873 and 1877 he advised against war. Nevertheless, the Nez Perce War began in 1877.

In the early stages of the war, Looking Glass remained aloof from the hostilities, convinced that nothing was to be gained by war. He was falsely accused of aiding the hostiles, however; an arrest warrant was issued, and a fight broke out. The Indians deserted their village, which was destroyed by the whites. Seething with hatred, Looking Glass joined the other nontreaty Nez Perce in their war.

At a council on July 15, 1877, Looking Glass persuaded the other combatants to cross the Lolo Trail and seek safety with the Crow tribe in

Plains country. If necessary they could continue on to join SITTING BULL in Canada and then return to their lands when the trouble had subsided. Looking Glass became war leader of all the bands and was responsible for guiding them. Encountering no resistance from whites along the route, Looking Glass proceeded confidently at a slow and leisurely pace, brushing aside concerns about the pursuing soldiers. The Nez Perce were overtaken on August 9 at Big Hole and suffered significant casualties before they escaped. Looking Glass was held responsible, and—in disgrace—was relieved of his leadership. In September, he again counseled a slower pace because the pursuing soldiers were far behind and his people needed rest. Once more he had his way and was reinstated as leader of the march.

This time, his decision proved fatal. The Indians were overtaken again in the Bear Paw Mountains, only thirty miles from Canada, and defeated. Looking Glass was the last casualty of the Nez Perce War, fatally shot in the head on October 5, 1877.

Laurence Miller

FURTHER READING
Hampton, Bruce. *Children of Grace: The Nez Perce War of 1877.* Lincoln: University of Nebraska Press, 2002.

Looking Horse, Arvol

Born: 1954; Cheyenne River Reservation, South Dakota
Tribal affiliation: Miniconjou Lakota (Sioux)
Significance: Arvol Looking Horse is a major American Indian spiritual leader, Lakota traditionalist, and spokesperson on cultural issues.
Arvol Looking Horse was born on the Cheyenne River Reservation in north central South Dakota, a region that is home to four of the seven bands of Lakota speakers who represent the western branch of the Dakota, Nakota, and Lakota Sioux Confederation known as the Seven Council Fires (*Oceti Sakowin*).

At the age of twelve, Looking Horse became the youngest person to assume the responsibilities of Keeper of the Sacred White Buffalo Calf Pipe, a hereditary post passed down through the generations. He represents the nineteenth generation of Pipe Keepers. the post is connected to one of the Sioux's most sacred legends—that of the White Buffalo Calf Woman. This is the story of how the Sioux received the gift of the sacred pipe as well as their seven sacred rites from a supernatural being

Chief Avrol Looking Horse shakes hands with Democratic presidential hopeful Dennis Kucinich at a rally in Des Moines, Iowa, in January, 2004. (AP/Wide World Photos)

around five centuries ago. Looking Horse's responsibilities as a modern Pipe Keeper include caring for the sacred bundle, serving as a spiritual adviser to his people, protecting and maintaining the nation's sacred traditions, and educating others about the traditional values and wisdom of indigenous peoples.

In 1994, as Pipe Keeper, Looking Horse interpreted the birth of a White Buffalo calf in Wisconsin as an important omen to both the Sioux and all other peoples of the world. Two years later, he inaugurated a special World Peace and Prayer Day to honor the Four Directions on the summer solstice. After 2000, Looking Horse began holding this ceremony at sacred sites in other parts of the world.

Although the Sioux by tradition have neither a single chief with centralized authority nor a formal religious hierarchy, the Keeper of the Sacred White Buffalo Calf Pipe Bundle is the highest honorary post in the Sioux Nation, and Looking Horse's pronouncements are therefore given serious consideration. A growing concern among many Sioux traditionalists and elders is the misuse and misappropriation of their ceremonies by both Indians and non-Indians. In May, 2003, Looking Horse responded to this concern with a proclamation that barred nonnatives from the centers of ceremonies and restricted the handling of the sacred rites to legitimate Lakota, Dakota, and Nakota medicine bundle keepers. These strict provisions of his directive met a mixed reaction. However, Looking Horse's edit led to further discussion on how best to resolve an important issue.

Looking Horse often speaks to audiences on Lakota spirituality and native rights issues such as religious freedom, environmental matters, and cultural survival. He has been one of the Native American voices calling for the return of remains and artifacts from museums and collections and for the protection of sacred sites. He has received invitations to give prayers, perform religious ceremonies, or speak at United Nations-sponsored conferences, in the U.S. Senate, and at the 1996 inauguration of President Bill Clinton. He has also made trips abroad to visit and confer with spiritual leaders of various faiths, such as the Dalai Lama and South Africa's Archbishop Desmond Tutu. His list of honors and recognition include an honorary doctorate from the University of South Dakota and the Canadian Wolf award for his peace efforts.

David A. Crain

MacDonald, Peter

Born: December 16, 1928; near Teec Nos Pos, Navajo Nation, Arizona
Tribal affiliation: Navajo
Significance: Peter MacDonald was one of the most important elected
    tribal leaders during the 1970's and 1980's and was active in the pan-
    Indian movement toward tribal self-determination.

Peter MacDonald's family embraced their Navajo heritage in the northwestern part of the huge Navajo Reservation that covers significant parts of Arizona and New Mexico. His father died when he was very young. Young Peter attended boarding schools but had to leave school in the seventh grade to work. MacDonald served in the Marine Corps as one of the renowned Navajo Code Talkers in the Pacific during World

War II. He then continued his studies at Bacone College, where he received his A.A. degree in 1951, and studied electrical engineering at the University of Oklahoma, where he received his bachelor's degree in 1957. Thereafter he worked for Hughes Aircraft Company in Southern California until 1965.

MacDonald returned to the Navajo Reservation in 1965 and became director of the Office of Navajo Economic Opportunity (ONEO). In this capacity he helped to design tribal self-determination in a political sense. MacDonald worked through the local governance chapter houses on the Navajo Reservation to empower the Navajo people after a century of paternalism. The people established home-improvement programs, physical fitness programs, Head Start programs, and a reservationwide Community Action Program.

In 1970, MacDonald ran successfully for the office of Navajo tribal chairperson. He served four terms in that office, in which he established a sustained pattern of economic and social development on the Navajo Reservation. His policies were based on facilitating reform efforts, protecting natural resources, and fostering interactive development among the Navajo people. He managed to obtain millions of dollars' worth of federal grants for the Navajo, and he fought to obtain more favorable mineral-lease arrangements with non-Navajo companies. In 1975 MacDonald was among the founders of the Council of Energy Resource Tribes (CERT) and was its first elected chairperson.

By the late 1980's, however, MacDonald was being accused of accepting bribes, and the tribal council removed him from office; in 1990 the council convicted him of taking bribes. His legal troubles grew, culminating in his being given a fourteen-year sentence by federal courts in 1992 for racketeering and fraud and, in a separate incident, instigating a riot. By 1996 a faction of the tribe led by Navajo president Albert Hale had decided to forgive MacDonald and began petitioning the federal government to release their former leader, by then in poor health.

In January, 2001, President

Peter MacDonald. (AP/Wide World Photos)

Bill Clinton commuted MacDonald's sentence, freeing the seventy-three-year-old former Navajo leader from a federal prison in Fort Worth, Texas. After leaving the prison, he said that he had no interest in returning to politics.

Howard Meredith

FURTHER READING
MacDonald, Peter, with Ted Schwarz. *The Last Warrior: Peter MacDonald and the Navajo Nation.* New York: Orion Books, 1993.

McGillivray, Alexander

Born: c. 1759; near present-day Montgomery, Alabama
Died: February 17, 1793; Pensacola, Florida
Also known as: Hippo Ilk Mico, Isti Atcagagi Thlucco (Great Beloved Man)
Tribal affiliation: Creek (Muskogee moiety)
Significance: A wealthy trader and skilled diplomat, Alexander McGillivray sought to unite the Creeks and thwart white incursions into Indian territory; he was party to the first treaty concluded with the U.S. government.

Alexander McGillivray was born into the Wind clan of the Creek Indians, the son of Scottish trader and planter Lachlan McGillivray and a French-Creek woman, Sehoy Marchand. At most McGillivray was one-fourth Indian. Until age fourteen, he resided with his mother at his father's trading post on the Tallapoosa River. He was then educated tutorially in Charleston, South Carolina, by the Reverend Farquhar McGillivray, a relative and Presbyterian minister. McGillivray also received business training at a countinghouse in Savannah, Georgia.

At the beginning of the American Revolution, McGillivray became a British agent and commissary to the southern Indians, which involved visits and residences among the various Creek groups. As Loyalists, Lachlan McGillivray and his son fled Georgia, the father returning to Scotland and Alexander, to the area of his birth in Alabama. The younger McGillivray helped to send out war parties to assist British and Loyalist troops during the war. McGillivray himself led raids, plundering Patriot plantations and stealing slaves.

McGillivray assumed leadership of the Creeks in 1783, when he summoned a gathering of representatives from thirty-four Creek towns, resulting in a repudiation of the Treaty of Augusta between Creeks and

Georgia. The treaty had ceded lands to Georgia between the Oconee and Tugaloo Rivers. McGillivray was elected chief and head warrior of all the Creeks.

McGillivray became a silent partner in the commercial firm of Panton, Leslie, and Company, which, under the protection of the Spaniards in the Floridas, had trade outlets at Pensacola and Mobile. McGillivray engaged extensively in the peltry trade and stock raising. He owned three plantations in the Alabama country and had sixty slaves. He worked diligently to strengthen the National Council of the Creeks. In 1784, McGillivray accepted a Spanish appointment as Indian commissary at fifty dollars per month. He hoped to involve the Spaniards in a frontier war against American settlements along the southern frontier. McGillivray's Creeks raided in western Georgia and along the Cumberland River. In 1787, the Spaniards stopped supplying arms to McGillivray and sought strict neutrality with the American government. McGillivray now decided to play the American and Spanish governments against each other.

In 1790, McGillivray led an Indian delegation of thirty Creeks, accompanied by a detachment of U.S. soldiers, to the federal capital in New York City. On August 7, on an extraordinary occasion, McGillivray and the other Creek chiefs met with the U.S. Senate, and on the spot, the Treaty of New York was signed and ratified. McGillivray and the Creeks agreed to come under the protection of the United States and to cede lands between the Ogeechee and Oconee Rivers but not to recognize any other claims by Georgia. In secret clauses, McGillivray received an annual salary of twelve hundred dollars from the U.S. government and was made a brigadier general in the American army. Abigail Adams, wife of the vice president, at the time commented that McGillivray "dresses in our own fashion, speaks English like a native . . . is not very dark, [and is] much a gentleman." The treaty had little immediate effect because McGillivray prevented surveys of the new boundary. He continued, however, as a pensioner of both the Spanish and U.S. governments.

McGillivray had at least two wives and two children, Alexander and Elizabeth. A very heavy drinker, he died of "gout in the stomach" at the home of William Panton in Pensacola and was buried in the garden of the estate.

Harry M. Ward

FURTHER READING
Caughey, John W. *McGillivray of the Creeks.* Norman: University of Oklahoma Press, 1938.

Coker, William S., and Thomas D. Watson. *Indian Traders of the Southeastern Spanish Borderlands: Panton, Leslie and Company and John Forbes and Company, 1783-1847.* Pensacola: University of West Florida Press, 1986.

Green, Michael D. "Alexander McGillivray." In *American Indian Leaders: Studies in Diversity,* edited by R. David Edmunds. Lincoln: University of Nebraska Press, 1980.

Wright, Amos J., Jr. *The McGillivray and McIntosh Traders on the Old Southwest Frontier, 1716-1815.* Montgomery, Ala.: NewSouth Books, 2001.

McIntosh, William

Born: c. 1775; Coweta, Georgia
Died: May 1, 1825; Acorn Town, Alabama
Also known as: Tustennugee Hutkee (White Warrior)
Tribal affiliation: Creek
Significance: William McIntosh led the pro-American faction of the Creeks during the early nineteenth century, signing treaties ceding much land to the United States.

Son of a Scottish father and Creek mother, William McIntosh was principal chief of the important Lower Creek town of Coweta. He and his followers sought a more centralized tribal government and good relations with the United States, even at the cost of ceding tribal lands. McIntosh adopted the lifestyle of a southern planter and moved easily in both Creek and white culture.

McIntosh was opposed by the Red Stick faction of Creek traditionalists and fought against them in the Creek War (1813-1814). McIntosh signed several treaties ceding Creek land, climaxing in the 1825 Treaty of Indian Springs, which ceded most of the tribe's remaining land east of the Mississippi. This violated a decree of the Creek National Council that prescribed the death penalty for any Creek who ceded tribal land without the council's consent. The council ordered McIntosh's execution. This was duly carried out by a party led by the former Red Stick MENEWA. McIntosh's brother and sons subsequently played major roles in Creek politics.

William C. Lowe

FURTHER READING
Griffith, Benjamin W., Jr. *McIntosh and Weatherford: Creek Indian Leaders.* 1988. Reprint. Tuscaloosa: University of Alabama Press, 1998.

McNickle, D'Arcy

Born: January 18, 1904; St. Ignatius, Montana
Died: October 18, 1977; Albuquerque, New Mexico
Tribal affiliation: Salish, Kutenai
Significance: After writing one of the first novels by an American Indian, D'Arcy McNickle worked as an administrator and political organizer and wrote important works of anthropology and history.

Born to a Scotch-Irish father and a French Canadian mother of Cree heritage, D'Arcy McNickle knew from an early age the problems of mixed identity that many Native Americans experience. As he grew up on a northwestern Montana ranch, McNickle, along with his family, was adopted into the Salish-Kootanai Indian tribe. McNickle attended Oxford University and the University of Grenoble in France after completing his undergraduate education at the University of Montana and became as firmly grounded in Native American culture as he was in the white world.

McNickle completed his formal education when the United States was gripped by the Depression and was among the writers who joined the Federal Writers' Project, with which he was associated from 1935 to 1936. His first novel, *The Surrounded* (1936), was an outgrowth of this association. This book focuses on how an Indian tribe disintegrates as the U.S. government encroaches upon and ultimately grabs tribal lands and then sets out to educate the Native American children in such a way as to denigrate their culture and integrate them into the dominant society. Like McNickle, the protagonist of this novel, Archilde, has a mixed identity, being the offspring of a Spanish father and a Native American mother.

In his children's book, *Runner in the Sun* (1954), McNickle deals with similar questions of identity centering on the inevitable conflicts between whites and Native Americans. The Native Americans strive in vain to preserve their culture and retain their grazing lands.

Such also is the focus of McNickle's posthumous novel, *Wind from an Enemy Sky* (1978), in which tribal lands are condemned for the building of a dam and the sacred medicine bundle is given to a museum for display. McNickle also produced several works of nonfiction that grew out of his tenure with the Bureau of Indian Affairs and his directorship of the bureau's division of American Indian development.

The Surrounded has strong autobiographical overtones. The novel focuses on Archilde, through whom the readers see the identity conflicts that trouble the racially mixed hero. Archilde is caught between the white and the Indian cultures, neither of which is unambiguously good or bad, making his position even more difficult.

One of the ways that the novel emphasizes this cultural conflict is by describing many characters and events as opposing pairs. Catharine LaLoup Leon and Max Leon, for example, each present to Archilde some of the positive aspects of Indian and white culture, respectively. The Indian dancing on the Fourth of July, full of ancient meaning and beauty, is contrasted with the white people's meaningless dance in a dark, bare hall. The novel expresses particular concern for the decline of Native American culture. McNickle describes in great detail the transformation of Mike and Narcisse as the older women prepare them for the dance, emphasizing the beauty of traditional culture. McNickle applies his expertise as an anthropologist to the detailed explanation of all the old dances, stressing each dance's particular meaning. This is contrasted with the scene at the Fourth of July dance, where white people come to laugh disrespectfully at the old men as they move slowly through the only dances that they are still allowed to do.

In *Wind from an Enemy Sky*, McNickle writes of the difficult period in American history during which the U.S. government attempted to subdue Native Americans peacefully. McNickle, a government employee for most of his life, presents a balanced view of what occurred during this period in one small Native American enclave in the Flathead Lake-St. Ignatius area of Montana.

On the surface, McNickle presents the story of a Native American extended family that includes Pock Face, who, carrying his grandfather's rifle, steals furtively into a canyon where white developers have built a dam on tribal land. The Little Elk Indians equate the damming of their river with its murder. The dam has an immediate negative impact upon fishing and farming on their tribal lands. As Pock Face and Theobald, his cousin, approach the dam, they spy a white man walking across its surface. Pock Face fires one shot. Jim Cooke, ironically on his last day of work before going east to marry, dies instantly.

The remainder of the story revolves around the government's efforts to mete out justice to the murderer. This surface story, however, provides the justification for a compelling subtext that illustrates the difficulties involved when one well-established culture attempts to impose itself upon another. *Wind from an Enemy Sky*, maintaining throughout an objective view of two disparate cultures, proffers a poignant political and social statement about culture and values in multiethnic settings.

Wind from an Enemy Sky is concerned largely with the inability of the Native American and dominant societies in the United States to communicate productively with each other. As McNickle presents it, Native American society is deeply suspicious of the dominant society that has, through the years, oppressed it. Promises made have seldom been promises kept. The suspicions that keep Indians from interacting productively with government agencies are spawned not by paranoia but rather by extensive bitter experience.

The dam the government built has diverted a river on which the Indians depend. The waters that the dam captures will nourish the fields of white homesteaders, to whom the government has sold Indian lands at $1.25 per acre. The Native Americans look upon these land sales as forms of robbery. Added to this justifiable charge is the charge that white officials have kidnapped Indian children and sent them to distant government schools against their will.

McNickle suggests the inevitability of tragedy in dealings between Native Americans and representatives of the dominant society. He also demonstrates how some Native Americans—Henry Jim and The Boy, for example—move into the white world or attempt to straddle the two worlds, placing them in impossible positions. For Henry Jim, it is impossible to shake the Native American heritage, which the dying man finally embraces again.

R. Baird Shuman
Updated by Kelly C. Walter

FURTHER READING

Bevis, William. "Native American Novels: Homing In." In *Recovering the Word: Essays on Native American Literature*, edited by Brian Swann and Arnold Krupat. Berkeley: University of California Press, 1982.

Edmunds, R. David, ed. *The New Warriors: Native American Leaders Since 1900*. Lincoln: University of Nebraska Press, 2001.

Oaks, Priscilla. "The First Generation of Native American Novelists." *MELUS* 5 (1978): 57-65.

Owens, Louis. "The 'Map of the Mind': D'Arcy McNickle and the American Indian Novel." *Western American Literature* 19 (Winter, 1985): 275-283.

_____. "The Red Road to Nowhere: D'Arcy McNickle's *The Surrounded* and 'The Hungry Generations.'" *American Indian Quarterly* 13 (Summer, 1989): 239-248.

Parker, Dorothy R. *Singing an Indian Song: A Biography of D'Arcy McNickle*. Lincoln: University of Nebraska Press, 1992.

Purdy, John Lloyd. *The Legacy of D'Arcy McNickle: Writer, Historian, Activist*. Norman: University of Oklahoma Press, 1996.

_____. *Word Ways: The Novels of D'Arcy McNickle.* Tucson: University of Arizona Press, 1990.

Ruppert, James. *D'Arcy McNickle.* Boise, Idaho: Boise State University Press, 1988.

_____. "Textual Perspectives and the Reader in *The Surrounded.*" In *Narrative Chance: Postmodern Discourse on Native American Indian Literatures,* edited by Gerald Vizenor. Albuquerque: University of New Mexico Press, 1989.

Vest, Jay Hansford C. "Feather Boy's Promise: Sacred Geography and Environmental Ethics in D'Arcy McNickle's *Wind from an Enemy Sky.*" *American Indian Quarterly* 17 (Winter, 1993): 45-68.

McQueen, Peter

Born: c. 1780; near Tallassee, Florida
Died: 1820; Florida
Also known as: Talmuches Harjo
Tribal affiliation: Creek, Seminole
Significance: Peter McQueen's band of Creek Red Sticks touched off the Creek War (1813-1814) by battling Alabama militia at Burnt Corn Creek.

Peter McQueen was born in the Upper Creek town of Tallassee, the son of a white father and Creek mother. Though he prospered as a trader, he was drawn to the Red Stick faction that sought to preserve the traditional lifestyle and resist white settlement. As he returned from Pensacola, West Florida, with munitions and supplies on July 27, 1813, McQueen and his party of warriors were attacked by Alabama militia at Burnt Corn Creek. McQueen turned back the militia in what is usually considered to be the first engagement of the Creek War.

The tide turned against the Red Sticks, however, and after 1814 McQueen led his followers into northern Florida, where continued friction led to General Andrew Jackson's invasion (the First Seminole War, 1817-1818). McQueen, now regarded as a Seminole, was defeated but evaded capture. He fled to southern Florida, where he died. His band survived to become followers of his grandnephew, OSCEOLA.

William C. Lowe

Mangas Coloradas

Born: c. 1791; present-day New Mexico
Died: January 19, 1863
Also known as: Red Sleeves, Dasoda-hae (He Just Sits There)
Tribal affiliation: Apache
Significance: Mangas Coloradas was an important war chief during the
    era of the so-called Apache Wars.

Along with his equally famous son-in-law, Cochise, a Chiricahua Apache,
Mangas Coloradas was a leader in the guerrilla warfare waged by the
Apaches against the Mexicans. Toward the end of his life, Americans re-
placed Mexicans as his adversaries.

A long peace was disrupted in 1860 when prospectors discovered
gold in the Mimbres Mountains, homeland of Mangas Coloradas's people. During a visit to negotiate peace, the great leader was bound to a
tree and whipped. He was released to return home with deep wounds.

The decisive event for both Cochise and Mangas Coloradas was probably the "Bascomb affair"—Lieutenant George N. Bascomb's charge
that the Chiricahua Apaches had kidnapped a "half-breed" boy. The
Chiricahuas blamed the Coyotero
Apaches. During the investigation,
prisoners were murdered on both
sides; retaliation replaced investigation and dialogue.

During the following summer, in
July of 1862, Mangas Coloradas and
Cochise were besieged by infantry
from Star Chief Carleton's command. In the fighting that ensued,
Mangas Coloradas was wounded in
the chest. Cochise took his father-
in-law to a surgeon in the Mexican
village of Janos. A strong, broad-
shouldered man, still towering over
six feet tall in his seventies, Mangas
returned to his Mimbres Mountains
later that year.

In January of 1863, perhaps reflecting on the "perpetual peace"
he had pledged in an 1852 treaty,

Mangas Coloradas. (Library of Congress)

Mangas Coloradas committed his final days to securing peace for his people. Although accounts vary, historians agree that he went alone and unarmed to discuss peace under a white flag with Captain Edmond Shirland of the California Volunteers. The great leader's body was found in a ditch the next day. His feet and legs had been burned by heated bayonets, his body was pierced by close-range multiple bullet wounds, and his head had been removed and defleshed to be sold. From that point, the Apaches went to war in earnest.

Tonya Huber

FURTHER READING
Sweeney, Edwin R. *Mangas Coloradas: Chief of the Chiricahua Apaches.* Norman: University of Oklahoma Press, 1998.

Mankato

Born: c. 1830; near present-day Minneapolis, Minnesota
Died: September 23, 1862; Wood Lake, Minnesota
Also known as: Mahkato (Blue Earth)
Tribal affiliation: Santee Lakota (Sioux)
Significance: Mankato was a leader of the Minnesota Uprising of 1862, an event which marked the end of the Indian wars in Minnesota.

Born on the Minnesota River, Mankato became a village chief in 1853 following the death of his father. With LITTLE CROW, he worked to maintain peace with white settlers, helping to negotiate the Treaty of Washington of 1858. By 1862, the failure of government officials to provide food and supplies as indicated in the treaties caused tensions. Faced with starvation, small groups of warriors attacked isolated settlers. Caught in the accelerating conflict, Mankato joined Little Crow in the Minnesota Uprising. After Little Crow was wounded on August 22, 1862, during the attack on Fort Ridgely, Mankato assumed command. He led attacks on New Ulm and Birch Coulee. He was killed in the Battle of Wood Lake on September 23, struck in the back by a cannonball. He was buried in the bluffs of the Yellow Medicine River so that whites could not find his body.

Charles Louis Kammer III

FURTHER READING
Carley, Kenneth. *The Dakota War of 1862.* 2d ed. St. Paul: Minnesota Historical Society Press, 2001.

Keenan, Jerry. *The Great Sioux Uprising: Rebellion on the Plains, August-September, 1862.* Cambridge, Mass.: Da Capo Press, 2003.

Mankiller, Wilma Pearl

Born: November 18, 1945; Tahlequah, Oklahoma
Tribal affiliation: Cherokee
Significance: After taking part in the Indian civil rights movement of the 1960's and later working to improve conditions among rural Indian communities, Wilma Pearl Mankiller gained national respect during the 1980's when she became the first woman to head a major Native American tribe.

Wilma Pearl Mankiller was born in 1945 in the W. W. Hastings Indian Hospital in Tahlequah, Oklahoma. Her father, Charley Mankiller, a full-blooded Cherokee, married her mother, Clara Irene Sitton, of Dutch-Irish descent, in 1937. Wilma was the sixth of their eleven children. The family lived on Mankiller Flats in Adair County, northeastern Oklahoma. Mankiller Flats was an allotment of 160 acres that had been given to John Mankiller, Charley's father, in 1907, when Oklahoma became a state. The name "Mankiller" was the Cherokee military title of Wilma's great-great-great-grandfather, Mankiller of Tellico, in the eighteenth century. Tellico, in eastern Tennessee, was part of the original Cherokee Nation. The Mankillers and most other Cherokee were forcibly moved to the Indian Territory, later the state of Oklahoma, on the infamous Trail of Tears in 1838 and 1839.

The first eleven years of Wilma's life were spent on Mankiller Flats and in traditional Cherokee culture. In 1956, however, the Mankiller family moved to San Francisco, California, as part of a government relocation plan to move American Indians to large cities and into mainstream American life. Life in San Francisco was a culture shock, especially for the Mankiller children, but they soon adjusted to their new life. On November 13, 1963, Wilma Mankiller was married to Hugo Olaya, a member of a wealthy Ecuadorian family who was then a student in San Francisco. Two daughters, Felicia and Gina, were born to the couple before differences in lifestyles led to a divorce in 1975. During the years of her first marriage, Mankiller earned a degree from San Francisco State College.

Mankiller's Cherokee background was revived, and her activist work was initiated, in 1969, when a group of American Indians occupied Alcatraz Island, in San Francisco Bay, to gain support for American Indian rights. Wilma and many others in her family participated in that occupation. Charley Mankiller, who had become a longshoreman and a union organizer in California, died in 1971. His body was returned to his native Adair County, Oklahoma, for burial. That burial seemed to be a signal for the Mankillers to return, one by one, to Oklahoma. Wilma returned after her divorce in 1975. Only two older brothers remained in California. In Oklahoma, Mankiller was able to emulate Nancy WARD, an eighteenth century Cherokee woman who had also lived in both the Indian and mainstream American worlds. Mankiller was able to combine the best of Cherokee tradition with the best of European-American civilization.

Mankiller had begun her work to improve American Indian life before she left California. In 1974, with Bill Wahpapah, she cofounded the American Indian Community School in Oakland. Her return to Oklahoma in 1975, however, marked the beginning of her full-time service to the Cherokee Nation. The Cherokee Nation, with 55,000 acres of northeastern Oklahoma and a population of about 67,000 people, ranks second only to the Navajo in size among American Indian tribes in the United States. When Oklahoma became a state in 1907, the traditional tribal government of the Cherokee was dissolved. This created a unique political organization, neither a reservation nor an autonomous government, with unique political and social problems. Mankiller now began directing her energy toward solving those problems.

Wilma Mankiller receives the Presidential Medal of Freedom from President Bill Clinton in 1998. (AP/Wide World Photos)

Mankiller's first regular job with the Cherokee Nation began in 1977, when she was hired as an economic-stimulus coordinator. Her job was to guide as many people as possible toward university training in such fields as environmental science and health, and then to integrate them back into their communities. Mankiller eventually became frustrated with the slow-moving male-dominated bureaucracy of the Cherokee Nation.

Before Europeans came to

North America, Cherokee women had occupied leadership roles in tribal affairs. The title of Beloved Woman was given to those who performed extraordinary service. The first Europeans to contact the Cherokee accused them of having a "petticoat government." After this contact, the influence of Cherokee women began to decrease. A significant development in 1971 helped to open the way for a return to more female participation in Cherokee affairs. A revision of the tribal constitution provided that, for the first time since Oklahoma statehood in 1907, the principal chief would be elected by the people of the tribe rather than be appointed by the president of the United States. An entirely new constitution in 1976 solidified that change and provided for the election of a new fifteen-member tribal council.

In 1979, after working for two years as an economic-stimulus coordinator, Wilma Mankiller was made a program-development specialist and grant writer. Her immediate success in this position, especially in writing grant proposals, brought her to the attention of the tribal council and Principal Chief Ross Swimmer. This phase of Mankiller's work was soon interrupted by tragedy. On November 9, 1979, she was seriously injured in a head-on collision on a country road. The driver of the other car was Sherry Morris, a woman who happened to be a close friend of Mankiller. Morris was killed. In her autobiography, *Mankiller: A Chief and Her People* (1993), Mankiller gives a moving account of that tragedy.

Within a year of the accident, Mankiller was afflicted with a rare form of muscular dystrophy. These back-to-back experiences caused her to reach more deeply into her Cherokee background and led to a change in her philosophy of life. In 1981, although still undergoing physical therapy, Mankiller was able to return to her work with the Cherokee Nation, and she did so with her old energy. In that year, she helped to establish the Cherokee Nation Community Development Department and became its first director.

The next step in Mankiller's career came in 1983, when Chief Ross Swimmer asked her to join his reelection ticket as his deputy chief. This request, by which Chief Swimmer recognized Mankiller's potential, was very unusual because Swimmer was a conservative Republican and Mankiller was a liberal Democrat. After first declining, Mankiller accepted the offer as a way to help her people. One of Mankiller's opponents for deputy chief was Agnes Cowan, the first woman to serve on the tribal council. Mankiller was surprised when gender became an immediate issue in the campaign. The hostility toward Mankiller ranged from having her automobile tires slashed to death threats. She fought that negative campaigning by conducting a very positive and cheerful campaign based primarily on her past service to the Cherokee people. The victory for the Swimmer-Mankiller ticket meant that, on August 14, 1983, Mankiller became the first female deputy chief in Cherokee history.

In 1984, Deputy Chief Mankiller participated in a momentous meeting—a reunion between the Cherokee Nation of Oklahoma and the Eastern Band of the Cherokee from North Carolina. The Eastern Band had descended from those who escaped the Trail of Tears by hiding in the mountains. This meeting, the first full tribal council since 1838, was held at Red Clay in Tennessee, the last capital of the original Cherokee Nation.

A major career surprise for Mankiller came in 1985, when President Ronald Reagan nominated Chief Swimmer as assistant secretary of the interior for Indian affairs. This meant that, on December 14, 1985, Mankiller was inaugurated as the first woman principal chief of the Cherokee Nation. Chief Mankiller immediately declared that economic growth would be the primary goal of her administration. She described her guiding theory as bubble-up economics, in which the people would plan and implement projects that would benefit the tribe in future years, even though the present generation might not benefit. Until the next scheduled election in 1987, however, Mankiller had to govern without a mandate from the people. She faced strong opposition that limited her real power.

In October of 1986, while considering whether to run for a full term, Mankiller married Charlie Soap, a full-blooded Cherokee whom she had first met in 1977. It was Soap who persuaded her to run in 1987, and she won in a runoff election. Because the Cherokee had now returned to the strong female leadership of their past, Mankiller described her election as a step forward and a step backward at the same time. Although Chief Mankiller's first full term was successful in terms of economic progress, her level of personal involvement was influenced by a resurgence of kidney disease, from which she had suffered for many years. This difficulty led to a kidney transplant in June, 1990. The donor was Wilma's older brother Don.

In her early years as Principal Chief, Wilma P. Mankiller produced many significant results, both tangible and intangible. The most important of the former is a tribal Department of Commerce, which was created soon after Mankiller's 1987 victory. This department coordinates the business enterprises of the tribe and tries to balance tribal income with the needs of tribal members, creating jobs and producing a profit.

The intangible results include a renewed spirit of independence for all Cherokee and a renewed confidence that Cherokee women can once again influence the destiny of the tribe.

In 1990, Chief Mankiller signed a historic self-governance agreement that authorized the Cherokee Nation to administer federal funds that previously had been administered by the Bureau of Indian Affairs in Washington. The same year saw a revitalizing of tribal courts and tribal police as well as the establishment of a Cherokee Nation tax commission. The most outstanding proof of Chief Mankiller's impact on the Cherokee Nation was her reelection victory in 1991, one year after her kidney transplant, with more than 82 percent of the votes. The same election put six women on the fifteen-member tribal council. In 1995, she resigned from her post as principal chief in order to focus on local concerns in Oklahoma.

Glenn L. Swygart

FURTHER READING

Edmunds, R. David, ed. *The New Warriors: Native American Leaders Since 1900.* Lincoln: University of Nebraska Press, 2001.

Mankiller, Wilma. *Mankiller: A Chief and Her People.* New York: St. Martin's Press, 1993.

Nabokov, Peter, ed. *Native American Testimony: A Chronicle of Indian-White Relations from Prophecy to the Present, 1492-1992.* Foreword by Vine Deloria, Jr. New York: Viking, 1991.

Van Viema, David. "Activist Wilma Mankiller Is Set to Become the First Female Chief of the Cherokee Nation." *People Weekly* (December 2, 1985): 91-92.

Wallace, Michele. "Wilma Mankiller." *Ms.* (January, 1988): 68-69.

Manuelito

Born: c. 1818; near Bears Ears Peak (now in Utah)
Died: 1894; Navajo Reservation, New Mexico
Also known as: Hastin Ch'ilhajinii (Man of the Black Weeds), Hashkeh Naabah (Angry Warrior), Pistol Bullet
Tribal affiliation: Navajo
Significance: A leader in the Navajo War of 1863-1866, Manuelito was the first commander of the Navajo police, established in 1872.

Manuelito, born in southeastern Utah, became a prominent warrior and married the daughter of a well-known leader. When his father-in-

Manuelito, as depicted by artist E. A. Burbank.
(National Archives)

law was killed by federal soldiers, Manuelito assumed his place.

A conflict in 1858 led to greater prominence. Federal soldiers at Fort Defiance in New Mexico demanded the use of pastures that had been reserved for Navajos. When troopers shot Navajo horses, Navajos undertook raids to replace the losses. The Navajos had chosen a leader to negotiate with the Federals; when he resigned, Manuelito was selected in his place.

Manuelito repudiated the previous agreements with the United States government, so soldiers burned his home. He in turn attacked Fort Defiance in April, 1860, and mauled a pursuing force. The post was abandoned in a treaty signed by Manuelito in February of 1861, but conflict erupted anew at Fort Fauntleroy in September, 1861, after a dispute over a horse race resulted in the slaughter of more than a dozen Navajos by soldiers.

The Navajo War of 1863-1866 was delayed by federal efforts to cope with Confederates, but scorched-earth tactics, including the destruction of Navajo refuges in Canyon de Chelly, soon forced most Navajo leaders to surrender. One of the last was Manuelito, who in September, 1866, led twenty-three starving warriors to join the other Navajos at Bosque Redondo, where many died from disease and lack of food.

Manuelito was one of the delegates who went to Washington in 1868 and secured a reservation of 3.5 million acres. Recognized as a prominent leader by U.S. administrators, in 1872 he became the commander of the new Navajo police. He was ruthless in maintaining order, but he represented the Navajos twice again in Washington and led a rebellion in 1875 against corrupt federal administration.

Manuelito advocated education for the Navajos; ironically, his son

died while at school. Depressed, Manuelito resigned as chief and succumbed to alcoholism. He died from measles and pneumonia.

Richard B. McCaslin

Martínez, Crescencio

Born: c. 1890; San Ildefonso, New Mexico
Died: June 20, 1918; Santa Fe?, New Mexico
Also known as: Ta'e or Te E (Home of the Elk)
Tribal affiliation: San Ildefonso Pueblo
Significance: Crescencio Martínez is considered by many to be the fa-
ther of watercolor painting among Puebloan Indians, leading to the
Southwestern School of Indian painting.

Crescencio Martínez began drawing sometime before 1910, using crayons he picked up while working as a janitor at the San Ildefonso Day
School. Edgar Hewett, excavating near San Ildefonso in about 1915,
hired Crescencio as a laborer and found him drawing on the ends of
cardboard boxes. Hewett gave him drawing paper and watercolors, and
bought many of his drawings. In 1916, Crescencio began painting the
summer and winter dances of his pueblo for a museum commission arranged by Hewett. The ease with which his work sold influenced the
men of his pueblo to turn to watercolor painting for income, and it was
his style they often followed.

Crescencio married Maximiliana (Anna) Martínez, a sister of potter
María Antonía MARTÍNEZ and herself an accomplished potter. Crescencio painted Anna's pots, as well as those of his mother, sister, and
sister-in-law. Other relatives were painters Alfonso Roybal, Romando
Vigil, and Alfredo Montoya.

Anna and Crescencio moved to Santa Fe during World War I, working for the Rocky Mountain Camp Company grooming horses. There
they continued potting and painting. Crescencio Martínez died of
pneumonia.

Cheryl Claassen

Martínez, Julián

Born: 1897; San Ildefonso, New Mexico
Died: March, 1943; San Ildefonso, New Mexico
Tribal affiliation: San Ildefonso Pueblo (Tewa)

Significance: Julián Martínez collaborated with his wife, María Antonía MARTÍNEZ, in making pottery prized by museums and collectors worldwide.

In 1908, Julián Martínez was one of several men from San Ildefonso hired to help with the excavations at Tyuonyi and Frijoles Canyon, led by Edgar Hewett, director of the Museum of New Mexico. When Hewett wanted a potter who could produce pottery based on fragments of prehistoric vessels found at the sites, Julián suggested that his wife, María, might attempt it. She agreed, on condition that Julián decorate the pots. María was an exceptional potter who, by simply coiling the clay, could make large, thin-walled pots of perfect symmetry. Julián proved to be an equally exceptional painter, decorating the pots with his own intricate and flawlessly executed designs based on his intensive study of both prehistoric and historic sources.

After producing polychrome pottery for several years, María and Julián began to experiment with the firing technique which finally resulted in the black-on-black ware (c. 1918-1920). Julián, by now the leading pottery decorator at San Ildefonso, developed his two most innovative design elements, the *avanyu* (plumed serpent) and his own adaptation of the prehistoric Mimbres feather design, for use on the black pottery.

Although Julián is best known for his designs on María's pottery, his paintings and graphics do appear in many major collections of American Indian art in museums throughout the United States.

LouAnn Faris Culley

FURTHER READING

Berlo, Janet C., and Ruth B. Phillips. *Native North American Art*. New York: Oxford University Press, 1998.

Spivey, Richard L. *The Legacy of Maria Poveka Martinez*. Rev. ed. Santa Fe: Museum of New Mexico Press, 2003.

Martínez, María Antonía

Born: April 5, 1887; San Ildefonso, New Mexico
Died: July 20, 1980; San Ildefonso, New Mexico
Also known as: Poveka (Pond Lily)
Tribal affiliation: San Ildefonso Pueblo
Significance: María Martínez revitalized the vanishing art of pottery among Pueblo peoples.

In 1908, María Martínez was asked by archaeologist Edgar Hewett to re-produce and decorate pottery in the style of that being unearthed near San Ildefonso. At that time, few women in the pueblo made pots. Hewett bought and reordered Martínez's simple polychrome reproductions, launching a revival in pottery-making in the pueblo and immeasurably helping its economy. Decorating her pots were Crescencio MARTÍNEZ; her sister Maximiliana; her husband, Julián MARTÍNEZ; her daughter-in-law Santana; and her son POPOVI DA.

Martínez's first son was born in 1904, and three other children followed. In 1909, she became the leader of an important women's ceremonial society. María worked all year forming, firing, slipping, and burnishing pottery; by 1915, she had far surpassed all other potters in the pueblo in skill and reputation. In 1921, she and Julián revealed their technique for making black-on-black pottery. In 1923, she initiated the practice of signing pottery—using the name "Marie" until the 1950's because white customers were more familiar with it. She earned about five thousand dollars from pottery sales in 1931, and one dollar per hour for teaching pottery classes. In the course of her seventy-year career, she won hundreds of prizes; showed at three World's Fairs; visited the White House four times; and received the Craftsmanship Medal, the Palmes Academiques Medal, the Jane Addams Award, and honorary doctoral degrees.

Cheryl Claassen

FURTHER READING

Berlo, Janet C., and Ruth B. Phillips. *Native North American Art.* New York: Oxford University Press, 1998.

Marriott, Alice. *Maria: The Potter of San Ildefonso.* 1948. Reprint. Norman: University of Oklahoma Press, 1987.

Perdue, Theda, ed. *Sifters: Native American Women's Lives.* New York: Oxford University Press, 2001.

Spivey, Richard L. *The Legacy of Maria Poveka Martinez.* Rev. ed. Santa Fe: Museum of New Mexico Press, 2003.

Massasoit

Born: c. 1580; near present-day Bristol, Rhode Island
Died: 1661; near present-day Bristol, Rhode Island
Also known as: Ousamequin (Yellow Feather)
Tribal affiliation: Wampanoag

Significance: From the landing of the *Mayflower* in 1620 to his death in 1662, Massasoit worked to preserve a peaceful relationship with the English colonists.

Massasoit was born about 1580 in Rhode Island. He became the grand sachem over the Wampanoag (also known as Pokanoket) towns along the coastal regions of Massachusetts and Rhode Island. Massasoit led the sachems of the individual towns, but he was not an authoritarian ruler.

Massasoit was responsible for the welfare of his people. When the Plymouth Colony was established in 1620, Massasoit determined that his people would be best served by friendly relations with the colonists. In March, 1621, Massasoit went to Plymouth. Soon trade and communication between the Wampanoags and the English were well established.

When the colonists held their first service of thanksgiving in November, 1621, they invited the Wampanoags. Massasoit and about ninety others went, taking with them five deer.

Until his death in 1661, Massasoit was able to maintain peace with the English; however, the increasing number of colonists soon caused the goodwill to dissolve, leading to the bloody King Philip's War (1675-1676), led by Massasoit's son.

Glenn L. Swygart

Engraved depiction of Massasoit meeting settlers of Plymouth Colony in 1621.
(Library of Congress)

FURTHER READING

Peirce, Ebenezer Weaver. *Indian History, Biography, and Genealogy: Pertaining to the Good Sachem Massasoit of the Wampanoag Tribe, and His Descendants.* Freeport, N.Y.: Books for Libraries Press, 1972.

Weeks, Alvin Gardner. *Massasoit of the Wampanoags.* Fall River, Mass.: The Plimpton Press, 1919.

Mato Tope

Born: c. 1795; place unknown
Died: July 30, 1837; place unknown
Also known as: Four Bears
Tribal affiliation: Mandan
Significance: Mato Tope accused whites of genocide when an epidemic of smallpox nearly wiped out his tribe.

There were two Mandan leaders known as Mato Tope, or Four Bears; they were father and son. Mato Tope the elder was born around 1795 and died in 1837; his son, who became chief after his father's death, died in 1861.

Mato Tope the elder was second chief of the Mandans when George Catlin visited in 1832 and painted his portrait. Catlin said at the time that the elder Mato Tope was one of his favorite artistic subjects and Native American friends. Karl Bodmer also painted the elder Mato Tope when he visited the Mandans two years after Catlin, and the portraits by the two men were widely reproduced.

The elder Mato Tope was selected head chief in 1837 just as a smallpox epidemic was sweeping in with an influx of transient whites. Smallpox descended on the Mandans with a virulence that ultimately killed all but thirty-one of some sixteen hundred people. Mato Tope succumbed to the disease on July 30, 1837. On the day he died, he is said to have raged against the smallpox epidemic that was killing him and his people and to have called upon his people to rise up and kill all white people. (Whether he actually made this speech has been debated by historians.) After the younger Mato Tope assumed tribal leadership, the Mandans attempted to find a strategy to resist further white encroachment, but they did not launch a major campaign against whites. The younger Mato Tope was a signatory of the 1851 Fort Laramie Treaty.

Matonabbee

Born: c. 1736; near Fort Prince of Wales, Hudson Bay, Canada (now in Manitoba, Canada)

Died: August, 1782; Fort Prince of Wales, Hudson Bay, Canada (now in Manitoba, Canada)

Tribal affiliation: Ojibwa (Chippewa)

Significance: As a guide for the Hudson's Bay Company, Matonabbee led the third Coppermine expedition in search of precious metals and the Northwest Passage.

Following his father's death, Matonabbee was adopted and educated by the Hudson's Bay Company governor, Richard Norton. With Norton's recall to England, Matonabbee joined relatives in a Chippewa hunting band roaming regions of present-day northern Manitoba, Saskatchewan, and eastern Northwest Territories.

At the age of sixteen, Matonabbee returned to Fort Prince of Wales, where he hunted animals for the British and accompanied them during several trading trips. After serving as an interpreter and guide, he rose to the position of chief of his tribe and became a respected ally of the Hudson's Bay Company. In 1770, Matonabbee found and aided the return of the stranded second Coppermine expedition under Samuel Hearne. Afterward, Hearne and Matonabbee made a third expedition, from 1771 to 1772, to search for metals and the Northwest Passage. During the expedition, Matonabbee led his men in a raid against a band of Inuit, their traditional enemies. After smallpox killed many of his people in 1782, Matonabbee committed suicide.

Mary E. Virginia

Means, Russell

Born: November 10, 1939; Pine Ridge Reservation, South Dakota

Tribal affiliation: Oglala Lakota (Sioux)

Significance: Russell Means has been a principal leader of the American Indian Movement (AIM).

Russell Charles Means was born on the Pine Ridge Reservation in South Dakota on November 10, 1939, and reared in Oakland, California, where his parents moved during World War II. In 1969, he was asked to join the American Indian Movement (AIM). He soon revealed talent as a media strategist, attracting national attention through actions such as painting Plymouth Rock red on Thanksgiving Day of 1971.

Russell Means listens to questions during a news conference at the Colorado Libertarian Party's convention in 2001. (AP/Wide World Photos)

By the time of the Trail of Broken Treaties occupation of the Bureau of Indian Affairs (BIA) headquarters building in Washington, D.C., in November, 1972, Means was one of AIM's primary leaders. He continued this role in subsequent confrontations, notably the armed standoff at Wounded Knee from February to May of 1973.

After Wounded Knee, Means was charged with forty-seven felonies, most of them dismissed when it was proved that the Federal Bureau of Investigation (FBI) and federal prosecutors had fabricated evidence with which to "neutralize" him. Meanwhile, he suffered four assassination attempts. He was finally imprisoned in 1978, after South Dakota obtained his conviction on the somewhat arcane charge of "criminal syndicalism." Means later resumed his activism, launching the occupation of Yellow Thunder Camp in the Black Hills (1981 to 1985) as part of an effort to recover Lakota treaty lands. In 1988, he became the first American Indian to pursue the U.S. presidency in an attempt to "inject Indian issues into the consciousness of the American public."

In the years prior to the Columbian quincentenary, Means also led a series of demonstrations in Denver, Colorado—the city in which commemoration of "Columbus Day" originated—to "protest celebration of the genocide of American Indians embodied in the Columbian legacy." He was successful in stopping the events planned for Denver in 1992. In 1995, Means published his autobiography, *Where White Men Fear to Tread*.

Ward Churchill

FURTHER READING

Edmunds, R. David, ed. *The New Warriors: Native American Leaders Since 1900*. Lincoln: University of Nebraska Press, 2001.

Matthiessen, Peter. *In the Spirit of Crazy Horse*. 2d ed. New York: Viking Press, 1991.

Means, Russell, and Marvin J. Wolf. *Where White Men Fear to Tread: The Autobiography of Russell Means*. New York: St. Martin's Press, 1995.

Smith, Paul Chaat, and Robert Allen Warrior. *Like a Hurricane: The Indian Movement from Alcatraz to Wounded Knee*. New York: New Press, 1996.

Weyler, Rex. *Blood of the Land: The U.S. Government and Corporate War Against the First Nation*. 2d ed. Philadelphia: New Society Publishers, 1992.

Medicine, Bea

Born: August 1, 1924; Standing Rock Reservation, Wakpala, South Dakota

Also known as: Beatrice Medicine

Tribal affiliation: Standing Rock Lakota (Sioux)

Significance: One of the few Native American women with an advanced degree in anthropology, Bea Medicine has specialized in studies of Lakota culture.

A Standing Rock Lakota elder, Bea Medicine taught in schools sponsored by the U.S. Indian Service and promoted ethnic studies programs and urban Indian centers throughout the United States and Canada. She holds a doctoral degree in anthropology from the University of Wisconsin at Madison and is professor emerita at California State University at Northridge.

Medicine has studied contemporary religious movements, Native American women's lives, pan-Indianism, Dakota ethnohistory, reservation culture, and Native American sovereignty. She did pioneering research on self-actualizing Plains Indian women in *The Hidden Half* (1983). She has argued that throughout North America, Native American men and traditionally women valued each other's contributions to traditional life, and that their complementary roles provided community stability and mutual satisfaction. Medicine has served as a cultural bridge between Native Americans and representatives of federal and state agencies and has mediated between Native Americans and anthropologists. Her publications include scores of articles on various aspects of Indian life and cultures, and she has received the prestigious Distinguished Service Award from the American Anthropological Association.

In her professional writings, Medicine sees from within Native American cultures while maintaining the distance of a trained anthropologist. With her uniquely hybrid perspective, she has functioned as a valuable observer of, and commentator on, Native American cultures. For example, she recognized that the Sun Dance had become a tourist attraction on the Lakota reservation by the 1950's, and during the political activism of the 1960's, she appreciated the insistence of American Indian Movement (AIM) activists such as Russell MEANS to restore the traditional skin piercing on the fourth day of the Sun Dance ritual "as a new badge of commitment." She has also praised Lakota women for making the traditional flesh offerings in the Sun Dance. She sees that many Lakota women have acted as revitalizers of traditional rituals, such as the Sun Dance, in which they have mentored younger women.

Medicine perceives that government prohibitions against Native American languages have severely damaged the communication skills of American Indians and Native Alaskans because languages are core expressive elements in cultures. However, she also believes that the persistence of native languages attests to the great vigor of native people and their cultures, as language is central to maintaining cultural continuity and native identity.

Joanna Yin

FURTHER READING

Medicine, Bea. *Becoming an Anthropologist and Remaining Native.* Urbana: University of Illinois Press, 2001.

_____, and Patricia Albers. *The Hidden Half: Studies of Plains Indian Women.* Lanham, Md.: University Press of America, 1983.

Menewa

Born: c. 1765; along the Tallopoosa River (now in Alabama)
Died: 1865; Indian Territory (now in Oklahoma)
Also known as: Hothlepoya, Crazy War Hunter
Tribal affiliation: Creek
Significance: As a leader of the Creek war faction, Menewa fought Andrew Jackson at the Battle of Horseshoe Bend.

As a young man in Tennessee, Menewa established a warrior's reputation for daring horse raids. He became a leader of the traditional Creek warrior faction, the Red Sticks. When William McINTOSH, leader of the White Sticks peace faction, committed a murder, white settlers burned Menewa's village.

Thereafter, Menewa joined the Red Sticks's principal leader, William WEATHERFORD, aiding TECUMSEH, leader of a pan-Indian rebellion. Menewa fought General Andrew Jackson during the Creek War and was shot eight times and left for dead at the Battle of Horseshoe Bend in 1814. After recovering from his wounds, he surrendered, forfeiting all of his lands.

The Creeks appointed Menewa executioner of McIntosh, who in 1825 had illegally ceded twenty-five million acres of Creek land. Thereafter, Menewa traveled to Washington with Creek leader OPOTHLEYA-HOLO and translator Paddy Carr for negotiations. In exchange for

A circa 1837 lithograph depiction of Menewa. (Library of Congress)

promises of peace, the Creeks were allowed to retain some of their lands. After supporting federal troops during the Seminole War of 1835-1842, Menewa was nevertheless forced to relocate to Indian Territory.

Mary E. Virginia

Metacomet

Born: c. 1638; Pokanokep, probably present-day Massachusetts
Died: August 12, 1676; near present-day Bristol, Rhode Island
Also known as: King Philip, Metacom
Tribal affiliation: Wampanoag
Significance: Wampanoag leader Metacomet is primarily known for waging King Philip's War against the English Puritan colonists in seventeenth century New England.

Metacomet, or Metacom, also widely known as King Philip, was one of the two sons of the Wampanoag chief MASSASOIT, who is believed to have died around 1661. Before his death he brought his sons, Metacomet (or Pometacom) and Mooanum (or Wamsutta), to a meeting with the English governor of the Massachusetts Bay Colony to renew their treaty of peace sometime near the year 1656.

In order to protect his sons and ensure their survival, he allowed the English governor to stand as godfather to them. The governor, in open court, gave the boys the names Philip and Alexander. Massasoit believed that the colonists could be bargained with and the peace maintained in this way. The colonists made some honest but misguided attempts to be fair to and to educate and Christianize the native peoples while trying to respect their human rights. Within a few years after the death of Massasoit, however, relations deteriorated rapidly, eventually resulting in hostilities.

Metacomet was suspicious of the Puritans from the start and disliked the fact that they so easily intruded on his territory and attempted to win the support and confidence of his people with gifts of trinkets, tools, and metal implements. At the same time, they destroyed woodlands to create pastures, farmland, and towns and engaged in missionary activity.

Metacomet succeeded his brother as sachem (leader) of his people in 1662 and honored his father's peace for nine years. In 1671, however, he was summoned to Taunton, Rhode Island; fined for actions viewed as hostile by the colonists; and ordered to surrender. He refused and continued to resist colonial expansion for four more years.

In 1675, three Wampanoags were executed for the murder of a Christian Wampanoag informer. The colonial government tried to apply its laws to the Indians, but this only served to enrage Metacomet. He allied with the Nipmuck and Narragansett tribes, which were nearly destroyed because of their taking part in the burning of outlying towns, where they killed everyone. Metacomet preferred not to battle in the open and was difficult to engage. He went to the Mohawks and French and asked for their support, but they refused, even though he made a trip to Albany, New York, to negotiate for peace.

Metacomet became an eloquent statesman for his people as he encouraged them to drive the invaders out. His public statements contributed to a growing tension and antagonism between the colonists and the Wampanoags. He was an able and crafty leader.

The tribe engaged in escalating conflicts with the colonists, leading to the infamous Swamp Fight, which set off a series of brutal battles. Metacomet led many of the raids, and the ensuing conflict of 1675 was thus called King Philip's War. It was among the bloodiest in early American history. More than six hundred colonists and hundreds more Indians are said to have died in this conflict. Connecticut was defensive from the start, but Massachusetts Bay and settlements in Rhode Island were vulnerable to attack. The whites retaliated and destroyed tribal cornfields, captured women and children—including Metacomet's wife and son, who were sold into slavery—and gave pardons to Indian deserters.

Metacomet was finally defeated, and the coastal tribes of New England were destroyed as independent, sovereign powers. He was shot and killed at Mount Hope, Rhode Island, near Bristol, by a party of vigilantes under Benjamin Church, on August 12, 1676.

Michael W. Simpson

FURTHER READING

Drake, James D. *King Philip's War: Civil War in New England, 1675-1676.* Amherst: University of Massachusetts Press, 2000.

Kawashima, Yasuhide. *Igniting King Philip's War: The John Sassamon Murder Trial.* Lawrence: University Press of Kansas, 2001.

Schultz, Eric B., and Michael J. Tougias. *King Philip's War: The History and Legacy of America's Forgotten Conflict.* Woodstock, Vt.: Countryman Press, 1999.

Miantonomo

Born: c. 1600; place unknown
Died: September, 1643; place unknown
Tribal affiliation: Narragansett
Significance: Miantonomo attempted to build an Indian alliance against the colonists in New England.

A nephew of Chief CANONICUS, Miantonomo became the principal Narragansett chief around 1632. He maintained alliances with the colonists of Massachusetts Bay and with Roger Williams's new colony at Providence Plantations, later Rhode Island, begun in 1635 with Narragansett aid. Miantonomo even attended church with some of the colonists.

Despite these signs of friendship, Miantonomo was suspected of provoking Indian hostility toward the New England colonies, largely because of statements by UNCAS, the founder of the Mohegan tribe, who made a specialty of betraying "hostile" Indians to the Puritan authorities. In 1642, Miantonomo was imprisoned briefly by the Puritans, who scolded and then released him. After that incident, Miantonomo attempted to build an anticolonial alliance. When word of the attempt got to Uncas, he turned Miantonomo over to the English, who sentenced him to die at the hands of Uncas's brother Wawequa in September, 1643.

Bruce E. Johansen

Micanopy

Born: c. 1780; St. Augustine region of Florida
Died: January 2, 1849; Fort Gibson, Indian Territory (now in Oklahoma)
Also known as: Sint-Chakkee
Tribal affiliation: Seminole
Significance: As principal chief of the Seminoles, Micanopy resisted removal during the Second Seminole War.

Though the Seminoles had no central government, Micanopy was regarded as the tribe's principal chief by virtue of his descent from a line of past chiefs. Micanopy was also one of the wealthiest Seminoles of his day, with considerable holdings of land and slaves. He was a strong opponent of U.S. influence in Florida, and he sought to protect Seminole ways after Florida passed to American control in 1819.

When federal representatives arranged the Treaty of Paynes's Landing in 1832 as a prelude to removing the Seminoles from Florida to Indian Territory (modern Oklahoma), Micanopy refused to sign. The government accepted the treaty even though tribal leaders regarded it as fraudulent, and in 1835 began to prepare to move the Seminoles out of Florida. Micanopy supported the efforts of younger tribal leaders such as OSCEOLA and WILDCAT (Micanopy's nephew) to rally resistance. In December of 1835, Seminoles under his and Osceola's leadership attacked Major Francis Dade's column as it moved from Tampa Bay into the interior. Dade was killed—by Micanopy, it was said—and only three of his men survived. The Second Seminole War was under way; it would last until 1842.

The Seminoles proved able warriors, but Micanopy came to doubt their ability to hold off the United States indefinitely. He surrendered to U.S. forces in June, 1837. He was subsequently kidnapped by Osceola, who was intent on continuing the struggle and aware of the chief's symbolic value. Micanopy was recaptured by American forces while under a flag of truce in December of 1837. He agreed to accept removal to the West. After a brief period of imprisonment, he was transported to Indian Territory in 1838. There he found the Seminoles assigned to the Creek Nation, an arrangement that created friction between the two tribes. In 1845, Micanopy negotiated an agreement that allowed the Seminoles to settle as a group within the Creek lands. Ten years later, after his death, the Seminoles formally separated from the Creeks and received their own land.

William C. Lowe

FURTHER READING

Missall, John, and Mary Lou Missall. *The Seminole Wars: America's Longest Indian Conflict.* Foreword by Raymond Arsenault and Gary R. Mormino. Gainesville: University Press of Florida, 2004.

Mills, Billy

Born: June 30, 1938; Pine Ridge, South Dakota
Tribal affiliation: Lakota (Sioux)
Significance: Billy Mills was the first—and through 2004, the only—
    American to win the Olympic gold medal in the 10,000-meter run.

William Mervin (Billy) Mills, orphaned at the age of thirteen and raised thereafter by his sister, did not allow the hardships he faced in his early life to hold him back. Breaking numerous high school track records and excelling at the Haskell Institute in Lawrence, Kansas, earned him a full athletic scholarship to the University of Kansas. His performance on the university's cross-country team was respectable but not outstanding. Upon graduation he was commissioned an officer in the U.S. Marine Corps, serving from 1962 to 1965. He briefly competed on the Marine Corps team, then quit running, feeling that he was not improving. His wife, Pat, soon encouraged him to come out of retirement, however,

Billy Mills edges out Tunisia's Mohamed Gamoudi to win the gold medal for the 10,000-meter event in the 1964 Olympic Games in Tokyo. (AP/Wide World Photos)

and he decided to try and make the U.S. Olympic Team, hoping to run in the 10,000-meter event at the upcoming Tokyo Olympics.

During the year preceding the 1964 Tokyo Olympics, Mills ran 75 to 100 miles a week, practicing in obscurity. He made the team but caused little interest at the Olympic trials. When he was running the actual race, on October 14, 1964, few in the audience—and few of the officials—paid much attention to this virtually unknown runner until the final lap, when Mills suddenly sprinted ahead of the leaders, Ron Clarke (who held the previous record) and Mohamed Gammoudi, and won by three yards. The stunned audience applauded wildly. He had set a new Olympic record of 28:24.4, and his race was one of the greatest upsets in Olympic Games history. In 1965 Mills ran in the National AAU Outdoor Championships 6-mile run and broke Clarke's world record. Mills's story was dramatized in the 1983 film *Running Brave* (the fact that a non-Indian actor, Robby Benson, was cast as Mills created controversy but did not bother Mills himself).

Later becoming an acclaimed speaker, Billy Mills has traveled to more than fifty countries and was voted one of the top five speakers in America by Toastmasters International (1996). He has been inducted into numerous halls of fame, including the World Sports Humanitarian Hall of Fame (1997). As national spokesperson for Running Strong for American Indian Youth, a project of Christian Relief Services, he works to improve the quality of life on reservations around the United States.

Tonya Huber

FURTHER READING

Oxendine, Joseph B. *American Indian Sports Heritage.* Lincoln: University of Nebraska Press, 1995.

Modesto, Ruby

Born: 1913; Martinez Reservation, California
Died: April 7, 1980; Martinez Reservation, California
Also known as: Nesha (Woman of Mystery)
Tribal affiliation: Cahuilla
Significance: Ruby Modesto was a Desert Cahuilla medicine woman who passed traditional knowledge along to younger generations.

An elder of the Desert Cahuilla in inland Southern California, Ruby Modesto grew up along the shore of the Salton Sea learning the traditional ways of her father's people. Her mother was a Serrano from the Morongo Reservation. She did not speak English or attend school until she was ten years old. As a member of the Dog clan, she inherited shamanistic teaching and traditions through clan relatives, including her father, grandfather, great-grandfather, and several uncles who were *puls,* or shamans. Around about the age of ten, she received her dream helper, Ahswit the Eagle. As a youngster she dreamed to such a high level that she required the help of a shaman to end the comatose states that she occasionally entered for days at a time.

Modesto's mother took her to the Moravian Church services on the reservation, and she followed Christianity for a long time; however, she eventually chose to be a *pul.* As a medicine woman, she specialized in healing individuals possessed by demons. She trained people in traditional crafts, language, and religion. She was a guest lecturer at colleges in the area and served as an informant to anthropologists.

Modesto explained the Medicine Path of the Cahuilla that recognizes a spirit in everything, including people, animals, rocks, and plants. A desert people, the Cahuilla respect the life in plants and see smoke as the spirit of a plant made visible: "Smoke is God's breath." Modesto believed in healing with dream power, herbs, massage, songs, feathers, and smoke. In the Cahuilla creation story, the creator presents the gifts of tobacco and the pipe. People cremated the dead on outdoor funeral pyres, from which spirits could be seen rising from bodies like smoke.

Modesto expressed her Cahuilla religion's gratitude for creation, thanking Mother Earth for "holding me on your breast. You always love me no matter how old I get." She passed on her gratitude for God's gifts through a traditional mentoring system in which she chose young persons.

Joanna Yin

FURTHER READING

Modesto, Ruby, and Guy Mount. *Not for Innocent Ears: Spiritual Traditions of a Desert Cahuilla Medicine Woman.* Angelus Oaks, Calif.: Sweetlight Books, 1980.

Momaday, N. Scott

Born: February 27, 1934; Lawton, Oklahoma
Also known as: Tsaoi-talee (Rock-Tree Boy)
Tribal affiliation: Kiowa
Significance: A professor of literature and Native American studies, N. Scott Momaday is best known for his innovative and influential works of autobiography and fiction.

Among the most widely read and studied Native American authors, N. Scott Momaday manifests in his writings a keen awareness of the importance of self-definition in literature and life. From 1936 onward, his family moved from place to place in the Southwest, eventually settling in Albuquerque, where Momaday attended high school. He entered the University of New Mexico in 1954 and later studied poetry at Stanford University. In 1963, he received his doctorate in English, and afterward he held teaching jobs at various southwestern universities.

In a semiautobiographical work, *The Way to Rainy Mountain* (1969), Momaday writes that identity is "the history of an idea, man's idea of himself, and it has old and essential being in language." Momaday defines his characters in terms of their use or abuse of language; usually his characters find themselves relearning how to speak while they learn about themselves. Even the title of one of Momaday's essays, "The Man Made of Words," indicates his contention that identity is shaped by language. "Only when he is embodied in an idea," Momaday writes, "and the idea is realized in language, can man take possession of himself."

The forces that shape language—culture and landscape—are also crucial in Momaday's works. To Russell Martin, Western writing is concerned with the harsh realities of the frontier that "could carve lives that were as lean and straight as whittled sticks." This harsh landscape is present in Momaday's work also, but he has a heartfelt attachment to it. Having a spiritual investment in a place, in Momaday's writing, helps a person gain self-knowledge. To an extent, issues of identity were important to Momaday as well. The son of a Kiowa father and a Cherokee mother, Momaday belonged fully to neither culture. Furthermore, much of his early childhood was spent on a Navajo reservation, where his father worked, and he grew up consciously alienated from the surrounding culture.

To combat rootlessness, the imagination and its expression in language is essential. "What sustains" the artist, he writes in *The Ancient Child* (1989), "is the satisfaction . . . of having created a few incomparable things—landscapes, waters, birds, and beasts." Writing about the efforts of various people to maintain traditional culture in the face of the modern world, Momaday occupies a central place in the American literary landscape.

A complex and richly evocative work, Momaday's *The Ancient Child* is the story of two Native Americans—a middle-aged painter and a young woman—who come to a fuller understanding of themselves. Native American folklore and mythology are woven into their story, lending cultural

Author N. Scott Momaday in Paris, prior to receiving the UNESCO Artist for Peace award in 2004. (AP/Wide World Photos)

and psychological depth to their quests for, essentially, rebirth.

Locke Setman, called "Set" throughout the novel, is in many ways a representative Momaday protagonist because he is cut off from his past and therefore lives an unexamined life. Brought up in an orphanage by an embittered academic, Set has a tenuous connection to the Kiowa culture of his ancestors. Eventually, when he is completely stripped of illusions, Set is drawn back to Kiowan tribal lands.

House Made of Dawn (1968), Momaday's first novel, is the story of an outcast who learns that his being is bound up in his culture. The novel, which relates the experiences of a mixed-race World War II veteran, was a signal achievement, winning the Pulitzer Prize in fiction for Momaday in 1969 and paving a way for other Native American novelists. It begins with Abel's return to his ancestral village. Although Abel is so drunk that he does not recognize his grandfather, his troubles run much deeper. He feels cut off from the Tanoan tribe yet unwilling to live in white America.

Momaday's later publications include *The Man Made of Words: Essays, Stories, Passages* (1997) and *In the Bear's House* (1999).

Michael R. Meyers

FURTHER READING

Coltelli, Laura. *Winged Words*. Lincoln: University of Nebraska Press, 1990.

Isernhagen, Hartwig. *Momaday, Vizenor, Armstrong: Conversations on American Indian Writing*. Norman: University of Oklahoma Press, 1999.

Martin, Russell, and Marc Barasch, eds. *Writers of the Purple Sage*. New York: Viking, 1984.

Momaday, N. Scott. "The Man Made of Words." In *The Remembered Earth: An Anthology of Contemporary Native American Literature*, edited by Geary Hobson. Albuquerque: University of New Mexico Press, 1980.

Ramsey, Jerold. *Reading the Fire*. Lincoln: University of Nebraska Press, 1982.

Trimble, Martha Scott. "N. Scott Momaday." *Fifty Western Writers: A Bio-Bibliographical Sourcebook*, edited by Fred Erisman and Richard W. Etulain. Westport, Conn.: Greenwood Press, 1982.

Velie, Alan R. *Four American Indian Literary Masters*. Norman: University of Oklahoma Press, 1982.

Vizenor, Gerald. *Manifest Manners*. Middletown, Conn.: Wesleyan University Press, 1994.

Montezuma, Carlos

Born: c. 1867; Superstition Mountains of central Arizona
Died: January 31, 1923; Fort McDowell Reservation, Arizona
Also known as: Wassaja (Signaling or Beckoning)
Tribal affiliation: Yavapai
Significance: Carlos Montezuma was one of the first American Indians to earn a physician's degree and practice European American medicine on reservations.

In the mid-1860's, Carlos Montezuma was born to Yavapai parents in central or southern Arizona. He received the name "Wassaja," meaning "signaling" or "beckoning." Wassaja's childhood was far from peaceful, as during that decade European Americans were mining and settling the area and indigenous peoples were maintaining warfare with one another. In 1871, Pimas attacked the Yavapais and abducted Wassaja to Mexico. He never saw his natural parents again, but a photographer named Carlos Gentile purchased the boy out of pity. Gentile had the boy christened "Carlos Montezuma" and took him to Chicago.

After schooling in Chicago and Galesburg, Illinois, and a brief stay in Brooklyn, Montezuma found himself back in Urbana, Illinois, as the ward of a Baptist minister, William Steadman. Under such tutelage he prepared for college, matriculated at the University of Illinois, and earned a degree in chemistry. After a brief period of uncertainty, Montezuma enrolled at the Chicago Medical College. By 1889, he had completed his medical training.

Even before finishing his training, Montezuma was in touch with Captain Richard Henry Pratt, the head of the assimilationist Carlisle Indian School. Pratt immediately took an interest in Carlos as living proof of the value of "civilizing" the Indians. Commissioner of Indian Affairs Thomas Jefferson Morgan did the same, and in 1889 he appointed Montezuma as a clerk and physician at Fort Stevenson in the Dakota Territory. From there, Montezuma moved on to the Western Shoshone Agency in Nevada and the Colville Agency in Washington. At each place, however, his philosophy of Indian rights clashed with that of government agents, missionaries, and tribal shamans. By 1893, he was in Carlisle, Pennsylvania as the school's physician, a post he kept until 1896, when he ventured into private practice. Montezuma had a happier time at Carlisle, although he suffered a romantic spurning from the prominent Sioux woman Zitkala-Sa (Gertrude Simmons BONNIN).

Once outside the U.S. Indian Service, Montezuma began to devote his energies to political activism on behalf of indigenous causes. He helped create the Fort McDowell Yavapai (or Mojave-Apache) Reservation in 1903. By 1905, he was attracting attention as a national Indian leader. Suspicious of the assimilationist agenda of the Bureau of Indian Affairs, Montezuma joined with other like-minded indigenous intellectuals to form a loose front insisting on tribal peoples' control of their destiny. Although he was never completely at ease with the progressivist Society of American Indians that emerged in 1911, Montezuma moved in and out of the organization over the next four years or so. By 1915, however, his political views took him out of the progressivist camp. Convinced that the Bureau of Indian Affairs was a fraud that deprived indigenous people of land and livelihood, Carlos sharpened his attack on the agency, calling for its abolition and ridiculing those indigenous leaders who cooperated with it. To this end, he began publishing a newsletter, *Wassaja*, in 1916. Over the next seven years, until his death, Montezuma crusaded for citizenship rights for Indians and economic protection of tribal people, especially in his native Arizona. His was not a call for a nativist resurrection of old tribal ways; instead, he sought political autonomy and the economic empowerment of his people in the context of modern America. When by 1918 the Society of American Indians was beginning to embrace his views, he rejoiced. His elation proved short-lived when the movement began to lose its clout nationally. Personal matters, such as his attempt to enroll as a San Carlos Apache (because some genealogical searching led him to believe his parents had ended up with that tribe), foundered as well.

By the summer of 1922, Montezuma's health had deteriorated significantly. He diagnosed his condition as tuberculosis and headed back to Arizona. There, shunning European American medicine, he lingered in a wickiup until his death on January 31, 1923. Several newspapers and indigenous leaders, as well as the Society of American Indians, eulogized him, but the memory of his passions faded quickly. Not until the late 1960's and early 1970's did scholars and indigenous leaders rediscover Carlos Montezuma and his earlier form of resistance to European American domination.

Thomas L. Altherr

FURTHER READING
Speroff, Leon. *Carlos Montezuma, M.D.: A Yavapai American Hero: The Life and Times of an American Indian, 1866-1923*. Portland, Oreg.: Arnica, 2003.

Mopope, Stephen

Born: August 27, 1898; near Red Stone Baptist Mission, Kiowa Reservation, Oklahoma Territory
Died: February 3, 1974; Fort Cobb, Oklahoma
Also known as: Qued Koi (Painted Robe)
Tribal affiliation: Kiowa
Significance: Stephen Mopope was one of the Kiowa Five artists who helped to define and establish the Oklahoma style of Native American painting during the 1930's.
Mopope was the son of a distinguished Kiowa family. He was a painter most of his life, though he also worked as a farmer. Two granduncles, Haungooah (Silverhorn) and Hakok, taught him as a youth to paint on tanned skins in the traditional way. He was an expert performer of tradi-

tional dances and songs, and later in life built his own dance ground to sponsor dances.

Mopope drew from that background to paint portraits, traditional costumes, and dances. He frequently portrayed dancers doing the same steps that he himself danced. He painted or participated in the making of murals for a number of public buildings, including the chapel of St. Patrick's Mission School in Anadarko, Oklahoma; the University of Oklahoma (with Monroe TSATOKE); Southwestern State University (Oklahoma); U.S. Navy Hospital in Carville, Louisiana; the Federal Buildings in Anadarko and Muskogee, Oklahoma; First National Bank of Anadarko; Fort Sill Indian School; and Northeastern State University (Oklahoma). His work is in the collections of the National Museum of the American Indian, University of Oklahoma Museum of Art, Oklahoma Historical Society Museum, and others.

Ronald J. Duncan

FURTHER READING
Berlo, Janet C., and Ruth B. Phillips. *Native North American Art.* New York: Oxford University Press, 1998.

Moses

Born: c. 1829; Wenatchee Flat (now in central Washington)
Died: March 25, 1899; near Wilbur, Washington
Also known as: Quelatikan (The Blue Horn)
Tribal affiliation: Kowachinook
Significance: A tribal leader and diplomat, Moses was associated with a number of chiefs of the Northwest, including CHIEF JOSEPH THE YOUNGER and KAMIAKIN, and he provided counsel during the wars of the 1850's.

A member of the Kowachinooks, Chief Moses eventually claimed to be a spokesperson for numerous Upper Columbia River groups, particularly the Yakimas, Spokanes, Kowachinooks, Methows, and Okanagans. Quelatikan acquired the biblical name Moses while attending the Spaulding mission school at Lapwai but never became a Christian. It was here that he met and became a lifelong friend of Chief Joseph, the famous Nez Perce warrior. Moses is best known for his leadership and counsel during the wars between Indians and whites in eastern Washington from 1855 to 1858, a time when he was closely associated with Owhi, KAMIAKIN, and Qualchien, local chiefs who had opposed Colonel George Wright's ef-

Moses. (National Archives)

forts to force Indians onto local reservations.

After Chief Moses refused to settle on the Yakima Reservation, the Moses-Columbia Reservation was established on April 19, 1879, but on July 7, 1884, the "Moses Agreement" was ratified in which Moses gave up claim to the area and eventually settled on the Colville Reservation in 1884. Moses was described as a proud, handsome, and physically imposing man, with great intelligence and judgment, who was opposed to war and enjoyed gambling. He died from Bright's disease on March 25, 1899.

John Alan Ross

Mountain Chief

Born: 1848; along Oldman River, Alberta, Canada
Died: 1942; Browning, Montana
Also known as: Ninastoko
Tribal affiliation: Blackfoot
Significance: Mountain Chief was the last hereditary leader of the Blackfoot (Siksika) tribe.

Historically, the Blackfoot people lived throughout the region between Canada's North Saskatchewan River and the headwaters of the Missouri River in what is now Montana. The tribe numbered about 9,100 members during the mid-nineteenth century—a figure that would be significantly reduced by epidemics of smallpox and measles during the next decade.

It was along the Oldman River (also known as the Belly River) in Alberta, Canada, that Mountain Chief was born as Ninastoko in 1848. His prowess as a warrior became apparent when, at the age of eighteen, he led a war party against the Crow Indians in a battle at Cypress Hills. He earned a reputation as an aggressive and brave warrior, particularly when facing the traditional enemies of the Blackfeet, such as the Crow,

Sioux, Gros Ventres, and Kutenai. In 1867, for example, he defeated the Kutenai chief, Cut Nose, in hand-to-hand combat. Six years later, he received a leg injury fighting against the Crow that left him with a permanent limp.

Recognizing the strength of the white communities moving into what was traditionally Indian land, Mountain Chief was willing to accede to reasonable requests for land grants. The tribe had historically been buffalo hunters, but with the animal having been driven to near extinction by the 1880's, it became necessary to develop other means of survival. A government treaty in 1886 ceded the Sweet Grass Hills, a region in Montana east of the Rocky Mountains which by then was a portion of the Blackfeet Reservation, to the United States in exchange for tools and training in agriculture and the raising of stock. The Sweet Grass Hills area had historically been a sacred area for the Blackfoot Confederation, a region rich in grassland and buffalo; the Blackfeet had brewed the grasses into a sweet tea, hence the origin of the place name.

White settlers continued to migrate into the shrinking reservation, a movement which was in part the result of rumors that precious metals could be found in the Rocky Mountain portion of the Blackfoot land. In 1895, Mountain Chief ceded the region that fifteen years later would become Glacier National Park. Ironically, rumors about gold and other metal deposits proved false.

Mountain Chief's negotiating work ultimately brought him into contact with four U.S. presidents: William McKinley, Theodore Roosevelt, William Howard Taft, and Woodrow Wilson. In his later years, Mountain Chief worked as a guide within Glacier National Park. He also helped General Hugh Scott prepare a record of the sign languages used by the Plains Indians.

After going blind during his last years, Mountain Chief died in his home in Montana in 1942, at the age of ninety-four. The immense territory over which the Blackfoot tribe had once roamed is now limited to three reservations in Alberta, Canada, and a fourth in northwest Montana over a region that straddles the U.S. boundary with Canada.

Richard Adler

FURTHER READING
Blackfoot Gallery Committee. *The Story of the Blackfoot People.* Tonawanda, N.Y.: Firefly Books, 2002.

Mountain Wolf Woman

Born: April, 1884; East Fork River, Wisconsin
Died: November 9, 1960; Black River Falls, Wisconsin
Also known as: Xehaciwinga, Haksigaxunuminka (Little Fifth Daughter)
Tribal affiliation: Winnebago
Significance: Mountain Wolf Woman's autobiography is a unique account of adaptation of traditional Winnebago lifeways to modern conditions.

In 1958, Mountain Wolf Woman spoke into a tape recorder in the presence of her adopted kinswoman, Nancy Oestreich Lurie, who then edited a translation from Winnebago into English to produce Mountain Wolf Woman's autobiography, *Mountain Wolf Woman, Sister of Crashing Thunder* (1961). The youngest of seven children, Mountain Wolf Woman was a member of an extraordinary Winnebago family: She was the younger sister of Crashing Thunder (Sam Blowsnake), who worked with anthropologist Paul Radin, supplying him with most of the material for the myth cycle called the Trickster (1956), Sam Blowsnake's autobiography *Crashing Thunder* (1926), and the ethnology *The Winnebago Tribe* (1923).

Mountain Wolf Woman's life involved her own education in traditional Winnebago culture and her work in preserving and passing on that culture to her descendants. Mountain Wolf Woman was married twice, the first time reluctantly to a husband chosen by her brother, and later to a man named Bad Soldier. She had eleven children and was the caregiver for many of her grandchildren and great-grandchildren. Mountain Wolf Woman embraced three major religious traditions in her life, weaving into an integrated philosophy Winnebago traditional beliefs and practices, Christian theology, and the peyote rituals of the Native American Church.

Helen Jaskoski

FURTHER READING
Lurie, Nancy Oestreich, ed. *Mountain Wolf Woman, Sister of Crashing Thunder: The Autobiography of a Winnebago Indian.* Foreword by Ruth Underhill. Ann Arbor: University of Michigan Press, 1961.

Mourning Dove

Born: April, 1888; near Bonners Ferry, Idaho
Died: August 8, 1936; Medical Lake, Washington
Also known as: Humishuma, Christine or Cristal Quintasket, Mrs. Fred
  Galler
Tribal affiliation: Okanagan
Significance: Mourning Dove's *Cogewea* was one of the first novels by an
  American Indian to be published in the United States.

Mourning Dove was one of the first American Indian writers to publish a novel. *Cogewea, the Half-Blood: A Depiction of the Great Montana Cattle Range* appeared in 1927. Mourning Dove's novel was extensively edited by her mentor, friend, and agent, Lucullus Virgil McWhorter, who believed that the text provided a good platform to protest the mistreatment suffered by Indians; however, the essential story, which draws upon the romance novel and Western genres in order to offer a realistic view of the Montana frontier, is substantially Mourning Dove's work.

Mourning Dove's love for Okanagan culture derived from the education in tradition she received from an elder who lived with the family when she was a young girl. Mourning Dove continued her study of Okanagan traditions as an adult and compiled a collection of tales which was first published under the title *Coyote Stories* (1933); it had been heavily edited, however, by Heister Dean Guie, who omitted important material and rewrote the text to address a juvenile audience.

Mourning Dove left many unpublished manuscripts when she died, and two works have been published posthumously. The collection of traditional tales was reedited by Donald M. Hines as *Tales of the Okanogans* (1976); this edition is more complete and closer to Mourning Dove's own lively style. *Mourning Dove: A Salishan Autobiography* (1993) was edited by Jay Miller from various unpublished manuscripts.

Helen Jaskoski

FURTHER READING
Mourning Dove. *Mourning Dove: A Salishan Autobiography.* Edited by Jay
  Miller. Lincoln: University of Nebraska Press, 1993.
Perdue, Theda, ed. *Sifters: Native American Women's Lives.* New York: Oxford University Press, 2001.
Sligh, Gary Lee. *Study of Native American Women Novelists: Sophia Alice Callahan, Mourning Dove, and Ella Cara Deloria.* New York: Edwin Mellen Press, 2003.

Murie, James

Born: 1862; Grand Island (now in Nebraska)
Died: 1921
Tribal affiliation: Skidi Pawnee
Significance: James Murie collaborated with anthropologists and later
  wrote his own anthropological works about the Pawnee.

James Murie, a Skidi Pawnee of mixed blood, was born in Nebraska in
1862. At that time, Nebraska was still a scene of Pawnee struggle with
their traditional enemies, the Sioux. As a youth, Murie was among the
first Native Americans to attend Hampton Institute in Virginia. Founded
to encourage secondary education for blacks, the institute had only recently been opened to Native Americans.

Murie's advanced training was gained not in school but by association with professional anthropologists who were interested in Pawnee
traditions but lacked language training to do fieldwork without a native
intermediary. Murie's situation paralleled that of other Native Americans, such as George HUNT (a Kwakiutl), who worked with Franz Boas;
George BUSHOTTER (a Sioux), who collaborated with James O. Dorsey;
and Cleaver Warden (Arapaho), who, like Murie, worked with George
A. Dorsey.

Murie's earliest contribution to anthropological studies was near the
beginning of the twentieth century, when he served as an informant to
Alice C. Fletcher, who wrote the first major works on the Pawnees, including, in 1904, a detailed description of their unique Hako Ceremony.

Thereafter, Murie became more involved in recording firsthand
data, including ceremonial texts, either on his own or working with
other anthropologists. The first product of his collaborative ventures
was a typescript entitled "The Pawnee: Society and Religion of the Skidi
Pawnee," written jointly with George A. Dorsey between 1905 and 1907.
By this date, Murie and Dorsey had begun a project that was unique for
its time. They recorded the autobiography of an elderly Skidi priest on
wax cylinders. These were transcribed and translated by Murie and
served as a basis for the first systematic study of phonemic distinctions
in Pawnee.

When he died in 1921, Murie's name as sole author had appeared on
one original work only—three volumes of transcribed Pawnee mythology. After 1912, however, he had written (during a period in which he
collaborated with anthropologist Clark Wissler, working at the same

time for the U.S. Bureau of American Ethnology) a major monograph entitled *Ceremonies of the Pawnee.* This would be published posthumously by the Smithsonian Institution.

Byron D. Cannon

Musgrove, Mary

Born: c. 1700; Coweta, Georgia
Died: c. 1763; St. Catharine's Island, Georgia
Also known as: Consaponaheeso, Coosaponakeesa, Creek Mary, Mary Bosomworth
Tribal affiliation: Creek
Significance: Mary Musgrove was instrumental in the founding and development of the colony of Georgia.

Mary Musgrove was a member of what was known as the Creek Confederacy. Her Creek name was Consaponaheeso, and she was given the significant title of "Beloved Woman" by her people. She was an active leader in the matrifocal spheres that influenced the politics in the traditional Creek society of her day. Her exploits included a march on Savannah over a Creek land dispute, which was a precursor to the "Red Stick Revolt." Her political prowess distinguished her as a chief by the Europeans who had to deal with her; they also bestowed on her the name of "Creek Mary" in admiration.

It is often said that Mary had a mistrust of whites because of her Creek nationalism. This apparently did not prevent her from marrying three white men. Her first husband was John Musgrove, Jr., the son of a key British military commander in the Carolinas during the eighteenth century. The two had children while operating a trading post on Yamacraf Bluff in Georgia, but they moved to South Carolina to live near his father. After his death, her second marriage was to another Englishman, Jacob Matthews, but it was short-lived. In 1749, she was married for the third and last time, to the Reverend Thomas Bosomworth, a minister of the Church of England. He was also the chaplain to General James Edward Oglethorpe's Highland Regiment, whose later military reign involved the expropriation of Creek lands in Georgia for the Crown of England. Bosomworth played an active role in assisting his general in obtaining Creek lands. The minister also transferred real estate to himself instead of the Crown.

As Carolyn Thomas Foreman implies in her treatise on Mary Musgrove, she was in a strategic position between her tribespeople, her husband's private interests, and Oglethorpe's competing claims. The plan fell through when Creek leaders denounced the enterprise and Mary and her spouse's duplicitous natures. The enterprising couple were jailed, a situation which did not deter either one from continuing to expropriate Creek lands for the British Crown. On the other hand, it has also been written that she was an advocate for the early "pan-Indianism," an intertribal movement that was espoused by the Shawnee leader TECUMSEH and his brother TENSKWATAWA, the Prophet.

Musgrave was a complex individual with a dual nature, one who engaged in what others have referred to as "sexual politics" through her interracial marital liaisons. It has been asked whether she was a heroine or a pawn, a patriot or a traitor to her Creek Nation. It is most likely that she was a player in the politics of this period, which saw the development of American colonialism at the expense of her Creek homeland. Mary Musgrove has emerged in the historical literature as a symbol of Creek patriotism, despite her marital commitments. She was in the forefront of Creek resistance to European conquest and colonization, and she was an extraordinary role model to many native liberationists.

M. A. Jaimes

FURTHER READING

Brown, Dee. *Creek Mary's Blood.* New York: Holt, Rinehart and Winston, 1980.

Churchill, Ward. "The Historical Novel and *Creek Mary's Blood." Journal of Ethnic Studies* 12, no. 3 (Fall, 1984): 119-128.

Foreman, Carolyn Thomas. *Indian Women Chiefs.* 1954. Reprint. Muskogee, Okla.: Hoffman Printing, 1966.

Green, Michael D. *The Politics of Indian Removal: Creek Government and Society in Crisis.* Lincoln: University of Nebraska Press, 1982.

Holm, Tom. "Indian Removal and Creek Government." *Journal of Ethnic Studies* 12, no. 3 (Fall, 1984): 129-130.

Martin, Joel W. *Sacred Revolt: The Muskogees' Struggle for a New World.* Boston: Beacon Press, 1991.

Perdue, Theda, ed. *Sifters: Native American Women's Lives.* New York: Oxford University Press, 2001.

Naiche

Born: c. 1857
Died: 1921; Mescalero, New Mexico
Also known as: Natchez
Tribal affiliation: Chiricahua Apache
Significance: Said to be GERONIMO's closest associate in war and captivity, Naiche was a leader of the Apache people during their late nineteenth and early twentieth century interactions with the U.S. government.

Reared by his father, COCHISE, to be loyal to his older brother Taza (Tahza, Tazi), Naiche was unprepared to assume the leadership role he inherited when Taza died unexpectedly. Along with Geronimo, Naiche led many of the Apache raiding parties in the Southwest during the 1880's. Although photographs reveal the deference with which Geronimo saluted Naiche, invariably placing Naiche on the right, interpreters believed Geronimo dominated. The two leaders were nearly inseparable in battle and in captivity for half a century.

In 1886, Naiche, Geronimo, Chihuahua, and NANA met with Lieutenant Marion Maus in the Sierra Madre to discuss surrender. Nine Apaches were held hostage, including Naiche's oldest wife, Nah-deyole, and their son, who would be known later as Paul. Naiche's other wives were E-clah-heh and Ha-o-zinne. Naiche and Geronimo fled but were taken prisoner and sent to Florida.

In 1891, Naiche became one of the first soldiers in Company I of the Twelfth Infantry. He would later serve as a scout searching for Apaches still living in Mexico's Sierra Madre. In 1893, he was moved to Oklahoma, still as a prisoner of war. He was instrumental in accomplishing the 1912 congressional legislation releasing the Apaches as prisoners of war.

Tonya Huber

Nakaidoklini

Born: c. mid-1800's; present-day Arizona
Died: August 30, 1881; Cibecue Creek, Arizona
Tribal affiliation: Apache
Significance: Nakaidoklini was an Apache prophet whose murder precipitated the final stage of the Apache Wars.

At the San Carlos Reservation in Arizona, Nakaidoklini prophesied the resurrection of dead warriors through the practice of a new dance. The ritual was performed with Nakaidoklini standing in the center of a group of dancing warriors, anointing them with sacred pollen. In June, 1881, he announced his intention of performing a dance designed to resurrect two chiefs who would aid Apaches in their struggles against whites.

After Nakaidoklini reputedly claimed that his resurrection dance would fail because of white presence in the region, Fort Apache's commander, Colonel E. A. Carr, was ordered to arrest or kill him. Failing to lure him to the reservation, on August 30, 1881, Carr led cavalry troops and twenty-three White Mountain Apache scouts to Nakaidoklini's village. Although he surrendered, the White Mountain scouts rebelled; fighting ensued and Nakaidoklini was killed.

In retaliation, Nakaidoklini's followers attacked Fort Apache, precipitating a new phase of Apache Wars.

Mary E. Virginia

Nampeyo

Born: c. 1860; Hano, First Mesa, Arizona Territory
Died: July 20, 1942; Hano, First Mesa, Arizona
Tribal affiliation: Hano, Hopi
Significance: Inspired by prehistoric Sikyatki Polychrome pottery, Nampeyo created her own style, known as Hano Polychrome, which revived the declining pottery tradition in the Hopi pueblos.

When the Fewkes Expedition of 1895 excavated Sikyatki, a prehistoric Hopi site, Nampeyo's husband, Lesou, was a member of the team. More than five hundred intact pots and thousands of fragments were recovered, all of which Nampeyo had an opportunity to study. She did not copy the Sikyatki patterns in her work but combined many of the elements and motifs, such as spiral bird beaks, wings, and feathers, with her own ideas to re-create the Sikyatki sense of form. She also experimented with different clays until she discovered the one that had been used by the prehistoric Sikyatki potters.

Among modern Hopi potters, the two most popular vessel shapes are the bowl and the jar. It was Nampeyo who revived the jar shape that was characteristic of Sikyatki Polychrome—a shallow jar with a short neck, an incurving rim, and a low, flattened shoulder that presents an interesting design field. Nampeyo had a highly developed sense of the appropriateness of design to vessel shape, and the placement of her decorative elements always complemented the form of the pot.

In the early 1900's, with the Fred Harvey Company promoting her work, Nampeyo inspired many other Hopi potters to work in the Hano Polychrome style. With her creative ability and technical mastery, she set the standards for a pottery tradition that has continued under the leadership of her daughters, granddaughters, and great-granddaughters.

LouAnn Faris Culley

FURTHER READING

Blair, Mary Ellen, and Laurence Blair. *The Legacy of a Master Potter: Nampeyo and Her Descendants.* Tucson, Ariz.: Treasure Chest Books, 1999.

Kramer, Barbara. *Nampeyo and Her Pottery.* Albuquerque: University of New Mexico Press, 1996.

Moses, L. G., and Raymond Wilson, eds. *Indian Lives: Essays on Nineteenth and Twentieth Century Native American Leaders.* Albuquerque: University of New Mexico Press, 1985.

Nana

Born: c. 1810
Died: 1895?; Fort Sill, Indian Territory (now in Oklahoma)
Also known as: Nané, Nanay
Tribal affiliation: Chiricahua Apache
Significance: Nana was said to have had the longest fighting career of any Apache warrior.

Nana, who married GERONIMO's sister, Nah-dos-te, was closely allied with the Mimbreño chief VICTORIO in fighting removal to reservations. Nana was one of only seventeen Apaches to escape the 1880 massacre of Victorio and his people living in the Sierre Madre.

The scalps of sixty-two warriors and sixteen women and children earned the Mexican force under Colonel Terrazas fifty thousand dollars.

Nana. (Library of Congress)

An additional sixty-eight women and children were sold into slavery. Nana, then seventy years old, gathered the survivors and stepped into the leadership role.

From July of 1881 through the next year, Nana terrorized New Mexico. After surrendering to General George Crook's forces in May, 1883, Nana and about 320 Apaches were marched from Sierre Madre to San Carlos. In May, 1885, Nana and about 140 Chiricahuas broke away from the reservation once more. Their flight into Mexico and subsequent raids ended March 25, 1886, when the leaders negotiated with Crook to return to the reservation. The terms of surrender were violated, and Crook resigned. Over the next four months, five thousand men were employed to "capture or destroy" thirty-eight Chiricahuas. Removed as a prisoner to Florida, Nana survived captivity to return to Oklahoma, where he died, probably in 1895 or 1896. He was buried in the Apache cemetery near Fort Sill.

Tonya Huber

Natawista

Born: c. 1825; Alberta, Canada
Died: March, 1893; Stand Off, Alberta, Canada
Also known as: Natawista Iksana, Madame Culbertson
Tribal affiliation: Blood
Significance: After marrying Major Alexander Culbertson, Natawista became an interpreter, diplomat, and trading post hostess.

When she was fifteen years old, Natawista accompanied her father, Men-Es-To-Kos, on a trading voyage from their home in Alberta to Fort Union on the Missouri River, near the North Dakota-Montana border. There she married Alexander Culbertson, the fort commander, in an Indian ceremony. Four of their children lived to adulthood; two daughters married white easterners, while two sons remained in the West to work as traders.

During the early years of her marriage, from 1840 to 1845, Natawista resided at Fort Union, acting as hostess and diplomat. In 1845, the Culbertsons moved farther north along the Missouri, establishing Fort Benton in Montana. There, Natawista functioned as an interpreter for several Indian tribes, including the Blackfoot, Blood, and Gros Ventre, while simultaneously acting as hostess to visiting white traders.

After his appointment as special agent to the Blackfoot Confederacy in 1847, Culbertson and Natawista traveled to Indian camps throughout the territory. Natawista again assisted her husband by acting as interpreter and diplomat. On several occasions, she diffused tensions and helped maintain peace.

Retiring to Peoria, Illinois, in 1858, the Culbertsons were married in a Roman Catholic ceremony. In Peoria they lived extravagantly for ten years before losing their fortune through failed investments, thereafter returning to the Upper Missouri River, where Culbertson resumed trading. During the 1870's, Natawista left Culbertson and returned to her native Alberta, where she remained until her death.

Mary E. Virginia

Natiotish

Born: unknown

Died: Probably July 17, 1882; Upper fork of Clear Creek, Arizona Territory

Also known as: Nantiotish, Nantiatish

Tribal affiliation: White Mountain Apache

Significance: Bitter over the death of the Apache prophet NAKAIDOKLINI, Natiotish led White Mountain Apache warriors in the Battle of Big Dry Wash in Arizona Territory 1882.

In 1881, fearing the influence of the prophet Nakaidoklini, who preached a religion in which dead warriors would be resurrected to fight in battles against whites, Fort Apache's commander ordered the prophet's arrest. A rebellion of White Mountain Apaches ensued and Nakaidoklini was killed.

Angered by Nakaidoklini's death, Natiotish led his militant band of White Mountain Apaches on a retaliatory raid on the San Carlos Reservation, July 6, 1882. Four policemen, including the chief of police, "Cibecue Charley" Colvig, were killed.

Thereafter, Natiotish's band relentlessly raided the Tonto Basin, pursued by U.S. Cavalry led by Captain Adna Chaffee. Natiotish planned an ambush for Chaffee at a canyon near General Springs on the Mogollon Rim on July 17, 1882. Warned by army scout Albert Sieber and reinforced by troops under Major Andrew Evans, Chaffee's forces outnumbered and outfought Natiotish. The Apaches suffered a major defeat in the battle, during which they had abandoned their typical guerrilla tactics. Twenty-seven Apache warriors, probably including Natiotish, were killed in the skirmish, which became known as the Battle of Big Dry

Wash. The survivors returned to the reservation and abandoned further resistance. Only the Chiricahuas and Mimbrenos under GERONIMO remained militant.

Mary E. Virginia

Neolin

Born: c. 1725
Died: c. 1775
Also known as: Delaware Prophet
Tribal affiliation: Lenni Lenape (Delaware)
Significance: Also well known as the Delaware Prophet, Neolin was an important religious leader during the mid-eighteenth century who was known for his renunciation of "white ways."

While little is known of Neolin's early life, he came into prominence as an Indian prophet during the 1760's during PONTIAC's efforts to unite tribes against the European invaders. His requirements for salvation were twofold: First, to renounce all white influence, especially liquor, and avoid all trade; second, to return to the traditional ways but without the evil practices of war dances and medicine-making. These laws were reportedly given to him by the Master of Life, whom he had met in heaven in a mystical experience. Neolin also devised a prayer stick for his people.

Pontiac believed that his efforts were strengthened by his adherence to Neolin's teachings. The Ottawa chief, most noted for the coordinated attack on English outposts in the Great Lakes area during the 1760's, captured eight British forts and forced the abandonment of a ninth. Neolin predicted Pontiac's defeat of the whites. After Pontiac was ultimately defeated, Neolin's reputation was greatly diminished; little is known of him after 1770.

Tonya Huber

FURTHER READING
Dowd, Gregory Evans. *A Spirited Resistance: The North American Indian Struggle for Unity, 1745-1815.* Baltimore: Johns Hopkins University Press, 1992.
_____. *War Under Heaven: Pontiac, the Indian Nations, and the British Empire.* Baltimore: Johns Hopkins University Press, 2002.
Hunter, Charles. "The Delaware Nativistic Revival of the Mid-Eighteenth Century." *Ethnohistory* 18 (1971): 39-49.

Wayne Newton performs his 25,000th show before a sold-out audience at the Sheraton Desert Inn in Las Vegas in 1996. (AP/Wide World Photos)

Newton, Wayne

Born: April 3, 1942; Norfolk, Virginia

Tribal affiliation: Powhatan and Cherokee

Significance: A singer, entertainer, and real-estate entrepreneur, Wayne Newton is perhaps the most acclaimed and popular entertainer known to Las Vegas.

Born in Norfolk, Virginia, in 1942, Wayne Newton got his Native American heritage from both his father, who was half Powhatan, and his mother, who was half Cherokee. At the age of five he began his singing career performing on local radio stations. As a teenager Newton had his own radio program in Phoenix, and at the age of sixteen he dropped out of school to perform with his brother Jerry.

They went on the road and met Bobby Darin, who helped sign Newton to a recording contract; Newton's brother had by now dropped out of the act. Newton, singing in a distinctively high voice, scored a hit with "Danke Schoen" in 1963 and followed it with "Red Roses for a Blue Lady." His only other major chart success did not come until the 1970's, with the hit "Daddy Don't You Walk So Fast." Newton began to concentrate on performing live and settled in Las Vegas. By the 1980's he had become Las Vegas's most popular and most highly paid entertainer. He sold out show after show, at one point earning up to a million dollars a month. He invested heavily in real estate. Newton surprised the world by having to file for bankruptcy in 1991, a situation caused in part by legal costs in a libel suit against NBC and in part by problematic investments and lavish spending. Amazingly, however, he turned his financial situation around and was back on his feet in relatively short order.

In the late 1990's Newton was living just outside Las Vegas on a 52-acre ranch called Casa de Shenandoah. In his free time he flew his helicopter or private jet to his 218-acre ranch 60 miles north of Las Vegas, where he raised Arabian horses. In addition to singing, Newton has occasionally appeared in films, including *Eighty Steps to Jonah* (1969); *License to Kill* (1989), in which he played a televangelist; and *The Adventures of Ford Fairlane* (1990), and he has made several television appearances.

Newton holds a genuine concern for the welfare of American Indians and in 1982 held a benefit on their behalf at the John F. Kennedy Center for the Performing Arts in Washington, D.C. In May, 1998, the first Native American Music Awards program named him its entertainer of the year.

Jennifer Raye James

FURTHER READING
Newton, Wayne, with Dick Maurice. *Once Before I Go.* New York: Avon, 1989.

Ninham, Daniel

Born: c. 1710
Died: August 31, 1778; Kingsbridge, New York
Tribal affiliation: Mahican
Significance: Daniel Ninham sought the return of Mahican lands and fought on the colonial side during the American Revolution.

Daniel Ninham was a leader of a Mahican band in Westenhuck, New York, who allied with Sir William Johnson and the British against the French in the last of several colonial wars in North America (1754-1763). He took part in the Battle of Lake George, September 8, 1755.

As the war with France neared its conclusion, Ninham traveled to England with other native leaders, principally Connecticut Mohegans, to seek return of lands they contended had been illegally taken by British colonists. The American Revolution intervened, and the legal actions filed by Ninham and others never were heard in court. Ninham joined the American patriots during the Revolution and was killed fighting on their behalf at Kingsbridge, New York, August 31, 1778.

Bruce E. Johansen

Ninigret

Born: c. 1600
Died: c. 1678; Wequapaug, Rhode Island
Also known as: Ninicraft, Nenekunat
Tribal affiliation: Niantic
Significance: Ninigret was sachem of the eastern branch of the Niantic of southern Connecticut; he skillfully avoided being drawn into the seventeenth century wars between the Indians and the English settlers.

In the early 1630's, Ninigret was principal sachem (chief or leader) of the eastern branch of the Niantics. The Eastern Niantics occupied the coastal region of western Rhode Island and were subject to the more numerous and powerful Narragansetts, to whom they paid tribute. Ninigret was notable for struggling to preserve his independence from the British while avoiding a war with them such as destroyed other New England tribes. He joined the British Mohegan-Narragansett attack on the Pequots in 1636-1637, but during the 1640's Ninigret repeatedly clashed with British authorities for his support of the Narragansetts in their war with the Mohegans. In 1653-1654, Niantic attacks on the

Montauks of Long Island brought more disputes with colonial authorities, and a small British army invaded Niantic country to chastise Ninigret. He evaded contact by hiding in swamps with his people. During King Philip's War of 1675-1676, Ninigret avoided participation until the later stages of the conflict, when his Niantics assisted the British. In contrast, the Narragansetts had chosen to fight the British and suffered terrible losses. Regarded by the British as a schemer, Ninigret was a cunning survivor who recognized the reality of British power and reluctantly accommodated himself to it.

Bert M. Mutersbaugh

Oakes, Richard

Born: 1942; St. Regis Indian Reservation, Franklin County, New York
Died: September 21, 1972; Santa Clara, California
Tribal affiliation: Mohawk
Significance: As a leader of the political activists who occupied Alcatraz Island in 1969, Richard Oakes helped call attention to the aspirations of Native Americans in the United States.

Born into a Mohawk family, Richard Oakes was raised on the St. Regis Indian Reservation near New York's Canadian border. As he grew up, he was not stimulated by his early education, which was conducted under the assumptions that Indian children should be assimilated into mainstream American culture. After quitting high school in 1959, he began to work as an ironworker—an occupation long closely associated with the Mohawk people.

Although Oakes obtained steady work, he did not think that his talents were being put to their best use and attributed the problem to American society having no place for Indians and lacking any understanding of them. During the late 1960's, he went to the West Coast. By then, he had visited the reservations of several tribes across the United States and become more poetically conscious. In the wake of the Civil Rights movement and mounting protests against U.S. involvement in the Vietnam War, political activism was increasing throughout American society. One manifestation was the founding of the American Indian Movement (AIM) in 1968. Oakes was sympathetic with the beliefs of AIM and met other Native Americans from different tribal backgrounds who shared his views.

On November 9, 1969, Oakes and thirteen other Indian activists chartered a boat in San Francisco Bay and sailed to Alcatraz Island, whose high-security federal prison had been shut down six years earlier. The closing of the prison technically relegated the island to the status of unused federal land. After the Indians seized the island, they realized that they could occupy it with little resistance. Eleven days later, more than eighty additional activists arrived on the island.

The Indian occupation of Alcatraz was less an attempt at political provocation than a symbolic statement that Native Americans were the original inhabitants of North America and should not be neglected. Assuming the name Indians of All Tribes, the occupiers announced that their goal was to transform Alcatraz into a Native American educational and cultural center. Moreover, they pointed out that the island's bleak and barren condition symbolized the condition of Indians throughout the United States.

Eventually, internal dissension among the occupiers and infiltration of the occupation by Bay Area hippies reduced the occupiers' morale, and rivals to Oakes's leadership arose. The accidental death of Oakes's thirteen-year-old stepdaughter on the island aggravated the dissension and prompted Oakes's departure. On June 11, 1971, the island was retaken by federal agents.

Afterward, Oakes remained resolute about the ideals that had led to his actions, saying that the Alcatraz occupation was inspirational and would help native peoples take control of their own destinies. He later went to Los Angeles to work in the Native American Studies Center at the University of California (UCLA), Los Angeles.

During a visit to Northern California in 1972, Oakes was killed in what appeared to be a random encounter with a man named Michael Murphy, who may not have even known who his victim was. Morgan claimed that he shot Oakes in self-defense and was exonerated by a jury, but many Indian groups protested against what they deemed an unjust verdict.

Nicholas Birns

FURTHER READING
Adam Fortunate Eagle. *Heart of the Rock.* Norman: University of Oklahoma Press, 2002.
Johnson, Troy R. *The Occupation of Alcatraz Island: Indian Self-Determination and the Rise of Indian Activism.* Urbana: University of Illinois Press, 1996.

Occom, Samson

Born: c. 1723; New London, Connecticut
Died: July 14, 1792; New Stockbridge, New York
Tribal affiliation: Mohegan
Significance: Samson Occom was one of the first American Indians educated by whites who successfully bridged both cultures as a missionary and teacher.

Samson Occom was caught up in the religious enthusiasm of the "Great Awakening" when he was about sixteen. When he was twenty, his mother went to the Reverend Eleazar Wheelock, a prominent evangelical minister, and asked him to teach her son how to read.

Wheelock's success in teaching the highly motivated Occom led him to establish a school for Indians, Moor's Indian Charity School. Wheelock taught the basics of a secular and religious education. "Husbandry" (farming) was taught to boys, and girls were taught what today would be called home economics. Among other things, Wheelock taught Occom and his other students Greek, Latin, and Hebrew, which he believed were essential for future missionaries. (The Protestant emphasis on interpreting the Bible individually meant that students should be able to read the original Greek, Latin, and Hebrew biblical texts.)

Unable to attend college because of weak eyes, Occom became a teacher and minister to the Montauk tribe on the eastern tip of Long Island from 1749 to 1764. He was the town's minister, judge, teacher, and letter writer, and was expected to offer hospitality to visitors. He taught his students the alphabet, spelling, and the like. He received twenty pounds a year from the London Society for the Propagation of the Gospel for his work. He married Mary Fowler (a Montauk) in 1751.

Occom was ordained as a Presbyterian minister in 1759 by the Long Island presbytery. Wheelock sent him on missions to the Oneida tribe in New York in 1761, 1762, and

Samson Occom. (Hulton|Archive by Getty Images)

1763. In 1764, he returned home to Mohegan, Connecticut, and in 1765 he accompanied the Reverend Nathaniel Whitaker to England to raise money for Wheelock's Indian school. In two years of preaching across Britain, Occom was able to raise twelve thousand pounds. Upon his return to America, Occom was unwilling to do missionary work among the Iroquois as Wheelock suggested, and was upset over Wheelock's use of the money raised for Indian students to found Dartmouth College in New Hampshire.

Occom severed his connection with Wheelock and became a poverty-stricken itinerant preacher to the New England tribes. His concern for protecting Indian lands helped cause a rift with his church. In 1773, he sought a land grant from the Oneida tribe to remove a selected group of New England Indians beyond the negative influence of whites. Although interrupted by the American Revolution, Occom was able to establish Brothertown in 1789, and he pastored to his people for the remainder of his life. Occom's published works include *Sermon Preached at the Execution of Moses Paul, an Indian* (1772) and *A Choice Selection of Hymns* (1774).

Jon Reyhner

FURTHER READING
Love, William DeLoss. *Samson Occom and the Christian Indians of New England.* Introduction by Margaret Connell Szasz. 1899. Reprint. Syracuse, N.Y.: Syracuse University Press, 2000.
Peyer, Bernd C. *The Tutor'd Mind: Indian Missionary-Writers in Antebellum America.* Amherst: University of Massachusetts Press, 1997.

Oconostota

Born: c. 1710; now in eastern Tennessee
Died: 1783; Overhill Cherokee Territory, Tennessee
Tribal affiliation: Cherokee
Significance: Oconostota helped to shape early Cherokee policy toward British and French colonists in what became the southeastern United States.

Oconostota was born on the western side of the southern Appalachian Highlands. As a young warrior, he so distinguished himself that by 1736, in his mid-twenties, he was the war chief of the Cherokee. During the eighteenth century, a time of rivalry in North America between the British and the French, most Cherokee leaders favored ties to the British;

Oconostota was an exception. When the smallpox epidemic of 1738 broke out, the French told the Cherokee that the British had planted the smallpox germ. Oconostota survived his bout with the disease, but for the rest of his life he blamed the British for his smallpox-pitted face.

Following the French and Indian War (1754-1763), Oconostota found it necessary to work for a mutually beneficial relationship with the British, including Cherokee neutrality during the American Revolution. Until his death in 1783, Oconostota tried to protect the rights of the Cherokee while maintaining peaceful relations with the new nation that was emerging from the American Revolution.

Glenn L. Swygart

FURTHER READING
Raphael, Ray. *A People's History of the American Revolution: How Common People Shaped the Fight for Independence.* New York: New Press, 2001.

Old Briton

Born: ?; Wabash River area, northwestern Indiana
Died: June 21, 1752; at Pickawillany, on the Miami River in Ohio
Tribal affiliation: Miami (Piankashaw band)
Significance: Old Briton attempted to change Miami trading partners and allies from the French to the English in the mid-eighteenth century.

Frustrated by high prices and chronic shortages of French trade goods, Old Briton hoped to persuade his people to break ties with the French and open trade with the British. Having met British traders in his earlier travels along the lower Wabash and on the Ohio River, he understood that political relations with the British would be advantageous. In the fall of 1747, after participating in a failed uprising against the French, Old Briton led his followers east and founded a new village, Pickawillany, on the Great Miami River in western Ohio.

Old Briton sent a delegation to Pennsylvania, which signed a treaty of friendship and alliance and initiated the desired trading relationship. Despite repeated French efforts to persuade or intimidate Old Briton back into the old relationship, he diplomatically put them off. Pickawillany grew into a major western trading center, with Weas, Piankashaws, Kickapoos, and Mascoutens bringing their furs to the British. A small, ineffective French attack on Pickawillany in the summer of 1751 stimulated Old Briton to organize a general Indian war against the French, which included his execution of three French soldiers and mutilation of a fourth, who was then sent back to Canada.

Recognizing the threat Old Briton posed to their empire, the French enlisted Charles Langlade (Ottawa/French) in the spring of 1752 to raise a force of Ottawas, Ojibwas, and others to destroy Pickawillany. On June 21, just after most Pickawillany warriors had left to hunt, Langlade attacked. Caught by surprise, Old Briton was outnumbered ten to one. Wanting to make an example of Old Briton, Langlade had him executed, after which his body was boiled and his remains eaten by some of the attackers. Pickawillany was abandoned, but by the end of the decade the British had expelled the French in war and the Miamis found themselves with no other trade partner but the British.

Sean O'Neill

One Bull

Born: c. 1853; place unknown
Died: 1947; place unknown
Also known as: Lone Bull, Henry Oscar One Bull
Tribal affiliation: Hunkpapa Lakota (Sioux)
Significance: One Bull was a principal source of historical information on his contemporary Sioux leader SITTING BULL, and he helped to revive the sacred rite of the Sun Dance on the Standing Rock Reservation during the 1930's.

One Bull was born into a prominent Lakota family, probably during the spring of 1853. His father, Makes Room for Him, was a noted headman of the Miniconjou Lakota, and his mother, Pretty Feather Woman, was a Hunkpapa Lakota and Chief Sitting Bull's oldest sister. In 1857, after losing his wife and infant son, Sitting Bull took One Bull and reared him in place of his dead son. According to Lakota custom, children raised under such circumstances are lavished with attention and raised especially carefully. One Bull's name came from a vision that Sitting Bull's father, JUMPING BULL, once had that gave "Bull" names to the men in his family.

When he was about fourteen years old, One Bull killed his first buffalo, an important event for Lakota youth and their families. In honor of this event, Sitting Bull gave away a fine horse in his nephew's honor, and One Bull distributed all the meat from his first kill to the old people in camp. One Bull was a skilled horseman and a fine marksman with a bow and arrow, so at a young age, he was recruited by several Lakota warrior societies. Around the age of sixteen he joined the prestigious Strong Heart Society, and by eighteen he was an accomplished warrior. He participated in numerous horse raids, sometimes accompanied by Sitting Bull or by his older brother, WHITE BULL.

At the age of twenty-three, One Bull took part in the Battle of the Little Bighorn (1876). The Hunkpapa camp was invaded by Major Marcus Reno's men, so the men in One Bull's camp were the first to respond. One Bull was especially courageous that day. He saved a wounded comrade, had his horse shot out from under him, and engaged in hand-to-hand combat. Afterward, he stayed at Sitting Bull's side when many Hunkpapa fled to Canada to escape retribution from U.S. troops, and he remained with his uncle during the latter's detention at Fort Randall in Dakota Territory during the early 1880's. In 1883, One Bull and Sitting Bull were moved to the Standing Rock Reservation, where they tried to follow the agent's advice by taking up sedentary farming.

One Bull was not present when Sitting Bull was killed by Indian police on December 15, 1890, but his wife was there. One Bull and his family and others close to Sitting Bull were detained at Fort Yates on suspicion they might instigate further trouble. After his release, One Bull sought to pick up the pieces of his life. He lived far enough from the agency offices to practice some traditional Lakota rituals that had been banned in 1883.

One Bull was known to have the ability to make rain, cause pleasant weather, and make other changes in the weather. During the late 1920's and into the 1930's, provided interviews to historians studying Sitting Bull. During the 1930's, he had a vision instructing him to revive the Sun Dance—one of the rituals banned by the federal government. Eventually, he obtained permission for the ritual and conducted the first Sun Dance at Standing Rock since 1882. In 1947, at the age of ninety-four, he died of jaw cancer.

Carole Barrett

Opechancanough

Born: c. 1545; near the York River, Virginia
Died: 1644 or 1646; Jamestown, Virginia
Also known as: Mangopeomen, Massatamohtnock
Tribal affiliation: Powhatan
Significance: Opechancanough was one of the earliest tribal leaders in the Southeast to plan and carry out a major offensive against European immigrants.

The limited available evidence suggests that Opechancanough, whose Algonquian name meant "he whose soul is white," was born around 1545, near the York River in Virginia. Although little is known about the first half of his life, some historians—based on largely circumstantial evidence—believe that Spanish explorers in the region may have taken him to Spain and Florida during the 1560's. If so, he may have returned when Spanish Jesuits attempted to establish a mission in Virginia in 1570.

A brother of POWHATAN, chief of a powerful Tidewater Virginia confederacy of tribes, Opechancanough first appeared in English documents as chief of the Pamunkey tribe when Jamestown was established in 1607. In that capacity he confronted the English adventurer Captain John Smith on several occasions. Most notably, it was Opechancanough who captured Smith and took the Englishman to his brother's village, where Smith claimed that Powhatan's daughter, POCAHONTAS, saved his life.

Shortly after Powhatan's death in 1618, Opechancanough became the great *werowance*, or chief, of the Powhatan Confederacy. Intent upon reversing his brother's accommodation to English encroachment on native lands, he developed a well-coordinated plan to exterminate the intruders.

Opechancanough's resolve was the product of many factors. He was alarmed both by the rapid expansion of English settlements accompanying the tobacco boom in the colony's second decade of settlement and by the deadly impact of European diseases on his people. He also resented English efforts to assimilate the natives into their culture.

Opechancanough used the murder of Nemattanow as a pretext for his all-out assault. This man, a highly regarded warrior and religious prophet whom the English called Jack of the Feathers, was killed by two settlers in March of 1622. While lulling the English into a false sense of security by permitting continued trade and promising that the sky would fall before he broke the peace, Opechancanough ordered an attack on March 22. The offensive claimed 347 English lives, almost a third of the population. In response, Virginia officials declared war on the natives, and a decade-long conflict resulted. The natives were driven deep into the Virginia interior.

From 1632 to 1644 there were sporadic skirmishes between Indians and whites as the English continued to expand their settlements. Still hopeful of at least slowing the encroachment, an aged, enfeebled, and nearly blind Opechancanough persuaded most tribes to participate in one more assault in 1644. Although he had to be carried into battle,

Opechancanough led his forces. While the attacks took more than four hundred English lives, the casualties were less devastating to the English colony because the total population had reached about eight thousand.

After the English settlers defeated the Powhatan Confederacy for a second time, a militia unit captured Opechancanough. He was murdered by a guard while in a Jamestown jail in the mid-1640's.

Larry Gragg

FURTHER READING

Rountree, Helen C. *Pocahontas, Powhatan, Opechancanough: Three Indian Lives Changed by Jamestown.* Charlottesville: University of Virginia Press, 2005.

Opothleyaholo

Born: c. 1798; Creek Nation, Georgia
Died: 1862; near Leroy Creek, Kansas
Also known as: Apotheyahola, Optothe Yoholo, Good Shouting Child
Tribal affiliation: Creek
Significance: Both in Georgia and after removal to Indian Territory, Opothleyaholo was a Creek tribal leader.

As a leader of the traditional Creek warrior faction, the Red Sticks, Opothleyaholo fought with principal Creek leader William WEATHER-FORD against General Andrew Jackson in the Creek Wars of 1813-1814. Thereafter, Opothleyaholo was one of several chiefs opposing an illegal treaty ceding twenty-five million acres of Creek land, signed by William McINTOSH, leader of the peace faction, the White Sticks.

In 1825-1826, Opothleyaholo led a Creek delegation to Washington, D.C., protesting removal. He signed the Treaty of Washington, ceding many, but not all, Creek lands. He signed a second treaty in Washington in 1832. Resisting removal to Indian Territory, in 1834-1835, Opothleyaholo tried to purchase land in Mexico. The Mexican government, however, was uncooperative, and in 1836, he and his people were forcibly relocated to Indian Territory. There he became a head chief for temporarily reunited Creek factions, counseling peace with whites. He supported the Union during the Civil War, fleeing to Kansas after defeat by Confederate forces. Opothleyaholo died shortly thereafter.

Mary E. Virginia

FURTHER READING
McBride, Lela J. *Opothleyaholo and the Loyal Muskogee: Their Flight to Kansas in the Civil War.* Jefferson, N.C.: McFarland, 2000.

Ortiz, Simon

Born: May 27, 1941; Albuquerque, New Mexico
Tribal affiliation: Acoma Pueblo
Significance: Simon Ortiz is a respected and widely read poet.
Ortiz spent his early years at Deetseyamah on Acoma Pueblo land. He is a member of the Eagle (Dyaamih hanoh) clan. He attended McCartys Day School in McCartys, New Mexico, St. Catherine's Indian School in Sante Fe, New Mexico, and Grants High School in Grants, New Mexico.

Following high school, Ortiz worked in uranium mines for Kerr-McGee, served in the U.S. Army, and studied at both the University of New Mexico, where he earned a bachelor's degree, and the University of Iowa, where he earned a master's degree in fine arts. He has taught at Sinte Gleska College in South Dakota and at the University of New Mex-

Poet Simon Ortiz discusses his work during an interview at the American Indian Community House in New York in 2003. (AP/Wide World Photos)

ico. Ortiz is the author of the books of poems *Going for the Rain* (1976), *A Good Journey* (1977), and *Fight Back: For the Sake of the People, for the Sake of the Land* (1980). He is also the author of a collection of short stories, *Fightin': New and Collected Stories* (1983), and edited a collection of native fiction, *Earth Power Coming* (1983). Ortiz' work reflects his Acoma Pueblo heritage; it has also been influenced by the social movements of the 1960's and 1970's.

Ortiz' later publications include *Men on the Moon: Collected Short Stories* (1999), a collection of his own short stories, and *Speaking for the Generations: Native Writers on Writing* (1998), which he edited.

T. J. Arant

FURTHER READING

Iftekharuddin, Farhat, Mary Rohrberger, and Maurice Lee, eds. *Speaking of the Short Story: Interviews with Contemporary Writers.* Jackson: University Press of Mississippi, 1997.

Rader, Dean. "Luci Tapahonso and Simon Ortiz: Allegory, Symbol, Language, Poetry." *Southwestern American Literature* 22, no. 2 (Spring, 1997).

Osceola

Born: c. 1804; Tallassee on the Tallapoosa River, near present-day Tuskegee, Alabama

Died: January 30, 1838; Fort Moultrie, Charleston, South Carolina

Also known as: Assiola (Black Drink Singer), Tallassee Tustenuggee, Billy Powell

Tribal affiliation: Creek, Seminole

Significance: Allegedly a participant in the First Seminole War, Osceola became a leader of the Seminoles, who refused to be moved west of the Mississippi; he initiated the Second Seminole War.

Osceola later insisted, and some historians maintain, that both his father (name unknown) and mother (Polly Copinger) were Creeks and that his mother later married an Englishman, William Powell. A 1991 study by Patricia R. Wickman, however, provides impressive evidence that Powell was indeed Osceola's father, that Copinger's grandfather (James McQueen) and father were white, and that the boy also had black ancestors, as did many children who were born in the Upper Creek town of Tallassee. Nevertheless, Osceola was considered to be an Upper Creek, like his mother.

Osceola's mother's uncle, Peter McQueen, was chief of the village where Osceola was born and became a leader of the Red Sticks during the Creek War of 1813-1814. As that conflict escalated, many Creeks fled from Alabama into Florida. Among the refugees were Osceola and his mother, who followed McQueen and became separated from Powell during the migration. Osceola was captured by Andrew Jackson's troops during Jackson's 1818 campaign in Florida, but he was released because of his youth. He is believed to have fought against Jackson in the First Seminole War.

Osceola. (National Archives)

Osceola settled in central Florida after Jackson's campaign and, like many dislocated Creeks, became known as a Seminole. He was never a hereditary chief, nor was he apparently ever elected to such a post; however, in the controversy surrounding the signing of the treaties of Payne's Landing in 1832 and of Fort Gibson in 1833, both of which provided for the relocation of the Seminoles to the West, he emerged as a leader of those who opposed removal.

A heated clash with Wiley Thompson, the federal Indian agent for central Florida, made Osceola an outlaw. Abolitionists later wrote that Thompson aided two slave catchers in capturing one of Osceola's wives, who was a mulatto, but there is no evidence for this tale. Instead, the conflict apparently originated when Thompson called a council at Fort King to confirm the earlier treaties. Most of the Seminoles who were present silently refused to sign the documents placed before them, but Osceola allegedly plunged a knife through the agreement. Again, no contemporary account supports this story.

Other confrontations in the summer of 1835 led Thompson to have Osceola imprisoned in shackles, but Osceola was released when he agreed to support removal. Rather than abide by his agreement with Thompson, Osceola organized Seminole resistance and killed Charley

Emathla, a chief who had supported emigration. Osceola and his follow-ers then attacked a baggage train during December, 1835. Later that same month, he killed Thompson, while allies ambushed a force of more than a hundred regulars and killed all but three of them. On New Year's Eve, 1835, a large party led by Osceola attacked another detachment of regulars and punished them severely in the First Battle of the Withla-coochee, where Osceola was wounded slightly but escaped capture.

This began the Second Seminole War, which would last until 1842. Until his capture in 1837, Osceola was the primary target of army opera-tions because the U.S. military recognized his importance as a leader in the resistance. Participants in the campaigns against him noted that many of his followers were black. They would have supported him in-stead of the hereditary chiefs, and his desire to protect them may have been part of his motivation for continuing to fight long after his health began to fail. His evasion of army columns and bold attacks made him something of a folk hero in the United States, but it also earned him the hatred of military leaders, especially after he liberated more than seven hundred Indians held in a detention camp in June, 1837.

In October, 1837, General Thomas S. Jesup, frustrated by Osceola, treacherously accepted his request for a parley under a flag of truce. The Seminole leader, who was then suffering from malaria, and more than eighty of his followers were captured at their camp near Fort Peyton in a flagrant violation of the truce. Despite the public outcry, he was taken to Fort Mellon at St. Augustine, where two of his wives and two children, as well as his half sister and others, joined him. These two wives may have been the two sisters he had married in accordance with Creek custom, though there appear to have been others.

After several other Seminoles escaped, Osceola and his group were transferred on New Year's Eve, 1837, to Fort Moultrie at Charleston, South Carolina. There his health declined rapidly, and he died on Janu-ary 30, 1838. Allegations vary as to the cause of his death, but most agree that his depression contributed to his rapid demise. Wickman says that quinsy, or tonsillitis complicated by an abscess, was the immediate cause of Osceola's death, and both malaria and recurring fevers were contrib-uting factors in his declining health.

Osceola was buried outside Fort Moultrie on Sullivan Island with mil-itary honors, but before interment his head was removed by Frederick Weedon, the physician who had attended him during his fatal illness. It was displayed in a medical museum maintained by Valentine Mott of the Medical College of New York until the building was allegedly de-stroyed by fire in 1866.

The betrayal of Osceola destroyed any realistic hope of unity among the Seminoles. The war continued sporadically until 1842, when most of the surviving Seminoles moved West, as his family had after his death. Only a few remained in the swamps. The circumstances of Osceola's fight, capture, and death, which were often misrepresented, made him a folk hero to many. No fewer than twenty towns in the United States now bear his name, as do three counties, two townships, one borough, two lakes, two mountains, a state park, and a national forest.

Richard B. McCaslin

FURTHER READING

Boyd, Mark F. "Asi-Yaholo or Osceola." *Florida Historical Quarterly* 30 (July, 1951): 249-305.

Covington, James W. *The Seminoles of Florida*. Gainesville: University Presses of Florida, 1993.

Goggin, John M. "Osceola: Portraits, Features, and Dress." *Florida Historical Quarterly* 33 (January-April, 1955): 161-192.

Hartley, William, and Ellen Hartley. *Osceola: The Unconquered Indian*. New York: Hawthorn Books, 1973.

Mahon, John K. *History of the Second Seminole War, 1835-1842*. Gainesville: University Presses of Florida, 1967.

Missall, John, and Mary Lou Missall. *The Seminole Wars: America's Longest Indian Conflict*. Foreword by Raymond Arsenault and Gary R. Mormino. Gainesville: University Press of Florida, 2004.

Wickman, Patricia R. *Osceola's Legacy*. Tuscaloosa: University of Alabama Press, 1991.

Oshkosh

Born: 1795; Old King's Village on the Fox River near present-day Green Bay, Wisconsin

Died: August 20, 1858; Keshena, Wisconsin

Also known as: Oshkusi, Oiscoss (His Hoof, His Nail, or the Brave)

Tribal affiliation: Menominee

Significance: Oshkosh was first appointed chief by federal agents during mediation of a land dispute; he helped to negotiate removal of the Menominee Indians.

Oshkosh, descendant of chiefs, originally allied with the British during the War of 1812, fighting with Chief TOMAH in the battle at Fort Mackinaw, Michigan, and at Fort Stephenson, Ohio. In 1827, he was appointed chief by U.S. agents Lewis Cass and Thomas McKenney as they mediated a border dispute between the Chippewa and the Menominee and a subsequent disagreement between the Menominees and a group of New York Iroquois, led by Eleazar WILLIAMS, who wished to settle on Menominee land.

Oshkosh retained leadership throughout his life. He aided the United States during the BLACK HAWK War of 1832 and afterward continued to ensure Menominee compliance with white authority. Menominee land claims were continuously eroded, and removal was completed when Wisconsin became a state in 1848 and Oshkosh signed the Treaty of Lake Powahekone ceding the last Menominee lands to the federal government. Oshkosh died in 1858 in a drunken brawl and was succeeded by his son. The town of Oshkosh, Wisconsin, is named for him.

Mary E. Virginia

Otherday, John

Born: 1801; Swan Lake (now in Minnesota)
Died: 1871; Sisseton Sioux Reservation, South Dakota
Also known as: Angpetu Tokecha, Other Day
Tribal affiliation: Wahpeton Lakota (Sioux)
Significance: As an army scout and protector of whites, John Otherday was honored by the U.S. government.

As a young man, Otherday was reputedly a heavy drinker and a brawler, having killed other Sioux in arguments. After becoming a Christian, he married a white woman, adopted the name John, and settled on the Minnesota Sioux Reservation.

On several occasions, Otherday aided whites. After the Spirit Lake Uprising of 1857, he rescued white female captives and assisted in the search for Sioux raiders. During LITTLE CROW's uprising of 1862-1863, he led white settlers to safety. In retaliation, Little Crow burned Otherday's home.

As a U.S. Army scout, Otherday worked for General Henry Hastings Sibley, aiding his search for Little Crow. In reward for his services, he was granted $2,500 by the U.S. government, which was presented during a ceremony in Washington, D.C. With his reward he purchased a ranch, which quickly failed. He thereafter returned to the Sioux reservation, where the U.S. government built him a house. He died in 1871, a victim of tuberculosis.

Mary E. Virginia

FURTHER READING
Stillwell, Larry. *Flash Point of Deceit: The U.S.-Dakota War of 1862.* Moorhead, Minn.: Gold Fire, 1999.

Ouray

Born: c. 1820; northern Mexico, in present-day southern Colorado
Died: August 24, 1880; Ignacio, Colorado
Also known as: Willie Ouray, Ure
Tribal affiliation: Ute
Significance: Ouray led central Colorado (Uncompaghre) Utes from the mid-1860's to 1880, persuading them to conciliate rather than fight with encroaching whites.

Ouray was the son of a Ute-Apache union. His band ranged the mountains of central Colorado and hunted buffalo on the Great Plains east of the Rockies. Ouray spent his youth near Taos, New Mexico, as a shepherd; there he learned the Spanish language and culture, possibly as an Indian captive. He then rejoined his mother's Ute band, where he gained prominence as a warrior and hunter, and was useful as an interpreter.

Ouray was a minor signatory on the 1863 treaty ceding parts of southern Colorado to the United States but was a leading chief of the Uncompaghre (central Colorado) Utes by the time an 1868 treaty was signed. During the 1870's, other Utes began to resent his influence, the preferential treatment he obtained from the U.S. government, and his autocratic and often tyrannical leadership. He successfully thwarted more than one plot by subchiefs, including his own brother-in-law, to kill him.

In 1873, Ouray cooperated in obtaining the necessary signatures to ratify a new agreement ceding more lands, for which he was given special concessions as well as an annual salary of one thousand dollars, a home, and a four-hundred-acre ranch at a new agency. Here, Ouray appeared to adopt the whites' lifestyle, wearing broadcloth suits, riding in a carriage, and living in a cabin with standard American furniture. Despite continued antagonism by some northern Colorado Utes who accused Ouray of betraying his people for a salary, he could not be dislodged from his band leadership or the U.S. government's insistence on using him as head chief for all Utes.

In 1879, Utes of northern Colorado attacked and besieged U.S. troops in what they believed was a defense of their reservation. They

Ouray. (National Archives)

killed their unpopular agent and massacred agency workers. Ouray was instrumental in halting the attack and aiding the government in freeing white women who were taken prisoner. Whites used this incident to expel the Utes from Colorado. The Northern Utes were removed to Utah, and the U.S. government renegotiated the 1873 agreement with the Uncompaghre and Southern Utes. A three-fourths tribal ratification was required, and it was believed that only Ouray could obtain these signatures.

After obtaining his own band's signatures, Ouray traveled to the Southern Utes' agency at Ignacio, Colorado, to obtain the remainder. On the way he became sick, and he died on August 24, 1880. A negotiator bribed the Utes for the remaining signatures, and in 1881 Ouray's band was ultimately removed to Utah. Ouray had recognized the inevitability of the loss of Indian land to incoming whites, gaining as much as possible through peaceful means while he could and keeping his people relatively free of disastrous warfare.

Robert Jones
Sondra Jones

FURTHER READING

Decker, Peter R. *"The Utes Must Go!: American Expansion and the Removal of a People.* Golden, Colo.: Fulcrum Publishing, 2004.

Rockwell, Wilson. *The Utes: A Forgotten People.* Ouray, Colo.: Western Reflections, 1998.

Simmons, Virginia McConnell. *The Ute Indians of Utah, Colorado, and New Mexico.* Niwot: University Press of Colorado, 2000.

Smith, P. David. *Ouray, Chief of the Utes.* Ouray, Colo.: Wayfinder Press, 1986.

Parker, Arthur Caswell

Born: April 5, 1881; Cattaraugus Indian Reservation, Collins Township, New York

Died: January 1, 1955; Naples, New York

Also known as: Gawasowaneh, Big Snowsnake

Tribal affiliation: Seneca

Significance: Arthur Parker was a leading Native American figure in the fields of archaeology, anthropology, and museum directorship and was also a prolific author.

Born on New York's Cattaraugus Indian Reservation with one-quarter part Seneca parentage, Parker was a great-nephew of Ely Samuel PARKER, the secretary to General Ulysses S. Grant during the Civil War. He was also a distant relative of the early nineteenth century Iroquois prophet HANDSOME LAKE.

After studying at Dickinson Seminary in Pennsylvania, Parker enrolled at Harvard University, where he came to know Frederick Ward Putnam, a leading museum director. Although Parker never finished his degree at Harvard, he became a field archaeologist for Harvard's Peabody Museum in 1903. He also did part-time work at the American Museum of Natural History and was appointed state archaeologist for the New York State Museum in Albany in 1906. In his new position, he took the lead in excavating several Iroquois sites and organized the New York State Archaeological Survey as he built the State Museum into a major center for archaeological study. Meanwhile, he wrote *The Archeo-logical History of New York* (1922).

In 1925, Parker was appointed director of the Rochester Museum of Arts and Sciences, a post that he held for almost two decades. He was also a prolific writer, with roughly five hundred published and unpublished manuscripts, ranging from books to journal and magazine articles, radio scripts, plays, and others. His personal bibliography eventually included fourteen books, among them *Erie Indian Village* (1913), *Code of Handsome Lake* (1913), *Life of General Ely S. Parker* (1919), *Seneca Myths and Folk Tales* (1923), and *Last of the Senecas* (1952).

Bruce E. Johansen

FURTHER READING
Parker, Arthur. *Parker on the Iroquois.* Edited by William N. Fenton. Syracuse: Syracuse University Press, 1968.
_____. *The History of The Seneca Indians.* 1926. Port Washington, N.Y.: Ira J. Friedman, 1967.
_____. *The Code of Handsome Lake, the Seneca Prophet.* New York State Museum Bulletin No. 163. Albany, N.Y.: 1913.
Porter, Joy. *To Be Indian: The Life of Iroquois-Seneca Arthur Caswell Parker.* Norman: University of Oklahoma Press, 2001.

Parker, Ely Samuel

Born: c. 1828; near Pembroke, New York
Died: August 31, 1895; Fairfield, Connecticut
Also known as: Donehogawa, Hasanoanda (the Reader, or Coming to the Front)
Tribal affiliation: Seneca
Significance: Ely Samuel Parker was a Seneca chief who became a member of Ulysses S. Grant's staff during the Civil War; he was the first Indian to be appointed commissioner of Indian affairs.

Parker was born on the Tonawanda Seneca reservation in western New York. He was a member of the Wolf clan, in keeping with the Seneca and Iroquois custom of remaining in the clan of one's mother. Parker's mother was Elizabeth Parker (Gaontgwutwus). His father, William Parker (Jonoestowa), had a white mother but served as the chief of the Tono-wanda Seneca. His maternal grandfather, Jimmy Johnson (Sosehawa), was high priest of the Six Nations of the Iroquois and a nephew of RED JACKET, a noted Seneca leader.

Ely Samuel Parker. (Library of Congress)

Educated in a missionary school and two local academies, Parker was pressed into service at an early age as an emissary for Seneca leaders who were negotiating with President James K. Polk's administration and the U.S. Senate over land titles. These negotiations and some related court cases were eventually settled in favor of the Seneca. Parker also helped Lewis H. Morgan with his landmark study of the Iroquois, the first scientific work on the tribe. On September 19, 1851, Parker became a sachem. He assumed the title of Donehogawa, which signified the traditional role of keeper of the western door of the council house. At this time he was formally entrusted with keeping the silver medal given to Red Jacket by George Washington in 1792, though Parker had worn it previously.

After serving as an emissary for the Seneca, a role that he periodically repeated before the Civil War, Parker studied law, but he was not admitted to the bar because he was not a U.S. citizen. In 1849, he joined a state engineering party. He learned this profession as he worked; there is no record of his attending Rensselaer Polytechnic Institute, as some sources assert. A few years later, he became an engineering officer for the state militia, and he was active in the Masons. He failed to obtain a promotion from the state, so he resigned and secured an appointment as a civil engineer with the federal government. He directed the construction of a customhouse and marine hospital at Galena, Illinois, from 1857 to 1859, then supervised several other federal projects in the area. It was at this time that he became acquainted with Ulysses S. Grant.

Parker lost his federal appointment in the scramble for offices after Abraham Lincoln's election. His attempt to obtain a commission in the Corps of Engineers at the outbreak of the Civil War proved fruitless, allegedly because of his race. He returned to the reservation in New York, where he farmed and unsuccessfully applied for citizenship, the lack of which he believed was preventing him from receiving a military commission. Although he did not become a citizen, on May 25, 1863, Parker was appointed an assistant adjutant general with the rank of captain on the staff of General John E. Smith, a former Galena jeweler who was in command of a division for Grant at Vicksburg. Traditionally, a sachem could not hold a military title, but this restriction was waived since Parker would not be fighting another tribe.

In September, 1863, he was transferred to Grant's staff as an assistant adjutant general. Grant became a lieutenant general and went east in the spring of 1864; he took Parker along, and in August, 1864, appointed him as his military secretary, with the rank of lieutenant colonel of volunteers. Parker earned a brevet as a colonel of volunteers before Confederate general Robert E. Lee surrendered in April, 1865, at Appomattox, where Parker had the honor of writing the final copy of the terms of surrender. Allegedly, Lee was momentarily taken aback by the swarthy appearance of Parker, but he recovered his composure and declared that it was nice to have a "real American" present for such a historic occasion. For his Civil War service, Parker was brevetted a brigadier general of volunteers in 1865, to date from April 9—the day on which Lee capitulated.

Parker was one of several negotiators who met with Indians at Fort Smith, Arkansas, in September, 1865, and he was often asked to repeat this role immediately after the war. In July, 1866, when Grant became general-in-chief, Parker became his aide-de-camp. When the volunteers were mustered out, Grant secured the rank of lieutenant in the regular army for Parker, and this was quickly followed by brevets up to brigadier general. Grant took office as president in 1869 and appointed Parker as commissioner of Indian affairs, the first Indian to hold that office. Parker worked zealously to promote peaceful settlements of Indian problems within the "Quaker Peace Policy" adopted by Grant, which earned Parker some powerful enemies. In 1871, the House of Representatives tried him for defrauding the government. He was acquitted of all charges, but the experience prompted him to resign on August 1, 1871.

Although he remained very active in veterans' organizations, Parker never again worked for the federal government. He had married Minnie Orton Sackett, who was twenty years his junior, in 1867; after he resigned, they settled in Fairfield, Connecticut, where one of her close friends resided. Maude T. Parker (Ahweheeyo), their only child, was born at Fairfield in 1878. Parker invested in a variety of enterprises; various setbacks eliminated his fortune, though he retained his real estate. In 1876, he accepted an appointment as superintendent of buildings and supplies for the New York City Police Department. He held this post until his death in August, 1895, at the home of his wife's friend in Fairfield. Bright's disease killed him, but he also had diabetes and suffered several strokes.

Parker was buried initially in Fairfield, but in January, 1897, his body was removed to a plot at Forest Lawn Cemetery in Buffalo, where Red Jacket's remains had been interred in 1884 in a ceremony at which Parker spoke. Ironically, Parker's final resting place was within the shadow of a heroic statue of his illustrious ancestor, which had been commissioned after his own suggestion for a design commemorating the decline of the Iroquois Confederacy was rejected.

Richard B. McCaslin

FURTHER READING

Armstrong, William H. *Warrior in Two Camps: Ely S. Parker, Union General and Seneca Chief.* Syracuse, N.Y.: Syracuse University Press, 1978.

Parker, Arthur C. *The Life of General Ely S. Parker, Last Grand Sachem of the Iroquois and General Grant's Military Secretary.* Buffalo, N.Y.: Buffalo Historical Society, 1919.

Yeuell, Donovan. "Ely Samuel Parker." In *Dictionary of American Biography.* Vol. 14, edited by Dumas Malone. New York: Charles Scribner's Sons, 1943.

Parker, Quanah

Born: c. 1845; near Cedar Lake, Texas
Died: February 23, 1911; Fort Sill Reservation, near Lawton, Oklahoma
Also known as: Kwahnah (Sweet Odor)
Tribal affiliation: Quohada Comanche
Significance: Although a fierce warrior and battle leader, Quanah Parker became an outspoken advocate of Indian assimilation and aided his people in the transition from freedom to reservation life.

Quanah Parker was the son of a Nacona Comanche chief named Peta Nocona and a white woman named Cynthia Ann Parker. A mixed band of Comanches, Paiutes, and Kiowas captured Cynthia Ann (age nine at the time), her younger brother, and her older female cousin in 1836 during a raid on Parker's Fort in what is now east-central Texas. Cynthia Ann's brother and cousin escaped captivity within a few years, but a Comanche family adopted Cynthia Ann and reared her as a Comanche. At the age of seventeen or eighteen she married Peta Nocona and in due course gave birth to Quanah; another boy, named Pecos; and a daughter named Topasannah (Prairie Flower).

In December, 1860, a Texas Ranger named Sul Ross (later a governor of the state) led a force of 120 men against a Comanche camp on the Pease River near the present Oklahoma-Texas border. In a running fight, the Rangers killed a number of Comanches and captured others—among them Cynthia Ann and her daughter. Quanah's father died at the hands of Sul Ross himself during the battle, and his brother died shortly afterward, leaving the fifteen-year-old boy without close relatives. He was adopted by the Quohada Comanches and quickly proved himself an able warrior.

The Quohadas were a nomadic people who hunted buffalo from Kansas into Mexico, but their primary territory was the Llano Estacado (Staked Plain), especially the area that is now the Texas panhandle. Although Texas records do not mention Quanah by name during the next decade, he almost certainly participated in some of the Comanche raids that resulted in many deaths and much property damage in the Southwest during the 1860's. Many of the young white men being in the Confederate army during the early part of the decade, the frontier became especially vulnerable to Comanche raids. During the 1860's, Quanah apparently distinguished himself in raids and became a subchief. The raids of the 1860's pushed back the frontier more than one hundred miles and left many hundreds of white settlers dead. In 1866, the federal

Comanche chief Quanah Parker, leader of the second Battle of Adobe Walls in 1874. (National Archives)

government enacted legislation to deal with the "Indian problem," which resulted in the Medicine Lodge Treaty of October, 1867, which specifically targeted the Plains Indians and directly affected Quanah.

Representatives of the U.S. government met with leaders of the Arapahoes, Eastern Apaches, Cheyennes, Comanches, and Kiowas on Medicine Lodge Creek in southern Kansas on October 19, 1867. Many of the chiefs at the negotiations signed the treaty between October 21 and 27, agreeing to take their people to reservations in Oklahoma and Texas. Quanah Parker was not among those who signed the agreement. He and other Comanche subchiefs vowed they would never be confined to reservations, and they led their bands to the Llano Estacado in the Texas panhandle. For the next seven years they raided incessantly throughout the Southwest. General William Tecumseh Sherman, army commander in the region, attempted to force the recalcitrant chiefs and their people to relocate to the reservation, but with little success. Quanah and other leaders managed to evade the army units put into the field against them. Colonel Ronald Slidell Mackenzie led many expeditions against the Comanches from 1868 to 1873, but usually failed to find his adversaries. Indians and whites committed many atrocities against each other during the raids and battles during this period.

On June 27, 1874, Quanah's band fought a hard battle at Adobe Walls in the Texas panhandle. Many of the Comanche bands had come under the influence of a medicine man named ISATAI, who claimed to have spoken with the Great Spirit in heaven. The Great Spirit had told him that if the Indians did a Sun Dance they would be immune to bullets and would drive the whites from their lands. Quanah and Isatai were instrumental in organizing a large-scale attack on a group of buffalo hunters at Adobe Walls. The attack ultimately failed, and many Indians died despite Isatai's promises. After the battle, many of Quanah's allies agreed to go to the reservations after an ultimatum from the federal government. Only Quanah's band and a few others remained at large. The U.S. Army consequently launched a three-pronged campaign against the recalcitrant bands that eventually forced them onto the reservations.

On June 2, 1875, Quanah led his band into Fort Sill, Oklahoma, and surrendered to Mackenzie. Quanah, who had been the fiercest opponent of white settlement on the Texas plains, immediately became the most outspoken Comanche advocate of Indian assimilation into white culture. In time, he became the principal chief of the Comanche nation. From that position, he advocated Indian education in American-style schools and Indian technical education. Quanah became friends with many wealthy and influential white men, including Theodore Roosevelt, in whose inaugural parade he rode in 1905. He used his influence to fight for Indian rights for the remainder of his life.

Quanah later became a judge for Indians accused of crimes and a deputy sheriff. He also became a successful capitalist as a rancher and as an investor in the stock market. Ironically, he made considerable profits from railroad investments—strange for the man who had done much to retard the building of railroads in the Southwest. As recognition for his efforts in white-Indian relations, he became a favorite speaker at social gatherings throughout the Southwest and eventually had a Texas town named for him.

Quanah's popularity with many whites probably derived from the fact that he himself was half white. After his surrender, Quanah became fascinated with his mother's people. He arranged to have her remains disinterred and buried on his reservation, with the intention of being buried beside her. He visited many of his mother's surviving relatives, including her brother, who had been captured with her. His unique white-Indian heritage, coupled with his positions of leadership in both cultures, allowed Quanah Parker to become a major force in reconciling the differences between the two cultures.

Paul Madden

FURTHER READING

Carter, Robert G. *On the Border with Mackenzie.* Washington, D.C.: Enyon, 1935.

Dees, Mary R. *Quanah Parker's Strange Encounters: A Biography.* DeSoto, Tex.: Marmor Publishing, 1997.

Exley, Jo Ella Powell. *Frontier Blood: The Saga of the Parker Family.* College Station: Texas A&M University Press, 2001.

Hagan, William T. *Quanah Parker, Comanche Chief.* Norman: University of
   Oklahoma Press, 1993.
Jackson, Clyde L., and Grace Jackson. *Quanah Parker: Last Chief of the Co-
   manches.* New York: Exposition Press, 1963.
Neeley, Bill. *The Last Comanche Chief: The Life and Times of Quanah Parker.*
   New York: J. Wiley, 1995.
Richardson, Rupert N. *The Comanche Barrier to South Plains Settlement.*
   Glendale, Calif.: Arthur H. Clark, 1933.
Tilghman, Zoe A. *Quanah: The Eagle of the Comanches.* Oklahoma City:
   Harlow, 1938.
Wallace, Ernest, and E. Adamson Hoebel. *The Comanches: Lords of the
   South Plains.* Norman: University of Oklahoma Press, 1952.

Passaconaway

Born: c. 1568; place unknown
Died: c. 1665; place unknown
Also known as: Bear Cub
Tribal affiliation: Pennacook
Significance: Passaconaway was the principal Indian leader in southern
   New England during early English colonization.

The leader of the powerful Pennacook Federation during the beginning of the European settlement of New England, Passaconaway was
born and lived most of his life at Pennacook, near the site of present-day
Concord, New Hampshire.

   During the early colonization, Passaconaway was the principal chief
of a number of Pennacook bands in the area that the colonials called
southern New England. His influence spread westward to the fringes of
Mohawk Country and southward toward the expanding British settlements. Passaconaway fought British encroachment, and his warriors
made occasional small-scale attacks. In 1642, colonial troops moved on
his village. Passaconaway was not there at the time, but his wife and son
were taken prisoner. He negotiated their release and in 1644 pledged a
cessation of hostilities. The son, Wannalancet, was principal chief after
Passaconaway.

   Passaconaway's later life is obscure. He died in the mid-1660's, probably 1665 or 1666.

Bruce E. Johansen

Pawhuska

Born: c. 1760; Little Osage River (now in central Missouri)
Died: August 25, 1825; present-day Vernon County, Missouri
Tribal affiliation: Osage
Significance: Pawhuska participated in 1808, 1818, and 1825 treaties
  ceding Osage land in Missouri and Arkansas.

Pawhuska is thought to have been born in a Great Osage tribal village located on the Little Osage River in what is now Truman Reservoir in central Missouri. Pawhuska was a tribal leader when Zebulon Pike established Camp Independence in Osage territory in 1806. He later agreed to ceding all Osage lands in Missouri at the Treaty of Fort Clark in 1808.

The name Pawhuska, which means "white hair," was derived from an incident in which Pawhuska captured the French General St. Clair's wig during a skirmish. From that point on, Pawhuska wore the wig as a medicine symbol. While a young man, he managed to displace the Osage hereditary chief, Tawagahe. Pawhuska retained power through the help of white traders such as Pierre Chouteau. Later, through alliances with other tribal leaders such as Cashesegra, and continued white influence, Pawhuska signed all pivotal nineteenth century treaties ceding Osage land rights.

Pawhuska regarded white traders highly and allowed them to live among the Osage when the need arose. When the United States acquired Osage territory, his advice and counsel was sought by President Thomas Jefferson. As a result of Pawhuska's close relationship with the Chouteau trading family, the Osage, during the War of 1812, remained loyal to the United States.

Pawhuska was instrumental in the establishment and continued development of several religious missions to the Osage. He was buried in Osage style in a large tomb on Blue Mound, Vernon County, Missouri.

Burl E. Self

Peltier, Leonard

Born: September 12, 1944; Grand Forks, North Dakota
Also known as: Gwarth-ee-lass
Tribal affiliation: Ojibwa (Chippewa)/Lakota (Sioux)
Significance: Leonard Peltier is a political activist who has protested the
  mistreatment of Indians and whose controversial imprisonment has
  drawn worldwide criticism.

An active member of the American Indian Movement (AIM), Leonard Peltier has become, for many Indians and non-Indians alike, a symbol of injustice. Many believe that he received drastically unfair treatment from the Federal Bureau of Investigation (FBI) and the American judicial system. In 1977, Peltier received two life sentences for murdering two FBI agents during a 1975 shoot-out at the Pine Ridge Indian Reservation in South Dakota—an accusation he steadfastly denies.

Leonard Peltier in 1986. (AP/Wide World Photos)

Though not politically active as a young man, Peltier became involved in AIM and devoted to its causes after meeting Vernon BELLECOURT, an AIM leader. As a result, Peltier took part in a number of demonstrations, including the Trail of Broken Treaties in 1972, to draw attention to the plight of Indians. AIM's activities also drew the attention of the FBI, which intensified its Counterintelligence Program (COINTELPRO) and attempted to neutralize AIM under the guise of national security. At the Pine Ridge Reservation, a hotbed of discontent and rivalry among Indian factions, the FBI became embroiled in controversy.

On June 26, 1975, the FBI entered the reservation, apparently to issue a warrant. A confrontation ensued, resulting in the deaths of two agents and one Indian. Of the four Indians accused of murder, only Peltier was indicted and convicted of aiding and abetting in the deaths of the agents, even though a plethora of evidence pointed to his innocence. In the ensuing years, evidence supporting Peltier's innocence and indicating that FBI coercion occurred has mounted.

Despite repeated attempts to reopen the case, Peltier remained in prison through 2004. Since his trial and incarceration, Amnesty International, the National Association of Christians and Jews, Archbishop Desmond Tutu of South Africa, and many others have unsuccessfully petitioned for his release. In 1996, Native American activist Dennis BANKS agreed to lead the Bring Peltier Home campaign.

Sharon K. Wilson
Raymond Wilson

FURTHER READING
Peltier, Leonard. *Prison Writings: My Life Is My Sun Dance*. Introduction by Arvol Looking Horse. New York: St. Martin's Press, 1999.

Pemisapan

Born: 1550; place unknown
Died: June 1, 1586; Dasamonquepeuc (now in North Carolina)
Also known as: Wingina
Tribal affiliation: Roanoc/Secotan
Significance: Pemisapan was the first North American Indian to greet English explorers in the New World, and he was one of the first victims of the hostility that developed between the English and the American Indians during Sir Walter Ralegh's attempt to establish the first English colony.

Nothing is known for certain about the early years of the life of Pemisapan. He was a son of Ensinore and was known originally as Wingina. At some point, his father became *manamatowick*, or king, of the tribes inhabiting what is now called Roanoke Island, North Carolina, and the western neighboring mainland to the Neuse River. As ruler of the Roanoc or Secotan nation, Ensinore exercised his power through local subkings and warriors called *weroances*.

As a young male of his class, in an Algonquian-speaking Eastern Woodlands culture, Wingina would have have been trained in military and political leadership and hunting skills and would have probably undergone an initiation ritual into manhood called the *huskanaw*. Initiates between ten and fifteen years of age would be taken into the woods for months, given hallucinogenic drugs fashioned from roots, occasionally beaten, and usually caged.

Prior to 1582, Ensinore retired as *manamatowick* in favor of Wingina, and his other son, Granganimeo, became a *weroance* of Roanoke Island. Competition for resources in what was a subsistence economy that centered on hunting, fishing, and the cultivation of corn, squash, beans, gourds, and pumpkins was keen, and warfare with neighboring Neiosioke and Pamlico nations occurred quite frequently. In 1582, the Neiosiokes allegedly fell upon some Roanocs while at a peaceful get-together, murdering the men and taking some thirty women and children as slaves. At the time of the first reconnaissance expedition by the English in 1584, Wingina was recuperating from severe wounds sustained in battle with either the Neiosiokes or Pamlico at his mainland town of Secotan. (He had reportedly sustained two wounds to his body, one going straight through his thigh.) It was his brother Granganimeo who made the initial contact with the English explorers, Philip Amadas and Arthur Barlowe.

Initial contact proved friendly, and Amadas and Barlowe, who had been dispatched to the New World by Sir Walter Ralegh, took back to England with them (undoubtedly with Wingina's consent) two younger Indians: Manteo and Wanchese.

The following year, however, the English returned and brought back Manteo and Wanchese, but they also established a military colony under command of Captain Ralph Lane, who built a redoubt on Roanoke Island, which he called Fort Ralegh. Relations began to deteriorate after Lane's superior, Sir Richard Grenville, before returning to England, massacred the Roanocs at the village of Aquascogoc in retaliation for the theft of a silver cup. The English awed the Indians with their firearms, armor, and steel weapons, but they did not grow their own food; the English depended on the Roanocs and other Indians to supply them with food, which strained the resources of an already fragile economy. The imperious and arrogant attitude of some Englishmen, Lane among them, and cultural miscommunications contributed to an increased atmosphere of mistrust.

Despite requests by the Roanocs for the English to assist them in waging war against their Neiosioke and Pamlico enemies, Lane refused to get involved, and this may have been interpreted as a sign of gross ingratitude on the part of the newcomers. As European diseases such as smallpox began taking a toll on the indigenous population and Roanoc society began to unravel, an anti-English party (that included Wanchese) began to emerge. Wingina himself seemed to vacillate, but for the time being appeared to listen to the *weroances* who favored cooperating with the English. Notable among them were Ensinore and Granganimeo, who believed that Lane and his men were actually long-dead ancestors who had returned to life.

Changes occurred early in 1586. In March, Granganimeo succumbed to what was probably smallpox or measles. Wingina changed his name to Pemisapan. Then, on April 20, 1586, the aged Ensinore sickened and died—also likely because of smallpox or measles—and the last effective pro-English voice was eliminated from the ruling council, a fact that was not lost on Lane, who gathered information from Indians such as Manteo, who remained friendly to the English.

Having long suspected Pemisapan's true intentions, Lane was convinced that the chieftain was concocting a plot to annihilate Fort

Ralegh's garrison. Lane had heard that Pemisapan was going to attempt to assemble at least seven hundred warriors from the Roanoc, Weampemeoc, Chawanoac, and other adjacent nations to burn the fortress on June 10, 1586. Lane later said the story was based on intelligence passed on to him by Skyco, a young *weroance* of the Chawanoac nation (allied to Pemisapan) whom Lane was holding hostage.

There had been debate as to whether the plot actually existed or whether, at best, Lane was breaking under the strain and had become delusional. Thomas Hariot, a scientist who accompanied the expedition, of which he would write his own account, was highly skeptical and had always asserted that Pemisapan had acted honorably.

Lane was determined to make a preemptive strike, an ambush, and on June 1, 1586, sailed from Roanoke Island to the mainland town of Dasamonquepeuc, where Pemisapan was known to be staying. Upon encountering Pemisapan and his *weroances* in the village, Lane ordered his men to fire by uttering the prearranged command "Christ, our victory!" Pemisapan was among those who fell, but within a few moments he got up again and ran toward the woods. Shot again before he reached the underbrush, he was pursued and eventually slain by a soldier named Edward Nugent, who returned to Dasamonquepeuc to present Lane with Pemisapan's severed head.

Pemisapan's fate might be seen as a prototype of the antagonism that still haunts American Indians and Europeans. Though Pemisapan's assassination might have eased the threat to Lane's colony temporarily, the English left with Sir Francis Drake's fleet three weeks later. It is probable that Lane's actions made things more difficult for the second Roanoke Island settlement (the Lost Colony) of 1587-1588, and perhaps even ensured its ultimate failure.

Raymond Pierre Hylton

FURTHER READING

Durant, David N. *Ralegh's Lost Colony: The Story of the First English Settlement in America.* New York: Atheneum, 1981.

Hulton, Paul. *America 1585: The Complete Drawings of John White.* Chapel Hill: University of North Carolina Press, 1984.

Miller, Lee. *Roanoke: Solving the Mystery of the Lost Colony.* New York: Penguin, 2002.

Morison, Samuel Eliot. *The European Discovery of America: The Northern Voyages, A.D. 500-1600.* New York: Oxford University Press, 1971.

Quinn, David Beers. *Set Fair for Roanoke: Voyages and Colonies, 1584-1606.* Chapel Hill: University of North Carolina Press, 1985.

Rountree, Helen C. *The Powhatan Indians of Virginia: Their Traditional Culture.* Norman: University of Oklahoma Press, 1989.

Rountree, Helen C., and E. Randolph Turner III. *Before and After Jamestown: Virginia's Powhatans and Their Predecessors.* Gainesville: University of Florida Press, 2002.

Stick, David. *Roanoke Island: The Beginnings of English America.* Chapel Hill: University of North Carolina Press, 1986.

Peña, Tonita

Born: June 10, 1893; San Ildefonso Pueblo, New Mexico
Died: September, 1949; Cochiti Pueblo?, New Mexico
Also known as: Quah Ah (Little Bead or Pink Shell)
Tribal affiliation: San Ildefonso Pueblo, Cochiti
Significance: An influential artist, Tonita Peña painted scenes of traditional dances and women's work.

At San Ildefonso Day School, between 1899 and 1905, Tonita Peña was encouraged by teacher Esther B. Hoyt to use crayons to depict dances. Later, archaeologist Edgar Hewett kept her supplied with good paper and watercolors and was her patron until his death. In 1905 Tonita was moved to Cochiti Pueblo to be reared by her aunt. While she was attending Saint Catherine's Indian School in Santa Fe, the elders of Cochiti arranged her marriage at the age of fourteen. Two years and two children later, her husband died. Peña returned to St. Catherine's after a second arranged marriage (to Felipe Herrera, by whom she had another child, Joe H. Herrera), and she resumed painting. After the death of her second husband, she married a third time, in 1922, and bore five children. In addition to mothering, housekeeping, cooking, dancing, and farming, she painted by kerosene lamp. She taught pottery at local Indian schools and collaborated on murals for the Works Progress Administration. She painted scenes of women's work and pueblo dances on paper, wood, masonite, and canvas, using watercolors, casein, pen and colored ink, and oils. Painters Joe H. Herrera (her son) and Pablita Velarde cite her influence on their careers. Upon her death, all of her possessions, including paintings, were burned.

Cheryl Claassen

FURTHER READING

Trenton, Patricia, ed. *Independent Spirits: Women Painters of the American West, 1890-1945.* Berkeley: University of California Press, 1995.

Peratrovich, Elizabeth W.

Born: July 4, 1911; Petersburg, Alaska
Died: December 1, 1958; Juneau, Alaska
Also known as: Kaaxgal-aat
Tribal affiliation: Tlingit
Significance: Elizabeth W. Peratrovich championed the first explicit anti-discrimination law in the United States, the 1945 Alaskan Anti-Discrimination Act.

Before the mid-twentieth century, American Indians had gradually obtained certain rights through the years. The Dawes Severalty Act of 1887 offered citizenship to those American Indians who had "severed their tribal relationship and adopted the habits of civilization." In 1924 the U.S. Congress granted national citizenship and the right to vote to all Native Americans. However, Indians still faced discrimination in nearly all aspects of life. During the 1940's Alaska was still a territory rather than a state, but it was there that a significant advance in civil rights was made in 1945.

Born Elizabeth Wanamaker, Peratrovich attended elementary school in her hometown of Petersburg, then high school in Ketchikan. She then went to Washington State to attend the Western College of Education at Bellingham. She married Roy Peratrovich in Bellingham in 1931. They moved back to Alaska with their family ten years later.

The Peratroviches became active in the Alaska Native Brotherhood (ANB) and the Alaska Native Sisterhood (ANS). (The ANB had been founded in 1912 to gain Alaska Natives the right to vote, which they won in 1922. It continued to be an activist civil rights organization.) When they moved to Juneau from Klawock, Alaska, Elizabeth was grand camp (chapter) president of the ANS, and Roy was grand president of the regional ANB.

When Indian schoolchildren were denied admission to the public school in Juneau, the ANB sued the district and was able to force the school to integrate. In Juneau the Peratroviches also were shocked to encounter signs reading "No Natives Allowed" and "No Dogs or Indians Allowed." They were outraged when they were prohibited from buying a house in the neighborhood of their choice. The Peratroviches took the discrimination issue to the Alaskan territorial legislature and lobbied daily. An anti-discrimination bill had been proposed, and Elizabeth's articulate descriptions of discrimination were reported to have been the testimony that gained the 11-to-5 vote in favor of the bill. It outlawed discrimination in housing, public accommodations, and restaurants in Alaska, and it was the first explicit anti-discrimination law in the United States.

The act was signed into law on February 16, 1945. Because her eloquent testimony was credited with passage of the measure, in 1988 February 16 was officially designated "Elizabeth W. Peratrovich Day" in Alaska. Peratrovich lost her battle with cancer at the age of forty-seven, but her victory against discrimination is celebrated on February 16 every year.

Tonya Huber

Petalésharo

Born: c. 1797; place unknown
Died: c. 1833; place unknown
Tribal affiliation: Pawnee
Significance: Petalésharo ended the use of human sacrifice in the Pawnee Morning Star Ceremony.

"Petalésharo" seems to have functioned as a title, as well as a personal name, during the early eighteenth century among the Pawnee; several outstanding warriors used the name, and it is sometimes difficult to attribute biographical details to one individual.

The best-known person to claim the title distinguished himself not only as a warrior but also as an humanitarian. He aggressively curtailed the Pawnee use of human sacrifice in certain rituals. Until his time, the Pawnee would raid another tribe for a girl about thirteen years old, treat her well for a year, then sacrifice her in the Morning Star Ceremony. During one such ceremony in the late 1820's, Petalésharo is said to have protested by rescuing a young woman from sacrifice. Petalésharo cut the bonds that held the woman to a sacrificial cross, carried her to a horse to escape, then fed and protected the woman before taking her home.

During the fall and winter of 1821, Petalésharo toured the urban areas of the Northeast, including Washington, D.C., where he spoke at a conference attended by President James Monroe and Secretary of War John Calhoun. He also attended a New Year's reception at the White House. He probably died during a smallpox epidemic around 1833.

Bruce E. Johansen

Pictou Aquash, Anna Mae

Born: March 27, 1945; near Shubenacadie, Nova Scotia, Canada
Died: December, 1975; Pine Ridge Reservation, South Dakota
Tribal affiliation: Micmac
Significance: After being found murdered on the Pine Ridge Reserva-
tion in South Dakota, activist Anna Mae Pictou Aquash became a
symbol of the struggle for Native American rights.

Anna Mae Pictou was born in Nova Scotia to Mary Ellen Pictou and
Francis Thomas Levi. Shortly after she was born, her father left her
mother, and her early childhood was consequently spent in poverty. In
1949, her mother married Noel Sapier, a traditionalist Micmac, who
would help Anna Mae to appreciate her native culture. After Sapier
died in 1956, Anna Mae attended a nonreservation school, where she
confronted anti-Indian racism for the first time. Her mother abandoned the family around this time, and Anna Mae dropped out of
school to work as a harvester so she could support her siblings.

During the early 1960's, Anna Mae married fellow Micmac Jake
Maloney and moved to Boston, Massachusetts. Their marriage ended in
1969. In 1968, Pictou worked as a volunteer for the Boston Indian
Council, where she became involved with the American Indian Movement (AIM). In 1970, she joined national AIM leader Russell Means in
taking over the *Mayflower II* in Plymouth, Massachusetts, to protest the
celebration of Thanksgiving.

In 1971, Pictou met Chippewa artist Nogeeshik Aquash. They worked
together for AIM and participated in the Trail of Broken Treaties march
to Washington, D.C., during the following year. In April, 1973, they
joined other AIM members in occupying the settlement at Wounded
Knee, South Dakota. That month she and Aquash were married in a traditional Sioux ceremony by Nicholas and Wallace Black Elk.

In 1975, Pictou and fellow AIM member Leonard PELTIER joined
other traditionalists at Pine Ridge Reservation in South Dakota to lend
support to the Lakota who were fighting against the corrupt tribal
chairman Dick Wilson and his police force. On June 26, 1975, a firefight
erupted between agents of the Federal Bureau of Investigation (FBI)
and members of AIM, in which two FBI agents and one Native American
were killed.

In September, 1975, Pictou was arrested during a raid at the Rosebud
Reservation in South Dakota, but she eventually escaped her captors.
She was recaptured in Oregon and sent back to Rosebud but again fled

in November, 1975. On February 24, 1976, her frozen body was found on a Lakota ranch. An autopsy ruled that her cause of death was exposure. Because her body had deteriorated, identification was difficult. Her hands were severed and sent to the FBI in Washington, D.C., for positive identification. The family asked for second autopsy, which reclassified the death as a homicide. A bullet hole at the base of the skull indicated that she had been shot in an execution.

For years afterward, it was unclear who had killed Pictou Aquash. Although she had been arrested a number of times during her association with AIM, some people suspected her of being an FBI informant. However, it was also known that many AIM members were "snitch-jacketed" by the FBI—that is, the agency leaked information indicating that certain persons were informants who actually were not. Representatives of both the FBI and AIM denied having had anything to do with Pictou's death.

In March, 2003, two former AIM members, Arlo Looking Cloud and John Graham, were charged with the first-degree murder of Pictou Aquash, committed in the perpetration of a kidnapping. Looking Cloud was convicted in February, 2004, and sentenced to life in prison. Graham was scheduled to appear in court in December, 2004.

Pegge Bochynski

FURTHER READING
Bataille, Gretchen M., ed. *Native American Women.* New York: Garland Publishing, 1993.
Brand, Joanna. *The Life and Death of Anna Mae Aquash.* Toronto: James Lorimer, 1978.

Pitchlynn, Peter Perkins

Born: January 30, 1806; in present-day Mississippi
Died: January 17, 1881; Washington, D.C.
Also known as: Hatchootucknee
Tribal affiliation: Choctaw
Significance: As leader and representative of the Choctaw Nation, Peter Perkins Pitchlynn worked for his people's rights in tribal consolidation, relocation, government reimbursement, and involvement in the Civil War.

Peter Pitchlynn was the son of John Pitchlynn, a Choctaw interpreter for the United States. The Choctaw tribe had fairly readily accepted whites, and as the younger Pitchlynn grew up, interaction with them was quite commonplace. He was educated at Nashville University and returned to the Choctaw Nation where he headed, in 1824, the lighthorse force. Members of this force served as judges, juries, and sheriffs, riding across the Choctaw lands settling difficulties between parties and individuals. The United States provided a permanent annuity for this organization, beginning in 1825.

After the Choctaws adopted a constitution in 1860, Pitchlynn was elected to the central executive position, or principal chief, and served in that capacity from 1864 to 1866. Pitchlynn had argued, unsuccessfully, for Choctaw neutrality during the Civil War, but as principal chief he was able to sign an armistice ending Choctaw involvement in the war as a member of the Confederacy.

Pitchlynn also handled matters involving the so-called Net Proceeds, U.S. government money paid to the Choctaw Nation from sales of ceded Choctaw land. These funds, appropriated in 1859, were almost totally lost or dissipated during the confusion surrounding the Civil War. The fact that the Choctaw had joined the Confederacy, against the counsel of Pitchlynn, lost them their claim to much of the money.

Pitchlynn also served at the Fort Smith Council, which required the Choctaws to either abolish slavery and accept the freedmen into the tribe as equals or provide other appropriate provisions for them. Pitchlynn served as a delegate in Washington, and while there he fought both against the forced consolidation of Choctaws with neighboring tribes and against the removal of the Choctaws to the Oklahoma Territory.

Ruffin Stirling

FURTHER READING

Debo, Angie. *The Rise and Fall of the Choctaw Republic.* 2d ed. Norman: University of Oklahoma Press, 1961.

Hauptman, Laurence M. *Between Two Fires: American Indians in the Civil War.* New York: Free Press, 1995.

Plenty Coups

Born: c. 1849; near Billings, Montana
Died: May 3, 1932; Pryor, Montana
Also known as: Aleekchea'ahoosh (Many Achievements)
Tribal affiliation: Crow

Significance: Plenty Coups allied the Crows with the U.S. Army against other Indian tribes.

Plenty Coups, whose Crow name means "Many Achievements," was the principal chief of the Crows during the latter stages of the plains wars. He spearheaded the Crows' decision to cooperate with the U.S. Army in its pursuit of the Cheyennes, Sioux, Arapahoes, and other "hostiles." Plenty Coups's Crows provided scouts for George Armstrong Custer in his 1876 defeat at Little Bighorn.

Plenty Coups was groomed for chieftainship from an early age, and uncommon attention was paid to him as a child by the Crows. When Plenty Coups was nine years old, one of his brothers was killed by the Sioux, creating a lifelong enmity.

After Little Bighorn, the Crows under Plenty Coups continued to support the U.S. Army as it drove the Cheyennes and Sioux into subjugation. Crow warriors aided in the pursuit of SITTING BULL into Canada, the hounding of the Northern Cheyennes, and the surrender of CRAZY HORSE. Plenty Coups urged his people to become farmers and ranchers, and he abandoned his tipi for a log farmhouse. Plenty Coups also opened a general store so that the Crows could buy trade goods at fair prices.

Plenty Coups traveled to Washington, D.C., several times after 1880 to ensure trade and aid for the Crows. He was noted for his sagacity in business dealings. During World War I, Plenty Coups encouraged young Crow men to leave the enforced idleness and alcoholism of the reservation and join the U.S. Army. After the war, in 1921, he was chosen to represent all American Indians at the dedication of the Tomb of the Unknown Soldier in Arlington, Virginia. In 1928, his health failing, Plenty Coups willed his personal real estate, about 200 acres, to the U.S. government for the future use of the Crow people. Plenty Coups died May 3, 1932. The Crow council at the

Plenty Coups around 1908. (Library of Congress)

time so revered him that its members refused to name another principal chief in his place.

Bruce E. Johansen

FURTHER READING
Hoxie, Frederick E. *Parading Through History: The Making of the Crow Na-
    tion in America, 1805-1935.* New York: Cambridge University Press,
    1995.

Pocahontas

Born: c. 1596; Werowocomoco (near present-day Jamestown, Virginia)
Died: March, 1617; Gravesend, Kent, England
Also known as: Matoaka
Tribal affiliation: Powhatan, Algonquin
Significance: Pocahontas confronted cultural barriers between the Pow-
    hatan and English settlers; while she came to symbolize for white
    Americans the possibility of cultural unity, for many Native Americans
    she symbolizes the loss of traditional cultures.

Pocahontas, also called Matoaka, was the daughter of POWHATAN, chief
of the Powhatans of what is today the tidewater region of Virginia. The
Powhatan Confederacy, as it has traditionally been known by historians,
was a group of approximately thirty Algonquian-speaking tribes organized in large part by Powhatan in the last years of the sixteenth century. Pocahontas was born at Werowocomoco, north of what would become Jamestown along the York River, which was home to her father
and the center of Powhatan culture.

The most memorable extant story of Pocahontas's early life is contained in Captain John Smith's 1624 work *The Generall Historie of Virginia, New-England, and the Summer Isles.* Here, Smith reported that in
1608 Pocahontas saved his life as he was about to be killed on the orders
of her father. As numerous Powhatans were ostensibly preparing to kill
Smith, Pocahontas, "when no intreaty could prevail, got his head in her
armes, and laid her owne upon his to save him from death." This apparent act of salvation led to a brief peace between the struggling colonists
and Powhatan. Pocahontas brought food to the English at Jamestown
through the starvation winters of 1608 and 1609, and she persuaded her
father to assist the settlers also.

Pocahontas was kidnapped in 1613 by Captain Samuel Argall and
taken to Jamestown and then to Henrico; she was held hostage for En-

Seventeenth century painting of Pocahontas by William Sheppard. (Library of Congress)

glish prisoners of the Powhatan. While among the English colonists, she converted to Christianity and was baptized, taking the name Lady Rebecca. In 1614, Chief Powhatan and Virginia governor Sir Thomas Dale agreed to the marriage of Pocahontas to the English settler John Rolfe; the peace agreement between Powhatan and the English settlers that followed can in part be attributed to the marriage. The couple's son, Thomas, was born the following year.

In 1616, Governor Dale saw in the young Pocahontas an advertising opportunity for the Virginia Company, and Pocahontas—together with several other Powhatans—was compelled to sail with her husband and son for England, arriving in Plymouth on June 3. She was warmly received at court and throughout English society. While in England, she also became reacquainted with John Smith, who had returned there in 1609. Preparing to return to her native land in 1617, she contracted smallpox and died at Gravesend, England, in March. John Rolfe also died in England, five years later. Their son Thomas eventually returned to Virginia after receiving his education in England, and he became a prominent citizen in the colonies.

Since the beginning of the nineteenth century, when the United States began looking to the past to assess its history and culture, Pocahontas has held a central position in colonial mythology. Beginning in the early nineteenth century, writers looked upon the John Smith salvation episode as a romantic symbol of the birth of the nation; the episode was the centerpiece of numerous of the "Indian plays" so popular in the first half of the nineteenth century. The portraits to be found here bolstered the stereotyped image of the "noble savage" that one finds so frequently in European American literature of the day. The standard American histories since 1800 have likewise all included the salvation tale.

The story of Smith's salvation by Pocahontas has been disputed since the mid-nineteenth century, when Charles Deane and Henry Adams suggested that Smith invented the whole episode. Leo Lemay argues convincingly in favor of the tale's veracity, however; Lemay carefully adjudicates the controversy, determining that the evidence lies heavily in favor of Smith and against his doubters. A larger question has emerged in the light of ethnographic scholarship: Did Smith misconstrue (or pretend to misconstrue) the event he witnessed? Studies have suggested that ritual salvations of the sort Smith describes were fairly commonplace events among the Algonquian-speaking peoples, and several similar tales survive, including at least one which Smith himself quite likely would have read. Though Smith believed that Powhatan was fattening him up for sacrifice, in fact the event that he made famous was likely to have been part of a ritual of adoption into Powhatan culture, in which Pocahontas played the role of Smith's sponsor. Smith himself tells us that two days later Powhatan approached him to say that he was now regarded as one of the Powhatans.

This question of interpretation—perhaps more troublesome than the question of the tale's veracity—will probably intrigue scholars for some time to come. The event, which has often been taken by white interpreters as a symbol of the blessing of the colonial settlement of America, in this more recent reckoning comes to symbolize instead the failure of European Americans to comprehend the cultures they encountered in the New World. Wishing to uncover forgiveness among the very populations that had been so devastated by European Americans, nineteenth century writers seized upon the romantic tale of Pocahontas-as-savior.

Along with other mytho-historical Native American figures such as SQUANTO and SACAGAWEA, Pocahontas came to symbolize for European Americans the innocence of the land as well as the possibility of a union of white and Native American ideologies. (European Americans ignored the fact that any such union would most likely take place on the terms of whites and at the expense of Native American culture.) Pocahontas's apparent salvation of Smith, her conversion to Christianity, and her marriage to a prominent white citizen all contribute to her central status in the mythology of early European contact with Native Americans.

Jeff Abernathy

FURTHER READING

Allen, Paula Gunn. *Pocahontas: Medicine Woman, Spy, Entrepreneur, Diplomat.* San Francisco: HarperSanFranciso, 2003.

Barbour, Philip L. *Pocahontas and Her World.* Boston: Houghton Mifflin, 1970.

Davis, Richard Beale. *Intellectual Life in the Colonial South, 1585-1763.* 3 vols. Knoxville: University of Tennessee Press, 1978.

Lemay, Leo. *Did Pocahontas Save Captain John Smith?* Athens: University of Georgia Press, 1992.

Mossiker, Frances. *Pocahontas: The Life and the Legend.* New York: Alfred A. Knopf, 1976.

Perdue, Theda, ed. *Sifters: Native American Women's Lives.* New York: Oxford University Press, 2001.

Rountree, Helen C. *Pocahontas, Powhatan, Opechancanough: Three Indian Lives Changed by Jamestown.* Charlottesville: University of Virginia Press, 2005.

_____. *Pocahontas's People: The Powhatan Indians of Virginia Through Four Centuries.* Norman: University of Oklahoma Press, 1990.

Smith, John. *The Generall Historie of Virginia, New-England, and the Summer Isles.* London: J. D[awson] and J. H[aviland] for Michael Sparkes, 1624.

Young, Phillip. "The Mother of Us All: Pocahontas Reconsidered." *Kenyon Review* 24 (1962): 391-415.

Pokagon, Leopold

Born: c. 1775; near present-day Bertrand, Michigan
Died: July 8, 1841; Cass County, Michigan
Also known as: Pocagin
Tribal affiliation: Potawatomi, Ojibwa (Chippewa)
Significance: Leopold Pokagon was a forceful advocate of peace and a convert to Roman Catholicism.

Leopold (Leo) Pokagon sold the site of Chicago to whites in 1832 as part of the Treaty of Tippecanoe. A Chippewa who was captured and reared by Potawatomis in what is now Michigan, Pokagon—like many of his people—was converted to Catholicism by Jesuits as a young man. Once he became a chief, he requested a Jesuit to live in his village along the St. Joseph River, where Michigan borders Indiana. Stephen Badin, a Jesuit, soon took up residence there.

The place and date of Leo Pokagon's birth are not known exactly, but he was probably born about 1775 near Bertrand, Michigan. As the civil chief of his tribe, Pokagon worked to keep his people out of TECUMSEH's Rebellion and the War of 1812—even as Topenebee, the tribe's war chief, advised taking a much more aggressive stance toward the invading whites. Twenty years later, Pokagon also rebuffed BLACK HAWK's urgings to ally for war, as Topenebee allied with the Sauk and Fox leader. Despite his alliance with white settlers, Pokagon was forced to relocate his village to Dowagiac, Michigan. Remarkably, even after whites had seized much of the land near southern Lake Michigan that had belonged to his people, Pokagon continued friendly relations with them. Pokagon was known as a forceful advocate of peace and an orator of rare abilities. Jesuit letters of the time indicate that Pokagon himself called the people to prayer. He died in 1841 in Cass County, Michigan.

Bruce E. Johansen

Pokagon, Simon

Born: c. 1830; St. Joseph Valley, Michigan
Died: January 28, 1899; near Hartford, Michigan
Tribal affiliation: Potawatomi
Significance: Simon Pokagon was widely regarded as the best-educated Indian of his generation; his writings on Indian culture were published in many magazines.

Simon Pokagon was a son of Leopold POKAGON, who had sold the site of

Chicago to whites in 1832. His father died when Simon was ten years old; Leopold was succeeded in the chieftainship of his band by his son Paul, who died; another son, Francis, then became chief, until his death. The younger brother, Simon, then inherited the office of chief.

Pokagon, who was born in St. Joseph Valley, Michigan, spoke only Potawatomi until age fourteen but later studied English at Notre Dame University and Latin and Greek at Oberlin College. Pokagon mastered five languages and became an accomplished writer and organist. He was sometimes called the best-educated American Indian of his time.

Pokagon also used his education to advantage when meeting with presidents Abraham Lincoln and Ulysses S. Grant on behalf of the Potawatomis. He spoke at the Chicago World Exposition (1893) and composed poetry and several articles on Native American customs and beliefs. He also wrote an autobiographical romance in the Potawatomi language and later translated it into English: *O-Gi-Maw-Kwe Mit-I-Gwa-Ki (Queen of the Woods)*. The book was published in 1899, the year Pokagon died near Hartford, Michigan. A monument to Simon Pokagon and his father, Leopold, was erected in Chicago's Jackson Park.

Bruce E. Johansen

Pontiac

Born: c. 1720; along Maumee River (now in northern Ohio)
Died: April 20, 1769; present-day Cahokia, Illinois
Also known as: Obwandiyag
Tribal affiliation: Ottawa
Significance: In 1763, in the wake of the French defeat during the French and Indian War, Pontiac envisioned a pan-Indian confederation to drive the British from Indian land.

Pontiac was born in present-day northern Ohio, the son of an Ottawa father and a Chippewa (Ojibwa) mother. According to Ottawa custom, which allowed polygamy, presumably he married on several occasions, though only one wife, Kantuckeegan, and their two sons, Otussa and Shegenaba, have been identified. Pontiac, a large, imposing warrior, was esteemed for his strategic skills as well as for his intelligence and eloquence. By 1755 he had become an Ottawa war chief.

The four colonial wars culminating in the French and Indian War (1754-1763) had pitted the French and their Indian allies against the British. Although the British had occasionally courted Indian alliance,

Pontiac. (Library of Congress)

Indians had disdained them, preferring the French, who practiced fair trade, provided lavish tribute, and established few permanent settlements on Indian land. The English scorned Indian culture, but the French were historically more tolerant, frequently marrying Indians and being welcomed into tribes.

The Ottawas, like most of their Great Lakes neighbors, were primarily fur traders who shared a congenial and mutually beneficial relationship with the French. During the French and Indian War, Pontiac fought with the French, helping to defeat General Edward Braddock and his British troops at Fort Duquesne (later Fort Pitt), modern-day Pittsburgh.

French defeat in 1763 proved disastrous for frontier Indian tribes, whose fate was suddenly thrust into British hands. Westward settlement was unimpeded with the removal of the French, and Indians faced new threats from migrating settlers. Furthermore, the British, through an unsympathetic commander in chief, Lord Jeffrey Amherst, alienated Indians by abandoning the French policy of bestowing gifts; Amherst viewed the practice as extravagant. The Indians, in the meantime, had grown dependent on European tools and weapons; French gunpowder had enabled them to supply vast quantities of fur as well as meat for their tribes. Indians faced genuine hardship when the British refused them supplies of gunpowder. In addition, Amherst, who during the war had fostered Indian addiction to alcohol, afterward prohibited its sale.

In 1763, Pontiac, hoping to seize the initiative during the postwar confusion and possibly encouraged by promises of French aid, planned an offensive strike to drive the British from the frontier. In the meantime, another leader, NEOLIN—who was known as the Delaware Prophet—was formulating his own plans for a unification of Indian tribes. Claiming to be the recipient of visions from the spirit world, Neolin denounced European technology and alcohol and proposed a return to traditional Indian customs. Like Pontiac, Neolin envisioned a pan-Indian alliance; unlike Pontiac, he was an advocate of peaceful methods.

On April 27, 1763, Pontiac convened a general war council during which he finalized his war plans. In a single massive assault, he intended to capture British forts ranging across the frontier. To that end, he delivered a general call to arms in the form of red wampum, to which several tribes responded, including the Chippewas, Delawares, Hurons, Illinois, Kickapoos, Miamis, Mingoes, Potawatomis, Senecas, and Shawnees. On May 8, Pontiac and three hundred warriors entered Fort Detroit, concealing weapons and ready for an offensive strike. Realizing his plans had been revealed to the fort commander, Major Henry Gladwin, Pontiac withheld his battle signal. The next day, however, he and his men laid siege to the fort, and they continued it successfully for six months. During that time, nine other British forts were captured by Indians, and the British suffered more than two thousand casualties.

Fearing collapse of their frontier defense, the British mustered their strength and successfully counterattacked. By late 1763, the Indian resistance was weakening. Protracted warfare was inimical to Indians, who were accustomed to short strikes, and French support had failed to materialize. As the winter drew near, warriors became concerned about providing food, as the long disruption of their hunting and fishing threatened hardship for their families. Moreover, at Fort Pitt, soldiers under the command of Captain Simeon Ecuyer precipitated a devastating epidemic by distributing blankets infected with smallpox, a disease to which Indians had little resistance.

In late autumn, Pontiac ended his siege of Fort Detroit. Independent tribes remained hostile, however, engaging in battle throughout 1764. By July, 1765, Pontiac tentatively agreed to peace, formalizing his agreement in a treaty signed at Oswego in 1766 and thereby earning British pardon. Afterward he returned to his village along the Maumee River. His peace treaty angered many Indians, however, who were reluctant to end hostilities. Consequently, Pontiac, his family, and a small group of supporters were driven from their village.

In April, 1769, Pontiac traveled to a trading post at Cahokia, Illinois. There he was murdered by a Peoria Indian named Black Dog, whom the British may have paid to assassinate the great leader in an effort to curb future rebellions. Pontiac's murder precipitated a war among the Indians, as several tribes united against the Illinois Indians to avenge his death.

Prior to the American Revolution, Pontiac and his pan-Indian alliance provided the greatest native threat to British expansion in the New World. Several more Indian leaders over the coming century attempted rebellion, including LITTLE TURTLE in 1790-1794 and TECUMSEH in 1809-1811, sustaining a tradition of Indian rebellions beginning in the early seventeenth century and lasting until the Battle of Wounded Knee in 1890.

Mary E. Virginia

FURTHER READING

Dowd, Gregory Evans. *A Spirited Resistance: The North American Indian Struggle for Unity, 1745-1815.* Baltimore: Johns Hopkins University Press, 1992.

_____. *War Under Heaven: Pontiac, the Indian Nations, and the British Empire.* Baltimore: Johns Hopkins University Press, 2002.

Leach, Douglas E. *Arms for Empire: A Military History of the British Colonies in North America, 1607-1763.* New York: Macmillan, 1973.

_____. "Colonial Indian Wars." In *History of Indian-White Relations*, edited by Wilcomb E. Washburn. Vol. 4 in *Handbook of North American Indians.* Washington, D.C.: Smithsonian Institution Press, 1988.

Peckham, Howard H. *Pontiac and the Indian Uprising.* Princeton, N.J.: Princeton University Press, 1947.

Sosin, Jack M. *Whitehall and the Wilderness: The Middle West in British Colonial Policy, 1760-1775.* Lincoln: University of Nebraska Press, 1961.

Popé

Born: 1630?; San Juan Pueblo (now in New Mexico)
Died: 1690; place unknown
Tribal affiliation: San Juan Pueblo
Significance: Popé inspired and led the Pueblo Revolt against Spanish colonists in New Mexico in 1680.

Little is known of the early life of Popé, a medicine man of the San Juan Pueblo in seventeenth century New Mexico. As an older man, Popé became an ardent opponent of the Spanish regime. The Spanish, whose colony was established in 1598, became more oppressive as more settlers arrived. Franciscan missionaries forced the Pueblos to abandon their own religion in favor of Christianity, while *encomenderos* exploited Pueblo labor. During the 1670's, drought and famine brought Pueblo resentment and desperation to a peak. In 1675, signs of unrest prompted Governor Juan Francisco Trevino to punish the Pueblos by arresting and flogging forty-seven Pueblo medicine men, including Popé. Popé then moved from San Juan to Taos, where he began to organize a general revolt against the Spanish.

Popé had brilliant organizational and leadership skills. He preached a millenarian message in which he promised that the ancient gods would return, bearing gifts of prosperity, as soon as the Christians and their gods were dead. Popé offered land and liberation from Spanish slavery for warriors who would fight the Spanish. Spreading his message through the Pueblos, Popé engineered a coordinated attack on the Spanish, beginning on August 10, 1680. Franciscans living in the Pueblos were massacred, and Santa Fe was besieged. By August 20, the surviving Spanish and a group of loyal Indians fled south to El Paso.

As the leader of the Pueblos, Popé urged the destruction of all vestiges of Christianity and promised the return of prosperity as soon as the Pueblos revived their own ancient religion. Drought, internal dissension, and attack from neighboring tribes continued to disrupt Pueblo life. Popé's influence waned, and he died in 1690. The Spaniards returned to reconquer New Mexico between 1692 and 1694, though they never subjected the Pueblo to such harsh exploitation as they had before the revolt of 1680.

Lynne Getz

FURTHER READING

Knaut, Andrew L. *The Pueblo Revolt of 1680: Conquest and Resistance in Seventeenth-Century New Mexico.* Norman: University of Oklahoma Press, 1995.

Roberts, David. *The Pueblo Revolt: The Secret Rebellion That Drove the Spanish Out of the Southwest.* New York: Simon & Schuster, 2004.

Popovi Da

Born: April 10, 1923; San Ildefonso Pueblo, New Mexico
Died: October 17, 1971; Santa Fe, New Mexico
Also known as: Antonio Martínez
Tribal affiliation: San Ildefonso Pueblo (Tewa)
Significance: Popovi Da, the son of María and Julián MARTÍNEZ, continued the pottery renaissance that they had begun at San Ildefonso, adding many significant contributions of his own.

In 1948, Popovi Da (Red Fox) legally changed his name from Antonio

Martínez to his Tewa name and opened a studio of Indian art at San Ildefonso, where he sold outstanding examples of Indian arts, including his mother's pottery. By 1950, he was helping with the decorating of his mother María's pottery, and by 1956 his experiments with polychrome ware had resulted in the revival of a style that had been seldom seen since the mid-1920's. Popovi, who had studied at the Institute of American Indian Art in Santa Fe in the early 1930's, had developed an innovative approach to design and technique and was now winning awards for his work at the Gallup Ceremonial and elsewhere.

From 1961 to 1964, he developed two new pottery types: sienna ware and black-and-sienna ware. Both types involved a complicated two-firing process. One of the most beautiful new finishes Popovi created was the gunmetal ware, fired in the same way as the black ware but in a hotter fire for a longer period of time. Popovi was also the first contemporary Pueblo potter to set turquoise stones into his pottery.

Popovi Da was a religious, community, and business leader as well as an outstanding artist. He served several terms as governor of San Ildefonso, was chairman of the All-Pueblo Council, and was a member of the New Mexico Arts Commission.

LouAnn Faris Culley

FURTHER READING
Spivey, Richard L. *The Legacy of Maria Poveka Martinez*. Rev. ed. Santa Fe: Museum of New Mexico Press, 2003.

Porter, Pleasant

Born: September 26, 1840; Creek Nation, near Clarkesville, Alabama
Died: September 3, 1907; Vinita, Cherokee Nation, Oklahoma
Also known as: Crazy Bear, Talof Harjo
Tribal affiliation: Creek
Significance: As a principal chief, Pleasant Porter sought acculturation and accommodation between his Creek people and whites.

The grandson of a Creek chief, Tulope Tustunugee, Pleasant Porter also had black ancestry. Born in Alabama, he moved to Indian Territory, where he became a respected leader. During the Civil War, along with most Creeks, he supported the Confederacy, becoming a lieutenant in the Confederate Second Creek Regiment. He was wounded in battle.

After the war, he was active in tribal politics, a leader of a faction of mixed-blood Creeks who supported an imposed constitutional government and acculturation to white customs. He served as a prominent member of the Council of the Creek Nation, and in that capacity he traveled on several occasions to Washington, D.C. For nearly twenty years after the Civil War, Porter was also Creek school superintendent, establishing an exemplary Creek educational system.

In 1889, Porter supported the Dawes Commission in ceding Creek lands to the United States for white settlers. In 1902, he ceded all Creek lands in support of the allotment policy by which individual tribal members would receive private allotments. He was principal chief when Indian Territory became Oklahoma in 1907. He died of a stroke in the same year.

Mary E. Virginia

Porter-Locklear, Freda

Born: October 14, 1957; Lumberton, North Carolina
Tribal affiliation: Lumbee
Significance: One of a handful of American Indian women who holds a doctorate in her field, Freda Porter-Locklear has used her mathematical training to perform mathematical studies of groundwater purification and to apply this knowledge.

Freda Porter-Locklear grew up in Pembroke, North Carolina, and attended Pembroke State University, where many of North Carolina's Lumbee Indians have studied. After earning her undergraduate degree she went on to North Carolina State University, then Duke University, receiving her doctorate in mathematics in 1991 with a thesis on properties of semilinear hyperbolic systems as investigated by computer numerical analysis. Since then she has taught at Pembroke (1991-1994) and at the University of North Carolina at Chapel Hill (1994-1996), where she also pursued postdoctoral studies and worked on a three-year summertime grant from the American Indian Science and Engineering Society (AISES).

Porter-Locklear's professional activity has dovetailed with her American Indian activism in areas of technology. While teaching at Pembroke she founded a chapter of AISES and acted as its program adviser. She has applied mathematical methods to groundwater studies, with particular focus on water problems in Indian communities. This work resulted in a presentation in 1997 at a conference in Colorado on math, science, and technology education in service of American Indian communities, and in 1998 in a paper on natural bioremediation of ground-water. Not content with theoretical approaches, she founded her own company in Pembroke, Porter Scientific, to deal with these problems in the field. Porter-Locklear is married to a Lumbee, Milton Locklear; they have two sons.

Robert M. Hawthorne, Jr.

Posey, Alexander Lawrence

Born: August 3, 1873; near Eufaula, Creek Nation (now in Oklahoma)
Died: May 27, 1908; North Canadian River, Oklahoma
Tribal affiliation: Creek (Tuskegee)
Significance: Alexander Lawrence Posey's Fus Fixico letters combined political satire, local color, and dialect humor in the tradition of Mark Twain.

Alexander Posey grew up in a large rural Oklahoma family, speaking Creek as his first language but educated in English at the Creek national public school and at Bacone Indian University. He was the first American Indian owner/editor of a daily newspaper; he published the weekly *Indian Journal* of Eufaula, Oklahoma. He was active in Creek politics and helped prepare the census of Creek Indians for the Dawes Severalty Act (General Allotment Act) allotments. Posey accepted the Dawes Act but sympathized with traditionalists who foresaw the damage that allotment would do to Creek life. His life was cut short in 1908 when he drowned near Eufaula. He was survived by his wife, Minnie Harris Posey (Lowena), and his children, Wynema Torrans and Yohola Irving.

In the "Fus Fixico" letters, Posey's major contribution to American literature, fictional characters reflect on the pressing issues of allotment and Creek independence. Posey was reluctant to editorialize, so he created the personas of Hotgun, Fus Fixico, Chinubbie Harjo, Tookpafka Micco, Kono Harjo, and Wolf Warrior, who became voices of skepticism, tradition, advocacy, or resistance as Posey sought to educate his readers about the changes being imposed upon the Creek people. The letters transcend local concerns and exhibit an economy of style and superb rendering of dialect in their trenchant political commentary.

Helen Jaskoski

Poundmaker

Born: c. 1842; near Battleford, Northwest Territories (now in Canada)
Died: July 4, 1886; near Gleichen, Alberta, Canada
Also known as: Opeteca Hanawaywin
Tribal affiliation: Cree
Significance: Poundmaker fought in the Second Riel Rebellion.

Poundmaker, whose followers included Plains Cree and some Assini-
boines, fought with Louis RIEL, Jr., and other Métis in the Second Riel
Rebellion. Poundmaker had initially urged peace, but his young warriors pushed him into raids on settlements and a brief (but successful)
battle with three hundred soldiers.

Riel had become a Métis spokesman by 1870 (Métis people are of
mixed French and Indian descent); he joined with other Indians to
block surveyors from entering the Red River Country. Riel and his allies, including Poundmaker's people, prevented a newly assigned governor from taking up residence in the area; they also seized Fort Garry, a
Hudson's Bay Company outpost near St. Boniface. After that, the Métis
and their allies established a provisional government. Two attempts to
recapture the fort failed as the Métis sent a delegation to Ottawa to argue their case for independence.

Poundmaker pledged to assist Riel and his followers to the end. The
uprising was short-lived: The newly constructed railroad allowed the Canadian government to transport a large number of troops into the area
in a short time. Riel's second rebellion was crushed in a few days, and
Poundmaker was arrested and sent to prison.

Riel was tried for sedition and hanged on November 16, 1885. Afterward he became a martyr and folk hero to many Métis and French Canadians. Poundmaker died the next year.

Bruce E. Johansen

FURTHER READING
Jenish, D'Arcy. *Indian Fall: The Last Great Days of the Plains Cree and the
Blackfoot Confederacy.* Toronto: Viking, 1999.
Flanagan, Thomas. *Riel and the Rebellion: 1885 Reconsidered.* 2d ed. Buf-
falo: University of Toronto Press, 2000.

Powhatan

Born: c. 1550; Powhata (near present-day Richmond, Virginia)
Died: April, 1618; Powhata, near Richmond, Virginia
Also known as: Wahunsonacock
Tribal affiliation: Powhatan
Significance: Powhatan, the leader of a powerful confederacy, made significant contributions to the English settlement in North America. He provided the basis for a peaceful coexistence between the Indians and the English that ultimately enabled the Jamestown colony to thrive and expand.

Powhatan was born around the year 1550, but his exact birth date is unknown. It has been documented that Powhatan was at least partly of foreign extraction, that his father had come from the West Indies because he had been driven from there by the Spaniards. His given name was Wahunsonacock, but he came to be called Powhatan after the name of one of the tribes that was later to come under his rule. It is known that Powhatan had at least two brothers: OPECHANCANOUGH, who later became chief of one of Powhatan's most important tribes, the Pamunkeys, and who was the most formidable enemy of the English after Powhatan's death, and Opitchepan, who succeeded Powhatan.

Virtually nothing has been recorded about Powhatan's early childhood. When he was a young man, he inherited the leadership of six tribes upon his father's death, thus becoming a chief, or sachem. By force or threat of force, he expanded his reign to include thirty tribes. Powhatan's geographical jurisdiction encompassed most of tidewater Virginia. It began on the south side of the James River, extended northward to the Potomac, and included two tribes of the lower eastern shore of the Chesapeake Bay. In addition to the tribe from which he took his name, he controlled the Pamunkey, the Chickahominy, and the Potomac tribes. He and his people belonged to the Algonquian-speaking family that occupied the coastal areas from upper Carolina to New England and beyond. It has been estimated that Powhatan had between eight thousand and nine thousand people under his rule.

Early written English records state that Powhatan was tall, stately, and well proportioned. Although he was perceived as having a sour look, his overall countenance was described as majestic and grave. Powhatan possessed fabulous robes of costly skins and feather capes. He was always bejeweled with long chains of pearls and beads. The English described him as possessing a subtle intelligence—as well as being wily and crafty—and they had great respect for him. Powhatan's principal residence was set deep in a thicket of woods in the village of Werowocomoco, on the York River not far from Jamestown. It was approximately fifty to sixty yards in length and was guarded by four decorative sentries: a dragon, a bear, a leopard, and a giant man.

Powhatan's status as sachem brought with it many privileges, one of

Powhatan in a longhouse meeting, from a German engraving. (Library of Congress)

which was having many wives and, as a result, many children. He selected his favorite women to bear him children, and after they did so
they were free to leave and marry again. One of these women bore him
the most loved and most famous of his daughters, POCAHONTAS. It was
through her that Powhatan became personally involved with the first
English colony in America in 1607 and ultimately decided its destiny.

Powhatan's main goal as sachem of such a large number of tribes was
to create unity and foster harmony among them. Powhatan's people enjoyed political, economic, and artistic stability and prosperity under his
domain. Although his tactics may be deemed despotic by modern standards, his political system offered protection for its people against their
numerous and varied foes. The economy was a relatively sophisticated
one. Three crops of Indian corn were cultivated each year. Tobacco was
also grown. Their foodstuffs were richly supplemented by hunting and
fishing, which were carried out in an organized, communal fashion and
manifested the tribes' common goals and sense of unity. They hunted
wild turkey, beaver, and deer, which not only reinforced their food supply but also provided them with important items for clothing and tools.
For fishing, they employed equipment such as the weir, net, fishhook,
spear, and arrow.

Upon the arrival of the English, Powhatan sought to maintain the
peace, prosperity, and strength of his people. His approach was based
on the assumption that it would be possible for the two groups to coexist
peacefully and that neither would prosper through the extinction of
the other. In seeking coexistence, Powhatan's wisdom, wiles, and capacity for negotiation were put to the test, and in spite of many trials and
tribulations, he never wavered from this goal. He instinctively sought to
guard his people against the disruptive temptations presented by the
English.

The Englishmen certainly possessed weaponry that was far more sophisticated than that of the Indians. When Powhatan met the English
Captain John Smith, his instincts and political acumen told him that
Smith was trying to deceive him. He decided that Smith should be put
to death. At the last minute, however, he relented; Smith claimed that
Pocahontas intervened in his behalf, and the Englishman's life was
spared. Powhatan then attempted to trade with Smith and the English
in order to obtain muskets. He sent a generous quantity of badly
needed food to the starving colonists and, in return, demanded can-
nons, muskets, and a millstone for grinding corn. Smith returned to
Jamestown a free man, laden with food supplies, only to break his bar-
gain with Powhatan by sending him bells, beads, and mirrors instead of

the items he requested. Powhatan felt deceived and refused the next request for food.

Powhatan adopted a wait-and-see stance. He recognized, resisted, and outwitted a variety of attempts to subjugate him or his people. For example, when Powhatan was asked to participate in a coronation ceremony which would make him a subject of the English king, he reacted with some rancor. He did not see the wisdom or the logic of one king serving another. He did, however, accept all the gifts that were presented to him. These included a huge bed, a red silk cape, and a copper crown. The English, for their part, continued to try to use the Indians while biding their time and building up their strength with supplies from England.

When Powhatan realized that Smith was never going to trade his weapons, he made a deal with Captain Christopher Newport, who was not on friendly terms with Smith. The Indians traded twenty wild turkeys for twenty English swords. The result was favorable for Powhatan: The deal created further demoralization and internal strife among the members of the Jamestown community, while at the same time it strengthened and fortified the unity of Powhatan's people.

Despite his desire for arms, Powhatan's humanitarian side prevailed on most occasions. When a fire destroyed the Jamestown warehouse that contained the colonists' food, Powhatan sent not only food but also his daughter Pocahontas to serve as ambassador. When Pocahontas was kidnapped by an English captain, and one of the ransom demands was the return of all captured prisoners and pilfered guns, Powhatan again reacted in a shrewd manner. Although Pocahontas was known to be his favorite daughter, and he had often said that she was as dear to him as his own life, he knew that the English had always been her friends. Believing that they would not harm her, he made no attempts to rescue her. When it was announced by the English that she was engaged to marry an English planter, John Rolfe, he blessed the impending marriage. He promised friendship, sent two of his sons to attend the wedding bearing many gifts, and returned the prisoners—but not the guns.

This act began an era of peace between the Indians and the English known as the Peace of Pocahontas, which lasted until the time of Powhatan's death in 1618. The sachem had achieved his goal without compromising his personal dignity or jeopardizing the strength and peace of his tribes.

There are many theories as to why Powhatan allowed the Jamestown colony to survive rather than simply wiping it out at the first sign of trouble. Given the large numbers of people under his rule, it is quite obvious that, had he so wished, he could have easily destroyed the colony in spite of its superior weaponry. He had no apparent reason to do so, however, and perhaps he thought that fair play and a cautious approach in his relations with the English could be mutually advantageous.

The English colony did not seem to pose any real threat to Powhatan at the time of their initial landing in the spring of 1607. It was composed of a group of quarrelsome, power-hungry men who were incapable of unifying even their small group. The colony's rate of growth was extremely slow, and Powhatan had no way to imagine the devastation that the future would bring. There were only about 350 people in the colony at the time of Powhatan's death. Since its founding, the colonists had suffered such grave misfortunes that it was only with Powhatan's help that they had survived; he, in turn, reasoned that the English could help him. Their sophisticated weaponry not only would facilitate daily chores such as hunting but also would provide his people with better protection against their foes and further reinforce his own authority. This interdependence would have the potential to lead to an alliance if such a situation presented itself.

The deceit and double-crossing that was exchanged between the two sides was probably only the normal politicking of two astute leaders. Although Powhatan was often a victim of English deceit, he did not allow resentments to interfere with the formation of a long-lasting peace treaty. It is highly doubtful that he allowed sentimental considerations to interfere with his political decisions. Although there is no denying that Powhatan loved Pocahontas, he also knew that her ability to deal with the English could prove fruitful to him; thus he sent her to negotiate the return of the Indian prisoners in the Jamestown camp. He knew that Smith would yield to Pocahontas what he would yield to no one else.

Anne Laura Mattrella

FURTHER READING

Chatterton, E. K. *Captain John Smith.* New York: Harper and Brothers, 1929.

Craven, Wesley Frank. *White, Red, and Black: The Seventeenth Century Virginian.* Charlottesville: University Press of Virginia, 1971.

Fishwick, Marshall W. *Jamestown: First English Colony.* New York: Harper and Row, 1965.

Fritz, Jean. *The Double Life of Pocahontas.* New York: G. P. Putnam's Sons, 1983.

Gerson, Noel B. *The Glorious Scoundrel: A Biography of Captain John Smith.* New York: Dodd, Mead, 1978.

Rountree, Helen C. *Pocahontas, Powhatan, Opechancanough: Three Indian Lives Changed by Jamestown.* Charlottesville: University of Virginia Press, 2005.

Willison, George F. *Behold Virginia: The Fifth Crown.* New York: Harcourt, Brace, 1951.

Pretty Shield

Born: March, 1857; south-central Montana
Died: 1932; Crow Reservation, Montana
Tribal affiliation: Crow
Significance: Pretty Shield was a prominent Crow medicine woman whose firsthand account of life on the plains before white settlement became a classic in Native American studies.

Born to Kills-in-the-Night and renowned warrior Crazy-Sister-in-Law, Pretty Shield was the fourth of eleven children. When she was three years old, her mother, a Mountain Crow, sent her away to be raised by a widowed aunt, Strikes-with-an-Ax, a River Crow woman who had lost her two young daughters. Because the survival of the Crow people was tied to the migration of the buffalo, Crow clans moved often. The nomadic nature of tribal life limited contact between Mountain and River Crow communities, and Pretty Shield saw her natural mother only the few times each year when the two clans met.

Strikes-with-an-Ax proved to be a wise mentor for Pretty Shield and taught her what was expected of all Crow women: how to set up lodges, cook, dress skins, and dig for roots, among other duties. Following in the footsteps of her grandmother, a respected healer, Pretty Shield also learned about the curative properties of herbs. Her own calling as a medicine woman was affirmed when she had her first medicine dream after the death of one of her children.

Although Pretty Shield enjoyed a happy childhood, life on the plains was often precarious, and war with other tribes was a constant threat. Led by chief PLENTY COUPS, the Crow engaged in skirmishes with the Lakota, Cheyenne, Arapaho, and Blackfeet. Crow warriors were frequently outnumbered by their opponents, and casualties were high.

White encroachment onto Native American land proved to be another danger to traditional Crow life. Diseases such as smallpox, introduced by white settlers, wiped out whole villages, and Pretty Shield's own father died from smallpox when she was seventeen. Clashes between Indian tribes and the U.S. Army also increased. Because the government was fighting against the Sioux, the Crows' enemy, for control of the sacred Black Hills, the Crows occasionally allied with U.S. forces.

In June, 1876, Pretty Shield's husband, Goes-Ahead, was a scout for General George Crook, who was ordered to stop the marauding Lakota led by CRAZY HORSE. The battle between Crook's forces and Crazy Horse's warriors took place on June 17 on Montana's Rosebud River, where the Sioux defeated government troops. Forced to retreat to their base camp, Crook and his soldiers were prevented from backing up George Armstrong Custer's army at the Little Bighorn eight days later. Pretty Shield noted that her husband and other Crow scouts deserted Crook shortly after his defeat at Rosebud.

Despite the Crows' alliance with the U.S. government, the U.S. government broke its treaties with the tribe and encouraged white settlement on Crow land. Robbing native peoples of their traditional livelihood, white hunters and traders indiscriminately slaughtered buffalo, and ranchers seized tribal lands. Finally, in 1904, the borders of the Crow reservation were fixed, and the tribe became ranchers and farmers. Although Pretty Shield lamented the destruction of her culture, she spent the rest of her life helping to reconcile her people to their new way of life.

Pegge Bochynski

FURTHER READING
Linderman, Frank B. *Pretty Shield: Medicine Woman of the Crows.* New York: John Day, 1972.

Pushmataha

Born: June, 1764; British Indian territory in present-day Noxubee County, Mississippi
Died: December 24, 1824; Washington, D.C.
Also known as: Apushamatahubib (Warrior's Seat Is Finished)
Tribal affiliation: Choctaw
Significance: The most powerful Choctaw leader of the early nineteenth century, Pushmataha allied his people with the United States during the Creek War (1813-1814) and the War of 1812.

Few hard facts are known about Pushmataha's early life. He fostered the legend that he had sprung fully grown from an oak tree split by lightning. This story may have been a way of covering up his relatively humble origins. His position among his fellow Choctaws was attributable to

Pushmataha. (Library of Congress)

his personal achievements as a warrior, hunter, athlete, and orator. He became the chief of the Six Towns district of the Choctaw Nation, and by the early nineteenth century he was the most influential of the Choctaw leaders.

Pushmataha greatly influenced the course of Choctaw relations with the United States. In 1804, he met with President Thomas Jefferson, signing a treaty that ceded a small tract of Choctaw land in return for guarantees of friendship and assistance. Within the tribe, he emphasized the need for education.

Pushmataha proved himself to be a loyal ally of the United States. In 1811, he used his considerable oratorical abilities to blunt TECUMSEH's appeal for a pan-Indian alliance against American expansion. He raised a large contingent of Choctaws for service in the Creek War of 1813-1814. He and his warriors later fought against the British at New Orleans. As a reward, he was made a brigadier general in the U.S. Army.

As Choctaw lands came under increasing white pressure, Pushmataha continued to seek accommodation. In the 1820 Treaty of Doak's Stand, he agreed to the cession of a large portion of tribal lands in western and central Mississippi; in return the Choctaws received extensive lands west of the Mississippi River. In late 1824, hoping to prevent further cessions, he visited Washington to meet directly with President James Monroe. He became ill, however, and died. He was buried there with the honors due his military rank.

FURTHER READING

Lincecum, Gideon. *Pushmataha: A Choctaw Leader and His People.* Tuscaloosa: University of Alabama Press, 2004.

Queen Anne

Born: c. 1650; junction of Pamunkey and Mattapony Rivers, present-day Virginia

Died: c. 1725

Tribal affiliation: Pamunkey Powhatan

Significance: As leader of the Pamunkey tribe, a member of the Powhatan Confederacy, Queen Anne aided white Virginia settlers against hostile tribes.

Queen Anne's husband, Totopotomoi, was principal chief of the Pamunkey tribe. With his death in battle as an ally of whites against other Indian tribes in 1656, Queen Anne assumed leadership of the Pamunkeys. In 1675 she traveled to Williamsburg to respond to governor William Berkeley's request for her aid in suppressing Bacon's Rebellion—a rebellion within Virginia ostensibly caused by Berkeley's failure to protect western Virginians from hostile Indians.

In full Indian attire, Queen Anne appeared at the Colonial Council, where she initially refused Berkeley's request, citing his earlier failure to protect her husband and her tribe. After promises of future aid, she reluctantly provided the governor with assistance. Afterward, in tribute, she was presented with a silver-inscribed medal (now in the collection of the Association for the Preservation of Virginia Antiquities).

Quinney, John W.

Born: 1797; New Stockbridge, New York
Died: July 21, 1855; Stockbridge, Wisconsin
Also known as: Quinequan
Tribal affiliation: Mahican (Stockbridge)
Significance: John W. Quinney was a Mahican leader at the time the tribe relocated from the East to the Great Lakes area.

As a young man, John W. Quinney was taught to read and write English. He assisted Moravian missionaries in translating religious works into printed, phonetic Mahican (Stockbridge).

White encroachment in the early 1800's pushed the Mahicans from the Hudson River valley, and Quinney was instrumental in purchasing Menominee land in Wisconsin. The U.S. government was willing to grant citizenship to the Stockbridge, since the vast majority were Christianized. This would have effectively ended their existence as a separate tribe and ended their need for their own land. Quinney resisted American citizenship for his tribe.

Quinney was appointed grand sachem in 1852, although his family was not of the hereditary line of sachems; the appointment may have been largely honorary. He served until his death in 1855. Quinney was hostile to the Mohawk throughout his life and was resentful that his people were removed and the Mohawk were not.

Glenn J. Schiffman

Rain in the Face

Born: c. 1835; forks of the Cheyenne River, North Dakota
Died: September 14, 1905; Standing Rock, North Dakota
Also known as: Amarazhu, Iromagaja
Tribal affiliation: Hunkpapa Lakota (Sioux)
Significance: During the Sioux Wars of the 1860's and 1870's, Rain in the Face was a leading war chief.

His name came from childhood incidents in which blood, along with red and black war paint, streaked his face. Not a hereditary chief, Rain in the Face earned his reputation and status in war. During the war for the Bozeman Trail (1866-1868), Rain in the Face was a leading war chief, participating in numerous raids. At Fort Trotten, North Dakota, he was severely wounded.

Arrested in 1873 for the murder of a white surgeon, Rain in the Face,

Rain in the Face. (National Archives)

though admitting his guilt, was aided by a white guard, who permitted his escape. He thereafter participated in the war for the Black Hills (1876-1877) and in the last great Indian victory, the Battle of the Little Bighorn, during which he was reputed to have killed George Armstrong Custer. At war's end, he retreated with SITTING BULL to Canada, returning with him to Montana in 1880 and surrendering at Fort Keogh. Rain in the Face had seven wives and numerous children.

Mary E. Virginia

FURTHER READING

Ostler, Jeffrey. *The Plains Sioux and U.S. Colonialism from Lewis and Clark to Wounded Knee.* New York: Cambridge University Press, 2004.

Red Bird

Born: c. 1788; near Prairie du Chien, Wisconsin
Died: February 16, 1828; Prairie du Chien, Wisconsin
Also known as: Wanig Suchka, Zitkaduta
Tribal affiliation: Winnebago
Significance: The leader of the brief Winnebago Uprising, Red Bird was war chief of a small, militant group of Winnebagos.

Born at the forks of the Mississippi and Wisconsin Rivers, Red Bird succeeded his father as war chief of the Prairie La Crosse Winnebagos. As lead prices rose during the 1820's, federal officials seeking to obtain rich Indian lands attempted to discourage Indians from mining and selling lead to traders. Consequently, tensions escalated, and in 1826 warriors killed members of a French trading family. In 1827, two warriors were accused of murder; rumors of their imminent execution reached Red Bird's village. Authorized by tribal council, Red Bird and two other warriors killed two white settlers and scalped an infant. On June 30, Red Bird also attacked a Mississippi boatman who had kidnapped and raped several Indian women. Subsequently, federal troops, Illinois volunteers, and white volunteer miners massed at Fort Snelling. When other Winnebagos failed to join the uprising, Red Bird surrendered to white forces, expecting immediate execution. His trial met with several delays, however, and Red Bird died of dysentery shortly before charges against him were dropped because of a lack of witnesses.

Mary E. Virginia

Red Cloud

Born: 1822; Blue Creek, near North Platte (now in Nebraska)
Died: December 10, 1909; Pine Ridge, South Dakota
Also known as: Makhpia-sha
Tribal affiliation: Oglala Lakota (Sioux)
Significance: Red Cloud led the Lakota Sioux through a difficult period, effectively resisting the onrush of the American westward advance and later helping the Sioux make the transition to reservation life.

Red Cloud was born into the Oglala subtribe of the Teton branch of Lakotas (Sioux) on the High Plains of what is now Nebraska. His father, a headman in the Brule subtribe, was named Lone Man, and his mother was Walks-as-She-Thinks, a member of the Saone subtribe. There is disagreement over the origins of the name Red Cloud. Some sources contend that it was a family name used by his father and grandfather, while others claim that it was coined as a description of the way his scarlet-blanketed warriors covered the hills like a red cloud.

Very little is known about Red Cloud's early life. His father died when he was young, and he was reared in the camp of Chief Old Smoke, a maternal uncle. He undoubtedly spent his boyhood learning skills that were important to Sioux men at the time, including hunting, riding, and shooting. Plains Culture Indians sometimes conducted raids against enemies, and Red Cloud joined his first war party and took his first scalp at the age of sixteen. Thereafter, he was always quick to participate in expeditions against the Pawnee, Crow, or Ute. Other Oglala frequently retold Red Cloud's colorful exploits in battle. During a raid against the Crow, he killed the warrior guarding the ponies and then ran off with fifty horses. This was a highly respected deed among Plains Indians, whose horses were central to their way of life. On an expedition against the Pawnee, Red Cloud killed four of the enemy—an unusually high number in a type of warfare in which casualties were normally low.

In the early 1840's most Oglala bands camped around Fort Laramie on the North Platte River, where they could obtain a variety of goods from white traders. Red Cloud was part of a band known as the Bad Faces, or Smoke People, under the leadership of his uncle, Old Smoke. Another band in the area, the Koya, was led by BULL BEAR, the most dominant headman among the Oglala and commonly recognized as their chief. The two groups frequently quarreled. One day in the fall of 1841, after young men of both sides had been drinking, a member of the Bad Faces stole a Koya woman. Bull Bear led a force to the Bad Face camp and shot the father of the young man who had taken the woman. The Bad Faces retaliated, and when a shot to the leg downed Bull Bear, Red Cloud rushed in and killed him. This event led to a split among the Oglala that lasted for many years. It also elevated Red Cloud's standing among the Bad Faces, and shortly after the incident he organized and led a war party of his own against the Pawnee.

Soon after recovering from wounds suffered in that raid, Red Cloud married a young Lakota woman named Pretty Owl. Sources disagree as to whether he thereafter remained monogamous or took multiple wives, a common practice among prominent Sioux. Nor is there agreement on how many children he fathered, although five is the number most often accepted by scholars. Over the next two decades, Red Cloud's reputation and status continued to grow. By the mid-1860's he was a ruggedly handsome man of medium stature with penetrating eyes and a confident and commanding presence. He was also a band headman and a leading warrior with a growing following among the Bad Faces. Sioux social and political structure was very decentralized; no one person had authority over the whole group. Instead, certain leaders were recognized as chiefs on the basis of ability and achievement. An important member of his band, at this time Red Cloud was not yet a chief.

In the several decades before the Civil War, traders began operating in Sioux territory; they were followed by wagon trains, telegraph construction, and further encroachments by whites. The Sioux welcomed most of the traders and at least tolerated most of the wagon trains, even though whites disrupted hunting by killing indiscriminately and chasing animals away from traditional hunting grounds. By the closing years of the Civil War, American traffic across the northern Plains increased

even further. The discovery of gold in the mountains of Montana in late 1862 enticed more whites to cross Sioux land, leading to friction and occasional clashes. The final straw came when the government sent soldiers in to build forts and protect passage along a popular route known as the Bozeman Trail, which linked Montana with the Oregon Trail.

In 1865 many Sioux, including Red Cloud, took up arms in resistance. Several Lakota leaders signed a treaty in the spring of 1866 that would open the Bozeman Trail, but Red Cloud and his many followers held out, insisting on the removal of soldiers. The government tried

Red Cloud. (National Archives)

to ignore Red Cloud for a time, but the Sioux almost completely closed down travel and obstructed efforts to construct the forts. These actions represented the high point in Red Cloud's career as a military strategist. He led his men to a number of victories, most notably the annihilation of Captain William J. Fetterman and eighty-two soldiers in an incident known to whites as the Fetterman massacre and to Indians as the Battle of a Hundred Slain. In November of 1868, when, after negotiations, the army withdrew the troops and abandoned the forts, Red Cloud finally ended the war.

This victory increased Red Cloud's standing among his people, although he still was not the Sioux's exclusive leader. The U.S. government, however, assumed that he was the head chief and dealt with him as such. In the late 1860's, there was talk of creating a reservation for the Lakota, and Red Cloud surprised everyone by announcing that he would go to Washington, D.C., and talk about the idea. Some have argued that he was motivated by a desire to gain the status among the Sioux that he already enjoyed in the view of federal officials. On the other hand, he may have realized that since some white Westerners opposed granting a reservation—preferring the extermination of Indians—a reservation, if combined with the withdrawal of troops from all Sioux lands, might be the best compromise he could achieve.

Red Cloud and twenty other Sioux leaders were escorted to the nation's capital in 1870 with great ceremony. Red Cloud did not win everything he wanted, but he clearly emerged as the most famous Native American of his time. He was applauded by many Easterners who sympathized with Indians and saw Red Cloud as a symbol of justifiable response to white advance.

In 1871 Red Cloud settled on the newly created reservation, at the agency named after him. Then, only a few years later, gold was discovered in the Black Hills portion of the reserve, and the government pressured the Sioux to sell the area. When negotiations broke down, events quickly escalated into the Sioux War of 1876-1877. With one eye on the government, Red Cloud publicly opposed the armed action undertaken by some Lakota to stop the flood of prospectors onto their lands, but privately he seemed to sanction such moves. Red Cloud frequently became embroiled in political battles with federal agents on the reservation. He tried to win whatever provisions and concessions he could to ease his people's suffering, and he resisted government efforts to break down traditional cultural and political life. When many Sioux became involved in the controversial Ghost Dance in 1889-1890, Red Cloud avoided early commitment to, or open encouragement of, participation. Many dancers, however, believed that they had his support anyway. Red Cloud's frequent compromise position and his seeming cooperation with government agents sometimes made him suspect among some of his people, and, as a consequence, his influence steadily eroded. He died on the reservation on December 10, 1909.

Red Cloud emerged as a military and political leader at a dramatic and tragic time in the history of the Lakota Sioux. Once powerful nomadic buffalo hunters, their lives were being changed forever. The relentless westward advance of whites constricted their land base, destroyed the buffalo upon which their economy depended, and ultimately brought about their impoverishment. Moreover, government attempts to destroy traditional Sioux ways of life on the reservation, while never completely successful, resulted in severe cultural disruption.

For a time, Red Cloud resisted militarily as effectively as any Native American leader ever had. Then, when American domination became clear, he attempted to balance the two worlds of Indian and white, hoping to win the best results possible for his people under the circumstances. This was a difficult task, and he did not satisfy everyone. He was attacked from both sides—by whites for not doing more to encourage his followers to assimilate into the white world, and by some Sioux for being too willing to give in to government authorities.

Red Cloud stood as a symbol to many Indians (and some whites) of strong defense of homelands and culture, while to other whites he epitomized the worst in Indian treachery and savagery. For both sides, the name Red Cloud conveyed immense power. During the 1960's and 1970's, with the rise of the Red Power movement and a rejuvenation of Indian culture, he again became a symbol—this time to a generation of young Indian (and sometimes white) political activists who found inspiration in what they saw as his defiance in the face of unjust authority.

Larry W. Burt

FURTHER READING

Cook, James H. *Fifty Years on the Old Frontier.* New Haven, Conn.: Yale University Press, 1923.

DeMallie, Raymond J., ed. *The Sixth Grandfather: Black Elk's Teachings Given to John G. Neihardt.* Lincoln: University of Nebraska Press, 1984.

Hyde, George E. *Red Cloud's Folk: A History of the Oglala Sioux Indians.* Norman: University of Oklahoma Press, 1937.

_____. *A Sioux Chronicle.* Norman: University of Oklahoma Press, 1956.

Larson, Robert W. *Red Cloud: Warrior-Statesman of the Lakota Sioux.* Nor man: University of Oklahoma Press, 1997.

Olson, James C. *Red Cloud and the Sioux Problem.* Lincoln: University of Nebraska Press, 1965.

Paul, R. Eli, ed. *Autobiography of Red Cloud: War Leader of the Oglalas.* Helena: Montana Historical Society Press, 1997.

Robinson, Doane. *A History of the Dakota or Sioux Indians.* Aberdeen, S.Dak.: News Printing, 1904. Reprint. Minneapolis, Minn.: Ross and Haines, 1958.

Utley, Robert M. *The Last Days of the Sioux Nation.* New Haven, Conn.: Yale University Press, 1963.

Red Jacket

Born: c. 1756; near Canoga, New York
Died: January 20, 1830; Seneca Village, New York
Also known as: Sagoyewátha (He Causes Them to Be Awake)
Tribal affiliation: Seneca
Significance: An eloquent speaker known for his great wit and memory, Red Jacket participated in numerous treaty conferences, arguing against Seneca assimilation into white society.

Red Jacket was born about 1756 near Canoga, New York. His original name was Otetiani (Always Prepared), but upon his election as a merit chief shortly after the American Revolution he was given the Wolf Clan title Sagoyewátha (He Causes Them to Be Awake). To the whites, he was known as Red Jacket because of his fondness for red coats (first provided by the British).

At the Council at Oswego (1777), Red Jacket and CORNPLANTER urged Iroquois neutrality in the revolution. When the council decided to join the British cause, he followed the Iroquois custom of unanimity and joined the war effort at Oriskany (1777) and Cherry Valley (1778), but he fled both encounters. He later participated in the Schoharie Valley campaign (1780). His undistinguished war record did not prevent recognition of his oratorical skills, and he served as speaker for the women and chiefs at Buffalo Creek. From 1790 to 1794, he was present at seven major negotiations between Iroquois and U.S. officials. In 1792, George Washington presented him with a silver medal.

Initially he was open to the adoption of some white ways, but land sales, fraud, and frontier evangelists made him wary of whites. He took an increasingly conservative cultural position. At the same time, he signed treaties selling land and negotiated secretly with federal commissioners, receiving six hundred dollars and a hundred-dollar annuity at Big Tree in 1797. This apparent hypocrisy earned him the enmity of the prophet HANDSOME LAKE, who declared that Red Jacket would be undergoing eternal punishment for his role in the sale of Seneca land.

Red Jacket's harshest attacks were reserved for missionaries. Noting the absence of beneficial effects of preaching in white communities, he wondered why Christians were unable to reach agreement on their religion. He was so humiliated when his wife converted to Christianity that he left her briefly. Deposed as chief in 1827 by a minority of chiefs (all Christians), he was reinstated the following year. As leader of the pagan faction, he objected to tactics used to obtain Seneca acquiescence to land sales to the Ogden Land Company and Seneca removal to Kansas. Red Jacket sent remonstrances to the governor of New York and President John Quincy Adams, and he personally visited Adams, securing an investigation that upheld charges of fraud.

As vain as he was eloquent, and with a reputation for intemperance, he was disappointed in never being named a confederacy chief. This may have been a result of his conflict with Handsome Lake, or perhaps it reflected the Winnebagos' fear of concentrating too much authority in such a wily individual. He died on January 20, 1830, ironically receiving a Christian burial. His remains were reburied in 1884 (along with those of other prominent Senecas) by the Buffalo Historical Society.

Joy A. Bilharz

FURTHER READING

Densmore, Christopher. *Red Jacket: Iroquois Diplomat and Orator.* Syracuse, N.Y.: Syracuse University Press, 1999.

Parker, Arthur Caswell. *Red Jacket: Seneca Chief.* Reprint. Lincoln: University of Nebraska Press, 1998.

Swatzler, David. *A Friend Among the Senecas: The Quaker Mission to Cornplanter's People.* Mechanicsburg, Pa.: Stackpole Books, 2000.

Red Shoes

Born: c. 1700; New Stockbridge, New York
Died: June 22, 1748
Also known as: Shulush Homa
Tribal affiliation: Choctaw
Significance: The Choctaw leader Red Shoes was an advocate of peace and trade with whites.

Red Shoes rose to prominence during the period of factionalism in the Choctaw tribe that culminated in civil war between 1746 and 1750. The Choctaw were allied with the French, fighting against the English and their Chickasaw allies. Red Shoes was awarded a French medal for his loyal service soon after the Natchez Revolt of 1729. Soon afterward, however, he became an advocate of peace with the Chickasaw and trade with English merchants from South Carolina. His reasons may have included a chronic shortage of trade goods from the French, his marriage connections with the Chickasaw, or the fact that his wife suffered a rape at the hands of the French. Whatever the reason, Red Shoes was received with ceremony by the English at Charleston in 1738.

Red Shoes attempted to sway other Choctaw towns away from their dependence on the French and ultimately contributed to serious political divisions in the tribe. French diplomats, desperate to reestablish their influence before losing their loyal allies to either an English alliance or unpredictable neutrality, conspired to induce other Choctaw war chiefs to assassinate Red Shoes. He was murdered on June 22, 1748, while escorting an English trader from the Creek towns to Choctaw territory.

Red Shoes was probably from the village of Couechitto. His name derives from the Choctaw title for war chief, *soulouche oumastabe*, or red shoe killer.

Thomas Patrick Carroll

Red Tomahawk, Marcellus

Born: c. 1850; present-day Standing Rock Reservation, North Dakota
Died: August 7, 1931; Standing Rock Reservation, North Dakota
Also known as: Ospecannonpa-luta, Tacanhpi-luta
Tribal affiliation: Sihasapa (Blackfoot) Lakota (Sioux)
Significance: A Sihasapa Lakota warrior whose profile was later used in the design of the North Dakota state highway symbol, Marcellus Red Tomahawk is best known as the Indian policeman who killed SITTING BULL.

Marcellus Red Tomahawk served as a sergeant on the Indian Police Service detailed to arrest Sitting Bull at the Ghost Dance outbreak in late 1890. Earlier that year, the U.S. government had banned the Ghost Dance on Sioux reservations. Meanwhile, the Northern Paiute prophet WOVOKA in Nevada had a vision that fallen warriors and buffalo would return to drive away the white men. Although white settlers panicked

Marcellus Red Tomahawk. (National Archives)

because of perceived threat, the peaceful Ghost Dance movement forbade the use of weapons and consisted of the community dancing hand in hand in a circle protected by Ghost Dance shirts believed to be bullet-proof.

During the Ghost Dance scare, KICKING BEAR and SHORT BULL, mystics of the Miniconjou Tetons, asked Sitting Bull, at the Standing Rock Reservation, to join them at nearby Pine Ridge Reservation. Sitting Bull, a Hunkpapa Lakota, had had a vision of white men falling within his camp circle before his forces defeated George Armstrong Custer at the Battle of the Little Bighorn in 1876. He envisioned his own death when he saw a meadowlark alight on a hillock beside him and heard it say, "Your own people, Lakotas, will kill you."

The Pine Ridge Reservation Indian agent, D. F. Royer, called for Army troops. At Standing Rock, James McLaughlin ordered Sitting Bull arrested. Forty-three "metal breasts"—Indian police—led by Lieutenant Bull Head botched the operation in the predawn of December 15, 1890. When the fifty-nine-year-old Sitting Bull resisted arrest, he was fatally shot in the head. Seven of his people, including his son, and six Indian police officers died. Eight days later, at Wounded Knee on the Pine Ridge Reservation, government troops killed perhaps two hundred Sioux who were traveling to a Ghost Dance celebration. The victims included many unarmed women and children.

Red Tomahawk afterward became known as the man who killed Sitting Bull on that occasion. He survived the event and lived to collect a government pension of twenty dollars per month.

In 1923, Red Tomahawk was chosen by the state of North Dakota to pose for the Indian profile that was to be adopted as the state's official highway symbol. Since then, his profile has appeared on highway signs throughout North Dakota. In 1929, at about the age of eighty, Red Tomahawk made a goodwill visit to Washington, D.C. He was invited by General Charles Summerall, President Herbert Hoover's army chief of staff, who had visited Red Tomahawk in North Dakota during the previous year. It was reported that politicians and socialites admired Red Tomahawk's natural dignity and noble posture. Red Tomahawk died two years later at his home in North Dakota.

Joanna Yin

Reifel, Ben

Born: September 19, 1906; Rosebud Reservation, South Dakota
Died: January 2, 1990; Sioux Falls, South Dakota
Tribal affiliation: Rosebud Lakota (Sioux)
Significance: Ben Reifel served five terms in Congress after several years in various capacities in the Bureau of Indian Affairs.

Ben Reifel, who would become a congressman from South Dakota, was the son of a German father and a Sioux mother. Reifel did not pass the eighth grade until he was sixteen and did not go to high school. His father could "see no reason for it," and he told Ben that he was needed on the farm. The young man read whatever he could find, and his passion for education grew. Finally the young man ran away from home, hiking 250 miles to enroll in high school.

Despite his late start in formal education, Reifel earned a bachelor's degree from South Dakota State University in 1932. He joined the army reserves as a commissioned officer while in college and was called to duty in World War II. At the end of the war, he was appointed Bureau of Indian Affairs (BIA) superintendent at the Fort Berthold Agency, North Dakota.

Reifel returned to college at Harvard University for a master's in public administration and then became one of the first American Indians to earn a doctoral degree, also at Harvard. When he returned to the Dakotas, he held several BIA posts including the superintendency at Pine Ridge, where he was the first head Indian agent of native blood. His career at the BIA culminated when he was appointed area director of the office in Aberdeen, South Dakota.

In 1960, Reifel retired from the BIA to run for Congress. He won on his first run for public office (as a Republican) and served five terms before retiring in 1970. On his retirement, Reifel, who had fought so hard to get a formal education, was awarded an honorary degree from the University of South Dakota.

Bruce E. Johansen

Renville, Joseph

Born: c. 1779; near present-day St. Paul, Minnesota
Died: March, 1846; Lac Qui Parle, Minnesota
Tribal affiliation: Lakota (Sioux)
Significance: Joseph Renville was an influential white sympathizer among the Minnesota Sioux.

Born and reared until age ten in an Indian village south of present-day St. Paul, Minnesota, Renville was the son of a French trader and a Sioux woman. After being sent to Montreal at the age of ten to receive a Roman Catholic education, he returned to Minnesota a few years later to become a trader. At the age of nineteen he was employed by the Hudson's Bay Company.

During his young adulthood, Renville was a guide and interpreter for Zebulon Pike, traveling with him as he sought the headwaters of the Mississippi River and aiding him in establishing peace treaties with the Sioux.

Renville served as a captain for the British army during the War of 1812. While living in Canada, both during and after the war, he was an interpreter for the British government.

After returning to Minnesota shortly after the war, he helped found the Columbia Fur Company. At his trading post at Lac Qui Parle, Renville trained an armed company of Sioux to guard against attacks by the hostile Ojibwas. In 1834, he helped found a Presbyterian mission at Lac Qui Parle, and in 1837 he aided missionaries in translating the Bible into Sioux. Many of Renville's descendants, including his nephew, Gabriel Renville, continued his tradition of support for whites.

Mary E. Virginia

Ridge, John Rollin

Born: March 19, 1827; Eastern Cherokee Nation (now Rome, Georgia)
Died: October 5, 1867; Grass Valley, California
Also known as: Chees-quat-a-law-ny, Yellow Bird
Tribal affiliation: Cherokee
Significance: John Rollin Ridge became a leading journalist, a noted poet, and a spokesperson for the plight of Indians in the late nineteenth century.

John Rollin Ridge was the son of a white woman and the Cherokee John Ridge, who, like his father, Major RIDGE, was initially a strong opponent of the removal of the Cherokee to the west, but later became an active supporter of the relocation of his tribe to the Indian Territory.

The younger Ridge endured a controversial and often violent childhood. Both his father and his grandfather became involved in a bitter conflict over the removal of the Cherokee with the faction of their tribe led by John Ross, and they were murdered in 1839, together with a third man, in Indian Territory in retaliation for their support of the move west.

Lured by the prospect of quick riches in the gold fields of California, Ridge moved to that state in 1850. Not successful as a prospector, he became involved in journalism. His pen name was Yellow Bird, a translation of his Indian name; essays written by him on the Indians in the nineteenth century and printed in newspapers and magazines have been compiled and published as *A Trumpet of Our Own* (1991).

During his lifetime, his most notable literary achievement was *The Life and Adventures of Joaquin Murieta, the Celebrated California Bandit* (1854), a fictionalized account of a Robin Hood-style character. Ridge was also a noted poet, and a compilation of his poetry was published in 1868, a year after his death.

Richard B. McCaslin

FURTHER READING

Dale, Edward Everett, and Gaston Litton. *Cherokee Cavaliers: Forty Years of Cherokee History as Told in the Correspondence of the Ridge-Watie-Boudinot Family.* Foreword by James W. Parins. 1939. Reprint. Norman: University of Oklahoma Press, 1995.

Jahoda, Gloria. *The Trail of Tears.* New York: Wings Books, 1995.

Parins, James W. *John Rollin Ridge: His Life and Works.* Lincoln: University of Nebraska Press, 2004.

Walker, Cheryl. *Indian Nation: Native American Literature and Nineteenth-Century Nationalisms.* Durham, N.C.: Duke University Press, 1997.

Wilkins, Thurman. *Cherokee Tragedy: The Ridge Family and the Decimation of a People.* 2d rev. ed. Norman: University of Oklahoma Press, 1986.

Ridge, Major

Born: c. 1771; Hiwassee, present-day Tennessee
Died: June 22, 1839; Indian Territory, present-day Arkansas
Also known as: The Ridge
Tribal affiliation: Cherokee

Significance: Major Ridge, an influential Cherokee orator, fought against the Creeks and was a leading figure during the removal era.

Ridge was born in eastern Tennessee around 1771. His paternal grandfather was a Highland Scot, but Ridge was brought up as a Cherokee. As a young man, called The Ridge after the Blue Ridge mountains, he became prominent as a hunter and warrior, sometimes raiding against white settlers. Ridge became an outstanding orator among his people, who made him a member of their central council. The Cherokees had a "blood law" decreeing death for anyone who sold Cherokee lands without the full consent of the nation. When Chief Doublehead violated this law, Ridge and Alexander Saunders assassinated him in 1807.

Observing the comparative prosperity of whites, Ridge concluded that Indian prosperity lay in becoming civilized and competing with whites in farming and trade, rather than in war. Ridge did so with such success that he soon became a wealthy planter in western Georgia. Without any formal education, he learned to understand English and could speak it brokenly, but he preferred to use Cherokee and translators.

During the War of 1812, when combat broke out between the Creeks and both the American government and rival tribes, Ridge led a Cherokee force against the hostile Red Stick Creeks, defeated them in several battles, then joined the army of Andrew Jackson, who made him a major. Ridge played a prominent role in Jackson's victory at Horseshoe Bend.

For the rest of his life, Ridge was known as Major Ridge; he used Ridge as his family name, so that his son became John Ridge and John Rollin RIDGE was his son's son. John was one of the most articulate and best-educated Cherokees; with his cousin Buck Watie (who changed his name to Elias BOUDINOT), he attended the Foreign Mission School at Cornwall, Connecticut, where he fell in love and became engaged to Sally Northrup, the daughter of a prominent citizen. The townspeople objected to a mixed marriage, but when Major Ridge, dressed in an imposing uniform, came to town in a coach with liveried servants, they were impressed. After their marriage, John and Sally returned to Georgia, where John became prominent in Cherokee politics. Major Ridge was made speaker of the Cherokee Council.

In the late 1820's, Georgia began an ever-intensifying effort to drive the Cherokees out of the state and take over their property. The Ridges resisted removal for years, but it was a losing fight, as Georgia began confiscating Cherokee lands and selling them at lottery. Finally, despite his own prosperity, Ridge became convinced, like his son and nephew, that remaining in Georgia would only bring more persecution of the Cherokees and inevitable confiscation of their lands. He believed that the best solution would be to accept the best treaty they could get and make a fresh start west of the Mississippi. In 1835, he signed the Treaty of New Echota, though doing so without the full consent of the Cherokee Nation made him liable to the "blood law" under which he had helped kill Chief Doublehead. The Ridges and Boudinot moved west without incident in 1836, but the Cherokees who followed Principal Chief John Ross in resisting removal were rounded up in 1838 by troops sent by President Van Buren, held in concentration camps, and finally sent west under armed guard on a death march known as the "Trail of Tears." About one-third of them died on the way. Blaming the Ridge party, militant followers of Ross, without Ross's knowledge, condemned them to death and on June 22, 1839, murdered Major Ridge and his son and nephew.

Robert E. Morsberger

FURTHER READING

Ehle, John. *Trail of Tears: The Rise and Fall of the Cherokee Nation.* New York: Doubleday, 1988.

Jahoda, Gloria. *The Trail of Tears.* New York: Wings Books, 1995.

Wilkins, Thurman. *Cherokee Tragedy: The Ridge Family and the Decimation of a People.* 2d rev. ed. Norman: University of Oklahoma Press, 1986.

Riel, Louis, Jr.

Born: October 23, 1844; Red River Colony, Northwest Territories, Canada (now Winnipeg, Manitoba)

Died: November 16, 1885; Regina, Northwest Territories, Canada

Ethnic affiliation: Métis

Significance: Louis Riel, Jr., organized the Métis during two rebellions: one in 1870, which successfully created the province of Manitoba, and the other in 1885, which ended in tragedy and transformed Riel into a heroic symbol of the oppressed.

Louis Riel, Jr., was born the son of Louis Riel and Julie Lagimodiére in the Red River Settlement, south of Lake Winnipeg. It was an area with a large population of Métis—people of mixed Indian and French parentage. Riel himself was one-eighth Métis, through descent from his paternal grandmother. His mother was French, as was his father, a farmer and miller who had been brought up in Quebec. The thousands of

Métis, Indians, and French and English settlers along the Red River were isolated and forgotten peoples at the time of Riel's childhood. Many worked for the Hudson's Bay Company (a fur trading monopoly), engaged in the traditional Métis buffalo hunt, or eked out a living as fur trappers and traders and as farmers.

Young Riel was sent to complete his education at the College of Montreal in preparation for the priesthood (his parents hoped he would become the first Métis missionary priest). The college dismissed him for lack of effort, however, and Riel took a position in the office of a radical anticlerical and anticonfederation attorney. In 1868, he returned to Red River. The Métis community was experiencing harsh economic times; crops had failed for two successive years. The Riel family was fortunate in that, with some livestock, they were able to hold together.

Canadian prime minister John A. Macdonald was pushing to expand the country and to tie it together with a continental railroad. The Northwest Territories were a key part of his plans, and when the Hudson's Bay Company offered to sell its lands to the new nation, he jumped at the opportunity. Macdonald sent survey teams to the territory. This surveying was done without informing or consulting the ten thousand Métis, Indians, English, and French living in the area. In addition, the surveying procedures did not respect the irregular farms and plots of settled land that existed along the river. Riel, literate, bilingual, and articulate, joined with other Métis to form a national committee. He helped draw up a petition to seek redress, which included recognition of existing landholdings, civil and political rights, and guarantees of consultation and participation.

At the beginning of what would become known as the First Riel Rebellion, the Métis rejected the territorial governor, took over Fort Garry, and declared a provisional government on December 9, 1869. Riel soon became president, and he pressed the Macdonald government to address the group's concerns. The willingness of the Métis to use force chastened the government, which did not want to harm its tenuous political ties with Quebec by waging war against Roman Catholic, French-speaking Métis. The eagerness of Ontario's anti-Catholic Orange Order to fight the Métis heightened a sensitive situation. Riel exacerbated the climate of anxiety by ordering the execution of the Catholic-baiting Thomas Scott. This action enraged English-speaking Canadians, who put a price on Riel's head.

Macdonald prudently sought to settle the matter as quickly as possible. The result was the Manitoba Act of 1870, which granted virtually everything that was petitioned and incorporated the eastern portion of

Métis lands into the small new province of Manitoba. Riel himself was forced to flee to escape revenge for the Scott execution. He headed eastward through the United States. At times he furtively entered Canada, sustaining his ties to the Métis.

Riel also sought to sustain his ties to French-speaking Roman Catholicism. Priests regularly took him in and encouraged him. He traveled to New York and to Washington, D.C., hoping to form an alliance with the United States to encourage the annexation of the Northwest Territories. He became increasingly distraught at his lack of success, though he never wavered from the idea that he was a man of destiny. In 1876, he was overcome by a revelation that he interpreted as being a calling for him to revitalize the Catholic faith. His friends became disturbed at the design of this call, which spoke of changing the Sabbath to Saturday, polygamy, a married clergy, circumcision of males, and even brother-sister incest. Later he assumed the title of prophet and called for the transference of the papacy, first to Montreal and later to the Northwest. Friends committed him to psychiatric hospitals in Montreal and Quebec.

In 1875 the Canadian government finally granted him a pardon but insisted that he spend five years more in exile. He returned to the United States to seek work. Eventually he moved to a Métis and Indian community in Montana, involving himself in local politics and even taking American citizenship. By 1883, he had married Marguerite Monet, the daughter of a Métis hunter. He became a schoolteacher. In 1884, he was approached by a delegation of settlers from Saskatchewan—whites, "half-breeds" (people with mixed Indian and English ancestry), and Métis—with grievances concerning land rights. Riel viewed the call as part of a divine plan for which he had suffered since 1870. The events that became known as the Second Riel Rebellion began to unfold.

Riel not only agreed to help formulate a petition of grievances but also assumed a leadership role. He insisted that the Northwest lands belonged to the half-breeds and the Métis and that the lands should be held in trust for future generations. He also demanded compensation for the years of privation and exile he had suffered. The Macdonald government considered his request blatant extortion.

A force of Canadian regulars led by British officers marched on the Riel forces, which had mobilized on March 18, 1885. The government's anxiety and anger was stimulated by Indian attacks on white settlements. Riel, who had urged armed resistance, presumed that the government would attempt to negotiate, as it had in Manitoba. His Métis revolutionary army, however, attacked the Mounted Police at Duck Lake on March 26, an act which put negotiations out of the question.

Beginning May 9, the government army assaulted the Métis forces for four days. Riel avoided confrontation and prayed for divine intervention. He was captured and held for trial along with eighty-five others.

The government planned to make an example of Riel. He was taken for trial to Regina, in the territory of Saskatchewan, a setting in which conviction was guaranteed (he would have a six-person jury, all of whom would be Protestant Anglo-Saxons). The jury took only half an hour to register a guilty verdict. The jury foreman asked for mercy, because the jury believed the government bore responsibility in that it had not dealt responsibly or fairly with the Métis, half-breeds, and Indians in the territory. The court had no recourse under the law, however, but to sentence Riel to death by hanging.

Representatives of the Catholic church visited Riel and finally got him to renounce his personal theories on religion. His execution on November 16, 1885, made Riel a martyr. Louis Riel stands as a singular hero of Métis and native peoples in Canada.

Jack J. Cardoso

FURTHER READING

Bowsfield, Hartwell, comp. *Louis Riel: The Rebel and the Hero.* Toronto: Oxford University Press, 1971.

Davidson, William McCartney. *Louis Riel, 1844-1885: A Biography.* Calgary: Alberton, 1955.

Flanagan, Thomas. *Louis "David" Riel: Prophet of the New World.* Rev. ed. Toronto: University of Toronto Press, 1996.

_____. *Riel and the Rebellion: 1885 Reconsidered.* 2d ed. Buffalo: University of Toronto Press, 2000.

Howard, Joseph Kinsey. *Strange Empire: Louis Riel and the Métis People.* Toronto: J. Lewis and Samuel, 1974.

Howard, Richard. *Riel.* Toronto: Clarke, Irwin, 1967.

Osler, Edmund Boyd. *The Man Who Had to Hang: Louis Riel.* Toronto: Longman, Green, 1961.

Riel, Louis. *Diaries of Louis Riel.* Edited by Thomas Flanagan. Edmonton: Hurtig, 1976.

Stanley, George F. G. *The Birth of Western Canada.* 1936. Reprint. Toronto: University of Toronto Press, 1960.

_____. *Louis Riel.* Toronto: Ryerson Press, 1968.

Riggs, Lynn

Born: August 31, 1899; near Claremore, Indian Territory (now Oklahoma)
Died: June 30, 1954; New York, New York
Tribal affiliation: Cherokee
Significance: Lynn Riggs is the best known of Native American playwrights.

Lynn Riggs was born into an Oklahoma Cherokee family. His father was a cowboy, and young Lynn was at home with the open range. As a youth he drove a grocery wagon to make money and entertained himself with what he would later describe as "trashy lurid fiction." In his late teens, Riggs traveled on both coasts earning money as an office and factory worker, book salesman, and singer in motion-picture houses. Following these experiences, he attended the University of Oklahoma and, as a sophomore, taught freshman English classes.

Riggs's first play was a farce, *Cuckoo*, written in 1921. Growing up, he was deeply influenced by the speech, music, and folklore of his neighbors. This play and subsequent works are deeply colored by Cherokee community observations. In 1923 he toured the West, singing tenor in a Chautauqua quartet, and ended up joining a Santa Fe artists' colony. He published some poetry, and the colony produced his play *Knives from Syria.*

Riggs left the artists' colony and settled in New York to write. He was given a Guggenheim Fellowship in 1929 and spent a year in Paris writing the plays *Roadside* (later reworked as *Borned in Texas*) and *Green Grow the Lilacs.* Upon returning to New York, he experienced his first commercial success with a 1933 production of *Green Grow the Lilacs.* Later, Rodgers and Hammerstein acquired the play and transformed it into the Broadway production *Oklahoma!*

In later years, Riggs wrote several plays, but none achieved the artistic or commercial success of *Green Grow the Lilacs.* He lived for a time in Chapel Hill, North Carolina, and associated with playwright Paul Green, another American playwright who used folklore provocatively in drama.

David N. Mielke

FURTHER READING
Braunlich, Phyllis Cole. *Haunted by Home: The Life and Letters of Lynn Riggs.* Norman: University of Oklahoma Press, 1988.

Robertson, Robbie

Born: July 5, 1943; Toronto, Ontario, Canada

Tribal affiliation: Mohawk

Significance: Robbie Robertson was a leading singer-songwriter from the late 1960's to the late 1970's. Although best known for his work in the Band, he also organized the Red Road Ensemble, an all-Indian band that plays traditional music using rock-and-roll instruments.

Jaime Robbie Robertson was born to a Jewish father and a Mohawk mother. Although his earliest musical influences were country, then big-band music, he had already moved to rock music when he dropped out of high school in 1958 and joined a band. The Hawks, initially a backup band for rockabilly singer Ronnie Hawkins, began working on their own in 1963. The Hawks backed up Bob Dylan on his 1965-1966 world tour and renamed themselves simply the Band. Over the next decade, they produced distinctive folk-rock albums with bluesy overtones, especially in *Music from Big Pink* (1968), *The Band* (1969), and *Stage Fright* (1970). The Band documented their planned and generally ami-

Robbie Robertson, former member of the Band, answers questions after giving the keynote address at the South by Southwest Music conference in Austin, Texas, in 2002.
(AP/Wide World Photos)

cable breakup on Thanksgiving Day, 1976, with a concert filmed by director Martin Scorsese and released as *The Last Waltz* (1978).

Robertson has continued to work with Scorsese, composing the scores to *Raging Bull* (1980), *The King of Comedy* (1983), and *The Color of Money* (1986). He has also acted in feature films, most notably, *Carny* (1980). In 1994, Robertson organized the Red Road Ensemble and composed a collection of songs for *The Native Americans,* a television documentary series. The Red Road Ensemble later released *Contact from the Underworld of Redboy* (1998). Robertson has also been active in the attempt to gain a new trial for Leonard PELTIER.

Richard Sax

FURTHER READING

Helm, Levon, with Stephen Davis. *This Wheel's on Fire: Levon Helm and the Story of the Band.* Chicago: A Cappella, 2000.

Hoskyns, Barney. *Across the Great Divide: The Band and America.* New York: Hyperion, 1993.

Rocky Boy

Born: c. 1860; place unknown
Died: 1914; place unknown
Also known as: Stone Child
Tribal affiliation: Ojibwa (Chippewa)
Significance: Rocky Boy was a leader of nomad Chippewas, securing for them a land grant although they had refused to live on a reservation.

Rocky Boy was a leader of the "Chippewa nomads," who were left out of treaties in both the United States and Canada. During the nineteenth century, roughly 350 Chippewas had left the main group in Wisconsin and gone to hunt in Montana. They were not settled on a reservation, and thus they were excluded from all treaty negotiations. As more land was fenced, the nomads' life became untenable and they were often reduced to begging.

Stone Child, often called "Rocky Boy" by settlers, emerged as a leader as the nomads' situation became desperate. He lobbied the Bureau of Indian Affairs, and after a number of years of bureaucratic indecision, "Rocky Boy's Band" was granted a tract of land on the Fort Assiniboin military reserve in Montana. The land grant finally came in 1914, the year that Rocky Boy died.

Bruce E. Johansen

Rogers, Will

Born: November 4, 1879; near Oologah, Indian Territory (now in Oklahoma)

Died: August 15, 1935; Walakpa Lagoon, near Point Barrow, Alaska

Tribal affiliation: Cherokee

Significance: An internationally prominent humorist and satirist, Will Rogers functioned as a constructive social critic and humanitarian as well as an entertainer and journalist.

William Penn Adair Rogers was born November 4, 1879, in the Indian Territory of the United States of America near what eventually became Oologah, Oklahoma. Both of his parents came from the Indian Territory and contributed to his status as a quarter-blood Cherokee Indian. His father, Clement Van (Clem) Rogers, was a rough and wealthy rancher, farmer, banker, and businessman, in addition to being a prominent politician. His mother, Mary Schrimsher Rogers, was a loving woman who came from a financially successful and politically powerful family. Will was the youngest of eight children, three of whom died at birth, and the only male to survive childhood.

Rogers developed a lasting love for the life and basic skills of the cowboy, horseback riding and roping, in his early years. At home, he adored his affectionate mother but developed a complex and not completely positive relationship with his father. Rogers clearly loved his father, who provided a masculine establishment figure with whom to identify. At the same time, Will possessed a strong personality which eventually clashed with that of the elder Rogers. At the age of ten, disaster entered the young Oklahoman's life when his mother died. Around that same time, the closing of the open range heralded an end to the traditional cowboy's life. These conditions changed a relatively secure and happy child into a sad wanderer who sought desperately to replace the love and sense of purpose that had been taken from him.

Tension increased between Rogers and his father in the years following Mary Rogers's death. The elder Rogers was particularly infuriated by his son's uneven performance in school. Between the ages of eight and eighteen, Rogers attended six different educational institutions and left each one under questionable circumstances. His main interests during these years were playing the class clown and participating in theatrical activities. He also developed a growing fascination with trick roping. In 1898, after running away from the last school he attended, the eighteen-year-old embarked on a seven-year odyssey. He worked vari-

Will Rogers, from a 1922 Ziegfeld Follies publicity photo. (AP/Wide World Photos)

ously as a wandering cowboy, as the manager of the family ranch, and as a trick-rope artist in Wild West shows, then turned to vaudeville. His travels took him literally across the globe. Such behavior merely increased the elder Rogers's dissatisfaction with his son. The son, on the other hand, manifested guilt at not having lived up to the father's expectations and example of success.

Rogers maintained his sensitivity to his Cherokee Indian heritage throughout his teenage and early adult years. This sensitivity was evident in his militant reaction to any criticism of Indians or people of partial Indian ancestry. Furthermore, because of his own Indian background, he faced racial prejudice when he tried to establish relationships with women.

The year 1905 proved to be a crucial one for Rogers. He went to New York and entered vaudeville as a trick-rope artist. At the same time, he began making serious proposals of marriage to Betty Blake of Roger, Arkansas, whom he had first met in 1899. When Rogers and Blake were married in 1908, the Oklahoman had taken the first step in what proved to be one of the most successful entertainment careers in American history. Perhaps more important, however, these events assisted Rogers in overcoming the sadness which had enshrouded him since youth: His marriage helped to replace the female love and sense of belonging he had lost when his mother died, while his success in show business enabled him to establish a more positive relationship with his father and compensated Rogers for the loss of the cowboy life.

Will Rogers's career can be divided into four periods. During the first, from 1905 to 1915, he became a successful vaudevillian. He began his stage career with a trick-roping act, in which he lassoed simultaneously a moving horse and its rider. Gradually, the young performer began making comical remarks as his lariats whirled about. By 1911, he was a bona fide monologuist, making humorous comments about other artists and the theater world. Traveling the famous Orpheum Circuit, he used the same material each evening. Rogers also toured England and Western Europe several times. The Rogers family numbered five by 1915: Will and Betty, William Vann Rogers, Jr. (born 1911), Mary Amelia Rogers (born 1913), and James Blake Rogers (born 1915).

The next stage in Rogers's rise to prominence started in 1915, when he began performing in Florenz Ziegfeld's Midnight Frolic. The Midnight Frolic was staged on the roof of the New Amsterdam Theater in New York City, the home of the Ziegfeld Follies. Rogers encountered a problem working in the Midnight Frolic. Since it attracted many repeat customers, he had to struggle to present new material each night. Eventually, the daily newspapers provided him with constantly changing material concerning contemporary society upon which he could base his humorous monologues.

Rogers's career received a giant boost in 1916, when he joined the Ziegfeld Follies. Within two years, Rogers had finished developing the basic characteristics of his humor. Fittingly, it was at this time that the budding comedian became known as the Cowboy Philosopher and began each performance with his famous line: "Well, all I know is what I read in the newspapers." Proven comedic material was mixed with continually changing jokes about contemporary news, and neutrality on controversial topics was maintained by poking fun at all sides. Rogers's comical style also involved the projection of his personality. With his humor resting on these tenets, Will quickly assumed the characteristics of a cracker-barrel philosopher and satirist who functioned as a constructive social critic. As such, he became increasingly serious about what he said. An additional facet of Rogers's life emerged during World War I: his genuine humanitarianism. He pledged one-tenth of what he made during the conflict to the Red Cross and the Salvation Army, and he was extremely active in raising funds for both organizations.

The third stage of Rogers's career encompassed the years from 1918 to 1928. He became a national figure during this era, expanding into new fields of endeavor. Much of his success was a result of his physical appearance and bearing. Slender, athletic, six feet tall, with handsome facial features that reflected his Indian heritage, Rogers performed in cowboy regalia, chomping on an ever-present wad of chewing gum, and twirling ropes which he watched while making detached comments concerning contemporary events. His ungrammatical speech, Western accent, contagious smile, and unruly forelock merely added to the pretense of an illiterate, homespun yokel, perceptively satirizing society. This pose enabled Rogers to get away with saying things that other performers would never have considered saying.

In 1918, Samuel Goldwyn offered Rogers a starring role in the silent film *Laughing Bill Hyde.* The humorist hesitantly accepted, since the New Jersey shooting location of the film allowed him to continue working in the Ziegfeld Follies. *Laughing Bill Hyde* proved to be a reasonable success, and Goldwyn presented Rogers with a two-year contract to make motion pictures in California. He agreed to the arrangement and moved to Los Angeles. Rogers added another dimension to his work in 1919, with the publication of two books: *Rogers-isms: The Cowboy Philosopher on the Peace Conference* and *Rogers-isms: The Cowboy Philosopher on Prohibition.*

The move to California was not without its troubles. The newest Rogers baby, Fred Stone Rogers, died of diphtheria when he was eighteen months old. The numerous two-reel motion pictures that Rogers made for Goldwyn did not turn the aspiring actor into a star, and when his contract with Goldwyn was not renewed in 1921, Rogers himself made three two-reel pictures in which he played the leading role. A complex set of circumstances resulted in his losing a large amount of money in the venture. Faced with bankruptcy, the determined performer left Betty and the children in California while he returned to New York and the Ziegfeld Follies. Between 1921 and 1923, Rogers launched a banquet-speaking career and began a syndicated weekly newspaper column, in addition to his work for Ziegfeld. Two years of laboring around the clock in this fashion enabled him to pay off his debts.

Rogers continued to pursue a career in motion pictures despite his initial difficulties. Thus, in 1923, after he had taken care of his money problems, he returned to Los Angeles and signed a contract with the Hal E. Roach Studio to make a series of two-reel comedies. Thirteen films resulted from this agreement. They were more successful than the Goldwyn films, but Rogers was still not a great motion-picture success. He eventually reached the conclusion that the problem resided with the unwillingness of studios and directors to allow him to project his own personality. Frustrated, the humorist once again returned to New York and the Ziegfeld Follies. A third book, *Illiterate Digest*, composed mainly of weekly newspaper articles, appeared in 1924.

Rogers added still another dimension to his work in the mid-1920's. He began his one-person lecture tour in 1925, repeating it in 1926 and in 1927, and periodically thereafter. Additionally, the energetic satirist published a number of magazine articles for the *Saturday Evening Post* and *Life* (at that time a humor magazine). In 1926, he began his short daily syndicated newspaper column, which frequently appeared under the caption "Will Rogers Says." Two more books followed: *Letters of a Self-Made Diplomat to His President* (1926) and *There's Not a Bathing Suit in Russia and Other Bare Facts* (1927). These were collections of articles he had written for the *Saturday Evening Post*, as was his 1929 offering, *Ether and Me: Or, "Just Relax."*

During the 1920's, Rogers also expanded his humanitarian efforts. While in Europe during 1926, he traveled to Dublin, Ireland, and did a benefit for the survivors of a theater fire. The same year, he took similar action to assist survivors of Florida tornadoes and Mississippi River flood victims. His daily and weekly newspaper columns complemented these efforts, repeatedly appealing for public support.

The final phase in Rogers's professional evolution covered the years from 1929 to 1935. During this time, Rogers was catapulted into the elite arena of superstardom. His salary, popularity, and influence, along with the range of media he employed to communicate with his massive audiences all contributed to this achievement.

Rogers made his first sound motion picture, *They Had to See Paris*, in 1929 for Fox Film Corporation. It was successful, and Rogers became a star overnight. He soon signed a two-year contract with Fox to make five pictures. A leading figure in the development of sound films, in 1934 Rogers was voted the nation's most popular box-office attraction in a poll taken among independent theater owners. It is estimated that at the time of his death in 1935, Rogers was making one million dollars a year performing in motion pictures, a sum then unsurpassed by any screen personality.

Rogers made infrequent radio appearances during the 1920's; at first he did not feel comfortable with the medium. Nevertheless, he did seventy-five radio programs between 1927 and 1935. His radio appearances increased after 1930, when he did fourteen programs sponsored by E. R. Squibb. A longer but more sporadic series was sponsored by the Gulf Oil Corporation between 1933 and 1935. In time, Rogers became one of the most popular radio entertainers in the country; as early as 1930, he was receiving $350 per minute for his radio performances. The onset of the Depression in 1929 elicited a predictable response from Rogers. He devoted more and more time to benefits for victims of all sorts of natural disasters and the disadvantaged. These activities took him all over the United States and as far afield as Nicaragua.

Haphazard vacation plans in August of 1935 resulted in Rogers joining famous aviator Wiley Post on a flight in a newly constructed plane of Post's design. Plans called for the two to fly from Seattle, Washington, to Point Barrow, Alaska, with stops in between. The plane crashed on August 15, 1935, at Walakpa Lagoon, sixteen miles short of its destination. Both Rogers, age fifty-five, and Post were killed in what became one of the most famous air tragedies of the twentieth century.

Rogers's philosophy remained consistent throughout his career. He generally sided with the disadvantaged and weak against the powerful and wealthy on both domestic and international questions. This outlook in part reflected Rogers's early experiences. His Indian heritage, for example, exposed him to racial prejudice. Having experienced such prejudice, he became more understanding of society's disadvantaged people and more supportive of the weak and the poor. In the entertainment world, Rogers established several important precedents. His method of remaining neutral on controversial topics by criticizing all involved established an approach to satire which has been employed by succeeding generations of performers. His commitment to humanitarian activities set a standard which entertainers have followed. Finally, his reliance on contemporary news as the basis for his constantly changing material has been widely imitated.

S. Fred Roach

FURTHER READING

Croy, Homer. *Our Will Rogers.* New York: Duell Sloan and Pearce, 1953.

Day, Donald. *Will Rogers: A Biography.* New York: David McKay, 1962.

Keith, Harold. *Boy's Life of Will Rogers.* New York: Thomas Y. Crowell, 1938.

Ketchum, Richard M. *Will Rogers: His Life and Times.* New York: American Heritage. 1973.

Milsten, David Randolph. *An Appreciation of Will Rogers.* San Antonio, Tex.: Naylor, 1935.

Robinson, Ray. *American Original: A Life of Will Rogers.* New York: Oxford University Press, 1996.

Rogers, Betty. *Will Rogers: The Story of His Life Told by His Wife.* Garden City, N.Y.: Garden City, 1943.

Rogers, Will. *The Autobiography of Will Rogers.* Edited by Donald Day. Boston: Houghton Mifflin, 1949.

_____. *The Writings of Will Rogers.* 23 vols. Edited by Joseph A. Stout, Jr., Peter C. Rollins, Steven K. Gragert, and James M. Smallwood. Stillwater: Oklahoma State University Press, 1973-1984.

Rollins, Peter C. *Will Rogers: A Bio-Bibliography.* Westport, Conn.: Greenwood Press, 1984.

Trent, Spi M. *My Cousin Will Rogers: Intimate and Untold Tales.* New York: G. P. Putnam's Sons, 1938.

Wertheim, Arthur Frank, and Barbara Bair, eds. *The Papers of Will Rogers.* 3 vols. Norman: University of Oklahoma Press, 1996-   .

Roman Nose

Born: c. 1830
Died: September 17, 1868; Beecher's Island, Colorado
Also known as: Sauts (Bat), Wokini (Hook Nose)
Tribal affiliation: Southern Cheyenne
Significance: Roman Nose was a fearless leader, though not a chief, during battles with white settlers and Union Pacific Railroad workers during the 1860's.

Though some accounts of the story may vary, it was generally believed that a protective war bonnet, made for Roman Nose by a medicine man named Ice, could protect him against bullets and arrows in battle. His six-foot, three-inch bonneted frame led his warriors into many battles against railroad gangs laying rails along the Kansas frontier between 1864 and 1868. In 1866, at a council in Fort Ellsworth, Kansas, Roman

A 1901 drawing from Scribner's *magazine depicting the defeat of Roman Nose by Major George Forsyth's troops in 1868.* (Library of Congress)

Nose distinguished himself in his protestations against the Union Pacific Railroad on Indian hunting grounds. He vowed to stop the railroad. As the attacks against the railroad heightened, the government sent Major George A. Forsyth and fifty special scouts against the Cheyenne. Forsyth's forces tracked the Cheyennes to the Arickaree Fork of the Republican River, where Beecher Island is located.

Legend recounts that the night before the battle, as a guest in the home of a Sioux family, Roman Nose was served food lifted with a metal fork. This violated one of the laws that dictated the power of the bonnet. A purification ceremony would have restored the "medicine" to his bonnet, but his warriors called for him and he responded. Roman Nose announced his own death upon riding into the battle, and moments later he was struck down by gunfire. The battle went on for eight days.

Tonya Huber

Ross, John

Born: October 3, 1790; Turkey Town, Cherokee Nation (near present-day Center, Alabama)

Died: August 1, 1866; Washington, D.C.

Also known as: Coowescoowe

Tribal affiliation: Eastern Cherokee

Significance: As a leader of the Cherokee Nation during its ordeal of forced removal and civil war, John Ross is the supreme example of nineteenth century Native American statesmanship.

John Ross was born October 3, 1790, at Turkey Town, a Cherokee settlement near modern Center, Alabama. He was by blood only one-eighth Cherokee. His mother, Mollie McDonald, was the granddaughter of a Cherokee woman, but his father, the trader Daniel Ross, and all of his mother's other ancestors were Scottish. His father, while securing a tutor for his children and sending Ross to an academy near Kingston, Tennessee, did not want to stamp out his children's Cherokee identity, and his mother gave him a deep sense of loyalty to the tribe, to their ancient lands and traditions, and to the ideal of Cherokee unity. As a son of three generations of Scottish traders, Ross early showed an interest in business. In 1813, he formed a partnership with Timothy Meigs at Rossville, near modern Chattanooga, and two years later another with his brother Lewis Ross; during the Creek War of 1813-1814, when Cherokee warriors fought in Andrew Jackson's army, he did a lucrative business filling government contracts. During the Creek War, he served as adjutant in a company of Cherokee cavalry.

By the mid-1820's, his increasing involvement in the political affairs of the Cherokee Nation caused him to abandon business. In 1827 he settled at Coosa, Georgia, thirty miles from the new Cherokee capital at New Echota, and established himself as a planter, with a substantial house, orchards, and herds; quarters for his twenty slaves; and a lucrative ferry.

Ross served as a member of four Cherokee delegations to Washington between 1816 and 1825 and was president of the tribe's National Committee in 1818, when it resisted the attempt of Tennessee to persuade members of the tribe to surrender their lands in that state. In 1822, he was a cosigner of a resolution of the National Committee that the Cherokee would not recognize any treaty which surrendered Cherokee land. In 1823, Ross earned for himself the undying loyalty of the majority of the tribe when he rejected a bribe offered by federal commissioners and publicly denounced them in a meeting of the National Committee.

Ross was president of the convention that in 1827 produced the Cherokee constitution. This document, in its assignment of powers to three branches of government, its bicameral legislature, and its four-year term for the principal chief, was modeled on the Constitution of the United States. In 1828, Ross was elected principal chief, an office which he held until his death, and in 1829 he went to Washington on the first of many embassies which he undertook in that capacity.

The Cherokee established their republic within the context of an ongoing struggle to maintain their traditional claims against state governments, particularly that of Georgia. In 1802, Georgia had ceded to the United States its western territory (what later became Alabama and Mississippi) in exchange for a promise that all Native Americans would be removed from Georgia. A substantial number of Cherokee, accepting removal, surrendered their land rights and moved west. (One of them was the Cherokee genius SEQUOYAH, who gave his people a syllabary for their language.)

With the inauguration of Andrew Jackson, who was determined to send the Cherokee west, and the discovery of gold on Cherokee land, it was clear that removal was inevitable. Ross was determined to exhaust every legal and political recourse, however, before submitting to the superior physical might of the U.S. government. Though Jackson was willing to assert the power of the federal government—even if it meant war—to put down any movement in South Carolina for "nullification" of the Constitution, he declared that in the Cherokee case he would not interfere with state sovereignty. As a result, his Indian Removal Bill of 1830 included the provision that any Native American who chose not to remove was subject to state law. Georgia therefore refused to recognize the legitimacy of the Cherokee republic and made no effort to prevent white squatters from moving into the Cherokee country. These official attitudes and the chaos caused by the gold rush produced a state of anarchy in which, on one occasion, Ross himself barely escaped assassination.

John Ross. (Smithsonian Institution)

By 1833, pressure by the government of Georgia and by the Jackson administration was creating tension among the Cherokee themselves. John RIDGE, the son of an influential Cherokee family, and Elias BOUDINOT, the editor of the *Cherokee Phoenix*, were both working for acceptance of removal and were thus undermining the efforts of Ross, who wanted the tribe to resist removal, and if it were inevitable, to accept it only on the best possible terms.

In 1835, returning from a trip to Washington, Ross found his land and house occupied by a white man who was able to present a legal title granted by Georgia. In the same year, the Ridge faction signed the Treaty of New Echota, accepting removal. In spite of the fact that the treaty was signed by only a handful of Cherokee, in spite of opposition by the Cherokee who had already settled in the West, in spite of a protest signed by fourteen thousand Cherokee, and in spite of Henry Clay's opposition in the U.S. Senate, it was approved by the Senate in May, 1836, and signed by President Jackson.

Under the conditions of the treaty, the Cherokee were given two years to prepare for removal to Indian Territory (Oklahoma), and Ross spent that time in further hopeless efforts to persuade the government to give the entire Cherokee people opportunity to accept or reject the treaty. The removal itself was a disastrous and tragic event. It was flawed by looting, arson, and even grave robbing by white squatters. Disease was inevitable in the stockades that served as holding pens for Cherokees before they left. Of the thirteen thousand Cherokees who were removed, probably four thousand, including Ross's wife, died on the Trail of Tears.

In his first years in Oklahoma, Ross devoted his energies to uniting three Cherokee factions: his own Nationalist followers; the Ridge-Boudinot faction, which had accepted removal; and the Old Settlers, who had formed their own government and did not want to merge with the easterners. In July, 1839, a convention wrote a new constitution, virtually the same as that of 1827, and passed the Act of Union, which was ratified by all parties. In spite of Ross's efforts toward Cherokee unity, however, extremists in his own party exacted the traditional Cherokee penalty for selling tribal lands when they murdered Ridge and Boudinot. Ross was not involved in these crimes and did not condone them, but they were a source of great disharmony in the tribe as long as he lived, and they were the primary reason that he had difficulty negotiating a new treaty with the government in an attempt to guarantee Cherokee claims to their Oklahoma lands. Ross had opposed removal partly because he knew that if the government were allowed to confiscate the Georgia lands they could also confiscate lands in Oklahoma later. The government refused to agree to any guarantees because the followers of Ridge and Boudinot claimed that Ross was responsible for the murders. Finally, in 1846, the Polk administration signed a treaty acceptable to all parties.

On September 2, 1844, Ross married Mary Bryan Stapler, the daughter of a Delaware merchant, who bore him two children. The period from the 1846 treaty until the Civil War was a relatively happy time for Ross and for many Cherokees. He prospered as a merchant, raised livestock, and contributed much of his wealth to charities on behalf of poor Cherokee; under his guidance, seminaries and a Cherokee newspaper were established.

Though by 1860 Ross himself owned fifty slaves, he opposed slavery on principle, and during the 1850's the slavery issue was another source of tribal dissension. His full-blood followers opposed it, and the mixed-bloods favored it. When the Civil War began and agents were working among the Oklahoma tribes on behalf of the Confederacy, Ross favored neutrality and adherence to the 1846 treaty. Only when the neighboring tribes accepted a Confederate alliance and the Cherokee Nation was virtually surrounded was Ross willing to accept an alliance. Yet in June, 1862, when Union forces finally arrived from Kansas, he welcomed them, though he and his family were forced to leave the Cherokee country as refugees when the Union forces withdrew. His four sons by his first wife served in the Union Army, and one of them died in a Confederate prison.

For the next three years, Ross was in the East working to persuade the Lincoln administration to send federal troops to the Cherokee country and to feed the six thousand pro-Union Cherokee who had taken refuge in Kansas. The last year of the war was a particularly unhappy time for him because of the illness of his wife, who died in July, 1865. When

Ross died on August 1, 1866, he was in Washington negotiating a peace treaty with the U.S. government and fighting the efforts of the Cherokee faction that had been pro-South in the war to get federal approval for a permanently divided tribe. The treaty, which was proclaimed ten days after his death, was his last contribution to the cause of Cherokee unity.

Robert L. Berner

FURTHER READING

Eaton, Rachel Caroline. *John Ross and the Cherokee Indians.* Chicago: University of Chicago Press, 1921.

Jahoda, Gloria. *The Trail of Tears.* New York: Wings Books, 1995.

McLoughlin, William G. *After the Trail of Tears: The Cherokees' Struggle for Sovereignty, 1839-1880.* Chapel Hill: University of North Carolina Press, 1993.

Meserve, John Bartlett. "Chief John Ross." *Chronicles of Oklahoma* 13 (December, 1935): 421-437.

Moulton, Gary. *John Ross: Cherokee Chief.* Athens: University of Georgia Press, 1978.

Wardell, Morris L. *A Political History of the Cherokee Nation, 1838-1907.* Norman: University of Oklahoma Press, 1938.

Woodward, Grace Steele. *The Cherokees.* Norman: University of Oklahoma Press, 1963.

Ross, Mary G.

Born: August 9, 1908; Park Hill, Oklahoma
Tribal affiliation: Cherokee
Significance: Mary G. Ross had a career as one of the foremost aircraft and satellite systems engineers in the United States.

Mary Ross was born in Park Hill, which had served as the intellectual center of the Cherokee Nation until it became a part of the state of Oklahoma in 1907. Ross's great-great-grandfather, John Ross, served as the principal chief of the Cherokee Nation during the "Trail of Tears" and the redevelopment of the Cherokee Republic in the nineteenth century.

Ross attended public schools in Oklahoma. Then she received the B.A. degree in mathematics from Northeastern State University in Tahlequah, which is the present home of the Cherokee National Government Complex. She took a master's degree in mathematics from the

University of Northern Colorado at Greeley. For a time she taught math and science in high school.

During World War II, Ross went to work for the Lockheed Aircraft Company; she was the first woman ever to be hired by Lockheed as an engineer. She helped develop the P-38, the largest and fastest pursuit plane to that time. After the war, she continued to work at Lockheed as an engineer. Over the years, she helped design guided missiles, satellites for orbiting Earth, and satellites for traveling around other planets.

By the time Ross retired in 1973, she was a senior advanced systems staff engineer for Lockheed-Martin Missiles and Space Company. She was a pioneer in the research and development and application of the theories and concepts of ballistics, orbital mechanics, and astrophysics. In 1992, Ross was inducted into the Silicon Valley Engineering Hall of Fame.

Howard Meredith

Sacagawea

Born: c. 1788; cental Idaho
Died: December 20, 1812; Fort Manuel, Dakota Territory (now in South Dakota)
Also known as: Tsakaka gia (Bird Woman, Boat Pusher)
Tribal affiliation: Northern Shoshone
Significance: Sacagawea accompanied Meriwether Lewis and William Clark on their expedition into Northwest America, performing invaluable, perhaps critical services as a guide and interpreter.

The Lewis and Clark expedition was instructed by President Thomas Jefferson in 1803 to explore the vast continent northwest of the Mississippi River and to look for an overland route to the Pacific Ocean. It is from expedition diaries that historians have learned most of what is known about Sacagawea (also spelled Sakakawea or Sacajawea).

On October 27, 1804, the expedition reached the villages of the Mandan Indians in North Dakota, where it wintered. It was there that Meriwether Lewis and William Clark met Sacagawea and her French Canadian husband, Toussaint Charbonneau. At that time, Sacagawea was about seventeen years old and pregnant. She had belonged previously to the Hidatsa Indians, who had stolen her from her Shoshone home in Idaho. Charbonneau probably obtained her by gambling or barter when she was ten or twelve years old. She was one of Charbonneau's two or three Indian wives.

A statue of Sacagawea in Portland, Oregon, commemorates her contributions as a guide to the Lewis and Clark expedition. (Library of Congress)

Lewis and Clark hired Charbonneau as an interpreter and believed that Sacagawea would prove her usefulness if the expedition encountered the Shoshone later on. On February 11 or 12, 1805, Sacagawea gave birth to her first child, a boy christened Jean Baptiste.

The expedition set out again on April 7, 1805, following the Missouri River. Sacagawea apparently first proved her usefulness to the expedition on April 9, when she unearthed wild artichokes to eat. Sacagawea earned Lewis's respect on May 14, when the supply boat capsized and began to sink. Sacagawea was on board. As the boat was righted she calmly and deliberately pulled on board all the invaluable records and supplies that were near her—all the while holding her baby and balancing herself. On May 20, the leaders of the expedition named a river after her.

On July 22, Sacagawea first recognized her home country near present-day Helena, Montana. She assured Lewis and Clark that they were on the correct route to get to the Three Forks of the Missouri River. On July 28, she reaffirmed that the expedition was in Shoshone territory, having in fact reached the exact spot where she had lived five years earlier when the Hidatsa abducted her.

Lewis and Clark decided to follow the central tributary of the three rivers. On August 8, Sacagawea recognized the area as the Shoshones' summer home and assured the expedition that her people would be found on this river. Contact was made on August 15, and Sacagawea was reunited with her tribe. She acted as interpreter (her brother was now chief). Her presence likely helped to maintain the cordial relations between Indians and whites and facilitated Lewis and Clark's successful bargaining with the Shoshone to obtain twenty-nine horses, which were essential for the expedition to continue. Although Sacagawea probably could have remained with the Shoshone, she instead stayed with the expedition and accompanied it to the Pacific Ocean.

On the return trip, Sacagawea performed additional services for the expedition. On May 11, 1806, she aided communication with the Nez Perce as an interpreter. Sacagawea recognized several of the areas the expedition passed through and reassured Clark that they were taking the correct route. She recommended the Bozeman Pass through the Rocky Mountains. Although they could have taken any of three passes, the Bozeman Pass was the most direct route to the Yellowstone Valley. Clark acknowledged that she had been of great service to him as a guide through this part of the trip.

On August 17, 1806, the expedition reached Fort Mandan in central North Dakota, where Lewis and Clark parted company with Charbonneau and Sacagawea.

The rest of Sacagawea's life is undocumented and uncertain, and widely varying accounts of it have been written. Harold P. Howard's *Sacajawea* (1971) suggests, on the basis of what documentary evidence there is, that Sacagawea died at Fort Manuel, South Dakota, on December 20, 1812, during an Indian raid. She was buried there in an unmarked grave. She would have been about in her mid-twenties. (Other accounts have her dying as late as 1884, at the approximate age of ninety-six, on the Wind River Shoshone Reservation in Wyoming.)

Both Lewis and Clark wrote of their admiration and respect for Sacagawea and of what great services she provided to the expedition. Many historians no longer believe that Sacagawea's presence was vital to the success of the expedition, as earlier historians had claimed. Had the expedition been left to its own resources it would have found its way, communicated with the Indians, and bartered for the vitally needed horses, they contend.

At the very least, there is no question that Sacagawea's presence significantly eased the way for the expedition, and perhaps her presence was her greatest contribution. She was a vital young woman of courage, loyalty, energy, and endurance—a true heroine. As Elliot Coues comments in *A History of the Expedition Under the Command of Captains Lewis and Clark* (1893): "Clark very sensibly followed the advice of the remarkable woman, who never failed to rise to the occasion."

In 2000, the U.S. Mint honored Sacagawea, and American Indians generally, by placing her image on the face of a newly designed one-dollar coin. The gold-colored coin depicts her looking over her shoulder, with her infant son sleeping in a sling on her back.

Laurence Miller

FURTHER READING

Duncan, Dayton. *Out West: An American Journey.* New York: Viking, 1987.

Howard, Harold P. *Sacajawea.* Norman: University of Oklahoma Press, 1971.

Hunsaker, Joyce Badgley. *Sacagawea Speaks: Beyond the Shining Mountains with Lewis and Clark.* Guilford, Conn.: Two Dot Books, 2001.

Kessler, Donna J. *The Making of Sacagawea: A Euro-American Legend.* Tuscaloosa: University of Alabama Press, 1996.

Lewis, Meriwether, and William Clark. *A History of the Lewis and Clark Expedition.* Edited by Elliot Coues. 4 vols. 1893. Reprint. New York: Dover, 1965.

_____. *History of the Expedition of Captains Lewis and Clark, 1804-5-6.* 2d ed. 2 vols. Chicago: A. C. McClurg, 1903.

Moulton, Gary E., ed. *The Journals of the Lewis and Clark Expedition.* Lincoln: University of Nebraska Press, 1988.

Nelson, W. Dale. *Interpreters with Lewis and Clark: The Story of Sacagawea and Toussaint Charbonneau.* Denton: University of North Texas Press, 2003.

Perdue, Theda, ed. *Sifters: Native American Women's Lives.* New York: Oxford University Press, 2001.

Ronda, James P. *Lewis and Clark Among the Indians.* Lincoln: University of Nebraska Press, 1984.

Sainte-Marie, Buffy

Born: February 20, 1942; Piapot Reserve, Saskatchewan, Canada
Tribal affiliation: Cree
Significance: From the mid-1960's through the 1970's, Buffy Sainte-Marie was a popular folksinger who championed Native American causes.

Beverly "Buffy" Sainte-Marie was born to Cree parents on the Piapot Reserve at Craven, Saskatchewan, Canada, but she was orphaned within the first year of her life. She was adopted by a couple in Massachusetts who were part Micmac. She graduated from the University of Massachusetts in 1963 with a B.A. degree in philosophy, having honed her skills as a folksinger at coffeehouses in the "Five College" region of central Massachusetts. A brief guest appearance at the Gaslight Cafe in Greenwich Village months after her college graduation caused *The New York Times* to identify her as "one of the most promising new talents on the folk scene."

Sainte-Marie signed a contract with Vanguard Records, and her albums sold reasonably well throughout the next decade. Although her work has ranged from country music to folk songs in Spanish and French, Sainte-Marie's primary legacy is that of a protest writer, having written and performed antiwar ballads ("The Universal Soldier," also recorded by Donovan) as well as compelling and poignant songs about Native American cultural dilemmas ("Now That the Buffalo's Gone" and "My Country 'Tis of Thy People You're Dying"). In the film *The Strawberry Statement* (1971), Sainte-Marie's version of "The Circle Game" was used on the soundtrack (rather than that of Joni Mitchell, who wrote the song). Sainte-Marie's husky alto voice has been favorably compared to the voices of Edith Piaf and Billie Holiday.

Since releasing an album in 1996, Sainte-Marie has performed in concert and has given speaking engagements on a limited basis, while devoting most of her time to the Cradleboard Teaching Project.

Richard Sax

FURTHER READING

Oswalt, Wendell H. *This Land Was Theirs: A Study of Native Americans.* New York: Oxford University Press, 2005.

Samoset

Born: c. 1590
Died: c. 1653
Tribal affiliation: Pemaquid Abenaki
Significance: Samoset was the first Indian to greet the Plymouth pilgrims.

On March 16, 1621, clothed only in a breechcloth despite the bitter weather, Samoset astounded the Plymouth colonists when he walked into their settlement and called, "Welcome, Englishmen." A sagamore of the Pemaquid band of Abenaki Indians of Monhegan Island off the Maine coast, Samoset had apparently learned English from coastal fishermen. He and the Wampanoag chief MASSASOIT had been clandestinely observing the pilgrims since their arrival on Wampanoag land three months before.

The settlers clothed and fed Samoset, and he departed the next day with assurances that he would arrange a meeting with Massasoit. Several days later he returned with SQUANTO, a Patuxet Indian who had been enslaved and taken to England but, with the aid of a sympathetic Englishman, had returned to Massachusetts in 1619. Speaking fluent En-

Samoset. (Library of Congress)

glish, Squanto helped to negotiate an agreement between Massasoit and the Plymouth colony, thus launching friendly relations between the whites and the Indians.

In 1625, Samoset and another Pemaquid Indian, Unongoit, signed the first deed between the British and the Indians for the sale of Pemaquid lands, thereby initiating the Plymouth practice of purchasing Indian lands. In 1653, Samoset sold another thousand acres. He died shortly thereafter.

Mary E. Virginia

Sampson, Will

Born: 1934 or 1935; Okmulgee, Oklahoma
Died: June 3, 1987; Houston, Texas
Tribal affiliation: Creek (Muskogee)
Significance: Will Sampson became one of the best known of American Indian actors after his portrayal of Chief Bromden in *One Flew over the Cuckoo's Nest.*

Will Sampson was raised on the Creek reservation in Oklahoma, and as a young man he served briefly in the Navy. Before doing any acting, he worked as a rodeo cowboy and a forest ranger. He also had a successful career as an artist, painting Western scenes and characters. He continued painting and exhibiting his work after beginning his acting career.

Sampson was forty when an associate of Michael Douglas, the film's producer, found him for the role of Chief Bromden in the 1976 film version of Ken Kesey's novel *One Flew over the Cuckoo's Nest.* Sampson was very tall—6 feet, 7 inches—and his silent, mysterious presence as Bromden was important in establishing the mood of the film, set in an insane asylum. Sampson was nominated for an Academy Award. He went on to many more film and television appearances, including roles in *The Outlaw Josie Wales* (1975), Robert Altman's *Buffalo Bill and the Indians* (1976), *Insignificance* (1985), and the television films *The White Buffalo* (1977) and *Alcatraz: The Whole Shocking Story* (1980). Other television work included a recurring role in the series *Vegas.* Sampson also joined the American Indian Theater Company of Oklahoma. In addition to his painting and acting, Sampson was an educator regarding both art and Indian traditions, and he contributed to a number of causes important to American Indians, including the fight against alcoholism.

Sampson died of kidney failure at the age of fifty-three after having recently undergone a heart and lung transplant.

McCrea Adams

FURTHER READING

Kilpatrick, Jacquelyn. *Celluloid Indians: Native Americans and Film.* Lincoln: University of Nebraska Press, 1999.

Rollins, Peter C., and John E. O'Connor. *Hollywood's Indian: The Portrayal of the Native American in Film.* Expanded ed. Lexington: University Press of Kentucky, 2003.

Sassacus

Born: c. 1560; near present-day Groton, Connecticut
Died: c. July, 1637; New York
Tribal affiliation: Pequot
Significance: Sassacus was the principal Pequot sachem when the tribe was virtually destroyed in war with the English during 1636-1637.

A famous warrior, Sassacus was chosen "great sachem" of the Pequots of southern Connecticut when his father Tatobem was killed in 1633. His residence was a fortified village called Weinshaunks (now Groton, Connecticut) on the east bank of the Thames River. His short period as sachem was marked by continuing conflict with the Narragansetts to the east, a war with the English, and the secession of many dissatisfied Pequots. The largest seceding group established themselves as the Mohegans under the leadership of UNCAS, a former Pequot angry because he had been passed over for the sachemship.

The clash with the colonists grew out of the murders of several English fur traders, attributed to the Pequots. War began in 1636 when Pequot efforts at compensation failed and an English army entered Pequot country. In May, 1637, a joint English-Mohegan-Narragansett force struck a Pequot village by surprise and burned it, killing four hundred to seven hundred people. This event, and the superiority of English guns to bows and arrows, so demoralized the Pequots that they surrendered or fled by the hundreds, ignoring Sassacus's pleas to fight on. With forty loyal warriors and fifty pounds of wampum as a gift, Sassacus journeyed west to the Mohawk country in a desperate attempt to win military support from the Mohawks, the Pequots' traditional enemies. Instead, the Mohawks killed Sassacus and his men and sent Sassacus's scalp to the English. The Pequots' status as an independent tribe temporarily ended.

Bert M. Mutersbaugh

Satank

Born: 1800; probably in present-day Kansas
Died: June 8, 1871; probably in Indian Territory (now Oklahoma)
Also known as: Set-tank, Set-angia, Sitting Bear
Tribal affiliation: Kiowa
Significance: A Kiowa warrior and medicine man, Satank is best known for his role in signing the Medicine Lodge Treaty.

Born near the turn of the nineteenth century, Satank established himself as a leading warrior among the Kiowa by the 1830's. Thanks to his success in warfare, he became one of the few members of the elite warrior society known as the Koitsenko. At that time, the Kiowa were embroiled in intertribal warfare. As white hunters, traders, and settlers began moving onto the Great Plains, Satank shifted the focus of his activities to white settlements.

Two incidents gained Satank notoriety as an effective warrior. The first incident occurred during the summer of 1864. While camping outside Fort Larned, Kansas, Satank and other Kiowas came near the fort. Due to the language barrier and consequent failure to understand each other, a soldier raised his rifle, and Satank responded by shooting and killing him. The second incident was his leading of a Kiowa massacre of the Henry Warren wagon train in the spring of 1871. Another Kiowa leader, SATANTA, later boasted about this incident as a training mission for young warriors.

During the years between these incidents, the Kiowas, Comanche, Kiowa-Apache, Southern Cheyenne, and Arapaho attended the Medicine Lodge Treaty council at Medicine Lodge Creek, Kansas. Satank, Satanta, and seven other Kiowas signed the Medicine Lodge Treaty in October, 1867. During the council, several of the four hundred attending chiefs gave speeches. Satanta became known as the Orator of the Plains for his speech. However, Satank, has been described as the Indian who delivered the most impassioned speech. He expressed his desire for the wrongs to cease and peace and friendship to return.

The Medicine Lodge Treaty effectively forced the Kiowa people onto Fort Sill Reservation in what is now southwestern Oklahoma. In exchange for the Kiowas' abandoning their claim to their ancestral land, the federal government promised to provide them with food, clothing, homes, and schools. Within a year, the Kiowas were again relocated.

Satank himself soon became restless with the confinement of reservation life and often left the reservation for extended periods. When his son—also named Satank—was killed in Texas during the summer of 1870, he became heartbroken. In his grief, he developed even greater hostile feelings toward white settlers, and he killed and scalped a white man while retrieving his son's remains in Texas.

Throughout the following year, Satank joined Satanta, BIG TREE, and other Kiowa, Comanche, and Plains Apaches in raiding white settlements in northwestern Texas. In May of 1871 they attacked the Henry Warren wagon train, killing seven of its members. This incident became notorious as a massacre and brought to the nation's attention the inadequacy of federal protection of settlers along reservation borders.

U.S. Army general William T. Sherman was brought in for an inspection of frontier conditions and sent cavalry troops after the Indians responsible for the Warren massacre. Evading capture by the Army, Satank and his party returned to Fort Sill to request rations. At the fort, Satanta bragged about his part in the raid and named Satank, Big Tree, and other Kiowas fellow participants. As Sherman tried to arrest these men, the Kiowa chief KICKING BIRD pleaded for their release. The grounds near the agent's office became tense as armed Kiowa men and cavalry soldiers appeared. Kicking Bird suggested to Sherman that the men should be released if some stolen mules were returned. He then asked to have the mules brought and told Sherman they would comply with his terms. With the three men in custody, Sherman prepared to have them sent to Fort Richardson, Texas, to be tried for murder.

Satank, Satanta, and Big Tree were handcuffed and shackled for the journey to Fort Richardson. When Satank refused to climb into the wagon on his own, two guards put him in a second wagon. During the transport, Satank, while chanting his death song, worked his hands free of the handcuffs and pulled a concealed knife on an Army guard. In the struggle that ensued, Satank was shot several times. Mortally wounded, he was left to die on the road. He was later buried at Fort Sill, quietly and without ceremony. Meanwhile, Satanta and Big Tree were the first Indians to be tried for murder before a jury in a civil trial.

Teresa Neva Tate

FURTHER READING

Boyd, Maurice, ed. *Kiowa Voices: Myths, Legends and Folktales.* 2 vols. Fort Worth: Texas Christian University Press, 1981, 1983.

DeMallie, Raymond J., and Lynn Shelby Kickingbird. *The Treaty of Medicine Lodge, 1867: Between the United States and the Kiowa, Comanche and Apache Indians.* Washington, D.C.: Institute for the Development of Indian Law, 1976.

Hosmer, Brian C. "Satank." *The Handbook of Texas Online.* Red River Authority of Texas, 1999-2004 (http://www.tsha.utexas.edu/handbook/online).

Mayhill, Mildred P. *The Kiowas.* Norman: University of Oklahoma Press, 1962.

Robinson, Charles M. *The Indian Trial: The Complete Story of the Warren Wagon Train Massacre and the Fall of the Kiowa Nation.* Spokane, Wash.: A. H. Clark, 1997.

Sturtevant Nye, Wilbur. *Bad Medicine and Good: Tales of the Kiowas.* Norman: University of Oklahoma Press, 1962.

Satanta

Born: c. 1830
Died: October 11, 1878; Huntsville, Texas
Also known as: Guaton-bain (Big Ribs)
Tribal affiliation: Kiowa

Satanta. (National Archives)

Significance: Satanta was one of the major Kiowa leaders to sign the Medicine Lodge Treaty of 1867; later, he led raids against whites.

Chief Satanta was the son of To-quodle-kaip-tau (Red Tipi). He spent his youth on the southern plains south of the Arkansas River. One of his closest friends was SATANK. He was also close to his half brother, Black Bonnet, and his cousin, STUMBLING BEAR.

Satanta was distinguished by his red headdress; his red tipi, with red streamers; his *zebat*, or medicine arrow-lance; and his buffalo-hide shield, which was the last of the "sun shields." The shield was carried into more than a hundred fights. When Satanta went to war, he wore a buckskin shirt painted red on one side and yellow on the other. He was known well enough as a warrior to speak at length at the Medicine Lodge Treaty meeting in 1867, a treaty he signed. In this treaty, the Kiowa agreed to cede their lands and move to a reservation.

In 1871, Satanta, along with Satank and BIG TREE, led the Kiowa against the whites in the Red River valley. The leaders were arrested and sent to Fort Richardson for trial. Satank was killed trying to escape. The other two leaders were tried and sent to the Texas State Penitentiary at

Huntsville. In 1873, the two were paroled and returned to Fort Sill.

In 1874, the Kiowa, joined by the Comanche, Cheyenne, and Arapaho, went to war against the whites to protect the remaining buffalo herds from slaughter. In this first ecological war, the U.S. Army prevailed tactically, but the buffalo were saved from extinction. Satanta was sent back to the prison in Huntsville, while the other tribal leaders were sent to Fort Marion in Florida. Satanta died in prison in Huntsville. It never has been decided with certainty whether he died trying to escape or committed suicide. He was buried in the prison cemetery.

Satanta left eight children. His descendants numbered more than 150 in 1993, the year that Satanta was elected to the National Hall of Fame for Famous American Indians in Anadarko, Oklahoma.

Howard Meredith

FURTHER READING

Robinson, Charles M., III. *Satanta: The Life and Death of a War Chief.* Austin, Tex.: State House Press, 1998.

Scarface Charlie

Born: c. 1837; near the Rogue River, California
Died: December 3, 1896; Seneca Station, Indian Territory (now in Oklahoma)
Also known as: Chichikam Lupalkuelatko (Wagon Scarface)
Tribal affiliation: Modoc
Significance: Scarface Charlie was the chief adviser, interpreter, and battlefield tactician to Modoc chief CAPTAIN JACK; he performed honorably and brilliantly during the Modoc War of 1872-1873.

Scarface Charlie acquired his name when, as a child, he hitched a ride on the back of a stagecoach and fell off. He received a deep and prominent scar on his right cheek either from hitting a sharp rock or from the rim of a wheel of the stagecoach. His involvement in the Modoc conflict with white settlers and the army began around 1851, when, as a youth, he witnessed the murder by Modoc warriors of an emigrant party that had gotten lost.

Scarface Charlie is best known for his participation in the Modoc War of 1872-1873. He was involved in all the major battles of that war, serving as the most trusted friend, field commander, tactician, and interpreter for the Modoc leader, Captain Jack. Scarface Charlie was a man of peace and conciliation who opposed shedding blood at every meeting with his people. He was also a loyal warrior, brilliant field commander, and tactician. These two sides of him manifested themselves in many instances but are perhaps best seen in his performance during the Battle of Hardin Butte (Thomas-Wright Massacre) in 1873. Scarface Charlie fought what Richard Dillon referred to in *Burnt-Out Fires* (1973) as "perhaps the classic, most perfect battle in Indian war history." With only twenty-two warriors, he ambushed eighty military men. After killing twenty-seven and wounding seventeen, unwilling to annihilate the rest, he abruptly called a halt to further killing, telling the survivors that "all you fellows that ain't dead had better go home. We don't want to kill you all in one day." Under his command, the Modocs never lost a battle. The only battle the Modocs lost, which caused their defeat and surrender, occurred when Captain Jack displaced Scarface Charlie as commander.

Several Modocs, including Captain Jack, were executed for their role in the war, but Scarface Charlie was spared, according to one observer because he was "the Bismarck of the band . . . a warrior in arms against our troops and today there are no regrets that he should be pardoned and at large."

Scarface Charlie was appointed Modoc chief after Captain Jack's execution, and he and the remaining Modocs were sent to the Quapaw reservation in Indian Territory. Scarface Charlie refused to interfere with the customs of the Modocs, and he was removed as chief. From 1874 to 1876, he appeared in a tour organized by one of the white principals in the Modoc War to familiarize people of the Midwest and East with the war. Scarface Charlie converted to Christianity and died of tuberculosis on the reservation in 1896.

Laurence Miller

FURTHER READING

Quinn, Arthur. *Hell with the Fire Out: A History of the Modoc War.* Boston: Faber & Faber, 1997.
Riddle, Jefferson C. Davis. *The Indian History of the Modoc War.* Introduction by Peter Cozzens. Mechanicsburg, Pa.: Stackpole Books, 2004.

Scholder, Fritz

Born: October 6, 1937; Breckenridge, Minnesota
Tribal affiliation: Luiseño
Significance: Fritz Scholder broke the bounds of traditionalist Indian painting with his brightly colored portraits of contemporary Indians.

Fritz Scholder began painting at the age of thirteen. He was graduated with a bachelor of arts degree from Sacramento State University in 1960, and he earned a master of fine arts degree from the University of Arizona in 1964. He was encouraged to pursue painting by Sioux artist Oscar HOWE and by pop art painter Wayer Thiebaud and has been strongly influenced by European artists and styles, particularly Francis Bacon and Edvard Munch, as well as by American artist Georgia O'Keeffe.

Scholder was hired to teach at the Institute of American Indian Art, Santa Fe, in 1964, which he did until 1969. In 1967, he launched his famous "Indian series," with groups of pictures of monster Indians, Indians and horses, Dartmouth portraits, American portraits, contemporary Indians in Gallup, and Indian postcards. With these paintings, he began what one critic called the postmodern interrogation of the historically circumscribed image of the Indian, using post-Impressionist, expressionist, and pop art styles. The series was concluded in 1980, whereupon he vowed never to paint another Indian. During the 1990's, his figurative paintings became shamanistic, often featuring animals and female nudes. A prolific painter and excellent colorist, Scholder has sought acceptance as an artist who happens to be Indian rather than as an "Indian artist." His work has been shown in numerous countries and has been the subject of three documentary films.

Cheryl Claassen

FURTHER READING
Reno, Dawn E. *Contemporary Native American Artists.* Brooklyn, N.Y.: Alliance Publishing, 1995.

Seattle

Born: c. 1788; near present-day Seattle, Washington
Died: June 7, 1866; Port Madison Reservation, Washington
Also known as: Noah Seathl, Seathl
Tribal affiliation: Suquamish, Duwamish
Significance: As chief of the Suquamish, Duwamish, and other allied Puget Sound tribes, Seattle urged peaceful coexistence with U.S. settlers.

Seattle (or Seathl), chief of the Duwamish, Suquamish, and other allied Puget Sound tribes, was the child of Scholitza (daughter of a Duwamish chief), and Schweabe, a chief of the Suquamish. It was not uncommon for upper-class Duwamishes to intermarry with other tribes; such matrimonial ties were of political import. Born near the present-day city of Seattle (which bears his name) in 1788, Seattle won credibility among the tribes by providing leadership in time of war. The Duwamish (the "inside [the bay] people"), located at the outlet of Lake Washington along the Duwamish River, experienced extensive contact with white settlers by the 1840's. Seattle urged his people to befriend the immigrants, to allow them to settle on Indian land, and to seek employment among them. Seattle won the support of the tribes for the Point Elliott Treaty, which he signed on January 22, 1855. This provided for the creation of a reservation, submission to agency authorities, and land cessions.

The city of Seattle's "Pioneer Square" rose on the site of a Duwamish winter village. Within a year some Duwamish, Suquamish, Puyallup, Nisqually, and Taitnapam warriors attacked the infant city of Seattle, but the chief withheld his support from their actions. During the two-year conflict (1856-1858), Seattle assisted the Americans. A grateful citizenry named their new settlement in the chief's honor. Initially, Seattle was unwilling to accept this honor, because traditional belief held that after death a spirit would be troubled each time his name was spoken. To allay these fears, Seattle residents paid "a kind of tax" annually to compensate for his "broken sleep of eternity."

The Duwamish were not entirely happy with reservation life. It permitted only a subsistence economy and, because of close proximity to the Suquamishes, caused considerable tension. Starting in the summer of 1856, many Duwamishes resettled near their old home sites, some still living at Foster, Washington, near the city of Seattle, as late as 1910. Chief Seattle consistently urged peaceful coexistence during this time of potential antagonism.

Because of the influence of French Roman Catholic missionaries, Seattle was baptized (possibly taking the biblical name "Noah"). As a practicing Christian, Seattle instituted daily morning and evening prayers for his people, a practice continued after his death.

Chief Seattle, much beloved and admired by white settlers, was described as having "unimpaired sincerity," "an irenic spirit," and a "dignified" and "venerable carriage." He was often compared in character and appearance to Senator Thomas Benton. Following his death in 1866, he was mourned by all. The city of Seattle erected a monument over his gravesite in 1890.

C. George Fry

FURTHER READING
Jefferson, Warren. *The World of Chief Seattle: How Can One Sell the Air?*
Summertown, Tenn.: Native Voices, 2001.

Sequoyah

Born: c. 1770; Taskigi, near Fort Loudon (now in Tennessee)
Died: c. August, 1844; near San Fernando, Tamaulipas, Mexico
Also known as: George Guess (or Gist)
Tribal affiliation: Cherokee
Significance: Sequoyah's syllabary enabled Cherokees to become literate in their own language.

Sequoyah, a mixed-blood Cherokee, was born near Fort Loudon, about five miles from the sacred Cherokee capital of Echota. He was a member of the "over the hill" Cherokees, so named because they lived west of the Appalachian Mountains. He was probably the son of trapper and trader Nathaniel Gist (or Guess), who abandoned Sequoyah's mother while she was still pregnant. Growing up west of the mountains, the young man became a prosperous hunter and fur trapper-trader. On a hunting trip while still quite young, he damaged one of his legs in an accident and was disabled for life. His hunting career over, he became a craftsman; his silver ornaments became widely sought both by various Native American tribes and by white traders. While still a young man, Sequoyah moved from the over-the-hill region of Tennessee to Willstown, in present-day Alabama. He had little contact with the white people to the east until the 1790's, when he increasingly encountered white tradesmen. His knowledge of the white world was expanded during the War of 1812, during which he served as one of General Andrew Jackson's volunteers. With Jackson, he fought against the Red Sticks, a Creek faction that had allied itself with the British. In 1813, he participated in such battles as the attack on Tallaschatche, a Red Stick town. In 1814, he fought at the Battle of Horseshoe Bend, where Jackson and his forces decisively defeated the Red Sticks and effectively broke up their resistance to Anglo penetration of their region.

After the United States and his tribe signed the Cherokee Treaty of 1817, Sequoyah joined Chief John Jolly, who led a group of the Native Americans into Arkansas country, as provided by the treaty. With his new wife, Sally, Sequoyah took land in present Pope County, Arkansas, and began farming. In his new home, Sequoyah continued to work on a syllabary that he had started during the War of 1812.

Cherokee leader Sequoyah with the syllabary he
developed to write the Cherokee language.
(National Museum of the American Indian,
Smithsonian Institution)

This Cherokee intellectual became fascinated when he observed white soldiers using "talking leaves" (writings on paper) to communicate with family and friends over vast distances. Sequoyah then began to develop a system of writing for his people. In 1821, he completed the syllabary and "went public" with it. The table of characters included eighty-six syllables in the Cherokee language. Aside from a few characters he borrowed, he had little to do with English, a language he had never learned to speak or write. Once he had polished his work, he taught it to his young daughter and several of her friends. Then he took the children before the Cherokee National Council at Echota, where they demonstrated what they had so easily learned. Impressed, the Council sanctioned it for the whole nation. Because of the syllabary's simplicity, it could be mastered in a few days at most. Soon, hundreds and then thousands of Eastern Cherokees had become literate in their own tongue. In 1822, Sequoyah took his "talking leaves" back to the Western Cherokees still living in Arkansas, who were soon to migrate into present-day Texas and Oklahoma. His western tribesmen easily mastered the syllabary, just as their eastern kinsmen had.

Subsequently, the syllabary contributed much to expand Cherokee culture and improve the quality of their lives. Education took on added meaning once the writing system was in place. Soon, books were being translated into—or written in—the Cherokee language. The famed missionary Samuel Worcester founded a press and quickly translated the Bible for his flock.

While still promoting his syllabary, Sequoyah developed other interests. The 1820's found him with the Western Cherokee delegation to Washington, D.C., where, with his companions, he lobbied for the interests of his nation. Meanwhile, just as he had earlier developed a system of writing for his people, he also developed a numbering system that his people could understand. Before his work with arithmetic, Cherokees had "mental" numbers up to one hundred but could not add, subtract, multiply, or divide. With Sequoyah's new system, tribal members could easily do so.

Even as he worked on his writing and numbering systems, Sequoyah also developed as an artist. With his paintings he became a natural realist. He took nature—everything he saw around him—and reproduced it.

By 1830, his band had moved into what is now present-day eastern Oklahoma, and Sequoyah himself settled near present-day Sallisaw. There, he developed another small farm and also raised cattle and horses. On his new farmstead he found a salt lick, and soon he was able to add saltmaking to his list of practical accomplishments. The rugged Sequoyah also chopped enough wood to have a surplus, which he sold or bartered for other goods.

In the late 1830's, survivors of the Cherokee Trail of Tears reached Oklahoma. Sequoyah was one of the established leaders who helped them to reestablish their civilized way of life. Concurrently, he became a diplomat and helped bring peace—and stop a wave of violent assassinations—among three political factions: the old settlers (Western Cherokees); the Treaty Party, who had "given away" eastern lands to the whites; and the Ross Party, whose members had sworn to take vengeance on the Treaty Party.

Next, Sequoyah aided the Texas Cherokees, whom the whites had forced out of the Republic of Texas in 1839. He persuaded those who had earlier promised retaliation to settle peaceably in Indian country and redevelop their way of life. His advice probably saved hundreds of lives, for the military might of Texas was too strong to be overcome. Had the Texas Cherokees trekked back into the republic, massacre would have been the result.

In 1842, Sequoyah became interested in a new project. He traveled westward, looking for a Cherokee band that traditions said had moved well west of the Mississippi River before the time of the American Revolution. While searching for the missing band, Sequoyah became ill and died near the settlement of San Fernando, Tamaulipas, Mexico. Although the exact date of his death is disputed, it is agreed by most researchers that he died between 1843 and 1845.

Considered one of the ablest intellectuals ever produced by Native American societies, the man of the "talking leaves" was honored by the state of Oklahoma. Officials also placed his statue in Statuary Hall in Washington, D.C.

James Smallwood

FURTHER READING

Foreman, Grant. *Sequoyah.* Norman: University of Oklahoma Press, 1938.

Foster, George E. *Se-quo-yah: The American Cadmus and Modern Moses.* New York: AMS Press, 1979.

Hoig, Stan. *Sequoyah: The Cherokee Genius.* Oklahoma City: Oklahoma Historical Society, 1995.

Kilpatrick, Jack F. *Sequoyah: Of Earth and Intellect.* Austin, Tex.: Encino Press, 1965.

Mails, Thomas E. *The Cherokee People: The Story of the Cherokees from Earliest Origins to Contemporary Times.* Tulsa, Okla.: Council Oaks Books, 1992.

Smith, William Robert Lee. *The Story of the Cherokees.* Cleveland, Tenn.: Church of God, 1928.

Shábona

Born: c. 1775; Ohio or Illinois
Died: c. July 17, 1859; Morris, Illinois
Also known as: Chambly, Shabbona, Shabonee
Tribal affiliation: Potawatomi
Significance: Initially a loyal follower of TECUMSEH, Shábona advocated peace and accommodation with whites following the War of 1812.

Shábona's mother was a Seneca and his father an Ottawa who may have been PONTIAC's nephew. Traveling throughout Illinois in 1807, Shábona recruited tribes for Tecumseh's pantribal rebellion. During the War of 1812, Shábona supported the British, fighting with Tecumseh at the Battle of the Thames in 1813. In 1812, he rescued some white families at the Fort Dearborn Massacre.

Succeeding his wife's father as principal Potawatomi chief, Shábona thereafter advocated peace, becoming a federal ally. In 1827, he persuaded most Winnebagos to remain neutral during RED BIRD's Winnebago Uprising. Accused of spying for the federal government, he was taken prisoner. During the Black Hawk War of 1832, Shábona warned Chicago settlers of an impending attack. In retaliation, he was captured by Sauks and Foxes who killed his son and nephew.

Granted land in Illinois following the rebellions, his people were nevertheless forced to relocate west of the Mississippi River. His land was sold at auction. Some grateful settlers bought Shábona a farm near Seneca, Illinois, where he lived for the rest of his life.

Mary E. Virginia

Shikellamy

Born: ?
Died: December 6, 1748; Shamokin, present-day Sunbury, Pennsylvania
Also known as: Ongwaterohiathe, Takashwangarous
Tribal affiliation: Oneida
Significance: As representative for the Pennsylvania Iroquois, Shikel-
lamy helped negotiate their admittance into the Iroquois Confeder-
acy.

Shikellamy was born either French or Cayuga, or possibly a mixture of
the two. He was kidnapped by the Oneidas when he was two years old
and later adopted by them. He lived with them along the Schuylkill
River in Pennsylvania. James LOGAN, a leader of the Ohio Oneidas who
became known as Mingos, was Shikellamy's son.

Shikellamy rose to prominence among the Oneidas and was assigned
by the Iroquois council to represent Iroquois holdings along the Susquehanna Valley in Pennsylvania. At his post at Shamokin, he negotiated with leaders of tributary tribes, Pennsylvania officials, missionaries,
and members of the Susquehanna Land Company. Encouraging absti-
nence among his people, Shikellamy helped curb white distribution of
alcohol.

Shikellamy helped engineer the agreement in 1736 by which Pennsylvania Indians were incorporated into the Iroquois Confederacy.
When he sold Delaware lands to the colony of Pennsylvania, Shikellamy
initiated a period of unrest.

Mary E. Virginia

Short Bull

Born: c. 1845; Niobrara River (now in northern Nebraska)
Died: c. 1915; Pine Ridge Reservation, South Dakota
Tribal affiliation: Brule Lakota (Sioux)
Significance: Short Bull introduced the Ghost Dance to the Sioux and
preached a holy war against whites.

According to Chief He Dog, Short Bull grew up with the future Oglala
Sioux chief CRAZY HORSE, played with him as a boy, and later fought in
wars with him. They were made chiefs at about the same time.

By 1880, the Sioux had been effectively confined to reservations and
reduced to a sorry condition. Their crops and cattle died. A miserly
Congress skimped and dawdled in sending clothing and food rations.

Epidemics of measles, influenza, and whooping cough combined with hunger to ravage the reservation and cause many deaths. The Sioux were unable to hunt their own food and were forbidden to practice the traditional Sun Dance, an important source of spiritual help.

Into this atmosphere of despair and anger came news of a Paiute prophet or messiah, WOVOKA. He preached the peaceful coming of a new world of hope and life for the Indian. By 1891, this new world would push the whites back across the ocean. The buffalo would return, and all Indians, past and present, would live happily for eternity. In order for this millennium to occur, Indians had to pray, sing, and dance the Ghost Dance.

During the winter of 1889, Short Bull and ten other Sioux, as part of a chosen delegation, journeyed to Utah to see Wovoka. They returned in the spring of 1890, full of enthusiasm and hope. Short Bull and KICKING BEAR rose to prominence as the high priests of this new religion, representing themselves as the special vicars of Wovoka. They reinterpreted Wovoka's peaceful prophecies as a call to arms, however; they preached that the destruction of whites in a holy war was necessary to prepare for the new world. They wore ceremonial Ghost Shirts that would protect their wearers from the whites' weapons.

Short Bull (left) with Miniconjou Sioux chief Kicking Bear. (National Archives)

The new religion found many converts, especially on the Rosebud and Pine Ridge Reservations. Prominent Sioux chiefs, among them HUMP, BIG FOOT, and SITTING BULL, were attracted. Oglala and Brule Sioux spoke a fiery rhetoric and danced themselves into a trancelike condition. White settlers and the Pine Ridge agent began to panic and called for troops to restore order. Three thousand troops arrived.

Short Bull was arrested and imprisoned, and Hump was pacified. Sitting Bull was ordered arrested but was killed in the attempt. Big Foot surrendered at Wounded Knee, but tempers got out of hand. A skirmish broke out, and before it was over nearly three hundred Sioux and twenty-five soldiers had been killed. The Ghost Dance excitement faded away, and Short Bull fell into disrepute. Upon his release, Short Bull spent the rest of his days on the Pine Ridge Reservation and affiliated himself with the Congregationalists.

Laurence Miller

FURTHER READING

Mooney, James. *The Ghost-Dance Religion and the Sioux Outbreak of 1890.* Introduction by Raymond J. DeMallie. Lincoln: University of Nebraska Press, 1991.

Silko, Leslie Marmon

Born: March 5, 1948; Albuquerque, New Mexico
Tribal affiliation: Laguna Pueblo
Significance: One of the best-known American Indian writers, Leslie Marmon Silko writes fiction, essays, and poetry that transcend boundaries between oral and written language.

The tensions and cultural conflicts affecting many of Leslie Marmon Silko's characters can be seen as fictional renderings of Silko's experience. Born of mixed European American and Indian ancestry, Silko spent her formative years learning the stories of her white ancestors and their relationship with the native population into which they married. Her great-grandfather, Robert Marmon, had come to New Mexico's Laguna pueblo in the early 1870's as a surveyor and eventually married a Laguna woman.

Even more important to Silko's development as a writer was the later generation of Marmons—half European American and half Native American—who continued to transmit the oral traditions of the Laguna Pueblo people. One such source was the Aunt Susie of Silko's autobiographical writings. The wife of Silko's grandfather's brother, she was a schoolteacher in the Laguna Pueblo during the 1920's and years afterward passed on to the young Silko the oral heritage of her race. So intimate was Silko's imagination with the elements of Laguna culture that her father's family photographs serve as visual commentary on the sketches and stories of *Storyteller* (1981).

Like the Inuit woman in *Storyteller,* Silko attended the local school operated by the Bureau of Indian Affairs, but she remained there only a short time, moving on to Roman Catholic schools in Albuquerque, eventually receiving a B.A. in English from the University of New Mexico in 1969. Like her ancestors, she taught school at Navajo Community College in Tsaile, Arizona, where she wrote *Ceremony* (1977), her first novel. One of the best known of her works and one of the best novels written by a Native American, the book tells the story of Tayo, a World War II veteran, who tries to cope with the conflicts of his mixed-blood heritage.

Silko's short stories were beginning to appear during the early 1970's. She quickly gained a reputation as one of the leading writers in the Native American Renaissance—a literary movement that arose during the 1960's and featured works by Native American writers using tribal customs and traditions as literary material. Stories such as "Yellow Woman," in which a mortal is seemingly abducted by spiritual beings, and "Uncle Tony's Goat," which retells an old Laguna beast fable, are typical of Silko's handling of traditional indigenous material. One of her best stories, "Lullaby," treats the conflict of an elderly Navajo couple as they seek to come to terms with the dominant culture and how that conflict strengthens their traditional values.

A collection of Silko's autobiographical sketches, poems, family photographs, and short stories, *Storyteller* fuses literary and extraliterary material into a mosaic portrait of cultural heritage and of conflict between the two ethnic groups composing her heritage, the European American and the Native American. The title story, "Storyteller," presents that conflict from the point of view of a young Inuit woman who is fascinated with and repulsed by white civilization. Set in Alaska—the only major work of the author not in a Southwestern setting—the story follows her thoughts and observations as she spends her days amid these contrasting cultures. Silko's later publications have included *Gardens in the Dunes* (1999) and *Conversations with Leslie Marmon Silko* (2000).

Edward A. Fiorelli

FURTHER READING

Antel, Judith A. "Momaday, Welch, and Silko: Expressing the Feminine Principle Through Male Alienation." *American Indian Quarterly* 12, no. 3 (1988): 212-220.

Barnett, Louise K., and James L. Thorson, eds. *Leslie Marmon Silko: A Collection of Critical Essays.* Albuquerque: University of New Mexico Press, 1999.

Danielson, Linda. "Storyteller: Grandmother's Spider Web." *Journal of the Southwest* 30, no. 3 (1988): 325-355.

Hoilman, Dennis. "'A World Made of Stories': An Interpretation of Leslie Silko's *Ceremony.*" *South Dakota Review* 17, no. 4 (1979): 54-66.

Jaskoski, Helen. *Leslie Marmon Silko: A Study of the Short Fiction.* New York: Twayne, 1998.

Larson, Charles. *American Indian Fiction.* Albuquerque: University of New Mexico Press, 1978.

Lincoln, Kenneth. *Native American Renaissance.* Berkeley: University of California Press, 1983.

Rand, Naomi R. *Silko, Morrison, and Roth: Studies in Survival.* New York: Peter Lang, 1999.

Silverheels, Jay

Born: May 26, 1919; Six Nations Indian Reserve, Brantford, Ontario, Canada

Died: March 5, 1980; Woodland Hills, California

Also known as: Harry Smith, Harold J. Smith

Tribal affiliation: Mohawk

Significance: The foremost Indian actor of his era, Jay Silverheels helped other Indians become actors and worked to improve Indian images in Hollywood films.

Born Harry (Harold Jay) Smith on the Six Nations Indian Reserve in Canada, Silverheels became the most famous Indian actor in Hollywood between 1940 and 1970. He was one of ten children. His father, a farmer, was the most decorated Canadian Indian who fought in World War I. Silverheels was a superior athlete, participating in several sports, and he quit school when he was seventeen to play professional lacrosse in Toronto. He acquired the name Silverheels because he painted his lacrosse shoes silver and swiftly ran with his heels in the air, easily sidestepping opponents. Several years before his death, he legally changed his last name to Silverheels.

Comedian Joe E. Brown, who saw Silverheels play lacrosse, helped him become an actor in 1938. Silverheels performed as an extra in "B Westerns," frequently being shot off horses during battle scenes. During the 1940's, he acquired better roles and appeared in such films as *Captain from Castile* (1947), *Key Largo* (1948), and the classic *Broken Arrow* (1950). He made over thirty films and worked with such actors as Tyrone Power, Lee J. Cobb, Humphrey Bogart, Errol Flynn, Henry Fonda, James Stewart, and John Wayne.

Silverheels is best known for his role as Tonto in the television series

Jay Silverheels as Tonto in The Lone Ranger *television series.* (Hulton|Archive by Getty Images)

The Lone Ranger, appearing in 221 episodes between 1949 and 1957. Although he was still an example of Hollywood stereotyping, his character nevertheless possessed the wisdom and skill to save the Lone Ranger from life-threatening situations.

Later in his career, Silverheels continued to appear in television, films, and commercials. During the 1960's, he protested the way Indians were portrayed in films and founded the Indian Actors Guild and the Indian Actors Workshop. He also competed as a harness-racing driver. In 1979, Silverheels became the first Indian actor to have a star set in Hollywood's Walk of Fame. He died at the Motion Picture and Television Country House in 1980.

Sharon K. Wilson
Raymond Wilson

FURTHER READING

Kilpatrick, Jacquelyn. *Celluloid Indians: Native Americans and Film.* Lincoln: University of Nebraska Press, 1999.

Rollins, Peter C., and John E. O'Connor. *Hollywood's Indian: The Portrayal of the Native American in Film.* Expanded ed. Lexington: University Press of Kentucky, 2003.

Sitting Bull

Born: March, 1831; near the Grand River, Dakota Territory (now in South Dakota)
Died: December 15, 1890; Standing Rock Agency, South Dakota
Also known as: Tatanka Iyotanka, Slow
Tribal affiliation: Hunkpapa Lakota (Sioux)

Significance: Sitting Bull was one of the major Sioux tactical and spiritual leaders, perhaps equaled only by CRAZY HORSE, during their final struggles against confinement to reservations and white domination.

Sitting Bull (Tatanka Iyotanka) was probably born in March, 1831, a few
miles below the modern town of Bullhead, South Dakota. During his
first fourteen years, his Sioux friends called him Slow, a name he earned
because of his deliberate manner and the awkward movement of his
sturdy body. The youth grew to manhood as a member of the Hunkpapa
tribe, one of seven among the Teton Sioux, the westernmost division of
the Sioux Confederacy.

Sitting Bull's people thrived as a nomadic hunter-warrior society. As
an infant strapped to a baby board, he was carried by his mother as the
tribe roamed the northern plains hunting buffalo. At five years of age,
Slow rode behind his mother on her horse and helped as best he could
around the camp. By the age of ten, he was riding his own pony, wrapping his legs around the curved belly of the animal (a practice which
caused him to be slightly bowlegged for the remainder of his years).
Slow learned to hunt small game with bow and arrows and to gather berries. He reveled in the games and races, swimming and wrestling with
the other boys. It was an active and vigorous life, and Slow loved it.

As the boy grew older he learned more about the warrior dimension
of Sioux life. The Tetons concentrated most of their wrath on their
Crow and Assiniboine Indians. Sioux society centered on gaining prestige through heroic acts in battle. Counting coups by touching an enemy with a highly decorated stick was top priority. Slow had learned his
lessons well, and at the age of fourteen he joined a mounted war party
for the first time. He picked out one of the enemy and, with a burst of
enthusiasm and courage, he charged the rival warrior and struck him
with his coup stick. After the battle, word of this heroic deed spread
throughout the Hunkpapa village. The boy had reached a milestone in
his development; for the remainder of his life, he enjoyed telling the
story of his first coup. Around the campfire that night, his proud father,
JUMPING BULL, gave his son a new name. He called him Sitting Bull after
the beast that the Sioux respected so much for its tenacity. A buffalo bull
was the essence of strength, and a "sitting bull" was one that held his
ground and could not be pushed aside.

In 1857, Sitting Bull became a chief of the Hunkpapa. He had ably
demonstrated his abilities as a warrior, and his common sense and leadership traits showed promise of a bright future. While his physical appearance was commonplace, he was convincing in argument, stubborn,

An 1885 photograph of Sitting Bull. (Library of Congress)

and quick to grasp a situation. These traits gained for him the respect of his people as a warrior and as a statesman.

Sitting Bull's leadership qualities were often put to the test in his dealings with whites. During the 1860's, he skirmished with whites along the Powder River in Wyoming. He learned of their method of fighting, and he was impressed with their weapons. In 1867, white commissioners journeyed to Sioux country to forge a peace treaty. They hoped to gain Sioux agreement to limit their living area to present-day western South Dakota. While his Jesuit acquaintance Father Pierre De Smet worked to gain peace, Sitting Bull refused to give up his cherished hunting lands to the west and south and declined to sign the Fort Laramie Treaty of 1868. Other Sioux, however, made their marks on the "white man's paper," and the treaty became official.

Developments during the 1870's confirmed Sitting Bull's distrust of white people's motives. Railroad officials surveyed the northern plains in the early 1870's in preparation for building a transcontinental railroad that would disrupt Sioux hunting lands. In 1874, the army surveyed the Black Hills, part of the Great Sioux Reservation as set up by the treaty, and, in the next year, thousands of miners invaded this sacred part of the Sioux reserve when they learned of the discovery of gold there. The tree-covered hills and sparkling streams and lakes were the home of Sioux gods and a sacred place in the Sioux scheme of life. The whites had violated the treaty and disregarded the rights of the Sioux. Sitting Bull refused to remain on the assigned reservation any longer and led his followers west, into Montana, where there were still buffalo to hunt and the opportunity remained to live by the old traditions. As many other Sioux became disgruntled with white treatment, they, too, looked to Sitting Bull's camp to the west as a haven from the greedy whites. In this sense, he became the symbol of Sioux freedom and resistance to the whites, and his camp grew with increasing numbers of angry Sioux.

The showdown between Sioux and whites came in 1876. The U.S. government had ordered the Sioux to return to their reservation by February of 1876 or be forced to return. Few Indians abided by the order. The government therefore turned the "Sioux problem" over to the army with instructions to force all natives back to their agencies.

In the early summer of 1876, General Alfred H. Terry oversaw a major expedition against the Sioux. Sitting Bull had a premonition of things to come, dreaming of blue-clad men falling into his camp. Indeed, the Seventh Cavalry, under the command of George Armstrong Custer, attacked the Sioux camp on June 25, 1876, initiating the Battle of the Little Bighorn. There were additional cavalry forces in the area and on the way, but for the moment Custer's men were badly outnumbered. They had badly underestimated the numbers of Sioux and other Indians—there were probably about two thousand. Custer and his unit were surrounded and annihilated. The battle continued for another day as the Sioux fought forces under Major Marcus Reno and Captain

Frederick Benteen, then withdrew. Sitting Bull's leadership was crucial to the Indian victory over Custer, as was the work of others, including Crazy Horse and GALL.

The Sioux decided that it was time to leave the area and divide into smaller groups in order to avoid capture. Many additional soldiers were ordered into the northern plains, and they spent the remainder of the summer and fall chasing and harassing the fleeing Sioux. While other groups of Sioux eventually returned to their agencies, Sitting Bull led his people to Canada, where they resided until 1881. Even though the Canadian officials refused to feed the Sioux, the natives were able to subsist in their usual manner of hunting and gathering until 1881, when the buffalo were almost gone. Because of homesickness and a lack of food, Sitting Bull finally surrendered to U.S. officials, who kept him prisoner at Fort Randall for two years.

By 1883, Sitting Bull had returned to his people at the Standing Rock Agency in Dakota Territory. He soon became involved in activities that no one could have anticipated. In that year, the Northern Pacific Railroad sponsored a last great buffalo hunt for various dignitaries, and Sitting Bull participated. In the next year, he agreed to tour fifteen cities with Colonel Alvaren Allen's Western show. Sitting Bull was portrayed as the "Slayer of George Armstrong Custer," but he found this label inaccurate and distasteful. In 1885, Sitting Bull signed with Buffalo Bill Cody's Wild West Show and traveled in the eastern United States and Canada during the summer. He sold autographed photographs of himself and eventually gave away most of the money he made to poor white children who begged for money in order to eat. At the end of the season, the popular Buffalo Bill gave his Indian friend a gray circus horse and a large white sombrero as remembrances of their summer together.

During the latter part of the decade, Sitting Bull returned to Standing Rock, where he settled into reservation life. The Hunkpapa still cherished him as their leader, much to the dismay of agent James McLaughlin, who sought to break the old chief's hold over his people. McLaughlin and Sitting Bull clashed frequently. Sitting Bull was struggling to maintain the sense of nationhood and preserve the traditional values of the Lakota; the agent, backed by government policy, was systematically working to destroy the old ways and organizations and compel the Sioux to accept a new way of life and new values.

In 1890, WOVOKA, a Paiute prophet from Nevada, began to preach a message that many Indians prayed was true. He dreamed that he had died and gone to Heaven. There, he found all the deceased Indians, thousands of buffalo, and no whites. The Indian prophet taught that in order to achieve a return to the old ways of life, the Indians had only to dance the Ghost Dance regularly until the second coming of the Messiah, who would be in the form of an Indian. The Ghost Dance spread rapidly throughout much of the West, and soon Sioux were following Wovoka's teachings. Sitting Bull had his doubts about the new religion, but he realized that it disturbed the whites—and in particular agent McLaughlin—so he encouraged his people to dance.

The events that followed brought about the death of Sitting Bull as well as the military and psychological defeat of the Sioux. Worried Indian officials deplored the fact that the natives were dancing again. Sitting Bull, the symbol of the old culture, was still their leader, so McLaughlin decided to arrest him. He chose a number of Sioux who served in the agency police force to apprehend Sitting Bull. They came to his hut to seize him during the night of December 15, 1890, and a scuffle broke out. The fifty-nine-year-old chief was one of the first to be killed. In the dust and confusion of the struggle, fourteen others also died.

Two weeks later, other Sioux, who had left their reservation, were stopped at Wounded Knee Creek, and a fight broke out with the white soldiers who were trying to disarm them and force them back to the agency. This event is sometimes referred to as the "battle" of Wounded Knee, but it was truly a massacre, as the soldiers trained Hotchkiss guns (they could fire fifty rounds a minute) on the Sioux camp and killed the Sioux en masse, including women and children. When the shooting stopped on that cold December day, nearly two hundred Sioux had been killed, and the dream of a return to the old way of life was gone forever.

John W. Bailey

FURTHER READING

Adams, Alexander B. *Sitting Bull: An Epic of the Plains.* New York: G. P. Putnam's Sons, 1973.

Anderson, Gary Clayton. *Sitting Bull and the Paradox of Lakota Nationhood.* New York: HarperCollins, 1996.

Bailey, John W. *Pacifying the Plains: General Alfred Terry and the Decline of the Sioux, 1866-1890.* Westport, Conn.: Greenwood Press, 1979.

Johnson, Dorothy M. *Warrior for a Lost Nation: A Biography of Sitting Bull.* Philadelphia: Westminster Press, 1969.

Rosenberg, Marvin, and Dorothy Rosenberg. "There Are No Indians Left but Me." *American Heritage* 15 (June, 1964): 18-23.

Utley, Robert M. *The Lance and the Shield: The Life and Times of Sitting Bull.* New York: Ballantine Books, 1994.

Utley, Robert M. *The Last Days of the Sioux Nation.* New Haven, Conn.: Yale University Press, 1963.

Vestal, Stanley. *Sitting Bull: Champion of the Sioux, a Biography.* Boston: Houghton Mifflin, 1932. Rev. ed. Norman: University of Oklahoma Press, 1957.

Slocum, John

Born: 1830's; place unknown
Died: c. 1896; place unknown
Tribal affiliation: Northwest Salish
Significance: John Slocum founded the Indian Shaker Church.

John Slocum, a Skokomish (Coast Salish) man, was the founder of the Indian Shaker Church in the early 1880's. Previously, he had spent his adult years in gambling and drinking. Oral tradition, as recorded by many scholars who have studied the Shaker Church, recounts that in 1881 Slocum appeared to die. Then, in the presence of family and friends who had gathered to mourn his death, he awoke. He said that he had ascended to heaven and spoken to God. Slocum was told to return to Earth and start a movement that would save his people. Among other things, they were all to abstain from gambling and drinking.

Eventually Slocum himself resumed his old ways, however, and in a few years he experienced another bout of sickness and (in some accounts) another near-death. It was during this illness that his wife, Mary, underwent the shaking that was believed to have helped heal her husband. A belief in this type of healing then became an important element in the Shaker Church.

Daniel L. Smith-Christopher

FURTHER READING

Amoss, Pamela T. "The Indian Shaker Church." In *Northwest Coast,* edited by Wayne Suttles. Vol. 7 in *Handbook of North American Indians,* edited by William C. Sturtevant. Washington, D.C.: Smithsonian Institution Press, 1990.

Barnett, Homer G. *Indian Shakers: A Messianic Cult of the Pacific Northwest.* Carbondale: Southern Illinois University Press, 1957.

Ruby, Robert H., and John A. Brown. *John Slocum and the Indian Shaker Church.* Foreword by Richard A. Gould. Norman: University of Oklahoma Press, 1996.

Smohalla

Born: c. 1815; present-day Wallula, Washington
Died: c. 1907
Also known as: Smóqula (the Preacher), Smokeller, Waipshwa (Rock Carrier)
Tribal affiliation: Wanapam
Significance: Smohalla's teachings formed the basis of the Dreamer religion, which flourished among the tribes of the Pacific Northwest well into the twentieth century.

Smohalla (or Smóqula, "the Preacher") was one of a core of leaders among the Wanapam who resisted the United States' attempts to place them on reservations. This resistance culminated in the 1,500-mile Long March in 1877. He also was a spiritual leader who fused aspects of Christianity and native traditions into the Dreamer religion, which swept the northwestern United States before the better-known Ghost Dance of the Great Plains.

Early in his adult life Smohalla distinguished himself in battle, despite being a hunchback. He incurred the personal enmity of MOSES, leader of the neighboring Sinkiuses. The two men met in combat, after which Moses left Smohalla for dead. Smohalla was not dead, however; he made his way to a nearby river and floated downstream in a boat, beginning a journey that eventually took him down the Pacific Coast to Mexico, then back to Wanapam country through Arizona and other inland points.

Smohalla's reappearance among his people caused a degree of awe that was impressive for a spiritual leader. Smohalla came bearing teachings said to have been acquired on a visit to the Spirit World: that all native peoples should reject the whites' beliefs and artifices. He counseled native peoples to stay away from reservations and to restore traditional ways of life. The Dreamer religion included dances done in hypnotic rhythm to bells, drums, and other musical instruments.

Smohalla survived the Long March and lived until 1907. He was buried at the Satus graveyard in Washington State, and his nephew Puckhyahtoot (the Last Prophet) carried on his Dreamer religion.

Bruce E. Johansen

FURTHER READING
Ruby, Robert H., and John A. Brown. *Dreamer-Prophets of the Columbia Plateau: Smohalla and Skolaskin.* Foreword by Herman J. Viola. Norman: University of Oklahoma Press, 1989.

Snake, Reuben

Born: January 12, 1937; Winnebago Reservation, Nebraska
Died: June 28, 1993; Winnebago Reservation, Nebraska
Tribal affiliation: Winnebago
Significance: Reuben Snake served for twenty-eight years in Winnebago tribal government, first as a tribal council member, later as vice chairman and chairman, and later became president of the National Council of American Indians. He also was a lifelong member of the Native American Church and a pipe carrier who lectured to diverse audiences around the world.

Reuben Snake synthesized an extraordinary range of life experience into a personal force for commitment and consensus that served his Winnebago people, as well as Native Americans on a national and international level.

Snake began his adulthood as a member of the U.S. Army's elite Green Beret force during the mid-1950's. He was educated at Northwestern College in Orange City, Iowa; the University of Nebraska at Omaha; and Peru State College in Nebraska. Noted for humor that kept him in demand as a conference speaker, Snake often signed personal letters "Your humble serpent." He was active in efforts to broaden the scope of Native American religious freedom as well as tribal economic development.

Snake often used humor to drive home the point that Native American philosophy, especially the idea that all natural phenomena move in cycles and that all things are related, could help ameliorate the alienation of European people from nature. For example, during a speech he delivered at an event sponsored by the Lummi tribe in Seattle, Washington, in October, 1991, he proposed that every Indian "adopt two hundred and fifty white people. Bring them into the family. Teach them the right way to do things."

After Snake died from a heart attack and complications from diabetes in June, 1993, a report in *Indian Country Today* characterized him as "a warm-hearted bear of a man noted for his leadership in spiritual circles and the political arena," adding that he would be mourned by people across the United States who remembered "his booming voice, his ever-present wit, and his dauntless dedication to Indian people of many tribal nations." His strength lay in consensus building and conflict resolution. Susan Harjo, the director of the Morning Star Institution, said that Snake had a good way of bringing people to consensus and would see any negotiation through to the end, regardless of how long it took or how contentious the issue was.

Bruce E. Johansen

FURTHER READING
Little Eagle, Avis, and Jerry Reynolds. "Tribute to Reuben Snake: 'Humble Serpent' Journeys On." *Indian Country Today,* June 30, 1993.
Snake, Reuben. *Your Humble Serpent, as Told to Jay C. Fikes.* Santa Fe, N.Mex.: Clear Light, 1995.
Russo, Kurt, ed. *Our People, Our Land.* Bellingham, Wash.: Kluckhohn Center, 1992.

Spotted Tail

Born: c. 1823 or 1824; near present-day Pine Ridge, South Dakota
Died: August 5, 1881; Rosebud, South Dakota
Also known as: Sinte Gleska
Tribal affiliation: Brule Lakota (Sioux)
Significance: After a youth spent fighting whites, Spotted Tail came to advocate peace; he is widely considered one of the greatest Sioux leaders.

The name Spotted Tail is a result of a raccoon tail given to him while a young man by a white trapper. He wore this as a sacred object in his first battles, and after surviving, he took the name Spotted Tail.

Spotted Tail grew to be a warrior during wars with the Pawnee. In 1841, he selected a Brule girl for a wife who was also being courted by Running Bear (Mato Wakuwa), a Brule chief. They quarreled; Spotted Tail killed the chief and took the girl as his first wife. She bore him thirteen children.

At the September, 1855,

Spotted Tail. (National Archives)

battle of Bluewater Creek near modern Oshkosh, Nebraska, a severely wounded Spotted Tail fought a delaying action against advancing cavalry to allow the escape of women and children. Soon after, Spotted Tail was branded a murderer and his surrender demanded as a precondition to peace. On October 18, 1855, Spotted Tail surrendered to General William S. Harney at Fort Laramie, Wyoming. While a prisoner of war at Fort Leavenworth, Kansas, Spotted Tail came to realize that the number and power of whites were indeed frightening.

In 1870, Spotted Tail and RED CLOUD were invited to Washington to confer with President Ulysses S. Grant and other officials. While there, Spotted Tail did not lose the opportunity to scold the president over his failure to comply with the Laramie Treaty of 1868.

Throughout the plains war of 1876-1877, Spotted Tail remained the most popular spokesman of the Sioux people. In 1877, he was responsible for negotiating the final surrender of hostile Sioux bands at Fort Robinson, Nebraska. It was to Spotted Tail's camp at Rosebud, South Dakota, that his nephew CRAZY HORSE fled to avoid confrontation and arrest by General Crook.

Spotted Tail's last years were spent in advocating Brule social and economic needs. In June, 1880, he raided the Carlisle, Pennsylvania, Indian school and removed several Brule children, returning them to their parents in South Dakota. On August 5, 1881, Spotted Tail was shot and killed by CROW DOG, a political opponent. The Little Missouri Sioux winter count (record) for that year said, "This year that brave and wonderful chief was killed by Crow Dog." The Dakota court sentenced Crow Dog to hang. The case was appealed to the Supreme Court, however (*Ex parte Crow Dog*, 1883), and the Court concluded that state courts have no jurisdiction on Indian reservations. Crow Dog was released.

Burl E. Self

Spybuck, Ernest

Born: 1883; on the Potawatomi and Shawnee Reservation, Oklahoma Territory (now in Oklahoma)
Died: 1949; near Shawnee, Oklahoma
Also known as: Mahthela
Tribal affiliation: Shawnee
Significance: Ernest Spybuck was one of the first Native American artists of the twentieth century to create a narrative style of painting depicting tribal culture.

Spybuck began drawing and painting as a small child; he never received formal art training. His most frequent subjects were horses, cowboys, ranch scenes, roundups, Native American ceremonies, traditional dancers, and peyote scenes. His experience was limited to his hometown, and he was more than fifty years old before he traveled outside Pottawatomie County, where he was born.

Spybuck met M. R. Harrington of the Museum of the American Indian (Heye Foundation) in 1910 in Shawnee. The museum commissioned him to paint several works as an ethnographic series. He later did commissions for the Creek Council House and Museum in Okmulgee, Oklahoma, and the Oklahoma Historical Society Museum in Oklahoma City. In 1937, he participated in the American Indian Exposition and Congress in Tulsa.

Spybuck is known for genre painting that is illustrative of cultural life in the early twentieth century. He depicted clothing, housing, and activities in detail, portraying the acculturation between the Native American and white worlds. For indoor scenes he used a window technique to show what was happening inside a building or tipi. This also permitted him to show details such as the time of day and the season of the year to give a context to the ceremony or event represented.

Ronald J. Duncan

FURTHER READING
Penney, David. *North American Indian Art*. Foreword by George Horse Capture. New York: Thames & Hudson, 2004.

Squanto

Born: c. 1590; Patuxet (near present-day Plymouth Bay, Massachusetts)
Died: November, 1622; Chatham Harbor, Plymouth Colony (now Chatham, Massachusetts)
Also known as: Tisquantum
Tribal affiliation: Patuxet, Wampanoag
Significance: Squanto helped the first English settlers survive in America. Many a schoolchild has heard, around Thanksgiving each year, the saga of Squanto, the New England Indian who, according to the traditional account, helped the forlorn pilgrims stave off starvation by teaching them how to grow corn by fertilizing it with dead fish. For many indigenous activists, Squanto's magnanimous gesture represents one more example of the uncredited or thankless role indigenous peoples played in

furthering European American civilization in the Americas. Recently, however, historians have cast doubt on the origin of Squanto's agricultural knowledge. One argues rather convincingly that such fertilization techniques were unknown to indigenous people in New England and that Squanto learned the custom from the English in Newfoundland.

That irony aside, Squanto did play an important role in the first few years of English settlement in Plymouth. A member of the Patuxet tribe in eastern Massachusetts, Squanto was among twenty individuals that Thomas Hunt, a member of John Smith's 1614 expedition, captured for sale as slaves. Hunt took Squanto to Spain but was unable to sell his slave candidates. Somehow Squanto made his way to London, where he lived at the home of John Slany, treasurer of the Newfoundland Company, and endeared himself to English entrepreneurs, who saw Squanto as a valuable tool for establishing friendships back in Massachusetts. With his fluency in English and knowledge of European and indigenous customs alike, Squanto would make the ideal ambassador.

In 1619, Squanto returned to New England and proceeded to help the English win the trust of the Nemasket and Pokanoket tribes. In an attack on Martha's Vineyard, Squanto was captured again, but he apparently returned to the Pokanoket around present-day Narragansett Bay. In March, 1621, Squanto was instrumental in helping the Pokanoket and Plymouth English set up a treaty. Squanto then lived among the pilgrims and acted as a diplomat and interpreter. He also helped in obtaining seed corn and teaching planting techniques. Behind the scenes, however, Squanto tried to put the epidemic-ravaged remnants of his Patuxet tribe back together, incurring some English wrath. The pilgrims still protected him, because they could play him off against the Pokanoket (also known as the Wampanoag) chief, Massasoit. The next summer, 1622, Squanto died, and the English found themselves without the services of this capable man.

In 1994 the Disney Company released a popular feature film titled *Squanto: A Warrior's Tale* that offered a highly embellished account of Squanto's experiences in Europe. The Canadian-born actor Adam BEACH played Squanto.

Thomas L. Altherr

FURTHER READING
Brandon, William. *The Rise and Fall of North American Indians.* New York: Taylor Trade Publications, 2003. The chapter titled "Puritans and Indians" establishes Squanto's role in the complex relationships between the English and the Native Americans.

Hoxie, Frederick, ed. *Encyclopedia of North American Indians.* Boston: Houghton Mifflin, 1996. Includes the best researched and likely the most accurate account of Squanto. Covers all that is known of his 1614 capture and the next five years.

Sweet, David, and Gary Nash, eds. *Struggle and Survival in Colonial America.* Berkeley: University of California Press, 1981. Neal Salisbury's chapter, "Squanto, Last of the Patuxets," is an excellent essay on Squanto in the overall context of the colonial confrontations between Native Americans and the European immigrants.

Standing Bear

Born: c. 1829; place unknown
Died: September, 1908; on Niobrara River, Nebraska
Also known as: Mochunozhin
Tribal affiliation: Ponca
Significance: The civil rights case *Standing Bear v. Crook* rendered the decision that an Indian was a person within the meaning of U.S. law.

An 1858 treaty guaranteed the Ponca people a permanent home on the land of their ancestral Niobrara River in Nebraska. An 1868 treaty, however, established boundaries for the Sioux people that included the Ponca land. In 1875, the government agreed to rectify the error, but instead of returning the land, they appropriated money to compensate for the Sioux attacks and removed the Ponca to Indian Territory (Oklahoma). In 1879, Standing Bear and some thirty followers walked forty days to traverse the five hundred miles to the Omaha (Nebraska) Reservation.

General George Crook's garrison returned the Ponca people to Oklahoma. The return journey of fifty days and the following year on the Quapaw Reservation claimed the lives of nearly a fourth of the five hundred Poncas. Among the dead were Standing Bear's children. In January of 1879, desiring to bury his son on traditional Ponca land, Standing Bear and sixty-six followers set out for the Niobrara. When Standing Bear reached the Omaha Reservation, he was placed under guard by Crook, who was to return the Ponca to Indian Territory. Several attorneys, members of the public, and newspaper correspondent Thomas H. Tibbles protested the treatment of the Ponca people.

Attorneys A. J. Poppleton and John L. Webster served Crook with a writ of *habeas corpus* to determine by what authority he was holding the group. The U.S. attorney countered that the Indian peoples had no right to *habeas corpus* because they were not "persons within the meaning of the law." On April 18, 1879, Judge E. S. Dundy rendered the famous decision in the *Standing Bear v. Crook* case: An Indian was a person within the meaning of the law of the United States, and no authority existed for removing any of the prisoners to Indian Territory during time of peace. Standing Bear's speech climaxed the trial: "My hand is not the same color as yours, but if you pierce it, I shall feel the pain. The blood will be the same color. We are men, the same God made us. . . . All I ask is what is mine—my land, my freedom, my dignity as a man." To prevent other tribal peoples from using the decision as precedent to leave other reservations, the commissioner of Indian affairs ruled that Dundy's decision applied only to Standing Bear and his people.

In the winter of 1879-1880, Standing Bear toured the East with correspondent Tibbles and interpreters Francis and Susette La Flesche. His message was one of nonviolent resistance and justice. Although the government finally appropriated funds to the Ponca people, those in Indian Territory were never allowed to return to the Niobrara.

Tonya Huber

Further Reading

Dando-Collins, Stephen. *Standing Bear Is a Person: The True Story of a Native American's Quest for Justice.* Cambridge, Mass.: Da Capo Press, 2004.

Mathes, Valerie Sherer, and Richard Lowitt. *The Standing Bear Controversy: Prelude to Indian Reform.* Urbana: University of Illinois Press, 2003.

Standing Bear, Luther

Born: c. 1868; Pine Ridge, South Dakota
Died: February 19, 1939; Huntington Park, California
Also known as: Plenty Kill
Tribal affiliation: Oglala Lakota (Sioux)
Significance: The author of four books, Luther Standing Bear was one of the few early twentieth century Indians to provide accounts of the transition from the old ways to reservation life and to offer a firsthand account of Sioux history and traditions.

Born to a man who was probably a Brule band leader, Luther Standing Bear described himself nonetheless as an Oglala Sioux. According to his own account, Plenty Kill—as he was named as a child—grew up in the traditional Sioux manner at a time when the old life was being de-

Luther Standing Bear. (Library of Congress)

stroyed by white settlers and the U.S. cavalry. In 1879 he entered the Carlisle Indian School in Pennsylvania, where he was given the name Standing Bear and where he got his only formal education. In 1902 Standing Bear traveled with Buffalo Bill's Wild West Show, performing in the United States and England. He later moved to California, where he lectured and acted.

In 1928, Standing Bear published his first book, *My People, the Sioux*, primarily an autobiography highlighting his youth, Carlisle years, the Ghost Dance, and Wild West Show experiences. *My Indian Boyhood* (1931), written for an adolescent audience, is also autobiographical. *Land of the Spotted Eagle* (1933), perhaps his most important book, is an ethnographic description of traditional Sioux life and customs, criticizing whites' efforts to "make over" the Indian into the likeness of the white race. Standing Bear also collected versions of his tribe's tales and legends, publishing them in *Stories of the Sioux* (1934). In an essay written for the *American Mercury*, Standing Bear argues that loss of faith has left a void in Indian life and that the white man would do well to grasp some of the Indian's spiritual strength.

Lee Schweninger

FURTHER READING

Moses, L. G., and Raymond Wilson, eds. *Indian Lives: Essays on Nineteenth and Twentieth Century Native American Leaders.* Albuquerque: University of New Mexico Press, 1985.

Standing Bear, Luther. *Land of the Spotted Eagle.* Reprint. Lincoln: University of Nebraska Press, 1978.

Studi, Wes

Born: December 17, 1947; Nofire Hollow, Oklahoma
Also known as: Wesley Studie
Tribal affiliation: Cherokee
Significance: As a prominent film actor, Wes Studi has strived to portray
    Native American characters with poignance and authenticity.

Born Wesley Studie in rural Oklahoma, Wes Studi is the eldest of four
sons of Andy Studie—a ranch hand—and Maggie Studie—a house-
keeper. Before he started school, he could speak only Cherokee. He attended a boarding school located in Chilocco, Oklahoma. In 1967 he
was drafted into the U.S. Army and sent to fight in Vietnam, where he
served for eighteen months. Traumatized by his Vietnam War experi-

Wes Studi (right) with fellow cast member James McDaniel at the premier of the film
Edge of America *during the 2004 Sundance Film Festival in Salt Lake City, Utah.*
(AP/Wide World Photos)

ences, Studi returned to the United States unsure of what he should do next. Eventually he took advantage of the G.I. Bill and enrolled in Tulsa Junior College.

In 1972, Studi participated in the Trail of Broken Treaties protest in Washington, D.C. During this protest, he and other participants briefly occupied the Bureau of Indian Affairs building. Afterward, Studi continued to be active in Native American issues, and he was arrested at the 1973 protest at Wounded Knee, South Dakota. He was released from jail on the condition that he leave the state of South Dakota. By 1974, Studi was married to his second wife, Rebecca Graves, and working as a reporter for the *Tulsa Indian Times*. After divorcing Graves in 1982, Studi became a member of Tulsa's American Indian Theater Company.

During the late 1980's, Studi finally recognized that he had a passion for acting. After appearing in the 1988 Public Broadcasting System (PBS) production of *The Trial of Standing Bear*, he decided that it was time to move to Los Angeles so he could work as a full-time actor. He initially struggled to get roles but appeared in occasional commercials and was chosen for a small role in Kevin Costner's award-winning 1990 film *Dances with Wolves*. In 1992, he appeared as the vengeful Magua in the remake of *The Last of the Mohicans*. After receiving glowing reviews for his performance in that film, he was then given the opportunity to star as Geronimo in the 1993 film *Geronimo: An American Legend*. For that role, he studied the Apache language and did extensive background research.

By the mid-1990's, Studi was established as a respected actor who could be counted on to deliver strong performances in a variety of roles. Films showcasing his most memorable performances of this period include *Heat* (1995), *Crazy Horse* (1996), and *Deep Rising* (1998). In 2002-2003, he costarred with Adam Beach in the PBS adaptations of Tony Hillerman's Navajo mysteries *Skinwalkers*, *Coyote Waits*, and *A Thief of Time*. In addition to being an acclaimed actor, Studi is a sculptor and the author of several children's books.

Jeffry Jensen

Stumbling Bear

Born: c. 1832
Died: 1903; Fort Sill, Indian Territory (now in Oklahoma)
Also known as: Setimkia (Charging Bear)
Tribal affiliation: Kiowa

Significance: Initially a fierce warrior, Stumbling Bear embraced peace after signing the Medicine Lodge Treaty in 1867.

As a young man, Stumbling Bear was an important war chief. Along with his cousin KICKING BIRD, SATANTA, and SATANK, Stumbling Bear participated in Kiowa raids against Pawnees, Navajos, Sauks, and Foxes as well as whites. Against Colonel Christopher "Kit" Carson at the first Battle of Adobe Walls in 1864, Stumbling Bear was principal war chief.

During negotiations for the Treaty of Medicine Lodge in 1867, establishing reservations in Kansas, Stumbling Bear was the primary Kiowa spokesman. Upon signing the treaty, he abandoned hostilities and thereafter advocated accommodation with whites. During the Kiowa, Comanche, and Cheyenne uprising known as the Red River War, from 1874 to 1875, he called for peace—opposing the Kiowa war leader LONE WOLF. In 1872, Stumbling Bear and Kicking Bird were the major Kiowa representatives during negotiations in Washington, D.C. In appreciation of his services, the U.S. government, in 1878, built a home for him in Indian Territory.

Mary E. Virginia

Sweezy, Carl

Born: c. 1879; near Darlington, Oklahoma Territory (now in Oklahoma)
Died: May 28, 1953; Lawton, Oklahoma
Also known as: Wattan (Black)
Tribal affiliation: Arapaho
Significance: Carl Sweezy was one of the earliest to use the Native American narrative genre style of painting, and he developed it beyond ledger-book-style drawings.

Sweezy began drawing as a child and learned to do watercoloring in school. At the age of twenty, he became an informant for James Mooney, an anthropologist of the Smithsonian Institution, when the latter did a study of the Cheyenne and Arapaho. Mooney needed an artist to restore paint on old shields and to copy designs, and Sweezy did that for him. Mooney liked his work and encouraged him to continue his "Indian" style of painting. Although Sweezy's most prolific period was while he worked with Mooney, he continued painting the remainder of his life and retired in 1920 to dedicate himself completely to painting.

Sweezy's paintings are important ethnographically and represent important values. He portrayed such themes as hunting buffalo, riding horseback, the defeat of George Armstrong Custer, ceremonies, and portraits, including details of costumes. His paintings of the Sun Dance are some of the best early visual documentation of that ceremony, and his portraits give details of dress and ritual paraphernalia. His work has been included in many exhibitions, and it is included in the collections of the National Museum of the American Indian, the University of Oklahoma Museum of Art, and the Oklahoma Historical Society Museum, among others.

Ronald J. Duncan

Swimmer

Born: c. 1835
Died: March, 1899; Qualla Boundary, North Carolina
Also known as: Ayunini
Tribal affiliation: Cherokee
Significance: A storyteller and a doctor, Swimmer gained renown by relating hundreds of Cherokee stories and songs that anthropologist James Mooney later published.

Swimmer was born in the Big Cove community of the Cherokees' Qualla Reservation in North Carolina shortly before the federal government forced most Cherokees to relocate to what is now Oklahoma. He grew up under the tutelage of traditionalists. Raised to be a priest, a doctor, and a keeper of the traditions, he eventually was recognized as the regional authority among the Cherokee. Without his presence and active assistance, no tribal functions, including green-corn dances and ball games, could take place. He lived during the crucial years of the Eastern Band of Cherokee's formation during the late nineteenth century and became legendary as an expert on Cherokee traditions.

During the Civil War, when Swimmer was in his late twenties, he served in the Confederate Army in the North Carolina Highland Brigade commanded by Colonel William Holland Thomas. This unit consisted of both Cherokee and white soldiers. At the beginning of their service, the Cherokee soldiers performed rituals, which included consulting an oracle stone to learn their fate, and participated in a traditional war dance.

In 1887, Swimmer worked with the ethnologist James Mooney of the Smithsonian Institution to record hundreds of Cherokee stories. Swimmer was the principal source for the records on the Cherokees that Mooney created for the Bureau of American Ethnology and published in collections of sacred Cherokee formulas, old prayers, songs, and medicinal prescriptions for many diseases.

Swimmer's Cherokee songs dealt with such themes as love charms, hunting and fishing charms, bad dreams, herb gathering, divinations, preparations for medicines, and other subjects. Many hunters paid him five dollars each to learn his hunting songs, in the belief that no animal could be killed without them. Swimmer's Cherokee prayers touched on such themes as assistance to warriors, success in ball games, having influence in councils, driving away storms, and growing corn. Swimmer's original manuscript was a 240-page book, half filled with handwritten notes in the Cherokee language. Mooney asked to have this book copied and then purchased it from Swimmer.

Mooney wanted to record Cherokee lore when he realized that tribal traditions were vanishing before the spread of Christianity and Western culture. Swimmer agreed to permit the Cherokee songs to be written down in order to preserve them for future generations. He therefore set on his mission to preserve the history, lore, and rituals before they were to entirely disappear.

Swimmer never learned to speak English and earnestly held onto his Cherokee language and traditions. Up to the time of his death in 1899, he continued to wear the moccasins, turban, and rattle that were recognized as his badges of tribal authority. He was buried in the traditional Cherokee fashion, along the slope of a forested mountain. With his passing, many Cherokee traditions were no longer practiced, but they survived in the records that he helped to create.

Teresa Neva Tate

FURTHER READING

Mooney, James. *Myths of the Cherokee.* 1902. Ashville, N.C.: Historical Images, 1992.

_____. *The Sacred Formulas of the Cherokee.* (Smithsonian Institution. Extract from the seventh annual report of the Bureau of American Ethnology), Washington, 1891.

_____. *The Swimmer Manuscript: Cherokee Sacred Formulas and Medicinal Prescriptions* (Bulletin 99). Washington, D.C.: Smithsonian Institution, Bureau of American Ethnology, 1932.

Sword, George

Born: c. 1847; present-day western South Dakota
Died: c. 1910; Pine Ridge Reservation, South Dakota
Also known as: Miwakan
Tribal affiliation: Oglala Lakota (Sioux)
Significance: George Sword was an important Oglala political and religious leader who aided his people's transition to reservation life and who helped record information on traditional Lakota social and religious life for posterity.

A member of the Oglala branch of the Lakota or Teton Sioux, George Sword (Miwakan) was born around 1847 in what is now western South Dakota. As a boy, he distinguished himself in buffalo hunting and warfare—the two most important activities of Lakota men before they were put on reservations. While he was still a young man, the members of Sword's camp appointed him to serve as one of their magistrates (*wakiconze*). As he matured, he also acquired the spiritual powers of a holy man (*wicasa wakan*) and a medicine man (*pejuta wicasa*). Of his healing abilities, Sword once declared that he knew all the old customs of his people and had conducted all their traditional ceremonies, including the Sun Dance, which he regarded as the greatest ceremony of the Lakotas.

During the last third of the nineteenth century, as more and more white settlers sought to establish homesteads on Plains Indian lands, the U.S. government increasingly pressured the Oglalas and other Lakota tribes to cede portions of their land and to relocate on reservations. Because of the high esteem in which Sword was held by his people, they chose him to be one of their representatives in several Lakota treaty delegations to Washington, D.C., and other eastern cities. One of the lasting impressions that these journeys made upon him was the apparent inevitability of white conquest of the Lakota. He went to Washington and other large cities, he said, and that showed him "that the white people dug in the ground and built houses that could not be moved. Then I knew that when they came they could not be driven away."

Sword's pessimistic forecast prompted him to submit to the federal government's reservation-based assimilation policy and to encourage other Lakotas to do likewise. As part of this strategy, in 1878, he accepted a commission as the captain of the Pine Ridge Reservation's Indian police and remained on the force until, as he stated, "Oglalas ceased to think of fighting the white people." Soon after his retirement, he served as a judge on the reservation's Court of Indian Offenses and later was ordained an Episcopal deacon.

Sword seems to have fully realized that reservation life would spell the end for many aspects of traditional Lakota life. In spite of this, however, he sought to preserve for future generations as much information about Lakota customs as possible. His most notable contribution to that end lay in helping the physician-anthropologist James R. Walker collect esoteric information about Lakota religious and social customs. Sword also served as one of Walker's principal informants, instructing the latter on the subtleties of Lakota metaphysics and language.

Sword's decision to submit to the federal government's assimilation policy did not undermine his Lakota identity. He acted in conformity with the traditional Lakota value that leaders utilize their talents for the welfare of their communities, so his roles as agency policeman, judge, and deacon, were practical transformations of his earlier roles as warrior, magistrate, and holy man. At the most fundamental level, Sword thus remained Lakota.

Harvey Markowitz

Tall Bull

Born: c. 1830
Died: July 11, 1869; Summit Springs Battlefield, Colorado
Also known as: Hotóakhihoois, Hotúaeka'ash Tait, Otóah-hastis
Tribal affiliation: Central Cheyenne
Significance: Tall Bull, the most noted Dog Soldier chief and leader, featured prominently in the Great Plains of the late 1860's.

When the famous treaty council met at Medicine Lodge Creek, in southern Kansas, in October, 1867, Tall Bull played a major role. He was one of the first Cheyenne leaders to visit the commission camp. Tall Bull declared at the council that the Cheyenne did not want war and had never done the whites harm.

In September of 1868, Tall Bull was with ROMAN NOSE in the fateful Beecher Island battle. He is reportedly the one who warned Roman Nose of the need for a purification ritual. Roman Nose was killed in the battle.

When George Armstrong Custer's troops destroyed BLACK KETTLE's village of so-called friendly Cheyennes on the Washita River the following year, Tall Bull led 165 lodges of Dog Soldiers and their families to establish a village on the Republican River. The village was attacked in the spring of 1869 by Major Eugene Carr, and twenty-five of Tall Bull's five hundred warriors were killed. During the retaliation that ensued, Tall Bull was killed by the commander of Carr's Pawnee scouts, Major Frank North, near Summit Springs in northeastern Colorado. Tall Bull's wife and six-year-old daughter were taken prisoner. The Battle of Summit Springs marked the end of the Dog Soldiers' power on the Great Plains.

Tonya Huber

Tallchief, Maria

Born: January 24, 1925; Fairfax, Oklahoma
Also known as: Ki-he-kah-stah (the Tall Chiefs)
Tribal affiliation: Osage (Wazhazhe)
Significance: A prima ballerina of the New York City Ballet for fifteen years, Maria Tallchief symbolized American ballet for an entire generation of theater and television audiences.

Elizabeth Marie (Betty Marie) Tall Chief was born on January 24, 1925, in Fairfax, Oklahoma, a small community on the Osage Indian Reservation. Oil discovered on the reservation—and the tribal leaders' insistence on holding their mineral rights in common—had made the Osage the wealthiest tribe in the United States. Betty Marie's father, Alexander Tall Chief, a full-blooded Osage, was a well-to-do real estate executive whose grandfather, Chief Peter Big Heart, had negotiated the tribe's land agreements with the federal government. Her mother, Ruth Porter Tall Chief, came from Irish, Scottish, and Dutch ancestry. Her paternal grandmother, Eliza Big Heart Tall Chief, often took young Betty Marie to secret tribal dance ceremonies (the government had outlawed these "pagan" rituals at the turn of the century), but it was Ruth Tall Chief's culture and ambitions that ultimately prevailed. Betty Marie began taking piano and ballet lessons at the age of three; by the time she started school, she was performing before nearly every civic organization in Osage County.

Concerned about the lack of educational and artistic opportunities on the reservation, Ruth Tall Chief persuaded her easygoing husband to move the family to Beverly Hills, California, in 1933. There, Betty Marie began a rigorous program of piano lessons and ballet classes, the latter taught by Ernest Belcher (whose talented daughter Marge would later team up with dancer/choreographer Gower Champion). Ruth Tall Chief was determined to groom her daughter for a career as a concert pianist, but it was dance that captivated both Betty Marie and her younger sister Marjorie. In 1938, Betty Marie and Marjorie began inten-

Maria Tallchief receives the National Medal of Art from President Bill Clinton in 1999. (AP/Wide World Photos)

sive training with David Lichine, Lichine's prima ballerina wife Tatiana Riabouchinska, and Bronisława Nijinska. Sister of the legendary dancer Vaslav Nijinsky, Nijinska was one of the foremost ballet teachers and choreographers in the United States. Both Tall Chief sisters impressed Nijinska, who cast them in her ballet *Chopin Concerto*, which was performed at the Hollywood Bowl in 1940.

After her graduation from Beverly Hills High School in 1942, Betty Marie Tall Chief made her professional debut with the New York-based Ballet Russe de Monte Carlo, one of the two leading ballet companies in the country at that time. Early in her five-year association with Ballet Russe, Betty Marie Europeanized her name to Maria Tallchief. Advancing rapidly from the corps de ballet to solo parts, she attracted favorable critical notice in a variety of classical productions, including Nijinska's *Chopin Concerto* in 1943 and, in 1944, Michel Fokine's *Schéhérazade* and George Balanchine's *Bourgeois Gentilhomme* and *Danse Concertante*. By 1946, Tallchief's repertoire also included principal roles in Leonid Massine's *Gaîté Parisienne* and two more Balanchine ballets.

Balanchine's brief stint as ballet master with the Ballet Russe (1944-1946) marked a turning point in Tallchief's career. Trained in the Russian Imperial School of Ballet, Balanchine was one of the most brilliant choreographers and teachers of the twentieth century. He quickly recognized the young dancer's potential, made Tallchief his protégée, and created roles designed to exploit her strength, agility, and great technical proficiency. On August 16, 1946, Tallchief was married to the forty-two-year-old Balanchine. The following spring, she made her European debut with the Paris Opera, where her husband was guest choreographer. When she returned to the United States, Tallchief joined Balanchine's new company, the Ballet Society, which in 1948 became the New York City Ballet (NYCB).

From 1947 to 1965, Tallchief was the prima ballerina of the NYCB and created roles in most of Balanchine's repertoire. Two of these roles were destined to become classics of the ballet theater. In 1949, composer Igor Stravinsky revised his score especially for Balanchine's new version of *The Firebird*, with Tallchief in the title role. Her electrifying performance as the mythical bird-woman dazzled critics and audiences alike; for the rest of her career, she would be more closely identified with this role than with any other. In 1954, Balanchine choreographed the NYCB's most popular and financially successful production, a full-length version of Peter Ilich Tchaikovsky's *The Nutcracker*, with Tallchief as the Sugar Plum Fairy.

During the 1950's and early 1960's, Tallchief reached the pinnacle of her success. She toured Europe and Asia with the NYCB, accepted guest engagements with other ballet companies, and gave numerous television performances. She played the famous Russian ballerina Anna Pavlova in a 1953 film, *Million Dollar Mermaid*, dancing the Dying Swan role from Balanchine's version of *Swan Lake*. Among the many honors awarded her, none pleased her more than those conferred by her home state: June 29, 1953, was declared Maria Tallchief Day by the Oklahoma State Senate, and the Osage Nation staged a special celebration during which she was made a princess of the tribe and was given the name Waxthe-Thonba, Woman of Two Standards. A triumphal tour of Russia in 1960 cemented her international stardom. Tallchief resigned from the NYCB in 1965 and retired from the stage a year later.

Tallchief's marriage to Balanchine (though not her friendship or their professional association) was annulled in 1952 on the grounds that he did not want children. By her own admission, their age difference and his obsession with Tallchief the artist rather than the woman doomed their marital relationship. A brief second marriage to airline pilot Elmourza Natirboff ended in divorce in 1954 when Natirboff insisted that she give up her career. In June, 1956, Tallchief was married to Henry D. Paschen, a Chicago construction company executive who accepted her career ambitions. She gave birth to their only child, Elise Maria, in 1959. Retirement in 1966 allowed Tallchief to settle permanently in Chicago with her husband and daughter.

During the 1970's and 1980's, Tallchief brought to the Chicago artistic world the same energy and determination that had characterized her own dancing. In 1974, she formed the Ballet School of the Lyric Opera. When financial problems forced the elimination of ballet from the Opera's budget, Tallchief engineered, in 1980, the creation of the Chicago City Ballet (CCB), using $100,000 in seed money from the state of Illinois and a building donated by her husband. Tallchief became artistic codirector (with Paul Mejia) of the new ballet company. Following the demise of the CCB in 1988, Tallchief returned to the Lyric Opera to direct its ballet activities. In 1989, she appeared in *Dancing for Mr. B.: Six Balanchine Ballerinas*, a documentary film for PBS.

Despite her assimilation into European-American culture, Tallchief remained proud of her American Indian heritage. In 1967, she received the Indian Council of Fire Achievement Award and was named to the Oklahoma Hall of Fame. A longtime member of the Association on American Indian Affairs, she frequently spoke to American Indian groups about Indians and the arts, and she participated in university programs to educate students about the first Americans. In 1991, Maria Tallchief became a charter member of the Honorary Committee of the National Campaign of the National Museum of the American Indian, whose members raised funds to assist the Smithsonian Institution in building the new museum on the National Mall in Washington, D.C. In 1997, Tallchief published her autobiography, *Maria Tallchief: America's Prima Ballerina*.

Constance B. Rynder

FURTHER READING

Gruen, John. *Erik Bruhn: Danseur Noble*. New York: Viking Press, 1979.

_____. "Tallchief and the Chicago City Ballet." *Dance Magazine* (December, 1984): HC25-HC27.

Hardy, Camille. "Chicago's Soaring City Ballet." *Dance Magazine* (April, 1982): 70-76.

Kufrin, Joan. *Uncommon Women: Gwendolyn Brooks, Sarah Caldwell, Julie Harris, Mary McCarthy, Alice Neel, Roberta Peters, Maria Tallchief, Marylou Williams, Evgenia Zukerman*. Piscataway, N.J.: New Century, 1981.

Livingston, Lili Cockerille. *American Indian Ballerinas*. Norman: University of Oklahoma Press, 1997.

Mason, Francis. *I Remember Balanchine: Recollections of the Ballet Master by Those Who Knew Him*. New York: Doubleday, 1991.

Maynard, Olga. *Bird of Fire: The Story of Maria Tallchief.* New York: Dodd, Mead, 1961.

Myers, Elisabeth. *Maria Tallchief: America's Prima Ballerina.* New York: Grosset & Dunlap, 1966.

Tallchief, Maria, with Larry Kaplan. *Maria Tallchief: America's Prima Ballerina.* New York: Henry Holt, 1997.

Tammany

Born: c. 1625; place unknown (probably present-day Pennsylvania)
Died: c. 1701; place unknown (probably present-day Pennsylvania)
Also known as: Tamanend (the Affable)
Tribal affiliation: Lenni Lenape (Delaware)
Significance: Tammany sold the Delawares' homeland to William Penn, who dubbed the land "Pennsylvania."

Tammany was a seventeenth century Unami Delaware (Lenni Lenape) leader. Little is known for certain about his life; fact and legend are probably inextricably linked. It is said that he greeted William Penn when Penn arrived in Pennsylvania. Tammany's name appears on two 1683 treaties (one of which sold to William Penn the land between Neshaminy and Pennypack creeks) and on another signed in 1697. Tammany was apparently friendly toward whites throughout his life, and the white settlers respected him. Well after his death, a number of societies during the American Revolution (and after) were named for Tammany (nicknamed "Saint Tammany"), who came to symbolize resistance to British colonial rule. The Society of St. Tammany, founded in New York in 1789, eventually evolved into the Democratic Party organization in New York.

Tonya Huber

Tapahonso, Luci

Born: 1953; Shiprock, New Mexico
Tribal affiliation: Navajo
Significance: Luci Tapahonso is a respected contemporary poet who has also pursued a career as an English professor, specializing in Native American literature.

Luci Tapahonso was born and raised on a farm in New Mexico, and her poetry reflects the issues and images of Navajo life in the Southwest.

While an undergraduate at the University of New Mexico, she was introduced to Laguna Pueblo author Leslie Marmon Sɪʟᴋᴏ, who encouraged Tapahonso to pursue her interests in creative writing. Tapahonso received a bachelor's degree in 1980 and a master's degree in 1983 from the University of New Mexico. She then taught at the University of New Mexico and moved to the University of Kansas in 1990.

As Tapahonso's career has developed, she has published widely, edited anthologies and journals, and produced volumes of poetry that are critically acclaimed and frequently taught on college campuses. Her publications include *One More Shiprock Night* (1981), *Seasonal Woman* (1982), *A Breeze Swept Through* (1987), *Saanii Dahataal: The Women Are Singing* (1993), *A Song for the Direction of North* (1994), *Bah and Her Baby Brother* (1994), *Hayoolkaal: Dawn—An Anthology of Navajo Writers* (1995), *Navajo ABC* (1995), and *Blue Horses Rush In* (1997). Beginning with *Saanii Dahataal*, Tapahonso's interest in Navajo culture, and especially in the Navajo language, became clearly evident. Although, as of the 1990's, she lived most of the year in Kansas, her poetry testifies to the affinity she feels for the northern Arizona and northern New Mexico homeland of her Navajo people.

Richard Sax

Fᴜʀᴛʜᴇʀ Rᴇᴀᴅɪɴɢ
Balassi, William, John F. Crawford, and Annie O. Eysturoy. *This Is About Vision: Interviews with Southwestern Writers.* Albuquerque: University of New Mexico Press, 1990.
Rader, Dean. "Luci Tapahonso and Simon Ortiz: Allegory, Symbol, Language, Poetry." *Southwestern American Literature* 22, no. 2 (Spring, 1997).

Tarhe

Born: 1742; near Detroit, Michigan
Died: November, 1818; Crane Town, near present-day Upper Sandusky, Ohio
Also known as: Crane, Le Chef Grue, Monsieur Grue
Tribal affiliation: Wyandot (Huron)
Significance: Although he initially resisted westward white settlement, Tarhe became an ally of the Americans during the War of 1812.

Tarhe was a shaman and chief of the Ohio Hurons known as the Wyandot. In his youth, he vigorously resisted American encroachment on western lands, fighting beside Shawnee leader CORNSTALK against the whites during Lord Dunmore's War in 1774. At the Battle of Fallen Timbers, during LITTLE TURTLE's War (1790-1794), he was one of thirteen chiefs who fought against the American General "Mad" Anthony Wayne. After being abandoned by their British allies, the Indians suffered devastating losses. Subsequently Tarhe acknowledged white military superiority and was a principal supporter of the Treaty of Greenville (1795), as a result of which Indians were forced from their lands. He was thereafter an ally of the Americans.

Tarhe, along with his close friend, Shawnee Leader CATAHECASSA, refused to join TECUMSEH in his attempts to organize a pan-Indian resistance to whites. During the War of 1812, Tarhe led his warriors in several battles against the British and earned the admiration of William Henry Harrison. Although he counseled accommodation, Tarhe was respected by most Indians in the Northwest Territory. His funeral was attended by many notable Indian leaders including the Seneca RED JACKET.

Tascalusa

Born: c. 1500; Mabila (now in Alabama)
Died: October 18, 1540; Mabila (now in Alabama)
Also known as: Tuskaloosa, Tuscaloosa, Tuscaluca, Taszaluza, Tastaluca, Black Warrior
Tribal affiliation: Choctaw
Significance: Tascalusa was the paramount chief of the Mobile Indians, who led his people first in diplomacy with Spanish explorer Hernando de Soto and then in opposition. The first-contact experience ended for the Mobile with a valiant but deadly battle, the largest and deadliest in sixteenth century North America between American Indians and Europeans, but it did stop de Soto's advance.

Not much is known of the early life of Tascalusa. The legendary parameters of Tascalusa's spare biography never entered the folk storehouse of Southeast Indian stories for a number of reasons. First, the Mobile Indians began to disappear as a tribe after 1540, eventually being absorbed into the Choctaw Nation in the early eighteenth century. Second, the North American Indian cultures in the path of de Soto's expedition suffered almost complete cultural annihilation, wiping out any form of oral history that might have been passed on about Tascalusa and his tribe. Third, Spanish versions of Tascalusa's life focus solely on his final days serving as the worthy counterpart to de Soto.

Tascalusa, whose name means "black warrior" in the Choctaw language, governed one of the most developed and complex of the Mississippian Indian cultures at the end of what had been an approximately eight-hundred-year period of growth and development before the first European contact in the sixteenth century. The hunter-gatherer society had metamorphosed into a more complex farming society that included one of the southernmost examples of moundbuilding. The Mobile Indians, in their daily religious practices, paid religious honor to the sun, a behavior de Soto himself attempted to exploit by introducing himself to the Southeast Indians as the "child of the sun."

Tascalusa appears to have been married, though there is no specific mention of him having a wife. There are, however, multiple references to groups of tribal women expressing both their homage to and their concern for him as he fought in the nine-hour Battle of Mabila. Tascalusa had a namesake son who was old enough to fight at Mabila and whose grisly death in combat is recounted by several different Spanish eyewitnesses. Interestingly enough, although all the Mobile men and virtually all the women were reported to have been dead or dying by nightfall on October 18, 1540, there is a single transcribed report of captured Indian women by a Spanish lieutenant that claims that Tascalusa was encouraged to leave the fortress walls of Mabila, repeatedly refused to do so, but finally relented and left with thirty men. This report, however, might simply be flawed understanding. The report assumed that many Indians, presumably twenty-five hundred or more, died outside the fortress walls of living trees and daub, even as another three thousand died inside the walls by the sword or lance; another thirty-five hundred died horrible deaths, either burned or suffocated in the huge structures to which de Soto and his men set fire and often blocked egress to the mostly women and children inside.

Tascalusa, as the leader of the largest village among North American Indian tribes of the Southeast of his day, made every attempt to remain a diplomat rather than become a warrior-leader. Indeed, he seems to have been well-prepared to play both roles. Tascalusa had welcomed de Soto initially and sent amicable, if somewhat cryptic and reserved, messages by courier to de Soto as the expedition moved west and north toward Tascalusa and his people.

On October 11, 1540, the two men finally met face-to-face. De Soto asked for several hundred men to serve as guides and carriers and seems to have asked for at least one hundred women as well, presumably for sexual favors. Tascalusa apparently provided a significant number of burden-carriers but told de Soto that the women would be provided at the next town to the north, the fortress town of Mabila. Over the next few days, Tascalusa traveled with de Soto toward Mabila. Extremely tall, Tascalusa's stature was such that one of de Soto's lieutenants noted that only a pack horse would be large enough to support his impressive frame.

De Soto seems to have become suspicious as he approached the walled fortress of Mabila, since houses that were outside the tree-and-mud walls had been dismantled, which would have provided a more open plain for fighting. De Soto also seems to have received some information from a Christian missionary at Mabila, who reported to de Soto that the Indians were acting suspiciously and that an inordinate number of armed men were collecting within the huts and meeting halls of the town, including Tascalusa, who had been in one of the larger houses near the central plaza and had refused to emerge from the structure. The largest and bloodiest battle of the century on the North American continent soon ensued during all nine sunlight hours of October 18, 1540.

The Spaniards were not ready for the scope or organization of the Indian attack, so they gathered outside the gates of the city to regroup. The Spaniards fought for hours, then launched a four-pronged attack on both gates and two points of the wall of the city, entering the fortress to kill the remaining soldiers and set fire to all the houses inside the walls of Mabila.

Despite the extent of the battle, the ferocity of the ensuing firestorm was so complete that to this day, scholars debate the exact location of the battle, though it was most likely at what is now known as Choctaw Bluff in Clarke County, Alabama. Somewhere in south-central Alabama, there is an archaeological library of information embedded in the swampy earth, containing at minimum more than ten thousand skeletal remains, pottery, arrowheads, and the remnants of a remarkable village, palisaded with live (likely, pine) trees daubed into city walls.

Tascalusa and his entire retinue of subordinate chiefs died that day, but so did a number of significant officers on the Spanish side, notably de Soto's two nephews, Don Carlos Enriquez and Diego de Soto. De Soto died two years later of a fever, and his men hurriedly buried him in the Mississippi River so that his demigod stature would not be mitigated. Therefore, the Battle of Mabila and de Soto's confrontation with Tascalusa constitute the critical points not only in the lives of these two leaders but also in the history of their cultures in North America.

Tascalusa was the paramount chief of forces who engaged in the largest and most significant sixteenth century battle involving North American Indians and Europeans. His name has been given to both a city and a county in Alabama (Tuscaloosa), and his life is emblematic and representative of first-contact experiences with Europeans: With diplomacy, guile, and pitched and valorous battle, the Spaniards followed through by annihilating and then essentially ending the chiefdom-level leadership within tribal cultures that faced colonialist Europeans.

Richard Sax

FURTHER READING

Clayton, Lawrence A., et al., eds. *The De Soto Chronicles: The Expedition of Hernando De Soto to North America in 1539-1543*. Tuscaloosa: University of Alabama Press, 1996.

Duncan, David Ewing. *Hernando De Soto: A Savage Quest in the Americas*. Norman: University of Oklahoma Press, 1997.

Higginbotham, Jay. *Mauvila*. Mobile, Ala.: A. B. Bahr/Factor Press, 2000.

Hudson, Charles. *Knights of Spain, Warriors of the Sun: Hernando De Soto and the South's Ancient Chiefdoms*. Athens: University of Georgia Press, 1997.

Josephy, Alvin M., Jr. *Five Hundred Nations: An Illustrated History of North American Indians*. New York: Alfred A. Knopf, 1994.

Mancall, Peter C., and James Merrell, eds. *American Encounters: Natives and Newcomers from European Contact to Indian Removal, 1500-1850*. New York: Routledge, 1999.

Swanton, John R. *Final Report of the United States De Soto Expedition Commission*. 76th Congress, 1st Session, House Document no. 71. Washington, D.C.: Government Printing Office, 1939.

Trigger, Bruce G., and Wilcomb E. Washburn, eds. *The Cambridge History of the Native Peoples of the Americas*, vol. 1, pt. 1. New York: Cambridge University Press, 1996.

Wilson, James. *The Earth Shall Weep: A History of Native America*. New York: Grove Press, 1998.

Tavibo

Born: c. 1810; Mason Valley (present-day Nevada)
Died: c. 1870; place unknown (probably Nevada)
Also known as: the Paiute Prophet
Tribal affiliation: Paiute
Significance: Tavibo's prophecies about the destruction of whites helped lead to the founding of the Ghost Dance religion during the 1890's.

Tavibo was a shaman who may have participated in several Indian wars, including the Pyramid Lake War (1860), the Owens Valley War (1863), and the Bannock War (1875).

Tavibo received a series of visions prophesying the destruction of whites. The first of these visions proclaimed a natural catastrophe which would destroy all whites but spare the Indians. A second vision modified the first: An earthquake would kill all people, but Indians would be resurrected. In a third vision, only his followers would be resurrected. Tavibo's influence spread to neighboring Bannocks, Shoshones, and Utes. His prophecies formed the basis for the Ghost Dance religion of the 1890's, created by his son WOVOKA. In 1889, during an eclipse of the sun, Wovoka received a vision of Indian renewal echoing and further refining Tavibo's visions.

Mary E. Virginia

FURTHER READING
Hittman, Michael. *Wovoka and the Ghost Dance.* Edited by Don Lynch. Expanded ed. Lincoln: University of Nebraska Press, 1997.
Mooney, James. *The Ghost-Dance Religion and the Sioux Outbreak of 1890.* Introduction by Raymond J. DeMallie. Lincoln: University of Nebraska Press, 1991.

Tawaquaptewa

Born: c. 1882; Oraibi, Third Mesa, Arizona
Died: April 30, 1960; Oraibi, Third Mesa, Arizona
Tribal affiliation: Hopi (Bear Clan)
Significance: Tawaquaptewa tried to lead his clan and the Progressives through major civil strife in the Hopi Nation; he is blamed for the degradation of the ancient pueblo of Oraibi.

Appointed chief of Oraibi, the oldest continuously occupied settlement in America, in 1901, Tawaquaptewa represented one of two factions of Hopis, the Friendlies, or Progressives, led by Lololma of the Bear Clan. The Hostiles, or Traditionals, were led by the dynamic and irascible Yukioma. The factions arose over a dispute about how much the Hopi should depend on the federal government for assistance. Lololma had earlier signed an agreement with the Bureau of Indian Affairs that pledged government support for the Hopi in their efforts to keep Navajo from trespassing on the Hopi reservation. The Hostiles believed that such agreements would lead to increased government intervention and further degradation of their spiritual and ceremonial roots; they wanted the policing of their land to be done without outside assistance. In 1891, a Navajo murdered Lololma's nephew on the Hopi reservation. The bureau reluctantly arrested a Navajo suspect, then allowed him to escape, adding to the tension between the two factions.

In September of 1906, Tawaquaptewa attempted to force Lololma's allies, led by Yukioma, from Oraibi. The skirmish would have led to civil war if not for the efforts of the Reverend H. R. Voth, a Mennonite missionary. Tawaquaptewa and Yukioma agreed to a "push of war," a physical contest between the two chiefs, to settle the dispute. The contest, staged on September 6, eventually disintegrated into chaos as allies for each faction joined in, trying to push their respective leaders across the line. Yukioma eventually lost after what has been documented as "hours of bloodless struggle." He and his followers abandoned Oraibi that night, establishing a spiritual center at nearby Hotevilla.

In 1912, Yukioma, still chief of the now popular and powerful center of Hotevilla, was jailed by the Bureau of Indian Affairs for threatening the matron of a government Indian school. This left Tawaquaptewa as the undisputed leader of the Hopi, a role for which he was unqualified and unprepared. Having received a routine American education from 1906 to 1910 in California, he could not reconcile his newfound knowledge with Hopi spiritual traditions. Oraibians began to abandon traditional ceremonies and, by 1933, the pueblo numbered only 112 people. At his death in 1960 the Bear Clan disintegrated, and Oraibi was in ruins.

Richard S. Keating

Tecumseh

Born: March, 1768; Old Piqua, western Ohio
Died: October 5, 1813; Thames River, southeastern Canada
Tribal affiliation: Shawnee
Significance: Tecumseh was one of the first Indian leaders to attempt (and, to a degree, succeed in) the forging of an alliance among all Indians to resist the westward expansion of white settlements in North America.

Tecumseh was the fifth child of a Creek woman named Methoataske (Turtle Laying Eggs), who lived in a Shawnee village in western Ohio near modern Chillicothe. His name, Tecumseh, means "shooting star" in the Shawnee language. His father, Puckeshinwa, a Shawnee war chief, had married Methoataske during the French and Indian War (1756-1763). The couple later had four more children.

Puckeshinwa died in battle during PONTIAC's Rebellion in 1774. Tecumseh's oldest brother, Chiksika, attempted to provide for the family, but Methoataske often had to rely on the charity of her husband's kinsmen to survive. When the American Revolution began in 1776, Shawnee warriors participated in raids on U.S. settlements in Kentucky, provoking a war between U.S. citizens and the Shawnee. Many Shawnee subsequently moved west to avoid the horrors of war. Methoataske and her youngest children joined an exodus of more than one thousand Shawnee to southeastern Missouri. Tecumseh and his older siblings remained in Ohio, where they were cared for by their older sister, Tecumpease, and her husband.

Tecumseh grew to manhood during a turbulent time in his tribe's history. In the period between 1780 and 1782, George Rogers Clark led two U.S. military expeditions against the Indian villages along the Mad and Great Miami Rivers. In 1782, the Shawnee joined with other tribes to defeat a U.S. military attack led by Colonel William Crawford, with the Americans suffering large losses. In alliance with the British, the Shawnee also participated in an invasion of Kentucky in 1782. Growing to manhood during the turmoil of war profoundly influenced Tecumseh's subsequent development. The prolonged struggle magnified the importance of war chiefs and warriors among the Shawnee. Tecumseh, at the age of fourteen, took part in several of the battles against the Americans in 1782-1783.

After the Revolutionary War, the U.S. government concluded a series of treaties (of questionable legality) with minor Indian chiefs which transferred much Shawnee land in Ohio to the U.S. government. Many Shawnee leaders refused to recognize the legitimacy of the treaties and resisted white settlement in the region by force. Tecumseh

Portrait of Tecumseh painted by Mathias Noheimer.
(Library of Congress)

took part in the numerous raids on white settlements, usually in war parties led by Chiksika. Chiksika died from wounds he received in one of those raids (this one in Tennessee) in 1787. Most of the Shawnee returned to Ohio after Chiksika's death, but Tecumseh and a small band of warriors stayed in Tennessee and continued to raid white settlements. Tecumseh led the band, and his reputation as a sagacious warrior and a war chief began to grow.

Returning to Ohio in 1790, Tecumseh found that although many tribes were threatened by American expansion, they could not form a united front against their foes. As a result, the U.S. army defeated the individual tribes piecemeal, and the white frontier continued to expand westward.

In 1805, Tecumseh's younger brother, Lalawethika, fell into a trance. When he awakened, he reported that the Master of Life had shown him how the Shawnee and the other Indian tribes could rid themselves of the white man and reclaim their cultural heritage, along with their hunting grounds. The way to salvation was to give up all vestiges of the white man's culture—muskets, clothes, especially whiskey—and return to the life their fathers had lived. If they did this, the Master of Life would expel the whites and give the Indians their knowledge, which had been intended for the Indians all along.

Lalawethika took the name Tenskwatawa (Open Door) but was often simply called the Prophet. His message rapidly spread widely among not only the Shawnee but all the Indian tribes in the old Northwest Territory, and even beyond. By August, 1805, Tenskwatawa and several hundred Shawnee established a village near Greenville in western Ohio. He was joined by new converts from the Senecas, Wyandots, and Ottawas. The Prophet's message formed the basis for the first great American Indian revitalization movement, which eventually galvanized most of the major Indian tribes in the Ohio River valley, and many beyond.

Tecumseh at first played a role subordinate to the Prophet in the revitalization movement, content to allow his brother to unify the tribes under the aegis of the new religion. During the ensuing seven years, Tenskwatawa established a new center for his growing millennial movement at Prophetstown in western Ohio, where he was joined by converts from as far away as Iowa and Canada. Among the converts were many war chiefs and warriors who hoped the Prophet would lead them in a successful war against the Americans. Tenskwatawa was no warrior, however, and Tecumseh often spoke for him in strategy-planning sessions.

As the War of 1812 approached, Tecumseh began attempting to forge the growing Indian religious unity into political and military unity. Allying himself with the British, Tecumseh secured promises of military support from all the surrounding tribes and more distant tribes, including the Creeks. Alarmed at Tecumseh's activities, the U.S. government dispatched William Henry Harrison with a large force of regular and militia troops to Prophetstown to disperse the leadership of the Indian movement. Tecumseh was absent in 1812 when Harrison's men defeated the Indians at the Battle of Tippecanoe. Tenskwatawa's ineffective leadership in the battle led to his permanent decline in influence among the Indians. Tecumseh became the unquestioned leader of the Indian movement.

Despite some initial successes against the Americans, the Indians and the British ultimately found themselves pushed out of the United States by the Americans. Many of Tecumseh's Indian allies deserted him as the war wore on, and the promised aid from the British was always inadequate and slow in coming. Attempting to resist Harrison's invasion of Canada during the autumn of 1813, the British and Indians suffered an overwhelming defeat at the Battle of Thames, northeast of Detroit. After the British fled the battlefield, Tecumseh suffered a mortal wound. Without him, the Indian movement withered away and disappeared.

Paul Madden

FURTHER READING

Edmunds, R. David. *Tecumseh and the Quest for Indian Leadership.* Boston: Little, Brown, 1984.

Gilpin, Alec. *The War of 1812 in the Old Northwest.* East Lansing: Michigan State University Press, 1958.

Klinck, Carl F., ed. *Tecumseh: Fact and Fiction in Early Records.* Englewood Cliffs, N.J.: Doubleday, 1961.

Oskison, John. *Tecumseh and His Times.* New York: W. W. Norton, 1938.

Sugden, John. *Tecumseh: A Life.* New York: Henry Holt, 1998.

Tucker, Glenn. *Tecumseh: Vision of Glory.* Indianapolis: Bobbs-Merrill, 1956.

Teedyuscung

Born: c. 1700; near present-day Trenton, New Jersey
Died: April, 1763; Wyoming Valley, Pennsylvania
Tribal affiliation: Lenni Lenape (Delaware)
Significance: Teedyuscung was an eloquent defender of Indian land rights.

Teedyuscung's career was one of opposition to white English encroachment on Indian lands. He was born in New Jersey, where he lived in a small Lenni Lenape community. Encroaching English settlement led the group, in about 1730, to move to the Delaware River valley in eastern Pennsylvania. Along with other Indians, Teedyuscung protested the unfairness of the Walking Purchase of 1737 under which Pennsylvania seized land from the Indians. Complicating the Lenni Lenape claims to the land were land grants made by the Iroquois, who claimed the smaller tribe as their subjects.

Teedyuscung was converted to Christianity by Moravian missionaries, but he later gave up his involvement in the church to take up duties as war chief against the Iroquois. In 1754 the Lenni Lenape were expelled westward, with Iroquois cooperation. During the Seven Years' War (1755-1763), Teedyuscung was a leader of a group of warriors from several tribes living in Wyoming. Teedyuscung appeared at a number of important meetings, including the Albany Conference of 1754. He became a symbol of the unfairness of proprietary policy toward Indian land rights, and his speeches were published by Benjamin Franklin. While opposing settlement of the northeast Pennsylvania frontier, Teedyuscung was burned to death at home in Wyoming, likely a victim of arson/murder by land speculators.

Thomas Patrick Carroll

FURTHER READING
Wallace, Anthony F. C. *King of the Delawares: Teedyuscung, 1700-1763.* 1949. Reprint. Syracuse, N.Y.: Syracuse University Press, 1990.

Tekakwitha, Kateri

Born: 1656; Ossernenon, Mohawk Valley (near present-day Auriesville, New York)
Died: April 17, 1680; Sault St. Louis, New France (near present-day Montreal, Canada)
Also known as: Catherine Tagaskouita, Tegakwith (She Pushes with Her Hands), Lily of the Mohawks
Tribal affiliation: Mohawk
Significance: Kateri Tekakwitha, the first Indian nun, was beatified by the Roman Catholic Church in 1980.
The daughter of a Mohawk father and a Christian mother of the Erie tribe who had been taken captive by Mohawks, Kateri Tekakwitha was

orphaned at the age of four as a result of a smallpox epidemic. The epidemic almost claimed her as well, and the disease left her with a scarred face and failing eyesight. She was reared by extended family members in a Mohawk village in present-day upstate New York. Some family members were opposed to Christianity, while others espoused it. Tekakwitha became entangled in this conflict because she had desired to practice Christianity, but family members arranged a marriage for her with an anti-Christian young man.

Tekakwitha rebelled by escaping from her village and traveling north to the budding Roman Catholic Mohawk community of Kahnawake, along the St. Lawrence River. Once there, she was baptized and became known for her extreme devotion to Christianity, excessive self-mortification, fasting, and other forms of penance. Tekakwitha also ministered to the needs of the sick and elderly at Kahnawake, and, along with several other young women, desired to form a convent. The Jesuit missionaries did not allow them to do this, but they did permit Tekakwitha to take a "vow of perpetual chastity." Her health failing, the young woman died prematurely on April 17, 1680, according to Jesuit legend, while uttering the names of Jesus and Mary. It is also said that shortly after her death, her pockmarked faced became beautiful and miracles were performed in her name. There soon developed a devotion to her not only among Catholic Mohawks but also among French colonists in the adjacent communities.

Tekakwitha's birth and death places became pilgrimage sites, and by the end of the twentieth century, she had achieved the status of "Blessed Kateri Tekakwitha" within the Roman Catholic Church. She is a source of empowerment for many Indians who adhere to Catholicism. More than fifty biographies of her have been written, in at least ten languages, along with several plays, operas, films, and countless devotional tracts about her. The Kateri Conference is an annual meeting of Catholic Native Americans that draws thousands from all over North America.

Gretchen L. Green

FURTHER READING

Greer, Allan. *Mohawk Saint: Catherine Tekakwitha and the Jesuits.* New York: Oxford University Press, 2005.

Shoemaker, Nancy, ed. *Negotiators of Change: Historical Perspectives on Native American Women.* New York: Routledge, 1995.

Ten Bears

Born: 1792; southern Great Plains
Died: November 23, 1872; near Fort Sill, Indian Territory (now in Oklahoma)
Also known as: Parra-Wa-Samen
Tribal affiliation: Comanche
Significance: Ten Bears led efforts to preserve peace between the Comanche and white settlers moving into Comanche territory.

A member of the Yamparika Comanche, Ten Bears was born south of the Arkansas River on the wide southern Plains. By 1860, when conflicts were beginning between the Comanche and white settlers, Ten Bears was a chief and spokesman for his people. His peacemaking twice took him to Washington, D.C.

Ten Bears's most famous speech, was delivered in 1867 at the Medicine Lodge Treaty council in Barber County, Kansas. He forcefully defended the Comanche, declaring that most conflicts were initiated by U.S. soldiers. The most emotional part of the address was Ten Bears's appeal that the Comanche be allowed to live as their ancestors had lived—on the open plains, unrestricted by walls or fences. The treaty signed at the conclusion of the council, however—the last treaty ever made with the Comanche—restricted them to a reservation.

In 1872, Ten Bears made his second visit to Washington, D.C. He attended a reception given by President Ulysses S. Grant. The conclusion of the visit again brought sorrow to the Comanche and disgrace to their aged spokesman. The order was given, and agreed to by Ten Bears, that all Comanche temporarily move to within ten miles of Fort Sill, Oklahoma.

Soon after his return, Ten Bears died at the age of eighty at the reservation near Fort Sill. After a life of service to the Comanche, he had been abandoned by all except his son.

Glenn L. Swygart

Tendoy

Born: c. 1834; Boise River, Oregon Country (now in Idaho)
Died: May 9, 1907; Fort Hall, Idaho
Tribal affiliation: Bannock
Significance: Tendoy influenced his people to work peaceably with the white settlers of Wyoming.

When his father, Kontakayak, a Bannock war chief, died in combat with the Blackfoot, Tendoy (the Climber) became war chief of the Lemhi Bannock band. An ally of WASHAKIE, to whom he was related on his mother's side, Tendoy believed in accommodating white settlement in the highlands of what would become Wyoming.

Unlike many Bannocks, who became destitute with the demise of their hunting economy, Tendoy and his band prospered by maintaining a trading relationship with white settlers, miners, and others. Even during the Nez Perce War, he maintained that his people would prosper by seeking accommodation. In February, 1875, President Ulysses S. Grant issued an order allowing the Lemhi Bannocks to remain on their ancestral lands. In 1892, however, they were removed to Fort Hall, Idaho. After Tendoy died there, local residents built a monument in his honor.

Bruce E. Johansen

Tenskwatawa

Born: March, 1768; Piqua, Ohio
Died: November, 1837; present-day Argentine, Kansas
Also known as: Lalawethika (the Rattle), the Shawnee Prophet
Tribal affiliation: Shawnee
Significance: Tenskwatawa led a spiritual and cultural revival among the tribes of the Old Northwest during the first decade of the nineteenth century.

The son of Puckeshinwa, a great war chief of the Kispokotha Shawnee who was killed at the battle of Point Pleasant in 1774, Tenskwatawa was one of two surviving triplets. In his youth, he was known as Lalawethika ("the Rattle") because of his excessive boasting. He was blind in one eye because of a childhood accident.

Tenskwatawa accompanied his brother TECUMSEH to Fallen Timbers (1794) to fight against the American army of Anthony Wayne. In the years after the Indian defeat at Fallen Timbers, Lalawethika was trained in magic and medicine by Penagasha. In April, 1805, Lalawethika fainted in his lodge. When he recovered, he began to preach a new gospel given to him by the Master of Life.

Taking the name Tenskwatawa (the Open Door), he urged all Indians to renounce whiskey, sexual promiscuity, and the technology of European Americans. He advocated a return to the communal life of his Shawnee ancestors. Tenskwatawa's reputation was greatly enhanced when he successfully predicted a solar eclipse on June 16, 1806.

From 1804 until 1811, agents of the U.S. government negotiated numerous treaties with various tribes of the Old Northwest, under which the government purchased millions of acres of Indian land. Tenskwatawa and his brother Tecumseh challenged the validity of the treaties.

Indiana Governor William Henry Harrison became increasingly concerned about the growing strength of the intertribal cultural revival being led by Tenskwatawa, who attracted followers from many Indian nations to his village Prophetstown, on the banks of the Wabash River. Convinced that Tenskwatawa and Tecumseh posed a real threat to European American interests on the frontier, Harrison raised an army and marched to Prophetstown, arriving near the Indian village while Tecumseh was on a southern journey. Tenskwatawa encouraged his multitribal army to strike first. He promised them that the power of his magic would lead to victory.

The Indians struck the American army in the predawn hours of November 7, 1811. After hours of fierce fighting, they were defeated in what came to be known as the Battle of Tippecanoe. Following the battle, Prophetstown was burned, and Tenskwatawa was discredited as a religious leader.

During the first year of the War of 1812, Tenskwatawa attempted to continue to live with a small band of followers in the Wabash River Valley. American pressure forced him to flee to Canada. The defeat of the British and the death of Tecumseh shattered any hope of revitalizing Tenskwatawa's cultural movement.

Tenskwatawa lived in Canada until 1825, when he returned to live among the Ohio Shawnee. He aided Governor Lewis Cass of the Michigan Territory in his efforts to persuade the Ohio Shawnee to move west across the Mississippi. In 1827, he established his home on the Shawnee Reservation in Kansas, where he lived out the remainder of his life.

Thomas D. Matijasic

Tenskwatawa. (Hulton|Archive by Getty Images)

Thorpe, Jim

Born: May 22, 1888; Indian
Territory (near present-day
Prague, Oklahoma)
Died: March 28, 1953; Lo-
mita, California
Also known as: Wa-tho-huck
(Bright Path)
Tribal affiliation: Sauk, Fox
Significance: Jim Thorpe was
one of the greatest and most
versatile athletes in history.

James Francis Thorpe was
born near Prague, Oklahoma.
His Indian ancestry included
Sauk and Potawatomi blood,
and he was the great-grandson
of BLACK HAWK, the great war
chief of the Chippewa (Ojibwa). Thorpe was proud of his
heritage.

Jim Thorpe's athletic career
began in 1908 at the Carlisle
Institute in Pennsylvania under football coach Glenn "Pop"
Warner. On Thorpe's second
play on the varsity team, he ran
75 yards for a touchdown. Fol-

Jim Thorpe in his Carlisle football uniform.
(National Archives)

lowing two years of professional baseball, Thorpe returned to Carlisle for
the 1911 and 1912 football season, in both of which he was a first-team all-
American.

The versatility of Jim Thorpe was revealed at the 1912 Summer Olympics in Stockholm, Sweden, where he won both the pentathlon and the
decathlon. Although his gold medals were taken away because of his
earlier professional baseball career, they were eventually returned to his
family in 1982.

After many years of professional baseball and football, Thorpe retired from athletics in 1929. He died at his home in California in 1953.

Glenn L. Swygart

FURTHER READING

Birchfield, D. L. *Jim Thorpe, World's Greatest Athlete.* Parsippany, N.J.: Modern Curriculum Press, 1994.

Crawford, Bill. *All American: The Rise and Fall of Jim Thorpe.* Hoboken, N.J.: John Wiley & Sons, 2004.

Oxendine, Joseph B. *American Indian Sports Heritage.* Lincoln: University of Nebraska Press, 1995.

Tiger, Jerome R.

Born: July 8, 1941; Tahlequah, Oklahoma
Died: August 13, 1967; Eufaula, Oklahoma
Also known as: Kacha (Tiger)
Tribal affiliation: Creek, Seminole
Significance: Jerome R. Tiger added emotion, subtle colors, and delicate strokes to traditional Indian painting.

Jerome Tiger spent his first ten years in communal living with the numerous visitors to West Eufaula Indian Baptist Church Camp. Even after moving to Muskogee, Oklahoma, his family returned often to the camp and the Creek stomp dances. At fifteen, he became head of the art department at a local business, then left school to spend two years in the Navy. From 1962 until 1967, Tiger produced hundreds of paintings and sketches of the Creek stomp dance in all its phases (ribbon dance, stomp dance, taking medicine, stickball, meals), of Seminole individuals, of windswept Indians on the Trail of Tears, and of contemporary Indians in everyday activities.

Tiger learned about Indian art from his older brother, then attended Cooper School of Art in Cleveland (with funds from the Indian Relocation Act), where he developed his technical expertise. By 1966, his distinctive style—a delicate line on blue or brown posterboard using one or two tempera colors—was established. Tiger was also a boxer, and in 1966 he won the Golden Gloves middleweight title. His life was ended by a self-inflicted accidental gunshot wound days before he would have finished his first clay sculpture for casting. Before his untimely death, he won dozens of prizes at leading Indian art competitions. He rarely interacted with other Indian artists and never traveled outside Oklahoma. His brother Johnny and daughter Dana are artists.

Cheryl Claassen

FURTHER READING
Berlo, Janet C., and Ruth B. Phillips. *Native North American Art.* New
    York: Oxford University Press, 1998.

Tomah

Born: c. 1752; near present-day Green Bay, Wisconsin
Died: c. 1817; Mackinaw, Wisconsin
Also known as: Thomas Carron
Tribal affiliation: Menominee
Significance: Although he initially resisted Tecumseh's call for armed
    resistance, Tomah joined the British as they fought the Americans in
    the War of 1812.

Tomah, the son of an Indian man who was part French and a woman
who was probably Abenaki, was widely respected by the Menominee for
his intelligence and leadership. When the hereditary chief, Chakaucho
Kama, was judged incompetent, the tribal council appointed Tomah
acting head chief.

In 1805, Tomah became a guide for U.S. Army Lieutenant Zebulon
Pike, who was searching for the headwaters of the Mississippi River. Pike
was impressed with Tomah's apparent loyalty to whites. Indeed, when
the Shawnee chief Tecumseh visited the Menominee to solicit their support in the rebellion he was fomenting, Tomah refused to join. He was
apprehensive that his small tribe would fare poorly in a pan-Indian alliance. Tomah also feared white encroachment, however, and when it appeared that the Americans might be defeated in the War of 1812, he
aided the British. Along with his protégé, Oshkosh, Tomah and approximately one hundred braves helped defeat the Americans at Fort
Mackinaw, Michigan, and Fort Stephenson, Ohio.

With Tomah's death in 1817, Menominee resistance to white encroachment collapsed. Later, under Oshkosh's leadership, the Menominee fell victim to Indian removal.

Mary E. Virginia

Tomochichi

Born: c. 1650; Apalachukla (now in Alabama)
Died: October 15, 1739; Yamacraw (now in Georgia)
Tribal affiliation: Creek

Significance: Tomochichi went to England to plead the cause of American Indians; he inspired much public sympathy for Indian issues.

Possibly the son of a Creek father and Yamasee mother, originally from
the Chattahoochee River area, Tomochichi was banished by the Creeks
and established the village of Yamacraw, near Savannah, Georgia, along
with a number of followers. Tomochichi's importance grew with the arrival of the English in the colony of Georgia in 1733.

James Oglethorpe desired the cooperation of the Creeks in his settlement. Along with Mary MUSGROVE, Tomochichi forwarded Oglethorpe's
invitation for a meeting to the Upper and Lower Creeks, and with their
affirmative response, Tomochichi was regarded by the newly arrived English as an important connection with their powerful neighbors.

So great was Tomochichi's importance in the eyes of English and
Creek leaders that he was chosen, with English and Indian approval, to
head a diplomatic party of Creeks to England. The visit lasted from June
19 to October 31, 1734. Tomochichi, his wife Senauki, and seven others
were welcomed, and their visit was a social success. The visiting Indians
met King George II at Kensington Palace and made a speech of friendship and peace. Perhaps reflecting the Creeks' matrilineal society,
Tomochichi particularly addressed the Queen as the "common mother
and protectress of us and all our children." To the last, Tomochichi favored a Creek-English alliance.

Thomas Patrick Carroll

Trudell, John

Born: 1947; Niobrara, Nebraska
Tribal affiliation: Santee Lakota (Sioux)
Significance: John Trudell has been one of the central, and most controversial, figures of the American Indian Movement (AIM); he is
also a poet and musician.

John Trudell, who spent his early years on the Santee Sioux reservation
and in Omaha, Nebraska, was one of a core of American Indian activists
who were identified with the founding of the American Indian Movement (AIM) in 1968 and its turbulent years in the early 1970's. Trudell
came to national prominence in 1969 as a spokesman for Native Americans who were occupying Alcatraz Island. Trudell; his first wife, Lou;
and their two children spent most of their time on Alcatraz during the
1969-1971 occupation, and their third child was born there.

Trudell participated in many of AIM's initiatives during the early

1970's, including the Trail of Broken Treaties (1972) and the occupation of Wounded Knee in 1973. Beginning in 1976, he coordinated AIM's work on behalf of Leonard PELTIER, who was jailed after being convicted (falsely, many believe) for involvement in the 1975 shooting of two Federal Bureau of Investigation (FBI) agents on the Pine Ridge Reservation. Personal tragedy struck in 1979 when Trudell's wife Tina, three children, and mother-in-law were killed in an arson fire at their home on the Duck Valley Reservation, Nevada. The crime was never solved, and many activists, including Trudell himself, believed the fire was set as an act of retribution for Trudell's outspoken stands on issues affecting Native Americans. The fire occurred less than a day after he had burned an American flag while protesting in Washington, D.C.

John Trudell. (Hulton|Archive by Getty Images)

Later in his life Trudell also became a nationally known poet and singer. He released some self-produced recordings during the 1980's, then released two albums on Rykodisc in the early 1990's. His compositions with his Graffiti Band on the 1992 album *AKA Graffiti Man*, produced by Jackson Browne, mix the spoken word, rock and roll, and Northern Plains musical traditions. *Johnny Damas and Me* was released in 1994. Trudell has also appeared in the documentary film *Incident at Oglala* and performed the role of Jimmy Looks Twice in the feature film *Thunderheart* (1992). Both films examine the incidents surrounding the trial of Peltier. Trudell continued to be active in the American Indian Movement through the 1990's. In 1992, he played a role in an AIM protest that prompted cancellation of Denver's Columbus Day parade.

Bruce E. Johansen

Tsali

Born: c. 1770?; probably present-day North Carolina
Died: November 25, 1838; Bushnell, North Carolina
Also known as: Old Charlie, Charley
Tribal affiliation: Cherokee
Significance: Tsali is a legendary hero in Cherokee lore because his
  death allowed some of his people to remain in North Carolina when
  the federal government was trying to force all the members of the
  Cherokee Nation to leave their ancestral home.

Little is known about Tsali's early life, beyond the fact that he was a
Cherokee traditionalist who eventually lost his life resisting the removal
of his people from North Carolina to what is now Oklahoma. In 1836, a
few Cherokee leaders signed the Treaty of New Echota, which was protested by the majority of the members of the Cherokee Nation. The
treaty required all Cherokee people to give up their land and remove
west of the Mississippi River to Indian Territory.

Because only a small number of Cherokee had relocated by May,
1838, General Winfield Scott was sent to Tennessee with about seven
thousand soldiers force the remaining sixteen thousand or so Cherokee
to go west. The Army built stockades to hold people until they could be
marched west in what later became known as the Trail of Tears.

According to Nanhi, Tsali's wife, he and his family applied for U.S.
citizenship so they could remain on their land, but the military authorities disregarded the permits the Cherokees obtained. Compelled to
leave their home and pursued by troops, the resisting Cherokees fled to
the Smoky Mountains in North Carolina. In early August of 1838, Scott
learned that numerous Cherokees had eluded his troops and were hiding in the mountains. He then sent mounted soldiers to search for an estimated three hundred fugitive men, women, and children. Another
group called the Oconaluftee Cherokees helped the Army search. Because these people did not live within the Cherokee Nation boundaries,
they were not being removed. They eventually assisted the Army in the
capture of 140 fugitives. On October 30, 1838, Second Lieutenant A. J.
Smith received information that other fugitives were in the area; these
included Tsali and his family. After their camp was discovered, they all
surrendered without resistance. Of the twelve captured, five were men.

Tsali's youngest son, Wasitani (also known as Washington), later said
that a soldier struck his mother with a horsewhip for stopping to care
for her infant. To make better time, Smith ordered his troops to give

their horses to the Cherokee women and children. Tsali's wife and her infant child were put on a horse, but the horse startled and the child fell off and died. According to Wasitani, this incident provoked his family's renewed resistance to being relocating. Soon afterward, Tsali gave a signal, there was a fight, and two soldiers were killed. After Smith and a wounded soldier escaped, Tsali and his family took the remaining horses and fled into the mountains.

General Scott ordered the Fourth Infantry back to the North Carolina mountains to punish the Cherokees, whom he regarded as murderers. The infantry troops received help from other Cherokees remaining in North Carolina. Within two weeks, eleven of the twelve fugitives—all but Tsali himself—were captured. Four of the captured men were executed—three of them by Cherokee scouts. Tsali's youngest son was spared from execution because of his youth.

Eventually, Tsali was brought in by Cherokee scouts, tried by them, and shot. The important role that the other Cherokee refugees played in capturing and executing Tsali led to their being permitted to remain in their homeland. Tsali's story became an inspiration to later generations of Cherokees. Through the rest of the nineteenth century, the federal government tried to get the Quallatown Cherokees to move west, but it is thought that the legend of Tsali encouraged them to remain in the mountains.

Jennifer Shannon
Teresa Neva Tate

FURTHER READING

King, Duane H. *The Cherokee Indian Nation.* Knoxville: University of Tennessee Press, 1979.

Malone, Henry Thompson. *Cherokees of the Old South.* Athens: University of Georgia Press, 1956.

Tsatoke, Monroe

Born: September 29, 1904; Indian Territory (now near Saddle Mountain, Oklahoma)
Died: February 3, 1937; place unknown
Tribal affiliation: Kiowa
Significance: Monroe Tsatoke was a member of the Kiowa Five group of painters who contributed to the formation of the twentieth century Oklahoma styles of Native American painting.

Tsatoke was one of the Kiowas in a fine arts club organized in Anadarko, Oklahoma, by Susie C. Peters in early 1926. Students did drawing, painting, and beadwork. In the fall of that year, special classes were set up for them outside the regular academic curriculum at the University of Oklahoma, and they studied there the next two academic years. In addition to being an artist, Tsatoke was a good singer and served as chief singer at Kiowa dances for many years.

Although he painted standard images, such as warriors, he was best known for paintings of dance scenes, drummers, and peyote cult subjects. While seriously ill with tuberculosis, Tsatoke joined the Native American Church and became active in the peyote ceremony. He did a series of paintings that explored his religious experience, and he is known for exploring spiritual themes.

Tsatoke's work has been included in many exhibitions and has been collected by the National Museum of the American Indian, Oklahoma Historical Society Museum, University of Oklahoma Museum of Art, and Museum of New Mexico, among others.

Ronald J. Duncan

FURTHER READING
Berlo, Janet C., and Ruth B. Phillips. *Native North American Art.* New York: Oxford University Press, 1998.

Two Crows

Born: c. 1820; place unknown
Died: March 4, 1894; Blackbird Hills, Nebraska
Also known as: Cahae Numba, Lewis Morris
Tribal affiliation: Omaha
Significance: Famed for his wisdom and speaking skills, Two Crows served as a chief of the Omaha Indians and as a research informant for the kinship, customs, and social life of his people.

While a young man, Two Crows policed the Omahas during the annual buffalo hunts on the plains of present-day Nebraska. Described as a tall, strong Omaha warrior, he fought against the Sioux and Pawnee on numerous occasions to protect Omaha lands and hunting grounds. In 1847, he killed two Sioux men in battle, and he served as war chief of a raiding party against the Sioux in 1854. A true friend of the white people, Two Crows was instrumental in keeping the Omahas from entering into any battles with the U.S. Army.

Two Crows was particularly valued in the Omaha tribe as a man of great wisdom. He was a principal doctor in the Omaha buffalo dance society. Revered as a spokesman in Indian councils, Two Crows had the ability to see clearly through complex issues to arrive at reasonable solutions. Other leaders eagerly listened to him for insights and guidance in solving difficult problems and often looked to him for the final word in such matters. Two Crows spoke succinctly, with clarity and authority. Elected as one of seven chiefs in a tribal reorganization in 1880, he was one of the foremost Omaha chiefs for many years.

A famous story involving the wisdom of Two Crows centers around those who should inhabit Omaha lands. When white men took Omaha women for wives, many chose to settle on Omaha land because of its rich soil, plentiful water, and abundant timber. Many older Omahas labeled these settlers as "white Indians." As this trend increased during the 1880's, many older Omahas proposed that only pure-blooded Omahas should be allowed to dwell on Omaha land and that all others should leave. After this conclusion was reached during a Omaha council, Two Crows rose and offered his insights. He agreed with the decision of the older Omaha leaders. Then he pointed out that everyone would have to move off of Omaha land except for his family and that of another Omaha leader, Wajepa, as their families were the only ones left who were of pure Omaha blood. Virtually all other Omaha families had intermarried with members of other Indian tribes, particularly the Poncas and Sioux, or with white people. With that pronouncement, the issue was dropped by the Omaha Indian council.

Documented publications about the Omaha Indians are sparse. In 1984, R. H. Barnes published his insights about the history, kinship, social life, and customs of the people in *Two Crows Denies It: A History of Controversy in Omaha Sociology*. Barnes's book cites statements of Two Crows that contradict some of the research on the Omahas that was published by the Omaha Indian ethnographer James Owen Dorsey in *Omaha Sociology* in 1884. During the 1880's, Two Crows served as a research informant for anthropological studies and clarified the names and numbers of Omaha clan and subclan divisions, as well as Omaha relationship terminology and tribal marriage rules.

Alvin K. Benson

FURTHER READING
Barnes, R. H. *Two Crows Denies It: A History of Controversy in Omaha Sociology*. Lincoln: University of Nebraska Press, 1984.

Two Leggings

Born: c. 1844; along the Bighorn River, Montana
Died: April 23, 1923; Hardin, Montana
Also known as: Big Crane, His Eyes Are Dreamy
Tribal affiliation: Crow
Significance: Two Leggings provided invaluable insights regarding his
    life as a Crow warrior to anthropologist William Wildschut.

Two Leggings, originally known as Big Crane, was born along the Bighorn River in Montana. He received the name His Eyes Are Dreamy following an unusually long and failed vision quest. As a young Crow warrior, he participated in raids for horses against the traditional Crow

Two Leggings in 1908. (Library of Congress)

enemies, the Sioux. At that time, the Crow were peaceful toward white settlers.

Between 1919 and 1923, Two Leggings related his life story to a Montana businessman and anthropologist, William Wildschut. Under the sponsorship of the Heye Foundation of the Museum of the American Indian, Wildschut recorded Two Leggings's detailed observations regarding everyday Crow life and the life cycles of a Crow warrior. Wildschut's manuscript, entitled *Two Leggings: The Making of a Crow Warrior,* was edited by anthropologist Peter Nabokov and published in 1967. It is an invaluable source of anthropological data on the tribe. Two Leggings married Ties Up Her Bundle, and together they reared two adopted children, Red Clay Woman and Sings to the Sweat Lodge.

Mary E. Virginia

FURTHER READING

Hoxie, Frederick E. *Parading Through History: The Making of the Crow Nation in America, 1805-1935.* New York: Cambridge University Press, 1995.

Nabokov, Peter, ed. *Two Leggings: The Making of a Crow Warrior.* 1967. Reprint. Lincoln: University of Nebraska Press, 1982.

Two Moon

Born: c. 1847
Died: c. 1917; Northern Cheyenne Reservation (near present-day Lame Deer, Montana)
Also known as: Ishi'eyo, Ishaynishus
Tribal affiliation: Cheyenne
Significance: An ally of SITTING BULL and CRAZY HORSE in the Sioux Wars of the 1870's and a leader in the war for the Black Hills of 1876-1877, Two Moon also distinguished himself as an informant to the writer Hamlin Garland.

Sometimes confused with his uncle Two Moons, who was chief in the Bozeman Trail wars of 1866-1868 and an ally of RED CLOUD's Sioux people, the younger Two Moon fought with Sitting Bull and Crazy Horse in the Sioux Wars of the 1870's. Two Moon fought troops on the Powder River in Montana in March of 1876 and fought at the Battle of the Little Bighorn in June of 1876.

Two Moon surrendered to Colonel Nelson Miles in 1877 and served under Miles as an army scout in the Nez Perce War of 1877. Two Moon was also one of six Cheyennes who met L<small>ITTLE</small> W<small>OLF</small> and his followers in March, 1879, following their exodus from Indian Territory. Hamlin Garland's article "General Custer's Last Fight as Seen by Two Moon" (*McClure's Magazine*, 1898) was based on Two Moon's information.

Tonya Huber

F<small>URTHER</small> R<small>EADING</small>
Hampton, Bruce. *Children of Grace: The Nez Perce War of 1877.* Lincoln: University of Nebraska Press, 2002.
Ostler, Jeffrey. *The Plains Sioux and U.S. Colonialism from Lewis and Clark to Wounded Knee.* New York: Cambridge University Press, 2004.

Two Strike

Born: 1832; near Republican River (now in southern Nebraska)
Died: c. 1915; Pine Ridge Reservation, South Dakota
Also known as: Two Strikes, Nomkahpa (Knocks Two Off)
Tribal affiliation: Brule Lakota (Sioux)
Significance: Two Strike was a prominent leader of the Sioux during the time before the closing of the frontier at Wounded Knee in 1890.

Two Strike's Brule Sioux name, Nomkahpa, meant "Knocks Two Off." The name was earned in battle, after Two Strike knocked two Utes off their horses with a single blow of his war club. Two Strike figured prominently in the history of the Brules late in the nineteenth century, up to and including the "closing" of the frontier at Wounded Knee in 1890.

Two Strike. (National Archives)

Born near the Republican River in what would become Nebraska, Two Strike played an important role in raids on the Union Pacific Railroad during R<small>ED</small> C<small>LOUD</small>'s War (1866-1868). During the 1870's, Two Strike allied with S<small>POTTED</small> T<small>AIL</small> and tried to insulate his people from the European American invasion. During the 1880's, Two Strike became an advocate of the Ghost Dance. A month before the massacre at Wounded Knee, however, Two Strike heeded whites' advice to give up the dance and its promised delivery from white domination. After the slaughter of native people under BIG FOOT at Wounded Knee in late December of 1890, Two Strike led his people on an angry rampage with other Sioux. He desisted only after General Nelson Meils promised fair treatment for his people. Two Strike's people surrendered a second time on January 15, 1891. After the turn of the century, Two Strike lived quietly at Pine Ridge, where he was buried after his death in about 1915.

Bruce E. Johansen

Tyon, Thomas

Born: c. 1855; present-day Pine Ridge Reservation, South Dakota
Died: before 1915; probably Pine Ridge Reservation, South Dakota
Also known as: Gray Goose
Tribal affiliation: Oglala Lakota (Sioux)
Significance: Thomas Tyon was an interpreter and informant of James R. Walker, an agency physician who studied Lakota religion on the Pine Ridge Reservation.

Thomas Tyon explained Lakota religion to his friend, James R. Walker, who worked as a physician at Pine Ridge Reservation from 1896 to 1914. Walker interviewed nonliterate Lakotas to record their stories and gather information on Indian culture, and he published the material he collected in a four-volume anthropological study.

Tyon was a Christian of mixed blood and was literate in the Lakota language. He used the phonetic system developed by early missionaries to record information for the Lakota for Walker. In 1911 he wrote narratives based on material that he had learned from older Oglala holy men.

Tyon explained the significance and logistics of the major Lakota traditions, such as the pipe, the sweat lodge, crying for visions, and the Sun Dance. He recorded how White Buffalo Calf Woman gave the Lakota the pipe, promising that when they smoked it, she would appear to them as smoke, hear their prayers, and take the prayers to Wakan Tanka. Tyon also explained how the Sun Dance ceremony gave the tribe and celebrants wisdom through suffering. The red-clad Sun Dancers gave painful skin offerings or gazed at the sun as they danced around the central pole in the camp circle to thank the Sun for its fertility and to ask for another fruitful year. Of all the Lakota deities, the Lakotas most revered the Sun.

Joanna Yin

FURTHER READING

Walker, James R. *Lakota Belief and Ritual.* Edited by Raymond J. De-Maillie and Elaine A. Jahner. Lincoln: University of Nebraska Press, 1980.

Uncas

Born: c. 1606

Died: c. 1682; Uncas Hill (present-day Mohegan, Montville Township, Connecticut

Also known as: Wonkas (the Fox), Poquiam

Tribal affiliation: Mohegan

Significance: Uncas protected his people's interests in a period of conflict and change in seventeenth century New England by allying himself with the English.

Uncas was sachem of the Mohegan branch of the closely related Pequot and Mohegan peoples of southern Connecticut. When Tatobem, great sachem of the Pequots (the dominant group), died in 1633, Uncas was passed over in a struggle to succeed him. Uncas and his supporters seceded, establishing themselves as a small, entirely separate tribe. With Uncas as sachem, the Mohegans were located west of the Thames River, while the majority Pequots held the territory east of it.

During the Pequot War of 1636-1637, Uncas assisted the English, leading sixty warriors in a joint English-Mohegan-Narragansett attack that destroyed the Pequots as an independent people. As a reward, the Mohegan and the Narragansett were each allowed by treaty to incorporate captured Pequots as adoptees. The Mohegans adopted many more, and rivalry between the Mohegan and Narragansett for predominance then led to years of conflict. In these clashes Uncas skillfully cultivated English favor. In a battle in 1643 near Norwich, Connecticut, Uncas and four hundred Mohegans defeated a thousand Narragansetts and took prisoner their principal sachem, MIANTONOMO, executing him at English urging.

During King Philip's War (1675-1676), Uncas again assisted the English against their Indian enemies. The English considered Uncas wily and unscrupulous, but he was so consistently loyal that their alliance endured for more than forty years.

Bert M. Mutersbaugh

FURTHER READING
Oberg, Michael Leroy. *Uncas: First of the Mohegans.* Ithaca, N.Y.: Cornell
    University Press, 2003.

Victorio

Born: c. 1825; present-day southwestern New Mexico
Died: October 16, 1880; Tres Castillos, Mexico
Also known as: Bidu-ya, Beduiat, Lucero
Tribal affiliation: Mimbreño Apache
Significance: Victorio led his band in raids against U.S. and Mexican
    forces; his death and the destruction of his band marked the mid-
    point of the Apache Wars.

Victorio was born a Mimbreño Apache in what is today southwestern
New Mexico. Although some assert that he was a Mexican captive
reared as an Apache, contemporary and Apache sources agree he was
Apache by birth. In his formative years, Victorio experienced the encroachments of Mexican miners and then American prospectors and
ranchers onto Apache lands. He also absorbed the legacy of hatred en-
gendered by two hundred years of Apache-Mexican warfare.

Most of Victorio's life was spent in relative peace and accommodation with the United States.
He signed an 1853 provisional
compact with the United
States, and requested a reservation for his people in 1869.
The Mimbreños settled first at
Cañada Alamosa, were re-
moved to Tularosa River, and
then moved to Ojo Caliente in
1874. An 1877 attempt to con-
solidate Apaches on the San
Carlos Reservation in southeastern Arizona brought the
Mimbreños there under protest, and they suffered neglect
and conflict with the Chiricahua Apaches.

In September, 1877, Vic-
torio led more than two hun-

Victorio. (National Archives)

dred Apaches off the reservation and asked to be returned to New Mexico. When the United States decided to return them to San Carlos, Victorio and fifty warriors fled. Though still willing to surrender, when he learned of a warrant for his arrest he dropped negotiations and began a year-long war of escape and raiding that terrorized southern New Mexico, southeastern Arizona, and northern Mexico.

Meanwhile, U.S. troops actively pursued Victorio and his band. At first, Victorio experienced extraordinary successes against U.S. forces as a result of his intimate knowledge of the rough terrain; the addition of other renegade Apaches (including GERONIMO for a time), who swelled his ranks to several hundred; and his acknowledged military genius in picking and fortifying strategic positions.

The turning point in the war came in May, 1880, when Apache scouts ambushed Victorio's band, wounding him and killing nearly fifty, many of them his most able warriors. Soundly defeated for the first time, Victorio fled back to Mexico, where he clashed with Mexican troops. Although he twice more attempted to reenter the United States through Texas, U.S. forces repulsed him both times.

An army of almost three hundred Mexicans was organized in August to operate against Victorio. Warning U.S. troops away from Mexico, the Mexicans searched for Victorio until October 15, 1880, when they ambushed and trapped the Apaches on the barren upthrust known as Tres Castillos. By morning the battle was over, and Victorio lay dead by his own hand. His warriors were scalped, and their women and children were captive.

Victorio fought against placing his people on a hostile reservation, but like other leaders in the Apache Wars, he was doomed by the attrition of his finite band and the overwhelming numbers and firepower of his enemies.

Robert Jones
Sondra Jones

FURTHER READING
Ball, Eve. *In the Days of Victorio: Recollections of a Warm Springs Apache.* Tucson: University of Arizona Press, 1970.

Vizenor, Gerald R[obert]

Born: October 22, 1934; Minneapolis, Minnesota
Tribal affiliation: White Earth Chippewa (Ojibwa)

Significance: Gerald Vizenor is known for his provocative and theoretically sophisticated works of fiction, nonfiction, and poetry.

An original voice in postmodern literature, Gerald Vizenor is a brilliant novelist, poet, and essayist, as well as an influential critic. He has received the Josephine Miles PEN award for *Interior Landscapes,* 1990; the Illinois State University/Fiction Collective Prize, 1986; and the American Book Award,1988, for *Griever: An American Monkey King in China* (1987).

Vizenor, who claims a mixed Native American and European American heritage, belongs to the first generation of his family born off the reservation. When he was a child, his father was murdered, and his mother left him with foster families while she vanished for years at a time. Later, she returned and married an alcoholic who beat him. When he was eighteen, Vizenor escaped into the Army. In the Army, Vizenor traveled to Japan, one of the most important experiences of his life. Views of Mount Fuji, a romance with a Japanese woman, and his first visit to a brothel inspired him to write haiku. After his discharge from the Army, Vizenor stayed in Japan.

Vizenor later returned to the United States to study at New York University and the University of Minnesota, where he discovered writers such as Lafcadio Hearn, Jack London, and Thomas Wolfe. He also studied the Japanese verse form haiku in translation. Vizenor calls his discovery of Japanese literature his "second liberation." His haikus won for him his first college teaching job, and his continuing fascination with the haiku form is demonstrated in the collections *Two Wings the Butterfly* (1962), *Raising the Moon Vines* (1964), *Seventeen Chirps* (1964), *Empty Swings* (1967), and *Matsushima: Pine Islands* (1984).

In addition to being a writer, Vizenor worked as a social worker, a mental hospital orderly, a camp counselor, and a reporter for the *Minneapolis Tribune,* where he was a staunch advocate for human rights. As a reporter Vizenor organized civil rights protests

Gerald Vizenor.

and exposed illegal domestic operations by the Central Intelligence Agency. He wrote important articles about the funeral of Dane Michael White and the trial of Thomas James White Hawk. As a founding director of the American Indian Employment and Guidance Center, he combated the "new urban fur traders" and worked to get services for urban Indians who chose to leave the reservation. Vizenor also directed the first Native American studies program at Bemidji State University.

Published shortly before the quincentennial of Christopher Columbus's 1492 voyage, Vizenor's *The Heirs of Columbus* (1991) proclaims: "I am not a victim of Columbus!" The novel tells of the nine tribal descendants of Christopher Columbus, including Stone Columbus, a late-night talk radio personality, and Felipa Flowers, a liberator of cultural artifacts. For the heirs, tribal identity rests in tribal stories, and they are consummate storytellers. For some readers, *The Heirs of Columbus* might recall African American novelist Ishmael Reed's *Mumbo Jumbo* (1972).

Vizenor's imaginative autobiography *Interior Landscapes: Autobiographical Myths and Metaphors*, recounts his triumphs, tragedies, and confrontations with racism. Throughout his autobiography, Vizenor adopts the mythic identity of the Native American trickster, who uses humor and stories to reinvent his world. "My stories are interior landscapes," Vizenor writes, and, as trickster autobiography, these stories about Vizenor's life enable him to mold his experience of his own life.

Wordarrows: Indians and Whites in the New Fur Trade (1978) is Vizenor's collection of autobiographical short stories. It stems from Kiowa novelist N. Scott MOMADAY's belief that storytelling is a means of situating oneself in a particular context in order to better understand individual and collective experiences. Vizenor's stories recount cultural "word wars" in which Native Americans cannot afford to be victims in "one-act terminal scenarios," but must become survivors, relying on their own words to preserve their sacred memories and represent the bitter facts. In *Wordarrows*, the trickster, a figure from Native American oral traditions who appears in most of Vizenor's writing, uses stories and humor to balance the forces of good and evil in the world.

Wordarrows describes the reality of urban Indians, who are denied services and shuttled between various government programs. Vizenor's persona, Clement Beaulieu, directs the American Indian Employment and Guidance Center in Minneapolis, where he is caught between politicians who want to restrict his radical activities and desperate Indians who need his help. At the center, Beaulieu encounters Marleen American Horse, who has been stereotyped as a drunken Indian. He helps her free herself from "the language of white people" so that she can create her own identity. He also meets Laurel Hole In The Day, a woman who struggles to move her family to a white neighborhood in the city. Ultimately, loneliness makes the parents turn to drink, lose their jobs, and return to the reservation.

Vizenor's later writings include the novels *Hotline Healers: An Almost Browne Novel* (1997) and *Chancers: A Novel* (2000).

Trey Strecker

FURTHER READING

Blaeser, Kimberly M. *Gerald Vizenor: Writing in the Oral Tradition.* Norman: University of Oklahoma Press, 1996.

Coltelli, Laura, ed. *Winged Words: American Indian Writers Speak.* Lincoln: University of Nebraska Press, 1990.

Isernhagen, Hartwig. *Momaday, Vizenor, Armstrong: Conversations on American Indian Writing.* Norman: University of Oklahoma Press, 1999.

Laga, Barry E. "Gerald Vizenor and His *Heirs of Columbus:* A Postmodern Quest for More Discourse." *American Indian Quarterly* 18, no. 1 (Winter, 1994): 71-86.

McCaffery, Larry, and Tom Marshall. "Head Water: An Interview with Gerald Vizenor." *Chicago Review* 39, nos. 3-4 (Summer/Fall, 1993): 50-54.

Velie, Alan. *Four American Indian Literary Masters: N. Scott Momaday, James Welch, Leslie Marmon Silko, and Gerald Vizenor.* Norman: University of Oklahoma Press, 1982.

Vizenor, Gerald. "Head Water: An Interview with Gerald Vizenor." Interview by Larry McCaffery and Tom Marshall. *Chicago Review* 39, nos. 3-4 (Summer/Fall, 1993): 50-54.

_____, ed. *Narrative Chance: Postmodern Discourses on Native American Indian Literatures.* Norman: University of Oklahoma Press, 1993.

Vizenor, Gerald, and A. Robert Lee. *Postindian Conversations.* Lincoln: University of Nebraska Press, 1999.

Waban

Born: c. 1604; present-day Concord, Massachusetts
Died: c. 1677; present-day Newton, Massachusetts
Tribal affiliation: Nipmuck
Significance: Waban adapted his tribal leadership capabilities to serve as town clerk and justice of the peace in the earliest of the Massachusetts "praying towns."

Most likely of the Nipmuck tribe, Waban was born around the beginning of the seventeenth century at or near the present-day site of Concord, Massachusetts. Nothing is known of the first half of his life, but by 1646, when he first encountered the missionary John Eliot, he had become a chief at Nonantum, a few miles west of Boston. There, on October 28, Eliot preached a sermon based on Ezekiel 37:9, beginning, "Then said he unto me, prophesy unto the wind." It happened that Waban means "the wind," a coincidence that impressed him favorably.

Even more impressive to the chief was Eliot's ability, cultivated over many years, to speak to the Indians in their own language. Eliot returned about every two weeks from his parish in Roxbury to teach Christianity to Waban and his people. By 1650, however, with white settlers encroaching on Nonantum, Waban asked the Massachusetts General Court for more space and received a tract on the Charles River in Natick; it became the first of Eliot's "praying towns." When Waban, who seems always to have been interested in the administration of justice, asked Eliot how the town should be governed, Eliot answered with a scheme he had learned from the Mosaic law: a judge for every ten people, a higher one for every fifty, and another for every hundred. An older Indian was chosen the highest ruler, Waban one of the leaders of fifty.

The settlement soon established a church for whose aspiring members a public confession of faith was required, but Waban's confession struck the white ministers as inadequate, and, although a believer, he did not gain full membership for many years. He was named town clerk, however, and later justice of the peace, as Natick developed into an Indian town of several hundred citizens.

The outbreak of King Philip's War in 1675 caused serious problems for the Natick Indians. Though only a handful of them were sympathetic to Philip's goal of reestablishing Indian control of the region by warfare, two hundred Natick Indians, among them Waban, were seized as a precautionary measure by order of the General Court and confined on Deer Island in Boston Harbor throughout the severe winter of 1676. Eliot visited them periodically and did his best to encourage them. Some months after the death of Philip the following August, the Praying Indians were resettled, but Natick never prospered as an Indian village thereafter.

In his seventies, Waban seems to have gone with a small group back to Nonantum. Shortly before his death around 1677, Waban became a full-fledged Christian, expressing his desire "not to be troubled about matters of this world." Today, two adjacent stations of the Massachusetts

Bay Transportation Authority Green Line through Newton to Boston
bear the names of the missionary and his first important Native American convert: Eliot and Waban.

Robert P. Ellis

Waheenee

Born: c. 1839; near Knife River (now in North Dakota)
Died: 1932?; Fort Berthold Reservation, North Dakota
Also known as: Buffalo Bird Woman, Waneehee-wea, Maxidiwiac, Mahi-
diwia
Tribal affiliation: Hidatsa
Significance: Waheenee was a Hidatsa woman who related her autobi-
ography during the early twentieth century.

Waheenee described her personal experience in the agricultural society of the Hidatsa, one of the settled, agricultural tribes of the Great
Plains. The Hidatsas hunted buffalo, grew crops, and lived in earthen
lodges in settled villages on the Upper Missouri River. Her grandmother was a child when Meriwether Lewis and William Clark arrived in
1804 and wintered across the Knife River from the thriving Five Villages
of Hidatsas and Mandans. Later, an 1834 attack by the Dakota and a
smallpox epidemic in 1837 devastated the Hidatsas and Mandans.

In 1906, Gilbert Wilson, a graduate student in anthropology, arrived
at Fort Berthold Reservation when Waheenee was in her sixties. Waheenee and her brother Wolf Chief told Wilson about their experiences,
and Waheenee's son George Goodbird translated their stories into English. Waheenee had learned many of her stories from her great-
grandmother White Corn and her grandmother Turtle. Waheenee lost
her biological mother when she was six but still had three mothers, as
her father had married four sisters, and her grandmother raised her.

Waheenee called herself a contented Indian girl who had been obedi-
ent to her mothers. She pointed out that while she had always had plenty
of work to do, she still had time to rest and visit friends and "was not given
tasks beyond my strength." Hidatsa women participated fully in the life of
the village, contributing to building houses, farming, raising children,
preparing food, weaving, and creating artistic designs. Their work wove
the social fibers of their villages together. Hidatsa cultivated corn, beans,
squash, and tobacco and became an important trader.

The matrilineal Hidatsa believed that each person enters the world
through the mother's clan—which gives membership and belonging—

and leaves through the father's clan—which confers rights and responsibilities. Clan relations structured ceremonial and social behavior by prescribing individual participation in life-cycle events, such as naming ceremonies, funerals, and the War Bonnet Dances that involved selected clan children each spring. The Hidatsas' origin stories, which Waheenee helped record, relayed cultural history by establishing ancestral relationships to specific cultural and sacred sites in North Dakota. Society bundles, representative objects that embodied cultural origins, reinforced group identity and anchored kinship ties. Age-graded societies regulated, as they do today, the transmission of ritual knowledge. The information that Wilson collected from Waheenee also explains the Hidatsas' cultural relationship with nature, including planting, cultivation, harvesting, and storing of crops, as well as traditional songs and prayers sung to honor and encourage the garden's yield.

Joanna Yin

FURTHER READING
Wilson, Gilbert L. *Buffalo Bird Woman's Garden: Agriculture of the Hidatsa Indians.* 1917. Reprint. St. Paul: Minnesota Historical Society, 1987.
_____. *Waheenee: An Indian Girl's Story Told by Herself.* 1921. Reprint. Lincoln: University of Nebraska Press, 1991.

Wapasha, Joseph

Born: c. 1822; place unknown
Died: 1876; Santee Agency, Nebraska
Also known as: Red Leaf
Tribal affiliation: Mdewakanton Lakota (Sioux)
Significance: Joseph Wapasha was the last of a line of prominent Sioux chiefs who were named Wapasha; they were all members of the same family.

The earliest known Mdewakanton Lakota chief named Wapasha was born around 1718 in present-day Minnesota. While he was chief, he spent much of his time making war or negotiating peace with the Chippewas. Later in his life, he made contact with the English when they withdrew trading relations following the murder of a merchant. Wapasha captured the culprit and set off to deliver him to his accusers. When the prisoner escaped, Wapasha offered himself as a substitute. The English refused the offer but made an ally. Wapasha died near Hokah, Minnesota.

Wapasha ("Red Leaf"), the son of the elder Wapasha, was born on the site of present-day Winona, Minnesota. He is the chief who met Zebulon Pike's 1805 expedition in search of the Mississippi River's source. Though he was generally an ally of immigrating Americans, the British claimed his loyalty in the War of 1812 but regarded him as suspect to the point of court-martial. He died of smallpox and was followed as tribal leader by his brother (some accounts say nephew), Joseph Wapasha.

In 1862, Joseph Wapasha became the Mdewakanton Sioux's principal chief. He continued the accommodationist policies of his two forebears of the same name. By the 1840's, however, white immigration to Minnesota had reached unprecedented levels, and friendliness was becoming more difficult to maintain without abject surrender.

Joseph Wapasha reluctantly surrendered to pressure to join in the Great Sioux Uprising that began in 1862 under LITTLE CROW. He and his people did their best to stay out of the hostilities, but after the war they were caught in the general colonists' fervor to rid Minnesota of Indians. Vigilantes drove Wapasha and his people to a reservation on the Upper Missouri River. They later moved to the Santee Agency in Nebraska, where Joseph Wapasha died in 1876.

Bruce E. Johansen

Ward, Nancy

Born: c. 1738; Chota (now in Tennessee)
Died: c. 1824; Polk County, Tennessee
Also known as: Nanye-hi (One Who Goes About)
Tribal affiliation: Cherokee
Significance: Nancy Ward was a chief of the Cherokee Nation and a staunch advocate of peace between Indians and European settlers.

Nancy Ward was born in the capital of the Cherokee Nation to an important Cherokee family. Nancy and her husband, King Fisher, fought against the Creeks in 1755 in the Taliwa battle. King Fisher was mortally wounded, and legend has it that Nancy fought so valiantly that the Cherokee declared her "Most Honored Woman"—a powerful distinction. Shortly after being widowed, Nancy married Bryant Ward, an English trader who had come to Chota. Nancy Ward is described as a strikingly beautiful woman with rose-colored skin. Because of this attribute, she was given the nickname "Wild Rose." She had two children by each of her husbands.

In 1775, the Cherokee met with English agents at Sycamore Shoals in what is now eastern Tennessee. The issues were whether more land should be sold to the English and what role the Cherokee should play in the English-American conflict. There was disagreement among the Cherokee chiefs as to which side to favor, but they needed weapons, and selling land to the English seemed to be the only way to obtain what they needed. Nancy Ward's voice was one of peace—in opposition to her cousin, DRAGGING CANOE, who desired weapons to drive the settlers east across the Appalachian Mountains. In 1776, it was decided to wage war against the white people. Nancy Ward prepared the ceremonial "black drink" that was purported to give the warriors success. She then informed the white settlers of the impending attack by releasing three white traders the Cherokees had held captive. Raids were carried out against settlements on the Holston River, and because of Nancy Ward, many lives were saved on both sides.

Nancy Ward was vocal in the 1781 peace talks between the Cherokee and white settlers at Long Island (near the present city of Kingsport, Tennessee). Though the consequences of the talks were short-lived, Nancy continued to speak for peace until her dying day. In her later years she moved to the Ocoee River area to be near her family. There she became a successful innkeeper. Nancy Ward died during the early to mid-1820's and is buried near Benton, Tennessee.

David N. Mielke

FURTHER READING
Bohrer, Melissa Lukeman. *Glory, Passion, and Principle: The Story of Eight Remarkable Women at the Core of the American Revolution.* New York: Atria Books, 2003.

Warren, William W.

Born: May 27, 1825; LaPointe, Michigan
Died: June 1, 1853; St. Paul, Minnesota
Tribal affiliation: Ojibwa (Chippewa)
Significance: Educated in both the English and Chippewa languages, William W. Warren wrote a detailed history of the Ojibwa.

William Whipple Warren was the son of Lyman Warren, a white blacksmith, fur trader, and Indian agent, and his Chippewa-French wife, Mary Cadotte. As a young boy, Warren attended both the LaPointe Indian School and the Mackinaw Mission School and later studied at the

Oneida Institute in New York. Thoroughly schooled in English, he returned to his people as a young man seeking to polish his Chippewa language skills. In 1845, he moved to Crow Wing, Minnesota, where he lived with his wife, Matilda Aiken.

With his considerable command of the Chippewa language, Warren was employed as a U.S. government interpreter. He was elected to the Minnesota State Legislature in 1850, where he earned a reputation for diligence. In 1852, he completed a one-volume history of the Chippewa people containing information he gathered during interviews with many of the tribal elders. Warren died of tuberculosis before finding a publisher for his *History of the Ojibways, Based upon Traditions and Oral Statements*, published posthumously in 1885.

Mary E. Virginia

Warrior, Clyde

Born: 1939; White Eagle, Oklahoma
Died: July, 1968; White Eagle, Oklahoma
Tribal affiliation: Ponca
Significance: One of the most dynamic young Indian leaders of the 1960's, Clyde Warrior was a Ponca activist, writer, and cofounder of the National Indian Youth Council.

Clyde Warrior was raised by his grandparents, who gave him a traditional Ponca upbringing. His first language was Ponca, and from his youth he was immersed in traditional Ponca life. By his late teenage years he was an accomplished powwow fancy dancer. He knew many old Ponca songs as well as many traditional songs of other Native American cultures.

While he was a student at Northeastern State University in Tahlequah, Oklahoma, he wrote an essay, "Which One Are You?," on what he called types of ineffective Indians: the Hood, the Joker, the Sellout, the Ultra-Pseudo-Indian, and the Angry Young Nationalist. He urged genuine and creative democratic leadership that would set guidelines and goals for the average Indian "based on true Indian philosophy geared to modern times."

Warrior became one of the most prominent leaders of the Indian youth movement that emerged during the early 1960's. In 1961, after the federal government's long history of broken treaties with Native Americans and relocation policies that had accelerated during the early 1950's, Native Americans from throughout the United States convened the

American Indian Chicago Conference. Inspired by the Civil Rights movement, Warrior was part of a new generation of Indians who openly rejected the trend toward assimilation and accommodation supported by
other Indian leaders, whom they called sellouts and "Uncle Tomahawks."

Radical members of the new movement issued a manifesto that
stressed the right of Indians to choose their own ways of life and their responsibility to preserve their heritage. Warrior instilled in young Indians ideas of native nationalism and cultural, social, and economic development. Later in 1961, Warrior helped to found the National Indian
Youth Council (NIYC) in Gallup, New Mexico. This organization published a monthly newsletter, *ABC: Americans Before Columbus*, which became a major vehicle of radical Indian thought. Warrior influenced the
direction of national Indian advocacy groups, helped provide organizational structure for an emergent generation of Indian youth, and articulated ideas of "Red Power" nationalism.

Warrior was president of NIYC during the mid-1960's. Under his
leadership, the organization's members learned techniques of legislative lobbying and litigation to win rights and resources owed to them
under federal treaties that had been ignored for decades. In 1965, they
began assisting in the fishing rights struggles of the Quillayute, Nisqually, Muckleshoot, and other tribes of the Pacific Northwest. By engaging in a series of direct confrontations ("fish-ins") with state and federal authorities, they succeeded in reaffirming Indian treaty rights in
the region. The NIYC raised national awareness of Native American
rights and helped inspire the establishment of the American Indian
Movement (AIM) in 1968. This new organization continued the strategy of direct confrontation in support of Native American rights.

On February 2, 1967—the same day on which older Indians were telling President Lyndon Johnson that his proposed bill to reform federal
oversight of Indian affairs was inadequate—Warrior testified at a hear-
ing of the President's National Advisory Commission on Rural Poverty.
His "We Are Not Free" speech pleaded for Indian freedom, linking Indian poverty with the refusal of white people to allow Indians to determine their own destinies.

In 1968, Warrior died at the age of twenty-nine from liver failure
caused by alcoholism. In a traditional Ponca funeral, his relatives and
friends gathered for four days at his grandparents' home for services.
The Lakota writer Vine DELORIA, Jr., leader of the National Congress of
Indians, declared that he was thankful to have known "three great Indians—Clyde Warrior, Hank Adams, and Russell MEANS."

Joanna Yin

FURTHER READING

Smith, Paul Chaat, and Robert Allen Warrior. *Like a Hurricane: The Indian Movement from Alcatraz to Wounded Knee.* New York: New Press, 1997.
Steiner, Stan. *The New Indians.* New York: Harper & Row, 1968.

Washakie

Born: c. 1804; Bitterroot Valley (now in Montana)
Died: February 10, 1900; Bitterroot Valley (now in Montana)
Also known as: Pinquana
Tribal affiliation: Shoshone
Significance: Washakie led the Eastern Shoshone in numerous battles against tribal enemies but remained friendly to whites, offering assistance to settlers and allying with the U.S. Army against hostile tribes.

Washakie was born in the southern Bitterroot Valley of Montana to a Flathead father and a Shoshone mother. Following his father's death in a Blackfoot raid, young Washakie roamed with his family among the Lemhi and Bannock Shoshones. Through Washakie's powerful leadership skills against Blackfoot hostility, he soon rose to tribal prominence.

Washakie then joined the Eastern Shoshones, who quickly accepted him as their leader; he soon gained renown for his kind and helpful treatment of white settlers. As Oregon Trail migration escalated during the 1840's, he consistently aided the immigrants, even to the point of recovering stolen property and assisting wagon trains at the Green River crossing. While acknowledging that whites depleted the available game, Washakie vowed never to war against them. For example, Washakie developed extensive relations with the Mormons, who helped achieve peace between him and Walkara, a Ute chief. Such was Washakie's friendship with the Mormons that when the U.S. Army sought his aid to defeat the "treasonous" sect in 1857, Washakie refused. While earning praise for this type of honest loyalty toward whites, he simultaneously became a feared warrior among his Indian enemies.

Washakie's band dominated the Upper Green and Sweetwater Rivers in southwestern Wyoming and later laid claim to the Wind River country. Tribal disputes soon arose over this game-rich area. In 1866, the Crow came against Washakie's band in a bloody five-day battle; Chief Washakie emerged from the fight with the Crow chief's heart on the end of his lance and thus gained control of the Wind River Valley.

Two years later, Washakie formalized his claim to the valley by signing

Washakie. (National Archives)

a treaty with the U.S. government. In reaction to the treaty and Washakie's friendship with the whites, some tribal warriors began agitating for a new chief. Washakie responded by mysteriously leaving his tribe. Two months later he returned with seven enemy scalps and challenged any warrior to better his feat. None accepted the challenge, and Washakie remained chief.

In 1874, Washakie successfully joined with the U.S. Cavalry against the marauding Arapaho; in 1876, he fought with the cavalry against the Sioux. In these campaigns, Washakie's leadership and fighting skills proved invaluable. For his valor, Washakie received high praise and a silver-mounted saddle from President Ulysses S. Grant.

Washakie spent his remaining life encouraging his people to accept the advancing white settlers and to take advantage of government assistance through the reservation system. Prior to his death, Washakie was baptized by John Roberts, an Episcopal missionary who later presided over Washakie's funeral. The highly respected chief was buried with full military honors at Fort Washakie, Wyoming.

Andrea Gayle Radke

FURTHER READING
Hebard, Grace Raymond. *Washakie: Chief of the Shoshones.* Introduction by Richard O. Clemmer. Lincoln: University of Nebraska Press, 1996.

Watie, Stand

Born: December 12, 1806; near Rome, Georgia
Died: September 9, 1871; Indian Territory (now in Oklahoma)
Also known as: Dagataga, Degadoga (He Stands on Two Feet)

Tribal affiliation: Cherokee

Significance: Stand Watie helped establish the *Cherokee Phoenix*, was a signer of the treaty accepting removal to Indian Territory, and was a Confederate brigadier general in the Civil War.

Born on December 12, 1806, in northwestern Georgia, to a full-blooded Cherokee father and half-blood mother, Watie was called Dagataga, but when his parents converted to Christianity, they changed their name from Oo-wa-tie to Watie and renamed their second son Isaac S., which he later turned to Stand. With his older brother Galegina ("Buck"), he attended the Moravian mission schools at Spring Place, Georgia, and Brainerd, Tennessee. While Buck went on to study in Connecticut at the Foreign Mission School and to change his name to Elias BOUDINOT (one of the school's benefactors), Stand took up farming. At the age of twenty-two, he also became clerk of the Cherokee Supreme Court, and later he became a lawyer. After Boudinot became editor of the Cherokee newspaper, the *Cherokee Phoenix*, Stand Watie sometimes assisted him, and in 1835, he joined him, their cousin John RIDGE, and their uncle Major RIDGE in signing the Treaty of New Echota, which required the Cherokees to give up their lands in Georgia and "remove" to comparable land in what is now Oklahoma. The signers were liable to the "blood law," which decreed death for any-one selling Cherokee land without the full consent of the nation, and Principal Chief John Ross and his followers, not at New Echota, repudiated the treaty.

After President Martin Van Buren had the Eastern Cherokees rounded up and removed west in 1838-1839 on the Trail of Tears, a death march that killed one-third of the tribe, militant followers of Ross murdered the Ridges and Watie's brother Boudinot. Watie himself was marked for death but escaped, offered ten thousand dollars for the murderers of his brother, and became leader of the anti-Ross party.

Stand Watie. (Library of Congress)

Before removal, Watie had several wives but no children; in 1843, the widower married Sarah Caroline Bell, by whom he had five children. When the Cherokees joined the Confederacy at the beginning of the Civil War, Watie raised the first regiment of Cherokee volunteers, the Cherokee Mounted Rifles. As a daring cavalry commander along the border of Indian Territory and at the battles of Pea Ridge and Wilson's Creek, Watie became the most outstanding Indian soldier in history and was promoted to brigadier general. During the war, he got revenge on his enemy John Ross by burning Ross's house. When the majority party of the Cherokees broke their alliance with the Confederate states in 1863, Watie remained loyal to the Confederacy and was elected principal chief by the tribe's southern faction. At the war's end, Watie was the last Confederate general to surrender, on June 23, 1865. After the war, Watie was a member of a Cherokee delegation to Washington, and he then went home to resume farming until his death on September 9, 1871.

Robert E. Morsberger

FURTHER READING

Cunningham, Frank. *General Stand Watie's Confederate Indians.* Foreword by Brad Agnew. Norman: University of Oklahoma Press, 1998.

Dale, Edward Everett, and Gaston Litton. *Cherokee Cavaliers: Forty Years of Cherokee History as Told in the Correspondence of the Ridge-Watie-Boudinot Family.* Foreword by James W. Parins. 1939. Reprint. Norman: University of Oklahoma Press, 1995.

Wauneka, Annie Dodge

Born: April 10, 1910; Navajo Nation, near Sawmill, Arizona
Died: November 10, 1997; Flagstaff, Arizona
Tribal affiliation: Navajo
Significance: A health educator and leader in the implementation of Navajo health programs, Annie Dodge Wauneka helped to educate her people about how to eradicate tuberculosis.

Annie Dodge was the daughter of Henry Chee DODGE, the first elected chairman of the Navajo tribal council, and K'eehabah, a Navajo wife and mother. Her father was also a government interpreter and a rancher, and by the time he was thirty years old, he was a wealthy man. The Dodge family lived in a house rather than a traditional Navajo hogan.

At the age of eight, Annie began her education at the government boarding school located in Fort Defiance. During her stay at the school she was exposed to common white diseases such as flu and trachoma. Many of her friends died, and those who did not were quarantined at the school with no classes. Annie helped the nurses to care for her class-mates, but it was a terribly long, sad year—and one that changed her life. Later, Annie attended the Albuquerque Indian School, where she improved her fluency in English—Indian children were not allowed to speak their native languages at this school. At the age of eighteen, she left the Albuquerque Indian School and returned home to tend the family's flock of sheep.

Dodge attended some of the important meetings that were going on between the Navajos and the officials of the Bureau of Indian Affairs (BIA). She came to understand the dynamics of tribal government and the courtesies involved in Indian and white negotiations. During this time, while traveling around the reservation with her father, she learned the extent of her people's poverty. Annie Dodge and George Wauneka had discussed marriage while both were still in school. They were mar-ried in October of 1929, approximately a year after Annie left the Albu-querque Indian School. They lived in a modern house on the Dodge es-tate at Sonsela Butte for two years. After that time, her father gave them his property in Tanner Springs. In return, Annie and George were to manage his huge cattle herd while running their own herds. The cou-ple reared six children: Georgia Ann, born in 1931; Henry, in 1933; Irma, in 1935; Franklin, in 1945; Lorencita, in 1947; and Sallie, in 1950.

Wauneka continued to attend the BIA meetings with her father in or-der to learn more about interpreting, and she accompanied him on vis-its to the hogans of Navajos who requested his help. She continually wit-nessed the results of disease, malnutrition, and despair among the poverty-stricken Navajos. In recalling her days at the Fort Defiance School, Wauneka remembered how the white administrators had tried to keep the students very clean. As she visited the hogans of the Navajos, with their dirt floors and roofs and their lack of running water, she saw how difficult it was for them to keep their children clean. She set out to improve living conditions for her people by educating them about germs and cleanliness. She began studying with the U.S. Public Health Service in order to learn strategies she could use in implementing a health-education program on the vast Navajo Reservation.

In 1951 Wauneka followed in her father's footsteps and became the first woman elected to the tribal council of seventy-four members. She competed against her husband in order to win her second term in 1954 and was reelected to a third term against another male opponent in

1959. Her work in public health made her the obvious choice to head the Navajo Tribal Council Health Committee. As she continued her work at the grassroots level with the health committee, Wauneka attended college and eventually earned her bachelor's degree in public health from the University of Arizona. In 1960, Wauneka began hosting a daily radio show from station KGAK in Gallup, New Mexico. The program, broadcast in the Navajo language, covered health improvement information as well as topics of general interest to the Navajo Nation.

In 1963, Annie Dodge Wauneka was one of thirty-one distinguished Americans selected to receive the Presidential Medal of Freedom Award that year. She was the first American Indian to receive this honor. Her citation read: "First woman elected to the Navajo tribal council; by her long crusade for improved health programs, she has helped dramatically to lessen the menace of disease among her people and to improve their way of life."

Darlene Mary Suarez

FURTHER READING

Bataille, Gretchen M., ed. *Native American Women: A Biographical Dictionary.* New York: Garland, 1993.

Gridley, Marion E., ed. *Indians of Today.* 4th ed. Chicago: Indian Council Fire, 1971.

Nelson, Mary Carroll. *Annie Wauneka.* Minneapolis, Minn.: Dillon Press, 1972.

Niethammer, Carolyn J. *I'll Go and Do More: Annie Dodge Wauneka, Navajo Leader and Activist.* Lincoln: University of Nebraska Press, 2001.

Waltrip, Lela, and Rufus Waltrip. *Indian Women.* New York: David McKay, 1964.

Weatherford, William

Born: c. 1780; near present-day Montgomery, Alabama
Died: March 9, 1824; Polk County, Tennessee
Also known as: Lamochattee, Lumhe Chate, Red Eagle
Tribal affiliation: Creek
Significance: As principal leader of the Creek war faction, the Red Sticks, William Weatherford fought the Americans during the Creek War, 1813-1814.

William Weatherford's father was a Scottish trader, and his mother was chief Alexander McGILLIVRAY's sister. In 1811, the Creek peace faction,

William Weatherford, meeting with General Andrew Jackson. (Library of Congress)

the White Sticks, refused Tᴇᴄᴜᴍsᴇʜ's appeal for Creek support of his pantribal alliance. Many Red Stick warriors, including Weatherford, sympathized with and were influenced by Tecumseh.

During the Creek War (1813-1814), approximately one thousand warriors under Weatherford's command successfully assaulted Americans at Fort Mims on August 13, 1813, killing five hundred settlers and releasing their black slaves. Subsequently, federal and state troops were mobilized under the command of General Andrew Jackson. At the Battle of Horseshoe Bend, March 27, 1814, Weatherford's forces suffered their final defeat. After surrendering several days later to Jackson, Weatherford was freed after promising to maintain peace thereafter. He died on his farm shortly before the remaining Creeks were forced to relocate to Indian Territory.

Mary E. Virginia

Fᴜʀᴛʜᴇʀ Rᴇᴀᴅɪɴɢ

Griffith, Benjamin W., Jr. *McIntosh and Weatherford: Creek Indian Leaders.* 1988. Reprint. Tuscaloosa: University of Alabama Press, 1998.

Weetamoo

Born: c. 1635; southwestern Massachusetts
Died: August 6, 1676; near present-day Taunton, Massachusetts
Also known as: Namumpum, Tatapanum
Tribal affiliation: Pocasset/Wampanoag
Significance: Weetamoo was a "squaw sachem," or female chief; such
   chiefs were sometimes found among the Algonquian peoples of New
   England.

Weetamoo was sachem of the Pocasset, whose territory lay east of Mt.
Hope Bay in southwestern Massachusetts. When King Philip's War
broke out in June, 1675, she resisted the urging of English emissaries to
remain neutral and joined METACOMET (King Philip), sachem of the
Wampanoag, with whom the Pocasset were affiliated. She provided ca-
noes that allowed Metacomet's people to escape an English force advancing into Mt. Hope Peninsula. Her band spent much of the war in
flight, sometimes in the Narragansett country, sometimes with Metacomet's forces. During the war she married the Narragansett sachem
Quinnapin. In August, 1676, her band was taken by surprise on the
bank of the Taunton River, near Taunton, Massachusetts, and Weetamoo drowned while trying to escape across the river on a raft. Her head
was cut off and set on a pole in Taunton.

Bert M. Mutersbaugh

FURTHER READING
Drake, James D. *King Philip's War: Civil War in New England, 1675-1676.*
   Amherst: University of Massachusetts Press, 2000.
Schultz, Eric B., and Michael J. Tougias. *King Philip's War: The History
   and Legacy of America's Forgotten Conflict.* Woodstock, Vt.: Countryman
   Press, 1999.

Welch, James

Born: November 18, 1940; Browning, Montana
Died: August 4, 2003; Missoula, Montana
Tribal affiliation: Blackfoot, Gros Ventre (Atsina)
Significance: James Welch's publication of several novels and a book of
   poetry earned him national recognition as an American Indian
   writer.

James Welch received his Indian bloodline from his mother, of the Gros

James Welch. (© Marc Hefty)

Ventre tribe, and from his father, of the Blackfoot tribe.
Although his parents had as
much Irish as Indian ancestry,
for the most part he grew up
in Indian territory. He attended Indian high schools
in Browning and Fort Bel-
knap, Montana.

In 1965, while Welch was a
student at the University of
Montana, his mother, a ste-
nographer at the reservation
agency, brought home copies
of annual reports from the
Fort Belknap Indian agents
for 1880, 1887, and 1897.
These documents excited
Welch, for they offered statis-
tics on the numerical decline
of Indians and showed how reservation agents had worked to
control Indians. Of greater interest was evidence that an agent had reported communication with Chief SITTING BULL who had been for a
time within a few miles of the house where Welch lived. This revelation
ignited Welch's interest in the history of his people.

"I wanted to write about that Highline Country in an extended way,"
wrote Welch in describing the impetus for his novel *Winter in the Blood*
(1974). Welch's book captures the feeling of vast openness of northeastern Montana's rolling plains. The novel is about a young Indian who
lacks purpose in life until he discovers how Yellow Calf saved and protected an Indian maiden, an intriguing, heroic tale of his Indian grandparents. The novel's locale is Welch's own parents' ranch, and it suggests Welch's own discovery of Indian forebears.

In *The Death of Jim Loney* (1979), Welch portrayed a young Indian tied
by heritage to his reservation, unable to find any opportunities there,
endlessly drinking at lonely bars. Welch said that he wrote only of situations that he had witnessed on Indian reservations. Lack of opportunity
on the reservation, he argued, led Indians whom he knew to alcoholic
despair. In *Killing Custer* (1994), Welch portrayed his people not as savages but as people justly defending their land, livelihood, and lives from

military massacre. Welch re-created nineteenth and twentieth century Indians living on the Western plains and engaged readers in their viewpoint.

Fools Crow (1986) dramatized Native American life on the plains of eastern Montana toward the end of the era of the free, nonreservation tribe. This novel follows an Indian coming to manhood, his free life, his romantic marriage, his daring attack on an enemy, and his struggle with the dilemma of whether to fight the white man and be slain or to submit to humiliating poverty and confinement on a reservation. The tales of Welch's paternal grandmother concerning the massacre at Marias River, Montana, provided basic material and a viewpoint from which to write. Welch's grandmother, a girl at the time of the massacre, was wounded but escaped with a few survivors. She spoke only her tribal language.

In 2000, the French government awarded Welch its medal of the Chevalier de l'Ordre des Art et des Lettres and the official status of knighthood. Welch's last novel to be published was *The Heartsong of Charging Elk* (2000). After battling lung cancer, Welch died of a heart attack in 2003.

Emmett H. Carroll

FURTHER READING

Barry, Nora. "A Myth to Be Alive: James Welch's *Fools Crow*." *MELUS* 17 (Spring, 1991): 3-20.

Bevis, William. "Dialogue with James Welch." *Northwest Review* 20 (1982): 163-185.

Gish, Robert F. "Word Medicine: Storytelling and Magic Realism in James Welch's *Fools Crow*." *American Indian Quarterly* 14, no. 4 (Fall, 1990): 349-354.

McFarland, Ronald E. "'The End' in James Welch's Novels." *American Indian Quarterly* 17, no. 3 (Summer, 1995): 319-327.

_____, ed. *James Welch.* Lewiston, Idaho: Confluence Press, 1986.

_____. *Understanding James Welch.* Columbia: University of South Carolina Press, 2000.

O'Connell, Nicholas. *At the Field's End: Interviews with Twenty Pacific Northwest Writers.* Seattle: Madrona, 1987.

Wild, Peter. *James Welch.* Boise State Western Writers Series. Boise, Idaho: Boise State University Press, 1983.

White Bird

Born: c. 1807; present-day Idaho
Died: 1892; Canada
Also known as: Penpenhihi, Peopeo Kiskiok Hihih (White Goose)
Tribal affiliation: Nez Perce
Significance: A skilled negotiator and marksman, White Bird was a major leader in the Nez Perce War of 1877.

Along with Joseph the Elder, White Bird refused to sign the Treaty of 1863, by which the Nez Perce would move to the Lapwai Reservation of Idaho. Although originally opposed to war, White Bird became a principal war leader as tensions peaked in 1877 after the Nez Perce were ordered to move to the reservation. As a skilled marksman, White Bird led his warriors against troops commanded by Colonel John Gibbon at the major Battle of Big Hole Valley, Montana, August 9, 1877.

After a six-day siege at the final Battle of Bear Paw, Montana, beginning September 30, White Bird, with approximately twenty other Nez Perce leaders and two hundred followers, retreated to Canada. There they joined Sioux chief SITTING BULL, already in exile after the Battle of the Little Bighorn (1876). Unlike Sitting Bull, however, White Bird remained in exile. He was later killed by the bitter father of two Indian patients who died after White Bird—in his role as a medicine man—had treated them.

Mary E. Virginia

FURTHER READING
Hampton, Bruce. *Children of Grace: The Nez Perce War of 1877.* Lincoln: University of Nebraska Press, 2002.

White Bull

Born: April, 1849; Black Hills (now in South Dakota)
Died: June 21, 1947; place unknown
Also known as: Bull Standing with Cow, Big in Center, Joseph White Bull
Tribal affiliation: Miniconjou Lakota (Sioux)
Significance: White Bull—whom some historians identify as the Lakota warrior who killed George Armstrong Custer—provided an important autobiographical account of his warring exploits through oral histories, pictographic drawings, and a brief written account in Lakota.

White Bull was a member of a prominent Lakota family. His father, Makes Room for Them, was an important headman of the Miniconjou, and his mother, Pretty Feather Woman, was SITTING BULL's sister. Although his brother, One Bull, was raised by Sitting Bull, White Bull and One Bull remained close throughout their lives. In fact, it was Sitting Bull's father, JUMPING BULL, who gave White Bull his first name, Bull Standing with Cow. As was common among the Lakota, this childhood name was eventually dropped and was replaced by Big in Center to commemorate his exploits in the Fetterman massacSre.

White Bull was born into the old Lakota world. As a child he was taught many skills that would prepare him to become a hunter and warrior. He learned how to care for and ride horses and to shoot with a bow and arrow. He was also encouraged to run and be quick. From an early age White Bull was recognized as a prolific buffalo hunter, and he often brought great quantities of meat back to camp to share with the older people. He was also known as a brave warrior and participated in many battles with the Lakotas' traditional foes and with the U.S. military during the period of the Plains Indian wars. He took part in the Fetterman massacre in 1866, the Wagon Box fight in 1867, the Battle of Rosebud Creek in 1876, and the Battle of the Little Bighorn in 1876, among others.

Sometime after the Battle of the Little Bighorn, White Bull went to live on the Great Sioux Reservation, as federal Indian policy dictated, and he also lived among the Miniconjou people at the Cheyenne River Agency. He learned how to read and write Lakota from Christian missionaries and wrote a short account of his life in the traditional days. His brother, One Bull, lived with Sitting Bull's people on the Standing Rock Reservation, but the brothers frequently visited each other.

White Bull gained notoriety during the 1930's, when he began to tell his war deeds to historians. Stanley Vestal and Usher Burdick both traveled to the Standing Rock Reservation to visit with White Bull and One Bull to gather information about their famous uncle, Sitting Bull. The old men talked of fighting and hunting with Sitting Bull, and the historians became interested in White Bull's own deeds of valor. His remarks gave rise to speculation that he was the warrior who killed Custer at Little Bighorn, and this information became the basis of a number of books.

White Bull and One Bull Both died in 1947, within months of each other.

Carole A. Barrett

FURTHER READING

Howard, James H., ed. and trans. *Lakota Warrior: Joseph White Bull.* Lincoln: University of Nebraska Press, 1998.

Vestal, Stanley. *Warpath: The True Story of the Fighting Sioux Told in a Biography of Chief White Bull.* Lincoln: University of Nebraska Press, 1984.

White Cloud

Born: c. 1830; Gull Lake (now in Minnesota)
Died: 1898; White Earth Reservation, Minnesota
Also known as: Wabanaquot
Tribal affiliation: Ojibwa (Chippewa)
Significance: A renowned peace chief, diplomat, and orator, White Cloud was also known for his addiction to alcohol.

The son of Wabojeeg, who had been appointed by the U.S. government, White Cloud succeeded his father as chief of the Minnesota Chippewa. He led his people to the White Earth Reservation in 1868, where they adopted sedentary agriculture and settled into a life of peace. White Cloud converted to Christianity in 1871.

Although a renowned politician and diplomat, White Cloud became dependent on alcohol and earned a reputation as a chief who accepted bribes and acted against the best interests of his tribe in favor of his own addiction. He became embroiled in controversy which weakened the tribe and threatened its unity after he sided with an influential white trader, who was liberally supplying him with alcohol, in a dispute against three Indian agents who were loyally serving the Chippewa. For nearly ten years, White Cloud's leadership was challenged and the trade issue was debated in the Chippewa tribal council. At numerous debates, White Cloud's oratory was honed to a fine edge; although he retained tribal leadership, the issue was a divisive one that permanently weakened Chippewa tribal unity.

Mary E. Virginia

White Eyes

Born: c. 1730; western Pennsylvania
Died: November, 1778; Pennsylvania
Also known as: Koquethagechton
Tribal affiliation: Lenni Lenape (Delaware)

Significance: White Eyes was an ally of the Americans during the American Revolution.

Named for his light-colored eyes, White Eyes played a diplomatic role in the American Revolution after becoming a friend of Colonel George Morgan, Indian agent of the Continental Congress. He signed a treaty in 1778 designed to incorporate the Delaware Nation as the fourteenth state of the United States.

White Eyes became principal chief of the Ohio Delawares in 1776. At the beginning of the American Revolution, he counseled neutrality, but he took up the patriot cause after the Delaware leader HOPOCAN sided with the British. In 1778, White Eyes was a party to the first treaty negotiated by the new United States, at Fort Pitt. The treaty was notable because it outlined a plan for a Delaware state with representation in Congress. The plan never materialized.

Two months after signing that treaty, White Eyes was acting as a guide for General Lachlin McIntosh in his expedition against Fort Sandusky. During the expedition, he was killed by American troops under confusing conditions, possibly by "friendly fire." To cover up the death of an ally, the soldiers reported that White Eyes had died of smallpox.

Bruce E. Johansen

White Hat, Albert

Born: November 18, 1938; St. Francis, South Dakota
Tribal affiliation: Sicangu Lakota (Sioux)
Significance: Albert White Hat, Sr., is a Lakota linguist, educator, and textbook author.

Albert White Hat was born in a small Lakota community on the Rosebud Sioux Reservation in South Dakota, where he grew up in two cultures. However, it was the more hidden Lakota world that would have the greatest impact on his life and thought. He has credited his mother, Emily Hollow Horn Bear White Hat, and his older brother, Isadore, with being his first Lakota language instructors. Through stories and personal example, they also taught him the philosophy and values of this heritage.

White Hat completed his basic and secondary education at the Jesuit-run St. Francis Indian School in his community. He later earned an associate of arts degree from the local tribal college. In 1961, he briefly lived in Cleveland, Ohio, to work for a steel company as a participant in the federal government's urban relocation program for Indians.

The major changes in Indian education and federal Indian policy that began during the late 1960's and 1970's affected White Hat's future career. For example, his old Jesuit school began altering its approach to Indian education by adding Lakota language instruction to its curriculum. In 1971, White Hat was hired by the school to teach Lakota courses at the middle and high school levels. In that same year, the new first tribal college came to his reservation with the establishment of Sinte Gleska College (later University). In 1983, Sinte Gleska hired White Hat as an instructor in its Lakota studies program.

As the number of Lakota language teachers on South Dakota reservation communities increased, the question of common approaches to instruction became a concern. Between 1981 and 1991, White Hat served as chairman of Lakotiyapi Okolakiciye, a committee of educators from tribal colleges, reservation schools, and the Rapid City school system whose task was to develop a standardized Lakota alphabet. Drawing on his teaching experience, White Hat wrote *Reading and Writing the Lakota Language* (1999). Because languages and the cultures in which they are spoken are closely interconnected, White Hat's textbook introduces the language by employing examples, anecdotes, and lessons on the philosophy and values of his Lakota community. The Lakota scholar Vine DELORIA, Jr., called White Hat's textbook "a real people's grammar" and a "masterpiece."

White Hat's teaching and research interests also include Lakota teachings and healing, traditions, oral history, ceremonial songs, and social activities. He has served as a language translator and cultural adviser for films, such as *Son of the Morning Star* (1991) and *Dances with Wolves* (1990). White Hat's contributions as a Lakota educator and linguist are recognized both locally and nationally. His honors include the Distinguished Service Award of the South Dakota Indian Education Association and recognition as Elder of the Year by the National Indian Educational Association. White Hat has also served as a representative on the Rosebud Sioux tribal council and was president of Sinte Gleska's board of directors from 1981 to 1983.

David A. Crain

White Man Runs Him

Born: c. 1855; place unknown
Died: c. 1925; Crow Agency, Montana
Also known as: Batsida Karoosh, Beshayeschayecoosis, Miastashede-karoos (White Man Runs Him)

Tribal affiliation: Crow

Significance: White Man Runs Him was George Armstrong Custer's chief scout during the Sioux Wars.

Beshayeschayecoosis's father was chased by a rifle-firing white man, thus acquiring the name White Man Runs Him; the young warrior inherited

White Man Runs Him in 1905. (Library of Congress)

his adult name from his father. Traditionally, the Crow and Sioux were enemies, and White Man Runs Him, in his youth, was a successful warrior who participated in numerous horse-stealing raids against the Sioux. During the 1870's, White Man Runs Him was chief Indian scout in Custer's Seventh Cavalry. While on a scouting foray, White Man Runs Him and four other scouts, in search of Sioux who had left the reservation, spotted them encamped on the banks of the Little Bighorn River. The sighting was reported to Custer, and the stage was set for the Battle of the Little Bighorn. Years later, some of White Man Runs Him's enemies, remembering his scouting activities, used his name derisively. He was often interviewed about his role in the Little Bighorn, but historians are not clear on what function the Indian scouts played during the actual battle. White Man Runs Him died in 1925; he was reburied in the Little Bighorn Battlefield Cemetery in 1929.

Moises Roizen

Further Reading

Hampton, Bruce. *Children of Grace: The Nez Perce War of 1877*. Lincoln: University of Nebraska Press, 2002.

Hoxie, Frederick E. *Parading Through History: The Making of the Crow Nation in America, 1805-1935*. New York: Cambridge University Press, 1995.

Wildcat

Born: c. 1810; present-day Yulaka, Florida
Died: 1857; Coahuila, Mexico
Also known as: Coacoochee
Tribal affiliation: Seminole
Significance: Beginning with the Second Seminole War, Wildcat was the most aggressive of the Seminole chieftains during their crusade against the U.S. Army; he was known for carrying a rifle and a scalping knife.

Wildcat was born in about 1810 in central Florida, where the Seminole, or Lower Creeks, had settled in the eighteenth century. A nephew of the Seminole principal chief, MICANOPY, Wildcat became the leader of those who strongly opposed white settlement in Seminole territory. When the Second Seminole War began in 1835, Wildcat was at the forefront.

In 1837, Wildcat was captured and put into a jail cell in St. Augustine but soon escaped through a small window 15 feet above the cell floor. Four years later, he was captured again near Fort Pierce. This time he urged his followers, including escaped slaves, or Black Seminoles, to give up the battle. In October, 1841, Wildcat left Florida aboard an American steamer sailing west.

For a brief time after leaving Florida, Wildcat lived with the Cherokee in Oklahoma. Fearing reprisals by the Creeks, however, he led his followers to Coahuila in northern Mexico, where large land grants were being given by the Mexican government. Wildcat died in Coahuila in 1857.

Glenn L. Swygart

FURTHER READING

Missall, John, and Mary Lou Missall. *The Seminole Wars: America's Longest Indian Conflict.* Foreword by Raymond Arsenault and Gary R. Mormino. Gainesville: University Press of Florida, 2004.

Williams, Eleazar

Born: May, 1788; St. Regis, New York
Died: August 28, 1858; near Hogansburg, New York
Tribal affiliation: Mohawk
Significance: Eleazar Williams was an influential missionary who used his position to persuade the Iroquois to establish a new empire west of Lake Michigan.

One of thirteen children of Thomas and Mary Rice Williams, Eleazar Williams was placed in the care of Nathaniel Ely at Long Meadow, Massachusetts, where he was trained as an Episcopalian missionary. Between 1809 and 1812, he continued his studies with the Reverend Enoch Hale at Westhampton, Massachusetts. Sponsored by the American Board of Missions, in 1812 he began proselytizing among the Iroquois.

During the War of 1812, Williams served the federal government as superintendent general of the North Indian Department. He was also a scout.

With the Ogden Land Company, fellow missionaries, and the War Department, Williams collaborated in a scheme to relocate the Iroquois empire west of Lake Michigan. After forging Iroquois council members' signatures, Williams left for Wisconsin in 1823, followed by the Oneidas and Mahicans, many of whom he had converted. Scorned by other Iroquois, Williams abandoned his plan in 1832.

Returning east in 1853, Williams claimed to be the lost dauphin of France, Louis XVII. The Reverend John Hanson wrote *The Lost Prince* in support of Williams's improbable claim.

Mary E. Virginia

Winema

Born: c. 1836; Link River, California
Died: May 10, 1932; Klamath Reservation, Oregon
Also known as: Toby Riddle
Tribal affiliation: Modoc
Significance: Fluent in English, Winema became an interpreter and mediator during the Modoc War of 1873.

Earning a reputation as a brave child, Winema once safely guided her canoe through dangerous rapids to save the lives of several companions. At the age of fourteen, she led warriors to victory during a surprise attack by a rival tribe. After marrying Frank Riddle, a white rancher, Winema was scorned by members of her tribe; however, her proficiency as an interpreter later enabled her to regain her status. On several occasions, she helped diffuse tensions and mediate quarrels between Modocs and whites.

Winema was shunned by her cousin, CAPTAIN JACK, leader of the Modoc Rebellion, after trying to persuade him to return to Oregon. In February of 1873, Winema warned a white peace commission of a murder plot by Captain Jack. Ignoring her warning, two members of the commission were killed; Winema rescued a third, Alfred Meacham.

Following the war, Winema became a celebrity, touring cities in a theatrical production about her life. She returned to the state of Oregon in 1890, and she was granted a pension by the federal government, most of which she donated to the Modocs.

Mary E. Virginia

FURTHER READING
Quinn, Arthur. *Hell with the Fire Out: A History of the Modoc War.* Boston: Faber & Faber, 1997.
Riddle, Jefferson C. Davis. *The Indian History of the Modoc War.* Introduction by Peter Cozzens. Mechanicsburg, Pa.: Stackpole Books, 2002.

Winnemucca, Sarah

Born: c. 1844; Humboldt Sink, Nevada Territory

Died: October 17, 1891; Henry's Lake, Idaho

Also known as: Thocmetony (Shell Flower), Sarah Winnemucca Hopkins

Tribal affiliation: Northern Paiute

Significance: Sarah Winnemucca is best known for her autobiography and for her determined efforts to gain justice for the Paiutes in their dealings with the federal government.

Sarah Winnemucca was born into a rapidly transforming world. Her people, the Northern Paiutes, were pursuing the nomadic hunting and gathering lives common among Great Basin people when their territory was invaded by miners, settlers, and the U.S. Army. Winnemucca responded to the disruption of the Paiute world by taking on extraordinarily diverse roles, including those of army scout, author, performer, interpreter, political activist, domestic servant, and primary school teacher. Her overriding talent and vocation was that of an intermediary, particularly between Paiutes and non-Indians.

Sarah Winnemucca came from a politically and spiritually influential Paiute family, which included her father, Winnemucca, and her grandfather, Truckee (for whom the Truckee River was named). When Sarah was a young girl, her family traveled widely to replace the livelihood disrupted by American expansion. In her travels, she acquired an unusual facility with languages and a knowledge of cultural differences. In addition to learning other Indian languages, Winnemucca learned Spanish during trips to California, where her family found work on ranches. She learned English when she was temporarily "adopted" by an Anglo-American family who treated her as something in between a daughter and a servant.

In 1878, Winnemucca put her linguistic aptitude to work when she served as an interpreter and scout for the U.S. Army during the Bannock War. She was also intermittently employed as an interpreter for federal Indian agents on the reservations to which the Paiute and neighboring Indian people were being sent. By the early 1880's, the government had scattered the Paiutes among reservations in Washington, southern Oregon, and Nevada, where they were subjected to severe corruption among agents as well as starvation and disease.

In 1880, Winnemucca took her people's plight to the American public. In addition to meeting with numerous government leaders, Winnemucca delivered lectures to audiences in California and cities throughout the Northeast. Living at Fort Vancouver for a year (1882), she met and married her fourth husband, Lieutenant Lewis H. Hopkins.

Winnemucca wrote her autobiography, *Life Among the Piutes: Their Wrongs and Claims* (1883), in which she attempted to gain support for the Paiutes in their struggles for land and freedom. Her efforts secured thousands of signatures on a petition asking that Paiutes be granted land in severalty. Though Congress passed the bill in 1884, Secretary of the Interior Edward Teller failed to implement it. Although Winnemucca's efforts were generally unsuccessful, she became renowned for her determination and resourcefulness.

Winnemucca returned to her brother's ranch in Lovelock, Nevada, where she started a school for Paiute children and taught for three years. Her husband died of tuberculosis in 1886, and shortly thereafter she moved to Henry's Lake, Idaho. She resided there with her married sister, Elma Smith, until her own death in 1891.

FURTHER READING

Brimlow, George F. "The Life of Sarah Winnemucca: The Formative Years." *Oregon Historical Quarterly* 53 (June, 1952): 103-134.

Canfield, Gae Whitney. *Sarah Winnemucca of the Northern Paiutes.* Norman: University of Oklahoma Press, 1983.

Egan, Ferol. *Sand in a Whirlwind: The Paiute Indian War of 1860.* Garden City, N.Y.: Doubleday, 1972.

Howard, O. O. *Famous Indian Chiefs I Have Known.* New York: Century, 1922.

Knack, Martha C., and Omer C. Stewart. *As Long as the River Shall Run: An Ethnohistory of Pyramid Lake Indian Reservation.* Berkeley: University of California Press, 1984.

Morrison, Dorothy Nafus. *Chief Sarah: Sarah Winnemucca's Fight for Indian Rights.* New York: Atheneum, 1980.

Peabody, Elizabeth P. *The Paiutes: Second Report of the Model School of Sarah Winnemucca, 1886-87.* Cambridge, Mass.: John Wilson and Son, 1887.

Walker, Cheryl. *Indian Nation: Native American Literature and Nineteenth-Century Nationalisms.* Durham, N.C.: Duke University Press, 1997.

Zanjani, Sally Springmeyer. *Sarah Winnemucca.* Lincoln: University of Nebraska Press, 2001.

Wooden Leg

Born: 1858; Cheyenne River, Black Hills of South Dakota
Died: 1940; Montana
Also known as: Kummok'quifiokta
Tribal affiliation: Northern Cheyenne
Significance: Wooden Leg's autobiography documents some of the most important events in Cheyenne history.

A group of Cheyenne and Sioux people near the Powder River in March of 1876 was attacked by troops led by Colonel Joseph J. Reynolds. Wooden Leg was with those who escaped to the shelter of SITTING BULL's encampment on the Little Bighorn River when George Armstrong Custer attacked. Following Custer's destruction, Wooden Leg's family did not follow the ill-fated group led by DULL KNIFE and LITTLE WOLF; Wooden Leg would live to write of the "Fort Robinson outbreak" by the Cheyenne imprisoned there. He was part of the Ghost Dance movement in 1890.

In his autobiography, he recounts these major historical events and explains the problems of adjusting to reservation living, especially the experience of monogamy and being forced to give up one of his wives. His survival at such a unique time in American Indian history and his apprehension of the need to record these events earned him an important place in history.

Tonya Huber

FURTHER READING
Marquis, Thomas B., trans. *Wooden Leg: A Warrior Who Fought Custer.* Introduction by Richard Littlebear. Lincoln: University of Nebraska Press, 2003.

Wovoka

Born: c. 1858; Mason Valley, Nevada
Died: September 20, 1932; Schurz, Nevada
Also known as: Jack Wilson
Tribal affiliation: Northern Paiute
Significance: Wovoka originated the messianic Ghost Dance religion, which was embraced by nearly sixty thousand Indians in 1889 and 1890.

Wovoka in 1892. (National Museum of the American Indian, Smithsonian Institution)

Wovoka was born near Walker Lake in western Nevada's Mason Valley. "The Cutter"—the meaning of the name Wovoka—would spend almost his entire life in this isolated valley.

Wovoka's father was TAVIBO, a Northern Paiute shaman and medicine man. His mother's identity is unknown. Orphaned at fourteen, Wovoka was taken in by the family of David and Mary Wilson, white ranchers who had settled in the valley. Devout Christians, the Wilsons introduced Wovoka to their theology. The works and words of the Christian messiah—especially Jesus' teachings about peace, love, and everlasting life in heaven—made an indelible impression upon the Indian teenager.

As a young man, Wovoka spent two years as a migrant worker in Oregon and Washington. In the Northwest, he met numerous Shaker Indians, disciples of a Squaxin religious leader named Squ-sacht-un (known to the whites as John SLOCUM). The Shakers told Wovoka that Squ-sacht-un, like Jesus, had experienced death and resurrection. He had returned from the spirit world with the message that God would exalt the Indians if they practiced righteousness and abandoned white vices. The testimony of these zealots had a profound effect upon the young Paiute.

Upon returning to his valley home, Wovoka began to identify himself more closely with his own people. When he was twenty, he left the Wilson ranch, moved back into an Indian wickiup, and wed a Paiute woman whom he called Mary. He then cultivated a reputation as a miracle-working religious leader. Using some shamanic techniques learned from Tavibo, he convinced many Paiutes that he had the power to heal the sick and control natural forces.

Wovoka's reputation as a wonder-worker was further enhanced by a mystical experience he underwent in 1887. One night, he lapsed into unconsciousness, and he remained in a deathlike state for two days. When he regained consciousness, he claimed that he had been taken up into heaven and had seen God. Angels had urged him to instruct Indians that Jesus was again among them, working miracles and teaching them to love one another and to live at peace with whites.

Wovoka mocked death a second time when he was about thirty. In late 1888, he fell ill with the dreaded scarlet fever and appeared to have died. Then, on January 1, 1889, he suddenly revived. The dramatic effect of his recovery was magnified by the fact that it had coincided precisely with a solar eclipse. Wovoka again asserted that he had seen God, who told him that within two years the earth would be regenerated and returned to the Indians, that the whites would disappear, that buffalo herds would return, and that all Indians—including their dead ancestors—would live forever in paradise. In the meantime, Indians were to practice pacifism and testify to their faith in Wovoka's prophecy by participating in a sacred ritual, the so-called Ghost Dance, which he taught them.

As a result of this second mystical experience, Wovoka was held in even greater esteem by the Nevada Paiutes, who regarded him as invulnerable to death. His people now called him their "Father" and revered him as the messiah sent by the Great Spirit to liberate Indians from white bondage.

The Paiutes of Mason Valley danced and soon went out as missionaries to spread Wovoka's gospel to other tribes. Many Great Basin and Plains tribes—including the Arapahos, Cheyennes, Utes, Shoshones, and Sioux—sent emissaries to talk to the Paiute prophet. They returned enthusiastic to start the dance among their own people. Beleaguered tribespeople who had lost hope now found it again in a ritual that promised to usher in a Native American millennium free of white people. By the summer of 1889, the messianic faith had spread beyond the Rockies eastward to the Mississippi.

The phenomenal expansion of the Ghost Dance among the Plains Indians alarmed the white authorities, who feared that militant Sioux chieftains might transform Wovoka's pacifistic religion into a massive Indian resistance movement. In an attempt to suppress the burgeoning revival, the U.S. Army began to round up many of the dance's promoters, including BIG FOOT, the leader of a small group of Hunkpapa Sioux. On December 29, 1890, the commander of the Seventh Cavalry started to disarm Big Foot's band of Ghost Dancers near Wounded Knee Creek, South Dakota; someone fired a rifle, and a bloodbath ensued. Soldiers shot as many as two hundred Indians, many of them women and children.

When the report of the Wounded Knee massacre reached Wovoka, he was stunned and saddened. He felt partly responsible for the tragedy, because the Sioux had embraced his teachings. After Wounded Knee, the appeal of his religion plummeted. The slaughter of the Sioux Ghost Dancers shattered the faith of tens of thousands in Wovoka's vision of an imminent Indian millennium.

The discredited prophet lived out his remaining forty-two years in Mason Valley as "Jack Wilson." A storekeeper named Ed Dyer befriended him, and Wovoka eked out a living by selling ceremonial objects. By 1900, he could no longer find enough disciples to form a Ghost Dance circle; few people continued to call him Father. Nevertheless, Wovoka never abandoned his conviction that he had visited heaven and talked to God. In 1932, at the age of seventy-four, he died at Schurz, on the Walker River Reservation in Nevada.

Ronald W. Long

FURTHER READING

Andrist, Ralph K. *The Long Death: The Last Days of the Plains Indians.* New York: Macmillan, 1964.

Bailey, Paul. *Wovoka: The Indian Messiah.* Los Angeles: Westernlore Press, 1957.

Hittman, Michael. *Wovoka and the Ghost Dance.* Edited by Don Lynch. Expanded ed. Lincoln: University of Nebraska Press, 1997.

Marty, Martin E. *Pilgrims in Their Own Land.* Boston: Little, Brown, 1984.

Mooney, James. *The Ghost-Dance Religion and the Sioux Outbreak of 1890.* Introduction by Raymond J. DeMallie. Lincoln: University of Nebraska Press, 1991.

Sherer, Joel. "Wovoka." In *Twentieth Century Shapers of American Popular Religion,* edited by Charles H. Lippy. Westport, Conn.: Greenwood Press, 1989.

Wright, Allen

Born: November 28, 1825; Attala County, Mississippi
Died: December 2, 1885; Boggy Depot, Indian Territory (now in Oklahoma)
Also known as: Kiliahote (Let's Kindle a Fire)
Tribal affiliation: Choctaw
Significance: A highly regarded scholar, Allen Wright served in several elected tribal offices and is credited with giving Oklahoma its name.

Born along the Yaknukni River in Mississippi, Allen Wright relocated to Indian Territory when he was seven years old. His mother died just before the relocation and his father soon after, so missionary Cyrus Kingsbury sponsored the boy's education at local academies. Wright was sent east to continue his education, earning a bachelor's degree at Union College, Schenectady, New York, in 1853 and a master's degree at Union Theological Seminary, New York, in 1855. He became a noted scholar in Latin, Greek, Hebrew, and English.

Ordained by the Presbyterian church in 1865, Wright returned to Indian Territory to work among his people. During the 1870's and 1880's, he translated numerous Indian works into English, including a Choctaw dictionary and the Choctaw and Chickasaw constitutions and code of laws.

In 1852, Wright was elected to the tribal house of representatives and to the senate. He was also the tribe's treasurer. After serving the Confederacy during the Civil War, he was elected to two terms as Choctaw tribal chief, 1866-1870, during which time he suggested the name Oklahoma for Indian Territory.

Mary E. Virginia

FURTHER READING
Debo, Angie. *The Rise and Fall of the Choctaw Republic.* 2d ed. Norman: University of Oklahoma Press, 1961.

Yellow Wolf

Born: 1856; Wallowa Valley, Oregon
Died: August 21, 1935; Colville Indian Reservation, Washington
Also known as: Hermene Moxmox (Yellow Wolf), Heinmot Hikkih (White Thunder or White Lightning)
Tribal affiliation: Nez Perce
Significance: Yellow Wolf was an important warrior in the Nez Perce tribe; he exhibited loyalty, courage, and skill during the Nez Perce War of 1877.

Yellow Wolf was born in the ancestral Wallowa Valley, Oregon. His mother, Yikjik Wasumwah, was a first cousin of Chief JOSEPH THE YOUNGER, so Yellow Wolf belonged to Joseph's band. Yellow Wolf's father, Seekumses Kunnin, was apparently a prosperous tribal member with many horses and cattle. Yellow Wolf remained with his parents until well into adulthood.

Yellow Wolf was not his chosen name, and he always considered it to be a nickname. He was named after the spirit which gave him a promise of its power as a warrior: Heinmot Hikkih (White Thunder). He received the name Yellow Wolf from a dream in which a yellow wolflike form stood in the air in front of him and called itself Hermene Moxmox (Yellow Wolf). Yellow Wolf's calling was as a warrior. The *kopluts*, or war club, he made as a boy, by direction of his spirit, gave him promise of war power because it had the same killing strength as thunder.

This prosperous and contented tribal life ended with the Nez Perce War in 1877, the result of the Wallowa Valley Nez Perce refusing to sign treaties to cede their land to the United States. The war was distinguished by the Nez Perce's masterful march to reach the safety of Canada. The Nez Perce outfought and outmaneuvered the army but were caught within two days of their objective. Yellow Wolf proved to be a loyal, resourceful, and courageous warrior. In September, 1877, Yellow Wolf was moved from a rear guard position to advance guard in order to deal with straggling soldiers before them. This change was recognition from his fellow warriors of their confidence in Yellow Wolf's ability to take care of the enemy single-handedly.

Yellow Wolf did not attend or participate in the peace negotiations because, according to tribal practice, he had not been a warrior long enough. Yellow Wolf refused to surrender. He and some other warriors escaped and made their way to SITTING BULL's Sioux camp in Canada in October, 1877. Yellow Wolf and other warriors left in June, 1878, to return to Wallowa Valley under the erroneous assumption that the area was now safe. While riding through land that brought back memories of happier times, Yellow Wolf realized that he had no place to go where he was not encircled by his enemies. He returned to the Nez Perce Agency in August, 1878. He was sent to Oklahoma, but the ravages of disease and weather led him to be resettled at the Colville Indian Reservation in northeast Washington. The reservation provided ample subsistence, and Yellow Wolf remained there until his death in 1935.

Laurence Miller

FURTHER READING

Beal, Merrill D. *"I Will Fight No More Forever": Chief Joseph and the Nez Perce War.* Seattle: University of Washington Press, 1963.

Hampton, Bruce. *Children of Grace: The Nez Perce War of 1877.* Lincoln: University of Nebraska Press, 2002.

McWhorter, Lucullus V. *Yellow Wolf: His Own Story.* Rev. and enlarged ed. 1940. Reprint. Caldwell, Idaho: Caxton Press, 1983.

Yellowtail, Robert

Born: c. 1889; Little Bighorn River, near Lodge Grass, Crow Indian Reservation, Montana

Died: June 18, 1988; Little Horn Ranch, Crow Indian Reservation, Montana

Tribal affiliation: Crow

Significance: As the preeminent Crow political leader during the twentieth century and the first Indian to served as a reservation superintendent, Robert Yellowtail made major contributions toward preserving Crow land and culture.

Born on a Crow reservation in Montana, Robert Yellowtail was taken at the age of four to a Crow Agency boarding school, where he was not allowed to speak his own language or be with members of his own tribe.

When the agent supervising the school noticed Yellowtail's potential for learning, he sent him to the Sherman Institute in Riverside, California. As Yellowtail grew up, he became committed to fight for the rights of his people. He eventually earned a law degree through extension classes from the University of Chicago.

In 1910, when Montana senator Thomas Walsh introduced a bill in Congress to open the Crow Indian Reservation to white homesteaders, Crow chief PLENTY COUPS asked Yellowtail to return home to help resist this new threat to Crow land. Yellowtail then spent the next seven years in a difficult legal and political struggle that resulted in a Crow victory. In 1919, he and Chief Plenty Coups led a Crow delegation to Washington, D.C., to lobby for the Crow Allotment Act, which secured Crow lands for the Crow. Yellowtail remained an activist for preserving Crow lands and winning for Native Americans civil rights, including full citizenship and the right to maintain the Indian culture and autonomy.

Under the administration of President Franklin D. Roosevelt, Yellowtail was appointed superintendent of Crow Reservation—a move that members of his tribe unanimously endorsed in an election. As the first Native American to manage a reservation, he restored a land-based economy, native culture, and pride to the Crow. Among his accomplishments was persuading white ranchers living on the reservation to return forty thousand acres of land. He also stocked the reservation with more than four hundred head of buffalo and some elk, drawing on surpluses in Yellowstone National Park, and he used federal funds to import fine herds of horses and cattle from Canada. He built the first Crow hospital as well as reservoirs, roads, and mountain trails. He also initiated logging, introduced the Shoshone Sun Dance, and revived the annual Crow Fair. However, much of the Crow land was still leased to non-Indians, and the reservation economy was still mostly controlled by whites.

In 1945, after serving eleven years as superintendent, Yellowtail resigned in order to concentrate his energy on fighting the damming of the sacred Bighorn River. Years of negotiations with the Eisenhower administration during the 1950's ultimately failed, and false information about Yellowtail's role in the development turned many of his people against him. In 1964, the dam was completed and, ironically, named Yellowtail Dam.

Meanwhile, Yellowtail wrote the Crow tribal constitution in 1948, and in 1952 he was named chairman of the Crow tribal council. In January, 1988—several months before he died—he prevented the Bureau of Indian Affairs from selling Crow coal at too low a price. A U.S. Supreme

Court ruling directed the Westmoreland Coal Company to pay the Crow a fee of thirty million dollars plus four million dollars per year.

As the most important Crow political leader of the twentieth century, Robert Yellowtail exemplified his people's traditional name, "The Sharp People"—alert and crafty as the Raven—during his long fight for Crow survival. He died half a year after the coal settlement, near the place at which he had been born. The Crows continue to live in southeast Montana on their ancestral lands with their language, culture, and family structures largely intact.

Joanna Yin

FURTHER READING

Bradley, Charles Crane, Jr. *The Handsome People: A History of the Crow Indians and the Whites.* Billings, Mont.: Council for Indian Education, 1991.

Graetz, Rick, and Susie Graetz. *Crow Country: Montana's Crow Tribe of Indians.* Billings, Mont.: Northern Rockies Publishing, 2000.

Yonaguska

Born: c. 1760; near the Tuckaseigee River, North Carolina
Died: c. 1839; Quallatown, North Carolina
Tribal affiliation: Cherokee
Significance: Under Yonaguska's leadership, a small band of Cherokees successfully resisted removal to Indian Territory and eventually became known as the Eastern Band of the Cherokee.

At approximately sixty years of age, Yonaguska fell ill and was mourned as dead. After regaining consciousness a few days later, he claimed to have visited the spirit world and was thereafter regarded by his people as a prophet. As spiritual leader and chief, Yonaguska denounced tribal use of alcohol. He also counseled his people to resist removal to Indian Territory, claiming that if they moved the government would soon desire their new lands.

In 1829, Yonaguska led fifty-one men and their families to a new home at the juncture of the Soco Creek and the Oconaluftee River in western North Carolina. They had separated from the Cherokee Nation through a provision in a treaty that allowed them to settle on an independent reservation. There they made a claim for U.S. citizenship.

Through the aid of William Holland Thomas, a white lawyer and adopted son of Yonaguska, their small tribe successfully fought removal.

Thomas represented his adopted tribe in Washington, using settlements won from treaty violations to purchase land for them. With Yonaguska's death in 1839, Thomas remained the principal advocate for Yonaguska's tribe, acting as its de facto chief. The tribe later became known as the Eastern Band of the Cherokee.

Mary E. Virginia

FURTHER READING
Ehle, John. *Trail of Tears: The Rise and Fall of the Cherokee Nation.* New York: Doubleday, 1988.

Young Bear

Born: c. 1868; Iowa
Died: 1933; Tama County, Iowa
Also known as: Maqui-banasha
Tribal affiliation: Fox
Significance: During the late nineteenth and early twentieth centuries, when official government policy called for Indian assimilation, Young Bear advocated revitalization of Indian traditions.

The last of several Fox chiefs to bear the name, Young Bear was the son of Pushetonequa. Fearing the diminution of Fox culture, Young Bear encouraged his people to restore their tribal customs. To that end, he recorded tribal legends and sponsored a revival of traditional arts and crafts. He bemoaned the U.S. government's intervention in educating Indian children, fearing that white education combined with racial intermarriage would result in the death of Fox culture.

Young Bear died in 1933, a year before President Franklin D. Roosevelt and his commissioner of Indian affairs, John Collier, instituted a policy of Indian revitalization embodied in the Indian Reorganization Act of 1934.

Mary E. Virginia

Young Man Afraid of His Horses

Born: c. 1830; place unknown (probably present-day South Dakota)
Died: 1900; Pine Ridge Reservation, South Dakota
Also known as: Tasunka Kokipapi (Young Man of Whose Horses They Are Afraid)

Tribal affiliation: Oglala Lakota (Sioux)

Significance: Realizing the futility of further resistance to white expansionism, Young Man worked for improved conditions on the Pine Ridge Reservation.

Young Man Afraid of His Horses's name, the same as his father's, was intended to convey the idea that, in war, the name's bearer was so powerful that even the sight of his horses inspired fear in others. Young Man was instrumental in helping to delay white expansion during the 1860's. Various tribes respected his leadership abilities and, in 1865, the Cheyenne inducted him into their Crooked Lances clan. A realist, Young Man tried unsuccessfully to warn his people of the falseness of the Ghost Dance prophecies.

After the massacre at Wounded Knee in 1890, Young Man—realizing the hopelessness of any further Sioux resistance—persuaded his people to surrender and accept General Nelson Miles's peace terms, which included confinement at Pine Ridge Reservation. In January of 1891, thirty-five hundred starving Sioux men, women, and children—wounded, sick, and demoralized—entered the reservation. Young Man Afraid of His Horses negotiated and won fairer treatment for them. White authorities respected him, but some Sioux felt he was an apologist; other Sioux understood that he was protecting their interests as best he could under the circumstances. He was seventy when he died at the Pine Ridge Reservation.

Moises Roizen

FURTHER READING

Gibbon, Guy E. *The Sioux: The Dakota and Lakota Nations*. Malden, Mass.: Blackwell Publishing, 2003.

Zotom, Paul

Born: 1853; southern Plains

Died: April 27, 1913; Oklahoma

Also known as: Podaladalte (Snake Head), the Biter

Tribal affiliation: Kiowa

Significance: Paul Zotom's pictographs on ladies' fans, his model tipis, and his shield covers provide valuable ethnographic and artistic data.

Paul Zotom was a warrior who, as a young man, participated in horse-stealing raids in Texas and Mexico. In 1875, he and seventy-one other Indians were captured and exiled to Fort Marion, Florida, for "rehabilitation." There, Zotom discovered his latent artistic talents: He was a graceful dancer, a gifted painter, and an accomplished orator. His decorated ladies' fans were in great demand. His drawing books chronicle Indian activities in the Great Plains and at the fort. In 1878, Zotom went to Paris Hill, near Utica, New York, to study for the Episcopalian ministry; he was baptized in October. Ordained deacon in 1881, Zotom returned to Indian Territory to convert the Kiowa but was unable to reconcile the cultural dualities he faced, and in 1894 he was dropped as a deacon and missionary. His spiritual needs were answered when he joined the Native American Church. Art became his passion and source of income. He made scale models of tipis for the 1898 Omaha exposition. His series of buckskin shield covers provides valuable ethnographic and artistic knowledge. Zotom died at the age of sixty in Oklahoma on April 27, 1913.

Moises Roizen

Arctic Culture Area

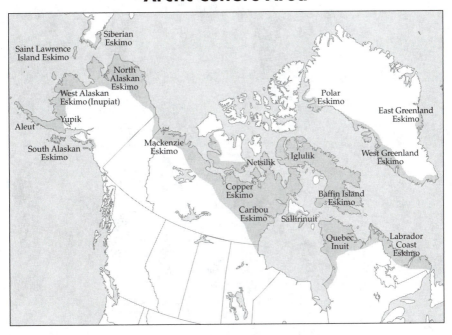

Subarctic Culture Area

565

Northwest Coast Culture Area

Eyak

Tlingit

Nishga
Gitksan
Tsimshian

Haida

Haisla

Bella Bella
Bella Coola

Kwakiutl

Nootka

Squamish
Semiahmoo
Cowichan
Makah   Nooksack
Quileute
Quinault   Clallam
Chehalis   Skokomish
Twana   Chemakum
Chinook   Duwamish
            Snoqualmie
            Puyallup
Clatskanie Klikitat
            Nisqually
Tillamook   Cowlitz
Siletz
Yaquina
Kalapuya
Alsea
Siuslaw
Coos   Umpqua
Tututni Takelma
       Chasta Costa
       Klamath

California Culture Area

Plateau Culture Area

Great Basin Culture Area

Northern
Paiute
(Paviotso)

Northern
Shoshone

Bannock

Eastern
Shoshone

Washoe

Western
Shoshone

Mono

Gosiute

Ute

Panamint

Southern
Paiute

Kawaiisu

Southwest Culture Area

Havasupai
Walapai
Mojave
Yavapai
Maricopa
Quechan
Cocopa
Tohono
O'odham
Pima

Hopi Navajo
Tiwa
Zuni Tewa
Jemez
Laguna
Acoma
Coyotero
Apache
Chiricahua
Apache

Jicarilla
Apache
Pecos
South
Tiwa
Mimbreño
Apache
Mescalero
Apache

Suma
Opata
Seri Jumano
Yaqui Tarahumara
Comarito

Lipan Apache
Karankawa
Coahuiltec
Tobosco

Lagunero
Zacatec

Plains Culture Area

Sarsi

Plains Cree

Blood
Blackfoot
Piegan

Atsina
Assiniboine

Crow

Hidatsa
Mandan
Yanktonai Lakota
(Sioux)

Arikara
Teton Lakota
(Sioux)

Cheyenne
Ponca

Santee Lakota
(Sioux)

Yankton Lakota (Sioux)

Omaha
Pawnee
Iowa

Oto

Arapaho
Kansa
Missouri

Osage

Kiowa

Quapaw

Comanche
Apache of
Oklahoma
Caddo

Wichita
Kichai

Tonkawa

Lipan Apache

Northeast Culture Area

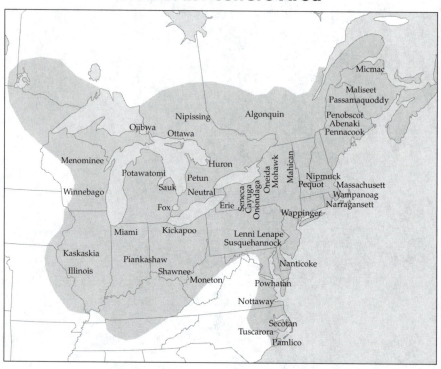

Southeast Culture Area

Manahoac

Saponi
Monacan
Tutelo

Yuchi
Chickasaw   Cherokee
        Coushatta   Cheraw
                                Catawba
        Tuskegee   Waccamaw

Caddo   Creek
        Tunica   Alabama   Hitchiti
        Ofo
Hasinai   Yazoo   Chiaha
        Natchez   Choctaw Tohome   Yamasee
        Houma   Guale
                Biloxi   Mobile
Atakapa   Apalachee
        Chitimacha

                        Timucua

                        Ais

                        Seminole
                        Calusa

List of Personages by Tribal Affiliations

Abenaki
Bruchac, Joseph, 71
Samoset, 442

Acoma Pueblo
Ortiz, Simon, 351

Algonquin
Pocahontas, 380

Anishinabe
LaDuke, Winona, 262

Apache
Betzinez, Jason, 36
Chatto, Alfred, 89
Cochise, 102
Delshay, 146
Eskiminzin, 166
Geronimo, 180
Juh, 244
Mangas Coloradas, 295
Naiche, 333
Nakaidoklini, 333
Nana, 335
Natiotish, 337
Victorio, 519

Arapaho
Left Hand the First, 270
Left Hand the Second, 271
Little Raven, 275
Sweezy, Carl, 480

Assiniboine
Little Assiniboine, 271

Bannock
Tendoy, 502

Blackfoot
Cobell, Elouise, 99
Crowfoot, 130
Mountain Chief, 326
Welch, James, 538

Blood
Charcoal, 87
Natawista, 336

Cahuilla
Antonio, Juan, 13
Costo, Rupert, 115
Modesto, Ruby, 319

Catawba
Hagler, 196

Cayuga
General, Alexander, 178
Logan, James, 280

Cherokee
Adair, John L., 1
Boudinot, Elias, 58
Boudinot, Elias Cornelius, 60
Bowl, 61
Bronson, Ruth Muskrat, 70
Bushyhead, Dennis Wolf, 79
Cher, 91
Chisholm, Jesse, 94
Cody, Iron Eyes(?), 106
Dragging Canoe, 153
Foreman, Stephen, 169
Green, Rayna, 193
Mankiller, Wilma Pearl, 297
Newton, Wayne, 339
Oconostota, 345
Ridge, John Rollin, 415
Ridge, Major, 416
Riggs, Lynn, 422

List of Personages by Tribal Affiliations

List of Personages by Tribal Affiliations

Wyandot
Clarke, Peter Dooyentate, 96
Tarhe, 490

Yahi
Ishi, 232

Yakima
Kamiakin, 252

Yavapai
Montezuma, Carlos, 322

List of Persons by Years of Birth

1880's
Cloud, Henry Roe, 97
Deloria, Ella Cara, 141
General, Alexander, 178
Gladstone, James, 187
Martínez, María Antonía, 304
Mountain Wolf Woman, 328
Mourning Dove, 329
Parker, Arthur Caswell, 359
Spybuck, Ernest, 472
Tawaquaptewa, 495
Thorpe, Jim, 505
Yellowtail, Robert, 558

1890's
Awa Tsireh, 20
Bronson, Ruth Muskrat, 70
Fools Crow, Frank, 168
Gilcrease, William Thomas, 186
Lame Deer, 267
Martínez, Crescencio, 303
Martínez, Julián, 303
Mopope, Stephen, 324
Peña, Tonita, 373
Riggs, Lynn, 422

1900
Hokeah, Jack, 219

1901
Crow Dog, Henry, 127

1904
Cody, Iron Eyes, 106
McNickle, D'Arcy, 291
Tsatoke, Monroe, 511

1906
Auchiah, James, 19
Bruce, Louis R., 70
Costo, Rupert, 115
Reifel, Ben, 414

1907
Blue Eagle, Acee, 55
Jones, Florence, 236

1908
Asah, Spencer, 17
Ross, Mary G., 437

1910
Wauneka, Annie Dodge, 534

1911
Peratrovich, Elizabeth W., 374

1912
Catches, Pete, 85

1913
Modesto, Ruby, 319

1915
Howe, Oscar, 225

1916
Dozier, Edward Pasqual, 152

1919
Silverheels, Jay, 461

1923
Hatathli, Ned, 207
Hayes, Ira Hamilton, 209
Popovi Da, 389

1924
Medicine, Bea, 311

1925
Tallchief, Maria, 485

1928
MacDonald, Peter, 286

1930
Cook-Lynn, Elizabeth, 110

1931
Bellecourt, Vernon, 32
Harris, LaDonna, 206

1932
Gorman, R. C., 190

1933
Campbell, Ben Nighthorse, 79
Deloria, Vine, Jr., 145

1934
Giago, Tim, 185
Momaday, N. Scott, 320
Sampson, Will, 443
Vizenor, Gerald, 520

1935
Deer, Ada Elizabeth, 135

1936
Bellecourt, Clyde H., 29

1937
Banks, Dennis, 21
Scholder, Fritz, 450
Snake, Reuben, 470

1938
Mills, Billy, 317
White Hat, Albert, 544

1939
Allen, Paula Gunn, 6
Heat-Moon, William Least, 210
Means, Russell, 308
Warrior, Clyde, 529

1940
Welch, James, 538

1941
Ortiz, Simon, 351
Tiger, Jerome R., 506

1942
Bruchac, Joseph, 71
Crow Dog, Leonard, 128

Green, Rayna, 193
Newton, Wayne, 339
Oakes, Richard, 342
Sainte-Marie, Buffy, 441

1943
Robertson, Robbie, 423

1944
Peltier, Leonard, 368

1945
Dorris, Michael, 150
Mankiller, Wilma Pearl, 297
Pictou Aquash, Anna Mae, 376

1946
Cher, 91
Cobell, Elouise, 99

1947
Hale, Janet Campbell, 197
Hogan, Linda, 218
Studi, Wes, 478
Trudell, John, 508

1948
Silko, Leslie Marmon, 459

1949
Harper, Elijah, 206

1951
Harjo, Joy, 203
Highway, Tomson, 217

1952
Greene, Graham, 194

1953
Crow Dog, Mary, 129
Tapahonso, Luci, 489

Variant Names

Abeel, John. *See* Cornplanter

Adoltay. *See* Big Tree

Adouette. *See* Big Tree

Affable, the. *See* Tammany

Agwelius. *See* Bruce, Louis R.

Aiionwatha. *See* Hiawatha

Akay na muka. *See* Gladstone, James

Aleekchea'ahoosh. *See* Plenty Coups

Alfonso Roybal. *See* Awa Tsireh

Allalimya Takanin. *See* Looking Glass

Amarazhu. *See* Rain in the Face

Angpetu Tokecha. *See* Otherday, John

Angry Warrior. *See* Manuelito

Anpetu Waste. *See* Deloria, Ella Cara

Antonio Martínez. *See* Popovi Da

Apayaka Hadjo. *See* Arpeika

Apotheyahola. *See* Opothleyaholo

Apushamatahubib. *See* Pushmataha

Apushwahite. *See* Looking Glass

Aquash, Anna Mae Pictou. *See* Pictou Aquash, Anna Mae

Arateva. *See* Irateba

Aripeka. *See* Arpeika

Ashishishe. *See* Curly

Assiola. *See* Osceola

Astoxkomi. *See* Crowfoot

Atsidi Sani. *See* Delgadito

Awa Tside. *See* Dozier, Edward Pasqual

Awoninahku. *See* Lean Bear

Ayonwatha. *See* Hiawatha

A-yo-went-ha. *See* Hiawatha

Ayunini. *See* Swimmer

Bad Heart Buffalo. *See* Bad Heart Bull, Amos

Barbon. *See* Barboncito

Bat. *See* Roman Nose

Batsida Karoosh. *See* White Man Runs Him

Bear Claw. *See* Charlot

Bear Cub. *See* Passaconaway

Bear Spirit. *See* Bear Hunter

Beautiful Bird. *See* Irateba

Beautiful Day. *See* Deloria, Ella Cara

Beaver. *See* Bent, George

Beduiat. *See* Victorio

Beshayeschayecoosis. *See* White Man Runs Him

Beshiltheeni. *See* Delgadito

Bidu-ya. *See* Victorio

Big Crane. *See* Two Leggings

Big in Center. *See* White Bull

Big Mouth. *See* Eskiminzin

Big Ribs. *See* Satanta

Big Snowsnake. *See* Parker, Arthur Caswell

Big Winnebago. *See* Crashing Thunder

Bird Woman. *See* Sacagawea

Bislahani. *See* Barboncito

Biter, the. *See* Zotom, Paul

Black Drink Singer. *See* Osceola

Black Hawk. *See* Blackbird, Andrew

Black Hoof. *See* Catahecassa

Black Warrior. *See* Tascalusa

Black. *See* Sweezy, Carl

Blessing Speaker

Blowsnake, Sam. *See* Crashing Thunder

Blue Earth. *See* Mankato

Blue Horn, the. *See* Moses

Boat Pusher. *See* Sacagawea

Bosomworth, Mary. *See* Musgrove, Mary

Bowles, Colonel. *See* Bowl

Brant, Mary. *See* Brant, Molly

Brave, the. *See* Oshkosh

Brave Bird, Mary. *See* Crow Dog, Mary
Bright Eyes. *See* La Flesche, Susette or Josette
Bright Path. *See* Thorpe, Jim
Buffalo Bird Woman. *See* Waheenee
Buffalo Bull Lodge. *See* Bull Lodge
Buffalo Lodge. *See* Bull Lodge
Bugonegijig. *See* Hole-in-the-Day
Bull Hump. *See* Buffalo Hump
Bull Standing with Cow. *See* White Bull
Bush, George. *See* Bushotter, George
By What One Plants. *See* Cornplanter

Cahae Numba. *See* Two Crows
Calichough. *See* Kalicho
Callicho. *See* Kalicho
Camaekin. *See* Kamiakin
Captain John. *See* Konkapot, John
Captain Konkapot. *See* Konkapot, John
Captain Pipe. *See* Hopocan
Carron, Thomas. *See* Tomah
Catherine Tagaskouita. *See* Tekakwitha, Kateri
Cetan Wakan Mani. *See* Little Crow
Chain Breaker. *See* Blacksnake
Chambly. *See* Shábona
Charging Bear (1832-1903). *See* Stumbling Bear
Charging Bear (1837-1918). *See* Grass, John
Charley. *See* Tsali
Chato. *See* Chatto, Alfred
Chebona Bula. *See* Blue Eagle, Acee
Chees-quat-a-law-ny. *See* Ridge, John Rollin
Cheucunsene. *See* Dragging Canoe
Chichikam Lupalkuelatko. *See* Scarface Charlie
Chief Joseph. *See* Joseph the Younger

Choukeka. *See* Decora, Spoon
Choukelea. *See* Decora, Spoon
Clem-hak-kah. *See* Charlot
Coacoochee. *See* Wildcat
Collichang. *See* Kalicho
Colonel Bowles. *See* Bowl
Colorado. *See* Colorow
Consaponaheeso. *See* Musgrove, Mary
Coosaponakeesa. *See* Musgrove, Mary
Cooswootna. *See* Antonio, Juan
Coowescoowe. *See* Ross, John
Corti, Espera. *See* Cody, Iron Eyes
Crane. *See* Tarhe
Crazy Bear. *See* Porter, Pleasant
Crazy Rattlesnake. *See* Arpeika
Crazy Snake. *See* Harjo, Chitto
Crazy War Hunter. *See* Menewa
Creek Mary. *See* Musgrove, Mary
Culbertson, Madame. *See* Natawista
Curly. *See* Crazy Horse

Dabuda. *See* Datsolalee
Dagataga. *See* Watie, Stand
Dahauson. *See* Dohasan
Dasoda-hae. *See* Mangas Coloradas
DeCorti, Espera. *See* Cody, Iron Eyes
Defender. *See* Giago, Tim
Degadoga. *See* Watie, Stand
Degonwadonti. *See* Brant, Molly
DeKaury. *See* Decora, Spoon
Delaware Prophet. *See* Neolin
Deskahe. *See* General, Alexander
Diwali. *See* Bowl
Donehogawa. *See* Parker, Ely Samuel

Eagle Lance. *See* Bad Heart Bull, Amos
Eagle Striking with Talons. *See* Kicking Bird
Eshkebugecoshe. *See* Flat Mouth
Etokeah. *See* Hump

Fire, John. *See* Lame Deer

Flat Nose. *See* Chatto, Alfred

Four Bears. *See* Mato Tope

Fox, the. *See* Uncas

Francis the Prophet. *See* Francis, Josiah

Galegina. *See* Boudinot, Elias

Galler, Mrs. Fred. *See* Mourning Dove

Ganeodiyo. *See* Handsome Lake

Gaspar Soiga. *See* Adario

Gawasowaneh. *See* Parker, Arthur Caswell

Gaynwawpiahsika. *See* Alford, Thomas Wildcat

Gist, George. *See* Sequoyah

Goci. *See* Cochise

Going-to-Run. *See* Betzinez, Jason

Gonwatsijayenni. *See* Brant, Molly

Good Shouting Child. *See* Opothleyaholo

Goodiarook. *See* Bedard, Irene

Goyathlay. *See* Geronimo

Grass Field. *See* Grass, John

Gray Goose. *See* Tyon, Thomas

Great Beloved Man. *See* McGillivray, Alexander

Great Sky. *See* General, Alexander

Grue, Le Chef. *See* Tarhe

Grue, Monsieur. *See* Tarhe

Guaton-bain. *See* Satanta

Guelle Plat. *See* Flat Mouth

Guess, George. *See* Sequoyah

Guipago. *See* Lone Wolf

Gwarth-ee-lass. *See* Peltier, Leonard

Hackibanzin. *See* Eskiminzin

Hágaga. *See* Crashing Thunder

Haiglar. *See* Hagler

Hakar Jim. *See* Hooker Jim

Haksigaxunuminka. *See* Mountain Wolf Woman

Hallalhotsoot. *See* Lawyer

Halpata Tastanaki. *See* Alligator

Halpatter Tustenuggee. *See* Alligator

Halpatter-Micco. *See* Bowlegs, Billy

Hancock, King. *See* Hancock

Harakontie. *See* Garakontie, Daniel

Harjo, Talof. *See* Porter, Pleasant

Hasanoanda. *See* Parker, Ely Samuel

Hashkeh Naabah. *See* Manuelito

Hastin Adiits'a'ii. *See* Dodge, Henry Chee

Hastin Ch'ilhajinii. *See* Manuelito

Hastín Daagii. *See* Barboncito

Hatchootucknee. *See* Pitchlynn, Peter Perkins

Having Indigestion. *See* Captain Jack

Hawk That Hunts Walking. *See* Little Crow

Hayo. *See* Francis, Josiah

He Brings Many Things with Him

He Causes Them to Be Awake. *See* Red Jacket

He Gets Mad Quickly. *See* Antonio, Juan

He Just Sits There. *See* Mangas Coloradas

He Stands on Two Feet. *See* Watie, Stand

He Who Combs. *See* Hiawatha

He Will Not Go. *See* Kamiakin

Hehaka Sapa. *See* Black Elk

Heinmot Hikkih. *See* Yellow Wolf

Henry Oscar One Bull. *See* One Bull

Hermene Moxmox. *See* Yellow Wolf

Hienwentha. *See* Hiawatha

Hillis. *See* Francis, Josiah

Hillishago. *See* Francis, Josiah

Hinmaton Yalatkit. *See* Joseph the Younger

Hippo Ilk Mico. *See* McGillivray, Alexander

His Eyes Are Dreamy. *See* Two Leggings

His Hoof. *See* Oshkosh

Little Bead. *See* Peña, Tonita

Little Bluff. *See* Dohasan

Little Boy. *See* Asah, Spencer

Little Chief. *See* Little Priest

Little Crow. *See* Little Raven

Little Fifth Daughter. *See* Mountain Wolf Woman

Little Mountain. *See* Dohasan

Logan, John. *See* Logan, James

Logan the Mingo. *See* Logan, James

Lone Bull. *See* One Bull

Lucero. *See* Victorio

Lumhe Chate. *See* Weatherford, William

Lyon, John. *See* Ignacio

McIntosh, Alex C. *See* Blue Eagle, Acee

Mack-aw-de-be-nessy. *See* Blackbird, Andrew

Madame Culbertson. *See* Natawista

Mahidiwia. *See* Waheenee

Mahkato. *See* Mankato

Mahthela. *See* Spybuck, Ernest

Mahtoiowa. *See* Conquering Bear

Makataimeshekiakiak. *See* Black Hawk

Makhpia-sha. *See* Red Cloud

Man of the Big Water. *See* Ganado Mucho

Man of the Black Weeds. *See* Manuelito

Man Who Goes in the Middle. *See* Gall

Man with Whiskers. *See* Barboncito

Mangopeomen. *See* Opechancanough

Many Achievements. *See* Plenty Coups

Many Guns. *See* Gladstone, James

Many Opposed to One. *See* Brant, Molly

Maqui-banasha. *See* Young Bear

Mary, Creek. *See* Musgrove, Mary

Mary Brave Bird. *See* Crow Dog, Mary

Massatamohtnock. *See* Opechancanough

Matihehlogego. *See* Hollow Horn Bear

Mato Wanartaka. *See* Kicking Bear

Mato Watakpe. *See* Grass, John

Matoaka. *See* Pocahontas

Maxidiwiac. *See* Waheenee

Metacom. *See* Metacomet

Miastashedekaroos. *See* White Man Runs Him

Michikinikwa. *See* Little Turtle

Mistahimaskwa. *See* Big Bear

Miwakan. *See* Sword, George

Mochunozhin. *See* Standing Bear

Moketavato. *See* Black Kettle

Morning Star. *See* Dull Knife

Morris, Lewis. *See* Two Crows

Mukatapenaise. *See* Blackbird, Andrew

Nah-dethy. *See* Betzinez, Jason

Namumpum. *See* Weetamoo

Nanay. *See* Nana

Nané. *See* Nana

Nantiotish. *See* Natiotish

Nanuntenoo. *See* Canonchet

Nanwica Kciji. *See* Giago, Tim

Nanye-hi. *See* Ward, Nancy

Natawista Iksana. *See* Natawista

Natchez. *See* Naiche

Nawat (1820-1864). *See* Left Hand the First

Nawat (1840-1911). *See* Left Hand the Second

Nazuha Hoksina. *See* Howe, Oscar

Nee-gon-we-way-we-dun. *See* Bellecourt, Clyde H.

Nenekunat. *See* Ninigret

Nesha. *See* Modesto, Ruby

Neshapanasumin. *See* Journeycake, Charles

Rock-Tree Boy. *See* Momaday, N. Scott

Rotten Belly. *See* Arapoosh

Sagoyewátha. *See* Red Jacket
Sarah Winnemucca Hopkins. *See* Winnemucca, Sarah
Sastaretsi. *See* Adario
Sauts. *See* Roman Nose
Seathl. *See* Seattle
Set-angia. *See* Satank
Setimkia. *See* Stumbling Bear
Set-tank. *See* Satank
Shabbona. *See* Shábona
Shabonee. *See* Shábona
Shao-hyowa. *See* General, Alexander
Shawnee Prophet, the. *See* Tenskwatawa
She Pushes with Her Hands. *See* Tekakwitha, Kateri
Shell Flower. *See* Winnemucca, Sarah
Shot Close. *See* Crowfoot
Shulush Homa. *See* Red Shoes
Si Tanka. *See* Big Foot
Si'k-okskitsis. *See* Charcoal
Sint-Chakkee. *See* Micanopy
Sinte Gleska. *See* Spotted Tail
Sitting Bear. *See* Satank
Sitting Bull. *See* Jumping Bull
Smith, Harold J. *See* Silverheels, Jay
Smith, Harry. *See* Silverheels, Jay
Smokeller. *See* Smohalla
Smóqula. *See* Smohalla
Snake Head. *See* Zotom, Paul
Snaky-Headed. *See* Atotarho
Sour Belly. *See* Arapoosh
Spahecha. *See* Isparhecher
Spotted Elk. *See* Big Foot
Stands Fast. *See* Copway, George
Starved Bear. *See* Lean Bear
Stays Back. *See* Little Assiniboine
Stone Child. *See* Rocky Boy
Sweet Odor. *See* Parker, Quanah
Swift. *See* Bruce, Louis R.

Tacanhpi-luta. *See* Red Tomahawk, Marcellus
Tadodaho. *See* Atotarho
Ta'e. *See* Martínez, Crescencio
Tahatan Wakan Mini. *See* Little Crow
Tahca Ushte. *See* Lame Deer
Tahgahjute. *See* Logan, James
Takashwangarous. *See* Shikellamy
Talker, The. *See* Lawyer
Tallassee Tustenuggee. *See* Osceola
Talmuches Harjo. *See* McQueen, Peter
Talof Harjo. *See* Porter, Pleasant
Tamanend. *See* Tammany
Tamela Pashme. *See* Dull Knife
Tanacharison. *See* Half-King
Tandinbilnojui. *See* Juh
Taoyateduta. *See* Little Crow
Tashunca-uitko. *See* Crazy Horse
Tastaluca. *See* Tascalusa
Tasunka Kokipapi. *See* Young Man Afraid of His Horses
Taszaluza. *See* Tascalusa
Tatanka Cante Sica. *See* Bad Heart Bull, Amos
Tatanka Iyotanka. *See* Sitting Bull
Tatapanum. *See* Weetamoo
Te'e. *See* Martínez, Crescencio
Tegakwith. *See* Tekakwitha, Kateri
Tekahionwake. *See* Johnson, Emily Pauline
Tene-angop'te. *See* Kicking Bird
Thaonawyuthe. *See* Blacksnake
Thayendanegea. *See* Brant, Joseph
Thocmetony. *See* Winnemucca, Sarah
Thunder in the Mountains. *See* Joseph the Younger
Tiger. *See* Tiger, Jerome R.
Tipi Sapa. *See* Deloria, Philip Joseph
Tisquantum. *See* Squanto
Toby Riddle. *See* Winema
Tohauson. *See* Dohasan
Tonto. *See* Silverheels, Jay

Time Line of Significant Events in American Indian History

Date	Event
c. 15,000-13,000 B.C.E.	Possible years of migration to the Americas by the ancestors of present-day Native Americans.
c. 12,000 B.C.E.	Estimate of when Paleo-Indians begin to migrate southward through ice-free corridors into the American interior.
c. 11,000 B.C.E.	Clovis Period begins across native North America; centers on hunting mega-fauna, especially the woolly mammoth.
c. 9,000 B.C.E.	Folsom Period emerges, centering on bison hunting.
c. 8,000 B.C.E.	Plano Period replaces Folsom, representing a transitional cultural period culminating in the Archaic.
c. 6,000 B.C.E.	Archaic Period begins, signaling a reliance on a variety of flora and fauna. Cultural innovations such as pottery, the bow and arrow, and the domestication of plants begin to appear across North America.
c. 1,000 B.C.E.	Agriculture appears in the Southwest; it gradually diffuses across North America.
c. 1,000 B.C.E.	Woodland Period emerges in eastern North America.
c. 1-500 C.E.	Complex societies flourish across North America.
c. 825-900	Athapaskan people, ancestors of the Navajo and Apache, invade the Southwest from the north, altering the cultural landscape of the Puebloan people.
c. 1007	Norsemen invade North America along the eastern seaboard and establish a short-lived colony.
1050-1250	Cahokia, near present-day St. Louis, is established as a great Mississippian trading and ceremonial center. The city may have contained as many as thirty thousand people.
1492	Christopher Columbus lands on Guanahani (the island of San Salvador), launching Europe's exploration and colonization of North America.
c. 1500	European-introduced diseases, warfare, and slavery begin to reduce native populations (from an estimated ten to eighteen million to approximately 250,000 in 1900).

Date	Event
1519-1521	Hernán Cortés conquers the Aztec Empire.
1582-1598	Spanish conquistadors invade and settle in the Southwest.
1585	Roanoke Colony is founded by the British (it lasts only until approximately 1607).
1599	Massacre at Acoma Pueblo. Vincente de Zaldivar attacks Acoma on January 21 because of its resistance to Spanish authority; eight hundred Acomas are killed.
1607	British Virginia Company establishes colony of Jamestown, affecting local indigenous populations.
1609	Henry Hudson opens the fur trade in New Netherlands.
1620	The Pilgrims colonize present-day Massachusetts.
1622-1631	Powhatan Confederacy declares war on the Jamestown colonists.
1629	The Spanish begin establishing missions among the Pueblos, leading to a 1633 revolt at Zuni.
1630	The Puritans colonize New England, carrying with them a religious belief that Native Americans are "children of the Devil."
1636-1637	Pequot War. The Pequot and their allies attempt to defend their homelands against the Puritans.
c. 1640	The Lakota (Sioux), forced in part by hostilities initiated by the fur trade, begin to migrate westward onto the Great Plains.
1642-1685	Beaver Wars. As the supply of beaver is exhausted in the Northeast, the Iroquois Confederacy launches a war against neighboring Native American nations to acquire their hunting territories.
c. 1650	Period of widespread migrations and relocations. Prompted by the diffusion of the gun and the horse, and by the increasing hostility of Europeans, many Native Americans migrate westward.
1655	Timucua Rebellion. Timucuan mission residents rebel against Spanish cruelty in Florida.
1655-1664	Peach Wars. The Dutch launch a war of extermination against the Esophus nation after an Esophus woman is killed for picking peaches.
1670	Hudson's Bay Company is chartered, launching a westward expansion of the fur trade.

Time Line of Significant Events in American Indian History

Date	Event
1670-1710	South Carolinians in Charleston encourage the development of a Native American slave trade across the Southeast.
1675-1676	King Philip's War. In response to English maltreatment, Metacomet (King Philip) launches a war against the English.
1676-1677	Bacon's Rebellion. Native Americans in Virginia fight a war of resistance but find themselves subject to Virginia rule.
1680	Pueblo (Popé's) Revolt. After decades of Spanish oppression, a Pueblo confederacy expels the Spanish from the Rio Grande region.
1682	Assiniboine and Cree begin to trade at York Factory, initiating European mercantile penetration of the Canadian west as far as the Rocky Mountains.
1689-1763	French and Indian Wars. King William's War initiates conflicts between the French and English that involve Native Americans and disrupt traditional patterns and alliances.
1692	Spanish reconquest of the Southwest (Nueva Mexico).
1695	Pima Uprising. Pimas burn missions in response to Spanish oppression.
c. 1700-1760	The horse diffuses across the Great Plains, prompting massive migrations and a cultural revolution.
1715-1717	Yamasee War. The Yamasee and their allies fight against the English for trading and other abuses.
1729	Natchez Revolt. Resisting French attempts to exact tribute, the Natchez go to war; the tribe is essentially destroyed, and many are sold into slavery.
1730	Articles of Agreement signed between the Cherokee Nation and King George II.
1740	Russia explores the Alaskan coast and begins trading operations.
1755	Some Iroquois settle near the Catholic mission of St. Regis, forming the nucleus of the Akwesasne Reserve.
1763	Proclamation of 1763. The Royal Proclamation of 1763 declares that Native Americans have title to all lands outside established colonies until the Crown legally purchases further land cessions.

Date	Event
1763-1764	Pontiac's War. Ottawa leader Pontiac constructs a multitribal alliance to resist the British.
1765	Paxton Riots (Paxton Boys Massacre). On December 14, 1765, seventy-five Europeans from Paxton, Pennsylvania, massacre and scalp six innocent Conestoga Mission Indians.
1768	Treaty of Fort Stanwix. The Iroquois Confederacy cedes lands south of the Ohio River (a later Fort Stanwix Treaty, 1784, changes the agreement).
1769	The California mission system is established.
1771	Labrador Inuit show missionaries where to build a trading post.
1774	Lord Dunmore's War. Lord Dunmore, the governor of Virginia, leads a fight against Shawnee led by Cornstalk.
1774	British defeat the Shawnee in the Battle of Point Pleasant in what is now West Virginia.
1774-1775	The first Continental Congress establishes an Indian Department.
1777-1783	The Iroquois Confederacy is dispersed by the American Revolution.
1787	Northwest Ordinance. The U.S. Congress establishes a legal mechanism to create states from territories.
1789	The Indian Department becomes part of the U.S. Department of War.
1790	First of the Trade and Intercourse Acts enacted; they attempt to regulate trade between Europeans and Native Americans.
1790-1794	Little Turtle's War. Shawnee and their allies under Little Turtle defeat Anthony St. Clair's troops in 1791 but eventually are defeated at the Battle of Fallen Timbers, 1794, by General Anthony Wayne.
1795	Treaty of Fort Greenville. Native Americans of the Old Northwest are forced to treat with the United States after Britain refuses to assist them in their resistance efforts.
1796	Trading Houses Act. On April 18, 1796, the United States establishes government-operated trading houses.
1799	Handsome Lake, the Seneca Prophet, founds the *Gaiwiio*, "the Good Word," also known as the Longhouse religion; it becomes a strong force among the Iroquois.

Time Line of Significant Events in American Indian History

Date	Event
1803	Louisiana Purchase. The United States acquires 800,000 square miles of new territory.
1804-1806	Lewis and Clark expedition. President Jefferson launches an expedition to collect information of national interest about the Louisiana territory purchased from the French in 1803.
1809	Treaty of Fort Wayne. The Delaware are forced to relinquish approximately 3 million acres of their land.
1809-1811	Tecumseh's Rebellion. Shawnee leader Tecumseh leads a multitribal force to resist United States incursions into their lands.
1811	Battle of Tippecanoe. William Henry Harrison and his forces attack and defeat Tecumseh's forces in Tecumseh's absence.
1812	War of 1812. Tribes of the Old Northwest are drawn into the European conflict.
1812	In August, the Hudson's Bay Company establishes the Red River Colony.
1813-1814	Red Stick civil war. Creeks fight a bloody civil war over disagreements about what their political relations with the United States should be.
1817-1818	First Seminole War. U.S. forces under General Andrew Jackson attack and burn Seminole villages.
1821	Sequoyah creates the Cherokee syllabary, the first system for writing an Indian language.
1823	*Johnson v. M'Intosh*. On February 28, 1823, the U.S. Supreme Court rules that Native American tribes have land rights.
1823	Office of Indian Affairs is created within the War Department.
1827	Cherokee Nation adopts a constitution.
1830	Indian Removal Act. At the urging of President Andrew Jackson, Congress orders the removal of all Native Americans to lands west of the Mississippi River. Removal proceeds from the 1830's to the 1850's.
1830	Treaty of Dancing Rabbit Creek. Choctaws cede more than 10 million acres of their lands in Alabama and Mississippi.
1830	Upper Canada establishes a system of reserves for Canadian natives.

Date	Event
1831	*Cherokee Nation v. Georgia.* U.S. Supreme Court rules that Native American tribes are "domestic dependent nations."
1832	Black Hawk War. Black Hawk, the Sauk and Fox leader, leads a war to preserve their land rights.
1832	*Worcester v. Georgia.* U.S. Supreme Court rules that only the federal government has the right to regulate Indian affairs.
1834	Department of Indian Affairs is reorganized.
1835	Texas Rangers begin raids against the Comanche.
1835-1842	Second Seminole War. The Seminole resist removal to Indian Territory.
1838-1839	Forced removal of Cherokees to Indian Territory becomes a "Trail of Tears" marked by thousands of deaths.
1839	Upper Canadian judge James Buchanan submits a report suggesting that Canadian natives should be assimilated into larger Canadian society.
1839	Taos Revolt. Taos Pueblos struggle against U.S. domination.
1848	Treaty of Guadalupe Hidalgo. United States acquires southwestern lands from Mexico.
1848-1849	California Gold Rush. Emigrants cross Native American lands, resulting in ecological destruction and spread of diseases.
1849	Metis Courthouse Rebellion. Metis resist Canadian domination.
1850	Period of genocide against California Indians begins and continues for some thirty years; thousands are killed.
1851	First Treaty of Fort Laramie. Great Plains Native Americans agree to allow emigrants safe passage across their territories.
1853	Gadsden Purchase. U.S. government purchases portions of Arizona, California, and New Mexico from Mexico.
1854-1864	Teton Dakota Resistance. The Teton Lakota and their allies resist U.S. intrusions into their lands.
1855	In the Northwest, Territorial Governor Isaac Stevens holds the Walla Walla Council and negotiates a series of treaties with Native American tribes.

Time Line of Significant Events in American Indian History

Date	Event
1855-1856	Yakima War. Led by Kamiakin, who refused to sign the 1855 treaty, Yakimas fight U.S. forces after the murder of a government Indian agent initiates hostilities.
1855-1858	Third Seminole War. Seminoles react to the surveying of their lands.
1858	British Columbia Gold Rush precipitates large-scale invasion of Indian lands.
1858	Navajo War. Manuelito leads the Navajo against U.S. forces to fight against whites' grazing their horses on Navajo lands.
1860	The British transfer full responsibility for Canadian Indian affairs to the Province of Canada.
1862	Minnesota Uprising. Little Crow carries out a war of resistance against federal authority because of ill treatment.
1863-1868	Long Walk of the Navajo. In a violent campaign, U.S. forces remove the Navajo from their homeland and take them to Bosque Redondo.
1864	Sand Creek Massacre. Colorado militiamen under John Chivington massacre a peaceful group of Cheyennes at Sand Creek.
1866-1868	Bozeman Trail wars. Teton Dakota and their allies resist the building of army forts in their lands.
1867	U.S. government purchases Alaska.
1867	Canadian Confederation. The Dominion of Canada is created.
1867	Commission Act. Legislation calls for the U.S. president to establish commissions to negotiate peace treaties with Native American nations.
1868	Second Treaty of Fort Laramie pledges the protection of Indian lands.
1868	Canadian government adopts an Indian policy aimed at the assimilation of Indians into Canadian society.
1868	Washita River Massacre. A peaceful Cheyenne camp is massacred by the U.S. Seventh Cavalry.
1869	First Riel Rebellion. Louis Riel leads the Metis in resisting Canadian domination; partly triggered by white surveying of Metis' lands.
1869	President U. S. Grant appoints Ely Samuel Parker the first Native American commissioner of Indian Affairs.

Date	Event
1870	Grant's Peace Policy. President Ulysses S. Grant assigns various Christian denominations to various Indian reservation agencies in order to Christianize and pacify the Indians.
1871	Congress passes an act on March 3 that ends treaty negotiations with Native American nations.
1871	*McKay v. Campbell.* U.S. Supreme Court holds that Indian people born with "tribal allegiance" are not U.S. citizens.
1871	Canada begins negotiating the first of eleven "numbered" treaties with Native Canadians.
1871-1890	Wholesale destruction of the bison on the Plains.
1872-1873	Modoc War. The Modoc resist removal to the Klamath Reservation.
1874	Canadian Northwest Mounted Police move to establish order in the Canadian West.
1874-1875	Red River War. Forced by starvation and Indian agent corruption, Kiowa, Plains Apache, Southern Cheyenne, and Arapaho raid European American farms and ranches to feed their families.
1875	Manuelito leads rebellion against corrupt administration of the Navajo Reservation in New Mexico.
1876	First Indian Act of Canada. The act consolidated Canadian policies toward its indigenous people.
1876	Battle of the Little Bighorn. General Custer and the Seventh Cavalry are annihilated by the Sioux, Cheyenne, and Arapaho camped along the Little Bighorn River.
1877	The Nez Perce are exiled from their homeland and pursued by U.S. forces as they unsuccessfully attempt to escape into Canada.
1877	Battle of Wolf Mountain. The last fight between the Cheyenne and the U.S. Army.
1877-1883	The Northern Cheyenne are forcibly removed to Indian Territory but escape north to their homelands.
1878	Bannock War. Because of settler pressures, the Bannock are forced to raid for food.

Time Line of Significant Events in American Indian History

Date	Event
1879	Carlisle Indian School, a boarding school with the goal of "civilizing" Indian youth, is founded by Captain Richard H. Pratt.
1880	Canadian officials modify the 1876 Indian Act, empowering it to impose elected councils on bands.
1882	Isparhecher leads the Creek in the Green Peach War in Alabama.
1885	Second Riel Rebellion. Louis Riel leads a second protest, then armed revolt, among the Canadian Metis and Cree; defeated, Riel is executed after the rebellion.
1887	General Allotment Act (Dawes Severalty Act). Provides for the dividing of reservation lands into individual parcels to expedite assimilation. (By the early twentieth century, the allotment policy is viewed as disastrous.)
1890	Wounded Knee Massacre. The Seventh Cavalry intercepts a group of Sioux Ghost Dancers being led by Big Foot to the Pine Ridge Reservation. When a Sioux warrior, perhaps accidentally, fires his rifle, the army opens fire; hundreds of Sioux, most unarmed, are massacred.
1897	Education Appropriation Act mandates funding for Indian day schools and technical schools.
1897	Indian Liquor Act bans the sale or distribution of liquor to Native Americans.
1903	*Lone Wolf v. Hitchcock.* U.S. Supreme Court rules that Congress has the authority to dispose of Native American lands.
1906	Burke Act. Congress amends the General Allotment Act to shorten the trust period for individual Native Americans who are proven "competent."
1906	Alaskan Allotment Act. Allows Alaska Natives to file for 160-acre parcels.
1907	Creek traditionalists in Oklahoma start the Smoke Meat Rebellion.
1910	Omnibus Act. Establishes procedures to determine Native American heirship of trust lands and other resources.
1912	Classification and Appraisal of Unallotted Indian Lands Act. Permits the Secretary of the Interior to reappraise and reclassify unallotted Indian lands.

Date	Event
1924	General Citizenship Act. As a result of Native American participation in World War I, Congress grants some Native Americans citizenship.
1928	Meriam Report outlines the failure of previous Indian policies and calls for reform.
1932	Alberta Metis Organization is founded by Joseph Dion.
1934	Indian Reorganization Act. Implements the Meriam Report recommendations, reversing many previous policies.
1934	Johnson-O'Malley Act replaces the General Allotment Act.
1936	Oklahoma Indian Welfare Act. Extends many of the rights provided by the Indian Reorganization Act of 1934 to Oklahoma Indian nations.
1944	National Congress of American Indians is founded to guard Native American rights.
1946	Indian Claims Commission Act. Provides a legal forum for tribes to sue the federal government for the loss of lands.
1950	Navajo and Hopi Rehabilitation Act is passed to assist the tribes in developing their natural resources.
1951	Indian Act of 1951. A new Canadian Indian Act reduces the powers of the Indian Affairs Department but retains an assimilationist agenda.
1951	Public Law 280 allows greater state jurisdiction over criminal cases involving Native Americans from California, Wisconsin, Minnesota, and Nebraska (extended to Alaska Natives in 1959).
1953	Termination Resolution. Congress initiates a policy (which continues into the early 1960's) of severing the federal government's relationships with Native American nations.
1955	Indian Health Service is transferred from the Department of the Interior to the Department of Health, Education, and Welfare.
1961	Chicago Indian Conference, organized by anthropologist Sol Tax, mobilizes Indian leaders to reassert their rights.
1961	National Indian Youth Council is founded by Clyde Warrior and others.

Time Line of Significant Events in American Indian History

Date	Event
1963	State of Washington rules against Native American fishing rights.
1964	American Indian Historical Society is founded in San Francisco to research and teach about Native Americans.
1966	Hawthorn Report examines the conditions of contemporary Canadian natives and recommends that Indians be considered "citizens plus."
1968	American Indian Civil Rights Act guarantees reservation residents many of the civil liberties other citizens have under the U.S. Constitution.
1968	American Indian Movement (AIM) is founded in Minneapolis by Dennis Banks and Russell Means.
1969	Canadian government's White Paper of 1969 rejects the Hawthorn Report's recommendations, arguing that Canadian natives' special status hinders their assimilation and urging the abolition of the Indian Affairs Department and Indian Act.
1969	President Richard M. Nixon appoints Louis R. Bruce commissioner of the Bureau of Indian Affairs.
1969	Two-year occupation of Alcatraz Island by Native American people begins.
1971	Alaska Native Claims Settlement Act marks the beginning of the self-determination period for Alaska Natives.
1972	Trail of Broken Treaties Caravan proceeds to Washington, D.C., to protest treaty violations.
1972	Native American Rights Fund (NARF) is founded to carry Indian issues to court.
1972	Indian Education Act enacted; it is intended to improve the quality of education for Native Americans (the act is revised in 1978).
1973	Wounded Knee occupation. More than two hundred Native American activists occupy the historic site to demonstrate against oppressive Sioux reservation policies.
1974	Navajo-Hopi Land Settlement Act facilitates negotiation between the two nations over the disputed Joint Use Area.

Date	Event
1975	Indian Self-Determination and Education Assistance Act expands tribal control over tribal governments and education.
1975	Political violence increases on the Pine Ridge Reservation; two FBI agents are killed in a shootout on June 26.
1975	James Bay and Northern Quebec Agreement is signed; Quebec Cree, Inuit, Naskapi, and Montagnais groups cede tribal lands in exchange for money and specified hunting and fishing rights.
1977	American Indian Policy Review Commission Report is released by Congress, recommending that Native American nations be considered sovereign political bodies.
1978	American Indian Freedom of Religion Act protects the rights of Native Americans to follow traditional religious practices.
1978	Federal Acknowledgment Program is initiated to provide guidelines for and assist tribes seeking official recognition by the federal government.
1978	Indian Child Welfare Act proclaims tribal jurisdiction over child custody decisions.
1978	The Longest Walk, a march from Alcatraz Island to Washington, D.C., protests government treatment of Indians.
1980	*United States v. Sioux Nation.* U.S. Supreme Court upholds a $122 million judgment against the United States for illegally taking the Black Hills.
1981	Hopi-Navajo Joint Use Area is partitioned between the Navajo and Hopi nations.
1982	Canada's Constitution Act (Constitution and Charter of Rights and Freedoms) is passed despite the protests of Indian, Metis, and Inuit groups.
1982	Indian Claims Limitation Act limits the time period during which claims can be filed against the U.S. government.
1985	Coolican Report declares that little progress is being made to settle Canadian native land claims.
1988	Indian Gaming Regulatory Act officially legalizes certain types of gambling on reservations and establishes the National Indian Gaming Commission.

Time Line of Significant Events in American Indian History

Date	Event
1989	U.S. Congress approves construction of the National Museum of the American Indian, to be part of the Smithsonian Institution.
1989	Violence erupts on St. Regis Mohawk Reservation in dispute over whether to allow gambling; under guard by state and federal law enforcement officers, the tribe votes to allow gambling on the reservation.
1990	The U.S. Census finds the Native American population to be 1,959,234.
1990	In *Duro v. Reina*, the U.S. Supreme Court holds that tribes cannot have criminal jurisdiction over non-Indians on reservation lands.
1990	Canada's proposed Meech Lake Accord (amendments to the 1982 Constitution Act) is sent to defeat in Canada by native legislator Elijah Harper; the accord provided no recognition of native rights.
1991	Tribal Self-Governance Act extends the number of tribes involved in the self-governance pilot project.
1992	Native Americans protest the Columbian Quincentenary.
1992	In a plebiscite, residents of Canada's Northwest Territories approve the future creation of Nunavut, a territory to be governed by the Inuit.
1992	Tim Giago changes the name of his *Lakota Times* to *Indian Country Today*—which became the nation's largest Indian newspaper.
1993	The International Year of Indigenous People.
1993	President Bill Clinton appoints Ada Elizabeth Deer commissioner of the Bureau of Indian Affairs.
1994	National Museum of the American Indian opens its first facility in New York's Heye Center (a larger museum is planned for the National Mall in Washington, D.C.).
1994	The National Congress of American Indians and the National Black Caucus of State Legislators ally themselves, agreeing that they face similar political and economic forces of oppression.
1996	Elouise Cobell files a class-action suit against the federal government to recover billions of dollars owed to Indians by the Department of the Interior.

Date	Event
1998	Canadian minister of Indian Affairs formally apologizes to Indian and Inuit peoples for past government attempts to destroy native cultures.
1998	*Smoke Signals*, with Adam Beach and Irene Bedard, is the first feature film written, directed, and produced entirely by Native Americans.
1999	Eastern portion of Canada's Northwest Territories becomes new territory of Nunavut.
2000	U.S. secretary of the interior Bruce Babbitt announces that the remains of Kennewick Man will be turned over to Washington State Native American tribes under the provisions of the Native American Graves Protection and Repatriation Act.
2001	Native Americans sue Secretary of the Interior Gale Norton over approximately $10 billion they claim was bilked from Native American trust funds of Indian land use royalties, administered by the Department of the Interior since 1887.
2003	Sioux leader Leonard Crow Dog opens the Sun Dance to non-Indians in Nebraska.
2004	National Museum of the Native American opens in Washington, D.C.

Subject Index

For alternative names of personages who are subjects of essays, see the Variant Names appendix that begins on page 589. Tribes are indexed in the List of Personages by Tribal Affiliations that begins on page 574.

ABC: Americans Before Columbus, 530
Ace Daklugie, 245
Actors; Banks, Dennis, 21-22; Beach, Adam, 24; Bedard, Irene, 27-28; Cody, Iron Eyes, 106; George, Dan, 179; Greene, Graham, 194-195; Means, Russell, 308-310; Rogers, Will, 425-430; Sampson, Will, 443; Silverheels, Jay, 461; Studi, Wes, 478
Adair, John L., 1
Adams, Abigail, 289
Adams, Hank, 530
Adams, Henry, 382
Adams, John Quincy, 411
Adario, 1-2
Adate, 149
Adobe Walls, Battles of, 231, 365, 480
Agona, 150
AIF. *See* American Indian Freedom Act
AIM. *See* American Indian Movement
AIO. *See* Americans for Indian Opportunity
AISES. *See* American Indian Science and Engineering Society
Alaska Native Brotherhood, 374
Alaska Native Sisterhood, 374
Alaskan Anti-Discrimination Act, 374
Alcatraz Island occupation; and Bellecourt, Clyde, 29; and Mankiller, Wilma, 297; and Oakes, Richard, 342; and Trudell, John, 508
Alexie, Sherman, 2-5
Alford, Thomas Wildcat, 5
Allen, Alvaren, 466
Allen, Paula Gunn, 6-9
Alligator, 9-10, 246
Allotment, 202, 226
Amadas, Philip, 371
American Horse, 10-12, 26
American Indian Chicago Conference, 530
American Indian Freedom Act, 30
American Indian Historical Society, 116
American Indian Movement, 21, 129, 369; and Bellecourt, Clyde H., 29; and Bellecourt, Vernon, 32; creation

of, 530; and Crow Dog, Leonard, 128; and Fools Crow, Frank, 169; and Means, Russell, 308; and Medicine, Bea, 311; and Oakes, Richard, 342-343; and Pictou Aquash, Anna Mae, 376
American Indian Science and Engineering Society, 391
American Revolution, 66; and Cayuga, 281; and Cherokee, 61, 346; and Creek, 288; and Delaware, 544; and Iroquois, 63, 66-67, 69, 112-113; and Lenni Lenape, 224; and Mahican, 341; and Miami, 277; and Mohawk, 68; and Mohegan, 345; and Ottawa, 387; and Senecas, 52; and Shawnee, 56, 85, 115, 497
Americans for Indian Opportunity, 207
ANB. *See* Alaska Native Brotherhood
Annawan, 12
ANS. *See* Alaska Native Sisterhood
Anthony, Scott, 50
Anthropologists; Bushotter, George, 77-78; Deloria, Ella Cara, 141-142; Dorris, Michael, 150-151; Dozier, Edward Pasqual, 152; Hewitt, John N. B., 211; Hunt, George, 227; Ishi, 232-233; McNickle, D'Arcy, 291-293; Medicine, Bea, 311; Murie, James, 330; Parker, Arthur Caswell, 359; Tyon, Thomas, 517
Antonio, Juan, 13-14, 177
Apache removal, 90
Apache Wars, 182-183, 519
Apes, William, 14-15
Aquash, Anna Mae Pictou. *See* Pictou Aquash, Anna Mae
Aquash, Nogeeshik, 376
Arapoosh, 15-16
Argall, Samuel, 380
Army scouts; Bad Heart Bull, Amos, 20; Big Bow, 39; Bloody Knife, 53-54; Chatto, Alfred, 89-90; Curly, 131; Gladstone, James, 187-188; Little Wolf, 279; Naiche, 333; Otherday,